Seventh Edition

An Introduction to Theories of Personality

B. R. Hergenhahn

Professor Emeritus
Hamline University

Matthew H. Olson

Hamline University

PEARSON
Prentice
Hall

Upper Saddle River, New Jersey 07458

Library of Congress Cataloging-in-Publication Data

Hergenhahn, B. R.,
  An introduction to theories of personality / B.R. Hergenhahn and Matthew
H. Olson.— 7th ed.
    p. cm.
  Includes bibliographical references and indexes.
  ISBN 0-13-194228-X
1. Psychology—History—Textbooks.   I. Olson, Matthew H.   II. Title.
  BF698.H45 2007

                                                  2005036544

Editorial Director: Leah Jewell
Senior Editor: Jeff Marshall
Editorial Assistant: Jennifer Puma
Media Editor: David Clevinger
Director of Marketing: Brandy Dawson
Senior Marketing Manager: Jeanette Moyer
Marketing Assistant: Alexandra Trum
Managing Editor: Joanne Riker
Assistant Managing Editor (Production):
  Maureen Richardson
Production Liaison: Jan Schwartz/
  Maureen Richardson

Manufacturing Manager: Nick Sklitsis
Manufacturing Buyer: Sherry Lewis
Interior Design: Pine Tree Composition
Cover Design: Bruce Kenselaar
Cover Illustration/Photo: Graphistock
Composition/Full Service Project Management:
  Mike Remillard
Cover printer: Phoenix Color Corporation
Printer/Binder: R. R. Donnelley & Sons

Credits appear on pages xxiii–xxiv which constitutes a continuation of the copyright page.

Pearson Education LTD., London
Pearson Education Singapore, Pte. Ltd
Pearson Education, Canada, Ltd
Pearson Education–Japan
Pearson Education Australia PTY, Limited

Pearson Education North Asia Ltd
Pearson Educación de Mexico, S.A. de C.V.
Pearson Education Malaysia, Pte. Ltd
Pearson Education, Upper Saddle River, New Jersey

PEARSON
Prentice
Hall

10 9 8 7 6 5

ISBN 0-13-194228-X

Dedicated to Matthew H. Olson. Loving husband to Marce, loving father to Mira, and an extremely helpful colleague and a very much appreciated friend to me through the years.   (B.R.H.)

Dedicated to the outstanding faculty of the Hamline University Psychology Department: Professors Dorothee Dietrich, R. Kim Guenther, Serena King, Charles LaBounty, and Robin Parritz (M.H.O.)

Contents

2   *Sigmund Freud*   21

3   *Carl Jung   63*

4   *Alfred Adler   95*

5   *Karen Horney   126*

6   *Erik H. Erikson*   153

7 *Gordon Allport*   184

8   *Raymond B. Cattell and Hans J. Eysenck*   *217*

9   *B. F. Skinner   260*

10 *John Dollard and Neal Miller* *292*

13 *George Kelly*   *403*

14   *Carl Rogers   438*

15   *Abraham Maslow*   *469*

16   *Rollo Reese May*   *502*

17   *A Final Word*   *529*

Preface

In addition to numerous minor changes, several substantial changes, including a new version of Chapter 12 (described below), were made in the seventh edition of this text and they are summarized below:

- All chapters were student tested, revised, and reorganized with attention to student comments and recommendations.
- All chapters now include brief introductions that relate them to other chapters or that set them in historical context.
- Suggestions for Further Reading appear in the Instructor's Manual rather than at the end of chapters in the text.
- Only three Questions for Discussion are included for each chapter in the text. Additional Questions for Discussion appear in the Instructor's Manual.
- Biographical information was updated and revised throughout.
- Chapter 1: Information on philosophy of science and psychology-as-a-science was updated and revised.
- Chapter 5: Karen Horney's contributions to contemporary feminist psychology was revised and updated.
- Chapter 11: Albert Bandura's current writings on human agency and self-efficacy were included.
- Chapter 12: The former chapter on E. O. Wilson and Sociobiology was eliminated and replaced with a new chapter featuring the work of David M. Buss and other evolutionary psychologists. The chapter presents all new material on human nature, mating strategies, love and jealousy, dysfunctional behavior, and psychological disorders. Substantial material on sex differences and cultural differences is included.

The seventh edition of this text continues to reflect our contention that it is in an Introduction to Theories of Personality course that the student experiences the full richness of psychology. In such a course, the student experiences everything from psychology's most rigorous scientists to its most mystical nonscientific thinkers. It is in such a course that the student reviews answers to questions such as: What, if anything, do all human beings have in common? What accounts for individual differences among people? How are the mind and body related? How much of what we call personality is inherited and how much of it results from experience? and, How much of human behavior is determined and how much of it is a function of free will? In such a course, the major theories of human motivation are reviewed and the major schools, paradigms, or "isms" within psychology are sampled: for example, psychoanalysis, behaviorism, humanism, and existentialism. It is in such a course that the student is exposed to the history of psychology, from Freud to the modern theorists, including Erikson, Allport, Cattell, Eysenck, Skinner, Bandura, Mischel, Buss, Kelly, Rogers, Maslow, and May. It is also in such a course that students encounter information that helps them make sense out of their own lives and their relationships with other people. Finally, in such a course, the nature of psychopathology and its treatment are explored. What other psychology course covers as much territory? Our answer is none, and therefore it is our belief that if a student were to take only one psychology course beyond the introductory course, it should be an Introduction to Personality course.

Although this text covers topics already mentioned, its main purpose is to summarize the major theories of personality. The text is built around the belief that it is misleading to search for the correct theory of personality. Rather, it is assumed that the best understanding of personality is derived from a variety of viewpoints. Thus, theories representing the psychoanalytic, sociocultural, trait, learning, sociobiological, and existential–humanistic paradigms are offered as different—yet equally valid—ways of approaching the study of personality.

We would like to express our appreciation to David M. Buss, whose guidance and patience made Chapter 12 possible. Thanks also to Leda Cosmides and John Tooby for providing a photo for that chapter. Thanks to the following individuals whose reviews of the sixth edition of this text were helpful as we wrote the seventh edition: Eros DeSouza, Illinois State University; Edward T. Asbury, Campbell University; Holiday E. Adair, California University of Pennsylvania; and Eugenia Cox-Fuenzalida, University of Oklahoma.

We would like to express our thanks to Professors Dorothee Dietrich, R. Kim Guenther, Charles LaBounty, and Robin Parritz, all of whom took on additional responsibilities in the Hamline University Psychology Department to provide Olson the time needed to work on this text. We express a special thanks to our star departmental assistant, Stephanie Goodsell, whose proofreading and editoral help was heroic. We would also like to thank Allen Esterson for continuing to share with us his scholarship on the deception involved in Freud's formulation of, and subsequent rejection of, his seduction theory. All comments, complaints, and inquiries should be directed to Olson at mholson@gw.hamline.edu.

B. R. Hergenhahn
Professor Emeritus
Hamline University

Matthew H. Olson
Hamline University

Credits

Photos

Notes

Chapter 3

From *Memories, Dreams, and Reflections* by C. G. Jung, edited by Aniela Jaffe, translated by Richard and Clara Winston, copyright 1961, 1962, 1963 by Random House, Inc. Reprinted by permision of Pantheon Books, a division of Random House, Inic.

Chapter 4

From *Born to Rebel* by Frank J. Sulloway, copyright ©1996 by Frank J. Sulloway. Used by permission of Pantheon Books, a Division of Random House, Inc.

Chapter 6

From *Childhood and Society* by E. H. Erikson, copyright 1985. Used by permission of W. W. Norton.

Chapter 8

H. J. Eysenck and M. W. Eysenck, *Personality and Individual Differences,* copyright ©1992, Kluwer Academic/Plenum Publishers. Reprinted with Kind permission from Springer Science and Business Media. From Cattell: *Personality and Learning Theory* (vol 1.), copyright ©1979, Springer Publishing

Company, Inc., New York, 10036. Used with permission of the publisher. From Mcrae and Costa, *Personality in Adulthood,* copyright ©1990, Guilford Publications Inc. Reprinted by permission of The Guilford Press.

Chapter 9

From *Beyond Freedom and Dignity* by B. F. Skinner. Copyright ©1971by B. F. Skinner Reprinted 2002 by Hackett Publishing Company Inc., by special arrangement with the B. F. Skinner Foundation. Reprinted by permission of Hackett Publishing , Inc. All rights reserved. From *Introduction to Theories of Learning* by Hergenhahn and Olson. Copyright ©2005. Reprinted by permission of Pearson Education Inc..

Chapter 12

Number of Partners as a Function of Time, from Buss & Schmitt (1993). *Psycological Review,* 100, pp. 204-232. With permission of David M. Buss and The American Psycological Association. From *Introduction to Theories of Learning* by Hergenhahn and Olson. Copyright ©2005. Reprinted by permission of authors and Pearson Education Inc..

Chapter 13

Reprinted from *Advances in Cognitive-Behavioral Research & Therapy,* Volume 4, by R. A. Neimeyer, edited by Philip C. Kendall, copyright 1985, Elsevier Science (USA), reproduced with permission from Elsevier.

Chapter 14

Excerpts from *On Becoming a Person* by Carl R. Rogers. Copyright ©1961 by Carl R. Rogers, renewed 1989 by David E. Rogers and Natalie Rogers. Reprinted by permission of Houghton Mifflin Company. All rights reserved.

Chapter 15

Reprinted with permission from *Psychology Today* magazine, Copyright © (1968 Sussex Publishers, Inc.). *Motivation and Personality,* 2/e by Maslow, ©. Reprinted by permission of Pearson Education, Inc., Upper Saddle River, NJ

Chapter 16

From *Psychology and the Human Dilemma* by Rollo May. Copyright © 1979 by Rollo May. Copyright © 1967 by W. W. Norton & Company, Inc. Used by permission of W. W. Norton & Company, Inc. Reprinted from *Love and Will* by Rollo May, by permission of W. W. Norton and Company, Inc. Copyright © 1969 by W. W. Norton and Company, Inc.

CHAPTER 1

WHAT IS PERSONALITY?

CHAPTER OUTLINE

The term *personality* comes from the Latin word **persona,** which means mask. Those defining personality as a mask view personality as one's public self. It is that aspect of ourselves we select to display to the world. This definition of personality implies that important aspects of a person remain concealed for some reason. Other definitions of personality range from the popular notion that personality allows a person to be socially effective (a person may be viewed as having a wonderful personality, a terrible personality, or no personality at all), to highly technical definitions involving mathematical formulations. Therefore, several definitions of personality exist. In fact, every theory of personality can be viewed as an attempt to define personality and these definitions differ markedly from one another.

Three Concerns of Personality Theory

Kluckhohn and Murray (1953, p. 53) observed that every human being is (1) like every other human being; (2) like some other human beings; and (3) like no other human being. We are like all other human beings insofar as there is a **human nature** that describes "humanness." One task of the personality theorist is to describe what all human beings have in common, what we come equipped with at birth—that is, to describe human nature. Next, we are like some other human beings insofar as we share a common culture. For example, it may be part of human nature to adorn one's body, to attempt to make sense of the universe and one's place in it, to seek a mate and produce offspring, to care for one's offspring, and to live cooperatively with one's fellow humans. It is culture, however, that determines how these needs are satisfied. In our culture, for example, if we want to marry, we must have only one wife or husband at a time. Lastly, each human is unique, with his or her own particular cluster of genes and his or her own particular cluster of personal experiences.

In describing personality, the personality theorist attempts to show how we are the same as other humans and how we are different from them. The former issue concerns human nature, and the latter concerns **individual differences.** It is one achievement to describe the components of human nature and the characteristics on

1

which humans differ; it is another to explain their origins, how they interact, how they change over time, and their functional significance. The goals of personality theory are to describe what humans are like and to explain why we are like that—to describe and explain both human nature and individual differences. This is a large order and no single theory has been completely successful at doing either. Rather, different theories emphasize different aspects of human nature and individual differences, and offer different descriptions, explanations, and methods for studying them. For this reason, perhaps, the best understanding of personality is provided by the composite of many theories of personality as opposed to any single theory.

Proposed Determinants of Personality

In this section we review some of the factors stressed by various personality theorists in their attempts to explain personality. We see that one theorist may emphasize one or more of the following factors, whereas other theorists minimize them or ignore them altogether.

Genetics

The most common lay explanation of personality is often based on genetics. When asked, our students tend to express the belief that personality characteristics are present for the same reasons that eye color, hair color, or physique are present. To ask why a person is shy is basically the same as asking why he or she is tall. Both characteristics, according to this viewpoint, are genetically determined. Common statements such as "He has an Irish temper," "She takes after her father," or "He has his uncle's artistic tendencies," imply a genetic explanation of personality because they all have an "It's in the blood" tone to them.

You should not be left with the impression that only nonprofessionals view personality characteristics as being influenced by heredity. Heredity may play a far greater role in determining personality than was previously suspected. For example, Thomas J. Bouchard, Jr., has studied identical twins separated at birth and reared apart. Bouchard consistently finds great similarity in the personalities of identical twins even when they had no contact with each other and were reared by distinctly different families. Bouchard (1984) concludes, "Both the twin studies and adoption studies . . . converge on the surprising finding that common family environmental influences play only a minor role in the determination of personality" (pp. 174–175). In other words, if children reared in the same family have similar personality characteristics, that fact seems to be explained more by their common genes than by their shared family experiences. Using the Multidimensional Personality Questionnaire to investigate the heritability of 11 personality traits, Tellegen et al. (1988) found that genetics was the single most influential variable in determining the extent to which a person possesses personality traits such as well-being, social potency, achievement, aggression, and traditionalism. Perhaps most surprising is the fact that religiosity was also found to be highly heritable (Waller, Kojetin, Bouchard, Lykken, & Tellegen, 1990). Waller et al. concluded, "Social scientists will have to discard the a priori assumption that individual differences in religious and other social attitudes are solely influenced by environmental factors" (1990, p. 141). After reviewing the work of Bouchard and others, Holden (1987) wrote the following:

> Although behavioral geneticists quibble about each others' methodologies, most appear to be in accord with the conclusion that the common environment seems to have a negligible role in creating personality similarities among family members. From the standpoint of the organism, it seems, there may be no such thing as a common environment for two given individuals unless those individuals also have all their genes in common. (p. 600)

The field of evolutionary psychology (Chapter 12) also stresses the role of genetics and evolved adaptations in its explanation of personality. In fact, all theories of personality are built on an inherited quality, whether it be physiological needs, described, for example, by Freud (Chapter 2), Skinner (Chapter 9), Dollard and Miller (Chapter 10), and Maslow (Chapter 15); the tendency toward self-actualization, described, for example, by Jung (Chapter 3), Horney (Chapter 5), Rogers (Chapter 14), and Maslow (Chapter 15); or social interest, as discussed by Adler (Chapter 4). Thus the question is not whether genes influence personality, but rather to what degree and in what manner.

The question of how much personality is influenced by inheritance is as old as psychology itself. **The nativism–empiricism controversy** (also called the nature–nurture controversy) exists in every major category within psychology, including personality theory. In general, the nativist claims that an important attribute, such as intelligence, is largely genetically determined. The nativist would say, for example, that the maximum level of intelligence that people can attain is determined at conception, and life's circumstances, at best, can help people to realize this genetically determined intellectual potential. The empiricist, conversely, believes that people's major attributes are largely created by experience. Intelligence, to the empiricist, is determined more by people's experiences than by their genetic endowment. To the empiricist, the upper limit of a person's intelligence is found in the environment, not in the genes.

The nativism–empiricism controversy manifests itself in many ways in personality theory, and we encounter it several times in this text.

Traits

Several personality theorists believe that what distinguishes people from one another are the traits they possess. Some traits, it is assumed, are learned (e.g., food preferences), and others are genetically determined (e.g., one's emotional makeup). Some exert a powerful influence in one's life (e.g., intelligence), and others have only a minor influence (e.g., fashion preferences). Trait theorists believe the traits one possesses remain relatively constant throughout one's life and, therefore, they believe one's behavior will tend to remain consistent across time and similar situations. The theories of Allport (Chapter 7) and Cattell and Eysenck (Chapter 8) stress the importance of traits in their explanations of personality.

Sociocultural Determinants

To a large extent, one's culture determines what are considered proper practices in courtship, marriage, childrearing, politics, religion, education, and justice. These, and other cultural variables, explain many important individual differences among humans, that is, differences among people of different cultures.

More specifically, some theorists say that one's personality can be viewed as a combination of the many roles one plays. If you were asked to start a blank sheet of paper with the words "I am" and then to list all of your qualities, you would have a rather extensive list. For example, you may be female, 19 years old, a college student, a Lutheran, from the Midwest, 5 feet 8 inches tall, a Republican, attractive, a Cancer, a psychology major, a departmental assistant, and so on. Each entry on your list has a prescribed role associated with it, and for each role, society has defined what is an acceptable range of behavior (norms). If you deviate from that range, you will confront social pressure of some type. Indeed, what is considered normal behavior and what is considered abnormal is, to a large extent, determined by how you behave relative to societal expectations.

Other sociocultural determinants of personality include the socioeconomic level of one's family, one's family size, birth order, ethnic identification, religion, the region of the country in which one was raised, the educational level attained by one's parents, and the like. One simply does not have the same experiences in a financially secure home as one would have in an impoverished home. These fortuitous circumstances into which a person is born (e.g., culture, society, and family) certainly have a major impact on personality. Again, this point is one that all personality theorists accept; it is just a matter of how much each one emphasizes it. The theories of Adler (Chapter 4), Horney (Chapter 5), and Erikson (Chapter 6) stress the importance of sociocultural determinants of personality.

Learning

Those emphasizing a genetic explanation of personality represent the nativistic side of the nativism–empiricism controversy. Those emphasizing the learning process in their explanations of personality represent the empiricistic side. An example is the learning theorist's contention that we are what we have been rewarded or punished for being; therefore, if our history of reward and punishment had been different, our personalities would be different. The difference between a successful person and an unsuccessful one, according to some learning theorists, is found in patterns of reward and punishment, not in the genes.

A powerful implication of this theoretical position is that one can control personality development by controlling the circumstances under which rewards and punishments are dispensed or withheld. Theoretically, according to this perspective, it is possible to create any type of personality by systematically manipulating reward and punishment. Those emphasizing the genetic basis of personality deny that personality is as pliable as the learning theorist suggests. The theories of Skinner (Chapter 9), and Dollard and Miller (Chapter 10) emphasize the importance of reward in the learning process. Bandura and Mischel (Chapter 11) also stress the learning process but deny the importance of reward in that process.

Considerable compatibility exists between those stressing sociocultural determinants in their explanations of personality and those stressing the learning process. Both accept **environmentalism.** One's personality is shaped by cultural expectations but it is through patterns of reward and punishment that those expectations are conveyed to children. That is, they both believe that personality results from one's life experiences.

Existential–Humanistic Considerations

Theories emphasizing existential–humanistic principles ask such questions as the following: What does it mean to be aware of the fact that ultimately you must die? What are the sources of meaning in human existence or in an individual's existence? According to what values is it best to live one's life and how are those values determined? How do the human needs for predictability and security relate to the human needs for adventure and freedom?

Such theories stress the importance of free will. Humans may be thrown by circumstances beyond their control into certain conditions of life, but how they value, interpret, and respond to those conditions is a matter of personal choice. For example, you may be born a male or a female, rich or poor, during peace, war, famine, or bountiful times. You may have been abused as a child, or you may have been raised under loving conditions. No matter what conditions you find yourself in or what experiences you have had, it is you who gives those conditions or experiences whatever meaning they have for you. It is you who is in charge of your life; therefore, you alone are responsible for the type of person you become. The theories of Kelly (Chapter 13), Rogers (Chapter 14), Maslow (Chapter 15), and May (Chapter 16) emphasize existential–humanistic considerations.

Unconscious Mechanisms

In many important respects, theories that emphasize unconscious mechanisms are the opposite of existential–humanistic theories. The primary concern of these so-called depth theories is to discover the underlying causes of behavior. According to this viewpoint, because the ultimate causes of behavior are unconscious and typically have their origins in childhood, the search for them is extremely complicated. Complex tools are needed in the search, tools such as dream and symbol analysis, free association, hypnosis, and the analysis of lapses of memory. According to this viewpoint, because what characterizes the unconscious mind can manifest itself in consciousness in any number of ways, one cannot really understand much about a person by studying his or her conscious experience. A personality theorist embracing this perspective does not ask a person why he or she acts in a particular way because the real causes of the behavior are typically not known to that person. To understand personality, one must somehow get beneath the arbitrary manifestations of the unconscious mind to the unconscious mind itself. In other words, one must get beneath a person's mask. The theories of Freud (Chapter 2) , Jung (Chapter 3), and Horney (Chapter 5) emphasize unconscious mechanisms in their analysis of personality.

Cognitive Processes

Currently there is considerable interest in cognitive processes within the realm of personality theory. Such processes determine how information from the environment is perceived, retained, transformed, and acted on by a person. Those theories stressing cognitive processes are typically interested in self-regulated behavior and focus on the importance of self-reward or self-punishment, which comes from goal attainment or nonattainment, rather than on rewards or punishments that come from sources outside the person. Cognitively oriented theories also tend to emphasize the importance of present experience and future goals in determining behavior and deemphasize the importance of the past. Theories emphasizing cognitive processes include those of Bandura and Mischel (Chapter 11) and Kelly (Chapter 13).

Personality as a Composite of Factors

Because almost every theory of personality contains elements of all of the explanations just reviewed, perhaps it is safe to say that personality is a function of all of them. The elements emphasized depend on which theory of personality one considers. Assuming that, the situation can be summarized as follows:

Genetics
Traits
Culture-society
Learning   Personality
Personal choice
Unconscious mechanisms
Cognitive processes

Questions Confronting
the Personality Theorist

Personality theorists are in the unique position in psychology of studying the entire person. Most other psychologists are concerned with only one aspect of humans such as child development, old age, perception, intelligence, learning, motivation, memory, or pathology. It is only the personality theorist who tries to present a complete picture of the human being.

The task is monumental and is related not only to developments in other aspects of psychology but to developments in other disciplines as well (e.g., medicine, neurophysiology, biology, sociology, anthropology, philosophy, and computer science). The personality theorists attempt to synthesize the best information from diverse portions of psychology and other disciplines into a coherent, holistic configuration. As personality theorists have attempted this synthesis through the years, they have addressed several questions related to human nature and individual differences. These are questions for which diverse answers exist; no matter what the answer, however, each personality theory addresses them directly or indirectly. We have already discussed the nativism–empiricism controversy that reflects one such question. Other important questions addressed by personality theorists follow.

What Is the Relative Importance of the Past, the Present, and the Future?

One question here is how childhood experiences are related to adult personality characteristics. A related question is: Are there critical irreversible stages of personality development? Freud, for example, said that personality was essentially fully developed by the end of the fifth year of life. Other theorists stress the importance of future goals for human behavior. Goal-directed or future-oriented behavior is also called **teleological behavior,** and it plays a prominent role in the theories of Jung (Chapter 3), Allport (Chapter 7), and Bandura and Mischel (Chapter 11). Both the learning theorists—for example, Skinner (Chapter 9)—and the existential–humanists—for example, May (Chapter 16)—tend to stress the importance of the present in their explanations of personality.

What Motivates Human Behavior?

Almost all theorists postulate a "master" motive for human behavior. That is, they specify what they believe is the major driving force behind most human behavior. Freud (Chapter 2), Skinner (Chapter 9), and Dollard and Miller (Chapter 10) postulate **hedonism,** or the tendency to seek pleasure and avoid pain. For Jung (Chapter 3), Horney (Chapter 5), Maslow (Chapter 15), and Rogers (Chapter 14) the master motive is **self-actualization,** or the impulse to realize one's full potential. For Adler (Chapter 4) it is striving for superiority. May (Chapter 16) and Kelly (Chapter 13) propose a search for meaning and the reduction of uncertainty. Buss (Chapter 12) postulates the predisposition to express evolved psychological mechanisms. For Bandura and Mischel (Chapter 11) it is the need to develop cognitive processes that are effective in dealing with the world.

How Important Is the Concept of Self?

Those theories that view human behavior as smooth running, consistent, and well organized need somehow to account for these characteristics of behavior. Several theories postulate the **self** as the organizing agent of personality. Also, it is often the self that is postulated as the mechanism providing individual consistency over time and across situations. The theories of Horney (Chapter 5), Allport (Chapter 7), and Rogers (Chapter 14) rely heavily on the concept of self. Other theorists claim that employing the concept of self simply switches all of the questions we have about the person to questions about the self. In other words, the self is viewed as a homunculus (i.e., a little person) inside the person who causes the person's actions. According to the opponents of the self concept, exactly how the self causes a person's actions remains a mystery. The concept of ego is often used in the same way as the concept of self and is criticized for the same reason. Skinner (Chapter 9) was a theorist who was highly critical of self theories.

How Important Are Unconscious Mechanisms?

The depth theories, such as those of Freud and Jung, focus on the unconscious mind. Theories that emphasize unconscious mechanisms confront questions such as, What is the relationship between the conscious and unconscious minds? How can the unconscious be investigated? Can persons ever become aware of their own unconscious motives and, if so, how?

Unconscious mechanisms are also important to many theorists stressing sociocultural determinants of personality (e.g., Adler, Horney, and Erikson) and to the evolutionary psychologists (e.g., Buss). Conversely, trait theorists (such as Allport, Cattell, and Eysenck), learning theorists (such as Skinner, Dollard and Miller, and Bandura and Mischel), and existential–humanistic theorists (such as Kelly, Rogers, Maslow, and May) either deny or minimize the importance of unconscious determinants of personality.

Is Human Behavior Freely Chosen or Is It Determined?

If all the influences acting on a person at any given time were known, would it be possible to predict that person's behavior with complete accuracy? If your answer is yes, you are a determinist. If your answer is no, you probably believe in free will. Notice this question assumes we could know all the factors influencing a person's behavior, and that is impossible. For example, imagine it is your task to determine what caused a person to commit a burglary. The possible causes would be numerous indeed and would include biological, social, and personal factors. More likely the cause of this, or any behavior, would be a combination of these and other factors. For this reason, even strict determinists realize their predictions about behavior must be probabilistic. Most personality theorists are determinists but, as we have seen, they stress different determinants of behavior.

The only theorists who reject the doctrine of **determinism** are the existential–humanists who believe that human behavior is freely chosen. For them, we are masters of our destiny. We are not necessarily the victims of our biography, culture, genes, traits, patterns of reward and punishment, or any other factors.

What Can Be Learned by Asking People about Themselves?

Examining the contents of one's mind is called **introspection.** This question concerns the extent to which introspective reports can be trusted. Answers to this question run the gamut, ranging from existentialists, who claim that introspection is the most valuable tool available for studying personality, to some learning theorists who claim that introspection is not only invalid but unnecessary. In between the two extremes are the theories of Freud and Jung, according to which introspective reports are useful only if they are interpreted by a trained analyst.

Uniqueness versus Commonality

We saw earlier that each person is unique because no cluster of genes or environmental experiences is the same for any two persons. It is also true that all human beings have a great deal in common. The fact that we share similar brains and sensory apparatuses and a culture with other humans means we respond as others do to many situations. To a large extent, what we find aesthetically pleasing, what makes us laugh or cry, and our beliefs concerning the supernatural are culturally determined. Thus it is possible to emphasize either the fact that each human being is unique, or the fact that each human has much in common with other humans. Both emphases are found in personality theories. The study of a single individual is called **idiographic** (id–ee–o–graf–ik) **research,** and the study of groups of individuals is called **nomothetic** (no–mo–thet–ik) **research.** Theorists such as Allport (Chapter 7), Skinner (Chapter 9), and Kelly (Chapter 13) use the idiographic approach because they emphasize the uniqueness of each individual. Theorists such as Cattell and Eysenck (Chapter 8) emphasize the nomothetic approach because they stress traits that many individuals have in common.

Are People Controlled Internally or Externally?

Where is the locus of control for human behavior? Some theorists stress internal mechanisms such as traits and self-regulatory systems, for example, Allport (Chapter 7), Cattell and Eysenck (Chapter 8), Horney (Chapter 5), Rogers (Chapter 14), and Maslow (Chapter 15); others stress external factors such as environmental stimuli and patterns of reward, for example, Skinner (Chapter 9) and Dollard and Miller (Chapter 10); still others emphasize the importance of both internal and external controls, for example, Bandura and Mischel (Chapter 11). Variables controlling a person's behavior internally are called **person variables;** those controlling externally are called **situation variables.** The determination of the relative importance of person and situation variables for human behavior is one of the primary concerns of current personality theorists. The question concerning internal versus external control is often posed in terms of subjective versus objective reality. A person variable would include a person's subjective awareness (consciousness) and the term situation variable is just another way of referring to the objective environmental circumstances a person experiences.

How Are the Mind and Body Related?

How can something purely mental such as the mind, thoughts, or consciousness influence something purely physical such as the brain, the body, or behavior, and vice versa? This classic philosophical question is still very much alive. One proposed answer is that no problem really exists because no mind exists; what we refer to as mental states are nothing more than subtle bodily responses. This position is called **physical monism** (materialism). Another answer is that mental events are merely the by-products of bodily responses and, therefore, can be, and should be, ignored in the analysis of human behavior. This position is called **epiphenomenalism.** Another proposed solution claims that an external event causes both bodily and mental events at the same time, but the two types of events are independent of each other. This position is called **parallelism.** Finally, some maintain that the mind influences the body and that the body influences the mind (such as when Freud maintains that pathogenic ideas can cause bodily ailments). This position is called

interactionism. We will see that virtually all positions on the mind–body question are represented among the various personality theorists.

What Is the Nature of Human Nature?

How a personality theorist answers this question determines the major thrust of his or her theory. Some answers include the following: The *empirical theory* states that people become what they experience, and the *rational theory* states that human behavior is, or can be, under the control of thoughtful, logical, rational thought processes. The *animalistic theory* states that humans possess the same impulses and instincts as other animals, particularly other primates. The *evolutionary psychological theory* claims that humans inherit behavioral tendencies from our evolutionary past but that these tendencies can be modified by rational thought or cultural influence. The *existential theory* states that the most important point about humans is our ability to choose courses of action and to assign meaning to the events in our lives. The *humanistic theory* claims humans are born basically good; if we engage in undesirable behavior it is because cultural, societal, or familial conditions have forced us to do so. The *mechanistic theory* states that humans are automatons who respond automatically to environmental events. The automatic response may be a simple response to an environmental stimulus or a response given after information from the environment has been processed through several information-processing systems. In either case the response is automatic and machinelike. In the latter case, the mechanistic theory of human nature likens humans to computers. Again, virtually all assumptions about human nature are found among the various theories of personality.

How Consistent Is Human Behavior?

Those theorists who stress traits, habits, genetics, or unconscious mechanisms in their explanations of personality assume a person's behavior should be consistent in similar situations and over time. For example, it is assumed a person who possesses the trait of honesty would be honest in most situations in which honesty or dishonesty is possible. Likewise, an aggressive person would be aggressive in a wide variety of situations. Traditionally most personality theorists assumed a person's behavior is consistent, and they saw their task as accounting for that consistency. More recently, however, it has been discovered that human behavior may not be so consistent. For example, after a careful review of studies investigating the consistency of behavior across time and across similar situations, Mischel (1968) concluded that human behavior is too inconsistent to be explained in terms of such things as traits. Evidence suggests that some persons are consistent in some ways but not in others, and these areas of consistency vary from person to person. The questions that personality theorists must now confront are, How consistent is human behavior? What constitutes consistency? What accounts for individual differences in consistency? What variables account for consistency and inconsistency? Efforts to answer these questions usually involve a discussion of the relative importance of person (internal) versus situation (external) variables and the interaction between them. We will address the question of behavioral consistency in Chapter 11.

How Do We Find the Answers?

Epistemology

Epistemology is the study of knowledge. It attempts to answer questions such as, What does it mean to know? What are the limits of knowledge? What are the origins of knowledge? Because science, at least in part, is a method of gaining knowledge, it can be considered an epistemological pursuit.

Science

Science combines two ancient philosophical positions on the origins of knowledge. One of these positions, called **rationalism,** contends that one gains knowledge by exercising the mind, in other words, by thinking, reasoning, and using logic. According to the rationalist, information must be sorted out by the mind before reasonable conclusions can be drawn. The other philosophical position, called **empiricism,** contends that sensory experience is the basis of all knowledge. In its extreme form, empiricism states that we know only what we experience. Thus the rationalist emphasizes mental operations whereas the empiricist equates knowledge with experience. Science combined the two positions, thereby creating an extremely powerful epistemological tool.

Scientific Theory

In the realm of science, empiricism and rationalism meet in **scientific theory.** A scientific theory begins with empirical observations. These observations may have been recorded by researchers in the past or they might be made by contemporary scientists concerned with a specific problem or phenomenon. Next, through reason, logic, and sometimes insight, one looks for a pattern or theme that organizes or explains the observations. In turn, the organizational scheme that one uses to make sense of the empirical observations should point to other phenomena that can be explained similarly. Thus, in science, observations are made (empiricism) and then they are organized in some meaningful way (rationalism). Next, the scientist must verify if the groupings are, in fact, meaningful. If they are, they should indicate where to look for additional information. Stanovich (2004) summarizes the dynamic role of scientific theory as follows:

> A theory in science is an interrelated set of concepts that is used to explain a body of data and to make predictions about the results of future experiments. Hypotheses are specific predictions that are derived from theories (which are more general and comprehensive). Currently viable theories are those that have had many of their hypotheses confirmed. The theoretical structures of such theories are thus consistent with a large number of observations. However, when a data base begins to contradict the hypotheses derived from a theory, scientists begin trying to construct a new theory that will provide a better interpretation of the data. Thus, the theories that are under scientific discussion are those that have been verified to some extent and that do not make many predictions that are contradicted by the available data. They are not mere guesses or hunches. (pp. 20–21)

The process just described is represented in the following diagram:

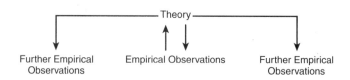

Note that we do not say that evidence "proves" or "disproves" a scientific theory. Evidence that confirms a scientific hypothesis is said to "support" the theory while contradictory evidence either " fails to support" or "refutes" the theory. Theories that have been tested and confirmed many times without significant refutation may attain high status among scientists, but they are never proven in the sense that we can prove a mathematical theorem.

We can see that a scientific theory comes into existence to explain several observations (its **synthesizing function**), and when it exists, it must be able to suggest other places where the researcher may seek additional information. A theory's ability to generate new research is called its **heuristic function.**

As an example of the foregoing, imagine that young Freud is talking with a friend when the friend realizes he has missed his dental appointment. This incident registers in Freud's sensitive mind. Later, Freud observes his friend's other lapses of memory and notes they all have something in common: They serve to protect the individual from painful or anxiety-related experiences. Freud speculates that many disturbing thoughts are repressed; that is, they are held in the unconscious mind, thereby preventing the discomfort that would be caused by their conscious recognition. The theoretical notion of the repression of disturbing thoughts serves two purposes: It helps to make sense out of previously disjointed observations, and it generates hypotheses about the processes and mechanisms of repression. For example, if disturbing thoughts are repressed, the unconscious mind will be a veritable storehouse of such thoughts, which could be released under the appropriate circumstances. In other words, if one could tap the contents of the unconscious mind with such devices as hypnotism, dream analysis, or free association, one should find an abundance of repressed memories.

Synthetic Function versus Heuristic Function

Which role of a scientific theory is more important? Is a theory that provides an imaginative and elaborate synthesis of empirical observations but generates little research preferred to one that is simple, even dull, but generates abundant research? Hall and Lindzey (1978) answer these questions in the following way:

> However vague and poorly developed the theory, and however inadequate its syntax and empirical definitions, if it can be shown to have had a generative effect upon significant areas of research we would have to conclude that it passes the crucial test. Thus, the payoff question that overrides, and actually makes trivial, all

questions of formal adequacy is the matter of how much important research the theory has produced. (p. 20)

Principle of Verification

The feature of scientific theories that most differentiates them from nonscientific explanations, including conjectures that the layperson often refers to when he or she uses the term "theory," is the **principle of verification.** As Stanovich (2004) indicates in the previous passage, informal "hunches," opinions, and passionate beliefs held by the layperson do not have the same status as scientific theories because they have not been and sometimes cannot be objectively verified. All scientific explanations must be capable of being tested by objective, empirical methods, for example, by experimentation. Furthermore, this test must be available to any interested person. That is, scientific propositions must be capable of *public* verification. No matter how interesting a theory may be, without the potential for public empirical validation it is not a scientific theory. Marx and Goodson (1976) make this point, "If there is no way of testing a theory it is scientifically worthless, no matter how plausible, imaginative, or innovative it may be" (p. 249).

Optimally, scientific theories, in addition to their ability to synthesize (explain) observations, should be internally consistent, precise, testable, parsimonious, and heuristic. Few, if any, personality theories meet all these criteria, but this does not necessarily render such theories useless. Even personality theories containing terms and propositions too general to verify directly often generate research hypotheses that are capable of empirical verification. It is this ultimate concern with the empirical verification of its terms and propositions that differentiates the efforts of the personality theorists from those of pseudoscientists.

Science and Personality Theory

Scientific theories differ in their rigor. In such sciences as physics or chemistry, theories are highly developed. The terms used in them are precisely defined, and a high correspondence exists among the words, signs, and symbols in the theory and the empirical events it purports to explain. The use of complex mathematics is common in such theories. In psychology, theories exist in almost all stages of development. In areas such as psychophysics, cognition, and learning, psychology has theories that rival those in the physical sciences in terms of rigor. Many theories in psychology are in their infant stages, however, containing terms that are not precisely defined. Also, the relationship between their terms and empirical events is not a tight one. Most personality theories are in the latter category. In fact, some theories of personality make no claim to being scientific in the sense that they can be tested under highly controlled conditions. Such theories claim that their verification comes either from everyday experience or from clinical practice. Stanovich (2004) cautions, however, that while case studies and anecdotes may be important in early stages of theory development, "It is . . . wrong to cite a testimonial or a case study as support for a *particular* theory . . ." (p. 54). This is because, unlike controlled experimentation, case studies and anecdotes do not allow researchers to rule out alternative theories or explanations for phenomena under scrutiny.

To say that most personality theories lack scientific rigor is not the same thing as concluding that they are not useful. Each personality theory provides us with a different viewpoint. In the final analysis, we may learn more about some topic by viewing it from a variety of angles than we would by burrowing in deeply from one angle.

Kuhn's View of Science

Thomas Kuhn (1922–1996) in his influential book, *The Structure of Scientific Revolutions* (1996), indicated that most scientists accept a "viewpoint" concerning their subject matter as they carry out their research. This viewpoint guides their research activities and to a large extent determines what is studied and how it is studied. Kuhn called a viewpoint shared by many scientists a **paradigm.** For example, years ago most physicists accepted a Newtonian viewpoint regarding their work but now most follow an Einsteinian viewpoint. The dominant paradigm in physics shifted from Newton's theory to Einstein's theory.

In psychology, no one paradigm ever guided all psychological research; rather, several paradigms have always existed simultaneously. In addition, the term *paradigm,* as it applies to psychology, corresponds to groups of interrelated theories commonly called a "school of thought" or an "ism" instead of to a single theory, as is the case in physics. In either case, a paradigm can be considered a way of looking at and investigating a certain subject. Therefore, different scientists exploring the same subject matter go about their work differently, depending on which paradigm guides their research activities.

The most important point regarding paradigms is that it is not necessary to consider one correct and the others incorrect; they all simply generate different research methodologies.

How do these ideas relate to personality theory? Personality is a complex topic, and many approaches to its study exist. In fact, these approaches are paradigms, and everything that has been said applies to them. In the remainder of this text, we sample paradigms that guide research in the area of personality. These six paradigms are listed along with the theorists who have been chosen to represent them.

Psychoanalytic Paradigm
Sigmund Freud
Carl Jung

Sociocultural Paradigm
Alfred Adler
Karen Horney
Erik Erikson

Trait Paradigm
Gordon Allport
Raymond B. Cattell and Hans J. Eysenck

Learning Paradigm
B. F. Skinner
John Dollard and Neal Miller
Albert Bandura and Walter Mischel

Evolutionary Paradigm
David M. Buss

Existential–Humanistic Paradigm
George Kelly
Carl Rogers
Abraham Maslow
Rollo May

Note that each paradigm is named for its central theme. The psychoanalytic paradigm focuses on the analysis of the psyche, and the sociocultural paradigm focuses on the study of societal-cultural factors influencing personality. The trait paradigm emphasizes the importance of the various traits that persons possess, and the learning paradigm focuses on the importance of learning for personality development. The evolutionary paradigm emphasizes the inherited tendency to engage in certain social behaviors, and the existential–humanistic paradigm focuses on free choice and personal responsibility.

Again, do not attempt to find the paradigm that is most correct. All paradigms provide useful information about personality; the information generated by one paradigm is just different from that generated by others. To attempt to build a house with only one tool such as a hammer, a saw, or a screwdriver would be ineffective. Likewise, attempting to understand personality using only one theoretical orientation would leave huge gaps in one's understanding. This text offers a variety of theories that collectively may provide a far greater understanding of personality than any one of them taken alone could do.

Popper's View of Science

We have just reviewed Kuhn's philosophy of science with his emphasis on the concept of paradigm. It is also important to examine Karl Popper's philosophy of science because it has special relevance to personality theory. According to Popper (1902–1994), if a theory can account for everything that could possibly happen, the theory cannot be considered scientific. Such a theory explains everything and, therefore, it explains nothing. To be scientific, a theory must make **risky predictions.** That is, it must make predictions that have a chance of being incorrect. If a theory does generate predictions (hypotheses) that are not confirmed, the theory is considered invalid and should be revised or abandoned. Thus, according to Popper's **principle of falsifiability** (also called the principle of refutability), all scientific theories must be falsifiable. In sympathy with Popper, Dawes (2001) argues that there should be some evidence that would lead us to doubt or reject the theory. If all evidence is simply interpreted as supporting it, then it is termed *irrefutable,* which is a hallmark of pseudoscience, not of science. The implications that can be tested and potentially refuted may not follow immediately from a statement of the basic ideas of the theory, but at some point in the inferential chain that results from these ideas, there must be some link that can be tested empirically, where the implications need not be found true. (p.96, emphasis added)

History has been plagued by pseudoscientific explanations of personality. At one time or another all of the following have had wide popular appeal: astrology, numerology, palmistry, phrenology, physiognomy, and graphology. Although popular, all of these explanations of personality violate the principles of verification and falsifiability. That is, their claims are so general and nebulous that no test is available to clearly demonstrate their truth or falsity. Astrology, for example, cannot be considered scientific because each horoscope is so general as to apply to almost anyone. If astrology made highly specific, potentially false predictions about the major events in the lives of individuals, then the predictions could be objectively evaluated, but it does not do so.

Self-Correction in Science

Scientific theories risk refutation, and it is this that allows for progress in science. An irrefutable theory prevents researchers from eliminating explanations that are incorrect and discovering more accurate ones. Marx and Goodson (1976) describe the implications of Popper's principle of falsifiability:

In real scientific life theories typically contribute not by being right but *by being wrong.* In other words, scientific advance in theory as well as experiment tends to be built upon the successive correction of many errors, both small and large. Thus the popular notion that a theory must be right to be useful is incorrect. (p. 249)

Popper's principle of falsification is especially important in the realm of personality theory. Many theories of personality are extremely difficult, if not impossible, to falsify. Hergenhahn and Olson (2005) give an example:

Freud's theory . . . makes no risky predictions. Everything that a person does can be "explained" by Freud's theory. If, for example, Freud's theory predicts that on the basis of early experience a man should hate women but is found to love them, the Freudian can say that he is displaying a "reaction formation." That is, he really does hate women on the unconscious level, and he is simply going overboard in the opposite direction to reduce the anxiety that his recognition of his true hatred of women would cause. Astrology suffers the same fate since there is no conceivable observation that could be made that would refute its claims. Contrary to common belief, if every conceivable observation agrees with a theory, the theory is weak, not strong. (p. 27)

Further examples of the problem Freud's theory has with the principle of falsification will be presented in the next chapter.

Obviously, a theory's ability to generate *predictions* (hypotheses) is vitally important in Popper's philosophy of science; without predictions falsification would not be possible. Unfortunately, in the realm of personality theory the concern is often with *post*diction rather than prediction. Hall and Lindzey (1978) say, "Most personality theorists have been oriented toward after-the-fact explanations rather than toward the generation of new predictions concerning behavior" (p.16).

Many theories of personality cannot pass the test of falsifiability and, therefore, according to Popper, are not scientific. Remember, however, that personality is enormously complex and has many subjective components that cannot be observed or measured directly. Also, the systematic, objective study of personality is relatively new compared to the subject matters of the older, more established sciences. Finally, to say that a theory is not scientific is not to say that it is useless. Popper (1963) made the following observation:

Historically speaking all—or nearly all—scientific theories originate from myths, and . . . a myth may contain important anticipations of scientific theories. . . . I thus [believe] that if a theory is found to be non-scientific, or "metaphysical" . . . it is not thereby found to be unimportant, or insignificant, or "meaningless," or "nonsensical." (p. 38)

We believe that although the theories that follow vary in terms of their scientific rigor, all of them contribute to our understanding of personality; and, as Popper suggested, even those that are now seen as nonscientific or even mythical may someday lead to more rigorous scientific explanations.

Summary

The definition of personality varies with the assumptions and beliefs of those studying it. Thus, there are at least as many definitions of personality as there are theories of personality. The personality theorist attempts to describe what all humans have in common (human nature), what some have in common, and the uniqueness of each individual (individual differences). The authors of the present text assume that a comprehensive explanation of personality would specify the relative importance of genetics, traits, sociocultural determinants, learning, existential–humanistic considerations, unconscious mechanisms, and cognitive processes. Each personality theorist must implicitly or explicitly address a number of basic questions, such as: What is the relative importance of the past, present, and future? What motivates human behavior? How important is the concept of self? How important are unconscious mechanisms? Is human behavior freely chosen or is it determined? What can be learned by asking people about themselves? What should be emphasized, human uniqueness or commonality? Are people controlled internally or externally? How are the mind and body related? What is the nature of human nature? How consistent is human behavior?

The most objective way to answer questions such as those above is to employ scientific method. Scientific theory combines empiricism and rationalism by insisting that first empirical observations be made of the phenomena of interest, and then precise explanations are formulated that attempt to explain the observations. In addition to explaining observations, a good scientific theory will generate additional research (its heuristic function). In the realm of science, all terms and propositions must be capable of public, empirical verification. The principle of verification is what differentiates scientific from pseudoscientific explanations.

Kuhn observed that most scientists embrace a general paradigm that determines their research topics and methodologies. The physical sciences are usually dominated by a single paradigm but in psychology several paradigms have always existed simultaneously. The paradigms that have guided research on personality include the psychoanalytic, sociocultural, trait, learning, sociobiological, and existential–humanistic. Popper's philosophy of science features the principle of falsifiability. According to this principle, in order for a theory to be considered scientific, it must generate predictions that run a real risk of being disconfirmed. If the predictions generated by a theory are so general that most any outcome confirms them, the theory, according to Popper, is not scientific. Many theories of personality fail Popper's test of falsifiability and therefore, according to his definition, are not scientific. However, Popper observed that nonscientific theories often precede scientific theories and, therefore, nonscientific theories can be useful.

Experiential Exercises

1. Place the words "I am" at the top of a blank sheet of paper and proceed to list the characteristics that are true about you at the moment. For example, I am a woman, a Christian, a psychology major, a mother, a waitress. Briefly describe the culturally prescribed role associated with each item on your list. Do you believe a person who either refuses to play a socially prescribed role, or is incapable of doing so, will experience social pressure of some type? Explain.

2. Formulate your own theory of personality. Indicate what your theory stresses. For example, what assumption about human nature does it make? Does it stress the im-

portance of the past, present, or future? Unconscious mechanisms? Would you place it within the existential–humanistic paradigm? If not, which one? Is your theory falsifiable? Save your theory and compare it to the one you will be asked to formulate at the end of this book.

3. How does the consistency–inconsistency controversy apply to your personality? Are there some aspects of your personality that you consider consistent over time and across situations and some you consider inconsistent? Give examples of each. Attempt to account for both the consistent and inconsistent aspects of your personality.

Discussion Questions

1. Give an example of how each of the following might influence a person's personality: genetics, traits, sociocultural determinants, learning, existential–humanistic considerations, unconscious mechanisms, and cognitive processes.
2. What is determinism? Give examples of the types of determinism represented among the personality theories. What is the alternative to believing that human behavior is determined?
3. Describe Popper's principle of falsifiability and explain why, in terms of this principle, astrology and Freud's theory of personality cannot be considered scientific.

Glossary

Determinism. Belief that all behavior is caused and is therefore not free.

Empiricism. Contention that an attribute is determined by experience rather than by genetics. Within epistemology, it is the belief that all knowledge is derived from sensory experience.

Environmentalism. Belief that the determinants of behavior are found in the environment instead of in the person.

Epiphenomenalism. Contention that mental events are the by-products of bodily events. Bodily events cause mental events but mental events cannot cause bodily events. Mental events, therefore, can be ignored in the analysis of human behavior.

Epistemology. Study of the nature of human knowledge.

Hedonism. Contention that the major motive in life is to seek pleasure and avoid pain.

Heuristic function of a theory. Theory's ability to generate new information.

Human nature. Those qualities that characterize all humans. One task of the personality theorist is to specify the nature of human nature.

Idiographic research. Intense study of a single person.

Individual differences. Important ways in which humans differ from one another. One of the tasks of the personality theorist is to describe and explain individual differences.

Interactionism. Contention that the mind influences the body and the body influences the mind. That is, the mind and the body are causally related.

Introspection. Self-examination. Directing one's thoughts inward to discover the truth about one's self.

Mind–body problem. Problem of specifying how something mental (cognitive) can influence something physical, such as the body and vice versa.

Nativism. Contention that an attribute is determined by genetics rather than by experience.

Nativism–empiricism controversy (also called the nature–nurture controversy). Argument concerning the extent to which an attribute, such as intelligence, is influenced by inheritance as opposed to experience. Nomothetic research. Study of groups of individuals.

Paradigm. Term used by Kuhn to describe a theoretical viewpoint shared by many researchers.

Parallelism. Contention that an environmental event causes both mental and bodily reactions at the same time. According to this proposed answer to the mind–body question, bodily and mental phenomena run parallel to each other and are therefore not causally related.

Person variables. Variables contained within persons thought to be responsible for their behavior. Traits, habits, memories, information-processing mechanisms, and repressed early experiences exemplify person variables.

Persona. Latin word meaning mask.

Physical monism (also called materialism). Contention that no mind–body problem exists because no mind exists. No mental events occur, only physical events.

Principle of falsifiability (also called principle of refutability). Popper's contention that a scientific theory must make risky predictions; that is, it must make predictions that could conceivably be false and, if so, would refute the theory.

Principle of verification. The stipulation that scientific propositions must be capable of objective, empirical testing that is available to any interested person.

Rationalism. Belief that knowledge can be gained only by exercising the mind, for example, by thinking, deducing, or inferring.

Risky predictions. Predictions that run the risk of being incorrect. According to Popper, for a theory to be considered scientific it must make risky predictions.

Science. Epistemological pursuit that combines the philosophical schools of empiricism and rationalism.

Scientific theory. Combination of the philosophical schools of rationalism and empiricism, with two major functions: (1) to synthesize (explain) many observations, and (2) to generate new information.

Self. Concept employed by several personality theorists to account for the facts that human behavior is smooth running, consistent, and well organized. The concept of self has also been used to explain why we are aware of ourselves as individuals.

Self-actualization. Situation that exists when a person is acting in accordance with his or her full potential.

Situation variables. Those variables found in the environment thought to be responsible for behavior.

Synthesizing function of a theory. A theory's ability to organize and explain several otherwise disjointed observations.

Teleological behavior. Purposive behavior.

SIGMUND FREUD

CHAPTER OUTLINE

Freud (1966b, pp. 284–285) observed that humans have had three major blows to their self-esteem. The first came from Copernicus, who demonstrated the earth was not the center of the universe, as humans had so egotistically believed. In fact, Copernicus demonstrated the earth was not even the center of our solar system, a fact that was not easily digested.

The second blow came from the work of Charles Darwin, who demonstrated humans were not the product of "special creation," but were descended from and continuous with the so-called lower animals.

As the dust caused by Darwin's revelations was settling, our self-esteem was salvaged by the belief that humans were rational animals. Although we descended from lower animals, somewhere in the process of evolution we became qualitatively different from them by becoming dependent on our intellect. Animals were driven by instinct; only human behavior was rationally determined.

It was Freud who dealt the third blow to human self-esteem by demonstrating that human behavior is primarily instinctive and motivated mainly by unconscious processes. In other words, according to Freud, most humans are anything but rational animals. Whether we agree with Freud's theory or not, Freudian concepts have completely revised the way we view human nature.

Biographical Sketch

Sigmund Freud was born on May 6, 1856, in Freiberg, Austria (now Pribor, Czech Republic). As we see shortly, however, it is possible that Freud was born on March 6 instead of May 6. When Freud was 4 years old, he and his family moved to Vienna, where he continued to live for nearly 80 years. His father, Jakob, was a not-too-successful wool merchant and a strict authoritarian father. At the time of Freud's birth, his father was 40 years old, and his mother, who was his father's third wife, was a youthful 20. Freud was the first of eight children born to his mother, Amalie Nathansohn Freud, in the course of 10 years. One son, however, died at the age of 7 months when Sigmund was 2 years old. It is interesting to note that Amalie was Jakob Freud's third wife, not his second as has been commonly believed. Examination of the town records of Freiberg in 1968 revealed that Jakob's second wife was a woman named Rebecca, about whom practically nothing is known. Years earlier it was also discovered by examining the birth register of Freiberg that Sigmund Freud's official birthday was March 6, 1856, not May 6 as is commonly reported. Ernest Jones, Freud's official biographer, suggests that the discrepancy reflects only a clerical error, but others see it as more significant. For example, Balmary (1979) believes that Freud's parents reported the birthdate of May 6 to conceal the fact that Freud's mother (Amalie) was pregnant with Sigmund when she married Jakob. In her book, *Psychoanalyzing Psychoanalysis: Freud and the Hidden Fault of the Father* (1979), Balmary speculated that both "family secrets" (the fact that Amalie was Jakob's third, not his second wife, and that Freud's mother was pregnant when she married) had a significant influence on Freud and his subsequent theorizing. Jakob had two sons by his first wife (Sally Kanner) and was a grandfather when Sigmund was born. It is interesting to note that Jakob Freud's sons by his first marriage were about the same age as Sigmund's mother. In fact, one of Freud's first playmates was the son of his half-brother. This playmate, Freud's nephew, was a year older than Freud. Sigmund and his mother had a strong relationship, the effects of which Freud felt throughout his life. In fact, Freud attributed much of his success to his mother's faith in him. Freud's mother died on September 12, 1930, at the age of 95, only 9 years before her son's own death.

Freud was an outstanding student and graduated at the head of his high school class. At home, his brothers and sisters were not allowed to study musical instruments because doing so disturbed his studies. He entered medical school at the University of Vienna when he was 17 years old, but it took him almost 8 years to finish a 4-year medical program, mainly because he pursued many interests outside of medicine. Freud chose medical school because medicine was one of the few careers open to a Jew in Austria at that time. Although not interested in becoming a physician, he saw the study of medicine as a vehicle for engaging in scientific research.

Freud hoped to become a professor of neurology and published several highly regarded articles on the topic. He soon discovered, however, that advancement within the academic ranks would be extremely slow for a Jew, and this realization, along with the fact that he needed money, prompted him to enter private practice as a clinical neurologist on April 25, 1886. About 5 months later, on September 13, 1886, he was finally able to marry Martha Bernays, to whom he had been engaged since 1882. During their 5-year engagement, Freud wrote more than 400 letters to his fiancée.

Sigmund Freud, age 16, with his mother, Amalie Nathansohn Freud, in 1872.

They remained married until Freud's death. They had six children, three daughters and three sons. One daughter, Anna, became a famous child analyst in London.

The Cocaine Incident

In 1884, Freud began experimenting with cocaine after hearing from a German army physician that the drug enhanced the endurance of soldiers. Taking the drug himself, Freud found it relieved depression and increased his ability to concentrate; furthermore, it appeared to have no negative side effects. Impressed with the drug, Freud took it freely himself and gave it to Martha, his sisters, his friends, and his colleagues. Eventually Freud published six articles on cocaine, recommending it as a stimulant, local anesthetic, cure for indigestion, and harmless substitute for morphine. One of Freud's associates, Carl Koller, learned from Freud that cocaine could be used as an anesthetic during eye operations, and Koller presented a paper describing an experiment in which it was successfully used as such. Koller's paper caused a sensation and brought him worldwide fame almost overnight. Freud deeply regretted just having missed receiving this professional recognition himself.

Although cocaine was of value in eye surgery, Freud's other beliefs concerning the "magical substance" were soon proven false. Freud treated one of his close friends with cocaine to terminate his addiction to morphine, and the friend became addicted to cocaine instead. Reports of cocaine addiction began to pour in from all over the world, and cocaine came under heavy attack from the medical community. Because Freud was closely associated with the harmful drug, his medical reputation suffered considerably. To a large extent, it was this cocaine episode that created the skepticism with which Freud's later ideas were met by his medical colleagues. Although Freud avoided addiction to cocaine, he did become addicted to nicotine. For most of his adult life he smoked an average of 20 cigars a day.

Early Influences on Freud's Theory

Freud's Visit with Charcot

In 1885, Freud received a small grant that allowed him to study with the famous French neurologist **Jean-Martin Charcot** (1825–1893) who was experimenting with hypnotism. At that time, Charcot was at the peak of his career and in French medicine was considered second in prominence to only Louis Pasteur. By endorsing the use of hypnotism, Charcot dramatically reversed the negative attitude toward the phenomenon held by members of the medical community since, in the 1770s, Franz Anton Mesmer (1734–1815) had claimed it resulted from the rearrangement of animal spirits within the body. After hypnotizing a patient, Charcot demonstrated that various types of paralyses could be created and removed artificially through the inducement of the hypnotist. Thus he demonstrated that physical symptoms could have a psychological origin as well as a physical or organic origin. Charcot was so im-

Jean-Martin Charcot demonstrating hypnotism.
(Culver Pictures, Inc.)

pressed by the mind's ability to create and remove physical symptoms that he wondered if his discovery could eventually explain faith healing (Sulloway, 1979, p. 30).

Charcot's observations had clear implications for the treatment of **hysteria.** Hysteria is a term used to describe a wide variety of symptoms such as paralysis, loss of sensation, and disturbances of sight and speech. Originally, it was assumed that hysteria was exclusively a female disorder (*hystera* is the Greek word for uterus). Because it was often impossible to find anything organically wrong with hysteric patients, the medical community tended to view them as malingerers, and the physicians who agreed to treat them were typically discredited. Charcot's research indicated that the physical symptoms of hysteric patients could be psychogenic, and therefore the disease must be taken seriously even if symptoms could not be explained in terms of organic dysfunction. Thus Charcot did much to make the treatment of hysteria respectable. Charcot also convincingly demonstrated that, contrary to what most physicians had believed, hysteria was not an exclusively female disorder. By showing the psychogenic nature of bodily symptoms, Charcot provided a new approach to studying hysteria, an ailment that had puzzled the medical community for centuries. Freud soon explored the implications of this approach. Freud was so impressed by Charcot that he named his first son, Jean-Martin, after him.

Freud's Visit with Bernheim

After Freud returned from his visit with Charcot, he attempted to use hypnotism in his private practice but was only partially successful. In an effort to improve his skills as a hypnotist, Freud returned to France in 1889. This time, however, he visited **Hippolyte Bernheim** (1840–1919) in Nancy, France. Like Charcot and his colleagues, members of the "Nancy School" were experimenting with hypnosis as a means of treating hysteria. Freud learned information from this visit that profoundly influenced both his later theorizing and his therapeutic method. Bernheim hypnotized persons, and while they were under hypnosis he had them perform various acts. While still under hypnosis, he instructed them not to remember what they had done under hypnosis when they awoke. This created **posthypnotic amnesia;** that is, the person was unable to recall what he or she had done while hypnotized. Bernheim demonstrated that the amnesia was not complete, however. He showed that if the hypnotist insisted strongly and convincingly the memory would return, it would do so. To facilitate this recall, Bernheim placed his hand on the forehead of the awake person as he insisted the events that occurred during the hypnotic session be remembered. Freud learned from Bernheim that persons can have memories they are not aware of; however, under pressure these memories can be retrieved.

A second important lesson that Freud learned from Bernheim involved **posthypnotic suggestion.** To exemplify this phenomenon, Bernheim hypnotized a woman and told her that after waking and a specified period of time had expired, she would walk over to the corner of the room, pick up the umbrella that was found there, and open it. After being aroused from the hypnotic trance and after the designated period of time had expired, she did exactly that. When questioned as to why she had opened the umbrella, the woman said she wanted to see if it belonged to her. Freud learned from this that behavior can be caused by ideas of which a person is totally unaware. Thus Freud learned from his visit with Bernheim that behavior can be caused by unconscious ideas, and that these ideas can be brought into consciousness under the right circumstances.

Freud got many of the ideas that were later to characterize psychoanalysis from Charcot and Bernheim; many others he got from Josef Breuer.

Josef Breuer and the Case of Anna O

Freud first met **Josef Breuer** (1842–1925) at the University of Vienna when both men were engaged in neurological research in the late 1870s. Breuer was 14 years older than Freud and, like Charcot, was a highly regarded physician and researcher. Breuer gave Freud advice, friendship, and loaned him money. Breuer's wife also became a good friend of Freud and his wife, and they named their first daughter, Mathilde, after her. Most important for the development of psychoanalysis, however, was Breuer's treatment of a young woman anonymously referred to as Fräulein Anna O.

Anna O. was 21 years old when Breuer began treating her in December 1880, and her treatment continued until June 1882. Anna O.'s symptoms included paralysis of various parts of her body, problems with vision, periodic deafness, a nervous cough, periodic aversion to nourishment and liquids, suicidal impulses, an occasional inability to speak in her native German language while retaining an ability to speak in English, and various hallucinations. Anna O.'s condition was diagnosed as hysteria.

Much to his amazement, Breuer found that if Anna O. traced a symptom to its original occurrence it disappeared either temporarily or permanently. Breuer found that Anna O. was able to discuss the origins of her various symptoms while she was either hypnotized or when she was very relaxed. Working several hours each day for more than a year, Breuer systematically removed each of Anna O.'s symptoms in this manner. Anna O. herself called this laborious procedure the "talking cure" or "chimney sweeping;" Breuer called it **catharsis.** Aristotle had originally used this term to describe the emotional release and feeling of purification that an audience experiences while viewing a drama. It turned out that most of Anna O.'s symptoms originated from a series of traumatic experiences she had as she was nursing her dying father.

Several important facts were learned from Breuer's treatment of Anna O. Perhaps most important was that her condition improved when she openly expressed her feelings. Breuer also observed that as treatment continued, Anna O. began transferring to him the feelings she had toward her father. This phenomenon, in which a patient responds to the analyst as if he or she were an important person in the patient's life, is called **transference.** Freud considered transference a vital part of effective psychoanalysis. Likewise, Breuer was becoming emotionally involved with Anna O. The phenomenon of an analyst forming an emotional attachment to a patient was later called **countertransference.** Because of the considerable amount of time Breuer was spending with Anna O. and the deep feelings they were developing toward each other, Breuer's marriage began to suffer; as a result, he decided to stop seeing his patient. Anna O. was so disturbed by this that she was thrust into hysterical (i.e., imaginary) childbirth. Ernest Jones (1953), Freud's official biographer, described what happened next:

> Though profoundly shocked, he [Breuer] managed to calm her down by hypnotizing her, and then fled the house in a cold sweat. The next day he and his wife left

for Venice to spend a second honeymoon, which resulted in the conception of a daughter. (p. 225)

As we will see throughout this chapter, recent scholarship has uncovered several discrepancies in the history of psychoanalysis as it has been presented by those involved. Jones's account of the events surrounding Breuer's termination of the treatment of Anna O. is an example. As entertaining as Jones's account may be, it has been found to be incorrect. In his biography of Breuer, Hirschmüller (1989) notes that Breuer did not end his treatment of Anna O. abruptly, but planned it carefully with her mother; there was no hysterical pregnancy and therefore no need to hypnotize Anna O. and leave in a "cold sweat;" the Breuers went to Gmunden, not Venice, on their "secondary honeymoon" and their daughter was born *before* they left; and finally, contrary to what Jones claimed, Breuer did not give up treating hysteria after his experience with Anna O.

There is another historical inaccuracy concerning the case of Anna O. In *Studies on Hysteria* (1955), which Breuer coauthored with Freud, Breuer concluded that his treatment of Anna O. was successful. It turns out, however, that this was not exactly true.

Jones (1953, p. 223) identified Anna O. as Bertha Pappenheim (1859–1936) and we review some of the details of her life next.

The Fate of Bertha Pappenheim

Through some clever detective work, Ellenberger (1972) was able to discover what happened to Bertha Pappenheim after Breuer terminated her treatment. Documents uncovered by Ellenberger indicate that she was admitted into a sanatorium in 1882, still suffering many of the same ailments described earlier by Breuer. While at the sanatorium, she was treated with substantial amounts of morphine, and the record shows that she continued to receive injections of morphine after her release from the sanatorium several months later. Little is known about the next few years of her life, but she eventually emerged as a social worker in the late 1880s. Her accomplishments thereafter were truly impressive: She was the director of an orphanage in Frankfurt for 12 years (1895–1907); she founded a league of Jewish women (1904); she founded a home for unwed mothers (1907); she traveled to the Near East, Poland, Russia, and Rumania to help orphaned children and to help solve the problems of prostitution and white slavery; she became a leader in the European feminist movement; and she became a playwright and an author of children's stories. In addition, she was an outspoken opponent of abortion.

Throughout her professional life, Bertha Pappenheim maintained a negative attitude toward psychoanalysis and never allowed any of the girls under her care to be psychoanalyzed. A hint of her feminism is seen in the following statement made by her in 1922 (quoted by Jones, 1953, p. 224): "If there is any justice in the next life women will make the laws there and men will bear the children." By the time she died in March 1936, she had become an almost legendary figure and tributes to her came from prominent persons throughout Europe. In 1954, the German government issued a stamp bearing her picture in her honor as part of a series of stamps paying tribute to "helpers of humanity." The relationship between Pappenheim's ultimate success and her early experiences, including her treatment by Breuer, is still being debated (see, e.g., Kimble, 2000; Rosenbaum & Muroff, 1984).

The Development of Free Association

Influenced by what he had observed during his visits with Charcot and Bernheim, Freud tried hypnosis in his practice but was not satisfied with the results. Freud eventually gave up hypnosis because he found that not all his patients could be hypnotized. One of his patients, Frau Emmy Von N., became furious with him over his constant interruptions while trying to hypnotize her. She expressed the desire simply to be allowed to speak her mind without being interrupted.

Next, Freud tried hand pressure, a technique he learned from Bernheim, instead of hypnosis. He would place his hand on his patients' foreheads and instruct them to begin talking when he released the pressure. Although this technique was somewhat successful, he eventually abandoned it and settled on **free association,** which he called "the fundamental rule of psychoanalysis."

Freud's experiences with hypnosis and hand pressure and his recollection of an essay by Ludwig Borne, which had been given to him when he was 14, gradually evolved into the technique of free association. The following quotation from Borne's essay, entitled "The Art of Becoming an Original Writer in Three Days," contains the seeds of what later became the technique of free association:

> Take a few sheets of paper and for three days on end write down, without fabrication or hypocrisy, everything that comes into your head. Write down what you think of yourself, of your wife, of the Turkish War, of Goethe, of Fonk's trial, of the Last Judgment, of your superiors—and when three days have passed you will be quite out of your sense with astonishment at the new and unheard-of thoughts you have had. (quoted in Freud 1955c, p. 265)

Breuer and Freud worked on several cases of hysteria and in 1895 published the book *Studies on Hysteria,* which is usually considered the beginning of the psychoanalytic movement. Although their book is now regarded as having monumental significance, it then was met with negative reviews, and it took 13 years to sell 626 copies. Breuer and Freud, who had been extremely close friends, soon parted company because of Freud's insistence that sexual conflicts were the cause of hysteria. Breuer agreed that sexual conflicts were often the cause of mental disorders, but disagreed with Freud's contention they were the only cause.

Freud began his highly influential self-analysis in 1897. He began this self-analysis for both theoretical and personal reasons; for example, he had a dread of railroad travel and was preoccupied by thoughts of his own death. The main vehicle in his self-analysis was the interpretation of his dreams. This analysis finally resulted in what many consider Freud's greatest work, *The Interpretation of Dreams,* published in 1900. As with his earlier book, written with Breuer, this one also met with considerable criticism; it was 8 years before 600 copies were sold, for which Freud received the equivalent of $209. Eventually, however, the importance of the book was realized, and it was translated and published throughout the world.

It was after the publication of *The Interpretation of Dreams* that the psychoanalytic movement began to gain momentum. International recognition finally came when Freud and a few of his close followers were invited by G. Stanley Hall to give a series of lectures at Clark University in 1909. Although Freud did not care much for the United States and never returned, he looked on his visit to Clark University as significant in the development of the psychoanalytic movement.

In 1923, Freud was diagnosed with cancer of the mouth, which was linked to smoking, a habit he did not abandon even after his cancer was detected. From 1923 to his death in 1939, Freud underwent 33 operations. Although in constant pain because of his refusal to accept pain-reducing drugs, his mind remained alert and he worked on his theory until the end of his life.

When the Nazis came to power in 1933, they publicly burned Freud's books in Berlin, as a Nazi spokesman shouted, "Against the soul-destroying overestimation of the sex life—and on behalf of the nobility of the human soul—I offer to the flames the writings of one Sigmund Freud!" (Schur, 1972, p. 446). About this event Freud commented, "What progress we are making. In the Middle Ages they would have burnt me; nowadays they are content with burning my books" (Jones, 1957, p. 182). Freud resisted leaving Vienna even after it was invaded in 1938. Finally, after his daughter Anna had been arrested and interrogated by the Nazis, he agreed to go to London. Four of his sisters were later killed by the Nazis in Austria. In London, the Freuds took up residence at 20 Maresfield Gardens in Hampstead, North London. Here, in great pain, Freud continued to write, see patients, and occasionally attend meetings of the London Psychoanalytic Society.

Freud had reached an agreement with his physician, Max Schur, that when Freud's condition became hopeless, Schur would assist him in dying. Peter Gay (1988) describes Freud's final days:

> Schur was on the point of tears as he witnessed Freud facing death with dignity and without self-pity. He had never seen anyone die like that. On September 21, Schur injected Freud with three centigrams of morphine—the normal dose for sedation was two centigrams—and Freud sank into a peaceful sleep. Schur repeated the injection, when he became restless, and administered a final one the next day, September 22. Freud lapsed into a coma from which he did not awake. He died at three in the morning, September 23, 1939. (p. 651)

Instincts and Their Characteristics

For Freud, all aspects of the human personality are derived from biological instincts. This point cannot be stressed too much. No matter how lofty the thought or the accomplishment, it ultimately relates to the satisfaction of a biological need. Freud's theory is a hedonistic one: It assumes that humans, like other animals, continually seek pleasure and avoid pain. When all the bodily needs are satisfied, one experiences pleasure; when one or more needs are not satisfied, one experiences discomfort. The main motive for humans, then, is to obtain the steady state that one experiences when all of one's biological needs are satisfied.

An **instinct** has four characteristics: (1) a source, which is a bodily deficiency of some kind; (2) an aim, which is to remove the bodily deficiency, thereby reestablishing an internal balance; (3) an object, which is the experience or object that reduces or removes the bodily deficiency; and (4) an impetus, which is determined by the magnitude of the bodily deficiency. For example, a person experiencing the hunger instinct will need food (source), will want to eliminate the need for food (aim), and will seek and ingest food (object). The intensity with which these activities occur will depend on how long the person has gone without food (impetus).

Life and Death Instincts

All the instincts associated with the preservation of life are called the life instincts, and the psychic energy associated with them collectively is called the **libido.** In Freud's earlier writings, he equated libido with sexual energy but in light of increased evidence to the contrary and because of severe criticism from even his closest colleagues, he expanded the notion to include the energy associated with all of the life instincts including sex, hunger, and thirst. Freud's final position was that libidinal energy is expended to prolong life. Freud also referred to the life instincts collectively as **eros.**

The death instinct, named **thanatos,** stimulates a person to return to the inorganic state that preceded life. Death is the ultimate steady state because there is no longer a struggle to satisfy biological needs. Quoting Schopenhauer, Freud claimed "the aim of all life is death" (1955a, p. 38). The most important derivative of the death instinct, or the death wish as it is sometimes called, is aggression that, according to Freud, is the need for self-destruction turned outward to objects other than the self. Cruelty, murder, and other forms of aggression were thought by Freud to derive from the death instinct. Even though Freud never developed thanatos as fully as eros, it is nonetheless an important part of his theory.

Divisions of the Mind

The Id

The mature adult mind has three divisions: an **id,** an **ego,** and a **superego.** At birth, however, the entire mind consists of only the id (from the German *das es,* meaning "the it"). The id consists of pure, unadulterated, instinctual energy and exists completely on the unconscious level. The id cannot tolerate the tension associated with a bodily need and therefore demands the immediate removal of that tension. In other words, the id demands immediate gratification of bodily needs and is said to be governed by the **pleasure principle.**

The id has two means of satisfying bodily needs: **reflex action** and **wish fulfillment.** Reflex action is responding automatically to a source of irritation. For example, an infant may sneeze in response to an irritant in the nose or reflexively move a confined limb, thereby freeing it. In both cases, reflex action effectively reduces tension. Coughing and blinking are also examples of reflex action.

Wish fulfillment is more complicated. In addition to the characteristics of instincts described earlier, instincts can be considered mental representations of physiological needs. It is within the id and via the concept of instinct that Freud came to grips with the mind–body question. The mind–body question asks how biological events and psychological events are related to each other. It is a question that every theory with a cognitive component eventually must address.

Freud's answer to the mind–body question was as follows. A biological deficiency (a need) triggers in the id an attempt to reduce the tension associated with that need by imagining an object or event that will satisfy the need. For example, the need for food will automatically trigger in the id a food-related image that has the effect of temporarily reducing the tension associated with the need for food; this is called wish fulfillment. At this point, Freud becomes quite mystical. Because the id is entirely unconscious, what images does it conjure in response to the various needs? Certainly, it cannot conjure a hamburger in response to the hunger drive because it never experienced a hamburger or anything else that is directly related to the reduction of the hunger drive. The alternative seems to be that the id has available to it the inherited residuals of experience from preceding generations. If so, it has available to it the images of things that consistently satisfied the needs of humans through many past generations. It is the latter view that Freud accepted and in so doing he embraced Lamarck's notion of the **inheritance of acquired characteristics,** about which we say more later.

Because wish fulfillment can never really satisfy a bodily need except on a temporary basis, another component of the personality must develop to make real satisfaction possible and that component is the ego. As we have seen, the id attempts to reduce needs through hallucinations (mental pictures of objects that could satisfy a need). These, along with reflex actions, are called the **primary processes.** The primary processes of the id, however, are ineffective in ultimately alleviating the need. The id cannot distinguish between its images and external reality. In fact, for the id, its images are the *only* reality.

The Ego

Eventually, the ego (from the German *das ich,* meaning "the I") develops and attempts to match the images of the id with objects and events in the real world. Freud called this matching process **identification.** The ego is governed by the **reality principle** and operates in the service of the id. In other words, the ego comes into existence to bring the person into contact with experiences that truly satisfy his or her needs. When the person is hungry, the ego finds food; when the person is sexually aroused, the ego finds appropriate sexual objects; and when the person is thirsty, the ego finds liquid. The ego goes through the process of **reality testing** to find appropriate objects. Because the ego is aware of both the images of the id and external reality, it operates on both the conscious and unconscious level. The realistic efforts of the ego that bring about true biological satisfaction are called **secondary processes,** which contrast with the ineffective primary processes of the id. The relationship between the id and the ego is summarized in the diagram below.

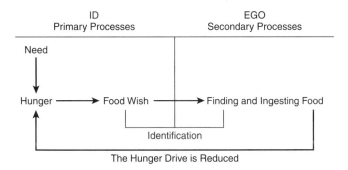

Within Freudian theory, it is important to realize that the ego operated in the service of the id.

> The ego must on the whole carry out the id's intentions, it fulfils [sic] its task by finding out the circumstances in which those intentions can best be achieved. The ego's relation to the id might be compared with that of a rider to his horse. The horse supplies the locomotive energy, while the rider has the privilege of deciding on the goal and of guiding the powerful animal's movement. But only too often there arises between the ego and the id the not precisely ideal situation of the rider being obliged to guide the horse along the path by which it itself wants to go. (Freud, 1966a, p. 541)

The Superego

If the only two components of the personality were the id and the ego, we would have a hedonistic, animalistic person who, when in a need state, would seek immediate gratification of needs (id) from appropriate environmental objects (ego). The superego, a third component of the personality, makes this process more complicated, however. The superego (from the German *das überich,* meaning "the over I") is the moral arm of the personality. It develops primarily from the internalized patterns of reward and punishment that the young child experiences. That is, depending on the values of the parents, certain things the child does or says are rewarded and thereby encouraged; other things the child does or says are punished and thereby discouraged. Those experiences that bring reward and punishment are gradually internalized, and the superego is said to be fully developed when self-control replaces environmental or direct parental control.

The fully developed superego has two subdivisions. The **conscience** is the internalized experiences for which the child had been consistently punished. Engaging in these behaviors now, or even thinking about engaging in them, makes the child feel guilty or "naughty." The second subdivision of the superego is the **ego ideal** that is the internalized experiences for which the child had been consistently rewarded. Engaging in these behaviors now, or even thinking about engaging in them, makes the child feel successful or proud. Although Freud believed the superego was strongly influenced by internalized personal experiences, he also believed it was influenced by historical or phylogenetic experiences. We see examples of the latter later.

The superego constantly strives for perfection and is, therefore, as unrealistic as the id. Any experience that violates the internalized values of the child is not tolerated by the superego; now, the job of the ego becomes more complicated. Not only must the ego find objects and events that satisfy the needs of the id, it also must find objects and events that do not violate the values of the superego. If, for example, the need to urinate arises while one is on a city bus, the id would demand immediate gratification through urination. The ego would allow this to happen by causing, in the case of a boy, the pants to be unzipped and so on. Urinating on a city bus, however, would in all likelihood violate an internalized value of the superego and considerable guilt or anxiety would be experienced as the result of this behavior. The ego, aware of both the needs of the id and of the superego, would probably, in this case, cause the person to get off the bus at the next stop and enter a washroom in which urination would satisfy all the components of the personality. It is no wonder the ego is called the executive of the personality. Freud (1966a) described the enormous task of the ego:

> We are warned by a proverb against serving two masters at the same time. The poor ego has things even worse: it serves three severe masters and does what it can to bring their claims and demands into harmony with one another. . . . Its three tyrannical masters are the external world, the super-ego and the id. . . . [On the one hand it] attempts to mediate between the id and reality. . . . On the other hand it is observed at every step it takes by the strict super-ego, which lays down definite standards for its conduct . . . and . . . if those standards are not obeyed, punishes it with tense feelings of inferiority and of guilt. Thus the ego, driven by the id, confined by the super-ego, repulsed by reality, struggles to master its economic task of bringing about harmony among the forces and influences working in and upon it; and we can understand how it is that so often we cannot suppress a cry: 'Life is not easy!' (pp. 541–542)

Cathexis and Anticathexis

Freud's most influential teacher at the University of Vienna was the renowned physiologist Ernst Brücke (1819–1892) who, along with Hermann Von Helmholtz (1821–1894) and a few other physiologists, had revolutionized the field of physiology by purging physiology of all subjective, nonscientific concepts and terminology. Their goal was to explain all physiological events in terms of known, measurable, verifiable physical events. That is, living systems were viewed as dynamic energy systems that obey the laws of the physical universe. **Vitalism,** or the belief that life consists of some vital force that cannot be reduced to physical events, was strongly opposed by these individuals. For them, there was no "ghost in the machine" that existed independently of physiological events and the laws that governed them. It was in this "Helmholtzian school of medicine" that Freud received his early training; this positivistic training had a strong and lasting influence on him. In fact, one of Freud's first endeavors in psychology was entitled *Project for a Scientific Psychology*. This was an effort to explain psychological phenomena entirely in terms of neurophysical processes. Although the *Project* was completed in 1895 (the same year Freud published *Studies on Hysteria* with Breuer), Freud considered it a failure, and it was not published in his lifetime (it was first published in 1950 in German, and 1954 in English). Although Freud later employed subjective (nonphysiological) terminology in his theory of personality, the positivism of the Helmholtzian school remained highly influential in that he continued to avoid vitalistic and teleological concepts in explaining human behavior.

Following his practice of naming his children after individuals who had deeply impressed him, Freud named his fourth son Ernst after Brücke.

One Helmholtzian concept that Freud adopted was the **principle of conservation of energy.** This principle states that within a system, energy is never created or lost but only rearranged or transformed from one place or form to another. The principle did not originate with Helmholtz, but he was the first to apply it to living organisms. For example, Helmholtz demonstrated that the total energy expended by an organism equaled the amount of energy associated with the food and oxygen it consumed.

Freud applied the principle of conservation of energy to the human mind. According to Freud, each person is born with more or less the same amount of **psychic energy** and that amount remains more or less the same from birth to death. This energy, however, can be transformed and rearranged, and it is how the energy is distributed at any given time that determines a person's personality characteristics.

Freud used the term **cathexis** (from the Greek *kathexo,* meaning to occupy) to describe the investment of psychic energy in the thoughts of objects or processes that will satisfy a need. The energy itself never leaves the body, but if considerable energy is invested in the image of an object, an intense longing occurs for it in the form of thoughts, images, and fantasies. These thoughts and feelings continue until the need is satisfied, at which point the energy dissipates and is available for other cathexes. Again, if only the id and the ego existed, humans would be animalistic. That is, a need would arise, an image (wish) of an object that would satisfy that need would form, and that wish would be endowed with energy, thereby creating a tension that would continue until the need was satisfied. There would be no regard for other people and no differentiation between acceptable and unacceptable objects with which to satisfy needs. As we have seen, however, with the development of the superego comes the need to inhibit certain primitive desires. This requires the expenditure of energy to prevent unacceptable cathexes. Freud called the energy expended to prevent undesirable cathexes an **anticathexis.** Because the emergence of an unacceptable cathexis would cause anxiety, the ego and the superego often team up to create an anticathexis powerful enough to inhibit the strong primitive cathexes of the id. In such cases, the original need does not disappear. Instead, the original cathexis is displaced to other, safer objects.

Anxiety

According to Freud, our most overwhelming experience of anxiety occurs when we are separated from our mother at birth. Freud called this experience the *birth trauma* because we suddenly go from an environment of complete security and satisfaction to one in which the satisfaction of our needs is far less predictable. The feeling of helplessness following birth is, according to Freud, the basis of all subsequent feelings of anxiety.

The function of anxiety is to warn us that if we continue thinking or behaving in a certain way, we will be in danger. Because anxiety is not pleasant, we will do what is necessary to reduce it. That is, we will tend to terminate those thoughts or actions that cause anxiety. Freud distinguished three types of anxiety. **Reality anxiety** is caused by real, objective sources of danger in the environment and is the easiest type of anxiety to reduce because doing so solves problems objectively, such as leaving a building that is on fire. **Neurotic anxiety** is the fear that the impulses of the id will overwhelm the ego and cause the person to do something for which he or she will be punished. Examples include becoming overly aggressive or giving in to one's sexual desires. Generally, this fear is one of becoming animal-like. **Moral anxiety** is fear that the person will do something contrary to the superego and thus experience guilt. For example, if one has learned that being honest is good, then even thinking of being dishonest would cause moral anxiety. Neurotic anxiety is the fear that one will be punished externally (by other people) for impulsive actions whereas moral anxiety is the fear that one will be punished internally (by feelings of guilt) if the dictates of one's superego are violated. Thus anxiety controls our behavior by causing us to avoid threatening experiences in the environment, to inhibit the impulses of the id, and to act in accordance with our internalized values.

One of the ego's biggest tasks is to avoid or reduce anxiety. In addition to anticathexis, the ego has several other processes available to it for use in its battle against anxiety; these processes are referred to collectively as the ego-defense mechanisms.

Ego-Defense Mechanisms

If normal, rational approaches of the ego to reduce or remove anxiety are ineffective, the ego may revert to irrational methods called **ego-defense mechanisms.** All ego-defense mechanisms have two things in common: (1) they are unconscious; that is, the person is unaware that he or she is using them, and (2) they falsify or distort reality. Freud's daughter Anna (1966) was mainly responsible for elaborating the ego-defense mechanisms, and we consider several of them.

Repression

This is the most basic defense mechanism because for any of the other defense mechanisms to occur, **repression** must occur first. Concerning the importance of repression, Freud said, "The theory of repression is the cornerstone on which the whole structure of psycho-analysis rests" (1966c, p. 14). Repression is the mechanism by which the ego prevents anxiety-provoking thoughts from being entertained on the conscious level. These thoughts can be either those innately part of the id, in which case their repression is referred to as **primal repression,** or they can be memories of painful experiences from one's lifetime, in which case their repression is referred to as **repression proper.** In either case, the ego keeps the potentially anxiety-provoking thought in the unconscious with an anticathexis whenever it threatens to reach consciousness. It is important to realize what Freud considered to be innately part of the id. The primary drives that we share with other animals are inherited as part of the id but, according to Freud, more is contained in the id than physiological needs. As we mentioned earlier, Freud was an ardent Lamarckian. That is, he believed we inherit memories of what our ancestors had learned from their experiences. Freud believed our id comes well stocked with inherited prohibitions because of the punishment our ancestors received for engaging in certain behaviors. Many of the events that cause anxiety in our lifetimes do so because of the experiences of our ancestors. Thus we can fear castration, believe we have been sexually attacked as children by an adult, and avoid incest not necessarily because we have learned to do so in our lifetimes but because these thoughts are part of our **phylogenetically inherited endowment.** Consider the following quotation:

> The experiences of the ego seem at first to be lost for inheritance; but when they have been repeated often enough and with sufficient strength in many individuals

in successive generations, they transform themselves, so to say, into experiences of the id, the impressions of which are preserved by heredity. Thus in the id, which is capable of being inherited, are harboured residues of the existence of countless egos. (Freud, 1961b, p. 38)

Thus, if our ancestors were consistently punished for certain activities, we are born with the tendency to inhibit those activities. The impulse to engage in those tendencies (e.g., incest or violence) continues to exist in the id, however, and energy must be expended to inhibit them and related impulses. Another way to state Freud's position is to say that he believed at least part of human morality is inherited. In *Totem and Taboo* (1958) Freud said, "I have supposed that the sense of guilt for an action has persisted for many thousands of years and has remained operative in generations which can have no knowledge of that action" (pp. 157–158). Freud's belief in Lamarck's concept of the inheritance of acquired characteristics is also stated in his last book, *Moses and Monotheism* (1964a):

> We become aware of the probability that what may be operative in an individual's psychical life may include not only what he has experienced himself but also things that were innately present in him at his birth, elements with a phylogenetic origin— an archaic heritage. (p. 98)

For Freud, the mechanism of repression was of vital importance because repressed thoughts do not stop having an influence on our personality; they simply are not readily available in consciousness. The whole purpose of procedures such as dream analysis, free association, hypnosis, and the analysis of slips of the tongue or memory lapses (which we discuss later) is to attempt to discover repressed thoughts so their effects on one's personality can be determined. Not all material in the unconscious mind is repressed, however. An abundance of information exists that is simply not relevant to a person at any given moment, such as names, telephone numbers, or dates. Although the person is not momentarily aware of this kind of information, he or she can easily become aware of it when needed. Such information is said to exist in the **preconscious.**

Displacement

As we saw earlier, **displacement** is the substitution of one need satisfier for another. For example, the ego may substitute an available object for one that is not available, or it may substitute a nonanxiety-provoking object or activity for one that does cause anxiety. With displacement, what a person truly desires is repressed and is replaced by something safer.

In his book *Civilization and Its Discontents* (1961a), Freud indicated that civilization itself depends on the displacement of libidinal energy from one object to another. When a displacement results in something advantageous to civilization, it is called **sublimation,** such as when sexual impulses are displaced into such activities as painting, writing, building, or just plain hard work. "Sublimation of instinct," wrote Freud, "is an especially conspicuous feature of cultural development; it is what makes it possible for higher psychical activities, scientific, artistic or ideological, to play such an important part in civilized life" (1961a, p. 63).

All impulses can be displaced, even those associated with the death instinct. For example, the impulse toward self-destruction can be displaced to the destruction of others, and an aggressive impulse directed toward a threatening person such as a boss or a parent can be displaced to less threatening objects such as other cars on the street while driving home, children, household pets, or, quite commonly, to athletic teams opposing the hometown team. These are examples of **displaced aggression,** one of Freud's most influential concepts.

Identification

Freud used the term **identification** in two ways. The one we have already covered is the process by which the ego attempts to match objects and events in the environment to the subjective wishes of the id. The term *identification* is also used to describe the tendency to increase personal feelings of worth by affiliating oneself psychologically with a person, group, or institution perceived as illustrious. The feelings of pride when the home team wins a game or when one's country wins a gold medal in the Olympics are examples. Choices of fashion, music collection, reading material, and even mannerisms can also exemplify identification if they bring a person closer psychologically to individuals perceived as successful, powerful, or attractive. Wearing T-shirts or jackets with team, business, or institutional logos also exemplifies identification.

The child also identifies with his or her parents (internalizes their values), thereby eliminating the punishment that comes from having contrary values. This is primarily how the superego develops.

Denial of Reality

This mechanism involves the denial of some fact in one's life despite abundant evidence for its reality. Examples include the refusal to believe a loved one has died; the refusal to acknowledge the negative attributes of a loved one; the refusal to believe that one's poor driving was the cause of an accident; the tendency for some severely overweight and underweight individuals to deny they have a weight problem; and the tendency for people addicted to substances such as alcohol, nicotine, or cocaine to believe such substances will not harm them or that they could easily quit their habits. By definition, a person using the mechanism of **denial of reality** is not in touch with at least some aspect of reality and this could impair normal functioning.

Projection

This mechanism is the one by which something that is true of the person and would cause anxiety if it were recognized is repressed and projected onto someone or something else instead. For example, the statement "I want to go to bed with him" may be true, but because it causes anxiety it is converted into "He wants to go to bed with me." Also, the statement "I failed the test because I was unprepared," although perhaps true, is converted into statements such as, "Our textbook is terrible," "She's the worst teacher I've ever had," or "The test had trick questions."

In general, **projection** is repressing anxiety-provoking truths about oneself and seeing them in others instead, or by excusing one's shortcomings by blaming them on environmental or life circumstances.

Undoing

Here a person performs an unacceptable act, or thinks about doing so, and then engages in ritualistic activities designed to atone for or "undo" the unacceptable act or thought. With **undoing,** it is as if the person is attempting to magically undo one act with another. "It is a kind of negative magic in which the individual's second act abrogates or nullifies the first" (A. Freud, 1966, p. 33). For example, after killing King Duncan, Lady Macbeth compulsively washes her hands as if to absolve herself of the heinous act. Likewise, a man, after physically abusing his wife, may attempt to undo the abuse by profusely apologizing to her, expressing his true love for her, or by buying her a gift, such as flowers.

Reaction Formation

This mechanism is the one by which objectionable thoughts are repressed and their opposites expressed. For example, the person who is most attracted to sexual materials may become the town censor, or the mother who really does not care much for her child may become overprotective. Freud believed that the clue in determining the difference between a **reaction formation** and true feelings is the degree to which the feelings are emphasized. People displaying a reaction formation tend to be more intense and extravagant in their emotions, as when a boyfriend insists, "I love you, I love you, I love you more than anything in the world," or when someone says, "You should meet my mother. She is absolutely wonderful beyond belief." In Shakespeare's *Hamlet,* the lady doth protest too much, and in so doing reveals her guilt.

The following is a letter written to Masserman, a famous psychologist who did work on alcoholism using cats as experimental subjects. The letter was written by an antivivisectionist who claimed to be terribly concerned with what Masserman was doing to his research animals. See if you can find evidence in the letter that its author was basically a violent person, and that his or her affiliation with the antivivisectionists was, therefore, a reaction formation.

> I read [a magazine article . . . on your work on alcoholism]. . . . I am surprised that anyone who is as well educated as you must be to hold the position that you do would stoop to such a depth as to torture helpless little cats in the pursuit of a cure for alcoholics. . . . A drunkard does not want to be cured—a drunkard is just a weak minded idiot who belongs in the gutter and should be left there. Instead of torturing helpless little cats why not torture drunks or better still exert your would-be noble effort toward getting a bill passed to exterminate the drunks. They are not any good to anyone or themselves and are just a drain on the public, having to pull them off the street, jail them, then they have to be fed while there and it's against the law to feed them arsenic so there they are. . . . If people are such weaklings the world is better off without them. . . .
>
> My greatest wish is that you have brought home to you a torture that will be a thousand fold greater than what you have, and are doing to the little animals. . . . If you are an example of what a noted psychiatrist should be I'm glad I am just an ordinary human being without letters after my name. I'd rather be myself with a clear conscience, knowing that I have not hurt any living creature, and can sleep without seeing frightened, terrified dying cats—because I know they must die after you have finished with them. No punishment is too great for you and I hope I live

to read about your mangled body and long suffering before you finally die—and I'll laugh long and loud. (Masserman, 1961, p. 35)

Rationalization

Through this mechanism, the person rationally explains or justifies behaviors or thoughts that may otherwise be anxiety provoking. The ego excuses through logic (although faulty) outcomes that would be disturbing if they were not explained in some way. The so-called sour grapes **rationalization** is quite common. Aesop, in about 500 B.C., told of a fox who saw clusters of grapes hanging from a trellised vine. It tried everything in its power to reach them but nothing worked. Finally, the fox turned away, saying, "The grapes were probably sour anyhow." Minimizing something to which one has aspired but failed to obtain is a common form of rationalization called "sour grapes." Likewise, something that at first was not overly attractive may be glorified after it is obtained. This has been called a "sweet lemon" rationalization.

Intellectualization (Also Called Isolation of Affect)

Here an idea that would otherwise cause distress is stripped of its emotional content by intellectual analysis. Thus, a disturbing thought is not denied consciousness but is denied the accompanying negative emotion. Using **intellectualization,** it is possible to ponder topics such as death, separation from a loved one, severe illness, or personal loss without the negative emotions typically associated with such events. For example, attempting to understand the medical nature of cancer in a logical, detached manner can minimize the emotional impact of a loved one having the disease. Likewise, the negative emotions associated with the death of a loved one can be minimized by emphasizing the thought that death is the inevitable consequence of life. Finally, one can minimize the distress typically associated with his or her house burning down by intellectually stressing the futility in becoming emotionally attached to material things.

Regression

With this mechanism, the person returns to an earlier stage of development when he or she experiences stress. For example, a child may revert to bed-wetting or thumb-sucking when a new sibling is born. We have more to say about **regression** in our discussion of the psychosexual stages of development to which we turn shortly.

The ego-defense mechanisms described above were those described by Freud and his colleagues and were summarized by his daughter Anna in her book *The Ego and the Mechanisms of Defense* (1966). In that book, however, Anna Freud offered two defense mechanisms of her own: altruistic surrender and identification with the aggressor.

Altruistic Surrender

Here a person minimizes the frustration and anxiety associated with making responsible decisions in life by vicariously identifying with another person perceived as superior and then living in accordance with that person's values.

Identification with the Aggressor

Here a person internalizes the values and mannerisms of a feared person, thereby reducing him or her as a threat. This mechanism may explain why some hostages develop affection toward their captors. Anna Freud believed that this mechanism was instrumental in the development of the superego: "What else is the superego than identification with the aggressor?" (quoted in Young-Bruehl, 1988, p. 212).

It should be made clear that everyone uses the ego-defense mechanisms and doing so in some moderation often facilitates normal functioning. Using one or more of them extensively, however, can be dysfunctional.

Cramer (2000, 2001) discusses the ego-defense mechanisms within the context of contemporary cognitive and developmental psychology. Cramer also discusses the circumstances under which the ego-defense mechanisms are adaptive.

Psychosexual Stages of Development

Freud believed every child goes through a sequence of developmental stages, and the child's experiences during these stages determine adult personality characteristics. In fact, Freud believed that for all practical purposes, the adult personality is formed by the end of the fifth year of life.

Each stage has an **erogenous zone** associated with it, which is the greatest source of stimulation and pleasure during that particular stage of development.

To make a smooth transition from one psychosexual stage to the next, the child must be neither undergratified nor overgratified, both of which cause the child to be fixated at that stage. A **fixation** occurs when a substantial amount of psychic energy remains cathected in images of objects that can satisfy the needs corresponding to a particular stage of development. Again, a fixation can occur either because the needs corresponding to a stage are consistently frustrated (undergratified) or are satisfied too often and too easily (overgratified). An example of the latter is an infant who is breast-fed whenever it shows the least sign of hunger or discomfort. Fixation and regression go hand in hand, because, when a person regresses, he or she tends to go back to the stage at which that person had been fixated. In addition, persons who are fixated at a certain stage will, as an adult, display personality characteristics corresponding to that stage. We see examples of this next.

Oral Stage

The **oral stage** occurs during about the first year of life, and the erogenous zone during this stage is the mouth. During the early oral stage (less than 8 months old) pleasure comes mainly from the mouth, lips, and tongue through the activities of sucking and swallowing. According to Freud, an adult who is fixated at the early oral stage engages in an abundance of oral activities such as eating, drinking, smoking, and kissing. This person also engages in activities that are symbolically equivalent to those oral activities such as collecting things, being a good listener (taking in knowledge), or being what is labeled a gullible person, that is, a person who "swallows" anything he or she hears. Such a person is called an **oral-incorporative character.**

In the later oral stage (from 8 months to about 1 year) experience is concentrated on the teeth, gums, and jaws, and pleasure comes from activities such as biting and devouring. An adult fixated at the late oral stage may be a fingernail biter and also would like eating. This person also would engage in activities symbolically equivalent to biting such as sarcasm, cynicism, and ridicule. Such a person is called an **oral-sadistic character.**

Anal Stage

The **anal stage** occurs during about the second year of life, and the erogenous zone is the anus-buttocks region. During this stage, the child must learn to control his or her physiological processes so they function in accordance with the demands of society. That is, the child must be toilet trained.

In the first part of the anal stage, pleasure derives from feces expulsion. Fixation at this level may result in an adult having physical problems such as a lack of sphincter control or enuresis. Symbolically, the person would be overly generous, wanting to give away nearly everything he or she owns, and may also tend to be creative. Such a person is called an **anal-expulsive character.**

In the later anal stage, pleasure comes from feces possession. Fixation here may manifest itself physically, in a problem with constipation, or symbolically in stinginess, parsimony, orderliness, and a tendency toward perfectionism. Such a person is called an **anal-retentive character.**

Phallic Stage

This stage occurs from about the third year of life to about the fifth year, and the erogenous zone is the phallus or penis. Although the phallus is a male organ, Freud believed the **phallic stage** described the development of both male and female children. Freud believed the clitoris was a small penis and, therefore, activity related to it such as clitoral masturbation was viewed as masculine in nature. The phallic stage is one of the most complicated and controversial of Freud's stages. It is during this stage when our subsequent adjustments to members of the opposite sex are determined. The phallic stage is the scene of the Oedipus complex, the resolution of which, Freud believed, has a profound influence on adult life.

The **Oedipus complex** is named after an ancient play by Sophocles entitled *Oedipus Rex* in which King Oedipus kills his father and marries his mother. According to Freud, both male and female children develop strong, positive feelings toward the mother because she satisfies their needs. For example, because of breast-feeding and sexual contact from bathing and grooming, both male and female children develop erotic feelings toward their mother. These feelings persist in the boy but typically change in the girl.

The boy begins to fear the father as the dominant rival for his mother's affection and this fear becomes **castration anxiety.** That is, the boy develops the fear of losing his sex organs because they are assumed to be responsible for the conflict between him and his father. According to Freud, it is not necessary for a male child to be overtly threatened with castration to develop castration anxiety. Boys may have the opportunity to observe that girls do not possess penises and assume that they once did. That is, boys may believe that girls lost their penises because their penises, like their own, were the source of trouble with their father. Also, according to Freud, castration anxiety could result from the phylogenetic memory of actual castrations that occurred in the distant past.

No matter what its source, castration anxiety causes a repression of the sexual desire for the mother and creates hostility toward the father. Next, the boy identifies with his father, thereby gaining vicarious satisfaction of his sexual impulses toward his mother. In a sense, the boy becomes the father and thereby shares the mother. By identifying with his father, the male child not only shares the mother, he also accepts his father's notions of right and wrong as his own, thereby completing the development of his superego. That is, his father's morality becomes his morality. This process exemplifies what Anna Freud meant by identification with the aggressor and describes what was for Freud the healthy resolution of the Oedipus complex.

The female version of the Oedipus complex is more complicated. Freud pondered calling the female version of the Oedipus complex the Electra complex after another play by Sophocles entitled *Electra,* in which Electra causes her brother to kill her mother, who had killed Electra's father. Freud rejected the idea, however, choosing instead to refer to the male and female Oedipal complexes.

As we have seen, female children also start life with a strong attraction to their mothers. This attraction is reduced, however, when the girl discovers she does not possess a penis. Whereas a male child assumes that female children once had penises and had lost them, the female child assumes that all other children possess penises but for some reason she was deprived of one. The female child holds the mother responsible for purposely depriving her of this valued organ. The rejection of the mother is coupled with an attraction to the father whom she knows possesses the valued organ that she wants to share. Her positive feelings toward the father, however, are mixed with envy because he has something that she does not and she is said to have **penis envy.** Freud leaves the girl suspended between the mother and father with positive and negative feelings toward both.

Unlike castration anxiety in boys that is quickly repressed, Freud believed penis envy, in one form or another, could last for years. According to Freud, the female's sexuality changes from masculine to feminine when she fantasizes about having her father's baby. It is this fantasy that explains the female impulse to reproduce rather than any maternal instinct. Of course, this impulse symbolically generalizes to other men and represents the healthy resolution of the female Oedipal complex. For Freud, the final resolution of the female Oedipal complex occurs when the female eventually has a baby, especially a male baby.

The phallic stage is further complicated by the fact that both male and female children are bisexual. As we have seen, both male and female children begin with a strong sexual attraction to their mother. This attraction typically persists in males and results in heterosexual development. However, because of his strong attraction toward his mother, the male child also imagines his father as a love object and has erotic fantasies about him. Likewise, although penis envy causes the female child to turn from the mother to the father, the strong positive feelings she has toward her mother are not completely abandoned. Because male and female children identify with both their mothers and fathers, they possess both masculine and feminine characteristics; that is, they are bisexual. Freud considered bisexuality to be universal and normal. It is when life's circumstances cause these natural impulses to become exaggerated that homosexuality results. According to Freud, all humans have the potential to become homosexual.

Regression to the phallic stage for the male may include displaying many of the father's characteristics and, also typically, brashness and an overconcern with masculinity and virility. Regression to the phallic stage for the girl may exemplify penis-envy-related activities. These activities may include seeking to share a penis—for example, promiscuity or seductiveness, or activities that symbolically castrate men, such as embarrassing, deceiving, or hurting them.

The first three psychosexual stages, called the pregenital stages, are by far the most important to personality development. As we mentioned earlier, Freud believed that the basic ingredients of the adult personality are formulated by the end of the phallic stage.

Latency Stage

The **latency stage** lasts from about the 6th year to about the 12th year. This is a time when sexual interests are repressed and displaced to substitute activities such as learning, athletics, and peer group activities. That is, during this stage libidinal energy is sublimated.

Genital Stage

This is the final stage of development and begins at puberty. At this time, the person emerges from the pregenital stages as the adult he or she is destined to become. The child is sometimes transformed from a selfish, pleasure-seeking child to a realistic, socialized adult, typically with heterosexual interests leading to marriage and perhaps childrearing. If, however, the experiences during the pregenital stages cause fixations, they will manifest themselves throughout the person's adult life. Supposedly, only psychoanalysis can dredge up the remnants of these early experiences, which otherwise would remain repressed into the unconscious, and cause the individual to face them rationally, thereby reducing their influence on his or her life.

In fact, the process of psychoanalysis can be viewed as a means of discovering repressed thoughts that are having a negative influence on one's life. The question is, How does one gain access to thoughts that have been actively held in the unconscious mind all one's life? It is to this question that we turn after summarizing Freud's views on feminine psychology.

Summary of Freud's Views on Feminine Psychology

There is no doubt that Freud considered the psychology of women more enigmatic than that of men. He once commented to his friend Marie Bonaparte, "The great question that has never been answered and which I have not yet been able to answer, despite my thirty years of research into the feminine soul, is 'What does a woman want?'" (quoted in Jones, 1955, p. 421). But Freud tried strenuously to understand women via many approaches. At times his proposed explanations emphasized the role of society in determining gender differences, saying that women are inferior to males because society oppresses them. Most consistently, however, he claimed that "anatomy is destiny;" that is, gender differences have a biological origin.

Freud persisted in viewing women as failed or inferior men. The cornerstone of his psychology of women remained penis envy. For males, the Oedipus complex is terminated by castration anxiety, causing them to identify with their fathers and to seek female partners in their adult lives. For females, penis envy commences the Oedipus complex, causing them to turn (partially) away from their mothers and toward their fathers as sex objects. This switch of affiliation causes the female erogenous zone to change from the clitoris to the vagina because of the latter organ's involvement in reproduction. According to Freud, it is only after the erogenous zone changes from the clitoris to the vagina that true feminine sexuality begins.

Freud believed that women could respond to their "castration" in three ways: (1) they could later withdraw from sexual activity altogether, becoming frigid; (2) they could cling to their masculinity and become homosexual or embrace feminism (which he believed is characterized by masculine aggressiveness); or (3) they could symbolically take their father as a sex object, leading to heterosexuality and childbearing.

Freud believed that because penis envy is not as intense as castration anxiety, females do not have the same need to engage in defensive identification as males. Remember, it is the defensive identification with their fathers that completes the development of the male superego. But what about the female? Freud believed the female does identify somewhat with her mother (mainly because of the fear of losing her love), but the identification is not nearly as intense and complete as it is for the male. The result, according to Freud, is that the female superego tends to be weaker than that of the male; that is, she is morally inferior. Even as Freud expressed his views on feminine psychology, he had many supporters and detractors. It is interesting to note that many of his supporters were female psychoanalysts (e.g., Jeanne Lampl-de Groot and Helene Deutsch). Likewise, many of his critics were male psychoanalysts (e.g., Ernest Jones). This is not to say, however, that all female analysts agreed with him and all male analysts disagreed with him. One of his most outspoken critics was Karen Horney, whose theory of personality we review in Chapter 5.

In the end, Freud essentially admitted defeat in his attempt to understand women. Following are his last words on the subject:

> That is all I [have] to say to you about femininity. It is certainly incomplete and fragmentary and does not always sound friendly. . . . If you want to know more about femininity, enquire from your own experiences of life, or turn to the poets, or wait until science can give you deeper and more coherent information. (1966a, p. 599)

Freud's views on feminine psychology have been harshly criticized for reflecting only the thought processes of his disturbed patients, the Victorian culture in which he practiced, his own personal biases, or for being scientifically incorrect. As valid as these and other criticisms may be, Freud has often been criticized for things he never said. Also, he sometimes held the same views as his so-called critics; for example, the view that it is often the societal oppression of women that contributes to their apparent inferiority to men. In order to provide a more objective appraisal of Freud's views on feminine psychology, Young-Bruehl (1990) collected all of his writings on the topic. She arranged these writings in chronological order so it can be observed how Freud's views on feminine psychology changed over the course of his career.

Tapping the Unconscious Mind

If repressed anxiety-provoking thoughts are effectively anticathected by the ego or superego, how can we come to know what they are? To say the least, it is not easy, but it is the business of psychoanalysis to attempt to do so. Freud employed several methods of determining the contents of the unconscious mind, and we examine a few of them.

Free Association

Earlier in this chapter we showed how the technique of free association gradually evolved. To stimulate free association (the fundamental rule of psychoanalysis), Freud instructed his patients as follows:

> You will notice that as you relate things various thoughts will occur to you which you would like to put aside on the ground of certain criticisms and objections. You will be tempted to say to yourself that this or that is irrelevant here, or is quite unimportant, or nonsensical, so that there is no need to say it. You must never give in to these criticisms, but must say it in spite of them—indeed, you must say it precisely because you feel an aversion to doing so. . . . Finally, never forget that you have promised to be absolutely honest, and never leave anything out because, for some reason or other, it is unpleasant to tell it. (1963, pp. 134–135)

The idea was that even in conscious expressions, there are hints as to the contents of the unconscious mind that the trained observer can detect. What is *not* said is as important as, if not more important than, what *is* said. Topics to which patients offer strong **resistance** provide the analyst with useful hints to problem areas in the unconscious mind. One reason that Freud abandoned hypnosis is because a hypnotized patient does not display revealing resistances. During the course of free association, resistance can take the form of telling carefully structured stories, long periods of silence, refusing to say something considered (by the patient) silly or embarrassing, avoiding certain topics, the tendency to report events in a highly intellectual, unemotional manner, "forgetting" important insights that had been gained from previous therapeutic sessions, and hiding important thoughts behind excessive emotion. In addition, if the therapeutic process appears dangerously close to revealing anxiety-provoking material, the patient may be late for an appointment or not show up at all.

Revealing the contents of the unconscious mind is difficult and requires a great deal of time. Typically a patient undergoing psychoanalysis is in therapy for four to six 50-minute sessions per week for several years. To facilitate the flow of ideas Freud had his patients lie on a couch in a dim room while he sat out of the patient's view. Freud remained out of sight for two reasons: (1) he did not want his gestures and expressions to influence the patient's thoughts, and (2) he could not tolerate being stared at for hours on end. At times Freud demonstrated a rather cavalier attitude toward his therapeutic sessions. Early in his career, he wrote a letter to his friend Wilhelm Fliess while one of his patients was under hypnosis (Masson, 1985, p. 21). Later, he confessed to taking naps during his afternoon sessions, presumably as his patients free associated (Masson, 1985, p. 303).

It should be realized that although Freud referred to his major therapeutic technique as "free association," he believed the reported associations to be anything but "free" in the sense of being random or accidental. Rather, the patient's associations reflect the complex ways that unacceptable impulses are repressed, displaced, and in other ways disguised. Thus a patient's associations may seem free, but to the trained analyst they reflect the complex interactions between the conscious and unconscious levels of the mind.

Dream Analysis

Freud considered his book, *The Interpretation of Dreams* (1965a), to be his most important contribution, and it was this book that finally brought Freud the professional recognition he had been seeking. Freud believed it was in dreams that the contents of the unconscious are most available, still hidden, or distorted but available. Indeed, Freud thought "The interpretation of dreams is the royal road to knowledge of the unconscious activities of the mind" (p. 608).

It is interesting to note that the notion of the Oedipus complex was supported when Freud began his own dream analysis. Although his father had been ill, and his death was imminent, Freud became extremely depressed when his father died. He was confused by his depression until the explanation came to him in a dream. After carefully analyzing the symbols contained in one of his dreams, Freud concluded that his extreme reaction to his father's death was explained by the fact that unconsciously he wanted his father to die, and therefore he felt guilty. Further analysis showed that Freud had sexual desires for his mother and viewed his father as a competitor for his mother's affection. As we have seen, Freud believed that such Oedipal impulses (lust for the mother and wanting the father dead) were universal among boys.

According to Freud, a dream is caused when the events of the day activate unacceptable impulses in the unconscious mind, causing them to seek conscious expression. At night, as the person sleeps, these impulses continue to seek conscious expression, but the ego realizes that if the contents of a dream are too threatening, they will cause the dreamer to awake prematurely. The ego, therefore, censors the impulses by driving them back into the unconscious. If these unacceptable impulses are ever to be consciously recognized they must be at least partially camouflaged. Freud referred to the various mechanisms that make impulses more acceptable by distorting their true meaning collectively as dream work. The two most important types of **dream work** are condensation and displacement.

Condensation occurs when a dream element represents several ideas at the same time. For example, one person in a dream can represent several people in the dreamer's waking life. **Displacement** occurs when an unacceptable dream-thought is replaced by a thought that is symbolically equivalent but is acceptable such as when penises become objects such as baseball bats or flagpoles; breasts become mountains, balloons, or cantaloupes; and sexual intercourse becomes dancing or horseback riding, to give but a few examples. Freud believed most of the symbols that occur in a particular person's dream are derived from events in that person's life. Freud did believe, however, that some dream symbols were universal. For example, kings and queens symbolize mothers and fathers; boxes, chests, and cupboards symbolize the womb; walking up or down staircases, ladders, or steps symbolizes sexual intercourse; haircutting, baldness, and decapitation symbolize castration; small animals symbolize children; and long, stiff objects symbolize the penis. The symbols that occur in a person's dream can come from events in the person's waking life, from his or her childhood, or from the phylogenetic heritage of the human species (again we see Freud embracing Lamarck's notion of the inheritance of acquired characteristics).

The dream work creates several disjointed symbols that have little meaning to the dreamer, and thus they are allowed past the censor and enter consciousness. The dream symbols no longer cause anxiety because they represent unacceptable wishes, but they do cause anxiety for another reason. Because the rational (secondary) processes of the ego seek to interact with the physical world in a logical, intelligible manner, the meaningless symbols attempting to enter consciousness after being acted on by the dream work cannot be tolerated. To make the material acceptable, the ego engages in what Freud called **secondary revision** (sometimes called secondary elaboration). That is, the ego synthesizes the symbols in some coherent fashion. It is this secondary revision that we recall as a dream. When we recall a dream, we describe its **manifest content** or about what it appeared to be. More important is the dream's **latent content** that consists of the repressed thoughts seeking expression.

Dream work and secondary revision act on a dream to make its content more acceptable but still the latent meaning is always there for the trained observer to discover. Because dreams always contain at least some threatening material, the patient and therapist must work quickly before their contents are repressed again. The nature of dreams and the process of repression explain why the memory of dreams is so short-lived.

Everyday Life

In 1901, Freud published a book entitled *The Psychopathology of Everyday Life* in which he gave numerous examples of **parapraxes,** that is, the manifestation of repressed thoughts in the course of everyday living. Being a determinist, Freud believed all human behavior had a cause, that nothing happened simply by chance—not even "accidents." Freud believed little "mistakes" such as temporary lapses of memory provided information about the unconscious mind. For example, one may forget a potentially painful visit to the dentist or psychoanalyst. One may forget a date altogether or show up on Saturday instead of on Friday, when the date actually was to occur. One may stop at a green light on the way to his or her mother-in-law's house.

Slips of the tongue that have come to be known as **Freudian slips** are also thought to reveal unconscious motives. Legend has it that once Freud was introduced as Dr. Sigmund Fraud. Zimbardo and Ruch (1977, p. 416) reported that a radio announcer, reading a commercial for Barbara Ann Bread, instead of saying "Barbara Ann for the best bread" read "Barbara Ann for the breast in bed."

Even actual accidents were thought by Freud to have meaning. After all, an automobile accident is a socially acceptable way of not getting somewhere. The main point here is that just because a thought is repressed does not mean it goes away; it is always there striving for expression, and these manifestations in everyday life are another way of getting a glimpse into the unconscious.

Humor

According to Freud, **humor** allows the expression of repressed thoughts in a socially approved manner. In his book *Jokes and Their Relation to the Unconscious* (1960) Freud indicated that through humor a person can express aggressiveness (e.g., practical jokes) or sexual desires without the fear of retaliation by either the ego or the superego. Jokes, then, are like dreams in that both allow the compromised expression of unacceptable impulses, and both employ condensation, displacement, and symbolization. The purpose of both jokes and dreams is to satisfy unacceptable impulses indirectly that would be shocking if expressed directly. A joke that is too blatant fails to be humorous just as a nightmare fails to preserve the sleep of the dreamer. In both cases, the impulses involved were not disguised enough. Also jokes, like dreams, are usually forgotten quickly, for they too deal with "dangerous" material. In fact, for a joke to be "funny," it must contain anxiety-provoking material. According to Freud, we laugh only at jokes that bother us. An examination of American humor shows sex, elimination, and death to be favorite topics, and this would indicate to a Freudian that they contain an abundance of repressed thoughts. The Freudians say one way to discover what has been repressed in a person's unconscious mind is to examine what he or she finds humorous.

Freud's View of Religion

When our ancestors were children they turned to their fathers for protection and guidance. Fathers tended to be revered, feared, and relied on. According to Freud, it is understandable that our ancestors created a God with the same characteristics as real fathers. According to Freud, these infantile conceptions of the father were generalized to an image of a deity who had to be blindly obeyed, just like a real father. This God protects his children from natural disasters such as earthquakes, storms, floods, volcanic eruptions, and disease. God, and the religions based on his existence, protect humans from feeling helpless and from feeling confused in light of the many apparent contradictions in life. Typically, religions teach that life continues after death; life after death can be perfect even if life on earth is not; good persons will eventually be rewarded and bad ones punished; the difficulties one may experience in his or her life serve a higher purpose, and therefore no need for despair exists; and, in general, the world is being governed by a providence of superior wisdom and infinite goodness who relates to humans with the intimacy of a loving father. Religions also teach it is God's will that humans inhibit their sexual and aggressive tendencies to live in harmony with their fellow humans. About the role of religion in the lives of so many humans, Freud said: "The whole thing is so patently infantile, so foreign to reality, that to anyone with a friendly attitude to humanity it is painful to think that the great majority of mortals will never be able to rise above this view of life" (1961, p. 22).

Perhaps, according to Freud, the uneducated masses will always need the illusions of religion to cause them to restrain their passions but educated, intelligent persons should live their lives according to scientific facts, not illusions. It is time, said Freud, to admit that our ancestors were wrong about religion; miracles never existed; natural disasters kill both believers and nonbelievers; no life after death occurs;

and the course of human history is explained by evolutionary principles rather than the unfolding of a divine plan. Furthermore, although civilization does require rules, regulations, and inhibitions, these should be justified on rational grounds rather than claiming that they are the will of a deity. In other words, humans should be shown how various sanctions ultimately work to their own self-interests and, for that reason, should strive to preserve them.

Freud hoped that religion would eventually be replaced by rational, scientific principles. Just as Freud took no pain-killing drugs during his 16-year bout with cancer, he believed that humans could and should confront reality without the aid of illusions:

> No belittlement of science can in any way alter the fact that it is attempting to take account of our dependence on the real external world, while religion is an illusion and it derives its strength from its readiness to fit in with our instinctual wishful impulses. (1966a, pp. 638–639)

Freud concluded his book *The Future of an Illusion* (1961c) saying, "Our science is no illusion. But an illusion it would be to suppose that what science cannot give us we can get elsewhere" (p. 71).

Freud's View of Human Nature

To Freud, humans were mainly biological organisms whose master motive was the satisfaction of bodily needs. Cultural achievements in the sciences, arts, and religion were regarded mainly as displacements away from the more direct (and natural) ways of satisfying our biological needs in general and our sexual needs in particular. Freud viewed humans as hedonistic creatures driven by the same impulses that drive nonhuman animals. Religion and civilization developed either because of our fear of the unknown, or because we needed protection against our own inborn aggressive tendencies.

Freud seemed to grow more pessimistic with age, a fact that many attribute to his worsening cancer of the mouth and throat. In his book *Civilization and Its Discontents,* he reacted to the commandment "Thou shalt love thy neighbor as thyself," as follows:

> What is the point of a precept enunciated with so much solemnity if its fulfillment cannot be recommended as reasonable? . . . Not merely is this stranger in general unworthy of my love; I must honestly confess that he has more claim to my hostility and even my hatred. He seems not to have the least trace of love for me and shows me not the slightest consideration. If it will do him any good he has no hesitation in injuring me, nor does he ask himself whether the amount of advantage he gains bears any proportion to the extent of the harm he does to me. Indeed, he need not even obtain an advantage; if he can satisfy any sort of desire by it, he thinks nothing of jeering at me, insulting me, slandering me and showing his superior power; and the more secure he feels and the more helpless I am, the more certainly I can expect him to behave like this to me. . . . Indeed, if this grandiose

commandment had run "Love thy neighbour as thy neighbour loves thee," I should not take exception to it. . . .

The element of truth behind all this, which people are so ready to disavow, is that men are not gentle creatures who want to be loved, and who at the most can defend themselves if they are attacked; they are, on the contrary, creatures among whose instinctual endowments is to be reckoned a powerful share of aggressiveness. As a result, their neighbour is for them not only a potential helper or sexual object, but also someone who tempts them to satisfy their aggressiveness on him, to exploit his capacity for work without compensation, to use him sexually without his consent, to seize his possessions, to humiliate him, to cause him pain, to torture and to kill him. Homo homini lupus [Man is a wolf to man]. (1961a, pp. 65–69)

Although pessimistic, Freud believed humans could, and should, live more rational lives, and the information that his theory provided could help them do so. To live rationally one must come to understand the workings of his or her own mind. Freud (1955b) said:

The news that reaches your consciousness is incomplete and often not to be relied on. . . . Even if you are not ill, who can tell all that is stirring in your mind of which you know nothing or are falsely informed? You behave like an absolute ruler who is content with the information supplied him by his highest officials and never goes among the people to hear their voice. Turn your eyes inward, look into your own depths, learn first to know yourself! (p. 143)

Modifications of the Freudian Legend

Few would doubt that Freud was one of the most influential figures in human history. Recently, however, several researchers have provided information that requires rather substantial changes in the traditional view of Freud and his ideas.

Freud's Revision of His Seduction Theory

In April 1896, Freud delivered a paper entitled "The Aetiology of Hysteria" in which he concluded that hysteria is caused by a sexual seduction that had been experienced by the patient in childhood. At this time, Freud reported the seducers as nursemaids, governesses, domestic servants, adult strangers, tutors, and in most cases brothers who were slightly older than the sisters they supposedly seduced; no mention was made of parents as seducers. Freud's address to his colleagues was met with total silence, and he was urged not to publish his findings because doing so would damage his professional reputation beyond repair. Despite the warnings, however, Freud published his article in 1896 (reprinted in Masson, 1984) and he continued to experience professional, emotional, and intellectual isolation. Even Wilhelm Fliess (1858–1928), Freud's closest friend at the time, was not supportive of Freud's seduction theory.

Freud abandoned his **seduction theory** in September 1897, although it was never scientifically refuted. The reasons for this abandonment are still a matter of speculation. In any case, Freud acknowledged that he had made a mistake in believing his patients that a real seduction had occurred in their childhoods. His revised position was that the seductions were often imaginary. Freud later claimed that this change from real to imagined seductions marked the beginning of psychoanalysis as a science, therapy, and profession. It was only at this time that Freud claimed his patients reported parents, usually the father, as their seducers. It is now believed that this change was designed to make Freud's clinical "observations" compatible with his newly proposed Oedipal theory. This exemplifies Freud's tendency to find support for whatever theoretical notions he was entertaining at the time. About this tendency, Esterson (1993) says, "It is difficult to escape the conclusion that both self-deception and dishonesty play a role in this story though at times it is scarcely possible to distinguish one from the other" (p. 31).

Jeffrey Masson, in his book *The Assault on Truth: Freud's Suppression of the Seduction Theory* (1984), explored possible reasons why Freud changed his belief from real to imaginary seductions and concludes he did so mainly because he lacked personal courage, not for any clinical or theoretical reasons. Masson, the former projects director of the Sigmund Freud Archives, bases his conclusion on several previously unpublished or newly discovered letters and other documents. Masson, himself a psychoanalyst, also concludes that psychoanalysis would be better off today had Freud not revised his seduction theory:

> By shifting the emphasis from an actual world of sadness, misery, and cruelty to an internal stage on which actors performed invented dramas for an invisible audience of their own creation, Freud began a trend away from the real world that, it seems to me, is at the root of the present day sterility of psychoanalysis and psychiatry throughout the world. (p. 144)

Masson (1984) provided a number of personal reasons that may have caused Freud to revise his seduction theory, reasons that are most unflattering to Freud in particular and to psychoanalysis in general. Masson believes that Freud's basic mistake was not accepting recovered memories of children's sexual seduction as reflecting actual events. But what if there were no recovered memories of any kind? There is now convincing evidence that Freud entered into the therapeutic situation with the strong conviction that repressed memories of infantile abuse existed in his patients, and he manipulated events during therapy in ways that caused his conviction to be confirmed. Furthermore, evidence indicates that it was Freud's interpretations and reconstructions of his patient's responses that were offered as evidence for his beliefs, rather than anything his patients actually said. For example, Esterson (1993) says, "A consideration of all the evidence . . . points to the conclusion that Freud's early patients, in general, did *not* recount stories of infantile seductions, these stories were actually analytic reconstructions which he foisted on them" (pp. 28–29). Esterson (1998, 2001) provides further evidence that none of Freud's patients during the time he was formulating his seduction theory reported that they had been sexually seduced in childhood. Similarly, Webster (1995) concludes, "There is no evidence that any of the patients who came to Freud without memories of sexual abuse had ever suffered from such abuse" (p. 517).

For additional support for the conclusions just cited by Esterson (1993, 1998, 2001) and Webster (1995) and for a discussion of other problems associated with

Freud's account of repressed memories see, for example, Cioffi (1974, 1998); Crews (1995); Gelfand and Kerr (1992); Israëls and Schatzman (1993); Powell and Boer (1994); Schatzman (1992); and Wilcocks (1994). Given the fact that Freud described the concept of repression as the "cornerstone" of psychoanalysis, these, and other, researchers are attacking the very foundation of psychoanalysis.

Not all contemporary accounts of Freud's development of his seduction theory and his subsequent abandonment of that theory are negative. For a more positive analysis and for rebuttals of most of the criticisms cited above, see Gleaves and Hernandez (1999); for a rebuttal of the claims made by Gleaves and Hernandez (1999), see Esterson (2002); and for a rebuttal of Esterson's rebuttal, see Gleaves and Hernandez (2002).

Obviously, concern about the reality of repressed memories is not only of historical interest. A number of contemporary researchers are concerned about the widespread search for repressed memories by current therapists. Elizabeth Loftus (1993), for example, wonders why so many individuals enter therapy without memories of abuse but leave with them. She speculates that often it is the suggestions made by therapists that make the difference.

> If therapists ask questions that tend to elicit behaviors and experiences thought to be characteristic of someone who had been a victim of childhood trauma, might they too be creating this social reality?
>
> Whatever the good intentions of therapists, the documented examples of rampant suggestion should force us to at least ponder whether some therapists might be suggesting illusory memories to their clients rather than unlocking distant memories. . . . What is considered to be present in the client's unconscious mind might actually be present solely in the therapist's conscious mind. (p. 530)

Researchers, such as Loftus, do not deny that many children are sexually abused or that therapy can help them deal effectively with such experiences. It is the notion of repression and the techniques used to recover "repressed memories" that are being questioned.

> Many tortured individuals live for years with the dark secret of their abusive past and only find the courage to discuss their childhood traumas in the supportive and empathic environment of therapy. We are not disputing those memories. We are only questioning the memories commonly referred to as "repressed"—memories that did not exist until someone went looking for them. (Loftus & Ketcham, 1994, p. 141)

In recent times, allegations of childhood sexual abuse based on recovered memories has become so widespread that the False Memory Syndrome Foundation (FMSF) was created in 1992 to investigate and assess such charges (see, e.g., False Memory Syndrome Foundation, 1992). The American Psychological Association (APA; 1995) approved the FMSF as a provider of information concerning so-called recovered memories of abuse.

Correcting Other Freudian Myths

Earlier in this chapter we saw examples of how the Freudians distorted their history to make it more interesting or flattering. In the same vein, Freud and his followers tended to paint Freud as a lonely, heroic figure who suffered discrimination because he was a Jew and because of the difficulty others had in accepting his bold, creative, original ideas. Henri Ellenberger has done much to demythologize the Freudian legend. According to Ellenberger (1970), the Freudian legend has two main features:

> The first is the theme of the solitary hero struggling against a host of enemies, suffering "the slings and arrows of outrageous fortune" but triumphing in the end. The legend considerably exaggerates the extent and role of anti-Semitism, of the hostility of the academic world, and of alleged Victorian prejudices. The second feature of the Freudian legend is the blotting out of the greatest part of the scientific and cultural context in which psychoanalysis developed, hence the theme of the absolute originality of the achievements, in which the hero is credited with the achievements of his predecessors, associates, disciples, rivals, and contemporaries. (p. 547)

According to Ellenberger, a careful reading of the facts indicates that Freud's career was only slightly hampered by anti-Semitism; that Freud experienced no more than the normal amount of hostility from his fellow physicians and not nearly as much as several more prominent physicians did; and that most of Freud's ideas concerning dreams, the unconscious mind, and sexual pathology were not original. Ellenberger (1970) said, "Much of what is credited to Freud was diffuse current lore, and his role was to crystallize these ideas and give them an original shape" (p. 548).

Freud and his early followers had a low tolerance for criticism and usually attributed it to a lack of understanding, resistance, or bigotry. Frank Sulloway in his book, *Freud, Biologist of the Mind: Beyond the Psychoanalytic Legend* (1979), however, concluded that most of the criticisms directed at psychoanalysis as it began to become popular were rational and justified. Sulloway summarizes those criticisms:

> In addition to the criticisms that had already been raised before Freud acquired a substantial following, common objections against psychoanalysis now began to include: (1) that psychoanalysts were continually introducing their assertions with the statement, "We know from psychoanalytic experience that. . .," and then leaving the burden of proof to others; (2) that Freud's disciples refused to listen to opinions that did not coincide with their own; (3) that they never published statistics on the success of their method; (4) that they persisted in claiming that only those who had used the psychoanalytic method had the right to challenge Freud; (5) that they saw all criticism as a form of "neurotic resistance"; (6) that psychoanalysts tended to ignore all work that had been done before them and then proceeded to make unwarranted claims about their own originality; (7) that they frequently addressed themselves to the wider lay audience as if their theories were already a proven fact, thus making their opponents seem narrow-minded and ignorant; (8) that so-called wild analysts, or individuals without proper training, were analyzing patients in irresponsible ways; and (9) that Freud's followers were becoming a sect, with all of the prominent features of one, including a fanatical degree of

faith, a special jargon, a sense of moral superiority, and a predilection for marked intolerance of opponents. In their contemporary context, such criticisms were considerably more rational and had far more merit than traditional psychoanalytic historians have been willing to admit. (p. 460)

Evaluation

Empirical Research

The many attempts to validate Freudian ideas experimentally have produced mixed results. In his review of numerous studies, J. McVicker Hunt (1979) found support for Freud's contention that early experience is important in molding adult personality but little support for the influence of specific psychosexual stages as Freud described them. In his review, Maddi (1996) found considerable support for the various mechanisms of defense postulated by Freud, especially repression. Maddi also found evidence that boys experience more castration anxiety than do girls. Silverman (1976), Blum (1962), and Hall and Van de Castle (1965) also found more castration anxiety in boys relative to girls and the reverse for penis envy. Kline (1972) reviewed more than 700 studies designed to test Freudian notions and concluded that Freudian theory could not be rejected on the basis of the research designed to test it because "Too much that is distinctively Freudian has been verified [and] there are few good experiments which actually refute the theory" (p. 350). Fisher and Greenberg (1977) reached a similar conclusion: "Scanning the spectrum of tests we have applied to Freud's theories, we are generally impressed with how often the results have borne out his expectations" (p. 393). Also, responding to the frequently made assertion that Freudian notions are too nebulous to be tested, Fisher and Greenberg said, "We have actually not been able to find a single systematic psychological theory that has been as frequently evaluated scientifically as have Freud's concepts!" (p. 396). Masling (1983) also reported numerous experiments that verify several Freudian notions.

Criticisms

Earlier we reviewed several criticisms of psychoanalytic theory that were made in Freud's day just as his theory was gaining widespread recognition. Many current critics of Freudian theory believe that those early criticisms are still valid. In addition, say the critics, Freudian theory can be criticized for being internally inconsistent; demonstrating male chauvinism (e.g., girls long to have a penis); overemphasizing sexual motivation; overemphasizing unconscious motivation; being too pessimistic about human nature (e.g., humans are basically aggressive and irrational); and equating the ultimate state of happiness with the tension-free state that results when all of one's biological needs are satisfied.

Critics also claim that, although a few Freudian concepts have been supported by empirical research, most of his important notions remain untestable. About psychoanalytic theory in general, Stanovich (2004) says:

Adherents of psychoanalytical theory spend much time and effort in getting the theory to explain every known event, from individual quirks of behavior to large-scale social phenomena, but their success in making the theory a rich source of after-the-fact explanation robs it of any scientific utility. (p. 26)

Dawes (2001) provides a specific example:

Consider [the] Freudian assertion that someone has an oral character "based on the young child's nursing and weaning." Such a character may be created by overindulgence, by deprivation, or by inconsistency between overindulgence and deprivation on the part of the mother. Then the person who suffers from this defect of oral character as an adult may either be excessively passive or "oral sadistic"—as indicated by excessive use of sarcastic humor, negative statements, skepticism, and so on.

 The problem is that there are six combinations of nursing and adult character that are meant to support the idea. But they constitute every conceivable combination. . . . The point is that no matter what occurs, we can interpret it as supporting the idea of childhood determination of adult psychopathology. Moreover, if we find one of the antecedents with none of the consequences, or vice versa, we can rationalize this negative result by simply assuming that we don't know enough, are inept at understanding what is there, or haven't searched diligently enough, and so forth. Psychoanalysis can claim special insight into the unique way in which the analyst's patient develops the [oral] character, but to an outside observer, the whole argument becomes irrefutable. And it is exactly to the outside observer whom the scientist must answer the "show me" challenge common to any type of valid scientific endeavor. (p. 97)

Most often Freudian theory attempts to explain events after they have occurred, as the preceding quotation exemplifies. That is, the theory engages in postdiction rather than prediction. As we saw in Chapter 1, if a theory does not generate risky predictions it cannot be falsified and, therefore, according to Popper, it is not scientific. From what has preceded, then, we can conclude that some aspects of Freud's theory are scientific (testable) but many others are not.

Contributions

Despite the many criticisms of Freud's theory, many would agree that its overall value is positive. Freud contributed to our understanding of personality by demonstrating the importance of anxiety as a determinant of human behavior; by showing that physical and physiological disorders can have psychological as well as physiological origins; by showing that conflicts originating in childhood have lifelong consequences; by showing the importance of childhood sexuality in personality development; by showing the many ways that persons defend themselves against unbearable anxiety; by showing that much "normal" behavior is determined by the same processes that determine "abnormal" behavior; by showing that many human problems result from the clash between the selfish, biological nature of humans and our need to live harmoniously with other humans in society; and by developing a technique for treating persons experiencing unbearable anxiety. Freud has provided us with a general framework with which to study personality. Although portions of Freud's theory may be incorrect or vague and difficult to test, it has raised questions that researchers have attempted to answer ever since.

As we pointed out at the beginning of this chapter, few people in history have had the impact on human thought that Freud has had. No major category of human existence has been untouched by his ideas. For example, he has influenced religion, philosophy, education, literature, art, and all of the social sciences.

What follows in this text can be understood mainly as a reaction to Freud. Some theories support and extend his thoughts, and others refute them, but it was Freud who was first, and that is always most difficult.

Summary

Freud shocked the world by demonstrating the importance of unconscious motivation in human behavior. Although originally intending to become a professor of neurology, Freud became increasingly interested in mental problems. Freud first believed cocaine to be a "magical substance" and used and prescribed it freely; when it was found to be addictive, however, Freud's medical reputation suffered considerably. From his visit with Charcot, Freud learned that physical disorders could have psychological as well as organic origins, and therefore hysteria should be viewed as a serious, treatable disorder. From Bernheim, Freud learned that behavior can be caused by ideas of which individuals are unaware. He also learned from Bernheim that unconscious ideas can be made conscious if certain procedures are followed. Freud learned from Breuer that when a patient openly discusses his or her problems, a release of tension called catharsis often occurs. Sometimes a patient responds to a therapist as if he or she were an important person in the patient's life, and this process is called transference. Also, the therapist sometimes becomes emotionally involved with the patient and this occurrence is called countertransference. After experimenting with several therapeutic techniques, Freud arrived at free association as a primary means of studying the unconscious.

According to Freud, instincts constitute the driving force behind personality. Instincts have a source, an aim, an object, and an impetus. Freud referred to the life instincts collectively as eros and to the energy associated with life instincts as libido or libidinal energy. A death instinct, called thanatos, is responsible for aggression that Freud believed was the tendency toward self-destruction turned outward.

The adult mind is divided into the id, the ego, and the superego. The id is the part of our mind we share with lower animals and is governed by the pleasure principle. The ego is the executive of the personality and is governed by the reality principle. The superego is the moral component of the personality and consists of the conscience and the ego ideal. When a physiological need arises, the id creates a mental image of an object that will satisfy that need. This is called wish fulfillment, which is, along with reflex action, a primary process. Because wishes cannot satisfy needs, the ego must seek out real objects in the environment that will actually satisfy that need. These problem-solving skills of the ego are called secondary processes.

The investment of psychic energy in the image of an object that will satisfy a need is called cathexis. If a desired object conflicts with the values of the superego, anxiety will be experienced, the ego will resist the id's attempt to invest energy in its image, and an anticathexis will occur. When an anticathexis occurs, the person will typically displace his or her desire to a substitute goal that does not cause anxiety. Freud discussed three types of anxiety: reality anxiety, which is the fear of actual dangers in the environment; neurotic anxiety, which is the fear of being punished for impulsive, animalistic actions; and moral anxiety, which is experienced when a value internalized in the superego has been violated.

The ego-defense mechanisms are unconscious processes that reduce anxiety by distorting or falsifying reality. Repression is the most basic ego-defense mechanism because all the other ego-defense mechanisms first employ repression. Repression keeps anxiety-provoking thoughts in the unconscious mind and thus out of a person's awareness. Displacement substitutes a nonanxiety-provoking goal for one that does cause anxiety. If the displacement involves a sexual impulse and contributes positively to society, it is called sublimation. If aggression is displaced from its primary goal to a safer one or one that is socially approved, it is called displaced aggression. Identification is affiliating oneself with someone or something that will enhance one's feelings of worth. Denial of reality involves the refusal to accept the reality of some event because to do so would cause anxiety. Projection involves seeing in other people, objects, or events qualities that are true about oneself but would cause anxiety if recognized. With undoing, a person performs some ritualistic activity in an effort to minimize or negate the anxiety caused by an unacceptable act or thought. Reaction formation is repressing anxiety-provoking impulses and exaggerating opposite impulses. Rationalization is giving "logical" explanations for behavior that would cause anxiety if it were not "explained away." With intellectualization, a potentially anxiety-provoking idea is stripped of its emotional component by the intellectual (rational) analysis of the idea. Regression is returning to a stage of development where fixation had occurred when stress is encountered. To the list of ego-defense mechanisms, Anna Freud added two: altruistic surrender, or the tendency to internalize another person's values and live in accordance with them, and identification with the aggressor, or the tendency to internalize the values of a threatening person in order to make him or her less threatening.

Freud believed each child goes through certain psychosexual stages of development, and the child's experiences during these stages determine what type of personality he or she will possess as an adult. During each psychosexual stage, an area of the body that is associated with maximum pleasure is called an erogenous zone. If, during any stage, either too much or too little gratification occurs, fixation results, which means as an adult the person will possess traits characteristic of that stage. The first psychosexual stage is the oral stage. Fixation at the oral stage results in either an oral-incorporative character or an oral-sadistic character. The second psychosexual stage is the anal stage. Fixation at the anal stage results in either an anal-expulsive character or an anal-retentive character. The third psychosexual stage is the phallic stage, which is the scene of the Oedipus complex. Typically during this stage boys experience castration anxiety and girls experience penis envy. It is the phallic stage, according to the Freudians, that largely determines adult sexual preferences. The fourth psychosexual stage is the latency stage during which time sexual interests are repressed and displaced to other activities such as learning and peer group activities. The final psychosexual stage is the genital stage from which the individual emerges as the adult he or she is destined to become after various experiences during the preceding psychosexual stages.

Freud tried several theoretical approaches to understanding women but most consistently claimed that "anatomy is destiny." That is, gender differences are ultimately biological in origin. In the end, however, Freud essentially admitted defeat in his effort to understand women.

Freud's major tools for investigating the unconscious mind were free association, dream analysis, analysis of everyday experiences, and humor. During free association, Freud noted that patients often resisted pondering certain ideas, and he assumed that those ideas were especially anxiety provoking to the patient. While analyzing dreams, he differentiated between a dream's manifest content, or its apparent meaning, and its latent content, or its true meaning. The mechanisms that distort dreams were called collectively dream work and included condensation and displacement. In everyday life, Freud noted that people tend to forget anxiety-provoking experiences, sometimes have "accidents" on purpose, and sometimes exhibit "slips of the tongue" that reveal their true (unconscious) feelings. Freud also noted that jokes were like dreams because both allow the indirect expression of thoughts that, if expressed directly, would cause unbearable anxiety.

Freud believed that the helplessness that our ancestors felt when confronting the power of nature and the uncertainties of life caused them to create a God that had the characteristics of a powerful, all-knowing, and benevolent father. Freud believed it dangerous for contemporary humans to go on basing their lives on the irrational wish fulfillments that constitute religion. It is better, according to Freud, to live in accordance with the objective facts provided by science. Freud was quite pessimistic about human nature. He believed humans are animals frustrated by the demands of civilization. According to Freud, humans are aggressive and selfish by nature. However, Freud did believe that it was possible for humans to live rational lives and that his theory could help them do so.

Recently the Freudian legend has been modified in several important ways. The reasons for Freud's abandonment of his seduction theory have been questioned. It has been suggested that the theory was correct and never should have been discarded. Others claim that none of Freud's patients who entered psychoanalysis without conscious memories of infantile sexual abuse ever recovered such memories during therapy. Rather, repressed memories were theoretical preconceptions that Freud foisted on his patients. In contemporary psychology, there is considerable skepticism concerning the existence of repressed memories, thus the very foundation of psychoanalysis is being challenged. It has also been discovered that Freud did not experience as much anti-Semitism nor rejection from the medical community as has been claimed. Finally, many of the ideas that were attributed to Freud were not original. The many attempts to validate Freud's ideas empirically have produced equivocal results. Critics say that many of Freud's most basic notions are incapable of falsification. Other criticisms include internal inconsistency, male chauvinism, overemphasis on sexual and unconscious motivation, being too pessimistic about human nature, and equating true happiness with the tension-free condition that occurs when all of one's biological needs are satisfied. Despite their possible shortcomings, Freud's ideas have influenced our understanding of every area of human existence. He has had a major influence on art, literature, philosophy, and science. His was the first comprehensive theory of personality, and all theories of personality since can be considered reactions to Freud's theory.

Experiential Exercises

1. Keep track of your dreams for about a week. As soon as possible following each dream write down as much of it as you can remember. Analyze the dreams as Freud would have. In other words, analyze the manifest content of each dream, assuming that a more basic latent content exists. Also, free-associate to your dreams, again assuming that the associations triggered by the dream's manifest content will reveal something about the dream's latent content. Summarize what you think your dreams reveal about the content of your unconscious mind.
2. Although, according to Freud, the ego-defense mechanisms function on the unconscious level, it is sometimes possible to detect one's own use of them by carefully observing one's behavior. Make a list of the ego-defense mechanisms you use and describe how you use them.
3. Observe your own behavior for about a week and note the following: appointments for which you were late or missed altogether; slips of the tongue; memory lapses; any "accidents" that you had; and any jokes you heard and found amusing. Analyze these everyday experiences with the idea they may reflect the contents of your unconscious mind. Summarize your conclusions.

Discussion Questions

1. Elaborate on the importance of the concept of instinct to Freud's theory.
2. Discuss the relationships among cathexis, anticathexis, and displacement.
3. Discuss Freud's view on the relationship between displacement and civilization.

Glossary

Altruistic surrender. An ego-defense mechanism postulated by Anna Freud by which a person internalizes the values of another person and lives his or her life in accordance with those values.

Anal-expulsive character. Character type that results from a fixation at the early anal stage. Such a person may have trouble with bowel control and may be overly generous.

Anal-retentive character. Character type that results from a fixation at the late anal stage. Such a person may suffer from constipation and may be stingy.

Anal stage. Second psychosexual stage that occurs about the second year of life during which time the anal area is the primary erogenous zone.

Anticathexis. Expenditure of energy to prevent a cathexis that would cause anxiety.

Anxiety. The general feeling of impending danger. *See also* Moral anxiety, Neurotic anxiety, and Reality anxiety.

Bernheim, Hippolyte (1840–1919). French neurologist from whom Freud learned that one's behavior can be determined by ideas of which he or she is unaware. He also learned from Bernheim that persons could become aware of unconscious ideas if pressured to do so.

Breuer, Josef (1842–1925). Physician who became Freud's close friend and coauthored *Studies on Hysteria* (1895). Breuer was the first to use the "talking cure" while treating hysteria, which later evolved into Freud's technique of free association.

Castration anxiety. Boy's fear that he is going to lose his sex organs because they are regarded as the source of difficulty between the boy and his father.

Catharsis. Emotional relief that results when a person is able to ponder pathogenic ideas consciously. Physical disorders are often relieved following catharsis.

Cathexis. Investment of psychic energy in the image of an object that will satisfy a need.

Charcot, Jean-Martin (1825–1893). French neurologist from whom Freud learned that physical disorders could have a psychological origin and that hysteria must, therefore, be taken seriously as a disease.

Condensation. Form of dream distortion in which one dream element represents several ideas at the same time.

Conscience. That part of the superego that results from the internalized experiences for which a child had been punished. This component of the personality is responsible for the experience of guilt. *See also* Ego ideal.

Countertransference. Phenomenon that sometimes occurs during therapy in which the therapist becomes emotionally involved with a patient.

Denial of reality. Some potentially anxiety-provoking aspect of reality is denied despite abundant information testifying to its existence.

Displaced aggression. Aggression directed toward a person or object less threatening than the one causing the aggressive impulse.

Displacement. Substitution of one cathexis that is anxiety-provoking with one that is not. Also a form of dream distortion in which an acceptable image is substituted for an unacceptable one—for example, when one dreams of mountains instead of breasts.

Dream work. Various mechanisms that distort a dream's latent content.

Ego. Executive of the personality whose job it is to satisfy the needs of both the id and the superego by engaging in appropriate environmental activities. The ego is governed by the reality principle.

Ego-defense mechanisms. Unconscious processes that falsify or distort reality to reduce or prevent anxiety.

Ego ideal. That portion of the superego that results from the internalized experiences for which a child has been rewarded. This component of the personality is responsible for the experience of success and pride.

Erogenous zone. Area of the body that is a source of pleasure.

Eros. All the life instincts taken collectively.

Fixation. Arrested development at one of the psychosexual stages because of the undergratification or overgratification of a need. Fixation determines the point to which an adult regresses under stress.

Free association. Called by Freud the fundamental rule of psychoanalysis, it entails instructing the patient to say whatever comes to his or her mind no matter how irrelevant, threatening, or nonsensical it may seem.

Freudian slip. Verbal "accident" that is thought to reveal the speaker's true feelings.

Genital stage. Final psychosexual stage and the one that follows puberty. It is a time when the full adult personality emerges and when the experiences that occurred during the pregenital stages manifest themselves.

Humor. According to Freud, humor is a socially acceptable way of expressing repressed, anxiety-provoking thoughts, for example, thoughts involving sex or aggression.

Hysteria. General term describing disorders such as paralysis of the arms or legs, loss of sensation, disturbances of sight and speech, nausea, and general confusion. Because hysteria has no known organic cause, its root is assumed to be psychological. Until Charcot, hysteria was generally assumed to be exclusively a female disease. *Hystera* is the Greek word for uterus.

Id. Component of the personality that is completely unconscious and contains all the instincts. It is the animalistic portion of the personality that is governed by the pleasure principle.

Identification. A term used in two ways by Freud: (1) the matching of an idinal image with its physical counterpart, and (2) the incorporation of another person's values or characteristics either to enhance one's self-esteem or to minimize that person as a threat.

Identification with the aggressor. An ego-defense mechanism postulated by Anna Freud by which the fear caused by a person is reduced or eliminated by internalizing the feared person's values and mannerisms.

Inheritance of acquired characteristics. Lamarck's contention that the information learned during a person's lifetime can be passed on to that person's offspring.

Instinct. For Freud, instincts were the stuff from which personality is shaped. An instinct is the cognitive reflection of a biological deficiency. Instincts have four characteristics—a source, an aim, an object, and an impetus—and can be divided into two categories—life and death.

Intellectualization (also called isolation of affect). The minimization of the negative emotions associated with an event by a detached, logical analysis of the event.

Latency stage. Psychosexual stage that lasts from about the 6th year to about the 12th year of life. It is a time when sexual activity is repressed and an abundance of substitute activities are engaged in, such as learning and athletics.

Latent content of a dream. A dream's true meaning that is disguised or distorted by dream work.

Libido. In Freud's earlier writings, libido was the psychic energy associated with the sexual instinct but later he expanded the concept of libido to include the energy associated with all the life instincts—for instance, hunger and thirst in addition to sex.

Manifest content of a dream. What a dream appears to be about to the dreamer.

Moral anxiety. The guilt experienced when one either does or ponders doing something that violates the values of one's superego.

Neurotic anxiety. Caused by the fear that the impulses of the id will overwhelm the ego, thereby causing the person to do something for which he or she will be punished.

Oedipus complex. Male Oedipus complex begins when a boy loves his mother and views his father as a dominant rival for her affection. The male Oedipus complex is resolved when he defensively identifies with his father, thus completing the development of his superego. The female Oedipus complex begins when the girl discovers she lacks a penis and blames her mother for the deficiency. The female Oedipus complex is partially resolved when she symbolically takes her father as a love object and desires a baby from him. This desire generalizes to other males, and the female Oedipus complex is more

completely resolved only if she ultimately gives birth to a child, especially a male child.

Oral-incorporative character. Character type that results from a fixation at the early oral stage. Such a person spends considerable time engaged in activities such as eating, kissing, smoking, and listening.

Oral-sadistic character. Character type that results from a fixation at the late oral stage. Such a person is orally aggressive and may be a fingernail biter and sarcastic.

Oral stage. First psychosexual stage and the one that occurs during about the first year of life at which time the mouth is the primary erogenous zone.

Parapraxes. Manifestations of repressed thoughts in everyday life such as slips of the tongue, "accidents," forgetfulness, and errors in writing and speaking.

Penis envy. Jealousy a female experiences because a male has a penis and she does not.

Phallic stage. Third psychosexual stage and the one that occurs from about the third to the fifth year of life, during which time the phallus is the primary erogenous zone. Because Freud believed the clitoris to be a small penis, he used the term "phallic stage" to describe the development of both male and female children. *See also* Oedipus complex.

Phylogenetically inherited endowment. Images we inherit that reflect the consistent experiences of our ancestors. With his acceptance of such images Freud demonstrated his acceptance of Lamarck's theory of the inheritance of acquired characteristics. *See also* Inheritance of acquired characteristics.

Pleasure principle. Hedonistic principle governing the id that demands the immediate reduction of any tension associated with an unsatisfied biological need.

Posthypnotic amnesia. Inability to remember what one has done while hypnotized.

Posthypnotic suggestion. Phenomenon whereby a person performs an act while awake that he or she was instructed to perform while under hypnosis. Typically, the person is unaware of the reason for performing such an act.

Preconscious. State of information that is in the unconscious mind but has not been repressed. Such information enters consciousness easily when it is needed.

Primal repression. Repression of those anxiety-provoking thoughts that are innately part of the id and therefore independent of personal experience.

Primary processes. Processes available to the id for satisfaction of needs. Those processes are reflex action and wish fulfillment (hallucinations). *See also* Reflex action and Wish fulfillment.

Principle of conservation of energy. Principle stating that the amount of energy within a system remains constant. Although the amount of energy in a system cannot be increased or decreased, it can be rearranged and transformed freely within the system.

Projection. Ego-defense mechanism by which an anxiety-provoking thought is attributed to someone or something else instead of recognizing it as one's own.

Psychic energy. More or less fixed amount of energy that Freud believed was available to drive the entire personality. According to Freud, psychic energy obeyed the principle of conservation of energy. *See also* Principle of conservation of energy.

Rationalization. Giving a rational, logical (but incorrect) excuse for behavior or thoughts that otherwise would cause anxiety.

Reaction formation. Inhibition of an anxiety-provoking thought by exaggerating its opposite. For example, a person inclined toward pornography may become a censor.

Reality anxiety. Caused by real, objective sources of danger in the environment. It is the easiest type of anxiety to reduce or prevent.

Reality principle. Principle governing the ego that causes it to do commerce with the environment in a way that satisfies both the id and the superego.

Reality testing. Process by which the ego finds environmental experiences capable of satisfying the needs of the id or superego.

Reflex action. Automatic reflexive response aimed at the removal of a source of irritation. Blinking to remove something from the eye is an example.

Regression. Returning to an earlier stage of development when stress is encountered.

Repression. Ego-defense mechanism by which anxiety-provoking thoughts are held in the unconscious mind, thereby preventing a conscious awareness of them. *See also* Primal repression and Repression proper.

Repression proper. Repression of those anxiety-provoking thoughts that result from painful experiences in one's lifetime.

Resistance. Patient's unwillingness to ponder and report anxiety-producing thoughts during the therapeutic process. Freud believed that resistance was highly informative because it suggested what were troublesome topics for the patient.

Secondary processes. Realistic processes by which the ego operates to bring about true need reduction as opposed to the temporary need reduction that results from the wish fulfillments of the id.

Secondary revision (also called secondary elaboration). Resynthesizing dream elements after they have been distorted by dream work. This resynthesizing gives the distorted dream elements enough meaning to be accepted into consciousness.

Seduction theory. Freud's early contention that hysteria results from an actual sexual seduction experienced during childhood. For reasons that are not entirely clear, Freud revised his theory to state that most seductions were imagined rather than real.

Sublimation. Displacement that results in a higher cultural achievement such as when an artistic or scientific activity is substituted for sexual activity.

Superego. Moral component of the personality that has two parts: the conscience and the ego ideal. *See also* Conscience and Ego ideal.

Thanatos. Name given to the death instinct. The source of aggression that Freud believed was self-destruction turned outward.

Transference. Phenomenon that sometimes occurs during therapy in which a patient begins to respond to the therapist as if he or she were an important person in the patient's life, such as the patient's mother or father.

Undoing. An ego-defense mechanism by which an attempt is made to atone for, or negate, an unacceptable act or thought by engaging in some form of ritualistic activity.

Vitalism. Belief that life cannot be explained in terms of physical events and processes alone; rather, some nonphysical, vital force must be postulated.

Wish fulfillment. The conjuring of an image of an object or event that is capable of satisfying a biological need.

CARL JUNG

CHAPTER OUTLINE

As we see in this chapter, Jung's theory of personality is complex. In fact, the picture of human nature that he portrays may be the most complicated developed by any personality theorist. As might be expected, Jung himself was a complicated person. The details of his life often appear to be contradictory. For example, Stern (1976) portrayed Jung as a prepsychotic (if not psychotic), opportunistic person with anti-Semitic and pro-Nazi leanings. On the other hand, Hannah (1976), a Jungian herself and a close friend, portrayed him as a brilliant, sensitive humanitarian who was anything but an anti-Semite or pro-Nazi. The Jung whom Hannah describes is indeed an uncommon, sometimes troubled person with many idiosyncrasies but these, in her opinion, are attributes of a genius, not of a madman. Jung's autobiography (1961) does not help much because it is, Jung confessed, a combination of myth and fact.

It appears that many truths about Jung's personal life, if they are ever to be known at all, will need to unfold in the future. What follows is a summary of those facts about Jung over which there is little or no disagreement. As far as Jung's theoretical notions are concerned, as with any other personality theorist, either his ideas are valid and useful or they are not. The personal experiences that gave rise to those ideas may be interesting in themselves but they are scientifically irrelevant.

Biographical Sketch

Carl Gustav Jung was born on July 26, 1875, in the Swiss village of Kesswyl but grew up in the university town of Basel. Religion was a strong theme running through Jung's early years. His father, Paul Jung, was a pastor in the Swiss Reformed Church, and his mother, Emilie Preiswerk Jung, was the daughter of a theologian. Jung's father viewed himself as a failure, and his religion was little comfort to him. As a child, Jung often asked his father penetrating questions concerning religion and life but was unable to obtain satisfactory answers. It became clear to Jung that his father accepted church dogma completely on faith and was never personally touched by real religious experience. According to Jung, these fruitless theological discussions alienated him from his father. Later in Jung's life, religion became a vital part of his theory, but it was the kind of religion that touched individuals emotionally and had little to do with specific churches or religious dogma.

Jung considered his mother to be the dominant member of the family, although he saw her as terribly inconsistent, which caused him to suspect that she was really two persons in one body. One person was kindly and extremely hospitable with a great sense of humor; the other was uncanny, archaic, and ruthless. Jung described how he reacted when his mother's second personality emerged: "[I was] usually struck to the core of my being, so that I was stunned into silence" (1961, p. 49). It is interesting the young Jung thought that he, like his mother, was really two different people. One person he labeled number one (the schoolboy), the other number two (the wise old man). Later, Jung realized that his number one self represented his ego or conscious mind, and his number two self represented his more powerful unconscious mind. Thus, as a boy, Jung experienced what he later considered the very essence of human existence: the interaction between the conscious and unconscious mind.

Perhaps because of the constant bickering of his parents, Jung began to isolate himself from his family in particular and the world in general. Increasingly his dreams, visions, and fantasies became his primary reality, and he developed the belief that this inner reality was furnishing him with secret knowledge that only a select few persons were given, and therefore it could not easily be shared with others.

Jung's Early Dreams, Visions, and Fantasies

Stone

When Jung was about 7 years old, he discovered a large stone with which he began to play an imaginary game. First he would perceive himself as sitting on the stone, which he was. Then, however, he would assume the perspective of the stone. Jung imagined himself to be the stone being sat on by a boy. Jung found that he could switch perspectives with ease. In fact, it was difficult for Jung to tell if he was sitting on the stone or if he was the stone being sat on: "The answer remained totally unclear, and my uncertainty was accompanied by a feeling of curious and fascinating darkness. But there was no doubt whatsoever that this stone stood in some secret relationship to me. I could sit on it for hours, fascinated by the puzzle it set me" (1961a, p. 20).

When Jung returned to this stone 30 years later, as a married, professionally successful man, the magic of the stone returned immediately: "The pull of that other world was so strong that I had to tear myself violently from the spot in order not to lose hold of my future" (1961a, p. 20).

Manikin

When Jung was 10 years old, he carved a wooden figure of a man from a ruler and kept it in a little wooden case. Jung dressed the figure in a coat, black boots, and a top hat and gave it a little stone of its own. This figure became a refuge for Jung and whenever he was troubled he would visit his secret friend. At school Jung would write in a secret language on little scrolls of paper, which he would later place in the pencil case containing the manikin. The addition of each scroll required a solemn ceremonial act. Jung never worried about explaining these actions because they provided him with a sense of security. "It was an inviolable secret which must never be betrayed, for the safety of my life depended on it. Why that was so I did not ask myself. It simply was so" (1961a, p. 22). Jung's "relationship" with his manikin lasted for about a year.

Phallus Dream

Although strange, the manikin and stone experiences were not frightening to Jung. In fact, as we have seen, the manikin provided him with an element of peace and security. Other mystical experiences of the young Jung were not as tranquil, however. A dream that Jung had when he was about 4 years old was terrifying to him. In this dream, Jung discovered a stone-lined hole in the ground, peered down, and saw a stone stairway leading downward. Jung descended and at the bottom found a round arch closed off by a lush green curtain. Pushing the curtain aside, Jung observed a rectangular chamber about 30 feet long. In the chamber was a platform on which was a rich, magnificent king's golden throne. Standing on the throne was an object 12 to 15 feet high and about 2 feet thick. The object consisted of skin and naked flesh, and on the top was a rounded head with no face or hair. On the top of the object was a single eye staring upward. This was obviously a giant phallus. Although the object did not move, it gave the appearance of being able to. Within his dream Jung was paralyzed with terror and he dreamed he heard his mother saying, "Yes, just look at him. That is the man-eater!" (1961a, p. 12). Jung's fear intensified, and he awoke sweating and terrified. For many nights following, Jung could not go to sleep for fear of having that or a similar dream again.

The phallus dream haunted Jung for years and it influenced his view of Christianity for many years. From his dream, Jung concluded that the giant phallus was the underground counterpart of the Lord Jesus:

> At all events, the phallus of this dream seems to be a subterranean God "not to be named," and such it remained throughout my youth, reappearing whenever anyone spoke too emphatically about Lord Jesus. Lord Jesus never became quite real for me, never quite acceptable, never quite lovable, for again and again I would

think of his underground counterpart, a frightful revelation which had been accorded me without my seeking it. (1961a, p. 13)

Jung was so shaken by the phallus dream that he did not mention it to anyone until he was 65 years old.

Throne Vision

One day, when Jung was about 12 years old he left school on a warm summer day. The new brightly glazed tiles on the roof of a nearby cathedral sparkled in the radiant sunshine. Jung was struck with the notion that God made that beautiful day and that beautiful church and was viewing his creations from his golden throne high above in the blue sky. Suddenly Jung was struck with the idea that if he did not stop thinking, a terrible thought would enter his mind. He was convinced that if he continued thinking he would commit the most terrible sin, and his soul would be damned for all eternity. The next few days were torture for Jung as he tried desperately to fend off the forbidden thought. Finally, Jung allowed himself to experience the forbidden thought:

> I saw before me the cathedral, the blue sky. God sits on His golden throne, high above the world—and from under the throne an enormous turd falls upon the sparkling new roof, shatters it, and breaks the walls of the cathedral asunder. So that was it! I felt an enormous, an indescribable relief. Instead of the expected damnation, grace had come upon me, and with it an unutterable bliss such as I had never known. I wept for happiness and gratitude. (1961a, pp. 39–40)

This vision had a profound effect on Jung. He now believed he knew what his father had not known about God. By taking the Bible's commandments as his guide, Jung's father had never directly experienced the will of God:

> [Jung's father] believed in God as the Bible prescribed and as his forefathers had taught him. But he did not know the immediate living God who stands, omnipotent and free, above His Bible and His Church, who calls upon man to partake of His freedom, and can force him to renounce his own views and convictions in order to fulfill without reserve the command of God. In His trial of human courage God refuses to abide by traditions, no matter how sacred. In His omnipotence He will see to it that nothing really evil comes of such tests of courage. If one fulfills the will of God one can be sure of going the right way. (1961a, p. 40)

Personal experiences, such as those just described, convinced Jung there are aspects of the human psyche that are independent of any individual's personal experience. Jung (1961a) summarized what he had learned from his fantasies:

> My fantasies brought home to me the crucial insight that there are things in the psyche which I do not produce, but which produce themselves and have their own life. . . . I understood that there is something in me which can say things that I do not know and do not intend, things which may even be directed against me. (p. 183)

Jung eventually dedicated his professional life to understanding the nature and origins of the many extraordinary psychological experiences he had had as a child.

Jung's Early Professional Life

Jung first wanted to study archaeology but a dream convinced him to follow in his paternal grandfather's footsteps and become a physician. Jung became aware of the new field of psychiatry during his medical studies at the University of Basel, where he attained his medical degree in 1900. In psychiatry, Jung believed he found his true calling. Jung's interest in unusual psychic phenomena never wavered and his dissertation for his medical degree was entitled "On the Psychopathology of So-Called Occult Phenomena," published in 1902. At this time, Jung was almost totally absorbed with the study of the occult. He attended séances, participated in experiments with mediums, and devoured books on parapsychology. In addition to his visions and his readings in parapsychology, personal experience also seemed to confirm the existence of the supernatural. For example, as Jung was at home studying in his room, he and his mother heard a loud noise and observed that a solid table had split from the rim to the center and not along the joints as would be expected. Two weeks later, after another loud blast, it was discovered that the blade of a butter knife had shattered into pieces. Examination by a cutler revealed no fault in the steel that would explain the explosion. Also Jung was entertaining a group by telling an imaginary story about a person he did not know, only to learn that he was clairvoyantly revealing true facts about the man. Lastly, Jung awoke one night with an extremely painful headache only to learn that one of his patients had shot himself in the head that very night.

Jung's first professional appointment was at the noted Burghölzli psychiatric hospital in Zurich where he worked under the supervision of Eugen Bleuler, who coined the term schizophrenia. Bleuler was interested in psychological tests and he encouraged Jung to experiment with the word-association test that had been used previously by Francis Galton (Darwin's cousin) and Wilhelm Wundt (the founder of the school of voluntarism). We have more to say about Jung's extensive use of the word-association test when we discuss complexes later in this chapter. In 1905, Jung was given a lectureship at the University of Zurich, where he lectured on psychopathology, psychoanalysis, and hypnosis. Also, Jung became clinical director of Burghölzli Hospital and head of the outpatient clinic. In 1909, Jung resigned his positions at the Burghölzli and his lectureship in 1914 to devote his time to his growing private practice, research, and writing.

On February 14, 1903, Jung married Emma Rauschenbach, the daughter of a rich industrialist, and they raised four daughters and a son. Emma herself became a practitioner of her husband's theory. During middle age Jung began a lengthy affair with a woman 13 years his junior. Her name was Toni Wolfe, and she was an attractive, well-educated former patient of Jung's. At first Jung's wife Emma was deeply upset but their situation eventually worked out. Stern (1976) described the situation:

> Jung's affair with Toni might have been less troublesome if he had not insisted on drawing his mistress into his family life and on having her as a regular guest for Sunday dinner. . . . Jung managed to maintain this asymmetrical triangle for several decades, drafting both women to serve his cause. Thus, Emma Jung was the first president of the Jungian "Psychological Club"; a few years after she resigned, Toni assumed the presidency. Both women published papers about Jungian psychology. (pp. 138–139)

Hannah (1976) describes the love triangle among Jung, Emma, and Toni Wolfe as follows:

> Jung had . . . to deal with perhaps the most difficult problem a married man ever has to face: the fact that he can love his wife and another woman simultaneously. . . . Jung was able to succeed in his effort to build his friendship with Toni into his life primarily because of his own scrupulous fairness to all parties. Of course there were the most painful difficulties for everyone concerned. . . . Jealousy is a human quality that is never missing in any complete human being, but, as Jung often said: "The kernel of all jealousy is lack of love." What saved the situation was that there was no "lack of love" in any of the three. Jung was able to give both his wife and Toni a most satisfactory amount, and both women really loved him. . . . Emma Jung even said years later: "You see, he never took anything from me to give to Toni, but the more he gave her, the more he seemed able to give me." . . . [Toni] also realized later that Jung's unswerving loyalty to his marriage gave her more than she could possibly have had without it. (pp. 118–120)

Jung's Relationship with Freud

Jung first became interested in Freud after reading *The Interpretation of Dreams*. Jung began to apply Freud's ideas to his own practice and eventually wrote a monograph entitled *The Psychology of Dementia Praecox* (1936) summarizing their effectiveness. Jung had found considerable support for Freud's notion of repression in his own word-association studies, and he reported this fact in his book and in several articles. In 1906, Jung initiated correspondence with Freud, and in February of the following year, the two met in Freud's home in Vienna. Their first face-to-face meeting was intense and lasted 13 hours. The two became extremely close friends, and when Jung returned to Zurich, a correspondence began that lasted about 7 years. On the basis of the kind words that Jung published about Freud's theory and because of the impression Freud had of Jung following their meeting, Freud decided Jung would become his successor. In 1911, Freud nominated Jung as the first president of the International Psychoanalytic Association and despite considerable opposition from the members, Jung was elected.

Jung traveled with Freud to America in 1909 to give a series of lectures at Clark University. Jung was invited primarily because of his experimentation with the word-association test. Aboard ship, Jung and Freud spent considerable time analyzing each others' dreams. Jung was surprised at the inability of Freud, the master of dream interpretation, to analyze several dreams. More surprising, however, was Freud's unwillingness to explore with Jung the private aspects of his (Freud's) life that might explain the symbolism of his dreams, saying instead, "I cannot risk my authority." Jung (1961a) described his reaction to Freud's assertion, "At that moment he lost it altogether. That sentence burned itself into my memory; and in it the end of our relationship was already foreshadowed. Freud was placing personal authority above truth" (p. 158). It was also during this trip to the United States that Jung first began to entertain doubts about the emphasis on sexual motivation in Freud's theory. His opposition to Freud was not expressed strongly, however, and the two remained close friends. Jung simply suggested to Freud that his theory might be

Photograph taken during the visit of Freud and Jung to Clark University, 1909. *Top row, from left to right:* Sandor Ferenczi, Ernest Jones (Freud's biographer), and A. A. Brill. *Bottom row, from left to right:* Carl Jung, G. Stanley Hall (then president of Clark University), and Sigmund Freud.

more palatable to American audiences if he played down the role of sex. Freud viewed this suggestion as a departure from scientific ethics.

It was not until about the time that Jung was elected president of the International Psychoanalytic Association in 1911 that Jung openly expressed doubts about Freud's interpretation of libidinal energy as primarily sexual. Jung's book *The Psychology of the Unconscious* (1953) and a series of lectures he gave at Fordham University entitled *The Theory of Psychoanalysis* (1961c) amplified the differences between Jung's conception of the libido and Freud's. The following exchange of letters exemplifies the early disagreement between Freud and Jung over the nature of the libido. First, on March 31, 1907, Jung wrote:

> Is it not conceivable, in view of the limited conception of sexuality that prevails nowadays, that the sexual terminology should be reserved only for the most extreme forms of your "libido," and that a less offensive collective term should be established for all the libidinal manifestations? (McGuire, 1974, p. 25)

On April 7, Freud responded to Jung as follows:

> I appreciate your motives in trying to sweeten the sour apple, but I do not think you will be successful. Even if we call the unconscious "psychoid," it will still be the

unconscious, and even if we do not call the driving force in the broadened conception of sexuality "libido," it will still be libido. . . . We cannot avoid resistances, why not face up to them from the start? (McGuire, 1974, p. 28)

The relationship between Jung and Freud became so strained that they agreed to stop their personal correspondence in 1912, and in 1914 Jung completely terminated the relationship when he resigned his presidency of the International Psychoanalytic Association and also withdrew as a member. The break was especially disturbing to Jung, who was then almost 40 years old. The separation from Freud caused Jung to enter what he called the "dark years," a period of about 4 years during which he explored in depth his own dreams and fantasies, an activity that brought him, in the opinion of many, to the brink of madness.

Jung's Creative Illness

Jung said, "After the parting of the ways with Freud, a period of inner uncertainty began for me. It would be no exaggeration to call it a state of disorientation. I felt totally suspended in mid-air, for I had not yet found my own footing" (1961a, p. 170). According to Ellenberger (1970), what Jung experienced during the "dark years" following the collapse of his relationship with Freud was a **creative illness** that Ellenberger defined as follows:

A period of intense preoccupation with an idea and search for a certain truth. It is a polymorphous condition that can take the shape of depression, neurosis, psychosomatic ailments, or even psychosis. . . . Throughout the illness the subject never loses the thread of his dominating preoccupation. It is often compatible with normal, professional activity and family life. But even if he keeps to his social activities, he is almost entirely absorbed with himself. . . . The subject emerges from his ordeal with a permanent transformation in his personality and the conviction that he has discovered a great truth or a new spiritual world. (pp. 447–448)

Disagreement exists concerning whether Jung went on a voluntary voyage of self-exploration during his creative illness (see, e.g., Van der Post, 1975) or if his journey represented a series of full-fledged psychotic episodes (see, e.g., Stern, 1976). In any case, Jung continued to maintain his psychiatric practice and his home life during his illness. In fact, according to Jung, it was his family and his patients that kept him sane. It was during his "confrontation with the unconscious" that Jung developed his previously described relationship with Toni Wolfe.

How strange it must have been for Jung to be engaged in this intense self-exploration at a time when he was treating psychotic patients. Strange or not, however, Jung appears to have learned a great deal about the human psyche from both sources:

It is of course ironical that I, a psychiatrist, should at almost every step of my experiment have run into the same psychic material which is the stuff of psychosis and is found in the insane. This is the fund of unconscious images which fatally confuse the mental patient. But it is also the matrix of a mythopoeic imagination which has vanished from our rational age. Though such imagination is present everywhere, it is both tabooed and dreaded, so that it even appears to be a risky experiment or a questionable adventure to entrust oneself to the uncertain path that leads into the depths of the unconscious. . . . Unpopular, ambiguous, and dangerous, it is a voyage of discovery to the other pole of the world. (1961a, pp. 188–189)

Jung emerged from his creative illness with his own theory of personality, a theory that bore only a remote resemblance to that of his mentor, Freud. The results of the long, agonizing search of his own psyche are to be found everywhere in his theory of personality.

Jung continued to develop his theory up to the time of his death, at the age of 86, on June 6, 1961, at his tower home in Bollingen, Switzerland. A prolific writer for six decades, Jung's *Collected Works* consists of 20 volumes. Among his many honors are eight honorary doctorates from institutions such as Harvard (1936), Oxford (1938), and the University of Geneva (1945). In 1938, he was named Honorary Fellow of the Royal Society of Medicine and in 1943 he became an Honorary Member of the Swiss Academy of Sciences. In 1944, the University of Basel established the Chair of Medical Psychology in his name. In 1948, the first C. G. Jung Institute was founded in Zurich and was soon followed by the founding of the International Analytical Psychology Association. Today, as we will see later in this chapter, Jungian professional groups exist throughout the world.

Libido and the Principles
of Equivalence, Entropy, and Opposites

Libido

Freud and Jung disagreed about the nature of the **libido.** At the time of his collaboration with Jung, Freud saw libido mainly as sexual energy. Jung believed this view was too narrow and instead defined the libido as general biological life energy that is concentrated on different problems as they arise. For Jung, libido was a creative life force that could be applied to the continuous psychological growth of the person. In the early years of life, according to Jung, libidinal energy is expended mainly on eating, elimination, and sex, but as the person becomes more proficient at satisfying these needs or as these needs become less important, libidinal energy is applied to the solution of more philosophical and spiritual needs. Thus for Jung, libido is the driving force behind the **psyche** (Jung's term for personality), which is focused on various needs whether those needs are biological or spiritual. Those components of the personality in which considerable libidinal energy is invested are said to be valued more than others. Thus, according to Jung, the **value** of something is determined by how much libidinal energy is invested in it.

Principle of Equivalence

Like Freud, Jung drew heavily on the physics of his day for his theory of personality. His use of the principles of equivalence, entropy, and opposites demonstrates this orientation. The **principle of equivalence** is the first law of thermodynamics that states the amount of energy in a system is essentially fixed (conservation of energy), and if it is removed from one part of a system it will show up in another. Applied to the psyche, this means that only so much psychic energy (libido) is available, and if one component of the psyche is overvalued, it is at the expense of the other components. If, for example, psychic energy is concentrated on conscious activities, then unconscious activities will suffer and vice versa. We have more to say about this concept later.

Principle of Entropy

The **principle of entropy** is the second law of thermodynamics and states a constant tendency exists toward equalizing the energy within a system. If, for example, a hot object and a cold one are placed side by side, the hot object will lose heat energy (and the cold one will gain) until their temperatures are equalized. Likewise, according to Jung, a tendency exists for all components of the psyche to have equal energy. For example, the conscious and unconscious aspects of the psyche would have equal energy and thus equal representation in one's personality. The psychic balance, however, is extremely hard to achieve and must be actively sought. If the balance is not sought, the person's psychic energy will not be balanced and thus personality development will be uneven. That is, certain aspects of the psyche will be more highly valued than others.

Principle of Opposites

The **principle of opposites** is found almost everywhere in Jung's writings. This principle is similar to Newton's contention that "for every action there is an equal and opposite reaction" or Hegel's statement that "everything carries within itself its own negation." Every concept in Jung's theory has its polar opposite. The unconscious is contrasted with the conscious, the rational with the irrational, feminine with masculine, the animalistic with the spiritual, causality with teleology, progression with regression, introversion with extroversion, thinking with feeling, and sensing with intuiting. When one aspect of the personality is developed, it is usually at the expense of its polar opposite; for instance, as one becomes more masculine, one necessarily becomes less feminine. For Jung the goal of life, in accordance with the principle of entropy, is to seek a balance between these polar opposites, thereby giving both expression to one's personality, which is more easily said than done. Such a synthesis is constantly aspired to but seldom accomplished.

Components of the Personality

Ego

According to Jung, the **ego** is everything of which we are conscious. It is concerned with thinking, feeling, remembering, and perceiving. It is responsible for seeing that the functions of everyday life are carried out. It is also responsible for our sense of identity and our sense of continuity in time. It is important not to equate the ego with the psyche. The conscious experience of the ego represents only a small portion of the personality; the psyche refers to both the conscious and the more substantial unconscious aspects of personality. Considerable similarity exists between Jung's concept of ego and Freud's.

Personal Unconscious

The **personal unconscious** consists of material that was once conscious but was repressed or forgotten, or was not vivid enough to make a conscious impression at first. The personal unconscious contains clusters of emotionally loaded (highly valued) thoughts that Jung called complexes. More specifically, a **complex** is a personally disturbing constellation of ideas connected by common-feeling tone (1973, p. 599). A complex has a disproportionate influence on one's behavior, in the sense that the theme around which the complex is organized recurs over again in one's life. A person with a mother complex will spend a considerable amount of time on activities that are either directly or symbolically related to the idea of mother. The same is true of a person with a father, sex, power, money, or any other kind of complex.

Jung's early claim to fame was a technique he used to study complexes. He took the **word-association test,** developed earlier by Francis Galton and Wilhelm Wundt, and redesigned it as a tool to tap the personal unconscious in search of complexes. It was this research on which he lectured at Clark University when he went there with Freud in 1909. Jung's technique consisted of reading to a patient a list of 100 words one at a time and instructing the patient to respond as quickly as possible with the first word that came to mind. Words such as *child, green, water, sing, death, long,* and *stupid* were used. How long it took the patient to respond to each word was measured with a stopwatch. Breathing rate was also measured, as was the electroconductivity of the patient's skin, which was measured with a galvanometer.

The following were used by Jung as "complex indicators," that is, factors that indicated the presence of a complex:

1. Displaying a longer-than-average reaction time to a stimulus word
2. Repeating the stimulus word back as a response
3. Failing to respond at all
4. Using expressive bodily reactions, such as laughing, increased breathing rate, or increased conductivity of the skin
5. Stammering
6. Continuing to respond to a previously used stimulus word
7. Reacting meaninglessly, for example, with made-up words
8. Reacting superficially with a word that sounds like the stimulus word (die–lie), for example
9. Responding with more than one word
10. Misunderstanding the stimulus word as some other word

Jung used his word-association test in many ways. For example, he found that male subjects tended to respond faster to stimulus words than female subjects did, and that educated people tended to respond faster than uneducated people. In addition, he found that members of the same family had remarkably similar reactions to stimulus words. The following shows the reaction of a mother and her daughter to several stimulus words (1973, p. 469):

Stimulus Word	Mother	Daughter
law	God's commandment	Moses
potato	tuber	tuber
stranger	traveler	travelers
brother	dear to me	dear
to kiss	mother	mother
merry	happy child	little children

Jung believed it was important to discover and deal with complexes because they require the expenditure of so much psychic energy, and therefore inhibit balanced psychological growth.

With his use of the word-association test, Jung demonstrated that it was possible to investigate the unconscious mind systematically. This accomplishment alone would have given Jung a prominent place in psychology's history.

Collective Unconscious

To understand the **collective unconscious,** Jung's boldest, most mystical, and most controversial concept, is to understand the heart of Jung's theory. The collective unconscious reflects the collective experiences that humans have had in their evolutionary past, or in Jung's own words, it is the "deposit of ancestral experience from untold millions of years, the echo of prehistoric world events to which each century adds an infinitesimally small amount of variation and differentiation" (1928, p. 162). Not only are fragments of all human history found in the collective unconscious but traces of our prehuman or animal ancestry are found there as well. Because the collective unconscious results from *common* experiences that all humans have, or have had, the contents of the collective unconscious are essentially the same for all humans. Jung said it is "detached from anything personal and is common to all men, since its contents can be found everywhere" (1966, p. 66). For Jung, the terms collective unconscious and transpersonal unconscious were synonymous.

These ancestral experiences that are registered in the psyche have been called at various times racial memories, primordial images, or, more commonly, archetypes. An **archetype** can be defined as an inherited predisposition to respond to certain aspects of the world. Just as the eye and the ear have evolved to be maximally responsive to certain aspects of the environment, so has the psyche evolved to cause the person to be maximally responsive to certain categories of experience that humans have encountered over and over again through countless generations. An archetype exists for whatever experiences are universal, those that each member of each generation must experience. You can generate a list of archetypes yourself by simply answering the question, What must every human experience in his or her lifetime? Your answer must include such experiences as birth, death, the sun, darkness, power, women, men, sex, water, magic, mother, heroes, and pain. Humans have an inherited predisposition to react to these and other universal categories of experience. Specific responses and ideas are not inherited; what is inherited is the tendency to respond to categories of common human experience in terms of emotionally charged myths. For example, when our ancestors experienced a bolt of lightning or a clap of thunder, it stimulated in them emotional responses that immediately took the form of myths. Jung (1966) explained:

One of the commonest and at the same time most impressive experiences is the apparent movement of the sun every day. We certainly cannot discover anything of the kind in the unconscious, so far as the known physical process is concerned. What we do find, on the other hand, is the myth of the sun-hero in all its countless variations. It is this myth, and not the physical process, that forms the sun archetype. The same can be said of the phases of the moon. The archetype is a kind of readiness to produce over and over again the same or similar mythical ideas. Hence it seems as though what is impressed upon the unconscious were exclusively the subjective fantasy-ideas aroused by the physical process. We may therefore assume that the archetypes are recurrent impressions made by subjective reactions. (p. 69)

Primitive humans responded to all of their emotional experiences in terms of myths, and it is this tendency toward myth making that is registered in the collective unconscious and passed on to future generations. What we inherit, then, is the tendency to reexperience some manifestation of these primordial myths as we encounter events that have been associated with those myths for eons. Each archetype can be viewed as an inherited tendency to respond emotionally and mythologically to certain kinds of experience—for example, when a child, a mother, a lover, a nightmare, a death, a birth, an earthquake, or a stranger is encountered.

The collective unconscious is by far the most important and influential part of the psyche and its inherited predispositions seek outward manifestation. When the contents of the collective unconscious are not recognized in consciousness, they are manifested in dreams, fantasies, images, and symbols. Because few people fully recognize the contents of their collective unconscious, most can learn about themselves by studying the contents of their dreams and fantasies. In fact, according to Jung, humans can learn a great deal about their future by studying these dreams because they symbolize basic human nature, as it someday is hoped to be understood. In that sense, the collective unconscious knows more than any single human or generation of humans knows. Jung gathered information about the archetypes from a wide variety of sources including his own dreams and fantasies, primitive tribes, art, religion, literature, language, and the hallucinations of psychotic patients.

Although Jung recognized the existence of many archetypes, he wrote extensively on only a few. These were the persona, the anima, the animus, the shadow, and the self. We consider each of these next.

Persona, Anima, Animus, Shadow, and Self

Persona

Persona is the Latin word for mask, and Jung used this term to describe one's public self. The persona archetype develops because of humans' need to play a role in society. Although all humans share the same collective unconscious, individuals exist at a particular time and in a particular place. Archetypes must manifest themselves within these social and cultural circumstances. That is, the expression given to the archetypes is influenced by social conventions and by the unique circumstances of a person's life. Thus the persona is the outward manifestation of the psyche that is allowed by a person's unique circumstances. The persona is the part of the psyche by which we are known by other people. Jung pointed out that some people equate their persona with their entire psyche and this is a mistake. In a sense, the persona is supposed to deceive other people, because it presents to them only a small part of one's psyche, but if people believe that they are what they pretend to be, they are deceiving themselves, and that is unfortunate. Jung said,

> The construction of a collectively suitable persona means a formidable concession to the external world, a genuine self-sacrifice which drives the ego straight into identification with the persona, so that people really do exist who believe they are what they pretend to be. [However] . . . these identifications with a social role are a very fruitful source of neuroses. A man cannot get rid of himself in favour of an artificial personality without punishment. Even the attempt to do so brings on, in all ordinary cases, unconscious reactions in the form of bad moods, affects, phobias, obsessive ideas, back-slidings, vices, etc. The social "strong man" is in his private life often a mere child where his own states of feeling are concerned; his discipline in public (which he demands quite particularly of others) goes miserably to pieces in private. His "happiness in his work" assumes a woeful countenance at home; his "spotless" public morality looks strange indeed behind the mask—we will not mention deeds, but only fantasies, and the wives of such men would have a pretty tale to tell. As to his selfless altruism, his children have decided views about that. (1966, pp. 193–194)

Jung described the situation in which the persona is valued too highly as **inflation of the persona.** As with all components of the psyche, if the persona is valued too highly, it develops at the expense of other components.

Anima

The **anima** is the female component of the male psyche that results from the experiences men have had with women through the eons. This archetype serves two purposes. First, it causes men to have feminine traits. "No man," said Jung, "is so entirely masculine that he has nothing feminine in him" (1966, p. 189). These feminine traits include intuition, tenderness, sentimentality, and gregariousness. Second, it provides a framework within which men interact with women. "An inherited collective image of woman exists in a man's unconscious, with the help of which he apprehends the nature of woman" (Jung, 1966, p. 190). Because men's collective experiences with women have involved interactions with them as mothers, daughters, sisters, loved ones, and perhaps as heavenly goddesses, all of these elements are reflected in the anima, and together they form a complex, idealized image of women. This image portrays women at once as perilous, loyal, seductive, dangerous, and challenging. Women are viewed as the source of good and evil, hope and despair, and success and failure. It is within this idealized framework that men form their interactions with women in their lifetimes. Also, according to Jung, this complex image of women has inspired the portrayal of women by artists, poets, and novelists through the years.

Animus

The **animus** is the masculine component of the female psyche. It furnishes the woman with masculine traits (such as independence, aggression, competitiveness, and adventuresomeness) and also with a framework that guides her relationship with men. As the anima furnishes men with an ideal of the woman, the animus furnishes women with an ideal of the man. This ideal comes from women's experience with men through the eons as fathers, sons, brothers, loved ones, warriors, and perhaps as gods. As with the anima, the complex animus with its many conflicting images is projected onto actual men in a woman's lifetime.

The anima provides males with female traits and with a basis for understanding women. The animus provides females with masculine traits and with a basis for understanding men. It is best, according to Jung, when both genders recognize and give expression to their characteristics of the other sex. The male who gives little or no expression to his feminine characteristics lacks sensitivity, feeling, intuition, and creativity. The female who gives little or no expression to her male characteristics is overly passive. Also, if a component of the psyche is not given adequate, conscious expression it is forced to manifest itself unconsciously, making its influence uncontrolled and irrational. Thus if a woman denies expression to her masculine traits or a man his feminine traits, those traits will manifest themselves in indirect ways such as through dreams and fantasies.

According to Jung, for a man to give too much expression to his feminine traits or for a female to give too much expression to her masculine traits is also undesirable. Jung said, "A woman possessed by the animus is always in danger of losing her femininity, her adapted feminine persona, just as a man in like circumstances runs the risk of effeminacy" (1966, p. 209). As everywhere in Jung's theory, a balance should be sought, in this case a balance between one's male and female characteristics.

Shadow

The **shadow** is the darkest, deepest part of the psyche. It is the part of the collective unconscious that we inherit from our prehuman ancestors and contains all of the animal instincts. Because of the shadow, we have a strong tendency to be immoral, aggressive, and passionate.

As with all of the archetypes, the shadow seeks outward manifestation and is projected onto the world symbolically as devils, monsters, or evil spirits. It can even be projected onto a person, as Jung found out when he asked one of his young patients the following question:

> "How do I seem to you when you are not with me?" . . . She said, "Sometimes you seem rather dangerous, sinister, like an evil magician or a demon. I don't know how I ever got such ideas—you are not a bit like that." (1966, p. 91)

Not only does the preceding quotation describe the projection of the shadow, it also exemplifies Jung's approach to psychotherapy. Jung's goal was to introduce his patient to the various components of his or her psyche, and when the components were known, to synthesize them into an interrelated configuration resulting in a deeper, more creative person. Unlike Freud, who thought the unconscious, irrational mind had to be made increasingly conscious and rational if humans were to become truly civilized, Jung believed the archetypes, for example, the shadow, should be recognized and then used rather than overcome. The animal nature of the shadow was, to Jung, a source of spontaneity and creativity. The person who does not use his or her shadow, according to Jung, tends to be dull and lifeless.

Self

The **self** is the component of the psyche that attempts to harmonize all the other components. It represents the human striving for unity, wholeness, and integration of the total personality. When this integration has been achieved, the person is said to be self-realized. We have more to say about the self when we consider "life's goal" later in this chapter.

Psychological Types

Attitudes

Jung thought there were two general orientations the psyche could take. One was inward, toward the subjective world of the individual; and the other was outward, toward the external environment. Jung called these orientations **attitudes;** the former he labeled **introversion,** and the latter he labeled **extroversion.** The introvert tends to be quiet, imaginative, and more interested in ideas than in other people. The extrovert tends to be sociable, outgoing, and interested in people and environmental events.

The attitudes of introversion and extroversion were first presented by Jung at the International Psychoanalytic Congress at Munich in 1913. They were later elaborated in his book *Psychological Types* (1971). Included in the many ways that Jung applied the concepts of introversion and extroversion was his explanation of why different personality theorists create different kinds of personality theories. For example, Freud was an extrovert and thus developed a theory that stressed the importance of external events, for example, sex objects. Adler's theory (as we see in Chapter 4) stressed the importance of internal feelings because Adler was an introvert (Jung, 1966, pp. 41–43). Jung could easily have given his own theory as an example of a personality theory created by an introvert instead of Adler's.

Functions of Thought

In addition to the attitudes or general orientations, the four **functions of thought** pertain to how a person perceives the world and deals with information and experience.

Sensing. Detects the presence of objects. It indicates that something is there but does not indicate what it is.

Thinking. Tells what an object is. It gives names to objects that are sensed.

Feeling. Determines what an object is worth to the person. Pertains to liking and disliking.

Intuiting. Provides hunches when factual information is not available. Jung said, "Whenever you have to deal with strange conditions where you have no established values or established concepts, you will depend upon the faculty of intuition" (Jung, 1968, p. 14).

Examples of the functions of thought are detecting the presence of an object in the environment (sensing), noting that the object is a stranger who is a member of the opposite sex (thinking), experiencing an attraction toward the person (feeling), and believing that the possibility of a long-term relationship with the person exists (intuiting).

Thinking and feeling are called **rational functions** because they make judgments and evaluations about experiences. In addition, thinking and feeling are considered polar opposites, because, as Jung said, "When you think you must exclude feeling, just as when you feel you must exclude thinking" (1968, p. 16). Likewise, sensing and intuiting, the **irrational functions,** are thought to be polar opposites. Sensing and intuiting are considered irrational because they both occur independently of logical thought processes. Sensing occurs automatically because of the sensory mechanisms of the body, and intuiting involves a prediction made in the absence of factual information.

Ideally, the attitudes and functions would be equally developed and all would work in harmony; this, however, is seldom the case. Usually, one attitude and one function become dominant, and the other attitude and the other three functions remain underdeveloped and unconscious. For the functions, the one opposite the dominant conscious one is the least developed, but the other two functions are subservient to the dominant function and in that way may become somewhat developed. For example, in a person whose thinking function is highly developed, the other three functions, especially feeling (the opposite of thinking), will be relatively undeveloped on the unconscious level and may be expressed in dreams, fantasies, or in odd and disturbing ways.

Eight Personality Types

By combining the two attitudes and the four functions, Jung described eight different types of people. Note, however, that these eight types probably never exist in pure form because each person possesses both attitudes and all four functions, and which is conscious and which is unconscious is a matter of personal development. The eight pure types are listed here with a brief description of each type's tendencies (summarized from Jung, 1971, pp. 330–405).

> **Thinking Extrovert.** Objective reality dominates, as does the thinking function of thought. Feeling, sensing, and intuiting are repressed. Intellectual analysis of objective experience is of utmost importance. The truth exists "out there" and everyone must follow it. Activities dependent on feelings such as aesthetics, development of close friendships, and introspective religious and philosophical experiences are minimized. This person lives according to fixed rules and expects everyone else to do the same. He or she is dogmatic and cold. Personal matters such as health, social position, family interests, and finances are neglected. Jung believed many scientists are thinking extroverts.
>
> **Feeling Extrovert.** Objective reality dominates, as does the feeling function of thought. Thinking, sensing, and intuiting are repressed. This type responds

emotionally to objective reality. Because the feelings experienced are externally determined, they tend to be appropriate to the situation such as those elicited at the theater, at concerts, or at church. Such a person is respectful of authority and tradition. There is always an attempt to adjust one's feelings to those appropriate to the situation and, therefore, this person's feelings seem feigned. For example, the choice of a "loved one" will be determined more by a person's age, social position, income, and family status than by the subjective feelings about that person. That is, it is the expected feeling to have toward that person under the circumstances.

Sensing Extrovert. Objective reality dominates, as does the sensing function of thought. Intuiting, thinking, and feeling are repressed. This type is buffeted about by sensory experience. He or she is a realist and is concerned only with objective facts. Because the life of this type is governed by just what happens, he or she makes an entertaining companion. There is little inclination to analyze situations or to dominate them. Once an experience has been sensed, there is little additional concern with it. Only the tangible, the concrete has value. He or she rejects subjective thoughts or feelings as guides for living for himself or herself and for others.

Intuiting Extrovert. Objective reality dominates, as does the intuiting function of thought. Sensing, thinking, and feeling are repressed. This type sees in external reality a multitude of possibilities. New experiences are sought with enthusiasm, pondered until their implications are understood, and then abandoned. There is little concern with the convictions and the morality of others and, therefore, this type is often viewed as immoral and unscrupulous. Careers are sought that allow the exploitation of new possibilities such as being an entrepreneur, stockbroker, or politician. Although socially useful, this type may waste considerable time moving from one project to another. Like the sensing extrovert, this type is irrational and is little concerned with logic. Meaningful communication with individuals in which the rational functions (thinking or feeling) dominate is very difficult.

Thinking Introvert. Subjective reality dominates, as does the thinking function of thought. Feeling, sensing, and intuiting are repressed. Because the life of this type is determined by subjective rather than objective reality, he or she appears to others to be inflexible, cold, arbitrary, and even ruthless. Such individuals will follow their own thoughts regardless of how unconventional and dangerous to others they may be. Support and understanding from others are of little value. He or she values only the few friends that understand his or her internal frame of reference. For this type, subjective truth is the only truth, and criticism, regardless of its validity, is rejected. Logical thought is employed only to one's own subjective experience. Jung described himself as a thinking introvert.

Feeling Introvert. Subjective reality dominates, as does the feeling function of thought. Thinking, sensing, and intuiting are repressed. Rather than directing intellectual processes toward subjective experience, as is the case with the thinking introvert, this type emphasizes the feelings that such experience provides. Objective reality is important only insofar as it elicits subjective images that can be privately experienced and valued. Communication with others is difficult because it requires at least two individuals to have the same subjective reality and its associated feelings. Such a person is considered egotistical and unsympathetic. The basic motives of this type are unassessible to others, and they are therefore viewed as cold and indifferent. For this type there is no need to impress or influence others. Like all introverts, all that is important is internal rather than external.

Sensing Introvert. Subjective experience dominates, as does the sensing function of thought. Intuiting, feeling, and thinking are repressed. As is the case with many artists, this type gives his or her own meaning to sensory experience. Because this type embellishes his or her sensory experiences with subjective evaluations, interactions with objective reality are unpredictable. Sensory experience is important only insofar as it elicits subjective images.

Intuiting Introvert. Subjective experience dominates, as does the intuiting function of thought. Sensing, feeling, and thinking are repressed. Here the implications of internal images are explored thoroughly. Such a person, often a mystic, a seer, or a daydreamer, produces new and strange ideas. Of all the types, this type is most aloof, distant, and misunderstood. He or she is often viewed as an eccentric genius. Important philosophical and religious insights are often produced by this type.

In Jung's typology, we see the principles of equivalence, opposites, and entropy in operation. Because only so much libidinal energy is available to a person, little will be left for the other components (principle of equivalence) if an abundance of this energy is invested in a particular component of the psyche. When something is conscious, its opposite is unconscious and vice versa (principle of opposites). A constant tendency exists for the libidinal energy to equalize itself across all components and levels of the psyche (principle of entropy). The components of the psyche that we have discussed in this section can be summarized as follows.

Attitudes	*Functions of Thought*		*Levels*
	Rational	*Irrational*	
Introversion	Thinking	Sensing	Conscious
Extroversion	Feeling	Intuiting	Unconscious

Stages of Development

Stages of development were not as important to Jung as they were to Freud, but he did talk about them in general terms. Jung's stages were defined in terms of the focus of libidinal energy. We saw earlier that Jung disagreed with Freud about the nature of the libido. Freud believed the libido was mainly sexual in nature and how it was invested within the first five years of life determined, to a large extent, what a person's adult personality would be like. Jung, conversely, thought that libidinal energy was directed simply toward whatever was important to the person at the time and what was important changed as a function of maturation. Jung's stages of development can be summarized as follows.

Childhood (From Birth to Adolescence)

During the early portion of this period, libidinal energy is expended on learning how to walk, talk, and other skills necessary for survival. After the fifth year, more and more libidinal energy is directed toward sexual activities and this focus of libidinal energy reaches its peak during adolescence.

Young Adulthood (From Adolescence to About Age 40)

During this stage, libidinal energy is directed toward learning a vocation, getting married, raising children, and relating in some way to community life. During this stage the individual tends to be outgoing, energetic, impulsive, and passionate.

Middle Age (From About Age 40 to the Later Years of Life)

This stage of development was the most important for Jung. The person is transformed from an energetic, extroverted, and biologically oriented person to one with more cultural, philosophical, and spiritual values. The person is now much more concerned with wisdom and with life's meaning. The needs that must be satisfied during this stage are just as important as those of the preceding stages, but they are different kinds of needs.

> Our life is like the course of the sun. In the morning it gains continually in strength until it reaches the zenith-heat of high noon. Then . . . the steady forward movement no longer denotes an increase, but a decrease, in strength. . . . But it is a great mistake to suppose that the meaning of life is exhausted with the period of youth and expansion. . . . The afternoon of life is just as full of meaning as the morning; only, its meaning and purpose are different. . . . What youth found and must find outside, the man of life's afternoon must find within himself. (1966, pp. 74–75)

Because it is during middle age that a person begins to determine the meaning of life, it is a time when religion becomes important. Jung believed every person possesses a spiritual need that must be satisfied, just as the need for food must be satisfied. Jung's definition of religion, however, included any systematic attempt to deal with God, spirits, demons, laws, or ideals. We saw earlier that Jung did not have much patience with the kind of religion that involved religious denominations and dogma that was to be taken on faith.

Jung believed that the general decline of the religious life among modern people has caused a disorientation in worldview. More specifically, he found that the absence of the meaning, or spiritual equilibrium, once provided by a religious worldview caused the neurotic complaints of his middle-aged patients.

> Of all my patients past middle life, that is, past thirty-five, there is not one whose ultimate problem is not one of religious attitude. Indeed, in the end every one suffered from having lost that which living religions of every age have given to their believers, and none is really cured who has not regained his religious attitude,

which naturally has nothing to do with creeds or belonging to a church. (quoted in Wehr, 1987, p. 292)

Life's Goal

According to Jung, life's primary goal is to achieve **self-realization,** or a harmonious blending of the many components and forces within the psyche. Although self-realization is never completely achieved, approximating it involves a long, complex journey of self-discovery. Self-realization and individuation go hand in hand. **Individuation** refers to the lifelong process of psychological maturity by which components of the psyche are recognized and given expression by a particular individual. Jung believed that individuation, or the tendency toward self-realization, is inherent in all living organisms, "Individuation is an expression of that biological process—simple or complicated as the case may be—by which every living being becomes what it was destined to become from the beginning" (quoted in Stevens, 1994, p. 62). The process of individuation describes a personal journey toward self-realization, but the process provides an important connection among all humans. Jung (1966) said:

> The more we become conscious of ourselves through self-knowledge, and act accordingly, the more the layer of the personal unconscious that is superimposed on the collective unconscious will be diminished. In this way there arises a consciousness which is no longer imprisoned in the petty, oversensitive, personal world of ego, but participates freely in the wider world of objective interests. . . . The complications . . . are no longer egotistic wish-conflicts, but difficulties that concern others as much as oneself. . . . We can now see that the unconscious produces contents which are valid not only for the person concerned, but for others as well, in fact for a great many people and possibly for all. (p. 178)

Elsewhere, Jung (1969) said:

> This process is, in fact, the spontaneous realization of the whole man. . . . The more he is merely "I," the more he splits himself off from the collective man, of whom he is also a part, and may even find himself in opposition to him. But since everything living strives for wholeness, the inevitable one-sidedness of our conscious life is continually being corrected and compensated by the universal human being in us, whose goal is the ultimate integration of conscious and unconscious, or better, the assimilation of the ego to a wider personality. (p. 292)

As self-realization is approximated, the self becomes the new center of the personality and is experienced as being suspended among the opposing forces of the psyche. Jung believed the self was symbolized by a **mandala,** which is the Sanskrit word meaning circle. The self is perceived as the center of the circle, or midway among the many polarities that make up the psyche. Jung found variations of the mandala in different cultures all over the world, indicating to him its universality. As with all archetypes, the self creates a sensitivity to certain experiences, which in this particular case is a sensitivity to symbols of balance, perfection, and harmony like the circle. The basic Taoist (yin-yang) diagram is a well known example of a mandala.

Where does that leave all of us who are not self-realized? According to Jung, we are in various degrees of trouble. The degree of our problem depends on how lopsided our development has been:

> Modern man does not understand how much his "rationalism" (which has destroyed his capacity to respond to numinous symbols and ideas) has put him at the mercy of the psychic "underworld." He has freed himself from "superstition" (or so he believes), but in the process he has lost his spiritual values to a positively dangerous degree. His moral and spiritual tradition has disintegrated, and he is now paying the price for this break-up in world-wide disorientation and dissociation. . . . As scientific understanding has grown, so our world has become dehumanized. Man feels himself isolated in the cosmos, because he is no longer involved in nature and has lost his emotional "unconscious identity" with natural phenomena. These have slowly lost their symbolic implications. Thunder is no longer the voice of an angry god, nor is lightning his avenging missile. No river contains a spirit, no tree is the life principle of a man, no snake the embodiment of wisdom, no mountain cave the home of a great demon. No voices now speak to man from stones, plants, and animals, nor does he speak to them believing they can hear. His contact with nature has gone, and with it has gone the profound emotional energy that this symbolic connection supplied. (Jung, 1964, pp. 84–85)

Jung believed more to life exists than merely being rational. In fact, he believed that ignoring the irrational part of the psyche has caused many of our current problems:

> [Contemporary man] is blind to the fact that, with all his rationality and efficiency, he is possessed by "powers" that are beyond his control. His gods and demons have not disappeared at all; they have merely got new names. They keep him on the run with restlessness, vague apprehensions, psychological complications, an insatiable need for pills, alcohol, tobacco, food—and, above all, a large array of neuroses. (Jung, 1964, p. 71)

Despite the current emphasis on rationality and science, archetypes continue to manifest themselves. They do so, however, within the technological context of modern times. An example is the phenomenon of flying saucers. Writing during the Cold War, Jung said the following about flying saucers:

> A psychic phenomenon of this kind would, like a rumour, have a compensatory significance, since it would be a spontaneous answer of the unconscious to the present conscious situation, i.e., to fears created by an apparently insoluble political situation which might at any moment lead to a universal catastrophe. At such times

men's eyes turn to heaven for help, and marvelous signs appear from on high, of a threatening or reassuring nature. (1978, p. 131)

Causality, Teleology, and Synchronicity

Causality

By **causality,** Jung meant the attempt to explain adult personality in terms of prior experiences, as was the case with Freud. According to Jung, not only is such an attempt incomplete, but it also gives one a feeling of despair and hopelessness. This theory maintains that what a person will become is a function of what the person already has been.

Teleology

Although Jung did not discount causality altogether, he thought teleology must be added to it to have a complete picture of human motivation. **Teleology** means that human behavior has a purpose; that is, our behavior is drawn by the future as much as it is pushed by the past. Jung said, "Causality is only one principle, and psychology cannot be exhausted by causal methods only, because the mind lives by aims as well" (1961b, p. 292). In other words, to truly understand a person, one must understand his or her goals and aspirations for future attainment on a personal level. Jung's general view of human motivation can be represented schematically as follows.

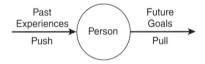

Synchronicity

Jung referred to **synchronicity** as meaningful coincidence, as when one dreams of a person and shortly thereafter the person appears, or when one fantasizes about an event and the event occurs. Progoff (1973) gives further examples of synchronicity:

> A person . . . has a dream or a series of dreams, and these turn out to coincide with an outer event. An individual prays for some special favor, or wishes, or hopes for it strongly, and in some inexplicable way it comes to pass. One person believes in another person, or in some special symbol, and while he is praying or meditating by the light of that faith, a physical healing or some other "miracle" comes to pass. (p. 122)

According to Jung, events such as those just described are of great importance to one's life, and they must be more clearly understood. Synchronicity is one of Jung's more complex concepts, and we discuss it only briefly here. For synchronicity to take place, two events must occur independently of each other. That is, the two events have their own causality but they are not causally related to each other. Then, at some point, an individual experiences them together, and in combination they have meaning to that person, whereas if they were experienced separately, they would not. It is this coming together in a meaningful way of two otherwise meaningless events that defines synchronicity. Progoff (1973) gave the following example of synchronicity from the life of Abraham Lincoln:

> There is a synchronistic event that occurred in the life of Abraham Lincoln that may say a great deal to us about the nature of Synchronicity and its future. During his early years, as we know, Lincoln found himself in a very difficult and conflicting situation. He had intimations of the fact that there was a meaningful work for him to do in the world. He realized, however, that that work would require him to develop his intellect and to acquire professional skills. In conflict with these subjective feelings was the fact that, in Lincoln's frontier environment, intellectual tools for professional study were very difficult to find. He had reason to believe that his hopes would never be fulfilled.
>
> One day a stranger came to Lincoln with a barrel full of odds and ends. He said that he was in need of money and that he would be much obliged if Lincoln would help him out by giving him a dollar for the barrel. The contents, he said, were not of much value; they were some old newspapers and things of that sort. But the stranger needed the dollar very badly. The story tells us that Lincoln, with his characteristic kindness, gave the man a dollar for the barrel even though he could not imagine any use that he would have for its contents. Some time later, when he went to clear out the barrel, he found that it contained almost a complete edition of Blackstone's *Commentaries*. It was the chance, or synchronistic, acquisition of these books that enabled Lincoln to become a lawyer and eventually to embark on his career in politics. (pp. 170–171)

Note that the two events that came together were not causally related to each other but had their own lines of causality. On the one hand, we had an ambitious Lincoln frustrated because of the lack of needed materials; conversely, we had a stranger with odds and ends who needed a dollar. Only when the two came together at a particular moment in Lincoln's life did they take on meaning. We might say that both Lincoln and the stranger were "lucky" to run into each other.

In a more complex way, the concept of synchronicity can be applied to the relationship between the collective unconscious and various experiences we have. As we have seen, each archetype can be regarded as a predisposition to respond emotionally to a certain class of environmental events. In fact, an archetype can be considered a *need* to have certain kinds of experiences. Under these circumstances, when we have an experience that gives symbolic expression to an archetype, the experience is as satisfying as finding food is to a hungry person. This explains why humans react emotionally to certain music, art forms, and various symbols in their lives. According to Jung, we all have archetypes, and when our experiences give them expression, the result is emotionally satisfying. Because the archetypes have one causal heritage and the environmental events that give them symbolic expression have another, their coming together is an example of synchronicity.

Research Techniques

We have already viewed Jung's research using his word-association test; this research was his most scientifically orthodox. The other sources of evidence he used to support his theory were more controversial. For example, he studied in depth his own dreams and visions. He studied the contents of the hallucinations of psychotic patients. He traveled to such places as Arizona, New Mexico, Tunis, Uganda, India, and Kenya to study the religions, rituals, myths, and symbols of various cultures. He studied theology, philosophy, history, mythology, literature, and poetry. He studied all forms of art and language. In short, he studied every major category of human existence, and everywhere he found support for his contention that humans are born with predispositions to respond to the world in certain ways. He believed that he found symbols corresponding to the content of the collective unconscious everywhere; symbols with powerful influences, yet not completely understood by those responding to them.

Psychotic Patients

It was during his years at Burghölzli that Jung realized that much could be learned about the psyche by studying psychotic patients. Jung (1961a) reflected:

> Through my work with the patients I realized that paranoid ideas and hallucinations contain a germ of meaning. A personality, a life history, a pattern of hopes and desires lie behind the psychosis. The fault is ours if we do not understand them. It dawned upon me then for the first time that a general psychology of the personality lies concealed within psychosis, and that even here we come upon the old human conflicts. Although patients may appear dull and apathetic, or totally imbecilic, there is more going on in their minds, and more that is meaningful, than there seems to be. At the bottom we discover nothing new and unknown in the mentally ill; rather, we encounter the substratum of our own natures. (p. 127)

Jung's encounter with a psychotic patient in 1906 exemplifies how we can learn about the psyche from mentally ill persons. Looking out the window, a patient called Jung over and told him that if he half-closed his eyes and looked at the sun, Jung would be able to see a phallus hanging from it. Furthermore, the patient told Jung that if he moved his head from side to side, the sun's phallus would swing back and forth. Finally, the patient asserted that it was the swinging of the sun's phallus that caused the wind (Jung, 1969, pp. 151–152). It was not until four years later that Jung discovered that the patient's hallucination may have reflected the contents of the unconscious mind. In 1910, Jung was reading a book about the rituals and visions of an ancient Greek religious cult. One of the visions described was that of the sun with a tube hanging from it, and the direction of the bending tube was determined by the direction of the wind. Because it was highly unlikely that the patient knew of the ancient vision, Jung was startled by the similarity between the two visions. In subsequent years, Jung learned that the sun-phallus or the divine phallus was a common theme in many primitive cultures. Because the many cultures displaying such a myth could not have communicated with each other, it must be, concluded Jung, a manifestation of the collective unconscious.

Jung's Analysis of Dreams

Like Freud, Jung viewed dreams as one of the most important sources of information about the unconscious mind. But Jung interpreted dreams differently than Freud. First, Jung disagreed with Freud's distinction between manifest and latent contents of a dream. To Jung, the content of a dream is just what it appears to be:

> I have long maintained that we have no right to accuse the dream of, so to speak, a deliberate [maneuver] calculated to deceive. Nature is often obscure or impenetrable, but she is not, like man, deceitful. We must therefore take it that the dream is just what it pretends to be, neither more nor less. (1966, p. 100)

Later Jung stated:

> The dream comes in as the expression of an involuntary, unconscious psychic process beyond the control of the conscious mind. It shows the inner truth and reality of the patient as it really is: Not as I conjecture it to be, and not as he would like it to be, but *as it is.* (1969, p. 139)

Jung's statements are a bit misleading, however, because the contents of dreams can include fragments of ancient symbols and myths and may require considerable knowledge of history, religion, and anthropology to comprehend them.

One of the most important functions of the dream, according to Jung, is to compensate for neglected parts of the psyche. For example, if the shadow is not given an opportunity to express itself consciously, it will manifest itself in dream content and the person's dreams will be characterized by demons, devils, monsters, and passionate, immoral impulses. In other words, the person will have an abundance of nightmares. One way, therefore, to detect undeveloped portions of the psyche is to analyze the contents of dreams.

Jung was not restricted by ordinary methods of science, and he felt no need to apologize because he believed traditional methods of science could not be applied to the richness of the human psyche. He thought one's methods had to be as complex and flexible as what was being studied, and to be sure, the methods of laboratory science did not qualify. According to Jung, the arena of human experience, not the laboratory, is the proper place to study the human psyche. Jung gave the student of the psyche the following advice:

> Anyone who wants to know the human psyche will learn next to nothing from experimental psychology. He would be better advised to abandon exact science, put away his scholar's gown, bid farewell to his study, and wander with human heart through the world. There, in the horrors of prisons, lunatic asylums and hospitals,

in drab suburban pubs, in brothels and gambling-hells, in the salons of the elegant, the Stock Exchanges, Socialist meetings, churches, revivalist gatherings and ecstatic sects, through love and hate, through the experience of passion in every form in his own body, he would reap richer stores of knowledge than text-books a foot thick could give him, and he will know how to doctor the sick with real knowledge of the human soul. (1966, pp. 246–247)

Jung's View of Human Nature

Certainly Jung's view of human nature is among the most complex ever described. The human psyche is embedded in the past, present, and future. It consists of conscious and unconscious elements, masculine and feminine traits, rational and irrational impulses, spiritualistic and animalistic desires, and a tendency to bring all these contradictory components and impulses into harmony with each other. Self-realization is achieved when such harmony is approximated, but self-realization must be sought; it does not occur automatically.

To Jung, the spiritual need must be satisfied, which usually happens during middle age, when many of the components of the psyche have been discovered. As we have seen, religion, broadly defined, was to Jung a major vehicle in the journey toward self-realization. If Freud was pessimistic about human destiny, Jung was optimistic. Jung's optimism, however, was contingent on humans coming to grips with their unconscious mind; if this is not accomplished, the projections of the unconscious mind, for example, the shadow, will continue to cause gross irrationality in our lives and perhaps even a third world war (1958, pp. 112–113).

Evaluation

Empirical Research

Empirical research designed to test Jung's theory has been relatively sparse, but there has been some. Research usually focuses on Jung's typology. For example, the Myers–Briggs Type Indicator Test (Myers, 1962) is a standardized pencil-and-paper test designed to measure where individuals fall along four of Jung's bipolar dimensions: being introverted versus extroverted, thinking versus feeling, sensing versus intuiting, and sensing versus judging. Using the Myers–Briggs test, Kilmann and Taylor (1974) and Carlson and Levy (1973) confirmed several Jungian predictions about how various types should differ in the areas of memory and judgment. Also, Carlson (1980) found that introverts and extroverts differ in their memories, the way they describe the world, and the way they describe themselves. Several other personality theorists have found Jung's concept of introversion–extroversion useful (e.g., Eysenck & Eysenck, 1985), and that concept is among the major personality dimensions measured by the popular Minnesota Multiphasic Personality Inventory (MMPI).

Criticisms

Jung's theory, like all theories covered in this text, has not gone uncriticized. He has been accused of being friendly toward occultism, spirituality, mysticism, and religion, all areas thought by many to emphasize the irrational. Jung believed that he was vastly misunderstood on this issue, however, and insisted that studying these topics in no way implied a belief in them. Rather, he studied them to gain information about the collective unconscious. Jung, like many contemporary personality theorists, believed that if a scientific method could not be applied to the study of a complex topic, the method should be discarded, not the topic. He thought personality was an example of such a topic.

Jung's theory also has been criticized for being incomprehensible, unclear, inconsistent, and even contradictory. Also, his concept of self-realization has been labeled elitist because it is possible for only highly intelligent, well-educated persons with an abundance of leisure time to arrive at the degree of self-insight necessary for self-realization. This restriction omits most people.

Finally, Jung's theory, like Freud's, has been criticized for being nonfalsifiable and therefore unscientific. Except for some research on psychological types and the functions of thought, little empirical research has been performed in an effort to validate the major components of Jung's theory. Jungian concepts such as the principles of equivalence, entropy, and opposites, as well as his notions of the collective unconscious and self-realization, go untested. Because Jung's theory makes few risky predictions it runs little risk of being proved incorrect. Jung would not be distressed by this observation, however. Except for his research using the word-association test, Jung sought validation for his theory not within controlled laboratory conditions but rather in the vast arena of human experience and within human intuition.

Contributions

On the positive side, Jung's theory can be credited with many original concepts in personality theory. His was the first modern theory to discuss the process of self-realization, which is currently so popular among personality theorists. His was the first modern theory to emphasize the importance of the future in determining human behavior. Related to this idea was his emphasis on the importance of purpose and meaning in one's life. This theme is now emphasized in the existential–humanistic theories of personality. Jung's theory was largely optimistic about human destiny rather than pessimistic, as Freud's theory was. Jung's theory stressed the attainment of selfhood as a master motive in human behavior, rather than the sexual impulses and early experiences that Freud stressed.

Somehow Jung's theory creates an image of the psyche that is believable in light of the times in which we live. He leaves us with an image of a psyche that is pushed by the past, pulled by the future, and attempts to make sense of itself in the present. It is a complex psyche struggling to give expression to its various components. Such a psyche causes a wide range of behaviors and interests, some of which might even be considered bizarre. Despite its criticisms, Jungian theory remains popular in contemporary psychology. According to Kirsch (2000) by the mid-1960s the popularity of Jungian psychology began to soar and Jungian professional groups began to spring up throughout all of Western Europe and the United States. In the 1970s Jungian groups formed in Latin America, Australia, and New Zealand and there was interest in South Africa, Japan, and Korea. In 1989, interest in analytic psychology spread to Eastern Europe and the former Soviet Union. Currently, there is also an emerging interest in China. So, concludes Kirsch, "today analytical psychology truly has an international character" (p. xxiv). For further evidence concerning the popularity of Jungian theory in contemporary psychology, see DeAngelis (1994).

Summary

Biographical information portrays Jung as a complex person who had a troubled childhood. He originally intended to study archaeology but a dream motivated him instead to study medicine. Although when they first met, Freud and Jung became close friends, theoretical differences between the two eventually caused them to terminate their association. A major disagreement between the two concerned the nature of the libido. Freud saw it as mainly sexual energy, and Jung saw it as general energy that could be directed at various problems as they arose, whether they be biological or spiritual.

Jung accepted the principle of equivalence that states the psyche consists of a finite amount of energy; the principle of entropy that states a constant tendency exists toward equalizing psychic energy among the various components of the psyche; and the principle of opposites that states for every mental process that exists, its opposite also exists. According to Jung, the psyche contains an ego (similar to Freud's concept of ego), a personal unconscious consisting mainly of repressed experiences from one's life, and the collective unconscious, which is a phylogenetic or racial memory. The personal unconscious contains clusters of interrelated thoughts called complexes, which Jung studied using his word-association test. The collective unconscious is made up of archetypes that are inherited predispositions to respond emotionally to certain categories of experience. Archetypes result from common human experiences through the eons. The more highly developed archetypes include the persona, the tendency to select only a part of ourselves to offer to the public; the anima, the female component of the male psyche; the animus, the male component of the female psyche; the shadow, the part of our psyche we share with nonhuman animals; and the self, each person's goal of psychic wholeness and harmony.

Jung postulated two major attitudes, or orientations, a psyche could manifest: introversion and extroversion. The introvert tends to be internally oriented whereas the extrovert tends to be externally oriented. In addition to the attitudes, Jung discussed four functions of thought: (1) sensing, which detects the presence of objects; (2) thinking, which tells us what an object is; (3) feeling, which tells us whether an object is acceptable or unacceptable; and (4) intuiting, which allows us to make guesses about objects or events in the absence of factual information. The thinking and feeling functions are rational, and the sensing and intuiting functions are irrational. By combining the two attitudes and the four functions, a description of eight personality types is possible: a thinking extrovert, a feeling extrovert, a sensing extrovert, an intuiting extrovert, a thinking introvert, a feeling introvert, a sensing introvert, and an intuiting introvert.

There are three stages of development: childhood (from birth to adolescence), during which time the skills necessary for survival are learned; young adulthood (adolescence to about 40 years old) when a person typically learns a vocation, gets married, and raises children; and middle age (from about age 40 to the later years), which was considered by Jung the most important time of life because philosophical and spiritual values are stressed and the meaning of life is sought.

Jung used the term individuation to describe the lifelong process by which the components of the personality are discovered and given expression within the context of an individual's life. The primary goal in life is to approach self-realization, a state characterized by a fully integrated and harmonious psyche. The self is symbolized by mandalas.

Jung accepted both causality by which he meant that personality is determined by past experience, and teleology, which states that what we do is determined by our anticipations of the future. In addition, he accepted synchronicity, or meaningful coincidence, as a major influence in a person's life. The main function of dreams, according to Jung, was to compensate for an unevenly developed psyche by giving expression to those portions of the psyche that are unable to manifest themselves more directly. Jung argued that the techniques used to study humans had to reflect human complexity and uniqueness. Scientific method, he said, was of only limited value in studying and understanding humans.

Empirical research has verified Jungian predictions concerning psychological types and the functions of thought but most of Jung's major concepts have not been empirically tested. In addition to being criticized for being, to a large extent, nonfalsifiable, Jung's theory has been criticized for being mystical, inconsistent, unclear, and contradictory. Conversely, Jung's theory has been praised for accounting for the multitude of human attributes, emphasizing the importance of the future for human behavior, describing the self-realization process, being optimistic about humans rather than pessimistic, and recognizing the importance of meaning for human existence.

Experiential Exercises

1. The following 20 items are from Jung's word-association test:

death	pity	unjust	anxiety
to sin	stupid	family	to abuse
money	book	friend	ridicule
pride	sad	happiness	pure
journey	to marry	lie	to beat

Respond to each word as quickly as you can. Using as many criteria specified in the chapter as possible, do you find any indication of a complex? If so, how would you describe that complex? Next, give the test to a close relative and see if you can detect a similar pattern of responding. Finally, give the test to a close friend and compare his or her reactions to your own and those of your relative. How do you explain the individual differences in responses to these words? Do you agree with Jung that a test such as this one can supply information concerning an individual's unconscious mind? Explain why you do or do not agree.

2. Describe how synchronicity has played a role in your life.

3. Assuming that Jung was correct in believing that dreams are compensatory, what do your dreams tell you about those aspects of your personality that are undeveloped? Jung thought that recurring dreams were of special relevance, so you may want to be especially attentive to such dreams in doing this exercise.

Discussion Questions

1. Describe the rise and fall of the relationship between Jung and Freud.
2. Explain the principles of equivalence, entropy, and opposites.

3. Describe Jung's concept of the collective unconscious. Be sure to include in your answer a description of the most fully developed archetypes.

Glossary

Anima. Female component of the male psyche.

Animus. Male component of the female psyche.

Archetype. Inherited predisposition to respond emotionally to certain aspects of the world. All the archetypes taken together make up the collective unconscious.

Attitudes. General orientations of the psyche when relating to the world. The two basic attitudes are introversion and extroversion.

Causality. Belief that a person's personality can be explained in terms of past experiences.

Childhood. Stage of development that lasts from birth to adolescence during which time libidinal energy is invested in learning the basic skills necessary for survival and sexual activities.

Collective unconscious. Collection of inherited predispositions that humans have to respond to certain events. These predispositions come from the universal experiences humans have had throughout their evolutionary past.

Complex. Set of interrelated ideas that are highly valued and that exist in the personal unconscious.

Creative illness. According to Ellenberger, a period of intense preoccupation with a search for a particular truth. This search is usually accompanied by depression, psychosomatic ailments, neuroses, and perhaps psychotic episodes.

Ego. For Jung, the ego is everything of which we are conscious and entails performing the functions related to everyday life.

Extroversion. Tendency to be externally oriented, confident, outgoing, and gregarious.

Feeling. Function of thought that determines whether an object or event is valued positively or negatively.

Functions of thought. Determines how a person perceives the world and deals with information and experience. The four functions of thought are sensing, thinking, feeling, and intuiting.

Individuation. Process whereby a person comes to recognize the various components of his or her psyche and gives them expression within the context of his or her life. A process that is prerequisite to approximating self-realization.

Inflation of the persona. Condition that exists when one's persona is too highly valued.

Introversion. Tendency to be internally oriented, quiet, subjective, and nonsocial.

Intuiting. Function of thought that makes hunches about objects or events when factual information is not available.

Irrational functions. Jung referred to sensing and intuiting as irrational functions because they do not involve logical thought processes.

Libido. According to Jung, the general life energy that can be directed to any problem that arises, be it biological or spiritual.

Mandala. Sanskrit word for circle. For Jung, the mandala is a symbol of wholeness, completeness, and perfection; that is, it symbolizes the self.

Middle age. Stage of development that lasts from about 40 to the later years of life during which time libidinal energy is invested in philosophical and spiritual pursuits. According to Jung, this stage of development is the most important.

Persona. Superficial aspect of the psyche that a person displays publicly. It includes the various roles one must play to function in a society.

Personal unconscious. Consists of material from one's lifetime that was once conscious and then repressed or material that was not vivid enough to make an initial conscious impression.

Principle of entropy. Second law of thermodynamics that states a constant tendency exists toward equalizing energy within a system.

Principle of equivalence. First law of thermodynamics that states the amount of energy in a system is fixed and, therefore, if some of it is removed from one part of the system, it must show up in another part.

Principle of opposites. Contention that each component of the psyche has an opposite.

Psyche. Term that Jung equated with personality.

Rational functions. Jung referred to thinking and feeling as rational functions because they involve making judgments and evaluations about experiences.

Self. State of the psyche if the individuation process has been completely successful. When the various components of the psyche are harmonized, the self becomes the center of all of the various opposing psychic forces. The emergence of the self, coming into selfhood, and self-realization were used synonymously by Jung.

Self-realization. State of balance and harmony that is reached when the various components of the psyche are recognized and given expression.

Sensing. Function of thought that detects the presence of objects.

Shadow. Deepest part of the collective unconscious that contains all the animalistic urges that characterized our prehuman existence.

Synchronicity. Meaningful coincidence. When two independent events come together in a meaningful way.

Teleology. Belief that a person's anticipations of the future must be considered if that person's personality is to be completely understood.

Thinking. Function of thought that names an object.

Value. Varies as the amount of libidinal energy invested varies. Those components of the personality that have an abundance of libidinal energy invested in them are valued more than components with less energy invested in them.

Word-association test. Research technique that Jung used to explore the complexes within the personal unconscious. It consisted of reading 100 words one at a time and having a person respond as quickly as possible with a word of his or her own.

Young adulthood. Stage of development that lasts from adolescence to about 40. During this time, libidinal energy is invested in learning a vocation, getting married, raising children, and participating in community life.

ALFRED ADLER

CHAPTER OUTLINE

In many ways, Adler's theory of personality is the opposite of Freud's. Freud viewed individuals constantly in conflict with one another and with society, whereas Adler viewed them seeking companionship and harmony. Freud ignored questions concerning life's meaning and the effects of future aspirations on one's life, whereas Adler made these questions a central part of his theory. Freud saw the mind as consisting of different components often in conflict with one another, whereas Adler viewed the mind as an integrated whole working to help attain the future goals of the person. So by choosing the term **individual psychology** for his theory, Adler by no means intended to imply that people are selfishly motivated to satisfy their own biological drives. Rather, he meant that although individuals are unique, they are characterized by inner harmony and a striving to cooperate with fellow humans.

Adler's theory is related to humanism because of its concern with the positive relationships among humans. His theory is related to existentialism because of its concern with questions concerning the meaning of human existence. Adler shared with the existentialists the belief that humans are future oriented (a belief shared by Jung), free to determine their own fate, and concerned with the meaning of life. Clearly, little similarity exists between Adler's individual psychology and Freud's psychoanalysis.

Biographical Sketch

Alfred Adler was born in a suburb of Vienna, Austria, on February 7, 1870. His father, Leopold, was a moderately successful grain merchant. Adler grew up under comfortable physical circumstances and was able to enjoy the open spaces, relative freedom from want, and a city (Vienna) that was one of the great cultural centers of Europe. In addition, he was able to share his love of music with his entire family.

Despite apparent physical comfort, however, Adler looked on his childhood as miserable. He thought of himself as undersized and ugly. He was the third of seven children and had a major rivalry with his older brother, who apparently was very athletic and a model child. Adler's mother seemed to prefer his older brother to him, but Adler got along very well with his father.

Adler's views of himself were not without foundation. He was a sickly child who was unable to walk until he was 4 years old. He suffered from rickets that prevented him from engaging in any strenuous physical activity.

> One of my earliest recollections is of sitting on a bench bandaged up on account of rickets, with my healthy elder brother sitting opposite me. He could run, jump, and move about quite effortlessly, while for me, movement of any sort was a strain and an effort. Everyone went to great pains to help me and my mother and father did all that was in their power to do. (quoted in Bottome, 1957, pp. 30–31)

When Adler was 5, he caught pneumonia and almost died. In fact, he heard the doctor say to his parents, "Your boy is lost" (Orgler, 1963). This illness, the death of a younger brother in a bed next to his when he (Adler) was 3, and being run over twice caused in him an awareness and a fear of death. He decided to become a physician when he grew up, believing that such a profession would provide a means of conquering death.

Contrary to what one may think, Adler remained a friendly, sociable child with a genuine love for people (traits he retained all his life). His unhappiness continued in school where he began as a poor student (especially in mathematics). One of his teachers counseled his parents to train him as a shoemaker because he apparently was not qualified for anything else. Eventually, however, Adler became one of the best students in his class.

Adler's childhood ambition was realized when he obtained his medical degree from the University of Vienna (Freud's alma mater) in 1895. He first specialized in ophthalmology (diseases of the eye) and later changed to general practice and finally to psychiatry. Two years after his graduation from medical school, he married Raissa Epstein, a rich Russian girl who came to Vienna to study. Raissa was a particularly liberated, domineering woman who was a militant socialist. It is interesting to note that, perhaps under his wife's influence, Adler's first publication came the year after he married Raissa, and it concerned the terrible working conditions of independent tailors and the need for socialized medicine for the poor. Marxism remained an influence in Adler's life and it influenced his theory of personality. From Marx, Adler learned that the social context within which one lives can significantly influence one's personality. Marx's philosophy also supported Adler's deep concern for common people.

The Adlers had four children. One daughter (Alexandra) and his only son (Kurt) became psychiatrists and continued their father's work in individual psychology. Adler's wife died on April 21, 1962, at the age of 89 in New York City.

Adler read Freud's book *The Interpretation of Dreams* and wrote an article defending Freud's theoretical position. On the basis of this defense, Adler was invited by Freud to join the Vienna Psychoanalytic Society in 1902. Adler accepted Freud's invitation, thereby becoming one of Freud's earliest colleagues. Adler became president of the society in 1910, just a year before his official break from the Freudian group. It appears now that joining the group may have been a mistake from the beginning because Adler had little in common with Freud. This incompatibility became increasingly obvious and, in 1911, while he was still president of the Vienna Psychoanalytic Society and after a 9-year association with Freud, he resigned from the society. The two men never met again. The differences between Adler and Freud that caused this separation were numerous and are reviewed at the end of this chapter, but the following quotation from Freud's biographer, Ernest Jones, lists a few of Adler's beliefs that were contrary to Freud's.

> Sexual factors, particularly those of childhood, were reduced to a minimum: a boy's incestuous desire for intimacy with his mother was interpreted as the male wish to conquer a female masquerading as sexual desire. The concepts of repression, infantile sexuality, and even that of the unconscious itself were discarded so little was left of psychoanalysis. (1955, p. 131)

Freud characteristically had a low tolerance for "defectors," and he remained hostile to Adler all his life. Adler was the pigmy in Freud's statement, "I made a pigmy great" (Wittels, 1924, p. 225). Adler said of Freud's theory that it was founded on the mythology of sex and that psychoanalysis was stimulated by the selfishness of a pampered child. Freud, who could not understand the grief a friend was suffering over the death of Adler, said, "I don't understand your sympathy for Adler. For a Jewish boy out of a Viennese suburb a death in Aberdeen is an unheard of career in itself and a proof of how far he had got on. The world really rewarded him richly for his service in having contradicted psychoanalysis" (quoted in Jones, 1957, p. 208). Fiebert (1997) provides interesting details concerning Adler's initial professional involvement with Freud, the sources of dissension between Adler and Freud, and the nature of the relationship between the two following Adler's "excommunication."

After breaking with the Freudians, Adler and his followers formed a group first called the Society of Free Psychoanalytic Research to express their contempt for the restrictive nature of the Freudian organization. However, they soon changed their name to Society for Individual Psychology because they did not want to be perceived as simply rebels against psychoanalysis. Because the term individual psychology can be easily misunderstood, the next section in this chapter clarifies its meaning.

Adler served as a physician in the Austrian Army during World War I and, following his release, he was asked by the government to open several child-guidance clinics in Vienna. This was one of Adler's early efforts to apply his theory to the problems of childrearing, education, and other everyday problems. Many of his books, articles, and lectures (of which there were hundreds) were directed either toward teachers or toward the general public. Adler's fame quickly spread and, in Vienna, he was surrounded by many students, friends, and admirers. Freud, disturbed by all this, proclaimed (incorrectly) that Adler's theory was actually nothing but psycho-analytic knowledge that Adler had labeled his own by changing its terminology.

In 1926, Adler first visited the United States and was warmly received by educators. In 1927, he was appointed lecturer at Columbia University, and in 1932 he became a professor of medical psychology at the Long Island College of Medicine in New York. In 1935, partially because of the Nazi takeover in Europe, Adler made the United States his permanent home. He died of a heart attack on May 28, 1937, in Aberdeen, Scotland, while on a lecture tour there.

One peak in the popularity of Adlerian psychology was in 1930 when 2,000 people attended the fifth International Congress of Individual Psychology in Berlin (Ansbacher, 1983). Another peak is more recent. According to Ansbacher:

> The Adlerian movement today numbers several thousand members in the United States, Canada, and European countries, especially Germany. It is composed of psychiatrists, psychologists, social workers, counselors, and educators, as well as lay people who accept the theory and apply the method of Adlerian psychology to family life and personal development. (1983, p. 76)

Adler's theory continues to be promoted today by the American Journal of Individual Psychology and by the American Society of Individual Psychology. Heinz and Rowena Ansbacher summarized many of Adler's ideas in two volumes (1956, 1979). Adler was a strong believer in bringing his ideas to nonprofessionals, a task perpetuated by Rudolf Dreikurs (1957, 1964).

Organ Inferiority and Compensation

In 1907, Adler published his now famous essay entitled "Study of Organ Inferiority and Its Physical Compensation." In this essay, Adler put forth the idea that people are especially vulnerable to disease in organs that are less developed or "inferior" to other organs. For example, some persons are born with weak eyes, others with weak stomachs, others with weak hearts, and still others with damaged limbs. These biological deficiencies cause problems in the person's life because of the stresses put on them by the environment. These organic weaknesses inhibit the person from functioning normally and, therefore, must be dealt with in some way.

Because the body acts as an integrated unit, a person can **compensate** for a weakness either by concentrating on its development or by emphasizing other functions that make up for the weakness. For example, someone with a frail body may work hard to overcome this frailty. Likewise, a blind person may concentrate on developing auditory skills. In both cases, a biological weakness is compensated.

In some cases, a person may **overcompensate** by converting a biological weakness into a strength. Two examples are Teddy Roosevelt, who was an extremely frail child, becoming a hardy outdoorsman, and Demosthenes, who overcame a speech impediment to become a great orator. At this early stage in the development of his theory, Adler emphasized biological inferiority, compensation, and overcompensation.

Feelings of Inferiority

In 1910, Adler shifted his emphasis from actual **organ inferiority** to subjective inferiority, also called **feelings of inferiority.** Now compensation or overcompensation was directed toward either real or imagined inferiorities. At this point in his theorizing, Adler left the biological sciences and entered psychology. Anything that caused inferiority feelings was worthy of study.

Adler pointed out that all humans start life with feelings of inferiority because we are completely dependent on adults for survival. Children feel completely helpless compared to the powerful adults on whom they depend. This feeling of being weak, impotent, and inferior stimulates in the child an intense desire to seek power, thereby overcoming feelings of inferiority. At this point in the evolution of Adler's theory, he stressed aggression and power as a means of overcoming feelings of inferiority.

Unfortunately, but mainly because of cultural conditions at the time that Adler was writing, he equated power and strength with masculinity and inferiority with femininity:

> Any form of uninhibited aggression, activity, potency, power, and the traits of being brave, free, rich, aggressive or sadistic can be considered masculine. All inhibitions and deficiencies, as well as cowardliness, obedience, poverty, and similar traits, can be considered as feminine. (1956b, p. 47)

According to Adler, every person has feelings of weakness (femininity) and an impulse to become strong (masculinity) and, in that sense, all humans are bisexual. For Adler, however, bisexuality was primarily psychological whereas for Freud it was primarily biological. That is, Adler did not believe that anatomy is destiny; rather, he believed that attitudes toward one's self and toward others are destiny.

In any case, at this stage in Adler's theorizing, to become more powerful meant to become more masculine and, consequently, less feminine. He referred to this striving to become more masculine as the **masculine protest.** Because both men and women seek to become powerful enough to overcome inferiority feelings, both attempt to approximate the cultural ideal of masculinity. In other words, both men and women engage in the masculine protest. Adler believed, however, that the cultural overvaluation of masculinity over femininity was not positive for either men or women:

> What I have said concerning the hatreds and jealousies between nations and groups also holds good of the bitter struggle between the sexes, a struggle that is poisoning love and marriage and is ever born anew out of the inferior valuation of woman. The idealized picture of overestimated masculinity imposes both on the boy and the grown-up man the obligation of appearing, if not being, superior to woman. This causes him to distrust himself, to exaggerate his demands on life and his expectations from it, and increases his sense of insecurity. On the other hand, a girl feels that she is valued less than a boy, and this may stimulate her either to exaggerated efforts to make up for her inadequacy and to fight real or apparent depreciation on all sides, or else may cause her to resign herself to her supposed inferiority. (1956c, p. 452)

The masculine protest occurs in any culture where power is associated with males and weakness with females. In any culture where females are perceived as powerful, the situation is reversed and there is a feminine protest. For Adler, then, sexuality was important because of what it symbolized within a culture rather than because of biological gender differences.

Feelings of Inferiority as Motivational

Are feelings of inferiority bad? No, said Adler. In fact, being human means feeling inferior. It is a condition common to all humans and, therefore, is not a sign of weakness or abnormality. In fact, such feelings are the primary motivating force behind all personal accomplishments. One feels inferior and is therefore driven to accomplish something. A short-lived feeling of success exists after such an accomplishment but in light of the accomplishments of others, one again feels inferior and again is motivated to accomplish more, and on it goes without end.

However, even though feelings of inferiority act as a stimulus for all positive growth, they also can create neurosis. A person can become overwhelmed by feelings of inferiority at which point he or she is prevented from accomplishing anything. Under these circumstances, feelings of inferiority act as a barrier rather than as a stimulus for positive accomplishment. Such a person is said to have an **inferiority complex.** According to Adler, all humans experience the feeling of being inferior but in some it stimulates neurosis and in others it creates a need to succeed. We have something to say about what makes the difference later in this chapter.

Striving for Superiority

Adler modified his theoretical position to state that it is not more aggression, power, or masculinity that we seek but superiority or perfection. Adler now referred to **striving for superiority** as the **fundamental fact of life.** Adler's theory had evolved from the point at which it emphasized compensation for organ inferiority, to that at which subjective inferiority was compensated through aggression and power, to that at which the fundamental fact of life is that all humans strive for superiority-perfection. What is the origin of this striving for perfection? According to Adler, it is innate to all humans:

> It runs parallel to physical growth. It is an intrinsic necessity of life itself. . . . All our functions follow its direction; rightly or wrongly they strive for conquest, surety, increase. The impetus from minus to plus is never-ending. The urge from "below" to "above" never ceases. Whatever premises all our philosophers and psychologists dream of—self-preservation, pleasure principle, equalization—all these are but vague representations, attempts to express the great upward drive . . . a fundamental category of thought, the structure of our reason . . . the fundamental fact of our life. (1930b, pp. 398–399)

In his final theoretical position, Adler retained striving for superiority as the master motive but he changed from striving for individual superiority to striving for a superior or perfect society. As we have seen, Adler believed that feelings of inferiority could result in positive growth or in an inferiority complex. Adler also believed that striving for superiority could be beneficial or harmful. If a person concentrates exclusively on his or her own superiority while ignoring the needs of others and of society, he or she may develop a **superiority complex.** A person with a superiority complex tends to be domineering, vain, boastful, arrogant, and depreciative of others. According to Adler, such a person lacks social interest (discussed in a later section) and is, indeed, undesirable.

Vaihinger's Philosophy of "As If"

In 1911, Hans Vaihinger (1852–1933) published *The Philosophy of "As If": A System of the Theoretical, Practical and Religious Fictions of Mankind.* Vaihinger's major premises were: (1) We can only be certain of sensations, that is, the subjective conscious elements provided by sensory stimulation and the relationships among them because we experience the physical world only indirectly through sensations; and (2) in order to make sense of our sensations we invent terms, concepts, and theories that give them meaning. According to Vaihinger, such inventions or fictions make all of civilized life possible. Thus, although the fictions by which humans live are figments of the imagination, they have great practical value:

> The principle of fictionalism is as follows: An idea whose theoretical untruth or incorrectness, and therefore its falsity, is admitted, is not for that reason practically valueless and useless; for such an idea, in spite of its theoretical nullity may have great practical importance. (Vaihinger, 1952, p. viii)

Although it is true that conscious experience consists only of sensations, there is an innate tendency to assign meaning to those sensations:

> Just as [the clam] when a grain of sand gets beneath its shining surface, covers it over with a self-produced mass of mother-of-pearl, in order to change the insignificant grain into a brilliant pearl, so, only still more delicately, the psyche, when stimulated, transforms the material of sensation which it absorbs into shining pearls of thought. (Vaihinger, 1952, p. 7)

What are these fictions invented by the imagination? According to Vaihinger (1952), they include all laws, generalizations, abstractions, models, theories, typologies, concepts, ideals, symbols, ideas, and even words. Vaihinger claimed that most communication among humans would be impossible without the use of fictions: "Most of the phrases of social intercourse are fictions, but [they are] *necessary* fictions, without which the more refined types of social intercourse would be impossible" (p. 83). By now it should be clear that for Vaihinger the term *fiction* is not derogatory; it refers to an expedient invention. Science would be impossible without such fictions as matter (e.g., atoms) and causality; mathematics would be impossible without such fictions as zero, perfect lines and geometric forms, imaginary numbers, and the concepts of infinity and the infinitesimal. Concepts of morality and jurisprudence would be impossible without the fictions of freedom and responsibility. Religion would be impossible without such fictions as gods or God, immortality, and reincarnation.

It is not possible to further summarize Vaihinger's philosophy here. Suffice it to say that he believed all discourse concerning so-called objective reality must necessarily employ "fictions" and the only criterion by which fictions can be judged is their fertility or practical value:

> Fictions have only a practical purpose and all the systems built up on elementary fictions are only more subtle and more elaborate fictions, to which no theoretical value must ever be attributed and which possess all the characteristics that we have so far always found in fictions. Theoretically they are valueless but practically they are important. (Vaihinger, 1952, p. 178)

Fictional Goals and Lifestyles

Adler embraced Vaihinger's philosophy enthusiastically and made it an important part of his theory. However, whereas Vaihinger was primarily interested in demonstrating how the use of fictions in science, mathematics, religion, philosophy, and jurisprudence made complex societal life possible, Adler applied the idea of fiction to the lives of individuals. From the interpretation of early experience, various worldviews can result. For example, the world can be perceived as an evil or dangerous place to be avoided, or as a pleasant or loving place to be embraced. It is important to emphasize that for Adler subjective reality was more important than physical reality. That is, it is the child's *perception* of the major events in his or her life that determines his or her worldview, not actual reality. If the child perceives the world to be a harsh, unpredictable place, he or she will adjust by creating life goals that incorporate those facts. If the child perceives the world as a warm, loving, predictable place, then those perceptions will be important in his or her adjustments to life. Because the important early experiences that mold a child's personality are those most vividly remembered through the years, they are the ones most likely to be reported as the person's earliest recollections. It was for this reason that Adler believed that one's earliest memories provide important information about one's life goals and one's lifestyle. We have more to say about the importance of first memories later in this chapter.

Coupled with feelings of inferiority, a child's worldview will determine his or her final goal, or **fictional finalism,** and his or her **lifestyle.** If a negative worldview develops, the child will believe that he or she must do battle with the world or escape from it in order to gain superiority. Here the goal will be to dominate, to defeat, to destroy, or to withdraw. If a positive worldview develops, the child will believe that he or she must participate in the world in order to gain superiority. Here the goal will be to join in, to create, to love, or to cooperate. Either type of worldview can manifest itself in a number of lifestyles. In turn, these lifestyles can manifest themselves in a number of professions. For example, a person with a negative worldview may become a ruthless businessperson or politician, a criminal, a hermit, or a domineering parent, teacher, or spouse. A person with a positive worldview may become a loving parent, spouse, teacher, physician, social worker, artist, writer, philosopher, theologian, or a politician whose goal is to improve the human condition.

The concept of fictional finalism, which Adler later called "a guiding self-ideal," or simply a "guiding fiction," gave Adler's theory a strong teleological (future-oriented) component but it did not ignore the past altogether. Now we can view the person as pushed by feelings of inferiority or imperfection toward perfection using his or her unique lifestyle as a means of attaining some future goal.

Adler emphasized that these future goals or ideals are convenient fictions invented to make life more significant than it otherwise would be. Healthy people, according to Adler, change fictions when circumstances warrant it. Neurotic persons, conversely, cling to their fictions at all costs. In other words, according to Adler, healthy individuals use fictional goals or ideals as tools in dealing with life. Life is unbearable without meaning so they invent meaning. Life is chaotic without a plan for living so healthy persons invent such a plan. For healthy persons, such goals, ideals, or plans are means of living a more effective, constructive life. For the neurotic, the idea that these are only tools is lost. The goals, ideals, or plans become ends in themselves, rather than means to an end. As such, they are retained even when they have become ineffective in dealing with reality. Thus, for Adler, an important difference between the healthy person and the neurotic is the ease with which fictional tools can be dispensed if circumstances warrant it. The healthy or normal person seldom loses sight of reality whereas for neurotic persons the fictional life plan becomes reality. Adler (1956a) explained:

> More firmly than the normal individual does the neurotic fixate his God, his idol, his personality ideal, and cling to his guiding line, and with deeper purpose he loses sight of reality. The normal person, on the other hand, is always ready to dispense with this aid, this crutch. In this instance, the neurotic resembles a person who looks up to God, commends himself to the Lord, and then waits credulously for His guidance; *the neurotic is nailed to the cross of his fiction.* The normal individual, too, can and will create his deity, will feel drawn upward. But he will never lose sight of reality, and always takes it into account as soon as action and work are demanded. The neurotic is under the hypnotic spell of a fictional life plan. (pp. 246–247 emphasis added)

We are reminded once again why Adler's theory is called individual psychology. The individual invents a worldview and derives a final goal or guiding self-ideal from that worldview. The individual then invents a lifestyle as a means of achieving that goal. All of this invention implies a great deal of personal freedom, an implication we explore further when we discuss the creative self later in this chapter.

Social Interest

Adler's earlier theory had been criticized because it portrayed humans as selfishly motivated to strive for personal superiority. With his concept of **social interest,** Adler put such criticism to rest. Social interest was, according to Adler, an innate need of all humans to live in harmony and friendship with others and to aspire toward the development of the perfect society. As we have seen, the attainment of the perfect society replaced perfection of the individual as the primary motive in Adler's theory. A well-developed social interest relates to almost all aspects of one's life:

It is almost impossible to exaggerate the value of an increase in social feeling. The mind improves, for intelligence is a communal function. The feeling of worth and value is heightened, giving courage and an optimistic view, and there is a sense of acquiescence in the common advantages and drawbacks of our lot. The individual feels at home in life and feels his existence to be worthwhile just as far as he is useful to others and is overcoming common, instead of private, feelings of inferiority. Not only the ethical nature, but the right attitude in aesthetics, the best understanding of the beautiful and the ugly, will always be founded upon the truest social feeling. (Adler, 1956c, p. 155)

However, what a person inherits, according to Adler, is the potential for social interest. If that potential is not realized, the person will live a most unfortunate life. Simply put, those without a well-developed social interest are neurotic or worse than neurotic. "In all human failure, in the waywardness of children, in neurosis and neuropsychosis, in crime, suicide, alcoholism, morphinism, cocainism, in sexual perversion, in fact in all nervous symptoms, we may read lack of proper degree of *social feeling*" (Adler, 1930b, p. 401).

According to Adler, each individual must solve three major problems in life, all of which require a well-developed social interest: (1) *occupational tasks*—through constructive work the person helps to advance society; (2) *societal tasks*—this requires cooperation with fellow humans. Adler said, "It was only because man learned to cooperate that the great discovery of the division of labor was made, a discovery which is the chief security for the welfare of mankind" (1964b, p. 132); (3) *love and marriage tasks*—the relationship between this task and the continuance of society is clear. Adler said, "On his approach to the other sex and on the fulfillment of his sexual role depends his part in the continuance of mankind" (1956c, p. 132).

What determines whether a person will have a well-developed social interest or not? Primarily the mother. According to Adler, the first major social situation the child encounters is in relation to the mother. The mother–child relationship acts as a model for subsequent social relationships. If the mother maintains a positive, cooperative atmosphere, the child will tend to develop social interest. If, however, the mother binds the child exclusively to herself, the child will learn to exclude other people from his or her life and will develop low social interest. For Adler, it is the nature of the mother's early interactions with her child that primarily determines whether or not the child will have a healthy, open attitude toward other people.

In the final version of Adler's theory, a person's fictional goal and lifestyle must take the improvement of society into consideration. If they do not, the person will be neurotic. For Adler, then, social interest was the index of normality.

Mistaken Lifestyles

Any lifestyle that is not aimed at socially useful goals is a **mistaken lifestyle.** We already have encountered two examples, the person who seeks personal superiority (superiority complex) and the person who is so overwhelmed by feelings of inferiority so as to accomplish nothing (inferiority complex). Both individuals lack social interest and, therefore, their lifestyles are mistaken or incorrect.

Adler delineated four types of people who were labeled according to their degree of social interest. The four types of people are: (1) the **ruling-dominant type** who attempts to dominate or rule people; (2) the **getting-leaning type** who expects everything from others and gets everything he or she can from them; (3) the **avoiding type** who "succeeds" in life by avoiding problems (such a person avoids failure by never attempting anything); and (4) the **socially useful type** who confronts problems and attempts to solve them in a socially useful way. The first three types have faulty or mistaken lifestyles because they lack proper social interest. Only the socially useful type can hope to live a rich, purposeful life.

Where do faulty lifestyles originate? Adler said they begin in childhood at the same time that a healthy lifestyle originates. Adler described three childhood conditions that tend to create a faulty lifestyle. The first is **physical inferiority** that can stimulate compensation or overcompensation, which is healthy, or can result in an inferiority complex, which is unhealthy. The second is **spoiling** or **pampering** that makes a child believe it is up to others to satisfy his or her every need. Such a child is the center of attention and grows up to be selfish with little, if any, social interest. **Neglecting,** the third condition, causes the child to feel worthless and angry and to look on everyone with distrust. Adler considered pampering as the most serious of parental errors:

> The most frequent difficulty is that the mother excuses the child from giving her any help or cooperation; heaps caresses and affection on him; and constantly acts, thinks and speaks for him, curtailing every possibility of development. Thus she pampers the child and accustoms him to an imaginary world which is not ours and in which everything is done for the child by others. (1956c, pp. 373–374)

Adler elaborated on how pampered children (and adults) view the world:

> The pampered child is trained to expect that his wishes will be treated as laws. . . . When he comes into circumstances where he is not the center of attention and where other people do not make it their chief aim to consider his feelings, he will be very much at a loss: he will feel that his world has failed him. He has been trained to expect and not to give. . . . When he has difficulties before him, he has only one method of meeting them—to make demands on other people. . . . Grownup pampered children are perhaps the most dangerous class in our community. (1958, p. 16)

According to Adler, pampering creates the Oedipus complex. "We could probably induce an [Oedipus] complex in any child. All we would need is for its mother to spoil it, and refuse to spread its interest to other people, and for its father to be comparatively indifferent or cold" (1958, p. 54). It is interesting to note that Adler viewed Freud's theory of personality as the creation of a pampered child:

> And, indeed, if we look closely we shall find that the Freudian theory is the consistent psychology of the pampered child, who feels that his instincts must never be denied, who looks on it as unfair that other people should exist, who asks always, "Why should I love my neighbor? Does my neighbor love me?" (Adler, 1958, p. 97)

The opposite of pampering is neglect, and it too gives the child an erroneous worldview. In the case of neglect, the child develops the impression that the world is a cold and unsympathetic place, and it is on this worldview that the child formulates his or her life's goal and lifestyle. According to Adler (1958), the neglected child

> has never known what love and cooperation can be: he makes up an interpretation of life which does not include these friendly forces. . . . He will overrate [the difficulties of life] and will underrate his own capacity to meet them . . . [and] will not see that he can win affection and esteem by actions which are useful to others. (p. 17)

Family experiences other than pampering and neglect can lead children to have distorted worldviews and, therefore, faulty lifestyles. According to Adler, other negative family experiences include failure to express a normal amount of tenderness or to consider sentimentality as ridiculous; excessive use of punishment, especially corporal punishment; establishment of standards of goals that are unattainable; excessive criticism of other people; and considering one parent superior to the other.

It is important to remember when considering the factors that may lead to a mistaken lifestyle that it is the child's perceptions that determine his or her personality, not reality. A pampered child who feels neglected will develop the worldview of a neglected child and vice versa. Adler said, "It is not the child's experiences which dictate his actions; it is the conclusions which he draws from his experiences" (1958, p. 123).

Creative Self

Hall and Lindzey called Adler's concept of the creative self his "crowning achievement as a personality theorist." They went on to say, "Here at last was the prime mover, the philosopher's stone, the elixir of life, the first cause of everything human for which Adler had been searching" (1978, pp. 165–166).

With his concept of the creative self, Adler stated that humans are not simply passive recipients of environmental or genetic influences. Rather, each person is free to act on these influences and combine them as he or she wishes. Thus no two people are ever the same even if the ingredients of their personalities are similar. We saw earlier that some persons with physical inferiorities compensate and become socially useful. Others develop an inferiority complex and accomplish nothing. To Adler, the difference is largely a matter of choice. According to Adler, heredity and environment provide a person only the "bricks which he uses in his own 'creative' way in building up his attitude toward life. It is his individual way of using these bricks—or in other words, it is his attitude toward life—which determines his relationship to the outside world" (1956d, p. 206). Elsewhere, Adler said:

> We concede that every child is born with potentialities different from those of any other child. Our objection to the teachings of the hereditarians and every other tendency to overstress the significance of constitutional disposition, is that the important thing is not what one is born with, but what use one makes of that equipment. . . . As to the influence of the environment, who can say that the same

environmental influences are apprehended, worked over, digested, and responded to by any two individuals in the same way? To understand this fact we find it necessary to assume the existence of still another force: the creative power of the individual. (1979, pp. 86–87)

For Adler, then, personality is essentially self-created. People assign meaning to their lives according to their perceptions of the world, themselves, and others. This is essentially an existential viewpoint.

Safeguarding Strategies

All neurotics have in common a self-centeredness, a concern with their own sense of security and superiority. That is, they lack social interest. According to Adler, neurotics know (or feel) that their goal of personal perfection is a mistaken one and may be exposed. Such public exposure would heighten the neurotic's already intense feelings of inferiority. Adler believed that neurotics use **safeguarding strategies** to protect what little self-esteem and illusions of superiority a mistaken lifestyle can generate. The feelings of self-esteem and superiority experienced by healthy persons are real because they are based on social interest and, therefore, they do not need to be supported by deceptive strategies. Adler's safeguarding strategies are similar to Freud's ego-defense mechanisms except, unlike ego-defense mechanisms, safeguarding strategies are used only by neurotics, can operate either on the conscious or unconscious levels, and protect persons from outside threats and the problems of life. Adler discussed three categories of safeguarding strategies: excuses, aggression, and distancing.

Excuses

The neurotic develops symptoms and uses them as excuses for his or her shortcomings:

> The patient . . . selects certain symptoms and develops them until they impress him . . . as real obstacles. Behind his barricade of symptoms the patient feels hidden and secure. To the question, "What use are you making of your talents?" he answers, "This thing stops me; I cannot go ahead," and points to his self-erected barricade. We must never neglect the patient's own use of his symptoms. . . . The patient declares that he is unable to solve his task "on account of the symptoms, and only on account of these." He expects from the others the solution of his problems, or the excuse from all demands, or, at least, the granting of "extenuating circumstances." (Adler, 1956c, pp. 265–266)

This safeguarding strategy consists of the "yes, but . . ." and "if only" excuses that protect a weak sense of worth and deceive neurotics, and those around them, into believing they are more worthy than they really are.

Freud too was well aware that patients often use their symptoms to gain attention and to rationalize ineffective behavior. Freud referred to these "benefits" of illness as pleasurable secondary gains.

Aggression

According to Adler, neurotics may also use aggression to protect their exaggerated sense of superiority and self-esteem. Neurotic aggression can take three forms: depreciation, accusation, and self-accusation. **Depreciation** is the tendency to overvalue one's own accomplishments and to undervalue the accomplishments of others. There are two common types of depreciation. The first is idealization or the use of standards so high in judging people that no real person could possibly live up to those standards; thus real people will be depreciated. Adler (1956c) gave the following examples of idealization:

> A short girl prefers tall men; or a girl falls in love only when the parents have forbidden it, while treating the attainable [partner] with open disdain and hostility. In the conversation and thoughts of such girls the limiting word "only" always crops up. They want only an educated man, only a rich man, only a real he-man, only platonic love, only a childless marriage, only a man who will grant his wife complete freedom. Here one sees the depreciation tendency so strongly at work that, in the end, hardly a man is left who would satisfy their requirements. Usually they have a ready-made, often unconscious, ideal to which traits of the father, a brother, a fairy-tale hero, a literary or historical character are admired. The more we become familiar with these ideals, the greater becomes our conviction that they have been posited as a fictional measure by which to depreciate reality. (p. 268)

A second type of depreciation is *solicitude* that is exemplified when neurotics act as if other people are incapable of caring for themselves. Using this strategy, neurotics constantly offer advice, demonstrate concern, and generally treat other people as children. Neurotics thereby safeguard their vulnerable feelings of self-esteem by convincing themselves that other people could not get along without them.

The second type of neurotic aggression discussed by Adler was **accusation,** or the neurotic's tendency to blame others for his or her shortcomings and to seek revenge against them. Adler believed that an element of revenge exists in all neuroses and that neurotic symptoms are often designed to make others suffer. Adler (1956c) said:

> In the investigation of a neurotic style of life we must always suspect an opponent, and note who suffers most because of the patient's condition. Usually this is a member of the family. There is always this element of concealed accusation in neurosis, the patient feeling as though he were deprived of his right—that is, of the center of attention—and wanting to fix the responsibility and blame upon someone. (p. 270)

Thus, according to Adler, a major goal of neurotics is to make those thought to be responsible for their misfortunes suffer more than they do.

The third type of neurotic aggression discussed by Adler is **self-accusation,** which involves

> cursing oneself, reproaching oneself, self-torture, and suicide. This may seem strange, until we realize that the whole arrangement of the neurosis follows the trait of self-torture, that the neurosis is a self-torturing device for the purpose of enhancing the self and depreciating the immediate environment. And indeed the

first stirrings of the aggression drive directed against one's own person originate from a situation in which the child wants to hurt the parents or wants to attract their attention more effectively. (1956c, p. 271)

Thus, in injuring themselves, neurotics really attempt to hurt or at least get the attention of other people. Also, guilt-inspired confessions are often used to inflict misery on other people. Adler gives the example of a domineering woman who confessed to her husband that she had deceived him with another man 25 years before. She accused herself of being unworthy and attributed the confession to guilt. Adler asked, "Who is so simple as to think that [this] is a case of the majesty of the truth vindicating itself after a quarter of a century?" (1956c, p. 272). According to Adler, the facts of the case show that the woman was attempting to hurt her husband by her confession and self-accusation because he no longer obeyed her.

Distancing

According to Adler, neurotics often escape from life's problems by **distancing** themselves from them. Adler discussed several ways in which neurotics do this: moving backward, standing still, hesitating, constructing obstacles, experiencing anxiety, and using the exclusion tendency. *Moving backward* involves safeguarding a faulty lifestyle by reverting to a more secure, less complicated time of life. This form of distancing often involves the use of disorders such as attempted suicide, fainting, migraines, refusal to take food, alcoholism, and crime to obtain the attention of others, to gain some control over them, and to avoid social responsibility.

About *standing still* Adler (1956c) said, "It is as if a witches' circle had been drawn around the patient, which prevents him from moving closer toward the reality of life, from facing the truth, from taking a stand, from permitting a test or a decision regarding his value" (p. 274). The disorders that Adler thought facilitate standing still include insomnia (with subsequent incapacity for work), a weak memory, masturbation, and impotence. *Hesitating* involves vacillating when faced with difficult problems. Adler believed most compulsions serve the purpose of occupying the neurotic long enough so that he or she is finally able to say, "It's too late now." Adler gave the following examples:

> Washing compulsion, . . . coming too late, retracing one's steps, destroying work begun . . . or always leaving something unfinished are found very often. Equally often one sees that the patient, under an "irresistible" compulsion toward some unimportant activity or amusement, delays a piece of work or a decision until it is too late. (p. 275)

Constructing obstacles creates distance that might be successfully overcome, whereas other forms of distancing remove the neurotic from the problems of life. According to Adler, neurotics can create relatively *minor* obstacles in their lives through such things as mild anxiety, certain compulsions, fatigue, sleeplessness, constipation, stomach and intestinal disorders, and headaches. These and other types of obstacles create a no-lose situation for the neurotic:

> The patient's self-esteem is protected in his own judgment, and usually also his prestige in the estimation of others. If [he is unsuccessful] he can refer to his difficulties and to the proof of his illness which he has himself constructed. If he [is]

Figure 4–1
Safeguarding Strategies

A summary of the various strategies used by neurotics to protect their fragile and false sense of superiority and self-esteem.

Excuses	Distancing
Aggression	Moving backward
Depreciation	Standing still
Idealization	Hesitating
Solicitude	Constructing obstacles
Accusation	Experiencing anxiety
Self-accusation	Using the exclusion tendency

victorious, what could he not have done if he were well, when, as a sick man, he achieved so much—one-handed so to speak! (1956c, p. 276)

Experiencing anxiety amplifies all of the distancing strategies. Neurotics are often fearful of undertakings such as leaving home, separating from a friend, applying for a job, or developing opportunities for relationships with members of the opposite sex. Insofar as these and other experiences cause anxiety, neurotics will attempt to distance themselves from them. The greater the amount of anxiety, the greater the distance sought. Using the *exclusion tendency* to avoid life's problems, the neurotic lives within narrow limits. "He tries to keep at a distance the real confronting problems of life and confines himself to circumstances in which he feels able to dominate. In this way he builds for himself a narrow stable, closes the door, and spends his life away from the wind, the sunlight, and the fresh air" (Adler, 1956c, p. 278). Living in a "narrow stable" would include being habitually unemployed as an adult, indefinitely postponing marriage, doing poorly in school, and maintaining close social ties only with one's family members. The various types of safeguarding strategies are summarized in Figure 4-1.

Goal of Psychotherapy

Healthy persons have a well-developed social interest; unhealthy persons do not. Those with faulty lifestyles, however, are likely to continue having them because lifestyles tend to be self-perpetuating. As we saw earlier, a lifestyle focuses a person on one way of looking at things, and this mode of perception persists unless the person runs into major problems or is made to understand his or her lifestyle through education or psychotherapy:

> Individual psychology considers the essence of therapy to lie in making the patient aware of his lack of cooperative power, and to convince him of the origin of this lack in early childhood maladjustments. What passes during this process is no small matter; his power of cooperation is enhanced by collaboration with the doctor. His "inferiority complex" is revealed as erroneous. Courage and optimism are awakened. And the "meaning of life" dawns upon him as the fact that proper meaning must be given to life. (Adler, 1930b, pp. 403–404)

By using an analysis of birth order, first memories, dreams, and mannerisms (all discussed shortly), Adlerians trace the development and manifestation of a mistaken lifestyle, one that necessitates therapy because it is ineffective in dealing with life's problems. The patient, with the therapist's help, seeks a new lifestyle that contains social interest and therefore will be more functional.

The Adlerian approach to therapy avoided criticism, blame, punishment, and an authoritarian atmosphere because these things typically amplified the patient's already strong feelings of inferiority. The therapist sits face to face with the patient and is informal and good humored. Patients are not allowed to use their neuroses, however, to gain the sympathy of the therapist as they once may have done with their parents or other persons. Although the therapist avoids pampering, he or she also avoids the opposite error of neglect. The Adlerian therapist believes that any insights gained should be explained with such clarity that they will be understood and accepted by the patient both intellectually and emotionally. The Adlerian therapist expects to see some improvement in the patient in about 3 months (with sessions once or twice a week) and considers it rare if the entire therapeutic process takes more than a year.

Adler was always interested in common people and a high percentage of his clientele were from the lower and middle classes, a rarity among psychiatrists of his time. Also extremely unusual was the fact that Adler worked directly with children. Adler typically treated children in the natural setting of their homes and insisted that their parents participate in the therapeutic process. As a result of his approach to treating children, Adler is considered one of the founders of group and family psychotherapy. Also, Adler insisted on treating problem children in front of a public audience in mental health clinics to help the child realize that his or her difficulty is a community problem.

As innovative and effective as Adlerian psychotherapy is, Adler always insisted that the prevention of disorders through proper childrearing and education was far easier and less costly than treating disorders later with psychotherapy.

Adler's View of the Unconscious

With his concept of the creative self, Adler denied the very foundation of Freudian psychoanalysis, that is, the importance of repressed traumatic experiences. Adler said, "We do not suffer the shock of [traumatic experiences] we make out of them just what suits our purposes" (1958, p. 14). As we have seen, once a worldview, a guiding fiction, and a lifestyle are formulated by an individual, all experiences are interpreted relative to them. Experiences compatible with a person's personality can be consciously pondered; those experiences incompatible are simply not understood. Thus, for Adler, compatibility with one's personality determined the difference between conscious and unconscious experience. If a person's personality changes, as is hoped will happen in therapy, many experiences previously not understood become understandable. We can only be aware of those experiences that make sense to us; all others are simply incomprehensible. We see in Chapter 13 that George Kelly explained the "unconscious" in essentially the same way as Adler did.

Methods of Research

Adler referred to birth order, first memories, and dreams as the three "entrance gates" to mental life, and he studied them extensively to discover the origins of a person's worldview, life goal, and lifestyle.

Birth Order

Adler contended that each child is treated differently within a family depending on the child's birth order and this differential treatment influences the child's world-view and thus his or her choice of a life's goal and lifestyle. "Above all," said Adler, "we must rid ourselves of the superstition that the situation within the family is the same for each individual child" (1964b, p. 229).

Adler concentrated his research on the first-born, secondborn, youngest, and the only child. The **first-born child** is the focus of attention until the next child is born, at which time he or she is "dethroned." According to Adler, the loss caused by the birth of a sibling is deeply felt by the first-born, because now the attention of the mother and father must be shared with a rival. Adler said, "Sometimes a child who has lost his power, the small kingdom he ruled, understands better than others the importance of power and authority" (1956c, pp. 378–379). The age of the first-born when the second child is born can make a substantial difference, however. If the first-born is old enough to have already developed a lifestyle and if that lifestyle is a cooperative one, then the first-born may develop a cooperative attitude toward the new sibling. If not, the resentment toward the new sibling may last a lifetime.

The **second-born child** has to be extremely ambitious because he or she is constantly attempting to catch up and surpass the older sibling. Of all the birth orders, Adler thought the second-born was the most fortunate. According to Adler, the second-born child behaves as if in a race, as if someone were a step or two in front, and he or she must rush to get ahead. Second-borns, Adler said, are "rarely able to endure the strict leadership of others" (1956c, p. 380).

The **youngest child** is, according to Adler, in the second worst position after the first-born. Adler stated that the reason for this

> generally lies in the way in which all the family spoils him. A spoiled child can never be independent. He loses courage to succeed by his own effort. Youngest children are always ambitious; but the most ambitious children of all are the lazy children. Laziness is a sign of ambition joined with discouragement; ambition so high that the individual sees no hope of realizing it. (1958, p. 151)

The youngest child, according to Adler, is the one most likely to seek a unique identity within a family such as becoming a musician in a family of scientists or vice versa.

The **only child** is like a first-born child who is never dethroned, at least by a sibling. The shock for the only child usually comes later (e.g., in school) on learning that he or she cannot remain the center of attention. The only child often develops an exaggerated sense of superiority and a sense that the world is a dangerous place. The latter results if the parents are overly concerned with the child's health. The only child is likely to lack a well-developed social interest and display a parasitic attitude, expecting others to offer pampering and protection:

> Only children are often very sweet and affectionate, and later in life they may develop charming manners in order to appeal to others, as they train themselves in this way, both in early life and later. . . . We do not regard the only child's situation as dangerous, but we find that, in the absence of the best educational methods,

very bad results occur which would have been avoided if there had been brothers and sisters. (Adler, 1964a, pp. 168–169)

Many factors can interact with the effects of birth order, bringing about results contrary to those generally expected. Such factors include the sex of older or younger siblings; the number of years separating them; and, most important, the way the child views his or her relations with other members of the family. For many reasons, then, all of Adler's remarks concerning the effects of birth order must be interpreted as describing only general tendencies. Adler intended them to be viewed this way.

We review the outcome of various attempts to empirically validate Adler's predictions concerning the effects of birth order on personality when we evaluate Adler's theory shortly.

First Memories

For Adler, the best way to identify a person's lifestyle is to obtain the person's earliest recollections of infancy or early childhood. These memories represent one's subjective starting point in life. It is irrelevant whether these memories are accurate or not. In either case, they reflect the person's interpretation of early experiences, and it is this *interpretation* of experience that shapes the child's worldview, life goal, and lifestyle. It is these interpretations of experience that are recalled as **first memories.** It follows that a close relationship among one's first memories, life's goal, and lifestyle must exist. Adler (1956c) explained:

> A depressed individual could not remain depressed if he remembered his good moments and his successes. He must say to himself, "All my life I was unfortunate," and select only those events which he can interpret as instances of his unhappy fate. Memories can never run counter to the style of life. If an individual's goal of superiority demands that he should feel, "Other people always humiliate me," he will choose for remembrance incidents which he can interpret as humiliations. Insofar as his style of life alters, his memories also will alter; he will remember different incidents, or he will put a different interpretation on the incidents he remembers.
>
> Most illuminating of all is the way the individual begins his story, the earliest incident he can recall. The first memory will show his fundamental view of life, his first satisfactory crystallization of his attitude. It offers us an opportunity to see at one glance what he has taken as the starting point for his development. (p. 351)

As we have seen, Adler's own first memories were of illness and death, and it was his concern about these matters that steered him in the direction of a medical career. Hertha Orgler (1963), Adler's friend and biographer, reported that Adler gave up his general medical practice after the death of several of his diabetic patients (before the discovery of insulin). Apparently his first memories of helplessness in the face of death were rekindled. Adler then turned to psychiatry, in which psychological death (of a mistaken lifestyle) and rebirth (the attaining of a new lifestyle with a healthy amount of social interest) were possible. Adler asked more than 100 medical physicians for their earliest memories, and most of them were of either serious illness or a death in the family.

Dream Analysis

Adler agreed with Freud on the importance of dreams but disagreed with Freud's interpretation of them. According to Freud, dreams allowed partial satisfaction of a wish that would be impossible to satisfy directly in a waking state. For Adler, dreams are always an expression of one's lifestyle and must be consistent with it. To Adler, however, the occurrence of dreams almost always suggests that the dreamer has a mistaken lifestyle. Dreams, according to Adler, offer emotional support for mistaken lifestyles. "Dreaming is the adversary of common sense. We shall probably find that people who do not like to be deluded by their feelings, who prefer to proceed in a scientific way, do not dream often or do not dream at all. Others, who are further away from common sense . . . have very frequent dreams" (1958, p. 101). Typically, dreams support a faulty lifestyle by creating an emotional state that will carry over into waking life and will justify actions compatible with the dreamer's faulty lifestyle. For example, if a student unconsciously wants to create a distance between him- or herself and an important examination, he or she may dream of being chased by criminals, fighting a losing war, or of being forced to attempt to solve insolvable problems. The student awakens from the dream experiencing such emotions as fear, discouragement, or helplessness, the very emotions that will support a decision to delay or avoid the forthcoming examination.

Adler (1958) said:

> The purpose of dreams must be in the feelings they arouse. The dream is only the means, the instrument, to stir up feelings. The goal of the dream is the feeling it leaves behind. . . . The style of life is the master of dreams. It will always arouse the feelings that the individual needs. We can find nothing in a dream that we shall not find in all the other symptoms and characteristics of the individual. We would approach problems in the same way whether we dreamed or not; but the dream offers a support and justification for the style of life. (pp. 98, 101)

Adler emphasized the self-deceptive and therefore the unhealthy nature of dreams. "In dreams we are fooling ourselves. Every dream is an auto-intoxication, a self-hypnosis. Its whole purpose is to excite the mood in which we are prepared to meet the situation" (1958, p. 101).

In summary, Adler believed that most dreams provide the self-deception necessary to maintain a mistaken lifestyle, and therefore people with healthy personalities dream little or not at all. That is, healthy persons require no self-deception and therefore do not require the irrational, emotional support provided by dreams.

Behavioral Mannerisms

In addition to analyzing birth order, first memories, and dreams, Adler also observed a client's characteristic ways of behaving in order to gain an understanding of his or her lifestyle. He observed such things as how a client walked, spoke, dressed, and where and how he or she sat. He also observed if a client was constantly leaning on something, the distance maintained between the client and other people, and eye contact or the lack of it. The goal was always to understand how the client viewed the world and him- or herself.

Summary of the Differences between Adler and Freud

The major differences between Adler and Freud can be summarized as follows.

ADLER	FREUD
Mind viewed as integrated whole	Mind viewed as consisting of warring factions
Emphasized conscious mind	Emphasized unconscious mind
Future goals important source of motivation	Future goals unimportant
Social motives primary	Biological motives primary
Optimistic about human existence	Pessimistic about human existence
Dreams analyzed to learn about lifestyles	Dreams analyzed to detect contents of unconscious mind
Humans free to determine their own personality	Personality completely determined by heredity and environmental factors
Minimized importance of sex	Maximized importance of sex
Goal of therapy to encourage lifestyle incorporating social interest	Goal of therapy to discover repressed early memories

Evaluation

Empirical Research

Most of the research generated by Adler's theory has explored the relationship between birth order and various personality characteristics. Many studies have found that first-born and only children have higher levels of educational aspiration and achievement than later-born children and are also more intelligent (e.g., Belmont & Marolla, 1973; Breland, 1974; Falbo, 1981; Wagner & Schubert, 1977). Generally it is found that first-borns are more responsible and achievement oriented and later-borns are more socially successful (e.g., Steelman & Powell, 1985). The proposed explanation for these results is that first-born and only children receive greater parental attention and are the objects of greater parental expectations. Falbo (1981) also found that last-born children typically have lower self-esteem than first-born children. This result is explained by the fact that last-born children typically have competent older siblings with which to compare themselves. Zajonc and Markus (1975) studied the relationships among birth order, family spacing, and family size and intellectual development. It was found that the fewer number of children in a family and the greater the spacing between children, the more intelligent each child is likely to be. Zajonc and his colleagues note that some researchers find a relationship between birth order and intelligence and others do not (Zajonc, 2001; Zajonc, Markus, & Markus, 1979; Zajonc & Mullally, 1997). According to Zajonc and his colleagues, whether or not a relationship exists between birth order and intelligence depends on the age at which children are tested. If a first-born is tested before age 11±2 years, no significant difference is found between his or her intelligence level and that of his or her younger siblings. If, however, the older child is tested after age 11±2 years, such a difference is found. The explanation for this discrepancy offered by Zajonc and his colleagues is that older children within a family often act as "parent surrogates" or "tutors" and younger children do not. Zajonc (2001) summarizes his explanation as follows:

> In his role as tutor, firstborn children gain an intellectual advantage. By virtue of rehearsal, by virtue of having to articulate an explanation or offer the meaning of a word, firstborns gain more verbal fluency more quickly than second-borns. However, younger siblings, if they are the last children in their families, will never act as tutors to older siblings. Last siblings are therefore in the same situation as are only children because neither group is offered the opportunity to be a tutor. (p. 491)

Downey (2001) focuses on the relationship between family size and intelligence. Downey notes that, "Across various measures of intellectual skills and educational achievement, individuals with the fewest siblings do the best" (p. 497). According to Downey, the explanation for this is straightforward: Parental resources (e.g., time, energy, and money) are finite and as the number of children in a family increases, the resources available to any one child necessarily decreases. According to Downey's "resource dilution model," family size rather than birth order per se is the most important variable in predicting the intellectual development of children.

Because the results of birth order studies are often contradictory, some researchers are highly critical of birth order research in general. For example, Ernst and Angst (1983) reviewed the studies on birth order between 1946 and 1980. The hundreds of studies reviewed investigated the relationship between birth order and such variables as intelligence, school and occupational achievement, aggressiveness, self-esteem, empathy, creativity, and various types of mental illness. Ernst and Angst concluded that research on birth order has been characterized by numerous methodological flaws and is "a sheer waste of time and money" (p. xi). Dunn and Plomin (1990) do not agree that birth order research is useless but they do say that birth order "plays only a bit-part in the drama of sibling differences" (p. 85). Somit, Arwine, and Peterson (1996) reach a similar conclusion.

Rodgers, Cleveland, van den Oord, and Rowe (2000) and Rodgers (2001) argue that there is no relationship between birth order and intelligence. According to Rodgers and his colleagues, when such a relationship is found, as it often is, it is an artifact of the research methodologies utilized. That is, when members of individual families are observed (within-family data) birth order effects on intelligence virtually disappear. In other words, no significant differences in intelligence are found among members of the same family. It is only when the mistake is made of comparing data across families (between-family data) that such an effect is found. Rodgers et al. discuss the problem involved in combining within-family and between-family data.

> To illustrate, imagine comparing the first-born child in a large middle-class White family in Michigan to the second-born child in a medium-sized affluent Black family in Atlanta to a third-born child in a small low-income Hispanic family in California. If differences between these children's intelligence are observed, it is impossible to tell whether they are due to [socioeconomic status], race, region of the country, birth order, family size, or other variables related to these. Yet, that is exactly the type of comparison that arises from cross-sectional [between-family] data. (p. 602)

Rodgers and his colleagues (2000) observe that even when using within-family data, the relationship between family size and the intellectual level of the children within the family remains significant. That is, there is a significant tendency for the intelligence of children to decrease as family size increases. However, contrary to Downey's "resource dilution model," Rodgers and his colleagues explain the relationship between family size and intelligence in terms of the intellectual and educational level of the parents involved. In any case, research on the relationship between family size and the intelligence of children within the family does not directly address the question of birth order. About the latter, Rodgers (2001) concludes, "The research community must be prepared for the real possibility that there simply are not any birth order–intelligence relationships" (p. 509).

Sulloway (1996) agrees that much birth order research has been poorly controlled and has involved hypotheses too nebulous to be objectively tested. When these problems are attended to, however, Sulloway believes the effects of birth order on personality are dramatic. As part of his massive historical undertaking, Sulloway studied how 3,890 scientists reacted to 28 scientific innovations when they were first reported (16 considered revolutionary, for example, the innovations provided by Copernicus, Darwin, and Freud, and 12 somewhat less radical). He found that those scientists who rejected the innovation in question were typically first-borns and those accepting it were typically later-borns. Sulloway says, "For the 28 innovations included in my survey, the odds are 2.0 to 1 in favor of laterborn adoption. The likelihood of this difference arising by chance is substantially less than one in a billion" (p. 42). Furthermore, as is shown in Figures 4-2 and 4-3, Sulloway found that this birth order effect was independent of sibship size and socioeconomic class. Sulloway found similar results when religious and social innovations were considered. In general, later-borns are much more receptive to innovation than first-borns. Of later-borns Sulloway says, "From their ranks have come bold explorers, the iconoclasts, and the heretics of history" (1996, p. xiv).

This finding has been consistent over time and across a wide variety of groups.

> For the past five centuries, the most consistent predictor of revolutionary allegiances turns out to be birth order. Compared with firstborns, laterborns are more likely to identify with the underdog and to challenge the established order. Because they identify with parents and authority, firstborns are more likely to defend the status quo. The effects of birth order transcend gender, social class, nationality, and—for the last five centuries—time. (Sulloway, 1996, p. 356)

Sulloway's research confirms the rather puzzling observation made over the last two decades that, "Siblings who grow up together are almost as different in their personalities as people plucked randomly from the general population" (1996, p. 352). The question is why this is so, and Sulloway offers a Darwinian answer. Within a family, siblings compete for parental resources, including affection. Without siblings to compete with, first-borns have everything to themselves and usually identify with parents and authority and grow up defending the status quo. The challenge of the later-born "is to find a valued family niche that avoids duplicating the

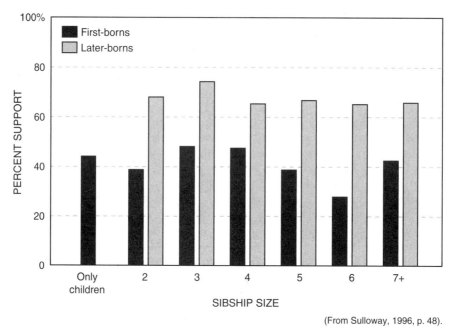

(From Sulloway, 1996, p. 48).

Figure 4–2 *Receptivity to Scientific Innovation by Birth Order and Sibship Size.*

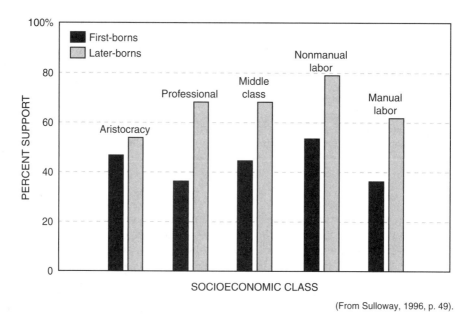

(From Sulloway, 1996, p. 49).

Figure 4–3 *Receptivity to Scientific Innovation by Birth Order and Socioeconomic Class.*

one already staked out by the parent-identified firstborn" (Sulloway, 1996, p. 353). This search for an unoccupied family niche by later-borns is facilitated by an openness to experience, or versatility, which, once developed, lasts a lifetime. Sulloway concludes, "From a Darwinian point of view, personality is the repertoire of strategies that each child develops in an effort to survive childhood" (p. 86).

Although Sulloway explained the effects of birth order within a Darwinian framework, the conclusion he reached was very much within the spirit of Adlerian analysis. "Families are best seen as containing an array of diverse niches, each occupied by a different individual and each presenting different vantage points of life. From these differing perspectives, family members experience the same events differently" (1996, p. 352).

Attempts to confirm Sulloway's conclusions about the relationship between birth order and personality have had mixed results. For example, Freese, Powell, and Steelman (1999) tested Sulloway's claim that first-borns are more conservative and supportive of authority than later-borns and found no support for it. However, Paulus, Trapnell, and Chen (1999) did find support for Sulloway's contention that later-born children are more rebellious than first-born children. J. R. Harris (2000) argues that the evidence suggests a compromise. Harris provides evidence for Sulloway's (and Adler's) contention that a child's position within a family influences the personality he or she develops *within the family*. However, when the child eventually leaves the family the coping strategies and other personality characteristics learned within the family constellation are no longer relevant. Harris concludes, "There is little or no transfer of training because patterns of behavior acquired at home are likely to be inappropriate or irrelevant outside the home" (p. 177).

Several attempts have been made to make other Adlerian concepts more measurable and thus more useful in counseling and therapeutic situations. For example, Crandall (1980, 1981, 1982) devised and utilized a scale for measuring level of social interest and found that social interest varies with one's social adjustment, among other things. Thorne (1975) devised a 200-item questionnaire called the Life Style Analysis, which is designed to determine a person's lifestyle. Rule (1972) and Rule and Traver (1982) devised and used an Early Recollection Questionnaire, and Altman (1973) created the Early Recollection Ratings Scale of Social Interest. Olson (1979) presented a collection of papers showing how early memories are used in clinical diagnosis and psychotherapy. Hafner, Fakouri, and Labrentz (1982) found more alcoholics than nonalcoholics described their earliest memories as threatening.

Criticisms

Difficult to Falsify. Like the theories of Freud and Jung, many of the terms in Adler's theory are not defined precisely enough to validate. Because they lack clear definition it is difficult, if not impossible, to determine the impact of such concepts as inferiority, superiority, social interest, and creative power on a person's personality. Adler's contention that "everything can also be different" (1956c, p. 194) makes it practically impossible to make a falsifiable prediction using his theory. As we have seen, Adler believed it was subjective reality that determines behavior, not objective reality. Therefore, if a person develops a personality unlike the one that is supposed to characterize, for example, his or her birth order, it can always be attributed to the person's unique perceptions of the situation. Also, Adler claimed that heredity and experience provide only the raw materials of personality and the creative self acts on those materials to mold a unique personality. The concept of creative self, then, makes it impossible to predict adult personality characteristics on the basis of either heredity or environmental experience.

Overly Simplistic.   Adler claimed that it is often a few early experiences that determine adult personality, and that if a person's interpretations of the world based on those experiences could be changed, an unhealthy lifestyle could be changed into a healthy one. Also, Adler relied almost exclusively on social factors in explaining personality, minimizing biological, hereditary factors. Finally, Adler contends that in the final analysis personality is, or could be, freely chosen by each person. Many modern personality theorists consider all of these Adlerian assumptions to be overly optimistic. Also, with his belief that all humans are born with the innate potential for social interest, Adler had trouble explaining the widespread occurrence of war, murder, rape, crime, and other human acts of violence. Many believe that the theories of Freud and Jung are far better able to explain the more unseemly aspects of human behavior.

Contributions

The Importance of Social Variables.   Although some consider Adler's emphasis on social variables a negative aspect of his theory, others consider that emphasis as Adler's most significant contribution. Adler vividly pointed out that the world each person lives in is a world of his or her own creation. Furthermore, the most important factor in formulating that worldview is the person's relationships with other people. For example, a person's family constellation is one variable that can influence his or her worldview. The importance of social variables for personality development were minimized by Freud and Jung.

Widely Influential.   Adler's terms "lifestyle" and "inferiority complex" have become part of everyday language. In the realms of personality theory and psychotherapy, we see Adler's influence in the contemporary emphasis on self-selected goals as determinants of behavior; social determinants of personality; family therapy, group therapy, and community psychiatry; the importance of subjective reality as opposed to objective reality; and personal freedom and responsibility in living one's life.

Several influential persons regard Adler's contribution to psychology greater than Freud's. For example, Albert Ellis says:

> Alfred Adler, more even than Freud, is probably the true father of modern psychotherapy. Some of the reasons are: He founded ego psychology, which Freudians only recently rediscovered. He was one of the first humanistic psychologists. . . . He stressed holism, goal-seeking, and the enormous importance of values in human thinking, emoting, and acting. He correctly saw that sexual drives and behavior, while having great importance in human affairs, are largely the result rather than the cause of man's non-sexual philosophies. . . .
> It is difficult to find any leading therapist today who in some respect does not owe a great debt to the Individual Psychology of Alfred Adler. (1970, p. 11)

Viktor Frankl stated that Adler's opposition to Freud

was no less than a Copernican switch. No longer could man be considered as the product, pawn, and victim of drives and instincts; on the contrary, drives and instincts form the material that serves man in expression and action.

Beyond this, Alfred Adler may well be regarded as an existential thinker and as a forerunner of the existential-psychiatric movement. (1970, p. 12)

Summary

Adler spent much of his childhood suffering from several physical ailments, feelings of inferiority, and in a losing competition with his older brother. He was one of Freud's earliest associates, but numerous differences caused them to terminate their relationship. Adler disputed Freud's notions of repression, infantile sexuality, and the importance of the unconscious. Adler's viewpoint, called individual psychology, stresses the wholeness and uniqueness of each person as he or she struggles to overcome feelings of inferiority by aspiring toward some future goal. Adler's theory is compatible with existentialism because of its concern with free will and the meaning of human existence; and with humanism because it stresses the innate goodness of humans.

In the earliest version of his theory, Adler believed that people were motivated to compensate for actual physical weaknesses by emphasizing those qualities that compensate for those weaknesses. In some cases, he thought a person could overcompensate and convert a weakness into a strength. Later, Adler extended his theory to include not only actual physical weaknesses but imagined ones as well. Now compensation or overcompensation was directed at the feelings of inferiority resulting from either real or imagined inferiorities. In his early writing, Adler equated inferiority with femininity and superiority with masculinity. The striving to become more masculine in order to become more powerful was called the masculine protest. According to Adler, feeling inferior is not necessarily bad; in fact, such feelings are the motivating force behind most personal accomplishments. Some individuals, however, are not stimulated to growth by their feelings of inferiority. Rather, they are overcome by them and the feelings become a barrier to personal growth; such individuals are said to have an inferiority complex.

Adler's final theoretical position was that humans are primarily motivated to seek superiority or perfection. The superiority sought is compatible with society, however, and not a selfish, individual superiority. A person who selfishly seeks personal superiority while ignoring the needs of others and of society is said to have a superiority complex.

Adler believed that persons must insert meaning into their lives by inventing ideals or fictional goals that give them something for which to live and around which to organize their lives. Such fictions are called fictional finalisms or guiding fictions. Healthy persons use such fictions as tools for living a more significant, effective life. For healthy persons, these fictions can easily be discarded if circumstances warrant. For neurotics, however, these fictions are confused with reality and therefore are retained at all costs. The means by which a person attempts to attain a fictional goal is called his or her lifestyle.

Adler theorized that all persons have an innate potential to live in harmony with other people; he called this need social interest. Each person must solve three major problems in life, and each requires a strong social interest: (1) occupational tasks, (2) societal tasks, and (3) love and marriage tasks. Adler believed that the nature of a child's interaction with the mother determines to what extent the child develops social interest. Any lifestyle not characterized by a strong social interest was labeled a mistaken lifestyle. Three types of people with a mistaken lifestyle are the ruling–dominant type, the getting–leaning type, and the avoiding type. The socially useful type has a strong social interest, and therefore his or her lifestyle is not mistaken. Three childhood conditions that can cause a mistaken lifestyle are physical inferiority, spoiling or pampering, and neglecting. Adler did not believe that personality is completely determined by biological inheritance, early experiences, or the environment. He believed each person is free to interpret life in any number of ways. The creative self allows us to be what we choose to be.

Because the feelings of self-esteem and superiority that are generated by a mistaken lifestyle are basically deceptive, they must be safeguarded. As the safeguarding strategies used by neurotics, Adler listed excuses; aggression consisting of accusation, depreciation, and self-accusation; and distancing consisting of moving backward, standing still, hesitating, constructing obstacles, experiencing anxiety, and using the exclusion tendency. The major goal of psychotherapy is to replace a mistaken lifestyle with one containing a healthy level of social interest. Adler's research methods included the study of birth order, first memories, and dream analysis.

Some of the major premises that differentiated Adler's theory from Freud's are Adler's emphasis on the conscious integrated mind, social motives, one's future goals, personal freedom, dreams as primarily supportive of faulty lifestyles, and his deemphasis on sexual motivation. In addition, Adler was optimistic about the human condition whereas Freud was pessimistic.

Adler's theory has been criticized for containing terms too nebulous to measure, making them nonfalsifiable, and for being too simplistic in its characterization of personality. The theory seems to overlook the baser side of human beings. Adler's theory has been praised for noting the importance of social variables in personality development and for introducing several terms, concepts, and methodologies that are useful in the therapeutic process and for understanding personality. Although there has been considerable research on the effects of birth order on various personality characteristics, the results have been equivocal. Sulloway appears to have amassed the most evidence supporting the argument that birth order is a powerful and predictable determinant of personality. However, the influence of birth order on personality is a hotly debated issue in contemporary psychology. The Adlerian concepts of social interest and first memories also show promise as topics of research.

Experiential Exercises

1. Adler believed that one's earliest memories provide the subjective starting point in one's life. List your earliest memories and discuss their possible relationship to your major goals in life.
2. Adler identified four basic types of people: the ruling type, the getting type, the avoiding type, and the socially useful type. Indicate which of the four types characterizes you best and give evidence supporting your conclusion.
3. According to Adler, each child is treated differently within a family depending on the child's birth order. Given your birth order, describe how your experiences may have been different than a child with a different birth order. Discuss how the experiences caused by your birth order may have influenced your adult personality. By interviewing acquaintances, determine whether or not persons with the same birth order have similar personality characteristics.

Discussion Questions

1. Why did Adler call his theory individual psychology?
2. Distinguish between feelings of inferiority and an inferiority complex.
3. Discuss Adler's concept of social interest. Give examples of how the concept is used by Adler in his theory.

Glossary

Accusation. Form of neurotic aggression that involves blaming other people for one's shortcomings and seeking revenge against those people.

Aggression. As a safeguarding strategy, aggression can take three forms: depreciation, accusation, and self-accusation. *See also* Accusation, Depreciation, and Self-accusation.

Avoiding type person. Person exhibiting the mistaken lifestyle of avoiding the attempt to solve life's problems, thereby escaping possible defeat. Such a person lacks adequate social interest.

Birth order. One of the topics that Adler studied in order to understand personality. He believed that different birth orders created different situations to which children must adjust and that this adjustment may have an influence on personality development.

Compensation. Making up for a weakness, such as organ inferiority, by emphasizing functions that substitute for the weakness.

Creative self. Free element of the personality that allows the person to choose between alternative fictional goals and lifestyles. It is the differential exercise of this creative power that is mainly responsible for individual differences.

Depreciation. Neurotic safeguarding strategy whereby one's accomplishments are overvalued and the accomplishments of others are undervalued. Depreciation can take the form of idealization, whereby standards used to judge people are so high that no real person could live up to them and is thus depreciated. Another form of depreciation is solicitude, whereby neurotics act as if other people could not get along without them.

Distancing. Safeguarding strategy used by neurotics that involves creating barriers between themselves and their problems in life. According to Adler, distancing can take the forms of moving backward or the use of childlike behavior in order to gain attention and control; standing still or the avoidance of failure by not attempting to do anything; hesitating or becoming involved in diversions until it is too late to confront a problem; constucting obstacles or the creation of minor obstacles so that they can be overcome, thereby increasing the neurotic's false feeling of worth; experiencing anxiety is caused by the neurotic's inability to solve life's problems; the greater the ineptitude, the greater the anxiety and therefore, the greater the need for distancing; and using the exclusion tendency or the neurotics' tendency to confine their lives to the few areas in which they can dominate.

Dream analysis. Adler believed that the primary purpose of dreams was to create emotions that could be used by dreamers to support their mistaken lifestyles. Dreams, then, were analyzed to learn about the lifestyles of the dreamers.

Excuses. Safeguarding strategy whereby neurotics use their symptoms as excuses for their shortcomings.

Feelings of inferiority. Feelings that one has of being inferior, whether or not these feelings are justified by real circumstances. Such feelings, according to Adler, can lead either to positive accomplishments or to an inferiority complex.

Fictional finalism. (also called a guiding self-ideal and guiding fiction). Fictional future goal to which a person aspires. This goal is the end to which the person is aspiring, and his or her lifestyle is the means to that end.

First-born child. This child is the focus of attention until the birth of a sibling "dethrones" him or her. The loss felt by the first-born child when the second child is born often creates bitterness that causes problems later in life. Adler considered this to be the most troublesome birth position.

First memories. A person's earliest recollections. Such recollections provide the basis for a person's worldview, fictional final goal, and lifestyle. Adler believed that as one's personality changes so do first memories.

Fundamental fact of life. Adler replaced his earlier contention that people seek power to overcome feelings of inferiority with the contention that they aspire to become superior or perfect. Adler referred to the latter contention as the fundamental fact of life. Adler's final position was that healthy persons aspire toward social rather than individual perfection. *See also* Striving for superiority.

Getting-leaning type person. Person exhibiting the mistaken lifestyle that expects everything to be given to him or her by others. Such a person lacks adequate social interest.

Individual psychology. Adler's term to describe his theory. The term individual was used to stress his belief that each person is an integrated whole striving to attain future goals and attempting to find meaning in life while working harmoniously with others.

Inferiority complex. Psychological condition that exists when a person is overwhelmed by feelings of inferiority to the point at which nothing can be accomplished.

Lifestyle. The primary means by which one attempts to attain his or her self-created or fictional goals in life.

Masculine protest. Attempting to become more powerful by being more masculine, and thereby less feminine. According to Adler's earlier theorizing, both men and women attempt to gain power by becoming more like the cultural ideal of the man.

Mistaken lifestyle. Any lifestyle that is not aimed at socially useful goals. In other words, any lifestyle that minimizes social interest.

Neglecting. Condition that causes the child to feel worthless and angry and to be distrustful of everyone.

Only child. This child is like a first-born child who was never dethroned. Only children, according to Adler, are often sweet, affectionate, and charming in order to appeal to others. Adler did not consider this birth position as dangerous as the first-born's position.

Organ inferiority. Condition that exists when some organ of the body does not develop normally. Such a condition can stimulate compensation or overcompensation, which is healthy, or can result in an inferiority complex, which is unhealthy. *See also* Compensation and Overcompensation.

Overcompensation. Process by which, through considerable effort, a previous weakness is converted into a strength. An example is when a frail child works hard to become an athlete.

Physical inferiority. Actual physical weakness. *See also* Organ inferiority.

Ruling-dominant type person. Person exhibiting the mistaken lifestyle that dominates and rules people. Such a person lacks adequate social interest.

Safeguarding strategies. Mechanisms neurotics use to preserve what little self-esteem and illusions of superiority a mistaken lifestyle can provide. *See also* Aggression, Excuses, and Distancing.

Second-born child. This child is very ambitious because he or she is constantly attempting to catch up and surpass the older sibling. Of all the birth orders, Adler believed that the second-born was the best.

Self-accusation. Form of neurotic aggression that involves wallowing in self-torture and guilt, the ultimate purpose of which is to hurt other people.

Social interest. Innate potential to live in harmony and friendship with others and to aspire to the development of a perfect society.

Socially useful type person. Person exhibiting a lifestyle containing a healthy amount of social interest. Such a lifestyle is not "mistaken."

Spoiling or pampering. Conditions that cause a child to believe it is the responsibility of others to satisfy his or her needs.

Striving for superiority. What Adler called "the fundamental fact of life." According to Adler's final theoretical position, it is not the search for the power necessary to overcome feelings of inferiority that motivates humans; rather, it is the constant search for perfection or superiority. However, Adler stressed the perfection of society rather than individual perfection. *See also* Fundamental fact of life.

Superiority complex. Psychological condition that exists when a person concentrates too much on his or her own need to succeed while ignoring the needs of others. Such a person tends to be vain, domineering, and arrogant.

Youngest child. According to Adler, the second-worst birth position after the first-born. This child is often spoiled and therefore loses courage to succeed by his or her own efforts.

KAREN HORNEY

Karen Horney was trained in the Freudian tradition, and all her work was influenced by that training. In fact, while at the Berlin Psychoanalytic Institute, she was psychoanalyzed by Karl Abraham and Hans Sachs, two of the most prominent Freudian analysts at that time. Early in her career, Horney even defended Freudian theory against attacks from such critics as Adler and Jung (Quinn, 1988, p. 151). As time went on, however, Horney found it more and more difficult to apply Freudian notions to her work. She completely disagreed with Freud's notions of the Oedipus complex and his division of the mind into the id, ego, and superego. She thought Freud's theory reflected a different country and a different time. To state it simply, Horney found that Freud's theory did not fit the problems people were having during the Great Depression in the United States. Sexual problems were secondary to several other problems that those special environmental conditions had created. Instead of sexual problems, people were worried about losing their jobs and not having enough money to pay the rent, buy food, or provide their children with needed medical care.

Horney reasoned that because such major differences exist in the types of problems that people experience from one country to another or from one time in history to another, they must be culturally rather than biologically determined, as Freud had assumed. So, although Horney was trained in the Freudian tradition and deeply influenced by that training, her theory ended up being quite different than Freud's. To Horney, what a person experiences socially determines whether or not he or she will have psychological problems and, if so, what type they will be. The conflict is caused by environmental conditions, not by opposing components of the mind (id, ego, and superego) as Freud had believed. As we shall see, Horney did not abandon Freud's theory completely but her viewpoint is much more compatible with Adler's than with Freud's.

Biographical Sketch

Karen Horney (pronounced "Horn-eye") was born Karen Danielson in a small village near Hamburg, Germany, on September 15, 1885 (the year Freud was studying hypnotism with Jean Charcot in Paris). Her father, Berndt Henrik Wackles Danielson, was a Norwegian sea captain, and her mother, Clotilde Marie van Ronzelen, was a member of a prominent Dutch-German family. Horney's mother was 18 years younger than the captain and was his second wife. The family consisted of four children from the captain's previous marriage as well as Horney's older biological brother, Berndt, who was considered the darling of the family. Horney's father was a tall, dashing, stern, God-fearing fundamentalist who strongly believed that women were inferior to men and were the source of evil in the world. He often clashed with Horney's mother who was proud, beautiful, intelligent, and free thinking. Horney had mixed feelings about her father. On the one hand, she felt intimidated by his stern, self-righteous manner and by his derogatory statements about her appearance and intelligence. Conversely, he added adventure to her life by taking her along on at least three lengthy sea voyages and by bringing her exotic gifts from around the world. Perhaps it was because of these fond memories that Horney began wearing a captain's cap when she was in her 30s. As an example of her father's negative side, Horney recalled that after reading the Bible at length, he sometimes exploded in a fit of anger and threw the Bible at his wife. The children referred to him as the "Bible thrower" (Rubins, 1978, p. 11). It is little wonder that Horney developed a negative attitude toward religion and a skepticism toward authority figures. After she was treated by a physician when she was 12, Horney decided to become a physician herself—a decision that was strongly supported by her mother and opposed by her father.

In 1906, when Karen was 21, she entered medical school at Freiberg, Germany, one of the few medical schools allowing women at the time. Shortly afterward she met Oskar Horney, an economics major on vacation from another institution, and was attracted to him because he was stern, intelligent, independent, and physically and emotionally strong. Karen married Oskar on October 31, 1909 (the year Freud and Jung gave a series of lectures at Clark University in the United States), and the union produced three daughters. By the time they married, Oskar had become a lawyer (as Karen's brother had also). By 1910 Horney was pregnant with Brigitte, the first of their three daughters. Shortly before the birth of Brigitte, Horney's mother died of a stroke. It was also about this time that Horney underwent her own psychoanalysis in preparation for a career as a psychoanalyst. Needless to say, these were tense times in Horney's life. Within the space of just a few years she experienced marriage, the death of her mother, childbirth, and psychoanalysis.

Horney's marriage to Oskar was never very happy. Horney had her first affair in early 1911, and that was only the beginning:

By early 1912, Oskar had ceased to play an important role in Karen's life. She felt that the great tensions and emotions were missing in their marriage and sought satisfaction of her needs elsewhere. . . . Within two years of their wedding, Karen and Oskar appear to have agreed on an open marriage, in which each pursued other relationships without concealment or deceit. . . . Karen and Oskar continued their liaisons discreetly and maintained the appearance of being a conventional family as their three daughters were growing up, but the vitality went out of their relationship within a year after Brigitte's birth. (Paris, 1994, p. 49)

In the above quotation we see signs of the promiscuity that characterized most of Horney's adult life. Several of her close acquaintances described her as being addicted to men, or as at least having a compulsion to be with them (Paris, 1994, pp. 148–149). Through the years Horney's lovers, who were almost always younger men, included her colleagues (sometimes married) and her students. There is evidence that Horney's sexual appetites extended to women (Paris, 1994, p. 241).

Although sexual promiscuity was a major theme in Horney's life, it apparently never became overly disruptive. In fact, it may have acted as a source of inspiration. About her numerous relationships, Paris (1994) says, "They were not . . . the main focus of Horney's life; her need for men was compulsive but not all-consuming. It did not interfere with her creative work but rather fueled her continuing search for psychological insight" (pp. 149–150).

It is interesting to note that although Horney felt essentially unwanted and unloved as a child, she was viewed by her own children as having a laissez-faire attitude toward them. Rubins (1978, p. 51) reported that during a Christmas dinner, the middle daughter, Marianne, leaned back too far in her chair. In an attempt to catch herself from falling she grabbed the tablecloth and took to the floor with her the entire Christmas dinner. Marianne's father (Oskar) beat her with a dog whip while the two other daughters cried, and Horney looked on without displaying any emotion.

The Horney marriage, such as it was, began to disintegrate in 1923, about the time that Karen's brother died of pneumonia at the age of 40. Shortly after her brother's death, the Horney family went on vacation. Karen went swimming alone and when she did not return for more than an hour, family members went looking for her. She was found clinging to a piling pondering whether to continue living or to take her own life. After much pleading she agreed to swim back to shore. This bout was but one of many with the deep depression that Karen experienced throughout her life. Also, about this time, Oskar's life was becoming extremely difficult. The firm that he worked for went bankrupt, his investments failed, and he borrowed heavily to survive financially. After a near-fatal attack of meningitis, the formerly successful Oskar was himself bankrupt, morose, and withdrawn. He became increasingly difficult to live with, and in 1926 Horney and her three girls moved into a small apartment. It was not until 1936 that Horney officially filed for a divorce, and the divorce did not become final until 1938.

Horney completed her medical studies in 1913 at the University of Berlin. She was an excellent student throughout her academic career and was often first in her class. From 1914 to 1918, she received psychoanalytic training at the Berlin Psychoanalytic Institute. In 1919, at age 33, she became a practicing psychoanalyst. From 1918 to 1932, she taught at the Berlin Psychoanalytic Institute, besides having a private practice.

In 1932, she accepted an invitation from Franz Alexander to come to the United States and become an associate director of the Chicago Institute of Psychoanalysis. Two years later, she moved to New York where she established a private practice and trained analysts at the New York Psychoanalytic Institute, where Horney reestablished a relationship with her old friend Erich Fromm. She had originally met Fromm at the Berlin Institute for Psychoanalytic Training in 1922 and there was a mutual attraction. Fromm was married at the time, however, and nothing romantic occurred. The two were together for awhile at the Chicago Institute of Psychoanalysis but apparently their intimate relationship did not begin until they both moved to New York in 1934. Rubins (1978) observes that the relationship was mutually beneficial because Horney "learned sociology from Fromm and he psychoanalysis from her" (p. 195). Fromm, who was 15 years Horney's junior, became highly successful and authored several influential books including *Escape From Freedom* (1941). The intimate relationship with Fromm lasted several years and even when it ended, a social and professional relationship continued for several more years. After Fromm, Horney's next romantic relationship was with Hans Baumgartner. Torn between marrying Hans or getting a cocker spaniel, Horney opted for the cocker spaniel (Paris, 1994, p. 145).

At the New York Psychoanalytic Institute, major differences between Horney and the traditional Freudians became apparent. Eventually the theses submitted by her students were routinely rejected because they reflected ideas contrary to traditional Freudian doctrine. Opposition to her ideas became strong enough to cause a restriction of her teaching duties and to bar her as a training analyst. Under such pressure Horney resigned from the New York Psychoanalytic Institute in 1941 and soon thereafter she founded and headed her own organization called the American Institute for Psychoanalysis, where she continued to develop her own ideas until her death from abdominal cancer on December 4, 1952.

Basic Evil, Hostility, and Anxiety

In her book *The Neurotic Personality of Our Time* (1937), Horney elaborated her contention that neuroses are caused by disturbed human relationships. More specifically, she maintained that the rudiments of neurotic behavior are found in the relationship between parent and child. This point agrees with Freud's theory because Horney also stressed the importance of early childhood experience in personality development. Horney, however, did not accept Freud's notion of the psychosexual stages of development. Like Adler, Horney believed the child starts life with a feeling of helplessness relative to the powerful parents. She believed the two basic needs in childhood are **safety** and **satisfaction,** and that the child is completely dependent on the parents for his or her satisfaction. The need for satisfaction refers to the child's needs for food, water, and sleep. At least minimal satisfaction of such physiological needs is necessary for the child's survival. According to Horney, however, the satisfaction of physiological needs is less important for personality development than the satisfaction of the need for safety. By the need for safety Horney meant the need for security and freedom from fear.

Although each child is in fact helpless and dependent on the parents during the early years, this need not necessarily create a psychological problem. Horney did not agree with Adler's earlier view that each child feels helpless and inferior and spends the rest of his or her life compensating or overcompensating for this feeling. She believed the condition of helplessness is a necessary but not a sufficient condition for the development of neurosis. Two possibilities exist: (1) The parents can demonstrate genuine affection and warmth toward the child, thereby satisfying the need for safety; or (2) the parents can demonstrate indifference, hostility, or even hatred toward the child, thereby frustrating the child's need for safety. The former condition leads to normal development, and the latter condition leads to neurotic development.

Horney called the behavior of parents that undermines a child's security the **basic evil.** Here is a sample list of such behaviors:

Indifference toward the child
Rejection of the child
Hostility toward the child
Obvious preference for a sibling
Unfair punishment
Ridicule
Humiliation
Erratic behavior
Unkept promises
Isolation of the child from others

A child who is abused by the parents in one or more of the preceding ways experiences **basic hostility** toward his or her parents. The child is now caught between dependence on the parents and hostility toward them, a most unfortunate situation. Because the child is in no position to change the situation, he or she must repress the hostile feelings toward the parents to survive. This repression of the child's basic hostility is motivated by feelings of helplessness, fear, love, or guilt (Horney, 1937, p. 73). The child who represses basic hostility because of feelings of helplessness seems to be saying, "I have to repress my hostility because I need you" (p. 74). The child who represses basic hostility because of fear seems to be saying, "I have to repress my hostility because I am afraid of you" (p. 74).

In some homes, real love for a child may be lacking but at least there is some effort to make the child seem wanted. For example, verbal expressions of love and affection may be substituted for real love and affection. The child, according to Horney, has little trouble telling the difference but clings to the "substitute" love because that is all there is. This child says, "I have to repress my hostility for fear of losing love" (Horney, 1937, p. 74). In our culture, the child may also repress basic hostility because of having been made to feel guilty about having any negative feelings about his or her parents. Such a child feels sinful and unworthy in feeling hostile toward the parents and therefore represses such feelings. The motto of this child is, "I have to repress hostility because I would be a bad child if I felt hostile" (p. 75).

Unfortunately the feeling of hostility caused by the parents does not remain isolated; instead, it generalizes to the entire world and all the people in it. The child is now convinced that everything and everyone is potentially dangerous. At this point, the child is said to experience **basic anxiety,** one of Horney's most important concepts. Horney described basic anxiety and its relationship to basic hostility as follows:

> The condition that is fostered or brought about by the factors I have mentioned . . . is an insidiously increasing, all-pervading feeling of being lonely and helpless in a hostile world. . . . This attitude as such does not constitute a neurosis but it is the nutritive soil out of which a definite neurosis may develop at any time. Because of the fundamental role this attitude plays in neuroses I have given it a special designation: the basic anxiety; it is inseparably interwoven with a basic hostility. (1937, pp. 76–77)

According to Horney, the origins of neurotic behavior are found in parent–child relationships. If the child experiences love and warmth, he or she will feel secure and probably develop normally. In fact, Horney thought that if a child were truly loved, he or she could survive a variety of negative experiences without ill effects: "A child can stand a great deal of what is often regarded as traumatic—such as sudden weaning, occasional beating, sex experiences—as long as inwardly he feels wanted and loved" (Horney, 1937, pp. 68–69). If, however, the child did not feel loved there would be hostility toward the parents, and this hostility would eventually be projected onto everything and everyone and become basic anxiety. According to Horney, a child with basic anxiety is well on the way to becoming a neurotic adult.

Adjustments to Basic Anxiety

Because basic anxiety causes feelings of helplessness and loneliness, the person experiencing it must find ways to keep it to a minimum. Originally, Horney (1942) described 10 strategies for minimizing basic anxiety that she called **neurotic trends** or neurotic needs. As you read through these neurotic needs, you will note they are needs that almost everyone has, which is an important point. The normal person, in fact, has many or all of these needs and pursues their satisfaction freely. In other words, when the need for affection arises, one attempts to satisfy it. When the need for personal admiration arises, one attempts to satisfy that need, and so forth. The neurotic person, however, does not pass easily from one need to another as conditions change. Rather, the neurotic person focuses on one of the needs to the exclusion of all the others. The neurotic person makes one of these needs the focal point of life. Unlike the normal person, the neurotic person's approach to satisfying one of these needs is out of proportion to reality, disproportionate in intensity, and indiscriminate in application, and when the need goes unsatisfied, it stimulates intense anxiety. "If it is affection that a person must have, he must receive it from friend and enemy, from employer and bootblack" (Horney, 1942, p. 39).

The 10 neurotic trends or needs are as follows (Horney, 1942, pp. 51–56):

1. **Need for Affection and Approval.** A person emphasizing this need lives to be loved and admired by others. "Center of gravity in others and not in self, with their wishes and opinions the only thing that counts; dread

of self-assertion; dread of hostility on the part of others or of hostile feelings within self" (p. 51).

2. **Need for a Partner Who Will Run One's Life.** A person emphasizing this need must be affiliated with someone who will protect him or her from all danger and fulfill all of his or her needs. "Overevaluation of 'love' because 'love' is supposed to solve all problems; dread of desertion; dread of being alone" (pp. 51–52).

3. **Need to Live One's Life Within Narrow Limits.** A person emphasizing this need is very conservative, avoiding defeat by attempting very little. "Necessity to be undemanding and contented with little, and to restrict ambitions and wishes for material things; necessity to remain inconspicuous and to take second place; belittling of existing faculties and potentialities, with modesty the supreme value" (p. 52).

4. **Need for Power.** A person emphasizing this need glorifies strength and despises weakness. "Domination over others craved for its own sake; . . . essential disrespect for others, their individuality, their dignity, their feelings, the only concern being their subordination; . . . indiscriminate adoration of strength and contempt for weakness; dread of uncontrollable situations; dread of helplessness" (pp. 52–53).

5. **Need to Exploit Others.** A person emphasizing this need dreads being taken advantage of by others but thinks nothing of taking advantage of them. "Others evaluated primarily according to whether or not they can be exploited or made use of; . . . pride in exploitative skill; dread of being exploited and thus of being 'stupid'" (p. 54).

6. **Need for Social Recognition and Prestige.** A person emphasizing this need lives to be recognized—for example, to have his or her name in the newspaper. The highest goal is to gain prestige. "All things—inanimate objects, money, persons, one's own qualities, activities, and feelings—evaluated only according to their prestige value" (p. 54).

7. **Need for Personal Admiration.** A person emphasizing this need lives to be flattered and complimented. This person wants others to see him or her in accordance with the idealized image he or she has of him- or herself. "Need to be admired not for what one possesses or presents in the public eye but for the imagined self; self-evaluation dependent on living up to this image and on admiration of it by others" (p. 54).

8. **Need for Ambition and Personal Achievement.** A person emphasizing this need has an intense interest in becoming famous, rich, or important, regardless of the costs. "Need to surpass others not through what one presents or is but through one's activities; self-evaluation dependent on being the very best—lover, sportsman, writer, worker—particularly in one's own mind, recognition by others being vital too, however, and its absence resented" (p. 55).

9. **Need for Self-Sufficiency and Independence.** A person emphasizing this need goes to great extremes to avoid being obligated to anyone and does not want to be tied down to anything or anyone. Enslavement is to be avoided at all costs. "Necessity never to need anybody, or to yield to any influence, or to be tied down to anything, any closeness involving the

danger of enslavement; distance and separateness the only source of security; dread of needing others, of ties, of closeness, of love" (p. 55).

10. **Need for Perfection and Unassailability.** A person emphasizing this need attempts to be flawless because of hypersensitivity to criticism. "Relentless driving for perfection; . . . feelings of superiority over others because of being perfect; dread of finding flaws within self or of making mistakes; dread of criticism or reproaches" (pp. 55–56).

Again, normal people experience most, if not all, of the 10 needs, and, when they do, put them in proper perspective. For example, normal people's need for power is not intense enough to cause a conflict with other needs, such as the need for affection. Normal people are in a position of satisfying all their needs because they do not have an intense emotional investment in any one of them. The neurotic, conversely, has made one of the needs a way of life. The neurotic's whole life is spent attempting to satisfy just one of the needs at the expense of all the others. Because it is important that many of the other needs be satisfied, the neurotic is locked into a vicious circle. The more one neurotic need is emphasized as a means of coping with basic anxiety, the more other important needs go unsatisfied. The more these other needs go unsatisfied, the more basic anxiety the neurotic feels, and the more anxious this person feels, the deeper he or she burrows into a single strategy to cope with the anxiety. And on it goes.

Moving Toward, Against, or Away from People

In her book *Our Inner Conflicts* (1945), Horney summarized her list of 10 neurotic needs into three major adjustment patterns. Each of the three patterns described the neurotic's adjustment to other people. These three patterns of adjustment are considered by many to be Horney's most significant contribution to personality theory.

Moving Toward People

This adjustment pattern includes the neurotic needs for affection and approval, for a dominant partner to control one's life, and to live one's life within narrow limits. This person, whom Horney called the **compliant type,** seems to say, "If I give in, I shall not be hurt" (Horney, 1937, p. 83):

> In sum, this type needs to be liked, wanted, desired, loved; to feel accepted, welcomed, approved of, appreciated; to be needed, to be of importance to others, especially to one particular person; to be helped, protected, taken care of, guided. (1945, p. 51)

It should be noted that, like the 10 neurotic needs, these major adjustments to other people also are based on basic anxiety that is, in turn, based on basic hostility. So, although a person may adjust to basic anxiety by **moving toward people** and by apparently seeking love and affection, the person is still basically hostile. Thus the compliant person's friendliness is superficial and is based on repressed aggressiveness.

Moving Against People

In most ways, this person is the opposite of the compliant type. This adjustment pattern combines the neurotic needs for power, for exploitation of others, for prestige, and for personal achievement. This person, whom Horney called the **hostile type,** seems to say, "If I have power, no one can hurt me" (Horney, 1937, p. 84):

> Any situation or relationship is looked at from the standpoint of "What can I get out of it?"—whether it has to do with money, prestige, contacts, or ideas. The person himself is consciously or semiconsciously convinced that everyone acts this way, and so what counts is to do it more efficiently than the rest. (1945, p. 65)

The hostile type is capable of acting polite and friendly, but it is always a means to an end.

Moving Away from People

This adjustment pattern includes the neurotic needs for self-sufficiency, independence, perfection, and unassailability. This person, whom Horney called the **detached type,** seems to be saying, "If I withdraw, nothing can hurt me" (Horney, 1937, p. 85):

> What is crucial is their inner need to put emotional distance between themselves and others. More accurately, it is their conscious and unconscious determination not to get emotionally involved with others in any way, whether in love, fight, cooperation, or competition. They draw around themselves a kind of magic circle which no one may penetrate. (1945, p. 75)

As with the 10 neurotic needs, the normal person uses all three adjustments to other people, depending on which one is appropriate at the time. Neurotic persons cannot. They emphasize one of the three adjustments at the expense of the other two. This causes further anxiety because all humans at various times need to be aggressive, to be compliant, and to be detached or withdrawn. The lopsided development of the neurotic causes further anxiety that then causes further lopsided development. Thus we have the vicious circle again.

Note that the three adjustment patterns are basically incompatible. For example, one cannot move toward people and away from people at the same time. For both the neurotic and the normal person, the three adjustment patterns are in conflict with each other. For the normal person, however, the conflict is not as emotionally charged as it is for the neurotic. Therefore, the normal person has far greater flexibility, being able to move from one adjustment mode to another as conditions change. The neurotic person must meet all of life's problems using only one of the three adjustment patterns whether that pattern is appropriate or not. It follows that the neurotic person is far less flexible and is therefore less effective in dealing with life's problems than the normal person is.

Real and Idealized Self

According to Horney, each human is born with a healthy **real self** that is conducive to normal personality growth. If people live in accordance with their real selves, they are on the road to **self-realization,** which means they will approximate their full potential and live in harmony with their fellow humans:

> You need not, and in fact cannot, teach an acorn to grow into an oak tree, but when given a chance, its intrinsic potentialities will develop. Similarly, the human individual, given a chance, tends to develop his particular human potentialities. He will develop then the unique alive forces of his real self: the clarity and depth of his own feelings, thoughts, wishes, interests; the ability to tap his own resources, the strength of his will power; the special capacities or gifts he may have; the faculty to express himself, and to relate himself to others with his spontaneous feelings. All this will in time enable him to find his set of values and his aims in life. In short, he will grow, substantially undiverted, toward self-realization. And that is why I speak . . . of the real self as that central inner force, common to all human beings and yet unique in each, which is the deep source of growth. (1950, p. 17)

If children experience loving satisfaction of their biological and security needs, they develop in accordance with their real selves and become normal, flexible, productive adults. If, however, the basic evil is experienced, children become alienated from their real selves. Such children view themselves as lowly and despicable; why else would they have suffered the abuse they did? This distorted view of one's self as unworthy displaces the real self as a frame of reference for living. Such a person creates an **idealized self,** which has little relationship to the real self.

According to Horney, when a person lives in accordance with an illusionary, idealized self instead of the real self, he or she is neurotic. The neurotic uses his or her idealized self as an escape from his or her real self that is viewed negatively. Unlike the real self, the idealized self is an unrealistic, immutable dream.

When a person's life is directed by an unrealistic self-image, that person is driven by what should be, rather than what is. Horney referred to this as the **tyranny of the should:**

> Forget about the disgraceful creature you actually are; this is how you should be; and to be this idealized self is all that matters. You should be able to endure everything, to understand everything, to like everybody, to be always productive—to mention only a few of these inner dictates. Since they are inexorable, I call them "the tyranny of the should." (1950, pp. 64–65)

The neurotic is locked into the illusion of the ideal self, an illusion that does not reflect reality and one that tends to be unchanging. The more intensely the neurotic chases the ideal, the further the person is driven from the real self and the more intense the neurosis becomes. Horney (1945) explained:

> A person builds up an idealized image of himself because he cannot tolerate himself as he actually is. The image apparently counteracts this calamity; but having placed himself on a pedestal, he can tolerate his real self still less and starts to rage against it, to despise himself and to chafe under the yoke of his own unattainable

demands upon himself. He wavers then between self-adoration and self-contempt, between his idealized image and his despised image, with no solid middle ground to fall back on. (p. 112)

For such a person, the only hope is a well-trained analyst or a highly disciplined self-analysis. (Horney's procedures for self-analysis are discussed later in this chapter.)

Normal people, conversely, have dreams, but they are realistic and changeable. Normal people experience both success and failure and both influence changes in their aspirations. Neurotic people experience mainly failure, because their ideals tend to be incompatible with their real selves. The feelings that neurotics experience cannot provide meaningful feedback concerning the effectiveness of their interactions with the environment and with people because those feelings are not genuine. The neurotic "feels what he should feel, wishes what he should wish, likes what he should like" (Horney, 1950, p. 159).

Externalization

According to Horney (1945):

> When discrepancies between the actual self and the idealized one reach a point where tensions become unbearable, [the person] can no longer resort to anything within himself. The only thing left then is to run away from himself entirely and see everything as if it lay outside. (pp. 115–116)

Horney referred to this tendency to view everything of importance occurring outside of oneself as **externalization,** defined as "the tendency to experience internal processes as if they occurred outside oneself and, as a rule, to hold these external factors responsible for one's difficulties. It has in common with idealization the purpose of getting away from the real self" (1945, p. 115).

Some similarity exists between externalization and the Freudian mechanism of projection, but, according to Horney:

> Externalization . . . is a more comprehensive phenomenon; the shifting of responsibility is only a part of it. Not only one's faults are experienced in others but to a greater or lesser degree all feelings. A person who tends to externalize may be profoundly disturbed by the oppression of small countries, while unaware of how much he himself feels oppressed. He may not feel his own despair but will emotionally experience it in others. What is particularly important in this connection, he is unaware of his own attitudes toward himself; he will, for example, feel that someone else is angry with him when he actually is angry with himself. Or he will be conscious of anger at others that in reality he directs at himself. Further, he will ascribe not only his disturbances but also his good moods or achievements to external factors. While his failures will be seen as the decree of fate, his successes will be laid to fortuitous circumstances, his high spirits to the weather, and so on. (1945, p. 116)

Because the neurotic removes himself or herself as a determinant of anything significant, it is only natural that experiences external to one's self will be overvalued, especially those with other people. If any major change is going to occur in the neurotic's life, so reasons the neurotic, it must result from changing other people. "When a person feels that his life for good or ill is determined by others, it is only logical that he should be preoccupied with changing them, reforming them, punishing them, protecting himself from their interference, or impressing them" (Horney, 1945, pp. 116–117).

The neurotic becomes completely dependent on external factors in maintaining his or her idealized image. When these external factors do not support the neurotic's idealized image, he or she feels a sense of rage, but that too must be externalized. According to Horney (1945, pp. 120–122), rage can be externalized in three ways: (1) If there are no inhibitions against hostility, anger is turned against others as either general irritability or as specific irritation concerning the faults in others that the neurotic really hates in him- or herself; (2) an incessant fear that the faults that one cannot tolerate in oneself will infuriate others; (3) the creation of bodily disorders such as intestinal maladies, headaches, fatigue, and so on.

Externalization does not help the neurotic's situation any; in fact, externalization makes the situation worse:

> Externalization is thus essentially an active process of self-elimination. The reason for its being feasible at all lies in the estrangement from the self that is inherent in the neurotic process anyhow. With the self eliminated, it is only natural that the inner conflicts, too, should be removed from awareness. But by making the person more reproachful, vindictive, and fearful in respect to others, externalization replaces the inner conflicts with external ones. More specifically, it greatly aggravates the conflict that originally set in motion the whole neurotic process: the conflict between the individual and the outer world. (Horney, 1945, p. 130)

Because the attempt at self-obliteration through externalization is destined to fail, the neurotic is forced to resort to what Horney called "auxiliary approaches to artificial harmony."

Auxiliary Approaches to Artificial Harmony

According to Horney, neurotic persons lie to themselves when they attempt to live their lives according to their idealized self-images and all of the "shoulds" associated with those images. To support that lie, they need to externalize whatever real feelings they may have, another lie. To support those lies, or to control the damage done by them, neurotics need to employ other lies, and on it goes. Horney (1945) explained:

> It is a commonplace that one lie usually leads to another, the second takes a third to bolster it, and so on till one is caught in a tangled web. Something of the sort is bound to happen in any situation in the life of an individual or group where a determination to go to the root of the matter is lacking. The patchwork may be of

some help, but it will generate new problems which in turn require a new makeshift. So it is with neurotic attempts to solve the basic conflict; and here as elsewhere, nothing is of any real avail but a radical change in the conditions out of which the original difficulty arose. What the neurotic does instead—and cannot help doing— is to pile one pseudo solution upon another. (p. 131)

Horney described seven unconscious devices neurotics use to deal with the inevitable conflicts that arise when one displaces one's real self with an idealized self. Horney viewed these devices as additional lies that neurotics use in attempting to live an illusionary life.

There is a similarity among what Freud called ego-defense mechanisms, what Adler called safeguarding strategies, and what Horney called auxiliary approaches to artificial harmony.

Blind Spots

This involves denying or ignoring certain aspects of experience because they are not in accordance with one's idealized self. For example, if one views oneself as extremely intelligent, one tends to overlook experiences that suggest one is not. Similarly, people who view themselves as pious or saintly will remain oblivious to any blatant acts of aggression in which they engage. Horney (1945) gave the following example:

> A patient . . . who had all the characteristics of the compliant type and thought of himself as Christlike, told me quite casually that at staff meetings he would often shoot one colleague after another with a little flick of his thumb. True enough, the destructive craving that prompted these figurative killings was at the time unconscious; but the point here is that shooting, which he dubbed "play," did not in the least disturb his Christlike image. (p. 132)

Horney's concept of **blind spots** is similar to Freud's ego-defense mechanism of denial of reality.

Compartmentalization

This involves dividing one's life into various components with different rules applying to each. For example, one set of rules applies to one's family life and another set to one's business life. Thus one can act in accordance with Christian principles at home and be ruthless in one's business dealings. The neurotic sees no conflict here because the situations are different. Horney (1945) elaborated on **compartmentalization:**

> There is a section for friends and one for enemies, one for the family and one for outsiders, one for professional and one for personal life, one for social equals and one for inferiors. Hence what happens in one compartment does not appear to the neurotic to contradict what happens in another. It is possible for a person to live that way only when, by reason of his conflicts, he has lost his sense of unity. (pp. 133–134)

Rationalization

According to Horney, **rationalization** is the type of self-deception that involves giving logical, plausible, but inaccurate excuses to justify one's perceived weaknesses, failures, or inconsistencies. Compliant types must offer such excuses for acts of aggression, and hostile types must offer them for acts of kindness.

Excessive Self-Control

This is guarding against anxiety by controlling any expression of emotion. The goal here is to maintain rigid self-control at all costs. Horney (1945) elaborated:

> Persons who exert such control will not allow themselves to be carried away, whether by enthusiasm, sexual excitement, self-pity, or rage. In analysis they have the greatest difficulty in associating freely; they will not permit alcohol to lift their spirits and frequently prefer to endure pain rather than undergo anesthesia. In short, they seek to check all spontaneity. (p. 136)

Arbitrary Rightness

Often the life of a neurotic is characterized by indecision, ambiguity, and doubt but the feelings generated by these characteristics are intolerable. By using **arbitrary rightness** as a protective device in ambiguous situations, the neurotic chooses one solution, one answer, one position and dogmatically declares that the problem is solved and the debate is over. The position taken by the neurotic becomes the "truth" and therefore cannot be challenged. The neurotic no longer needs to worry about what is right and wrong, or what is certain and uncertain.

Elusiveness

Elusiveness is the opposite of arbitrary rightness. The elusive neurotic seldom makes a decision about anything. If one is not committed to anything, one cannot be wrong, and if one is not wrong, one cannot be criticized. Horney (1945) described the characteristics of the elusive neurotic:

> They are vicious one moment, sympathetic the next; at times overconsiderate, ruthlessly inconsiderate at others; domineering in some respects, self-effacing in others. They reach out for a dominating partner, only to change to a "doormat," then back to the former variety. After treating someone badly, they will be overcome by remorse, attempt to make amends, then feel like a "sucker" and turn to being abusive all over again. Nothing is quite real to them. (pp. 138–139)

Cynicism

The elusive neurotic postpones making decisions whereas the cynic does not believe in anything. Cynics take pleasure in pointing out the meaninglessness of the beliefs of others. Horney believed that **cynicism** probably grew out of repeated failures associated with previous beliefs. By not believing anything, cynics are immune to the disappointment that comes from being committed to something shown to be false. Also, they are spared the difficult task of arriving at their own system of beliefs. They simply say *nothing* is worth believing. Also, by not accepting any moral

values these neurotics justify their Machiavellian approach to interpersonal relationships. Horney (1945) said of the cynical neurotic, "All that counts is appearance. You can do as you please as long as you don't get caught. Everyone is a
hypocrite who isn't fundamentally stupid" (p. 140).

Again, the difference between normal people and neurotics is one of degree.
Normal people will undoubtedly use each of these secondary adjustment techniques
at one time or another. Neurotics, however, will overuse one or more of them, thus
reducing their flexibility and efficiency in solving life's inevitable problems.

Feminine Psychology

Horney was trained as a Freudian psychoanalyst and, as we indicated earlier, was
herself psychoanalyzed by two of Freud's most ardent supporters (Karl Abraham
and Hans Sachs). Also, she taught at the Berlin Psychoanalytic Institute from 1918
to 1932. It is not surprising, then, that Horney's early work closely followed Freud's
teaching. For example, in an address entitled "The Problem of the Monogamous
Ideal" given in 1927, Horney analyzed the problems inherent in monogamous marriage from a strictly Freudian perspective. Her major point was that because males
symbolically marry their mothers and females symbolically marry their fathers, the
Oedipus complex necessarily manifests itself within marriage. On this point Horney
quoted Freud: "The husband or the wife is always a substitute" (1967, p. 85). Insofar as a child learned to inhibit his or her incestuous desires for his or her parent,
those inhibitions will manifest themselves in marriage:

> The manner and degree in which the influence of the early [Oedipal] situation will
> show itself [in marriage] will depend on the extent to which the incest prohibition
> still makes itself felt as a living force in the mind of the individual concerned. (Hor-
> ney, 1967, p. 86)

According to Horney, the incest prohibition typically has the same result in
marriage as it does in parent–child relationships. That is, "direct sexual aims give
place to an affectionate attitude in which the sexual aim is inhibited" (Horney, 1967,
p. 86). Thus Horney reached the conclusion that because maintaining a sexual relationship with one's spouse is symbolically the same as maintaining such a relationship with one's parent, the sexual aspect of marriage soon diminishes:

> I know personally of only one case in which this development [the transition from
> a sexual relationship to an affectionate one] has not supervened, the wife remain-
> ing permanently in love with her husband as a sexual object, and in this case the
> woman had, at the age of twelve, enjoyed actual sexual gratification with her father.
> (1967, p. 86)

According to Horney, the damage done by the resurrected Oedipal complex
in marriage can be minimized by seeking a marital partner as different from one's
mother or father as possible:

> It may be that the woman selected as wife must in no way recall the mother; in
> race or social origin, intellectual calibre or appearance she must present a certain

contrast to the mother. This helps to explain why marriages prompted by prudence or contracted through the intervention of a third party tend to turn out relatively better than genuine love matches. . . . We can perceive that there was a certain psychological wisdom in the institution of an intermediary to arrange marriages, such as obtains among the Eastern Jews. (1967, p. 87)

Thus perhaps the problems of monogamous marriage can be reduced but they cannot be eliminated: "It never has been and never will be possible to find any principle that will solve these conflicts of married life" (Horney, 1967, p. 98). For example, the possessiveness often displayed toward one's partner in marriage is "plainly [the] revival of the infantile wish to monopolize the mother or father" (1967, p. 91).

Horney's early analysis of marriage reflected many of the orthodox Freudian views of the male and female Oedipus complexes and therefore a belief that **anatomy is destiny.** Increasingly, however, Horney disagreed with Freud's contention that women are destined to possess certain personality traits simply because of their anatomy. She gradually developed the belief that cultural factors are more important in explaining the personality characteristics of both men and women than biological factors. Horney began writing articles on issues of special interest to women in 1923 and continued to do so until 1937. These articles, which also reflect Horney's transition from biological to cultural determinism, were compiled in *Feminine Psychology* (1967).

Horney's Explanation of Penis Envy

According to Freud, one of the most traumatic experiences in the psychological development of girls is their discovery they do not possess penises, although boys do. They react to this discovery by wishing to have a penis and being envious of more fortunate males. In this biological area, females must settle only for symbols, thus they wish to have male children who will finally furnish them (symbolically) with their own penises. According to Freud, anatomy is destiny and women are destined to be inferior to men (or at least feel inferior) and have a contempt for their own sex because they lack penises.

In her early writings, Horney accepted Freud's belief that anatomy is destiny, but did so with a few interesting twists. Horney found that in her treatment of male patients, they often displayed an envy of motherhood at least as strong as the supposed penis envy displayed by women:

From the biological point of view woman has in motherhood, or in the capacity for motherhood, a quite indisputable and by no means negligible physiological superiority. This is most clearly reflected in the unconscious of the male psyche in the boy's intense envy of motherhood. . . . When one begins, as I did, to analyze men only after a fairly long experience of analyzing women, one receives a most surprising impression of the intensity of this envy of pregnancy, childbirth, and motherhood, as well as of the breasts and of the act of sucking. (Horney, 1967, pp. 60–61)

Furthermore, "the 'womb envy' of the male must be stronger than the 'penis envy' of the female, because men need to depreciate women more than women need to depreciate men" (Paris, 2000, p. 166). Horney (1967) elaborated on why men might resent women and, therefore, feel the need to depreciate them.

One of the exigencies of the biological differences between the sexes is this: that the man is actually obliged to go on proving his manhood to the women. There is no analogous necessity for her. Even if she is frigid, she can engage in sexual intercourse and conceive and bear a child. She performs her part by merely being, without any doing—a fact that has always filled men with admiration and resentment. The man on the other hand has to do something in order to fulfill himself. The ideal of "efficiency" is a typical masculine ideal. (p. 145)

According to Horney, it is also this emphasis on performance that causes males to have "deeply hidden anxiety" about the size of their penises and attempt to "possess" as many women as possible. Typically, said Horney, males do not desire women who are their equals or superiors. "From the prostitute or the women of easy virtue one need fear no rejection, and no demands in the sexual, ethical, or intellectual sphere. One can feel oneself superior" (Horney, 1967, p. 146).

In her later writings, Horney completely rejected the biological determination of personality, including the Freudian notion of penis envy, and said instead that women often feel inferior to men because they are, indeed, culturally inferior to men. Because men control the power in culture, women may appear to wish to be masculine whereas all they are attempting to do is participate in those desirable experiences over which men have control. Horney said, "Our whole civilization is a masculine civilization. The State, the laws, morality, and the sciences are the creation of men" (1967, p. 55). Elsewhere, Horney said:

The wish to be a man, as Alfred Adler has pointed out, may be the expression of a wish for all those qualities or privileges which in our culture are regarded as masculine, such as strength, courage, independence, success, sexual freedom, right to choose a partner. (1939, p. 108)

Thus it is not penises that women envy and desire but the ability to influence and to participate in their culture freely.

Why does psychoanalysis seem to understand men better than women and to paint a more favorable picture of men than women? Horney answered, "The reason for this is obvious. Psychoanalysis is the creation of a male genius, and almost all those who have developed his ideas have been men. It is only right and reasonable that they should evolve more easily a masculine psychology and understand more of the development of men than of women" (1967, p. 54). Horney continued:

Like all sciences and all valuations, the psychology of women has hitherto been considered only from the point of view of men. It is inevitable that the man's position of advantage should cause objective validity to be attributed to his subjective, affective relations to the woman . . . the psychology of women hitherto actually represents a deposit of the desires and disappointments of men. (p. 56)

Horney (1939) concluded that Freud was a genius with limited intellectual vision:

It is one of the characteristics of a genius to have the power of vision and the courage to recognize current prejudices as such. In this sense as in others Freud certainly deserves to be called a genius. It is almost incredible how often he freed himself from venerable ways of thinking and looked upon psychic connections in a new light. It sounds like a banality to add that on the other hand no one, not even a genius, can entirely step out of his time, that despite his keenness of vision his thinking is in many ways bound to be influenced by the mentality of his time. (p. 37)

Psychotherapy

As far as psychotherapeutic techniques are concerned, Horney borrowed much from Freud. She commonly used dream analysis and free association. Both were used, however, to discover which major adjustment technique a patient was using (moving toward, against, or away from people). She also believed strongly in Freud's concept of transference. "Were someone to ask me," she said, "which of Freud's discoveries I value most highly, I should say without any hesitation: it is his finding that one can utilize for therapy the patient's emotional reactions to the analyst and to the analytical situation" (1939, p. 154). For Horney, what was revealed through transference was, once again, the patient's major adjustment technique. Thus the hostile type attempts to dominate the therapist; the detached type waits like a bystander while the therapist provides a miraculous cure; and the compliant type attempts to use his or her pain and suffering to gain sympathy and help from the therapist.

The tendency for neurotics to externalize is a major obstacle in psychotherapy. Horney (1945) explained:

> A patient with a general tendency to externalize offers peculiar difficulties in analysis. He comes to it as he would go to a dentist, expecting the analyst to perform a job that does not really concern him. He is interested in the neurosis of his wife, friend, brother, but not in his own. He talks about the difficult circumstances under which he lives and is reluctant to examine his share in them. If his wife were not so neurotic or his work so upsetting, he would be quite all right. For a considerable period he has no realization whatever that any emotional forces could possibly be operating within himself; he is afraid of ghosts, burglars, thunderstorms, of vindictive persons around him, of the political situation, but never of himself. He is at best interested in his problems for the intellectual or artistic pleasure they afford him. But as long as he is, so to speak, psychically nonexistent, he cannot possibly apply any insight he may gain to his actual living, and therefore in spite of his greater knowledge about himself can change very little. (pp. 129–130)

Goal of Psychotherapy

Like Adler, Horney believed that humans are born with a tendency toward positive growth but this tendency may be interfered with by social forces. According to Horney, we strive toward *self-realization,* which involves being productive and truthful, as well as relating to fellow humans with a spirit of mutuality. If nothing interferes with this innate tendency, humans develop as normal, healthy persons. Horney (1945) compared her optimistic view of humans with Freud's pessimistic view:

Freud's pessimism as regards neuroses and their treatment arose from the depths of his disbelief in human goodness and human growth. Man, he postulated, is doomed to suffer or to destroy. The instincts which drive him can only be controlled, or at best "sublimated." My own belief is that man has the capacity as well as the desire to develop his potentialities and become a decent human being, and that these deteriorate if his relationship to others and hence to himself is, and continues to be, disturbed. I believe that man can change and go on changing as long as he lives. (p. 19)

The goal of psychotherapy, then, is to bring the patient back in touch with his or her real self, that is, his or her capacity for positive growth and for warm, productive relationships with his or her fellow humans. The patient must first be convinced that he or she has been living in accordance with an illusion (idealized self) and doing so made life more frustrating than it needed to be. Gradually patients must be steered in the direction of self-realization by showing them their capacity for cooperative human relations, their true talents and creative powers, and their responsibilities. It is not enough that patients come to understand these qualities intellectually; they must understand them *emotionally* as well. The insights gained must become a living truth within the patient.

Horney described the characteristics she hoped would emerge in patients if psychotherapy were effective (1945, pp. 241–242): *responsibility,* making decisions in one's life and accepting the consequences of those decisions and recognizing obligations to other people; *inner independence,* living in accordance with one's own values and respecting the right for others to do the same thing; *spontaneity of feeling,* to be able to honestly experience one's own love, hate, happiness, sadness, fear, or desire; and *wholeheartedness,* "To be without pretense, to be emotionally sincere, to be able to put the whole of oneself into one's feelings, one's work, one's beliefs" (Horney, 1945, p. 242). When a person displays these characteristics, he or she is on the road to self-realization.

The goal of psychotherapy is not to create perfect human beings; rather, it is to help persons who have been diverted from their self-realization process to become "real" people again instead of fictitious ones. Real people have real problems, real anxiety, real failures, and real successes. Horney (1939) said, "The aim of analysis is not to render life devoid of risks and conflicts, but to enable an individual eventually to solve his problems himself" (p. 305).

Self-Analysis

Freud believed that to become an effective psychoanalyst one had to have intense training in psychoanalytic theory and then be psychoanalyzed oneself. With her book *Self-Analysis* (1942), Horney radically departed from Freudian tradition by claiming that individuals could engage in **self-analysis** if they were provided with proper knowledge and skills. Horney believed such knowledge could be partially acquired by reading the works of Freud and other analysts, such philosophers as Nietzsche and Schopenhauer, and such literary figures as Ibsen, Goethe, Shakespeare, and Dostoevsky. To assist in self-analysis, Horney presented her own theory concerning the origin of neuroses and the 10 neurotic trends or needs. She also provided numerous case studies in order to show how psychoanalysis typically proceeds and the complexities involved. It is interesting to note that according to Paris (2000), Horney's writing of *Self-Analysis* "was an out growth of the breakdown of her relationship with Erich Fromm" (p. 177).

According to Horney, three main tasks confront patients engaged in either professional psychoanalysis or self-analysis:

> The first is to express himself as completely and frankly as possible. The second is to become aware of his unconscious driving forces and their influence on his life. And the third is to develop the capacity to change those attitudes that are disturbing his relations with himself and the world around him. (1942, p. 93)

The success of therapy is determined by the extent to which these difficult tasks are accomplished. Therefore, effective therapy requires from the patient "a good deal of determination, self-discipline, and active struggle" (1942, p. 112).

For both self- and professional analysis, honest, free association is vital: "The process of free association, of frank and unresolved self-expression, is the starting point and continuous basis of all analytic work—self-analysis as well as professional analysis" (1942, p. 225). Closely associated with the use of free association is the problem of resistance. So important is the problem of resistance in self-analysis that Horney devoted an entire chapter to the topic (1942, chap. 10). For Horney the question was not whether a person working alone could overcome resistances, but to what extent he or she could overcome them:

> Can a person overcome his own resistances? This is the real question upon the answer to which hinges the feasibility of self-analysis. . . . Whether the job can be done depends, of course, on the intensity of the resistances as well as on the strength of the incentive to overcome them. But the important question . . . is to what extent it can be done rather than whether it can be done at all. (pp. 134–135)

Horney believed that the extent to which self-analysis is successful is largely determined by a person's ability to overcome resistances.

And what about transference, the phenomenon so important in professional analysis? In self-analysis the professional analyst is absent and therefore cannot be responded to as if he or she were a significant figure in the patient's life. Horney believed similar information could be gained by a person engaged in self-analysis if he or she would carefully observe his or her social interactions:

> There remains the fact that the analyst is not merely an interpreting voice. He is a human being, and the human relationship between him and the patient is an important factor in the therapeutic process. [The analyst–patient relationship] presents a unique and specific opportunity for the patient to study, by observing his behavior with the analyst, what his typical behavior is toward other people in general. This advantage can be fully replaced if he learns to watch himself in his customary relationships. The expectations, wishes, fears, vulnerabilities, and inhibitions that he displays in his work with the analyst are not essentially different from those he displays in his relations with friends, lover, wife, children, employer, colleagues,

or servants. If he is seriously intent upon recognizing the ways in which his pecu-liarities enter into all these relationships, ample opportunities for self-scrutiny are provided him by the mere fact that he is a social being. (1942, p. 135)

Freud, too, was aware that transference occurs in all human relationships: "Transference arises spontaneously in all human relationships just as it does be-tween the patient and the physician" (Freud, 1977, p. 51).

For Horney, then, effective self-analysis is certainly possible. How effective such analysis is, however, depends on the self-discipline and self-determination of the individual involved.

Comparison of Horney and Freud

Early Childhood Experience

Both Freud and Horney thought early childhood experiences were extremely im-portant. The reasons these experiences are important were different for the two, however. Freud believed there are universal stages of development, and fixation at any particular stage strongly influences one's adult personality. For Horney, it is the child's relationship to the parents that is important because it is this relationship that determines if the child will develop basic anxiety.

Unconscious Motivation

Both Horney and Freud emphasized the importance of unconscious motivation. For Horney, it is repressed hostility that leads to basic anxiety, which leads to neurosis. Thus the basis of all neurotic behavior is repressed basic hostility, which, of course, is unconscious.

Biological Motivation

Freud emphasized biological motivation. To him, all conflicts are derived from at-tempts to satisfy biological drives—especially the sex drive. Horney deemphasized biological motivation by stressing the importance of the child's need for a feeling of security. Thus we say that Freud's theory is biological and Horney's theory is social. For example, here is Horney's explanation of the Oedipus complex:

If a child, in addition to being dependent on his parents, is grossly or subtly in-timidated by them and hence feels that any expression of hostile impulses against them endangers his security, then the existence of such hostile impulses is bound to create anxiety. . . . The resulting picture may look exactly like what Freud de-scribes as the Oedipus complex: passionate clinging to one parent and jealousy to-ward the other or toward anyone interfering with the claim of exclusive possession. . . . But the dynamic structure of these attachments is entirely different from what Freud conceives as the Oedipus complex. They are an early manifestation of neu-rotic conflicts rather than a primarily sexual phenomenon. (1939, pp. 83–84)

Psychotherapy

Horney used Freud's methods of free association and dream analysis, and agreed with Freud on the importance of transference. Freud, however, used all of these concepts to uncover repressed traumatic memories whereas Horney used them to discover a neurotic's major adjustment technique. Also, whereas Freud discouraged analysis by individuals not professionally trained in psychoanalytic theory and technique, Horney actively encouraged self-analysis.

Is Anatomy Destiny?

Yes for Freud and for Horney early in her career, no for Horney later in her career.

Prognosis for Personality Change

Freud believed that personality is formulated early in life, and major changes thereafter are extremely difficult to make. Horney agreed that personality is strongly influenced by early experiences but that it remains changeable throughout life. Thus, she was more optimistic than Freud. "Our daring to name such high goals rests upon the belief that the human personality can change. It is not only the young child who is pliable. All of us retain the capacity to change, even to change in fundamental ways, as long as we live" (Horney, 1945, p. 242). Elsewhere, Horney said:

> Albert Schweitzer uses the terms "optimistic" and "pessimistic" in the sense of "world and life affirmation" and "world and life negation." Freud's philosophy, in this deep sense, is a pessimistic one. Ours, with all its cognizance of the tragic elements in neurosis, is an optimistic one. (1950, p. 378)

Evaluation

Empirical Research

Most of the research supporting Horney's theory is indirect. Horney believed that behavior disorders result when people attempt to live their lives in accordance with their idealized selves. Such people believe they are brilliant, great lovers, paragons of virtue, unselfish, or courageous. They also see the source of everything important in their lives as external to themselves (externalization). In other words, Horney believed a correlation exists between the irrational beliefs people have about themselves and psychopathology. Horney's suspicion has been confirmed in several areas. For example, people with several irrational beliefs about themselves are more likely to be depressed (Dobson & Breiter, 1983); to be socially ineffective (Hayden & Nasby, 1977); to have unhappy marriages (Eidelson & Epstein, 1982); and to be ineffective problem solvers (Schill, Monroe, Evans, & Ramanaiah, 1978).

Also, the rational–emotive therapy developed by Albert Ellis is based on the assumption that psychopathology results from the irrational beliefs held by patients. The rational–emotive therapist actively challenges the patient's erroneous beliefs and replaces them with more realistic thoughts and feelings. Considerable evidence exists that such therapy can be effective (Ellis & Greiger, 1977; Smith, 1983).

Criticisms

Unoriginal Contributions.   Like Freud, Horney emphasized the importance of early childhood experience, unconscious motivation, and defense mechanisms. Also like Freud, she used free association, dream analysis, and the analysis of transference in her approach to psychoanalysis. Like Adler, Horney deemphasized the biological origins of behavior disorders and instead emphasized their social origins. Adler's notion of safeguarding strategies is similar to Horney's auxiliary approaches to artificial harmony; both mask the person's real self. Both Horney and Adler believed that when a culture is male dominated, women will often attempt to become more masculine in order to gain power. Finally, both Jung and Horney employed the concept of self-realization that in both cases meant the natural impulse toward healthy personality development. One way to view Horney's theory, then, is as a blending of the theories of Freud, Jung, and Adler.

Little Empirical Support.   Often a personality theory contains language and concepts that are too nebulous to verify empirically. Furthermore, those personality theorists who were also clinicians claim that the true value of their theories is determined by subsequent enhancement of the therapeutic process. For them, empirical verification using controlled experimental procedures is irrelevant. Both of the preceding statements are true for Horney's theory, although, as we have seen, some indirect empirical verification of the theory exists.

Disregard of Healthy Persons.   Although Horney did discuss the natural tendency toward self-realization, she concentrated almost exclusively on understanding persons who had their tendency toward self-realization disrupted, namely, neurotics. Paris (1994) disagrees with this criticism, however, saying instead that Horney's mature theory had much in common with the humanistic theories of Rogers (see Chapter 14) and Maslow (see Chapter 15). Humanistic theories are primarily concerned with normal, healthy individuals.

Contributions

Original Ideas.   Although some have criticized Horney for borrowing too heavily from Freud, Jung, and Adler, others see her blending of these (and other) theories as a highly original and important contribution to the understanding of personality. For example, her concepts of the tyranny of the should and the major neurotic adjustment techniques, as well as her discussion of what happens when one becomes alienated from his or her real self, have had a significant influence on modern personality theory and therapeutic techniques (see, e.g., Carl Rogers, Chapter 14).

Self-Analysis.   Directly contrary to Freud and the other psychoanalysts at the time, Horney believed many persons could and should analyze themselves, and she hoped her writings would help them to do so. Horney's book *Self-Analysis* (1942) was one of the first self-help books in psychology, and it created quite a controversy. Now it is generally believed many troubled persons can improve their situations if given the proper information. However, most therapists believe, as Horney did, that severely disturbed persons must receive professional treatment.

Feminine Psychology. Horney's thoughts on feminine psychology were among the first in the field, and she appears to have anticipated many of the concerns of feminist scholars (Chodorow, 1989; Symonds, 1991; Westcott, 1986). Although Horney was strongly influenced by Freudian theory and agreed with much of it, she disagreed with almost every conclusion that Freud reached about women. It must be realized that departing from Freudian dogma at the time was no easy matter. In fact, those who did so were excommunicated just as if they had violated religious dogma. As you may remember, Horney learned from observing her father as a child how devastating blind belief in religious dogma could be; perhaps that was one reason she decided not to let Freud go unchallenged.

Summary

Although Karen Horney was trained in the Freudian tradition, she departed from that tradition in several important ways. She stressed the importance of early parent–child relationships in her theory of personality development. If these relationships are positive, warm, and based on genuine love, the child will tend to develop normally. Normal people are flexible and spontaneous, and their goals are tied realistically to their abilities. That is, they live in accordance with their innate tendency toward self-realization. If, however, parents react to a child with indifference, superficiality, or aggression, the child will feel basic hostility toward the parents that must be repressed because of the child's feelings of helplessness, fear, or guilt. The repressed hostility that the child feels for the parent is projected on the world in general, thereby becoming basic anxiety. Basic anxiety is the feeling of being alone and helpless in a hostile world.

In order to combat basic anxiety, persons adopt one of three major adjustment patterns relative to other people. They move toward, against, or away from them. Normal persons display all these adjustments toward people depending on the circumstances. The neurotic's life, however, is dominated by one of the adjustments, and therefore, the other two go unsatisfied, causing greater conflict and anxiety. For neurotics, the real self is displaced by the idealized self, and their lives are governed by a list of unrealistic "shoulds" instead of goals based on their own experiences. Neurotics engage heavily in externalization. That is, they view the source of all important events in their lives as external to themselves.

Besides the major adjustment patterns of moving toward, against, or away from people, Horney also postulated the following secondary adjustment techniques: blind spots, in which inconsistencies in one's life are ignored; compartmentalization, in which one applies different values to different situations; rationalization, in which one gives logical but erroneous explanations for wrongdoings or shortcomings; excessive self-control, in which one minimizes failure by living within a narrow, predictable range of events; arbitrary rightness, in which one takes a stand that becomes equated with truth and therefore cannot be challenged; elusiveness, in which one avoids failure by postponing decisions; and cynicism, in which one believes nothing is worth commitment.

Horney wrote many articles showing that much that had been written about the female personality reflected male biases and misunderstandings. In her early writings, Horney did accept a version of Freud's belief that anatomy is destiny. Later, however, she rejected this belief, emphasizing cultural determinates of personality instead. For example, Horney said that women often do aspire to be more masculine but it is not because they have penis envy. Rather, being masculine in a male-dominated society is the only way to gain power. Just as many psychological problems are caused by culture, so are many of the differences between men and women. Horney thought many female characteristics that Freud attributed to anatomy should be regarded as culturally determined.

For Horney, the goal of psychotherapy is to confront the patient with the fact that he or she is attempting to live an illusion (the idealized self). When this goal is accomplished, the therapist can help the patient to discover his or her real self and start on the road to self-realization.

Horney agreed with Freud that much behavior is unconsciously motivated but disagreed with him on the importance of biological motivation. Horney believed the social need for security was much more important than the need for biological satisfaction.

Horney's theory is supported by the finding that as the number of irrational beliefs people have about themselves increases, so does the tendency to be depressed, to be socially ineffective, to have unhappy marriages, and to be poor problem solvers. Also, the rational–emotive therapy of Albert Ellis has shown that patients show improvement when their irrational beliefs are actively challenged and replaced by more realistic beliefs and feelings.

Horney's theory has been criticized for being unoriginal, for stimulating little empirical research, and for ignoring the personality development of healthy persons. Among the contributions made by Horney's theory are listed its creative blending of Freudian, Jungian, and Adlerian theory, its encouragement of self-analysis, and its elaboration of feminine psychology.

Experiential Exercises

1. Describe your personality in terms of Horney's major adjustment techniques. Do you move toward, against, or away from people with about equal frequency? If not, which of the three do you emphasize? Using Horney's theory, attempt to explain why you use the major adjustment techniques the way you do.

2. Horney said that each person is born with a tendency toward self-realization, that is, toward normal, healthy growth. The tendency toward self-realization, however, can be disrupted by the basic evil, in which case the real self is displaced by an idealized self. The person living in accordance with an idealized self is, according to Horney, living an illusion. Are you living in accordance with your tendency toward self-realization or is your life governed by an idealized self? Explain.

3. Give an example of your use of externalization. Also, give examples of how you have used blind spots, compartmentalization, rationalization, excessive self-control, arbitrary rightness, elusiveness, and cynicism.

Discussion Questions

1. Explain why Freud's theory of personality is called a biological theory and why Horney's is called a social theory.
2. Differentiate between those childhood experiences that Horney thought conducive to normal development and those she thought conducive to neurotic development.

3. Describe the difference between the real and the idealized self. Explain the difference in the relationship between the real and the idealized selves for the normal person versus the neurotic person. Include in your answer a discussion of Horney's concept of the tyranny of the should.

Glossary

Anatomy is destiny. Contention of some personality theorists, Freud for example, that one's gender determines, to a large extent, one's personality characteristics.

Arbitrary rightness. Exemplified when issues arise that have no clear solution one way or the other, and a person arbitrarily chooses one solution, thereby ending debate.

Basic anxiety. Psychological state that exists when basic hostility is repressed. It is the general feeling that everything and everyone in the world is potentially dangerous and that one is helpless relative to those dangers.

Basic evil. Anything that parents do that undermines a child's security.

Basic hostility. Feeling generated in a child if needs for safety and satisfaction are not consistently and lovingly attended to by the parents.

Blind spots. Denying or ignoring certain aspects of experience because they are not in accordance with one's idealized self-image.

Compartmentalization. Dividing one's life into various components with different rules applying to the different components.

Compliant type person. Person who uses moving toward people as the major means of reducing basic anxiety.

Cynicism. Strategy in which a person believes in nothing and is therefore immune to the disappointment that comes from being committed to something that is shown to be false.

Detached type person. Person who uses moving away from people as the major means of reducing basic anxiety.

Elusiveness. Opposite to arbitrary rightness. The elusive person is highly indecisive.

Without commitments to anything this person is seldom, if ever, wrong.

Excessive self-control. Guarding against anxiety by denying oneself emotional involvement in anything.

Externalization. Belief that the causes of one's major experiences are external to oneself.

Hostile type person. Person who uses moving against people as the major means of reducing basic anxiety.

Idealized self. Fictitious view of oneself, with its list of "shoulds" that displaces the real self in the neurotic personality. *See also* Tyranny of the should.

Moving against people. Adjustment to basic anxiety that uses the tendency to exploit other people and to gain power over them. Horney referred to the person using this adjustment technique as the hostile type. *See also* Hostile type person.

Moving away from people. Adjustment to basic anxiety that uses the need to be self-sufficient. Horney referred to the person using this adjustment technique as the detached type. *See also* Detached type person.

Moving toward people. Adjustment to basic anxiety that uses the need to be wanted, loved, and protected by other people. Horney referred to the person using this adjustment technique as the compliant type. *See also* Compliant type person.

Neurotic trends (also called neurotic needs). Ten strategies for minimizing basic anxiety.

Rationalization. Giving "good" but erroneous reasons to excuse conduct that would otherwise be anxiety-provoking. Horney used this term in much the same way that Freud did.

Real self.   Self that is healthy and conducive to positive growth. Although each person is born with a healthy real self, the view of this real self can be distorted by the basic evil. The basic evil causes a person to view his or her real self negatively and then attempt to escape from it. Although the neurotic views his or her real self negatively, it remains a source of potential health and positive growth.

Safety.   Child's need for security and freedom from fear that Horney believed must be satisfied before normal psychological development could occur.

Satisfaction.   Meeting of such physiological needs as those for water, food, and sleep required for a child's biological survival.

Self-analysis.   Process of self-help that Horney believed people could apply to themselves to solve life's problems, and to minimize conflict.

Self-realization.   Innate tendency to strive for truthfulness, productivity, and harmonious relationships with fellow humans.

Tyranny of the should.   When one's idealized self is substituted for the real self, one's behavior is governed by several unrealistic "shoulds."

ERIK H. ERIKSON

CHAPTER OUTLINE

According to Freud, the job of the ego is to find realistic ways of satisfying the impulses of the id while not offending the moral demands of the superego. Freud viewed the ego as operating "in the service of the id" and as the "helpless rider of the id horse." The ego, according to this view, has no needs of its own. The id is the energizer of the entire personality, and everything a person does is ultimately reduced to its demands. As we saw in Chapter 2, Freud viewed enterprises such as art, science, and religion as mere displacements or sublimations of basic idinal desires.

The first shift away from Freud's position came from his daughter Anna in her book, *The Ego and the Mechanisms of Defense* (1966). Anna Freud suggested that instead of emphasizing the importance of the id, psychoanalysis should "acquire the fullest possible knowledge of all the three institutions [that is, id, ego, and superego] of which we believe the psychic personality to be constituted and to learn what are their relations to one another and to the outside world" (pp. 4–5). Erik H. Erikson was obviously influenced by his teacher, Anna Freud, but he believed she did not go far enough.

Erikson gave the ego properties and needs of its own. The ego, according to Erikson, may have started out in the service of the id but, in the process of serving it, developed its own functions. For example, it was the ego's job to organize one's life and to ensure continuous harmony with one's physical and social environment. This conception emphasizes the influence of the ego on healthy growth and adjustment and

153

also as the source of the person's self-awareness and identity. This contrasts sharply with the earlier Freudian view that the ego's sole job is to minimize the id's discomfort. Because Erikson stressed the autonomy of the ego, his theory exemplifies what has come to be called **ego psychology.** Although, as we saw in Chapter 4, there are those who credit Alfred Adler with the founding of ego psychology, it is an honor generally given to Erikson, perhaps because he actually emphasized the term ego in his theory. Indeed, Erikson's entire theory can be viewed as a description of how the ego gains or loses strength as a function of developmental experiences.

Biographical Sketch

Erik Erikson was born near Frankfurt, Germany, on June 15, 1902. Erikson's mother, Karla Abrahamsen, was a member of a prominent Jewish family in Copenhagen. In 1898, Karla, at 21, married a 27-year-old Jewish stockbroker, Valdemar Isidor Salomonsen. The marriage did not last the night and was probably unconsummated (Friedman, 1999, p. 29). Speculation concerning Valdemar's rapid departure ranges from his involvement in criminal activities causing him to become a fugitive, to the fact that he physically abused Karla, causing her to terminate the relationship (Friedman, 1999, p. 30). Karla never saw Valdemar after their wedding night, however, she retained his surname for legal purposes. When Erik was born four years later, the birth certificate listed Valdemar and Karla as his parents. Although Erik was technically legitimate, Valdemar was not his father. If Karla knew the identity of Erik's father she never revealed it (Friedman, 1999, p. 30). Later in life, Erik made several attempts to determine the identity of his biological father but was unsuccessful. Erik often proclaimed his biological father to be an artistically gifted gentile of Danish royality. This, however, was a family myth and was never substantiated (Friedman, 1999, p. 299).

Karla began a relationship with Erik's pediatrician, Theodor Homburger, and the two were married on Erik's third birthday, June 15, 1905. Erik went along on the honeymoon. Theodor's proposal came with one provision: Erik was to be told that Theodor was Erik's biological father. Karla agreed (Friedman, 1999, p. 33). A few years after the marriage, Theodor adopted Erik and legally he became Erik Homburger.

The fact that Dr. Homburger was not Erik's biological father was kept a secret throughout his childhood, but he still developed the feeling that somehow he did not belong to his parents and fantasized about being the son of "much better parents." Erikson used his stepfather's surname for many years and wrote his first articles using the name Erik Homburger. It was only when he became a U.S. citizen in 1939 that he changed his last name to Erikson. The circumstances of Erikson's birth created a problem in adopting an appropriate last name: "Erik's birth had resulted from an extramarital liaison of his mother's, and Erikson kept her secret until he was 68" (Hopkins, 1995, p. 796). Because "Erikson" was not the name of his biological father, his reason for choosing this name is a matter of speculation:

> One story has it that his children were troubled by the American tendency to confuse "Homburger" with "hamburger," and that he asked one of his sons for an

alternative; being Erik's son, he proposed Erikson. For Erikson's children such a name would be in accord with Scandinavian custom; but for Erikson it connoted that he was his own father, self-created. (Roazen, 1976, pp. 98–99)

In any case, "Homburger" was reduced to the middle initial of the name that Erikson then used to identify his works.

Erikson's sense of not belonging to his family was amplified by the fact that his mother, Karla, and his stepfather, Theodore, were Jewish. However, Erikson himself was tall, with blue eyes and blond hair. In school he was referred to as a Jew, whereas at his stepfather's temple, he was called a "goy" (the Yiddish word for gentile). Is it any wonder why the concept of "identity crisis" later became one of Erikson's most important theoretical concerns? Erikson was well aware of this influence on his later work: "No doubt my best friends will insist that I needed to name [the identity] crisis and to see it in everybody else in order to really come to terms with it in myself" (1975a, p. 26).

After graduating from a gymnasium, roughly equivalent to an American high school, he rebelled against his stepfather's desire for him to become a physician by studying art and roaming freely around Europe. Generally, Erikson was not a good student in school but did have artistic ability. Erikson (1964) said, "I was an artist then, which can be a European euphemism for a young man with some talent, but nowhere to go" (p. 20).

The year 1927 was a turning point in Erikson's life. In that year, at the age of 25, he was invited to Vienna by an old school friend, Peter Blos, to work at a small school attended by the children of Freud's patients and friends. He was hired first as an artist, then as a tutor, and finally, he was asked by Anna Freud if he would like to be trained as a child analyst. Erikson accepted the offer and received his psychoanalytic training under Anna Freud, for which she charged him $7 per month. The training, which included Erik being psychoanalyzed by Anna, lasted 3 years and was conducted almost daily. Anna Freud's particular brand of psychoanalytic theory, which differed in several ways from her father's, had a profound influence on Erikson, and in 1964 he showed his appreciation by dedicating his book *Insight and Responsibility* to her.

When Erikson joined the Freudian circle, Freud was 71 years old, and Erikson knew him only informally. It was only gradually that Erikson came to appreciate Freud's accomplishments. At the time, however, Erikson deeply appreciated the warm reception given to him by those associated with the psychoanalytic movement. The situation was perfectly suited to Erikson. He was asked to join a group of people who were still considered to be outside the medical establishment. By joining this group of "outcasts," he could maintain his identity as the "outsider." Conversely, because the group's function was to help disturbed people, he could at least indirectly satisfy his stepfather's desire for him to become a physician.

His graduation from the gymnasium, a Montessori diploma, and his training as a child analyst are the only formal training Erikson ever had. Because Erikson earned no advanced degrees, he is a clear example of Freud's contention that one need not be trained as a physician to become a psychoanalyst. Erikson graduated from the Vienna Psychoanalytic Institute in 1933. The fact that Erikson was granted full (rather than associate) membership in the Vienna Psychoanalytic Institute also made him a member of the International Psychoanalytic Association.

In 1929, Erik met Joan Serson. Joan was born in Canada and her father was an Episcopal minister. Her mother was from a wealthy railroad family in the United States. Joan obtained a BA in education from Barnard College and a MA in sociology from the University of Pennsylvania. Joan studied and taught modern dance at Columbia and the University of Pennsylvania as she pursued her PhD in education at Columbia. She planned a dissertation on the teaching of modern dance and went to Europe to conduct research. Joan eventually became a member of Freud's circle and even began to be psychoanalyzed by Ludwig Jekels, one of Freud's early disciples. During this time, Joan met Erik at a masked ball. They talked and danced throughout the night and soon thereafter she moved in with Erik and became pregnant. At first, Erik rejected the idea of marriage, but finally decided not to repeat the mistake his own father had made. They were married on April 1, 1930, and Joan became Erik's intellectual partner for the remainder of his long life.

In 1933, in response to the increasing Nazi threat, the Eriksons (now with two sons) moved first to Denmark and then to Boston, Massachusetts, where he entered private practice as a child analyst. Besides his private practice, Erikson was a research fellow under the supervision of Henry Murray in the Department of Neuropsychiatry at Harvard Medical School. Erikson enrolled at Harvard as a PhD candidate in psychology but dropped out of the program within a few months. Perhaps because he had already been voted a full member of the Vienna Psychoanalytic Institute, he considered further formal education unnecessary.

Between 1936 and 1939, Erikson held a position in the Department of Psychiatry at Yale University Medical School where he worked with both normal and emotionally disturbed children. At this time Erikson came in contact with anthropologists Ruth Benedict and Margaret Mead, and in 1938 he went on a field trip to the Pine Ridge Reservation in South Dakota to observe the childrearing practices of the Sioux Indians. Anthropological studies such as this one increased Erikson's awareness of the importance of social and cultural variables to personality development—an awareness that ultimately permeated his entire theory of personality.

In 1939, Erikson moved to California where he became a research associate at the Institute of Child Welfare at the University of California. By 1942, he was a professor of psychology but lost his professorship in 1950 when he refused to sign a loyalty oath. Later, when the University of California found him "politically reliable," he was offered his job back but refused to accept it because other professors had been dismissed for the same "crime."

In 1950, the same year he left the University of California, Erikson published his well-known book, *Childhood and Society,* which strongly emphasized the importance of social and cultural factors to human development. This book also greatly elaborated the functions of the ego that launched what is now called ego psychology. We have more to say about ego psychology later in this chapter.

Between 1951 and 1960, Erikson lived in Stockbridge, Massachusetts, where he was both a senior staff consultant at the Austen Riggs Center (a treatment center for disturbed adolescents) and a professor in the Department of Psychiatry at the University of Pittsburgh Medical School.

In 1960, Erikson returned to Harvard Medical School where he was a professor of human development and taught "The Human Life Cycle," an extremely popular undergraduate course. According to Erikson, his students renamed this course

"From Womb to Tomb." At Harvard, Erikson also led a seminar in which the lives of great or historical persons were analyzed. By now, colleges and universities throughout the world were inviting him to lecture. In 1962, he traveled to India to conduct a seminar on the life cycle. While there he became intensely interested in Mahatma Gandhi, whose nonviolent protest against British imperialism dramatically changed the British Empire.

As we see in this chapter, Erikson made several notable contributions to psychology. One is the application of his theory of development to the study of major historical figures. Such an endeavor has been labeled **psychohistory.** Erikson has analyzed such historical figures as Adolf Hitler, Maxim Gorky, Martin Luther, and Mahatma Gandhi. Erikson's book, *Gandhi's Truth* (1969), was awarded both a Pulitzer Prize and a National Book Award in philosophy and religion. Typically, all of Erikson's books sold well, but his last book, *The Life Cycle Completed: A Review* (1982), was mainly a summary of his previously published ideas, and was poorly received. Months after the publication of this book Erikson complained, "I have received only one letter saying, hey, thank you, that's a good book" (Friedman, 1999, p. 458).

Throughout most of his writings, Erikson insisted that a strong relationship exists between his theory and Freud's, but one gets the impression this is mostly a tribute to Freud. Although it is true there are some similarities between the theories, the differences between the two are more important. Erikson's theory, for example, is more optimistic about the human capacity for positive growth. We compare Erikson's theory to Freud's throughout this chapter, but for now we point out one common feature of the theories. Both have transcended the bounds of psychology and have influenced a variety of other fields such as religion, philosophy, sociology, anthropology, and history.

In 1970, Erikson retired from Harvard and the Erikson family divided its time between Marin County, California, and Cape Cod, Massachusetts. In 1987, Erikson moved back to Cambridge after the founding of the Erik Erikson Center, which was associated with Cambridge Hospital and Harvard Medical School. Erikson died on May 12, 1994, in Harwich, Massachusetts. Joan, Erik's wife and collaborator for over 60 years, died on August 3, 1997. She was cremated, as Erik had been, and was buried next to her husband. Erik and Joan were survived by their three children (Kai Erikson, Jon Erikson, and Sue Erikson Bloland).

Anatomy and Destiny

The closest Erikson came to traditional Freudian theory is in the chapter "The Theory of Infantile Sexuality" in his book, *Childhood and Society* (1985). In this chapter, Erikson summarized his research on 10-, 11-, and 12-year-old boys and girls in California. The children were instructed by Erikson to "construct on the table an exciting scene out of an imaginary moving picture" (p. 98). The children were to use toy figures and various-shaped blocks. Much to Erikson's surprise, in over a year and a half, about 150 children constructed about 450 scenes, and not more than about six were scenes from a movie. For example, only a few of the toy figures were given names of actors or actresses. But if the children were not following Erikson's suggestion in creating their scenes, what was guiding their activities? The answer to this question came when Erikson noted that the common themes or elements in the scenes created by boys were quite different from those created by girls.

Erikson observed, for example, that the scenes created by girls typically included an enclosure that sometimes had an elaborate entrance and contained such elements as people and animals. The scenes created by girls tended to be static and peaceful, although often their scenes were interrupted by animals or dangerous men. The scenes created by boys often had high walls around them and had many objects such as high towers or cannons protruding from them. The scenes created by boys also had relatively more people and animals outside the enclosure. The boys' scenes were dynamic and included fantasies about the collapse or downfall of their creation.

Examples of scenes created by boys and girls are shown in Figure 6–1. Erikson concluded that the scenes created by the children were outward manifestations of their genital apparatus. This tendency was so reliable that Erikson was surprised and uneasy when a departure from it occurred. For example, Erikson stated:

> One day, a boy arranged . . . a "feminine" scene, with wild animals as intruders, and I felt that uneasiness which I assume often betrays to an experimenter what his innermost expectations are. And, indeed, on departure and already at the door, the boy exclaimed, "There is something wrong here," came back, and with an air of relief arranged the animals along a tangent to the circle of furniture. Only one boy built and left such a configuration, and this twice. He was of obese and effeminate build. As thyroid treatment began to take effect, he built, in his third construction (a year and a half after the first) the highest and most slender of all towers—as was to be expected of a boy. (1985, p. 101)

It should be emphasized, however, that Erikson never said that biology was the only factor that determines how a person perceives and acts on the world. Social factors are also important. We are instructed by our culture how boys and girls are expected to act and think, and these cultural dictates obviously influence our outlook:

> Am I saying, then, that "anatomy is destiny"? Yes, it is destiny, insofar as it determines not only the range and configuration of physiological functioning and its limitations but also, to an extent, personality configurations. The basic modalities of woman's commitment and involvement naturally also reflect the ground plan of her body. . . . [But] a human being, in addition to having a body, is somebody, which means an indivisible personality and a defined member of a group. . . . In other words, anatomy, history, and personality are our combined destiny. (Erikson, 1968, p. 285)

Needless to say, Erikson's views of male–female differences have not gone uncriticized. One reaction came from Naomi Weisstein (1975) in her article, "Psychology Constructs the Female, or the Fantasy Life of the Male Psychologist (with Some Attention to the Fantasies of His Friends, the Male Biologist and the Male Anthropologist)." Weisstein argued that psychology does not know what either men or

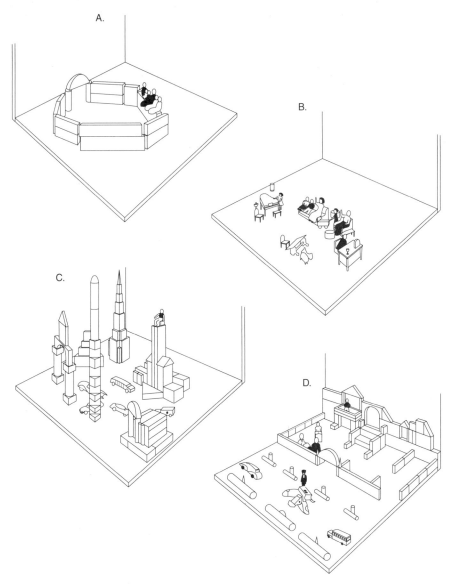

(From Erikson, 1950/1985, pp. 100-105.)

Figure 6–1 *A and B exemplify scenes created by girls, and C and D exemplify scenes created by boys.*

women are really like because it deals with only the cultural stereotypes of both. She insisted that what have been called biologically determined differences in behavior between the sexes are really better explained as the result of social expectations. She concluded that insofar as there are differences between the sexes, they are the result of cultural expectations and the prejudices of male social scientists.

Paula Caplan (1979) also criticized Erikson's contention that the type of sex organs one possesses influences how one interacts with the world. She was especially critical of Erikson's assertion that a woman's kinesthetic experience of her own inner space, that is, of her own uterus, determines even partially her personality characteristics. It was Erikson's belief that it is the female child's experience of this "inner space" that influences the configurations she produces during his play experiments. Caplan pointed out that Erikson's claim is impossible:

> The most important physiological factor to take into account is that there is no inner space. The walls of the uterus touch each other, as do the walls of the vagina. They are open only when separated by and filled with substances, as in intercourse or pregnancy. If girls' play constructions were to represent their uteri, they should look more like folded flapjacks than enclosures. Further, although the penis is external and erectable, so is the clitoris, although to a lesser degree. The movement of the ovum is as important for fertilization as that of the sperm, and although not as highly mobile as the sperm, both ovum and uterus move (the uterus contracts often in orgasm and delivery and certainly expands in pregnancy). So differences in play constructions should, if biologically based, be different in degree rather than in kind. (pp. 101–102)

Caplan repeated much of Erikson's research on play constructions; however, she used preschool children as her subjects. She justified using children who were younger than those used by Erikson because of Erikson's claim that gender differences in personality manifest themselves throughout the life span. Caplan (1979) summarized her results: "No sex differences were found in the frequency of constructions of simple enclosures, enclosures only in conjunction with elaborate structures or traffic lanes, height of structures, construction of a tower, or construction of a structure, building, tower, or street—all categories in which Erikson had reported sex differences" (p. 105). Caplan interpreted her results as indicating that there are no sex-determined personality characteristics. If these characteristics exist, they would be evident in her young subjects. Rather, she said, the personality differences between men and women that emerge later are due exclusively to differential socialization practices. Therefore, anatomy is definitely not destiny.

Erikson reacted to criticisms such as those just discussed in his essay entitled "Once More the Inner Space" (1975b). Essentially he said that (1) psychoanalytic truths are often disturbing and he can understand people being upset by them, and (2) biology is only one strong determinant of personality; culture is another.

Another important point should be made about Erikson's view of sexual differences. He did not say that males are better than females or vice versa. Rather, he said that there are important differences between males and females and that male traits and female traits complement each other. In some cultures, such as ours, the male role has been glorified relative to the female role but Erikson found this unfortunate. He believed that both men and women are hurt by current cultural stereotypes. Erikson stated that "Only a renewal of social creativity can liberate both men and women from reciprocal roles which, in fact, have exploited both" (1975b, p. 237).

Epigenetic Principle, Crises, Ritualizations, and Ritualisms

Epigenetic Principle

Erikson saw life as consisting of eight stages, which stretch from birth to death. According to Erikson, the sequence of the eight stages is genetically determined and is unalterable. Such a genetically determined sequence of development is said to follow the epigenetic principle, a term Erikson borrowed from biology. Erikson described this principle as follows:

> Whenever we try to understand growth, it is well to remember the epigenetic principle which is derived from the growth of organisms in utero. Somewhat generalized, this principle states that anything that grows has a ground plan, and that out of this ground plan the parts arise, each part having its special ascendancy, until all parts have arisen to form a functioning whole. (1968, p. 92)

Although, according to Erikson, personality unfolds across eight stages of development, all eight developmental stages are present in rudimentary form at birth. As each personality characteristic unfolds, it is incorporated into characteristics that developed during previous stages, thus creating a new configuration of personality characteristics. In other words, each stage, as it unfolds, builds on those that preceded it. Erikson (1985) said, "The strength acquired at any stage is tested by the necessity to transcend it in such a way that the individual can take chances in the next stage with what was more vulnerably precious in the previous one" (p. 263). According to the epigenetic principle, the personality characteristics that become salient during any particular stage of development exist before that stage and continue to exist after that stage. For social and biological reasons, however, the development of a certain personality characteristic becomes the focus of one stage as opposed to other stages.

Crises

Each stage of development is characterized by a crisis. The word "crisis" is used by Erikson as it is used by physicians, that is, to connote an important turning point. Thus the crisis characterizing each stage of development has a possible positive resolution or a negative one. A positive resolution contributes to a strengthening of the ego and therefore to greater adaptation. A negative resolution weakens the ego and inhibits adaptation. Furthermore, a positive crisis resolution in one stage increases the likelihood that the crisis characterizing the next stage will be resolved positively. A negative resolution in one stage lowers the probability that the next crisis will be resolved positively. Erikson did not believe a solution to a crisis is either completely positive or completely negative. Rather, he said the resolution of a crisis has both positive and negative elements. It is when the ratio of positive to negative is higher in favor of the positive that the crisis is said to be resolved positively. We say more about this in our discussion of the first stage of development to which we turn shortly.

In accordance with the epigenetic principle, a crisis exists in three phases: the *immature phase* where it is not the focal point of personality development; the *critical phase* where because of a variety of biological, psychological, and social reasons it is the focal point of personality development; and the *resolution phase* where the resolution of the crisis influences subsequent personality development. If the crises associated with the eight stages of development are resolved positively, normal personality development occurs. If one or more crises are resolved negatively, normal development is inhibited. In other words, each crisis must be positively resolved in the stage of development in which it is critical before a person is fully prepared to deal with the crises that dominate subsequent stages.

Although biology determines when the eight stages of personality development will occur, because the maturational process determines when certain experiences become possible, it is the social environment that determines whether or not the crisis associated with any given stage is resolved positively. For this reason, the stages proposed by Erikson are called **psychosocial stages of development,** to contrast them with Freud's *psychosexual stages.*

Ritualizations and Ritualisms

For Erikson, it is essential to realize that personality development occurs within a cultural setting. Rather than viewing humans as warring with their culture, as Freud did, Erikson emphasized the compatibility between individuals and their culture. In fact, to a large extent, the job of culture is to provide effective ways of satisfying both biological and psychological human needs. According to Erikson, a person's internal and external experiences must fit together, at least to some degree, if an individual is to develop and function normally in a particular culture. Erikson (1985) said, "Each successive stage and crisis has a special relation to one of the basic elements of society, and this for the simple reason that the human life cycle and man's institutions have evolved together" (p. 250).

The harmonious interplay between unfolding personality requirements and existing social and cultural conditions is made possible by **ritualizations.** According to Erikson (1977), ritualizations are recurring patterns of behavior that reflect those beliefs, values, customs, and behaviors sanctioned by a particular society or culture. Although it is ritualizations that make life meaningful within a particular society or culture, most individuals engage in them without knowing that they are doing so:

> [Each child must] be coaxed and induced to become "speciated" during a prolonged childhood by some form of family: he must be *familiarized by ritualization* with a particular version of human existence. He thus develops a distinct sense of corporate identity . . . We must realize from the outset that ritualization is an aspect of everyday life which is more clearly seen in a different culture or class or even family than in our own, where, in fact, ritualization is more often than not experienced simply as the only proper way to do things; and the question is only why does not everybody do it our way. (pp. 79–80)

Ritualizations, then, are culturally approved patterns of everyday behavior that allow a person to become an acceptable member of the culture. They include characteristic ways in which we relate to each other such as shaking hands, kissing, and hugging. They provide guides that set the boundaries between acceptable and unacceptable behavior. For example, you may be permitted to make bodily contact with a stranger at a dance but such behavior may not be tolerated under other circumstances. Likewise, it may be permissible for a woman to wear a bikini on a beach whereas such attire may cause a stir at work or at school. Ritualizations guide almost every aspect of social behavior and are the mechanisms by which persons of a certain culture become "socialized."

Erikson defined **culture** as "a particular version of human existence," suggesting that many equally valid versions exist. Indeed, Erikson believed that except for the requirement that ritualizations satisfy basic human needs, they are arbitrary. For example, many cultural variations exist for courting, mating, and childrearing practices, but these differences are less important than the fact that they all encourage reproduction and the perpetuation of the culture in which they occur. For some persons, the arbitrary nature of ritualizations is lost and their functional value is overlooked. For these persons, ritualizations take on a significance far beyond what is necessary. Erikson referred to such exaggerated or otherwise distorted ritualizations as **ritualisms.** Ritualisms are inappropriate or false ritualizations, and they are the causes of much social and psychological pathology. For example, a ritualization within a culture might encourage addressing certain accomplished persons with titles and thus encourage a sense of respect for their status. To idolize or worship such persons, however, would be an inappropriate exaggeration of that ritualization and would thus be a ritualism. A ritualism then is a ritualization that has become mechanical and stereotyped. Such empty ceremonies lack the power to bond people of a culture together, thus subverting the original purpose of the ritualization.

We discuss the ritualizations and the ritualisms associated with each stage of development in the next section.

Eight Stages of Personality Development

The most famous aspects of Erikson's work are his descriptions of the eight developmental stages through which he believes all humans pass and what happens to the ego during each of these stages. The first five stages of personality development proposed by Erikson closely parallel Freud's proposed psychosexual stages of development in the time at which they are supposed to occur. As to what is supposed to occur during these stages, however, little agreement exists between Erikson and Freud. The last three stages are Erikson's own and represent one of his major contributions to psychology. It should be noted that the epigenetic principle determines the exact order in which the stages must occur; however, when they occur cannot be specified exactly. Therefore, the ages associated with each of the following stages should be viewed only as approximations. We label each stage according to the developmental level at which it occurs and according to the crisis it features.

1. Infancy: Basic Trust versus Basic Mistrust

This stage lasts from birth through about the first year and corresponds closely to Freud's oral stage of psychosexual development. This is the time when children are most helpless and thus most dependent on adults. If those caring for infants satisfy their needs in a loving and consistent manner, the infants will develop a feeling of **basic trust.** If, however, their parents are rejecting and satisfy their needs in an inconsistent manner, they will develop a feeling of mistrust.

If care is loving and consistent, infants learn they need not worry about a loving, reliable parent and therefore are not overly disturbed when that parent leaves their sight:

> The infant's first social achievement, then, is his willingness to let the mother out of sight without undue anxiety or rage, because she has become an inner certainty as well as an outer predictability. Such consistency, continuity, and sameness of experience provide a rudimentary sense of ego identity which depends, I think, on the cognition that there is an inner population of remembered and anticipated sensations and images which are firmly correlated with the outer population of familiar and predictable things and people. (Erikson, 1985, p. 247)

The basic trust versus **basic mistrust** crisis is resolved positively when the child develops more trust than mistrust. Remember, it is the ratio of the two solutions that is important. A child who trusted everyone and everything would be in trouble. A certain amount of mistrust is healthy and conducive to survival. It is the child with a predominance of trust, however, who has the courage to take risks and who is not overwhelmed by disappointments and setbacks.

Erikson said that when the crisis characterizing a stage is positively resolved, a **virtue** emerges in one's personality. A virtue adds strength to one's ego. In this stage, when the child has more basic trust than basic mistrust, the virtue of **hope** emerges. Erikson defined hope as "the enduring belief in the attainability of fervent wishes, in spite of the dark urges and rages which mark the beginning of existence" (1964, p. 118). We can say that trusting children dare to hope, a process that is future oriented, whereas children lacking trust cannot hope because they must worry constantly whether their needs will be satisfied, and therefore are tied to the present.

Numinous versus Idolism.   The primary ritualization during this stage is the **numinous.** The numinous involves the various ways that mothers attend to their infants' needs in a particular culture. Although personal, these mother–infant interactions also reflect culturally sanctioned childrearing practices. For example, many mothers breast-feed their infants, but in the United States few do so in public. In a similar vein, it is not uncommon for mothers to babble inanely at their infants, imitating the babbling and cooing sounds the baby makes, rather than speaking to the infant as if he or she is a cognizant adult. As a result of these mother–infant interactions the child develops positive feelings toward the mother, and these feelings cause the infant to be socially responsive. Thus, the mother's warm, predictable caring for the child creates in the child a desire to seek interactions with persons other than the mother.

If the infant's normal reverence and respect for the mother become exaggerated, the ritualism of **idolism** results. Idolism occurs when normal respect and deep appreciation for a person become excessive admiration and idealization. Idolism steers the developing child in the direction of blind hero worship.

2. Early Childhood: Autonomy versus Shame and Doubt

This stage occurs from about the end of the first year to about the end of the third year and corresponds to Freud's anal stage of psychosexual development. During this stage, children rapidly develop a wide variety of skills. They learn to walk, climb, push, pull, and talk. More generally, they learn how to hold on and to let go. Not only does this apply to physical objects but to feces and urine as well. In other words, children can now "willfully" decide to do something or not. Thus children are engaged in a battle of wills with their parents.

The parents must perform the delicate task of controlling the child's behavior in socially acceptable directions without injuring the child's sense of self-control or autonomy. In other words, the parents must be reasonably tolerant but still be firm enough to ensure behavior that is socially approved. If the parents are overly protective or unjust in their use of punishment, the child will be doubtful and experience shame:

> This stage, therefore, becomes decisive for the ratio of love and hate, cooperation and willfulness, freedom of self-expression and its suppression. From a sense of self-control without loss of self-esteem comes a lasting sense of good will and pride; from a sense of loss of self-control and of foreign overcontrol comes a lasting propensity for doubt and shame. (Erikson, 1985, p. 254)

If the child develops more **autonomy** than **shame and doubt** during this stage, the virtue of **will** emerges. Erikson defined will as "the unbroken determination to exercise free choice as well as self-restraint, in spite of the unavoidable experience of shame and doubt in infancy" (1964, p. 119). Again, it is important to note that the positive resolution of the crisis characterizing this stage does not mean the child no longer experiences shame and doubt. Rather, it means the child's ego becomes strong enough to deal adequately with the inevitable experiences of shame and doubt.

Notice that the virtues emerging as the result of positive crises resolutions are ego functions. For example, the virtues of hope and will have some influence on the quality of one's life but little on survival. Persons without much hope or will do survive; that is, they are able to satisfy their biological (idinal) needs, but they probably are not as flexible, optimistic, or generally as happy as those with more hope and will.

Judiciousness versus Legalism. Autonomy is best served when one's will is freely exercised. Because each culture restricts some behaviors and allows others, however, the child must learn to discriminate between right and wrong, between what is acceptable and what is unacceptable. Erikson called **judiciousness** the ritualization by which the child learns what is culturally sanctioned and what is not. Through judiciousness the child learns the laws, rules, honored practices, and regulations that characterize the child's culture. Before this stage, it was the parents' responsibility to guide the child's behavior properly. Now, however, as the rules and regulations of a culture are internalized, the child begins to judge his or her own behavior as well as that of others. Children must learn to judge themselves as others judge them. As the superego develops, it is used by the child to make moral evaluations.

The perversion of the ritualization of judiciousness is the ritualism of **legalism,** which Erikson defined as "the victory of the letter over the spirit of the word and the law. It is expressed in the vain display of righteousness or empty contrition, or in a moralistic insistence on exposing and isolating the culprit whether or not this will be good for him or anybody else" (1977, p. 97). For the legalistic child or adult, the punishment and humiliation of transgressors is more important than the intent of the law that was transgressed.

3. Preschool Age: Initiative versus Guilt

This stage occurs from about the fourth year to about the fifth year and corresponds to Freud's phallic stage of psychosexual development. During this stage the child is increasingly capable of detailed motor activity, refined use of language, and vivid use of imagination. These skills allow the child to *initiate* ideas, actions, and fantasies, and to *plan* future events. According to Erikson, the child during this stage "is apt to develop an untiring curiosity about differences in sizes in general, and sexual differences in particular . . . his learning is now eminently intrusive and vigorous: it leads away from his own limitations and into future possibilities" (1959, p. 76).

In the preceding stages, children learn that they are people. Now they begin to explore what type of person they can become. During this stage, limits are tested to learn what is permissible and what is not. If parents encourage children's self-initiated behaviors and fantasies, the children will leave this stage with a healthy sense of **initiative.** If, however, parents ridicule the children's self-initiated behavior and imagination, they will leave this stage lacking self-sufficiency. Instead of taking the initiative, they will tend to experience **guilt** when pondering such behavior and therefore will tend to live within the narrow limits that others set for them.

If children develop more initiative during this stage than guilt, the virtue of **purpose** will emerge. Erikson defined purpose as "the courage to envisage and pursue valued goals uninhibited by the defeat of infantile fantasies, by guilt and by the foiling fear of punishment" (1964, p. 122). Children who have positively resolved the crises of the first three stages possess the virtues of hope, will, and purpose.

Authenticity versus Impersonation. In addition to playing with toys, children at this stage typically engage in a great deal of playacting, imitating, wearing costumes, and even pretending to be various types of animals. Such play provides them with an intermediate reality where they can explore the relationship between their inner and outer worlds. Both positive and negative roles are played to reconfirm the limits on behavior. Through the process of "trying on" various roles and reconfirming what is possible and what is not, children discover the "mix" of roles that is just right for him or her. Erikson referred to those activities as the ritualization of **authenticity.**

Exaggeration of the ritualization of authenticity results in the ritualism of **impersonation** that occurs when one confuses one's true self with one or more of the roles that one plays. Rather than a role becoming just a part of the true self or furnishing information about it, the child becomes the role he or she plays. What is lost in such a case is the rich blending of personality characteristics that have developed during previous stages into a unique, authentic person.

4. School Age: Industry versus Inferiority

This stage lasts from about the sixth year to about the eleventh year and corresponds to Freud's latency stage of psychosexual development. Most children attend school throughout this stage. It is during this stage that children learn the skills necessary for economic survival, the technological skills that will allow them to become productive members of their culture:

> The inner stage seems all set for "entrance into life," except that life must first be school life, whether school is field or jungle or classroom. The child must forget past hopes and wishes, while his exuberant imagination is tamed and harnessed to the laws of impersonal things—even the three R's. For before the child, psychologically already a rudimentary parent, can become a biological parent, he must begin to be a worker and potential provider. (Erikson, 1985, pp. 258–259)

School is the place where children are trained for future employment in and adjustment to their culture. Because survival requires the ability to work cooperatively with others, social skills are among the important lessons taught by the schools. The most important lesson that children learn during this stage is "the pleasure of work completion by steady attention and persevering diligence" (Erikson, 1985, p. 259). From this lesson comes a sense of **industry**, which prepares children to look confidently for productive places in society among other people.

If children do not develop a sense of industry, they will develop a sense of **inferiority** that causes them to lose confidence in their ability to become contributing members of society. Such children are more likely to develop a "negative identity," a concept that is explained in our discussion of the next stage.

Another danger associated with this stage is that children may later overvalue their positions in the workplace. For such people, work is equated with life, and they thus are blinded to the many other important aspects of human existence. "If he accepts work as his only obligation, and 'what works' as his only criterion of worthwhileness, he may become the conformist and thoughtless slave of his technology and of those who are in a position to exploit it" (Erikson, 1985, p. 261). According to Erikson, the skills necessary for future employment must be encouraged during this stage but not at the expense of other important human attributes.

If children's sense of industry is greater than their sense of inferiority, they will leave this stage with the virtue of **competence**. "Competence . . . is the free exercise of dexterity and intelligence in the completion of tasks, unimpaired by infantile inferiority" (Erikson, 1964, p. 124). Like the virtues discussed earlier, competence comes from loving attention and encouragement. A sense of inferiority comes from ridicule or lack of concern by those persons most important to the children.

Formality versus Formalism.   During this stage, children learn that to be a productive member of their community they must possess real (not imagined) skills and knowledge. Erikson called the ritualization corresponding to this stage **formality,** and it involves learning the appropriate ways of doing tasks. Whatever the child does, whether it be at school, at home, at work, or on the athletic field, he or she must learn to do it "properly."

The exaggeration of the ritualization of formality results in the ritualism of **formalism.** Formalism is demonstrated when an overconcern with technique, and a blindness to the purpose and meaning of a task, occur. The student whose only concern is with high grades exemplifies formalism. Erikson (1977) said of formalism:

> Whatever the name, it must express the fact that human striving for method and logic can also lead to that self-enslavement which makes of each man what Marx

called a "craft-idiot," that is, one who for the sake of a proficiency will forget and deny the human context within which it has a significant and maybe dangerous function. (p. 106)

5. Adolescence: Identity versus Role Confusion

This stage occurs between about 12 and 20 years of age and corresponds roughly to Freud's genital stage of psychosexual development. Erikson is best known for his description of this psychosocial stage, for it contains his well-known concept of **identity crisis.**

Erikson believed that this stage represents the transition period between childhood and adulthood. In the preceding stages, children were learning who they were and what it was possible for them to do, that is, the various roles that were available to them. During this stage, children must ponder the accumulated information about themselves and their society and ultimately commit themselves to some strategy for life. When they have done this, they have gained an identity and have become adults. Gaining a personal **identity** marks the satisfactory end of this stage of development. The stage itself, however, is viewed as a time of searching for an identity but not of having one. Erikson called the interval between youth and adulthood a **psychosocial moratorium.** Erikson (1964) vividly described what it is like to be in this period between childhood and adulthood:

> Like a trapeze artist, the young person in the middle of vigorous motion must let go of his safe hold on childhood and reach out for a firm grasp on adulthood, depending for a breathless interval on a relatedness between the past and the future, and on the reliability of those he must let go of, and those who will "receive" him. (p. 90)

Erikson used the term *identity* (sometimes called ego identity) in a variety of ways. For example, it is "a feeling of being at home in one's body, a sense of 'knowing where one is going,' and an inner assuredness of anticipated recognition from those who count" (Erikson, 1968, p. 165). Erikson made no apology for using the term identity in a variety of ways. Because it is a complex concept, he thought it must be approached from many angles.

If young adults do not leave this stage with an identity, they leave it with **role confusion** or perhaps with a **negative identity.** Role confusion is characterized by the inability to choose a role in life, thus prolonging the psychological moratorium indefinitely or to make superficial commitments that are soon abandoned. Negative identities are those roles that children are warned not to assume. Erikson defined negative identity as "an identity perversely based on all those identifications and roles which, at critical stages of development, had been presented to the individual as most undesirable or dangerous, and yet also as most real" (1959, p. 131). Erikson gave an example:

> A mother who is filled with unconscious ambivalence toward a brother who disintegrated into alcoholism may again and again respond selectively only to those traits in her son which seem to point to a repetition of her brother's fate, in which case this "negative" identity may take on more reality for the son than all his natural attempts at being good: he may work hard on becoming a drunkard. (1959, p. 131)

For Erikson, the concepts of role confusion and negative identity explained much of the unrest and hostility expressed by adolescents in this country. For example, the adolescent may lash out at those identities that do not fit him or her:

> The loss of a sense of identity often is expressed in a scornful and snobbish hostility toward the roles offered as proper and desirable in one's family or immediate community. Any aspect of the required role, or all parts, be it masculinity or femininity, nationality or class membership, can become the main focus of the young person's acid disdain. (Erikson, 1959, p. 129)

Why should an adolescent choose a negative identity if a positive one is not available? Erikson said because an adolescent would "rather be nobody or somebody bad, or indeed, dead—and this totally, and by free choice—than be not-quite somebody" (1959, p. 132).

If young adults emerge from this stage with a positive identity rather than with role confusion or a negative identity, they also will emerge with the virtue of **fidelity.** Erikson defined fidelity as "the ability to sustain loyalties freely pledged in spite of the inevitable contradictions of value systems" (1964, p. 125).

The stages preceding this provided the child with the qualities from which an identity could be derived. In this stage, the person must synthesize this information. The development of an identity marks the end of childhood and the beginning of adulthood. From this point on, life is a matter of acting out one's identity. Now that the person "knows who he or she is," the task of life becomes one of carrying "that person" optimally through the remaining stages of life.

Ideology versus Totalism.   The ritualization corresponding to this stage is **ideology.** The adolescent searches for an ideology that synthesizes all of the ego developments from the previous stages. The ideology furnishes a game plan for life; it gives life meaning. An identity cannot emerge until all previous ego functions are integrated, and commitment to an ideology allows such integration. A chosen ideology could be religious, political, or philosophical. The only stipulation is that acting in accordance with it furthers both individual and cultural goals.

The exaggeration of the ritualization of ideology results in the ritualism of **totalism.** Totalism involves the unquestioning commitment to overly simplistic ideologies. For example, adolescents may accept the values mouthed by various "heroes" in religious cults, musical groups, drug cultures, athletics, gangs, films, or political groups. According to Erikson, when adolescents overidentify with such groups or individuals it is because they seem to provide answers to life's most difficult questions. The simplistic thinking involved in totalism, then, can make life easier for the troubled adolescent and, if it is temporary, it may not be harmful. It is when totalism lasts beyond the time when an identity should be achieved that it becomes a problem.

It is important to remember that according to the epigenetic principle all crises exist in all stages of development. For example, the identity crisis exists in the young child as it does in the mature adult. However, it does so in the immature and resolution phases of the crisis, respectively. For biological, psychological, and social reasons, it is only during adolescence that the identity crisis exists in its critical phase.

6. Young Adulthood: Intimacy versus Isolation

This stage lasts from about 20 to about 24 years of age. For this and the remaining psychosocial stages, there is no corresponding Freudian psychosexual stage of development.

According to Erikson, "normalcy" for the young adult consists of, to a large extent, being able to love and work effectively; and on this point, he agreed with Freud:

> Freud was once asked what he thought a normal person should be able to do well. The questioner probably expected a complicated answer. But Freud, in the curt way of his old days, is reported to have said: "Lieben und arbeiten" (to love and to work). It pays to ponder on this simple formula; it gets deeper as you think about it. . . . We may ponder, but we cannot improve on "the professor's" formula. (Erikson, 1985, pp. 264–265)

Although Erikson agreed with Freud on the importance of love, he believed only the person with a secure identity can risk entering a loving relationship. The young adult with a strong identity eagerly seeks intimate relationships with others:

> The young adult, emerging from the search for and the insistence on identity, is eager and willing to fuse his identity with that of others. He is ready for intimacy, that is, the capacity to commit himself to concrete affiliations and partnerships and to develop the ethical strength to abide by such commitments, even though they may call for significant sacrifices and compromises. (Erikson, 1985, p. 263)

People who do not develop a capacity for productive work and **intimacy** withdraw into themselves, avoid close contacts, and thus develop a feeling of **isolation.** If individuals develop a greater capacity for intimacy than for isolation during this stage, they will also emerge with the virtue of **love.** Erikson defined love as "the mutuality of devotion forever subduing the antagonisms inherent in divided function" (1964, p. 129).

Affiliation versus Elitism.   Once an identity has been achieved and an ideology has been chosen that allows for the productive manifestation of that identity, a person can affiliate productively with fellow humans in work, friendship, and love. The ritualization characterizing this stage is **affiliation,** the various ways a culture sanctions caring, productive relationships between adults. The marriage ceremony and the subsequent honeymoon are two such sanctioning rituals. The wedding ceremony may involve the exchange of rings and a pledge of fidelity. We see in the wedding ceremony elements of the ritualizations from previous stages. For example, the ceremony casts a numinous (i.e., a feeling of reverence) spell; it has a judicious element in that certain rights are bestowed; the ceremony and subsequent marital relationship may reflect earlier experimentation with role playing; formality is reflected in the fact that the ceremony includes elements that must be performed according to accepted practice; and the mutual pledges taken by the man and woman affirm their identities as husband and wife. Affiliation further prepares individuals to live harmoniously with fellow humans within a culture.

The exaggeration of the ritualization of affiliation results in the ritualism of **elitism.** Those individuals who experience a sense of isolation rather than intimacy tend to surround themselves with small groups of like-minded individuals rather than forming deeply emotional relationships with healthy individuals. Their lives tend to be characterized by snobbery, status symbols, and membership in exclusive clubs; because such relationships are not truly intimate, they continue the person's sense of isolation within his or her culture.

7. Adulthood: Generativity versus Stagnation

This stage occurs from about age 25 to about 64 and is called middle adulthood. If one has been fortunate enough to develop a positive identity and to live a productive, happy life, one attempts to pass on the circumstances that caused such a life to the next generation. This can be done either by interacting with children directly (they need not be one's own) or by producing or creating experiences that will enhance the lives of those in the next generation. The person who does not develop a sense of **generativity** is characterized by "stagnation and interpersonal impoverishment" (Erikson, 1985, p. 267). If the ratio of generativity to **stagnation** is in favor of the former, one leaves this stage with the virtue of **care** that Erikson defined as "the widening concern for what has been generated by love, necessity, or accident; it overcomes the ambivalence adhering to irreversible obligation" (1964, p. 131).

Generationalism versus Authoritism.   The ritualization characterizing this stage is **generationalism** that involves the many ways in which older adults transmit cultural values to the next generation. Parents, teachers, physicians, and spiritual leaders are especially influential in conveying cultural values to children. Healthy adults are concerned with providing children with the same types of experiences they were fortunate enough to have, that is, with experiences that both facilitate personality growth and perpetuate cultural values.

The exaggeration of the ritualization of generationalism results in the ritualism of **authoritism.** Authoritism occurs when authority figures in a culture use their power not for the care and instruction of the young but for their own selfish purposes.

8. Old Age: Ego Integrity versus Despair

This stage occurs from about the age of 65 to death and is called late adulthood. Erikson defined **ego integrity** as follows:

> Only in him who in some way has taken care of things and people and who has adapted himself to the triumphs and disappointments adherent to being, the originator of others or the generator of products and ideas—only in him may gradually ripen the fruit of these seven stages—I know no better word for it than ego integrity. (1985, p. 268)

According to Erikson, the person who can look back on a rich, constructive, happy life does not fear death. Such a person has a feeling of completion and fulfillment. The person who looks back on life with frustration experiences **despair.** As strange as it may seem, the person experiencing despair is not as ready for death as the person with a sense of fulfillment because the former has not yet achieved any major goals in life.

Not only are the eight stages progressively related to each other, but the eighth stage is directly related to the first. In other words, the eight stages are interrelated in a circular fashion. For example, the adult's attitude toward death will directly influence the young child's sense of trust. Erikson said, "It seems possible to further paraphrase the relation of adult integrity and infantile trust by saying that healthy children will not fear life if their elders have integrity enough not to fear death" (1985, p. 269). If the person has more ego integrity than despair, his or her life will be characterized by the virtue of **wisdom** that Erikson defined as "detached concern with life itself, in face of death itself" (1964, p. 133).

Integralism versus Sapientism. If all has gone well in a person's life, that person realizes how instrumental he or she has been in perpetuating culture. That is, the person has a sense of immortality knowing that the culture he or she helped sustain will survive his or her own death. The ritualization of **integralism** involves the final unification of previous ritualizations. This last integration of the ritualizations puts life, and therefore death, into perspective:

> We can see now what rituals must accomplish: by combining and renewing the ritualizations of childhood and affirming generative sanction, they help to consolidate adult life once its commitments and investments have led to the creation of new persons and to the production of new things and ideas. And, of course, by tying life cycle and institutions into a meaningful whole, they create a sense of immortality not only for the leaders and the elite but also for every participant. And there can be little doubt that the ritualizations of everyday life permits, and even demands, that adults forget death as the inscrutable background of all life, and give priority to the absolute reality of world views shared with others of the same geography, history, and technology. By means of ritual, in fact, death becomes the meaningful boundary of such reality. (Erikson, 1977, pp. 112–113)

The exaggeration of the ritualization of integralism results in the ritualism of **sapientism** that Erikson defined as "the unwise pretense of being wise" (1977,

Table 6–1						
The Eight Stages of Development and Their Associated Crises, Virtues, Ritualizations, and Ritualisms	STAGE	APPROXI-MATE AGE (YEARS)	CRISIS	VIRTUE	RITUALI-ZATION	RITUALISM
	Infancy	Birth-1	Basic trust versus basic mistrust	Hope	Numinous	Idolism
	Early child-hood	1-3	Autonomy versus shame and doubt	Will	Judicious-ness	Legalism
	Preschool age	4-5	Initiative versus guilt	Purpose	Authenticity	Impersona-tion
	School age	6-11	Industry versus inferiority	Compe-tence	Formality	Formalism
	Adolescence	12-20	Identity versus role confusion	Fidelity	Ideology	Totalism
	Young adulthood	20-24	Intimacy versus isolation	Love	Affiliation	Elitism
	Adulthood	25-64	Generativity versus stagnation	Care	Generation-alism	Authoritism
	Old age	65-Death	Ego integrity versus despair	Wisdom	Integralism	Sapientism

p. 112). The older person experiencing despair instead of ego integrity may play the role of a person having all the answers, of being absolutely right; however, he or she is unable to place his or her life in the context of continuous cultural evolution. Such a life is viewed as having little meaning.

The eight stages of development and their associated crises, virtues, ritualizations, and ritualisms are summarized in Table 6–1.

Goal of Psychotherapy

Erikson stressed that his psychotherapeutic practices differ from those of traditional psychoanalysis because modern times have created different types of disorders. For example, Erikson explained that "the patient of today suffers most under the problem of what he should believe in and who he should—or, indeed, might—be or become; while the patient of early psychoanalysis suffered most under inhibitions which prevented him from being what and who he thought he knew he was" (1985, p. 279).

For Erikson, the main focus in the therapeutic process is the patient's ego that must be strengthened to the point at which it can cope with life's problems. "Rehabilitation work can be made more effective and economical if the clinical investigation focuses on the patient's shattered life plan and if advice tends to strengthen the resynthesis of the elements on which the patient's ego identity was based" (1959, p. 43).

Erikson believed the traditional technique of releasing the contents of the unconscious mind may do more harm than good. Erikson said the psychoanalytic method "may make some people sicker than they ever were . . . especially if, in our zealous pursuit of our task of 'making conscious' in the psychotherapeutic situation, we push someone who is leaning out a little too far over the precipice of the unconscious" (1968, p. 164).

Like Adler, Erikson had his patients sit across from him in an easy chair rather than lie down on a couch because the former creates a more equitable situation for the patient.

Briefly stated, the healthy person is one whose ego is characterized by the eight virtues resulting from the positive solution of each crisis in the eight stages of development. The purpose of psychotherapy is to encourage the growth of whatever virtues are missing, even if it means going back and helping the person to develop a sense of basic trust. For Erikson, the outcome of every crisis resolution is reversible. For example, the person leaving the first stage of development without basic trust may later gain it, and the person having it may lose it. Friedman (1999) summarizes Erikson's view of therapy as follows:

> Erikson characterized the premise that an early life experience invariabley determined subsequent psychological development as the "originology" fallacy. Most important, he felt that the clinician must always remember that the therapist–patient connection was essentially a relationship through which both parties gained by giving. Successful therapy was largely the practice of the Golden Rule—possibly no more and certainly no less. (p. 477)

Comparison of Erikson and Freud

The major areas in which Erikson and Freud differ are listed next.

Development

Freud concentrated his studies on the psychosexual stages of development coming before the age of 6 because he thought that most of what is important to personality development occurs by then. Erikson studied development as it occurs throughout life. Although Jung, too, believed that important developments occurred throughout one's life, Erikson's description of the development process was much more detailed.

Anatomy as Destiny

Freud emphasized the importance of biological differences between males and females for personality development. Erikson agreed that anatomical differences provide patterns of internal stimulation but insisted that such stimulation interacts with the social environment to produce personality characteristics. The term "penis envy" does not appear in Erikson's major work (1985). Elsewhere, Erikson (1968) argued that so-called penis envy, and the behaviors and attitudes supposedly associated with it, were necessitated by Freud's theory and therapeutic methods: "It must always be suspected that a special method bares truths especially true under circumstances created by the method" (p. 275). Erikson's theory and methods generated no support for Freud's concept of penis envy.

Ego Psychology

Under the influence of Anna Freud, Erikson shifted attention away from the id and toward the ego. Rather than viewing the individual as warring with society, Erikson viewed society as a potential source of strength.

As we have seen, Erikson believed that culture must provide ritualizations that help persons positively resolve the crises characterizing the various stages of development. The individual serves culture and culture serves the individual.

Unconscious Mind

Although Erikson's theory emphasized the conscious ego, he did not neglect unconscious mechanisms completely. In fact, although the ego gains strength from certain social experiences, the experiences themselves are largely unconscious. This use of the term unconscious, however, was far different from Freud's.

Dream Analysis

Although Erikson minimized the use of dream analysis in his practice, he did agree with Freud's contention that dreams provide information about the unconscious and that dream work creates dream symbols with more than one meaning. Furthermore, Erikson believed that free association is an effective way of studying dreams.

Most important to Erikson, however, was the ego's influence on dreams. Healthy egos remain powerful even during sleep and they make compromises with idinal impulses that produce dreams of success and achievement so that the dreamers can awake with a sense of competence and wholeness. Erikson also believed that dreams often suggest solutions to the dreamer's problems. In fact, during therapy a patient may dream dreams for the sole purpose of being analyzed by the dreamer's analyst, "Once we set out to study our dreams . . . we may well dream them in order to study them" (Erikson, 1977, p. 134). Furthermore, the patient may oblige the therapist by having just the type of dream the therapist is looking for:

> Patients . . . know that they will or should report their dreams, and this in the context of a therapeutic style: wherefore Jungian or Freudian patients, for example, seem to differ radically in their manifest dream imagery. Their dreams, in fact, can be seen to reflect the vision of the respective "schools"—a therapeutic communality, then, maybe seasoned with a bit of obliging "politic"? (Erikson, 1977, p. 134)

Thus, although Erikson agreed with Freud that dreams may provide information about unconscious, idinal desires, he chose to concentrate on the aspects of dreams that are constructive and teleological and therefore useful and refreshing to the dreamer. If dream analysis was used at all by Erikson, it was used to determine the strength of the dreamer's ego rather than as a way of discovering repressed, traumatic experiences. Erikson's approach to dream analysis was more similar to Adler's approach than it was to Freud's.

Psychotherapy

We have seen that Erikson considered people healthy if they successfully traverse the eight stages of life and thus acquire the virtues of hope, will, purpose, competence, fidelity, love, care, and wisdom. If people do not acquire these virtues, their egos will be weaker than they otherwise would be, and it is the job of the therapist to help provide the circumstances under which the virtues can develop. This is in marked contrast to Freud's belief that therapy facilitates the understanding of repressed memories using techniques such as dream analysis and free association.

Religion

Freud took a dim view of religion saying that it is merely a collective neurosis based on infantile fears and desires. Erikson totally disagreed. For him, religion is something that many people truly need. For centuries, humans have used religion to make the events of their lives more understandable and therefore less threatening. Without it, according to Erikson, the lives of millions of persons would be filled with uncertainty. In this respect, Erikson agreed with Jung and Adler.

According to Erikson, a key function of religion is to provide a "shared world image. For only a reasonably coherent world provides the faith which is transmitted by the mothers to the infants in a way conducive to the vital strength of hope" (Erikson, 1968, p. 106). In other words, for adults to instill hope in their children they must have faith in their world. Erikson did not believe, however, that religion is the only thing that can provide a world image conducive to trust, hope, and faith. Many people, he said, derive faith from such secular areas as science and social action (1985, p. 251).

We see that although Erikson called himself a Freudian, his theory had little in common with Freud's. In addition, his conception of human nature is in marked contrast to Freud's. Perhaps, as we have already suggested, Erikson's insistence that his theory is closer to Freud's than it really is reflects Erikson's deep appreciation that the Freudians took him into their camp, thus solving his own identity crisis.

Evaluation

Empirical Research

Like so many personality theories, Erikson's theory cannot be evaluated only on the basis of laboratory investigations, at least not yet. Erikson did not create his theory with the researcher in mind. He attempted to classify conceptually several items related to personality development, and one either believes they are clarified, or they are not; either his theory is a useful guide to understanding personality, or it is not. "The proof lies in the way in which the communication between therapist and patient 'keeps moving,' leading to new and surprising insights and to the patient's greater assumption of responsibility for himself" (Erikson, 1964, p. 75). The point is that Erikson believed there are ways other than laboratory investigations to evaluate a personality theory. Despite Erikson's thoughts about the need to verify his theory scientifically, others have taken it on themselves to do just that. For example, Ciaccio (1971) asked 120 male white children to make up stories about five pictures. The boys were equally divided into three groups consisting of 5-, 8-, and 11-year-old children. With the help of several judges, the stories the children told were categorized sentence by sentence according to which stage of development they best corresponded. The percentages of each child's sentences that expressed concern with the first five of Erikson's stages were recorded. The data tended to support Erikson's theory. The 5-year-old children showed the greatest number of themes corresponding to stage 2 (46 percent); next was stage 3 (42 percent). The 8-year-old children showed the greatest number of themes corresponding to stage 3 (56 percent), with stage 2 second (20 percent). The 11-year-old children showed the greatest number of themes corresponding to stage 4 (44 percent), with stage 3 second (26 percent).

By far, most of the research generated by Erikson's theory has involved the concept of identity. Several researchers have devised methods of quantifying the concept of identity so that it can be investigated experimentally (see, e.g., Bourne, 1978; Marcia, 1966; Rosenthal, Gurney, & Moore, 1981). Research using one or more of these objective measures of identity has found that identity achievers choose more difficult academic majors (e.g., chemistry, engineering, biology, and mathematics) than those chosen by nonachievers (e.g., anthropology, education, and physical education) (Marcia & Friedman, 1970); identity achievers have higher grades than nonachievers (Cross & Allen, 1970); identity achievers show greater tolerance for out-groups and higher levels of logical and moral reasoning than nonachievers (Cote & Levine, 1983; Rowe & Marcia, 1980; Waterman, 1982); many students achieve both occupational and ideological identities sometime between their freshman and senior years, indicating that adolescence is a time of profound psychosocial growth, just as Erikson had said (Adams & Fitch, 1982; Waterman, Geary, & Waterman, 1974); attainment of identity is far more likely if a sense of trust, autonomy, initiative, and industry have been attained in the earlier stages of development (Waterman, Buebel, & Waterman, 1970); the development of an identity greatly increases the probability of achieving an intimate relationship during middle age (Kahn, Zimmerman, Csikszentmihalyi, & Getzels, 1985; Schiedel & Marcia, 1985; Tesch & Whitbourne, 1982); and persons experiencing role confusion are much more affected by peer pressure than are identity achievers (Adams, Ryan, Hoffman, Dobson, & Nielsen, 1985).

Criticisms

Difficult to Test Empirically. We have seen that Erikson had little interest in testing his own theory empirically and what research he does report (e.g., his research on the play activities of boys and girls) lacks quantification and statistical analysis. Others, however, have had some success in verifying some Eriksonian concepts related to the stages of development and especially that of identity.

Overly Optimistic View of Humans. Although claiming a close affiliation with Freud's theory, Erikson painted a much rosier picture of humans than did Freud. Little in Erikson's theory describes an intense struggle to keep our animalistic nature in check. By emphasizing and expanding the functioning of the ego, Erikson concentrated on problems of identity, problem solving, and interpersonal relationships rather than on the taming of powerful sexual and aggressive instincts. To some critics, Erikson's portrayal of humans is too optimistic, unrealistic, and simplistic.

Support of Status Quo. Essentially Erikson defined a healthy person as one who adjusts to, accepts, and passes on to the next generation the elements of his or her culture. To many critics, this definition sounds like Erikson was advocating conformity. Indeed, Erikson insisted that ego development is enhanced by engaging in the cultural ritualizations that are available at various stages of development. In other words, Erikson insisted that healthy egos require the support of culturally sanctioned roles, and this insistence is taken by many as endorsement of those roles. For those seeing gross injustices, dangerous values, shallowness, and even stupidity in their culture, it makes little sense to define mental health in terms of adjustments to such an abnormal situation.

Excessive Moralizing. Erikson's definition of the positive adjustments to crises at various stages of development are in accordance with Christian ethics and with existing social institutions. The danger in this (as in all personality theories) is that Erikson may have been describing his own values rather than objective reality. Roazen (1980) elaborates:

> Confusing "ought" and "is" statements can lead to . . . undesirable consequences. . . . There is the danger of conservatism—throwing a mantle of morality over the pre-existing world and endorsing everything that already "is" with an ethical sanction. Erikson's message communicates too much of what we want to hear. His hopefulness is too often allied to social conservatism. (p. 339)

Roazen (1976) comments further on Erikson's moralizing:

> As one reflects on the implications of Erikson's ego psychology, with its deferential attitude toward the benefits of pre-existing social institutions, a consistent ethical mood does emerge; marriage, heterosexuality, and the raising of children are unquestionably part of what he takes the good life to consist of. (p. 171)

The criticism that Erikson's theory is too moralistic is closely related to the criticism that his theory supports the status quo.

Failure to Properly Acknowledge Influences on His Theory.   One criticism here concerns Erikson's insistence on being a "post-Freudian" when, in fact, little of substance is similar between his theory and Freud's. It has been suggested that Erikson continued to label himself a Freudian to avoid being "excommunicated" from psychoanalytic circles. In other words, it has been suggested that his motives were pragmatic and political. Conversely, Erikson, although giving perhaps too much credit to Freud, neglected to properly acknowledge theorists such as Adler and Horney who stressed the importance of social variables before Erikson.

Contributions

Expansion of Psychology's Domain.   Despite Erikson's lack of scientific rigor, his theory is considered by many to be one of the most useful ever developed. Henceforth, when you encounter the terms *psychosocial development, ego strength, psychohistory, identity, identity crisis,* and *life-span psychology,* keep in mind that they are concepts that were first articulated by Erikson and have since become an important part of psychology.

Considerable Applied Value.   Erikson's theory has been successfully used in such areas as child psychology and psychiatry, vocational counseling, marital counseling, education, social work, and business.

Development of Ego Psychology.   By developing and promoting ego psychology, Erikson encouraged the study of healthy people in addition to neurotics and psychotics; encouraged the study of personality development across the entire life span; and painted a dignified picture of humans. Also, by rejecting Freud's contention that society is necessarily a source of conflict and frustration and by stressing the positive influences of society instead, Erikson promoted the integration of psychology with such disciplines as sociology and anthropology.

Summary

Although Erikson had only the equivalent of a high school diploma, he was invited to work in a small school established to care for children who either were receiving therapy from Anna Freud or who had parents who were receiving therapy from Sigmund Freud. Erikson worked as a tutor for a while but eventually went into training to become a child analyst under the supervision of Anna Freud. Anna Freud's interest in the ego had a lasting effect on Erikson, who is usually credited with founding ego psychology. Ego psychology emphasizes the autonomous functions of the ego and deemphasizes the importance of the id to personality development.

Erikson agreed with Freud that one's gender markedly influences one's personality but he believed anatomical differences always interact with societal influences to produce individual differences. Furthermore, he did not believe that masculine traits are better or worse than feminine traits. Rather, he believed masculine and feminine traits complement each other.

The most widely known aspect of Erikson's theory is his description of the eight stages of personality development. According to Erikson's epigenetic principle, the stages unfold in a sequence that is genetically determined. Each of the eight stages is characterized by a crisis that can be resolved positively or negatively. The stages and the crises characterizing them are: (1) infancy—basic trust versus basic mistrust; (2) early childhood—autonomy versus shame and doubt; (3) preschool age—initiative versus guilt; (4) school age—industry versus inferiority; (5) adolescence—identity versus role confusion; (6) young adulthood—intimacy versus isolation; (7) adulthood—generativity versus stagnation; and (8) old age—ego integrity versus despair.

Society provides experiences that are conducive to the positive resolutions of the various crises; such experiences are called ritualizations. Distortions or exaggerations of ritualizations are called ritualisms. The ritualization characterizing the first stage is the numinous whereby the child's positive interactions with his or her mother make the child generally socially responsive. When the numinous is exaggerated, it becomes the ritualism of idolism or the excessive admiration of people. The ritualization characterizing the second stage is judiciousness through which the child learns the cultural definition of right and wrong. The exaggeration of judiciousness results in the ritualism of legalism that is a preoccupation with laws instead of what those laws are designed to accomplish. The ritualization corresponding to the third stage is authenticity that involves playing several roles to examine possibilities for living one's life. The exaggeration of authenticity results in the ritualism of impersonation whereby a person confuses a role he or she is playing with his or her true personality. The ritualization characterizing the fourth stage is formality that involves learning the correct way of acting in a culture. The exaggeration of formality results in the ritualism of formalism that is an overconcern with how tasks are done instead of why they are done. The ritualization characterizing the fifth stage is ideology that involves embracing a philosophy of life that synthesizes all previous ego developments. The exaggeration of ideology results in the ritualism of totalism, or the embracing of simplistic ideas because they seem to make life easier. The ritualization characterizing the sixth stage is affiliation that involves the sharing of one's life in caring, productive ways with fellow humans. The exaggeration of affiliation results in the ritualism of elitism where one's life is shared superficially with small groups of individuals similar to oneself. The ritualization characterizing the seventh stage is generationalism that involves all of the ways in which healthy adults help the younger generation adjust positively to their culture. The exaggeration of generationalism results in the ritualism of authoritism that involves the use of one's authority for self-serving reasons. The ritualization characterizing the eighth stage is integralism that involves a synthesizing of all the elements of one's life. The exaggeration of integralism results in the ritualism of sapientism that is the pretense of being wise.

If a crisis is resolved positively, a virtue will be gained that strengthens the ego. If the crises characterizing the eight stages of development are resolved positively, the person will live later years with the virtues of hope, will, purpose, competence, fidelity, love, care, and wisdom. Such a person was considered healthy by Erikson because he or she looks back on life with positive feelings and does not fear death. Children familiar with older people with these attributes are more likely to develop basic trust than basic mistrust.

One of the most important stages of development is the fifth stage because it is when the identity crisis occurs. It is during this stage that people attempt to learn who they are and where they are going in life. If people find answers to these questions they will leave this stage with an identity; if not, they will leave this stage with role confusion. It is also possible for people to develop a negative identity, which is the antithesis of a role that society has deemed desirable.

For Erikson, the outcomes of the experiences during the stages of development are reversible; that is, a favorable outcome can become unfavorable, and an unfavorable outcome can become favorable. In fact, Erikson viewed the therapeutic process mainly as a means of reversing the negative outcomes of various stages of development. For Erikson, the goal of therapy was to strengthen the conscious ego, rather than to understand the contents of the unconscious mind, as was the case with Freud. Many other differences exist between Freud's theory and Erikson's. For example, Freud viewed religion as a collective neurosis based on infantile desires, fear, and ignorance. Erikson, conversely, viewed religion as conducive to healthy adjustment.

Although Erikson believed no need exists to test his theory empirically, others have made attempts to do so. Most of the research generated by Erikson's theory has focused on the stages of development and on his concept of identity. These studies have tended to support predictions based on Erikson's theory. Erikson's theory has been criticized for being generally difficult to test empirically; portraying humans too simplistically or too optimistically; supporting the status quo; and for being too moralistic. Also Erikson has been criticized for not properly acknowledging those who influenced him. Erikson's contributions include the expansion of psychology's domain; the widespread usefulness of his theory; the development of ego psychology that is as concerned with healthy people as with unhealthy people; that his theory studies personality development across the entire life span; and that it stresses the fact that societal forces are conducive to personality development and are therefore not necessarily a source of conflict and frustration.

Experiential Exercises

1. Probably the most significant event in a person's life occurs when he or she gains an identity. Erikson believed this occurs toward the end of the fifth stage of development. The alternative to leaving this stage with an identity is to leave with role confusion. Drawing on the information in this chapter, would you say you have developed an identity or are you experiencing role confusion? Give evidence to support your answer.

2. Erikson asserted that one cannot experience true intimacy with another human until one has gained an identity. That is, two persons cannot share themselves in a deep, loving relationship unless they have both gained an identity. Respond to this assertion as it applies to your life and as it applies to the relationship of a close friend.

3. To minimize life's confusion, adolescents often idolize and overidentify with a teacher, a television or motion picture star, a rock star, an athlete, or even a friend. Was there someone in your adolescent years you idolized? If so, was this overidentification helpful? Harmful? Explain.

Discussion Questions

1. Compare ego psychology with traditional psychoanalytic theory.
2. Why are Erikson's stages of development labeled psychosocial rather than psychosexual?

3. Define ritualization and ritualism. List the ritualizations and ritualisms for each stage of development and give an example of each.

Glossary

Adolescence. The fifth stage of development.

Adulthood. The seventh stage of development.

Affiliation. Ritualization characterizing the sixth stage of development. This involves sharing one's identity with fellow humans in a caring, productive way, for example, by entering into an intimate relationship with someone who has also gained an identity.

Anatomy and destiny. Freud thought many important personality traits were determined by one's gender. Erikson believed the same but thought that one's culture was another powerful influence on one's personality. Although Erikson believed men and women have different personality characteristics, he did not consider one set of characteristics better than the other.

Authenticity. Ritualization characterizing the third stage of development. This involves playful role playing to discover possible ways of living one's adult life.

Authoritism. Ritualism that can occur during the seventh stage of development. This involves using power for selfish gains instead of helping others.

Autonomy. Sense of being relatively independent of external control, which arises if the crisis dominating the second stage of development is resolved positively.

Basic mistrust. Lack of trust in the world and the people in it, which arises if the crisis dominating the first stage of development is resolved negatively.

Basic trust. General feeling of trust in the world and the people in it, which arises if the crisis dominating the first stage of development is resolved positively.

Care. Virtue that arises when a person leaves the seventh stage of development with a greater sense of generativity than of stagnation.

Competence. Virtue that arises if a child leaves the fourth stage of development with a greater sense of industry than of inferiority.

Crisis. Conflict that becomes dominant during a particular stage of development that can be resolved positively thus strengthening the ego, or resolved negatively thus weakening the ego. Each crisis, therefore, is a turning point in one's development.

Culture. For Erikson, a version of human existence.

Despair. Lack of satisfaction with life and the fear of death, which characterize the person who has negatively resolved the crisis that dominates the eighth and final stage of development.

Early childhood. The second stage of development.

Ego integrity. The satisfaction with life and the lack of fear of death, which characterize the person who has positively resolved the crisis that dominates the eighth and final stage of development.

Ego psychology. Theoretical system that stresses the importance of the ego as an autonomous part of the personality instead of viewing the ego as merely the servant of the id.

Elitism. Ritualism that can occur during the sixth stage of development. This involves the superficial relationships with groups of like-minded individuals that people without identities seek.

Epigenetic principle. The innate biological principle that determines the sequence in which the eight stages of psychosocial development occurs.

Fidelity. Virtue that arises at the end of the fifth stage of development if one has a sense of identity instead of role confusion.

Formalism.   Ritualism that can occur during the fourth stage. This involves a preoccupation with how things work, or with one's work, and a disregard for the reason why things function as they do or why various types of jobs exist.

Formality.   Ritualization corresponding to the fourth stage of development. This involves learning how various things work in one's culture.

Generationalism.   Ritualization that characterizes the seventh stage of development. This involves the many ways in which healthy individuals help younger people to have experiences conducive to healthy personality growth.

Generativity.   Impulse to help members of the next generation that arises when the crisis dominating the seventh stage of development is resolved positively.

Guilt.   General feeling that develops in a child if the crisis dominating the third stage of development is resolved negatively.

Hope.   Virtue that arises if a child leaves the first stage of development with more basic trust than basic mistrust.

Identity (also called ego identity).   Sense of knowing who you are and where you are going in life that develops when the fifth stage of development is resolved positively. The emergence of an identity marks the end of childhood and the beginning of adulthood. Probably Erikson's most famous concept.

Identity crisis.   Crisis that dominates the fifth stage of development, which results either in the person gaining an identity (positive resolution) or in role confusion (negative resolution).

Ideology.   Ritualization characterizing the fifth stage of development. This involves embracing a philosophy of life that makes one's past, present, and future meaningful.

Idolism.   Ritualism that can occur during the first stage of development where instead of a child learning a warm, positive feeling toward others, he or she tends to worship them.

Impersonation.   Ritualism that can occur during the third stage of development. This involves confusing playing a role with one's true personality.

Industry.   Sense of enjoyment from work and from sustained attention, which arises if the crisis dominating the fourth stage of development is resolved positively.

Infancy.   The first stage of development.

Inferiority.   Loss of confidence in one's ability to become a contributing member of one's society, which arises if the crisis dominating the fourth stage of development is resolved negatively.

Initiative.   General ability to initiate ideas and actions and to plan future events, which arises if the crisis dominating the third stage of development is resolved positively.

Integralism.   Ritualization characterizing the eighth stage of development. This involves the wisdom to place one's own life in a larger perspective, that is, to see one's finite life as contributing to immortal culture.

Intimacy.   Ability to merge one's identity with that of another person, which arises if the crisis dominating the sixth stage of development is resolved positively.

Isolation.   Inability to share one's identity with that of another person, which results if the crisis dominating the sixth stage of development is resolved negatively.

Judiciousness.   Ritualization characterizing the second stage of development. This involves the many ways that children learn right from wrong.

Legalism.   Ritualism that can occur during the second stage of development. This involves a preoccupation with rules and regulations themselves instead of with what they were designed to accomplish.

Love.   Virtue that arises if one leaves the sixth stage of development with a greater sense of intimacy than of isolation.

Negative identity.   Identity contrary to the goals of society. Negative identities are all those roles that a child is warned not to assume.

Numinous.   Ritualization characterizing the first stage of development. This involves the many culturally determined ways in which mother and infant interact.

Old age.   The eighth stage of development.

Preschool age.   The third stage of development.

Psychohistory.   Term used to describe Erikson's use of his developmental theory of personality to analyze historical figures.

Psychosocial moratorium.   Time during the fifth stage of development when the adolescent is searching for an identity.

Psychosocial stages of development.   Erikson's eight stages of human development, so named to emphasize the importance of social experience to the resolution of the crises that characterize each stage.

Purpose. Virtue that arises if a child leaves the third stage of development with a greater sense of initiative than of guilt.

Ritualisms. Distorted or exaggerated ritualizations.

Ritualizations. Behaviors that reflect and thereby perpetuate the beliefs, customs, and values that are sanctioned by a particular culture.

Role confusion. The state produced by not acquiring an identity during the fifth stage of development. The state is characterized by an inability to choose a defining role in life and represents the negative resolution of the identity crisis.

Sapientism. Ritualism that can occur during the eighth stage of development. This involves the pretense of being wise.

School age. The fourth stage of development.

Shame and doubt. Feelings that develop instead of the feeling of autonomy when the crisis dominating the second stage of development is resolved negatively.

Stagnation. Lack of concern about the next generation that characterizes the person whose crisis during the seventh stage of development is resolved negatively.

Totalism. Ritualism that can occur during the fifth stage of development. This involves embracing simplistic ideas mouthed by various "heroes" because those ideas may temporarily make life more tolerable.

Virtue. Ego strength that arises when the crisis dominating a stage of development is resolved positively.

Will. Virtue that arises if the child leaves the second stage of development with a greater sense of autonomy than of shame and doubt.

Wisdom. Virtue that arises if a person has more ego integrity than despair during the eighth and final stage of development.

Young adulthood. The sixth stage of development.

GORDON ALLPORT

Gordon Allport was truly an eclectic theorist taking the best from a wide variety of other theories of personality. However, he was the first to criticize what he considered the worst in those theories. At one time or another, Allport took issue with psychoanalysis, behaviorism (stimulus–response [S-R] psychology), animal research designed to provide information about humans, and statistical methods of studying personality, such as factor analysis (see the theories of Cattell and Eysenck in the next chapter). Allport believed strongly that the principles governing the behavior of non-human animals or neurotic humans are different from those governing the behavior of healthy adult humans; therefore, little can be learned about one by studying the other. "Some theories of becoming are based largely upon the behavior of sick and anxious people or upon the antics of captive and desperate rats. Fewer theories have derived from the study of healthy human beings, those who strive not so much to preserve life as to make it worth living" (Allport, 1955, p. 18). We see in this statement a clear anticipation of what would become humanistic, or third-force, psychology (see Chapter 15). In fact, according to DeCarvalho (1991), Allport was the first to use the term *humanistic psychology*.

Allport battled with any viewpoint in psychology that obscured human individuality or dignity. If one had to isolate the dominant theme running through all of Allport's works, it is *the importance of the individual*. This theme put Allport in a position contrary to "scientific" psychology because it was considered the job of science to find the general laws governing all behavior. Science was interested in what is generally true, and Allport was interested in what is specifically true. Allport believed psychological research should have practical value, and in addition to his books on personality theory, he wrote: *The Individual and His Religion* (1950); *The Nature of Prejudice* (1958a); and *The Psychology of Rumor* (1947) with Leo Postman.

Biographical Sketch

Gordon Allport was born in Montezuma, Indiana, on November 11, 1897, making him the first American-born personality theorist we discuss. Allport was the youngest of four sons. His father, John Edwards Allport, was a physician, and his mother, Nellie Edith Wise Allport, was a teacher, and both had a strong, positive influence on him. In his brief autobiography, he said:

> My mother had been a school teacher and brought to her sons an eager sense of philosophical questioning and the importance of searching for ultimate religious answers. Since my father lacked adequate hospital facilities for his patients, our household for several years included both patients and nurses. Tending office, washing bottles, and dealing with patients were important aspects of my early training. . . . Dad was no believer in vacations. He followed rather his own rule of life, which he expressed as follows: If every person worked as hard as he could and took only a minimum financial return required by his family's needs, then there would be just enough wealth to go around. Thus it was hard work tempered by trust and affection that marked the home environment. (1967, pp. 4–5)

Allport credited his lifelong concern with human welfare and his strong humanistic psychology to experiences like those just described. Contrast Freud's view of human nature (see Chapter 2) with the one embraced by Allport:

> Normal men everywhere reject, in principle and by preference, the path of war and destruction. They like to live in peace and friendship with their neighbors; they prefer to love and be loved rather than to hate and be hated. (Allport, 1958a, pp. ix–x)

Although Allport was born in Indiana, he grew up in Cleveland, Ohio, where he attended public schools. At the urging of his older brother Floyd, a Harvard graduate (who also became a famous psychologist), Gordon Allport entered Harvard in 1915. He barely passed the entrance examination and his early grades were Cs and Ds. He worked hard, however, and finished the year with straight As. He graduated from Harvard in 1919 with a major in economics and philosophy.

Apparently not sure of what to do next and still seeking his personal identity, he spent the next year teaching English and sociology at Robert College in Istanbul, Turkey. Allport enjoyed teaching so much he decided to accept a fellowship offered to him by Harvard to do graduate work in psychology.

On his way back to the United States, Allport stopped in Vienna to visit one of his brothers. While there he had an experience that was to have a profound effect on his later theorizing. He wrote to Freud asking for permission to visit with him and permission was granted. Allport described his brief visit with Freud:

Soon after I had entered the famous red burlap room with pictures of dreams on the wall, he summoned me to his inner office. He did not speak to me but sat in expectant silence for me to state my mission. I was not prepared for silence and had to think fast to find a suitable conversational gambit. I told him of an episode on the tram car on my way to his office. A small boy about four years of age had displayed a conspicuous dirt phobia. He kept saying to his mother, "I don't want to sit there . . . don't let that dirty man sit beside me." To him everything was schmutzig [filthy]. His mother was a well-starched Hausfrau, so dominant and purposive looking that I thought the cause and effect apparent.

When I finished my story Freud fixed his kindly therapeutic eyes upon me and said, "And was that little boy you?" Flabbergasted and feeling a bit guilty, I contrived to change the subject. While Freud's misunderstanding of my motivation was amusing, it also started a deep train of thought. I realized that he was accustomed to neurotic defenses and that my manifest motivation (a sort of rude curiosity and youthful ambition) escaped him. For therapeutic progress he would have to cut through my defenses, but it so happened that therapeutic progress was not here an issue. (1967, pp. 7–8)

Allport learned from this experience that it is possible for "depth" psychology to dig so deeply that more important truths may be overlooked. Allport believed that he had perfectly valid, conscious reasons for visiting Freud and for telling him his little story, which were completely missed by Freud in his attempt to arrive at a "deeper" truth. About his visit with Freud, Allport (1968) said, "This experience taught me that depth psychology, for all its merits, may plunge too deep, and that psychologists would do well to give full recognition to manifest motives before probing the unconscious" (p. 384). As we see throughout this chapter, Allport believed the best way to discover a person's true motives is to ask the person about them.

Allport returned to Harvard where he earned his MA in 1921 and his PhD in 1922, at age 24. His early work was indeed indicative of what was to become Allport's own brand of personality theory. His first publication, coauthored with his brother Floyd, was titled "Personality Traits: Their Classification and Measurement" (Allport & Allport, 1921). His doctoral dissertation was titled "An Experimental Study of the Traits of Personality."

Allport's interest in personality traits was foreign to the psychology of his day. One dominant school of psychology at the time was structuralism that sought to study scientifically the elements of conscious thought and the principles by which those elements become associated. The founder and leader of structuralism was the illustrious and authoritarian Edward Titchener (1867–1927). Allport described his meeting with Titchener:

Standing at a frontier was a somewhat alarming business. The climax of my conflict came in connection with my single encounter with Titchener. I had been invited to attend the select gathering of his group of experimentalists, which met at Clark University in May, 1922, just as I was finishing my thesis. After two days of discussing problems in sensory psychology Titchener allotted three minutes to each visiting graduate to describe his own investigations. I reported on traits of personality and was punished by the rebuke of total silence from the group, punctuated by a glare of disapproval from Titchener. Later Titchener demanded of

Langfeld [Allport's thesis adviser] "Why did you let him work on that problem?" Back in Cambridge Langfeld again consoled me with the laconic remark, "You don't care what Titchener thinks." And I found that I did not. (1967, p. 9)

Allport viewed his encounter with Titchener as an important growing experience: "The whole experience was a turning point. Never since that time have I been troubled by rebukes or professional slights directed at my maverick interests" (1967, p. 9). Aided by a traveling fellowship, Allport spent the school year from 1922 to 1923 at the University of Berlin and the University of Hamburg, and the school year from 1923 to 1924 in England at Cambridge University. In 1924, he returned to Harvard, where he taught the first course on personality ever offered in the United States—Personality: Its Psychological and Social Aspects.

On June 30, 1925, Allport married Ada Lufkin Gould, who later became a clinical psychologist. They had one son, Robert Brandlee, who became a pediatrician. Except for a 4-year appointment at Dartmouth College from 1926 to 1930, Allport was at Harvard for his entire professional career. He died of lung cancer on October 9, 1967, a month before his 70th birthday.

Allport held many prestigious positions and received many honors. He was editor of the *Journal of Abnormal and Social Psychology* from 1937 to 1949. He served as president of the American Psychological Association (APA) in 1939 (at the age of 41), and of the Eastern Psychological Association in 1943. In 1936, he was one of the founders of the Society for the Psychological Study of Social Issues (SPSSI) and became its president in 1944. During World War II, he was a member of the Emergency Committee in Psychology, and was secretary of the Ella Lyman Cabot Foundation, which helped refugee psychologists escaping from Nazi Germany find work in the United States. In 1963, he received the APA's Gold Medal Award for Distinguished Contributions to Psychology, and in 1964 he received the APA's Distinguished Scientific Contribution Award. In 1966, he became the first Richard Clarke Cabat Professor of Social Ethics at Harvard. Allport's most prized honor, however, was two handsomely bound volumes of the publications of 55 of his former PhD students, given to him in 1963 with the dedicatory inscription "From his students— in appreciation of his respect for their individuality" (Allport, 1967, p. 24).

What Is Personality?

In his 1937 book *Personality: A Psychological Interpretation,* Allport introduced a uniquely American approach to the study of **personality.** From the very beginning, Allport was opposed to the established viewpoints of psychoanalysis and behaviorism. Allport's early theorizing was influenced mainly by Gestalt psychology, which he encountered in Germany after his graduation from Harvard, and by his strong humanistic tendencies developed early in his life. Gestalt psychology emphasized the wholeness and interrelatedness of conscious experience and also ignored the unconscious mind almost completely. Allport said Gestalt psychology was "the kind of psychology I had been longing for but did not know existed" (1967, p. 10). In fact, Allport distrusted science as a source of information about personality. He was more comfortable with the traditional descriptions of humans found in literature and philosophy. This is not to say that Allport ignored information provided by the scientific method; clearly he did not. He did not want to be restricted, however, to scientific method in his efforts to understand personality. He believed much useful nonscientific information had accumulated through the years, and that it would be foolhardy not to make use of that information. In fact, Allport did not want to be restricted to any particular approach or viewpoint in his attempt to understand personality: "Better to expand and refashion one's theories until they do some measure of justice to the richness and dignity of human personality, than to clip and compress personality until it fits one closed system of thought" (1937, p. vii).

In 1937, Allport reviewed the history of the word *personality*, beginning with its ties to the Latin word *persona,* which means mask. He then reviewed 50 definitions of personality before arriving at his own, now-famous, definition: "Personality is the dynamic organization within the individual of those psychophysical systems that determine his unique adjustments to his environment" (1937, p. 48).

In 1961, Allport changed the phrase "unique adjustments to his environment" to "characteristic behavior and thought" (p. 28). Because Allport's definition of personality acts as a summary of most of his major concepts, here we examine its key components more carefully.

Dynamic Organization

Personality, though always organized, is constantly changing, or dynamic. According to Allport, personality is never something that is; rather, it is something that is **becoming.** Although enough similarity exists within people to maintain their identity from one experience to another, in a sense they never are quite the same people they were before a particular experience. Allport borrowed this idea from the ancient Greek philosopher Heraclitus, who said, "Nothing is, everything is becoming," and "No man can step into the same river twice." It is the same with personality; it has organization and continuity within the person, but it is constantly changing or becoming something different.

Psychophysical Systems

According to Allport, "The term 'psychophysical' reminds us that personality is neither exclusively mental nor exclusively biological. The organization entails the operation of both body and mind, inextricably fused into a personal unit" (1937, p. 48).

Determine

According to Allport, personality is not an abstraction or a convenient fiction; it actually exists: "Personality is something and does something. . . . It is what lies behind specific acts and within the individual" (1937, p. 48). Allport believed a person is by no means simply a passive reactor to the environment. Rather, a person's behavior is generated from within by the personality structure.

Characteristic Behavior and Thought

As we mentioned, Allport revised his definition of personality in 1961 by deleting the phrase "unique adjustments to the environment" and replacing it with "characteristic behavior and thought." He did so because he believed the earlier statement placed too much emphasis on survival and thus on the satisfaction of biological needs. His revised definition covered all behavior and thought whether or not they were related to adaptation to the environment. One's dreams for the future, for example, are just as important as satisfying the hunger drive, but they have little or nothing to do with biological survival.

Both versions of Allport's definition of personality stressed the importance of individuality. In the 1937 definition, the word *unique* was used; in the 1961 definition, the word *characteristic* was used. Indeed, as we have seen, the emphasis on studying individual human beings rather than on the laws governing all human beings was a constant theme running through all of Allport's work. He repeatedly said that no two humans are the same, and therefore the only way to learn about a particular person is to study that particular person.

Character, Temperament, and Type

Allport distinguished among the terms **personality**, **character**, **temperament**, and **type.**

Character

Allport was bothered by the term **character** because it implied the moral judgment of a person, such as when it is said that a person has "a good character." Allport preferred "to define character as personality evaluated, and personality . . . as character devaluated" (1961, p. 32).

Temperament

Allport referred to temperament, intelligence, and physique as the **raw materials of personality** and all three are genetically determined. Temperament is the emotional component of the personality.

Type

A type is a category in which one person can be placed by another person. In other words, we use the word *type* when we describe other people. Types, therefore, are ways of categorizing people. If a person continually acts aggressively, we may say he or she is the aggressive type, which is to say that his or her behavior fits into this category. Personality, conversely, is something that is within a person causing him or her to behave in certain ways. We can say personality generates behavior patterns that can be described as types.

Criteria for an Adequate
Theory of Personality

In 1960, Allport described five characteristics that he believed a good theory of personality should possess.

1. **Views personality as contained within the person.** According to Allport, those theories that explain personality in terms of the various roles people play or in terms of behavior patterns elicited by environmental circumstances are inadequate. In other words, personality must be explained in terms of internal mechanisms rather than external mechanisms.

2. **Views person as filled with variables that contribute to his or her actions.** This statement, related to point 1, was made to show Allport's disdain of those behaviorists who assumed, for methodological reasons, that the human organism was empty. To those psychologists the proper way to study human behavior was to make a "functional analysis" of stimulating conditions (S) and responses to those conditions (R). Such psychologists prided themselves on studying the empty organism (B. F. Skinner led this group, and his theory is discussed in Chapter 9). Allport believed this position was especially distasteful and dehumanizing: "Any theory of personality pretending adequacy must be dynamic and, to be dynamic, must assume a well-stocked organism" (Allport, 1960, p. 26).

3. **Seeks motives for behavior in present instead of past.** Here Allport expressed his dissatisfaction with psychoanalytic theory that traces adult motives to childhood experiences: "People it seems, are busy leading their lives into the future, whereas psychology, for the most part, is busy tracing them into the past" (Allport, 1955, p. 51). According to Allport, neurotics may be prisoners of their past, and psychoanalytic methods may be useful in dealing with them, but the motives for healthy, mature adults are found in the present. Furthermore, healthy, normal adults are aware of their motives and can describe them accurately if asked to do so. We see in our discussion of functional autonomy, later in this chapter, that Allport viewed healthy adult motivation as independent of earlier experiences.

4. **Employs units of measure capable of "living synthesis."** According to Allport, the integrity of the total personality must never be lost. People are more than a collection of test scores or conditioned reflexes. Whatever units of measure are used to describe a person, they must be capable of describing the whole, dynamic personality:

   > To say that John Brown scores in the eightieth percentile of the "masculinity–femininity" variable, in the thirtieth percentile on "need for achievement" and at average on "introversion–extroversion" is only moderately enlightening. Even with a more numerous set of dimensions, with an avalanche of psychometric scores, patterned personality seems to elude the psychodiagnostician. (1960, p. 30)

   Allport's theory never lost sight of the whole person. As we shall see, the unit of measure that he believed made this possible is the "trait."

5. **Adequately accounts for self-awareness.** Humans are the only animals possessing self-awareness, and this fact, according to Allport, must be considered in any adequate account of personality. We explore Allport's attempt to deal with this difficult problem when we discuss the "proprium" later in this chapter.

Allport's Concept of Trait

We have seen that Allport believed an adequate theory of personality would employ units of measure capable of "living synthesis." For Allport, that unit was the trait. To help describe the various traits that people may possess, Allport and Odbert (1936) examined 17,953 adjectives that have been used to characterize people. Allport, however, certainly did not equate traits with names. Traits, for Allport, were actual biophysical structures.

Allport defined a trait as "a neuropsychic structure having the capacity to render many stimuli functionally equivalent, and to initiate and guide equivalent (meaningfully consistent) forms of adaptive and expressive behavior" (1961, p. 347). In other words, a trait causes a person to respond to similar environmental situations in a similar way. According to Allport, traits develop through a combination of innate needs and learning. He gave the following example:

> A young child finding that his mother is nearly always present to satisfy his wants, develops for her an early affective attachment (conditioning). But later other social contacts likewise prove to be conducive to this child's happy and successful adjustment: playmates, for example, or family gatherings, or crowds at the circus. . . . The child gradually comes to seek people, rather than to avoid them. A trait (not an instinct) of gregariousness develops. The child grows eager for social intercourse; he enjoys being with people. When isolated from them for some time, he misses them and becomes restless. The older he grows the more ways he finds of expressing this gregarious interest. He seeks to ally himself with groups of people at the lodge, at the theater, at church; he makes friends and keeps in touch with them, often entertains them, and corresponds with them. . . . Sociability has become a deep and characteristic quality of this individual's personality. Its expression is variable; a wide range of equivalent stimuli arouse it. (1937, pp. 292–293)

Traits account for the consistency in human behavior. Because no two people possess exactly the same pattern of traits, each confronts environmental experiences differently. A person possessing a strong trait of friendliness will react differently to a stranger than a person possessing a strong trait of suspiciousness. In both cases, the stimulus is the same but the reactions are different, because different traits are involved. Or, as Allport explained, "The same fire that melts the butter hardens the egg" (1961, p. 72).

People's traits organize experiences because people confront the world in terms of their traits. For example, if people are basically aggressive, they will be aggressive in a wide range of situations. Traits will guide their behavior because people can respond to the world only in terms of their traits. Traits, therefore, both initiate and

Figure 7–1

How one might react to various situations if one had a strong aggressiveness trait.

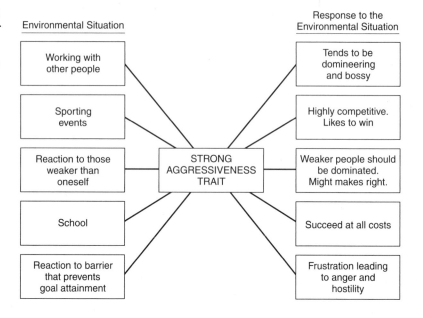

Environmental Situation

Response to the Environmental Situation

Working with other people

Sporting events

Reaction to those weaker than oneself

School

Reaction to barrier that prevents goal attainment

STRONG AGGRESSIVENESS TRAIT

Tends to be domineering and bossy

Highly competitive. Likes to win

Weaker people should be dominated. Might makes right.

Succeed at all costs

Frustration leading to anger and hostility

guide behavior. How a trait influences the way one will react to various situations is shown in Figure 7–1.

Traits cannot be observed directly, and therefore their existence must be inferred. Allport suggested the following criteria for assuming the existence of a trait:

> The *frequency* with which a person adopts a certain type of adjustment is one criterion of a trait. A second criterion is the *range of situations* in which he adopts this same mode of acting. A third criterion is the *intensity* of his reactions in keeping with this "preferred pattern" of behavior. (1961, p. 340)

Allport's theory predicts considerable cross-situational consistency in a person's behavior. The type of consistency displayed is assumed to be determined by the traits a person possesses. Although consistency of behavior is predicted or assumed by most personality theories, it has recently been found that a person's behavior is not nearly as consistent from one situation to another as it had been thought to be. We examine this consistency-versus-inconsistency controversy in more detail when we review social-cognitive theory in Chapter 11.

Interaction of Traits and Situations

In fairness to Allport, he never said that the possession of a trait or a pattern of traits necessarily caused a person to act the same in *all* similar situations. *Some* consistency in behavior must exist before a trait or pattern of traits is assumed to exist, but instances of inconsistency do not necessarily suggest such traits do not exist. For Allport, a person's traits create a possible range of responses to a given situation but it is the nature of the situation itself that determines which of the potential behaviors actually occur.

Allport (1961) described how he thought traits and situations interacted:

> We are forced . . . to the conclusion that while the situation may modify behavior greatly, it can do so only within the limits of the potential provided by the personality. At the same time, we are forced to concede that traits of personality must not be regarded as fixed and stable, operating mechanically to the same degree on all occasions. Rather we should think of traits *as ranges of possible behavior,* to be activated at varying points within the range according to the demands of the situation.
>
> It is wrong to say that Jim has y-amount of anxiety, or of extraversion, or of aggressiveness. Rather we should say that he has upper and lower limits of these traits. This would mean that he never shows more than x-amount and never less than z-amount. His exact location within the range at any given time will depend on what the situational cues bring forth. To put the matter slightly differently, we may conceive of [the] situation as "pulling" a person higher or lower on his scale of potentialities, but always within his particular limits. (pp. 180–181)

Even in the early version of his theory, Allport said, "Perfect consistency [of behavior] will never be found and must not be expected" (1937, p. 330). In 1961, he gave an example of how traits and situations interact to produce behavior: "The young teacher is not always 'friendly'; he is not uniformly 'ambitious' in every direction; his 'enthusiasm' surely depends on what and whom he is teaching" (p. 333).

Thus, Allport believed that different situations, although similar, can arouse trait-related behavior to varying degrees. Because of this belief, Zuroff (1986) concludes that Allport was an early interactionist, instead of a pure trait theorist. An interactionist is one who believes that behavior always results from the combined influence of person variables (e.g., traits) and situation variables. We will say more about person variables, situation variables, and the interactions between them in Chapter 11.

Traits Are Not Habits

Habits are more specific than traits. For example, one may have the habits of brushing one's teeth, putting on clean clothing in the morning, brushing one's hair, washing one's hands, and cleaning one's nails. One has all these habits, however, because one has the trait of cleanliness. In other words, a trait synthesizes a number of specific habits.

Traits Are Not Attitudes

Attitudes, like habits, are more specific than traits. A person has an attitude toward something, for instance, a certain person, a make of automobile, or travel. A trait, conversely, is more general. For example, if a person is basically aggressive, he or she will tend to act aggressively toward strangers, acquaintances, animals, world affairs, and the like. A second distinction between attitudes and traits is that attitudes usually imply evaluation; that is, attitudes are usually for or against something; they are either positive or negative; and they imply either acceptance or rejection of something. Traits, conversely, are responsible for all behavior and cognitions whether or not evaluation is involved.

Types of Traits

First, Allport distinguished between **individual traits** and **common traits.** As their names imply, individual traits are those possessed by a particular individual, and common traits are those shared by several individuals. The distinction between individual and common traits is determined mainly by what is being specified. Any group can be described by its traits. For example, a group can be described as friendly, aggressive, or intelligent. Likewise, any individual can be described by his or her traits; one can be described as friendly, aggressive, or intelligent. When traits are used to describe a group, they are called common traits; when they are used to describe an individual, they are called individual traits. Although recognizing the existence of both types of traits, Allport believed strongly that the personality theorist should focus on individual traits.

The distinction between individual and common traits is often confused by the assumption that an individual trait is one that only a single individual possesses. This assumption is incorrect. It is almost impossible to imagine any individual without some degree of friendliness, honesty, neatness, aggression, or any other trait. What Allport meant by individual uniqueness is the pattern of traits that an individual possesses. That is, one person may have a strong friendliness trait, a weak honesty trait, and a moderate aggressiveness trait. Another person may be moderate in friendliness, honesty, and aggressiveness. When the list of traits is extended and when it is realized that each trait can be possessed to almost any degree, the number of possible trait configurations is extremely large. What Allport meant by individual traits was a unique pattern of traits possessed by a particular individual. Furthermore, it is important to remember that a trait specifies a possible range of behaviors. For example, many people are aggressive but no two people are aggressive in exactly the same way and under exactly the same circumstances. It is because any trait can manifest itself in an almost infinite number of ways that Allport (1937) said, "Strictly speaking, no two persons have precisely the same trait" (p. 297). Thus individuals differ not only in the pattern of traits they possess but also in how any particular trait manifests itself in their personalities.

Borrowing his terms from the philosopher Wilhelm Windelband, Allport insisted the personality theorist use the **idiographic method** of research that is the intense study of a single case, and avoid the **nomothetic method** that studies groups of individuals and analyzes averages. Allport believed averages were merely abstractions and really described no single individual accurately. In other words, Allport believed the only way to learn about a particular person is to study that person, because no two people have exactly the same levels or configuration of traits.

Later in the evolution of his theory, Allport came to believe using the term *trait* to describe both group and individual characteristics was confusing. He therefore retained the term *common traits* to describe characteristics of groups but changed the term *individual trait* to **personal disposition,** which he defined as a "generalized neuropsychic structure (peculiar to the individual), with the capacity to render many stimuli functionally equivalent, and to initiate and guide consistent (equivalent) forms of adaptive and stylistic behavior" (1961, p. 373). Note that the definition of personal disposition is essentially the same as the earlier definition of trait.

Having decided on the study of personal dispositions, it was clear to Allport that not all dispositions a person possesses have the same impact on personality. He therefore distinguished among cardinal, central, and secondary dispositions.

Cardinal Dispositions

If a person possesses a **cardinal disposition,** it influences almost everything he or she does. When you think of Don Juan, for example, you think of a man possessed by romance, and when you think of Florence Nightingale, you think of a person driven by human compassion. Both individuals exemplify cardinal dispositions. Among the adjectives Allport (1937, pp. 302–303) used to describe the cardinal dispositions were: Christlike, Dionysian, Faustian, Machiavellian, Quixotic, and sadistic. Cardinal dispositions are observable in only a small number of people.

Central Dispositions

Think of a person you know quite well. Now pretend you have been asked to write an honest letter of recommendation for that person. Jot down the person's characteristics that you would mention in such a letter. Those terms on your list describe that person's **central dispositions** and summarize the consistencies in the person's behavior. Examples might be punctuality, neatness, creativity, and persistence.

Allport believed each person possesses surprisingly few central dispositions. "When psychology develops adequate diagnostic methods for discovering the major lines along which a particular personality is organized (personal dispositions), it may turn out that the number of such foci will normally vary between five and ten" (1961, p. 367).

Secondary Dispositions

Secondary dispositions apply to a more specific range of behaviors than either cardinal or central dispositions. Secondary dispositions are similar to habits or attitudes but are still more general than either. These include a person's idiosyncrasies such as preferences for certain types of food or clothing.

The Proprium

Earlier we saw that Allport defined personality as a "dynamic organization." We also saw that Allport believed personality consisted of biological as well as psychological structures such as personal dispositions. The fact that all of the diverse aspects of personality are continuous and are organized implies the existence of an organizing agent. In ancient times, this agent was called the soul. Later it was called the self, mind, or ego. Allport believed that these terms were too nebulous, and he renamed the organizer of the personality the **proprium.** The proprium includes all the facts about a person that make him or her unique.

This inward organization and self-awareness are not present at birth but rather, evolve slowly over time. Allport believed full propriate functioning characterizes only the final stage of an eight-stage developmental sequence that starts at birth and continues until adulthood.

1. **Sense of bodily "me" (first year).** Infants learn their bodies exist because of the many sensations they experience. Although the sense of bodily "me" is the first aspect of the proprium to evolve, it remains a lifelong anchor of our self-awareness. The sense of bodily "me" is used to distinguish what is part of oneself, and therefore, warm and intimate, and what is foreign to oneself. Allport (1961) vividly demonstrated the difference between what is perceived as belonging to oneself and what is not:

   > Think first of swallowing the saliva in your mouth, or do so. Then imagine spitting it into a tumbler and drinking it. What seemed natural and "mine" suddenly becomes disgusting and alien. Or, to continue this unpleasant line of thought for a moment, picture yourself sucking the blood from a prick in your finger; then imagine sucking blood from a bandage around your finger. What you perceive as belonging intimately to your body is warm and welcome; what you perceive as separate becomes instantly cold and foreign. (p. 114)

2. **Sense of self-identity (second year).** With this sense comes the realization that there is self-continuity over time. That is, children come to realize they are the same people although there are changes in their size and experiences. The development of language is directly related to the development of **self-identity.** Specifically, children learn their name, which acts as an anchor for their identity through a variety of experiences. "By hearing his name repeatedly the child gradually sees himself as a distinct and recurrent point of reference. The name acquires significance for him in the second year of life. With it comes awareness of independent status in the social group" (Allport, 1961, p. 115).

3. **Sense of self-esteem (third year).** This is the feeling of pride that emerges when children learn they can do things on their own. During this stage, children often seek complete independence from adult supervision.

4. **Sense of self-extension (fourth year).** During this stage children learn the meaning of the word *mine.* Now they realize that not only do their bodies belong to them but so do certain toys, games, parents, pets, sisters, and so on. At this time, the sense of self is extended to external objects.

5. **Emergence of self-image (fourth to sixth year).** During this stage, children develop a conscience that acts as a frame of reference for "the good me" and "the bad me." Now children can compare what they do with the expectations others have of them. It is also during this stage that children begin to formulate future goals for themselves.

6. **Emergence of self as a rational coper (sixth to twelfth year).** At this stage, children recognize "thinking" as a means of solving life's problems. In a sense, children begin to think about thinking.

7. **Emergence of propriate striving (twelfth year through adolescence).** At this stage, people become almost completely future oriented. Long-term goals are created that give organization and meaning to life. According to

Allport, the primary objective in life is not **need reduction,** as so many theorists would have us believe. Rather, it is **need induction** that is important. In other words, healthy adults create problems by formulating future goals that, in many cases, are unattainable:

> Propriate striving confers unity upon personality, but it is never the unity of fulfillment, of repose, or of reduced tension. The devoted parent never loses concern for his child; the devotee of democracy adopts a lifelong assignment in his human relationships. The scientist, by the very nature of his commitment, creates more and more questions, never fewer. Indeed, the measure of our intellectual maturity, one philosopher suggests, is our capacity to feel less and less satisfied with our answers to better and better problems. (Allport, 1955, p. 67)

The possession of long-range goals, regarded as central to one's personal existence, distinguishes the human being from the nonhuman animal, the adult from the child, and in many cases, the healthy personality from the sick.

8. **Emergence of self as knower (adulthood).** The final stage of development occurs when the self is aware of, unifies, and transcends the preceding seven aspects of the self. In other words, the **self as knower** synthesizes all of the propriate functions. In our daily experience it is most often the case that several, if not all, aspects of the proprium function simultaneously. Allport (1961) gave the following example:

> Suppose that you are facing a difficult and critical examination. No doubt you are aware of your high pulse rate and of the butterflies in your stomach (bodily self); also of the significance of the exam in terms of your past and future (self-identity); of your prideful involvement (self-esteem); of what success or failure may mean to your family (self-extension); of your hopes and aspirations (self-image); of your role as the solver of problems on the examination (rational agent); and of the relevance of the whole situation to your long-range goals (propriate striving). In actual life, then, a fusion of propriate states is the rule. And behind these experienced states of selfhood you catch indirect glimpses of yourself as "knower." (p. 137)

The term *proprium* refers to all eight aspects of the self. The development of the proprium is summarized in Table 7–1.

Conscience

According to Allport, the conscience emerges along with several aspects of the proprium, especially self-esteem, self-image, and propriate striving. Allport viewed conscience evolving in two stages. First a **must conscience** exists, which is the only type of conscience a child has. The must conscience evolves out of parental restrictions and prohibitions, which, after becoming internalized, guide behavior even when the parents are not present. On this point, Allport agreed with Freud: "There seems to be no doubt that this early stage of conscience is, as Freud argued, due to the internalization of tribal and parental values. Violation causes anxiety and guilt even though immediate punishment does not threaten" (1961, p. 135).

Table 7–1
Eight Stages in the Development of the Proprium and Functions Associated with Them

PERIOD OF DEVELOPMENT	PROPRIATE DEVELOPMENT
1. First year	Infant learns that he or she exists, through the many sensations experienced
2. Second year	Child learns that identity remains intact although circumstances change
3. Third year	Feeling of pride results from individual accomplishments
4. Fourth year	Child extends self-image by recognizing that certain objects belong to him or her
5. Fourth to sixth year	Child develops a conscience or a superego; now can deal with the concepts of right and wrong
6. Sixth to twelfth year	Child uses reason and logic to solve complex problems
7. Twelfth year through adolescence	Child formulates future goals and begins to organize his or her life around them
8. Adulthood	Individual who has synthesized the preceding stages of development emerges

Gradually must conscience is displaced by **ought conscience.** Must conscience is sustained by fear of punishment whereas ought conscience is tied closely to the person's proprium. For example, the young adult realizes that if certain long-term goals are to be attained certain experiences ought to be sought out and others avoided. Allport (1961) summarized the distinction between must conscience and ought conscience:

> There remain many "musts" in adulthood, but they spring now from a rational recognition of consequences and are seldom felt any longer as matters of conscience: I must obey traffic regulations. I must have the electric wiring repaired. I must not show her my true feelings. But, on the other hand, I ought to vote. I ought to write that letter. I ought to study harder. I ought to pursue the good as I see it. These are propriate value-judgments. No one will punish me if I fail to live according to my own preferred style. . . . Mature conscience, then, is a sense of duty to keep one's self-image in an acceptable shape, to continue one's chosen lines of propriate striving—in short, to build (and not tear down) one's style of being. Conscience becomes a kind of generic self-guidance. Emphasis has shifted from tribal and parental control to individual control. (p. 136)

Thus Allport agreed with Freud concerning the development of must conscience but disagreed with Freud's contention that the internalized values of authority figures guide a person's moral behavior throughout his or her life. Allport did agree that the morality of some adults is governed by infantile prohibitions and restrictions, but these adults are unhealthy. Normal adult morality is of the ought variety and is therefore rational, future oriented, and personal.

Functional Autonomy

As we have seen, most theories of personality also contain, either explicitly or implicitly, a theory of motivation. Allport had four requirements for an adequate theory of motivation.

1. **It must recognize the contemporary nature of motives.** As we have seen, Allport did not believe the child is the father of the man, as the psychoanalysts believed. According to Allport, for a motive to be a motive, it must exist in the present. "Whatever moves us," Allport said, "must move us now" (1961, p. 220).

2. **It must allow for the existence of several types of motives.** Allport believed that to reduce all human motivation to one factor, such as drive reduction or aspiring for superiority, was foolhardy. "Motives are so diverse in type that we find it difficult to discover the common denominator" (1961, p. 221).

3. **It must recognize the importance of cognitive processes.** To Allport, it was impossible to truly understand a person's motives without knowing his or her plans, values, and intentions. He believed that perhaps the best way to understand a person's personality structure is to ask, What do you want to be doing 5 years from now? Like Adler and Erikson, Allport emphasized the importance of conscious, cognitive processes as guides for behavior.

4. **It must recognize that each person's pattern of motivation is unique.** Just as no two people have the same configuration of traits, neither do they have the same configuration of motives. Because Allport believed traits initiated behavior, they can be equated with motives. Allport asked, "What is the relation between units of motivation and units of personality? I would suggest that all units of motivation are at the same time units of personality" (1960, p. 118).

Allport introduced a motivational concept he believed satisfied the foregoing requirements. This was **functional autonomy,** which he defined as "any acquired system of motivation in which the tensions involved are not of the same kind as the antecedent tensions from which the acquired system developed" (1961, p. 229). Allport believed the concept of functional autonomy to be so important that he referred to it as "a declaration of independence for the psychology of personality" (1937, p. 207).

Functional autonomy, which is probably Allport's most famous concept, simply means that the reasons why an adult now engages in some form of behavior are not the same reasons that originally caused him or her to engage in that behavior. In other words, past motives are not functionally related to present motives. Allport offered the following examples:

An ex-sailor has a craving for the sea, a musician longs to return to his instrument after an enforced absence, a miser continues to build his useless pile. Now the sailor may have first acquired his love for the sea as an incident in his struggle to earn a living. The sea was "secondary reinforcement" for his hunger drive. But now the ex-sailor is perhaps a wealthy banker; the original motive is destroyed and yet the hunger for the sea persists and even increases in intensity. The musician may first have been stung by a slur on his inferior performance into mastering his instrument; but now he is safely beyond these taunts, and finds that he loves his instrument more than anything else in the world. The miser perhaps learned his habit of thrift in dire necessity, but his miserliness persists and becomes stronger with the years even after the necessity has been relieved. (1961, p. 227)

A student who first undertakes a field of study in college because it is required, because it pleases the parents, or because it comes at a convenient hour may end up finding himself absorbed in the topic, perhaps for life. The original motives may be entirely lost. What was a means to an end becomes an end in itself. (1961, pp. 235–236)

Allport believed that when motives became part of the proprium they are pursued for their own sake and not for external encouragement or reward. Such motives are self-sustaining because they have become part of the person. To say that healthy adults pursue goals because they are rewarded for doing so was, to Allport, ridiculous. For example, Allport commented:

How hollow to think of Pasteur's concern for reward, or for health, food, sleep, or family, as the root of his devotion to his work. For long periods of time he was oblivious to them all, losing himself in the white heat of research. And the same passion is seen in the histories of geniuses who in their lifetimes received little or no reward for their work. (1961, p. 236)

Allport distinguished between two types of functional autonomy: (1) **Perseverative functional autonomy** refers to repetitious activities in which one blindly engages, and that once served a purpose but no longer do so. These activities occur independently of reward and independently of the past but are low-level activities of little importance. An example is when a man still rises at 7:30 each morning although he has been retired for some time. (2) **Propriate functional autonomy** refers to an individual's interests, values, goals, attitudes, and sentiments.

Allport suggested that propriate functional autonomy was governed by these three principles:

1. **Principle of organizing energy level.** This principle states that when one no longer needs to be concerned with survival and early adjustments in life, a considerable amount of energy becomes available to that person. Because this energy is no longer needed for basic adaptation, it can be diverted into propriate striving—for instance, future goals.
2. **Principle of mastery and competence.** There is an innate need for healthy adults to increase their efficiency and effectiveness and to aspire to greater mastery. In other words, according to Allport, healthy humans have a need to become better and better at more and more tasks. This is another case of drive induction, instead of drive reduction.
3. **Principle of propriate patterning.** The person's proprium is the frame of reference that determines what is pursued in life and what is not. This means that although motives become functionally independent of the past, they do not become independent of the proprium. In other words, all motives must be compatible with the total self (proprium). This ensures the consistency and the integration of the personality.

Not all behavior is caused by functionally autonomous motives. Much human behavior is stimulated by biological drives, reflex action, reward, and habit. Allport recognized this but believed behavior under the control of functionally autonomous

motives was characteristically human and therefore should be the personality theorist's focus of study.

The Healthy, Mature Adult Personality

Allport's theory did not grow out of psychoanalysis. In fact, he was not a psychotherapist and was not much interested in emotionally disturbed people. He believed strongly that the principles governing the healthy adult personality could not
be learned by studying animals, children, the past, or neurotics. According to Allport, the difference between a neurotic and a healthy person is that the former's motives lie in the past whereas the latter's lie in the present or future. Allport's
humanistic orientation is clearly seen in his following lament:

> We find today many studies of criminals, few of law-abiders; many of fear, few of
> courage; more on hostility than on affiliation; much on blindness in man, little on
> his vision; much on his past, little on his outreaching into the future. (1955, p. 18)

The concern that Allport had for studying healthy humans instead of neurotics
is remarkably close to the position taken later by Maslow (see Chapter 15). Maslow
attempted to correct the situation by exploring the lives of what he called self-
actualizing people. The list of characteristics that Maslow found such persons to
possess is similar to the following list of attributes Allport believed characterized the
normal, healthy adult.

1. **Capacity for self-extension.** Healthy adults participate in a wide range
   of events. They have many friends and hobbies and tend to be active politically or religiously.
2. **Capacity for warm human interactions.** Healthy adults are capable of
   intimate relationships with others without being possessive or jealous.
   Such people are compassionate as evidenced by their ability to tolerate
   major differences in values and beliefs between themselves and others.
3. **Demonstration of emotional security and self-acceptance.** Healthy adults
   have the tolerance necessary to accept the conflicts and frustrations inevitable in life. They also have a positive image of themselves. This is
   contrasted with the immature person who is filled with self-pity and has
   a negative self-image.
4. **Demonstration of realistic perceptions.** Healthy adults see events as they
   are, not as they hoped they would be. Such persons display good common
   sense when appraising a situation and in determining adjustments to it.
5. **Demonstration of self-objectification.** Healthy adults have an accurate
   picture of their own assets and liabilities. They also have a good sense of
   humor. Humor necessitates the ability to laugh at what one cherishes,
   including oneself. Persons who are not sure of themselves see nothing
   funny about jokes directed at them or at what they believe.
6. **Demonstration of unifying philosophy of life.** According to Allport, the
   lives of healthy adults are "ordered or steered toward some selected goal

or goals. Each person has something quite special to live for, a major intention" (1961, pp. 294–295).

Allport, like Jung and Erikson and, to a somewhat lesser degree, Adler, placed great importance on religion; and like Jung, Allport believed the importance of religion can be realized only in adulthood. Allport believed all healthy adults have a need for some unifying orientation, and although this orientation is commonly religious it does not need to be:

> Psychologically speaking we should point to the close analogy that exists between a religious orientation and all other high-level schemata that influence the course of becoming. Every man, whether he is religiously inclined or not, has his own ultimate presuppositions. He finds he cannot live his life without them, and for him they are true. Such presuppositions, whether they are called ideologies, philosophies, notions, or merely hunches about life, exert creative pressure upon all conduct that is subsidiary to them (which is to say, upon nearly *all* of a man's conduct). (Allport, 1955, pp. 95–96)

We have more to say about Allport's views on religion later but first we present Allport's view of the unhealthy individual.

Unhealthy Persons

According to Allport, the healthy person is one who displays the six characteristics listed above and who is in a constant state of becoming. Such a person is future oriented. The unhealthy person is one whose growth has been stifled. The motives of unhealthy persons are often found in his or her past rather than in the present or future. In his explanation of why some children develop into unhealthy adults, Allport essentially accepted Horney's position:

> All in all a generous minimum of security seems required in early years for a start toward a productive life-style. Without it the individual develops a pathological craving for security, and is less able than others to tolerate setbacks in maturity. Through his insistent demanding, jealousy, depredations, and egoism he betrays the craving that still haunts him. By contrast, the child who receives adequate gratification of his infant needs is more likely to be prepared to give up his habits of demanding, and to learn tolerance for his later frustrations. Having completed successfully one stage of development he is free to abandon the habits appropriate to this stage and to enter the mature reaches of becoming. Having known acceptance in an affectionate environment he learns more readily to accept himself, to tolerate the ways of the world, and to handle the conflicts of later life in a mature manner. (1955, p. 32)

To overcome his or her difficulties, the unhealthy person must experience the love that he or she missed early in life. This love can be provided by family, friends, or a therapist. In any case, "Love received and love given comprise the best form of therapy" (Allport, 1955, p. 33).

It is important to note that, according to Allport, the unhealthy person becomes healthy when he or she begins living in accordance with his or her proprium—that is, in accordance with his or her own personal goals, values, and aspirations. Health, therefore, is not defined in terms of adjustment to societal standards. In fact, conformity to societal standards can cause otherwise healthy persons to become unhealthy or such conformity can make unhealthy persons even more unhealthy. Allport explained why:

> Society itself is sick. Why then make a patient content with its injustices, hypocrisies, and wars? And to what society shall we adjust the patient? To his social class, thus making him provincial and depriving him of aspiration? To his nation, thus giving him no vision of mankind as a whole? It is doubtful that we can accept society (any society) as a standard for a healthy personality. A head-hunter society demands well-adjusted head-hunters as citizens, but is the deviant in this group who questions the value of decapitation necessarily an immature human being? (1961, p. 305)

The Nature of Prejudice

Allport began his book *The Nature of Prejudice* (1958a) with the following statement:

> Civilized men have gained notable mastery over energy, matter, and inanimate nature generally, and are rapidly learning to control physical suffering and premature death. But, by contrast, we appear to be living in the Stone Age so far as our handling of human relationships is concerned. (p. viii)

One factor interfering with positive relationships among humans is the inclination toward **prejudice.** Although the term *prejudice* now has negative connotations, that was not always the case. Allport (1958a) discussed the evolution of the term:

> (1) To the ancients, *praejudicium* meant a *precedent*—a judgment based on previous decisions and experiences.
> (2) Later, the term, in English, acquired the meaning of a judgment formed before due examination and consideration of the facts—a premature or hasty judgment.
> (3) Finally the term acquired also its present emotional flavor or favorableness or unfavorableness that accompanies such a prior and unsupported judgment. (p. 7)

Thus traditionally the term*prejudice* meant to prejudge and that prejudgment could be either positive or negative. Allport (1958a) found the following definition of prejudice acceptable: "*A feeling favorable or unfavorable, toward a person or thing, prior to, or not based on, actual experience*" (p. 7). Projecting positive attributes onto members of a group (e.g., members of one's family, religion, political party, gender, ethnic group, or nation) exemplifies *positive prejudice.* Projecting negative attributes onto members of a group exemplifies *negative prejudice.* In both cases, individuals are prejudged because of their group membership and without any knowledge of them as individuals.

Closely related to prejudice is the natural tendency for humans to generalize from their experience. From experience, categories, concepts, beliefs, and values are formed that guide subsequent behavior. That is, although an individual's experience is always with particular people or events, that experience must be generalized so past experience can guide future behavior. According to Allport (1958a), such generalization is natural and reasonable: "Overcategorization is perhaps the commonest trick of the human mind. . . . Life is so short, and the demands upon us for practical adjustments are so great, that we cannot let our ignorance detain us in our daily transactions" (p. 9). Allport continued, "Once formed, categories are the basis of normal prejudgment. We cannot possibly avoid this process. Orderly living depends upon it. . . . Open-mindedness is considered to be a virtue. But, strictly speaking, it cannot occur" (p. 19).

The generalization of experience into categories can have three results: (1) the categories can act as reasonable and effective guides for subsequent behavior; (2) the categories can be found to be incorrect and are revised so they can effectively guide subsequent behavior; (3) the categories can be found to be incorrect but are not revised. Although in all three cases prejudgment is involved, the latter is now most often associated with prejudice. That is, the negative categorization of a group of objects or persons is formed and thereafter is immune to modification in spite of experiences to the contrary. Such a categorization is referred to as a *stereotype*.

As an example of how stereotypic beliefs are maintained independent of the facts, Allport described a study in which letters were sent to hotel managers requesting hotel reservations. One letter was signed "Mr. Greenberg" and the other "Mr. Lockwood." Ninety-three percent of the managers offered accommodations to Mr. Lockwood and only 36 percent to Mr. Greenberg. Here we have an example of ethnic prejudice. Although none of the managers knew Mr. Greenberg, he was placed into a category toward which there was an attitude of hostility and rejection. The facts concerning Mr. Greenberg were not an issue; he was rejected because he belonged to a category of individuals *presumed* to have negative characteristics.

Allport (1958a) quoted a wit as defining prejudice as "being down on something you're not up on" (p. 8). It is as if the prejudiced person is saying, "My mind is made up, don't confuse me with the facts." Allport illustrated this point with the following dialogue:

Mr. X: The trouble with the Jews is that they only take care of their own group.

Mr. Y: But the record of the Community Chest campaign shows that they give more generously, in proportion to their numbers, to the general charities of the community, than do non-Jews.

Mr. X: That shows they are always trying to buy favor and intrude into Christian affairs. They think of nothing but money; that is why there are so many Jewish bankers.

Mr. Y: But a recent study shows that the percentage of Jews in the banking business is negligible, far smaller than the percentage of non-Jews.

Mr. X: That's just it; they don't go in for respectable business; they are only in the movie business or run night clubs. (1958a, pp. 13–14)

Like the natural inclination to form categories, another factor that facilitates the formation of negative prejudice is the tendency to form in-groups. That is, people tend to identify with their family, neighborhood, city, state, nation, ethnic group, religion, and gender, and in-groups imply out-groups. Although perceiving oneself as a member of one group does not necessarily imply a negative attitude toward individuals who are not members of that group, it often does so. Some families, religions, organizations, and even nations preach that its members are superior to nonmembers.

Group membership has its advantages. Life is easier if we are surrounded by individuals who share our beliefs, customs, and values. Conversely, life is more difficult when we confront individuals who are "different." However, it is possible to recognize differences without being hostile toward them:

> In summary, in-group memberships are vitally important to individual survival. These memberships constitute a web of habits. When we encounter an outsider who follows different customs we unconsciously say, "He breaks my habits." Habit-breaking is unpleasant. We prefer the familiar. We cannot help but feel a bit on guard when other people seem to threaten or even question our habits. Attitudes partial to the in-group, or to the reference group, do not necessarily require that attitudes toward other groups be antagonistic—even though hostility often helps to intensify the in-group cohesion. Narrow circles can, without conflict, be supplemented by larger circles of loyalty. This happy condition is not often achieved, but it remains from the psychological point of view a hopeful possibility. (1958a, p. 45)

Because of the natural tendencies to generalize from limited experience and to form in-groups, combating prejudice is a difficult task. The situation is further complicated by the tendency for humans to become aggressive when they are frustrated. Thus when an individual experiences personal or economic failure, he or she may seek a *scapegoat* to aggress toward, that is, someone or something to blame for his or her difficulties. With all of these natural tendencies facilitating the formation of prejudice, only a unified societal effort will overcome them. According to Allport, only if childrearing practices, the judicial system, educational practices, religious teachings, the media, politics, and other social agencies act to discourage prejudice, is there any chance of reducing its disruptive influence.

Allport believed that only a "One World" perspective in which people identify with all of humankind will allow peaceful coexistence among groups. That is, we must realize that although as individuals we are members of various groups, ultimately we are all members of the same group and, in a sense, we are all living in the same house—the earth. Allport (1958a) concluded his book with the following timely observation:

> America, on the whole, has been a staunch defender of the right to be the same or different, although it has fallen short in many of its practices. The question before us is whether progress toward tolerance will continue, or whether, as in many regions of the world, a fatal retrogression will set in. The whole world watches to see whether the democratic ideal in human relationships is viable. Can citizens learn to seek their own welfare and growth not at the expense of their fellow men, but in concert with them? The human family does not yet know the answer, but hopes it will be affirmative. (p. 480)

Religion

Freud viewed the need for religion as a characteristic of the weak or the neurotic whereas Allport believed a religious orientation often characterizes the healthy adult personality. Allport believed, however, that embracing some forms of religion was beneficial and embracing other forms was harmful. In other words, for Allport, there was healthy religion and unhealthy religion.

Extrinsic Religion

Extrinsic religion is unhealthy religion. It is immature and is often a carryover from childhood. Such religion constructs a deity who favors the interests of those who believe in him, "like a Santa Claus or an overindulgent father. Or the sentiment may be of a tribal sort: 'My church is better than your church. God prefers my people to your people'" (Allport, 1961, p. 300). Extrinsic religion is often embraced because it is superficially useful. For example, membership in a church can be used to make business contacts or to become a respected member of the community. Extrinsic religion tends to be a divisive factor in a person's life rather than a unifying theme. In fact, embracing extrinsic religion creates an individual who lacks most, if not all, of the criteria of a healthy, mature adult:

> Studies show that ethnic prejudice is more common among churchgoers than among nonchurchgoers. This fact alone shows that religion is often divisive rather than unifying. Extrinsic religion lends support to exclusions, prejudices, hatreds that negate all our criteria of maturity. The self is not extended; there is no warm relating of self to others, no emotional security, no realistic perception, no self-insight or humor. (Allport, 1961, p. 300)

Insofar as Freud criticized extrinsic religion, Allport agreed with him.

Intrinsic Religion

Intrinsic religion is healthy religion. Intrinsic religion motivates a person to seek and follow the value underlying all reality for its own sake and as an end in itself; directs the course of a person's life and development; facilitates the realization that many important experiences transcend one's own existence; provides a possible explanation for the many mysteries that characterize human existence, such as the fact that human behavior appears to be both free and determined, the simultaneous existence of good and evil, and the fact that the innocent often suffer; and creates a perspective within which to evaluate one's self and organize one's life. Intrinsic religion encourages an identification with all of humanity, not just with those who share one's beliefs. By providing a means by which a person can relate meaningfully to the totality of existence, intrinsic religion provides a unifying theme that characterizes the healthy, mature adult personality. With intrinsic religion in mind, Allport (1950) said, "A man's religion is the audacious bid he makes to bind himself to creation and to the Creator. It is his ultimate attempt to enlarge and to complete his own personality by finding the supreme context in which he rightly belongs" (p. 142). Allport himself was a devout Episcopalian and from 1938 to 1966, he offered a series of 33 meditations in the Appleton chapel at Harvard University (Allport, 1978).

In an effort to explore why churchgoers are often more prejudiced than nonchurchgoers, Allport and Ross (1967) created the Religious Orientation Scale (ROS). The scale included subscales that differentiated between a tendency toward extrinsic religion as opposed to intrinsic religion. Contrary to their expectations, Allport and Ross found that not everyone could be categorized as either intrinsically or extrinsically religious. Rather, they found that some people embraced *both* kinds of religion. These people were labeled *indiscriminately proreligious.* It was found that those categorized as indiscriminately proreligious were most prejudiced followed by those embracing extrinsic religion. Those embracing intrinsic religion were least prejudiced. The ROS has become a popular research tool, and we will discuss some of its recent applications when we evaluate Allport's theory at the end of this chapter.

Letters from Jenny

Given Allport's emphasis on the individual, how does one go about attempting to understand a specific person's personality? Allport believed that one of the best methods was to use **personal documents** such as diaries, autobiographies, letters, or interviews. Allport's most thorough use of personal documents to describe an individual's personality was a collection of 301 letters written by Jenny Grove Masterson (a pseudonym) during an 11-year period. The final version of this study was published as *Letters from Jenny* in 1965, although Allport had worked on the case for a number of years prior to that time.

Jenny was born in Ireland in 1868 and moved to Canada when she was 5. She had five younger sisters and one younger brother, all of whom were very dependent on her because her father had died when she was 18. Jenny outraged her family when she married a divorced railway inspector. She and her husband moved to Chicago, where she described life as boring. Her husband died in 1897, when she was 29 years old. Shortly after her husband's death, Jenny gave birth to her only child, whom she named Ross. She worked hard and devoted herself to Ross. When Ross reached puberty she enrolled him in an expensive boarding school. In order to afford this private school, she took a job as a librarian and lived primarily on milk and cereal in a small windowless room. Until Ross was 17, he and his mother were very close, but at that time he left home to go to Princeton. In his sophomore year Ross enlisted in the army, where he served in the Ambulance Corps. Before Ross went overseas to France, Jenny visited him at Princeton and met two of his friends, Glenn and Isabel. It was with Glenn and Isabel that Jenny was later to correspond.

When Ross returned home, he had changed completely and, except for finishing his degree at Princeton, his life was characterized by a series of failures and quarrels with his mother. The most intense quarrel followed Jenny's discovery of Ross's secret marriage. On this Allport commented, "On his first visit to her [Jenny] following her discovery she drove him out of her room with violent denunciations and a threat to have him arrested if he ever tried to see her again" (1965, p. 6). Following this encounter, Jenny contacted Ross's old friends, Glenn and Isabel, who were now married and teaching in an eastern college town. They offered "to keep in touch" with Jenny, and the result was 301 letters. The correspondence started in

March 1926, when Jenny was 58, and continued until October 1937, when Jenny died, at the age of 70. She outlived her son Ross by 8 years.

By 1928, Ross had abandoned his wife and begun a relationship with another woman named Marie. In a letter written in 1929, Jenny mentioned Ross's poor health. He suffered from an ear infection and, when they operated, the doctors found a tumor on the inner ear and an abscess on the outer tissue covering of the brain. Ross did not recover from his illness and died shortly afterward. In a letter written toward the end of 1929, Jenny blames Marie, who she refers to as a "chip" (whore), for Ross's death.

> My affairs. Oh, they are all in turmoil. The chip lady (although) all dissolved in tears, and of course heartbroken, is not too liquid to forget that material things count in this mundane sphere, and lo! she claimed Ross's clothes, and Ross's car. [She claims to be Ross's closest relative.] If she is Ross's nearest relative it is she who will receive the [Veteran's Administration's] compensation, and that would be tragic enough to make one die of laughter. She has only known him 6 months. February was the beginning of their "Great Romance"—dirty and low as they are made—the low contemptible street dog. She killed Ross—morally and physically. (Allport, 1965, pp. 73–74)

Following Ross's funeral and cremation, Jenny was reported to have said, "The body is consumed, now we'll have a good steak dinner" (recollection of Isabel, in Allport, 1965, p. 153).

In 1931, Jenny entered a home for women where she lived until her death. The superintendent of the home reported that she had become unbearably difficult during the year prior to her death. For example, she swept her dinner on the floor if it displeased her, and she hit one of her fellow boarders over the head with a pail. The superintendent considered moving her to an institution for the insane shortly before she died.

Allport had 36 judges read Jenny's letters in sequence and they, along with Allport, used 198 trait names to describe Jenny. But when synonymous traits were lumped together, it was observed that Jenny could be described accurately using eight trait names. They were:

1. Quarrelsome–suspicious
2. Self-centered
3. Independent
4. Dramatic
5. Aesthetic–Artistic
6. Aggressive
7. Cynical–Morbid
8. Sentimental

Using a computer, Jeffrey Paige (1966), one of Allport's students, performed a complex statistical factor analysis of Jenny's letters and isolated eight "factors" characterizing them.

1. Aggression
2. Possessiveness
3. Need for Affiliation

4. Need for Autonomy
5. Need for Familial Acceptance
6. Sexuality
7. Sentience (love of art, literature, etc.)
8. Martyrdom

On reviewing Paige's study, Allport concluded that the automated approach yielded about the same traits as did his "longhand" approach. There is probably no better example of what Allport meant by idiographic research than his analysis of Jenny's letters. It is because of this type of research that Allport has been accused of being more of an artist than a scientist.

Study of Expressive Behavior and Values

Besides his studies of religion, prejudice, rumor, and his extensive idiographic study of Jenny through her letters, Allport also investigated expressive behavior and values. His studies of both expressive behavior and values retained his emphasis on the importance of the individual. His research on expressive behavior, for example, investigated a person's unique facial expressions, style of walking, speech mannerisms, and handwriting (Allport & Cantril, 1934; Allport & Vernon, 1933). His *Study of Values,* first published with Vernon in 1931, is now in its third edition. To study values, Allport, Vernon, and Lindzey (1960) devised a scale that attempted to determine the extent to which a person emphasized certain values in his or her life. Allport observed that the scale of values actually combines nomothetic and idiographic methodologies: "We begin with an instrument that measures six common traits [values], but end with a profile that is strictly personal and individual" (quoted in Evans, 1976, p. 211). The following six values measured by the scale of values were first proposed by Eduard Spranger (1882–1963) in 1913 (Spranger, 1928).

1. *Theoretical.* The person emphasizing this value is primarily concerned with the search for truth.
2. *Economic.* The person emphasizing this value is very pragmatic and interested in the relevance of knowledge.
3. *Aesthetic.* The person emphasizing this value is strongly inclined toward artistic experiences.
4. *Social.* The person emphasizing this value gives high priority to developing and maintaining warm human relationships.
5. *Political.* The person emphasizing this value is primarily interested in attaining power.
6. *Religious.* The person emphasizing this value gives great importance to seeking unity and harmony in the universe.

Allport et al. (1960) reported that the scale produced the expected results; for example, clergymen scored highest on the religious value, art students scored highest on the aesthetic value, and business students scored highest on the economic value.

Evaluation

Empirical Research

Allport was the first to describe the personality in terms of traits, and therefore, the thousands of studies done involving personality traits are directly or indirectly derived from his theory. Also, Allport and his colleagues did more research to test their theoretical notions than any other personality theorists covered thus far in this text. As we have seen, Allport and Ross (1967) devised the Religious Orientation Scale (ROS) to measure kinds of religious commitments and their implications. Since its inception the ROS has been refined (Hood, 1970) and used in numerous other studies. For example, performance on the ROS has been found to be related to psychological health. Bergin, Masters, and Richards (1987) found that a high score on the intrinsic religion scale was negatively related to anxiety and positively related to self-control and effective personal functioning. The opposite relationships were found for performance on the extrinsic religion scale. Watson, Morris, and Hood (1990) found that people scoring high on the intrinsic scale had fewer personal problems than those scoring high on the extrinsic scale. Donahue (1985) and Wulff (1991) review several studies employing the ROS.

As we have seen, Allport and his colleagues also did extensive research on expressive behavior and provided one of the few tools by which to study human values. Although Allport's scale of values is more than 50 years old, this simple, straightforward instrument is still being used. For example, Huntley and Davis (1983) found that physicians scored high on theoretical and social values and businesspeople scored high on political and economic values. It is interesting that the value measures were obtained when the physicians and businesspeople were still undergraduate college students 25 years earlier. Allport's early interest in expressive behavior is now reflected in numerous experiments on nonverbal communication and body language. (See Harper, Wiens, & Matarazzo, 1978, for a review of such studies.)

Finally, as kind of a belated tribute to Allport, there has been a resurgence of interest in the use of idiographic techniques (e.g., the study of personal documents) in the study of personality (e.g., Bem & Allen, 1974; Hermans, 1988; Lamiell, 1981; Pelham, 1993; Runyan, 1983; Stewart, Franz, & Layton, 1988; West, 1983; Wrightman, 1981).

Criticisms

Lack of Scientific Rigor. Allport's theory was often criticized for being unscientific. Because all sciences seek to discover general laws, usually by using nomothetic methods, Allport's emphasis on the idiographic method, in which the single case is studied intensively, seemed unscientific. Furthermore, the study and understanding of unique individuals does not produce principles by which human behavior can be understood in general. For many, Allport's insistence on studying unique individuals is more like art than science. For example, the study of Jenny's letters may be interesting and pleasing but, unless it is possible to generalize what is found to other people, it has little scientific value.

Circularity. In Allport's theory, traits are inferred from behavior and then are used to explain the very behavior from which they were inferred. For example, if we say that Marce is aggressive because she hit Matt, we cannot then say that

Marce hit Matt because she is aggressive. Such circular reasoning tells us nothing about the cause of aggressiveness. Likewise, if a person acts suspiciously in a variety of situations, we conclude that he or she possesses the trait of suspiciousness. When then asked why he or she acts suspiciously we say it is because he or she possesses the trait of suspiciousness. In other words, it cannot be claimed that someone acts suspiciously because they are suspicious. For Allport traits were used to both describe and explain behavior—and that is circular.

Absence of Theory. Some claim that Allport did an admirable job of describing personality but failed to explain it. A person's personality is described in terms of traits or dispositions arranged in a hierarchy, but little is said about how specific traits or dispositions develop or change.

Denial of Important Facts about and Approaches to Study of Personality. Allport was criticized for assuming a discontinuity between animals and humans, between child and adult, and between normal and abnormal. He was criticized for placing too much emphasis on the conscious mind at the expense of the unconscious mind and for stressing internal causes of behavior at the expense of external causes. Probably Allport's most severely criticized concept was functional autonomy. When most, if not all, accepted viewpoints in psychology were attempting to determine the relationship between early experience and adult personality, Allport claimed that such a relationship did not exist.

On the matter of unconscious motivation, it is ironic that the very experience Allport had with Freud that caused Allport to mistrust depth psychology may in fact have supported it. Remember that during his visit with Freud, Allport attempted to disrupt the awkward silence by relating the story of the little boy he observed on the way to Freud's office who apparently had a strong aversion to dirt. On completing his story Freud inquired, "And was that little boy you?" Allport was flabbergasted and concluded that Freud had misinterpreted the significance of the whole incident. Allport told this story many times throughout his lifetime to demonstrate the ineffectiveness of psychoanalytic procedures. Faber (1970), however, suggested that Allport chose that particular story (of many that were possible) because of his preconception that Freud liked to hear "dirty" stories. Allport felt "naughty" in presuming to call on Freud, and he manifested this naughtiness by "pulling a dirty trick" on Freud. According to Faber, Freud saw through the entire situation and with his question attempted to put the conversation on a more honest level. Furthermore, Elms (1972) pointed out that Allport himself was a neat, orderly, punctual, and meticulous person. In fact, Allport was preoccupied with cleanliness and was known as "Mr. Clean Personality." According to Elms, Freud immediately saw Allport's "pathological" concern with dirt, and therefore his question to Allport was not as far off the mark as Allport suggested. Elms claimed Allport tried to change the topic immediately after Freud's question because Allport knew unconsciously that Freud was correct. Such insights demonstrate either that Allport was wrong in rejecting the importance of unconscious motivation, or that nothing exists that psychoanalytic theory cannot explain after the fact.

Inconsistency of Behavior Precludes Description in Terms of Traits. As we have seen, Allport deduced the existence of traits or personal dispositions from consistencies in behavior. Although Allport believed traits or personal dispositions allow a range of behaviors that are situationally determined, he still assumed considerable consistency in behavior across time and similar situations. Mischel (1968) examined

Allport's assumption and concluded, "With the possible exception of intelligence, highly generalized behavioral consistencies have not been demonstrated and the concept of personality traits as broad response predispositions is thus untenable" (p. 146). We say more about Mischel's conclusion and reactions to it in Chapter 11.

Behavioristic Critique.   The behaviorists believe behavior should be explained in terms of environmental stimuli. The postulating of inner mechanisms such as instincts, an unconscious or conscious mind, or traits just creates additional mysteries that need to be explained. Once it is known that certain environmental conditions tend to produce certain types of behavior, the explanation is complete. To say that traits (or anything else) intervene between the environment and behavior is, at best, irrelevant. We say more about the behavioristic position when we review Skinner's explanation of behavior in Chapter 9.

Contributions

Original Concepts and Methodologies.   Allport pioneered the social psychological studies of such complex topics as prejudice, religion, rumor, and values. Also, he did more than anyone to define and clarify the concept of trait. Furthermore, Allport showed that a great deal can be learned about a person by using the straightforward methods of self-reports, personal documents, and the observation of expressive behavior. "Too often," Allport said, "we fail to consult the richest of all sources of data, namely, the subject's own self-knowledge" (1962, p. 413). Allport was willing to use whatever method he believed contributed to an understanding of human behavior. "Whatever contributes to a knowledge of human nature" he said, "is an admissible method to science" (1942, p. 140). Allport then facilitated the spirit of eclecticism that characterizes much of contemporary psychology.

A Refreshingly New Way of Viewing Personality.   Like Adler's, Allport's theory can be considered a forerunner of the existential–humanistic theories that we review in Chapters 13–16. All such theories have in common the emphasis on the uniqueness of the individual, the belief that human motives are not merely biological in nature, that humans are future oriented, and that psychology should be socially relevant. Allport believed in all of these statements. In fact, Allport resisted many powerful trends in psychology because he believed they caused humans to lose their individuality. The healthy person that Allport envisioned creates tension in his or her life by creating future goals, is rational, possesses an "ought" rather than a "must" conscience, and if he or she is religious, intrinsic rather than extrinsic religion is embraced. Also, the healthy person, while belonging to various groups, ultimately identifies with all humankind. Allport's major concern, however, was with the dignity and uniqueness of each human being.

Summary

Allport was the first personality theorist from the United States. In his 1937 definition of personality, he emphasized that personality was dynamic, organized, and unique. He also said that personality was real in that it both initiates and guides behavior. He distinguished between personality and character that implies evaluation; temperament that along with intelligence and physique are the innate "raw materials" of personality; and type that is a classification used by one person to categorize another person. Allport theorized that traits provided the structure, the uniqueness, and the motivation that characterize a person's personality. Individual traits refer to those patterns of traits that characterize individuals and also the way in which a particular trait, such as aggressiveness, manifests itself in a particular individual's personality. What Allport originally called individual traits he later renamed personality dispositions to avoid their confusion with common traits. Common traits are those that characterize groups of individuals.

Nomothetic methods are used to examine what people have in common, and the idiographic method is used to discover what is true about the individual. Because not all personal dispositions have the same influence on one's behavior, Allport distinguished among cardinal dispositions that influence almost everything a person does; central dispositions, of which everyone has five to ten; and secondary dispositions that are only slightly more general than a complex habit.

Allport believed that the mature adult personality developed slowly through eight stages. The major attributes that emerge during each stage are (1) the bodily "me," (2) self-identity, (3) self-esteem, (4) self-extension, (5) self-image, (6) self as rational coper, (7) propriate striving, and (8) self as knower.

Allport distinguished between must conscience that exists when a child's or an unhealthy adult's moral behavior is guided by the internalized values of authority figures, and ought conscience that exists when a person's moral behavior is guided by personal values and propriate strivings. Allport's most controversial concept was functional autonomy, which stated that although one set of circumstances originally may have explained the existence of a motive, that motive can exist in an adult independently of those earlier circumstances. In other words, what was once a means to an end can become an end in itself.

Allport was not interested in studying animals, children, or neurotics. He was mainly interested in healthy, adult humans whom he believed displayed the following characteristics: (1) self-extension, (2) warm human interactions, (3) emotional security and self-acceptance, (4) realistic perceptions, (5) self-objectification, and (6) a unifying philosophy of life.

Like Horney, Allport believed that the unhealthy person is one whose positive growth has been stifled by a lack of childhood security. To overcome the damage done by the lack of security, the person must feel loved by family, friends, or a therapist. In addition to becoming unhealthy because of a lack of security, persons can also become unhealthy by conforming to the mores of society. This is because societies themselves can be sick. Religion too can be either healthy or unhealthy. Extrinsic religion is superficial and not conducive to personal growth; intrinsic religion involves the honest quest for meaning and a higher purpose in life, and can provide the type of unifying philosophy of life that characterizes the personalities of healthy persons.

Allport believed the natural tendencies to generalize, form in-groups, and aggress when frustrated contribute to the formation of negative prejudice. These tendencies can be overcome, however, through a unified societal effort. Also, Allport speculated that if humans would identify with all humankind, intergroup friction could be significantly reduced.

Letters from Jenny (1965) summarized Allport's major idiographic research project in which a woman's dispositions were studied through the 301 letters she had written during an 11-year period. Allport and his colleagues also did extensive research on expressive behavior and created a scale by which human values were measured. Allport's influence on current research on personality can be seen in the popularity of the concept of trait, a call for greater use of personal documents in assessing personality, a reemergence of idiographic research in general, and the popularity of experiments on nonverbal communication and body language.

Allport's theory has been criticized for being unscientific, being circular, not being a true theory, ignoring important facts about personality such as unconscious motivation and the importance of early experience, predicting that human behavior is more consistent than it actually is, and for postulating inner mechanisms that confuse rather than clarify our understanding of personality. Allport's theory has been praised for being the first to study such important topics as rumor, prejudice, traits, and values; showing the benefits of accepting at face value personal reports and documents; using expressive behaviors in assessing personality; and for doing much to promote what is now called existential–humanistic psychology.

Experiential Exercises

1. Apply Allport's criteria for a mature, healthy personality to yourself. First, list the criterion that characterizes you the most, then second most, and so on. Be sure to elaborate on your unifying philosophy of life, if such a philosophy characterizes your life. Using Allport's criteria, do you think you are a mature, healthy person? What, if anything, still needs improvement?

2. According to Allport, prejudice often involves the prejudgment of individuals because of their real or perceived group memberships. With this in mind, give an example of your own positive and negative prejudices. Do you agree with Allport's contention that an identification with all humankind can significantly reduce negative prejudice?

3. Allport distinguished between extrinsic religion and intrinsic religion. Review his distinction and then indicate if religion plays an important role in your life. If so, is it extrinsic or intrinsic religion?

Discussion Questions

1. First state Allport's definition of personality and then discuss each of the definition's major components.
2. Outline Allport's criteria for an adequate personality theory.

3. Explain why Allport had a negative attitude toward the use of lower animals, children, and neurotics as sources of information about personality.

Glossary

Attitude. Attitudes, like habits, are more specific than traits. One can, for example, have a favorable attitude toward boxing, but this may be only a single manifestation of the more general trait of aggressiveness.

Becoming. According to Allport, personality is never static; rather, it is always becoming something else.

Bodily "me." Attribute that emerges during the first stage in the development of the proprium. At this stage, infants learn that their bodies exist because of their sensory experience.

Capacity for self-extension. Participation in a wide range of events that characterizes the healthy, mature adult.

Capacity for warm, human interactions. Ability to have intimate relationships with others without being possessive or jealous. Such an ability characterizes the healthy, mature adult.

Cardinal dispositions. "Ruling passion" that influences almost everything a person does. Only a few individuals possess a cardinal disposition.

Central dispositions. Those qualities about a person that you would mention in a letter of recommendation. The 5–10 characteristics that summarize a particular person's personality.

Character. Description of a person that includes a value judgment. A person's character can be "good" or "bad" whereas a personality cannot be.

Common traits. Traits used to describe a group of individuals.

Emotional security and self-acceptance. Two of the characteristics of a healthy, mature adult.

Extrinsic religion. Superficial religion that is participated in for entirely selfish, pragmatic reasons. Allport considered such religion to be unhealthy.

Functional autonomy. Motive that existed once for some practical reason later exists for its own sake. In other words, a motive that was once a means to an end becomes an end in itself. Allport's most famous and controversial concept.

Habit. Specific mode of responding—for example, putting on clean clothing in the morning—that develops because a more general trait exists, for example, the trait of cleanliness.

Idiographic method. Research method that studies a single case in great detail and depth.

Individual traits. Either the unique patterns of traits possessed by an individual or the unique way that a particular trait manifests itself in the personality of a particular person. For example, a particular person's way of displaying aggressiveness. Later in the development of his theory, Allport changed the term individual trait to personal disposition.

Intrinsic religion. Religion that seeks a higher meaning and purpose in life and provides possible answers to the many mysteries that characterize human existence. Allport considered such religion to be healthy.

Must conscience. Moral guide used by children whereby their moral judgments are determined by the internalized values of authority figures such as the parents. The must conscience is similar to the superego postulated by Freud.

Need induction. Creation of needs rather than their reduction. Allport believed the healthy human lives in accordance with long-term goals that create more problems than they solve. Thus his theory is said to emphasize need induction rather than need reduction.

Need reduction. Satisfaction of a basic need. To many theorists, the elimination or reduction of needs is the primary goal in life. Allport did not agree.

Nomothetic method. Research method that studies groups of individuals and therefore concentrates on average performance, rather than on the performance of a single individual.

Ought conscience. Moral guide used by normal, healthy adults whereby their moral judgments are governed by their own personal values and propriate strivings.

Perseverative functional autonomy. Low-level habits retained even though they are no longer functional.

Personal disposition. Identical to an individual trait. The term individual trait was changed to personal disposition to avoid confusion with the term common trait.

Personal documents. To Allport, one of the best ways to study an individual's personality was to examine personal documents such as diaries, autobiographies, and letters.

Personality. According to Allport, personality is the dynamic organization within the individual of those psychophysical systems that determine characteristic behavior and thought.

Prejudice. Tendency to prejudge persons or objects in terms of how they are categorized as members of groups, rather than in terms of actual experience with them.

Principle of mastery and competence. Principle stating that an innate need exists for humans to aspire to greater mastery and competence.

Principle of organizing energy level. Principle stating that energy that was once used for survival can be changed into concern for the future when survival is no longer an issue.

Principle of propriate patterning. Principle stating that the proprium is the frame of reference that is used by a person in determining what is worth pursuing and what is not.

Propriate functional autonomy. Important motives around which one organizes one's life. Such motives are independent of the conditions that originally produced them.

Propriate striving. Attribute that emerges during the seventh stage in the development of the proprium. At this stage, the adolescent becomes almost completely future oriented.

Proprium. All the facts about a person that make him or her unique.

Raw materials of personality. Temperament, intelligence, and physique.

Realistic perceptions. Those accurate perceptions that characterize the healthy, mature adult.

Secondary dispositions. More specific than cardinal or central dispositions but still more general than habits and attitudes. A secondary disposition may be a person's preference for flamboyant clothing or for sweet food.

Self as knower. Attribute that emerges during the eighth and final stage in the development of the proprium. At this stage, the proprium is aware of, unifies, and transcends the preceding seven aspects of the proprium.

Self as rational coper. Attribute that emerges during the sixth stage in the development of the proprium. At this stage, the child begins to use complex mental operations (thinking) to solve problems.

Self-esteem. Attribute that emerges during the third stage in the development of the proprium. At this stage, the child develops a feeling of pride by doing things on his or her own.

Self-extension. Attribute that emerges during the fourth stage in the development of the proprium. At this stage, the child's self-identity generalizes to external objects.

Self-identity. Attribute that emerges during the second stage in the development of the proprium. At this stage, the child develops a self-identity; for example, realizing that he or she is the same person although conditions change.

Self-image. Attribute that emerges during the fifth stage in the development of the proprium. At this stage, the child develops a conscience and begins to formulate future goals.

Self-objectification. Honest appraisal of one's assets and liabilities that characterizes the healthy, mature adult. A person with self-objectification typically has a good sense of humor.

Temperament. One of the raw materials from which personality is shaped. Temperament is the emotional component of the personality.

Trait. Mental structure that initiates and guides reactions and thus accounts for the consistency in one's behavior.

Type. Category into which one person can be placed by another person. To label a person as an "aggressive type" is to place him or her in a descriptive category based on behavior.

Unifying philosophy of life. Unifying theme that holds together the life of a healthy, mature adult and gives it meaning. Such a theme is often religious in nature but, according to Allport, it does not need to be.

RAYMOND B. CATTELL AND HANS J. EYSENCK

CHAPTER OUTLINE

In this chapter, we explore the theories of Raymond B. Cattell and Hans J. Eysenck, both of whom were educated at the University of London. Both theories are based on sophisticated statistical techniques, and both place great importance on the role of genetic factors in personality. However, it is often the case in science that researchers with similar orientations examine similar sets of data using similar techniques but arrive at very different conclusions. As we will see, there are common ideas in the theories of Cattell and Eysenck, yet the theories differ in several significant ways.

Previous chapters introduced theories that attempted, in part, to improve on the Freudian tradition. These theories shared an interest in development from infancy through the later years, and with the exception of Allport's theory, they also traced many abnormal adult behaviors to problems or conflicts that occurred during childhood. In addition, these theories tended to focus on the idiosyncratic expression of each individual's personality, to deemphasize average group processes, and to place only minor emphasis—if any—on scientific methods.

The theories of Cattell and Eysenck represent distinct departures from the theories discussed in preceding chapters. Both emphasize the scientific discovery and measurement of basic psychological traits possessed by all people. Both use scientific rather than clinical methodology, and although both devote considerable time attempting to understand psychopathology, they are primarily concerned with explaining the personality of normal adults. And, as noted above, both are more interested in the contributions of biological and genetic factors than in developmental events.

Biographical Sketches

Raymond B. Cattell

Raymond B. Cattell was born in Staffordshire, England, on March 20, 1905. He remembered his childhood as a happy one, with an abundance of activities like exploring caves, swimming, and sailing. He did report considerable competition with his brother, however, who was 3 years older. England entered World War I when Cattell was 9 years old and the war had a major effect on his life. Seeing hundreds of wounded soldiers treated in a nearby house that had been converted into a hospital taught him life could be short and one should accomplish as much as possible while one could. As we will see, this sense of urgency about work characterized Cattell throughout his academic life.

At 16, Cattell entered the University of London, where he majored in physics and chemistry. He graduated in 1924, at 19, with high honors. Throughout his undergraduate years, Cattell became increasingly concerned with social problems and was aware that his background in the natural sciences had not prepared him to deal with those problems. These realizations prompted him to enter graduate school in psychology at the University of London, where he earned his PhD degree in 1929. In 1937, the University of London granted Cattell an honorary doctorate in science in recognition of his many accomplishments. While in graduate school, he worked with the famous psychologist-statistician Charles E. Spearman, who invented the technique of factor analysis and applied it to the study of intelligence. As we shall see, Cattell used factor analysis extensively in his study of personality.

After receiving his PhD, Cattell had great difficulty finding work doing what he had been trained to do, so he accepted a number of what he called "fringe" jobs.

He was a lecturer at the University of Exeter in England (1927–1932), and he was the founder and director of a psychology clinic in the school system in the city of Leicester, England (1932–1937). In 1937, he was invited by the prominent American psychologist Edward L. Thorndike to come to America to become his research associate at Columbia University. Cattell accepted Thorndike's invitation and remembered his first year in New York as depressing because he missed England deeply.

From 1938 to 1941, Cattell was the G. Stanley Hall Professor of Genetic Psychology at Clark University in Worcester, Massachusetts. In 1941, Gordon Allport invited Cattell to join the faculty at Harvard where, in the stimulating environment provided by Allport, Henry Murray, and Robert White, Cattell expanded the application of factor analysis from the study of intelligence to the more diverse problems of personality theory. He remained at Harvard as a lecturer until 1944.

Cattell never lost interest in applying the statistical technique of factor analysis to the study of personality. At the age of 40, in 1945, Cattell was offered a position at the University of Illinois as research professor and director of the Laboratory of Personality and Group Analysis. Without teaching responsibilities, Cattell was finally able to pursue his ambition of determining the structure of personality scientifically. Cattell's professional output while he was at the University of Illinois (1945–1973) was voluminous. Cattell pursued his goal until at least 11:00 P.M. every night and observed that his car was easy for him to find in the parking lot because it was the only one left.

Cattell married Monica Rogers on December 1, 1930, and had one son, who is now a surgeon. His wife left him a few years after their marriage because of their poverty and his total dedication to his work. He was married again, on April 2, 1946, to Alberta Karen Schuetter, a mathematician, with whom he eventually had three daughters and a son.

As already mentioned, early in life Cattell developed the belief that one should work hard and not waste time. Throughout his 70-year career, Cattell published more than 450 professional articles and more than 40 books. It is not only the quantity of Cattell's work that is impressive but the quality as well. His work at the Laboratory of Personality and Group Analysis won him worldwide recognition as a personality theorist.

In 1953, Cattell wrote an essay on the psychology of the researcher, which won the Wenner-Gren prize given by the New York Academy of Sciences, and he held the Darwin Fellowship for Genetic Research. The scope of Cattell's research interests is evident when one considers he published articles in American, British, Australian, Japanese, Indian, and African journals.

In 1973, Cattell established the Institute for Research on Morality and Self-Realization in Boulder, Colorado, where he pursued his lifelong interest in social problems. In 1977, Cattell became a visiting professor at the University of Hawaii at Manoa, as well as professor emeritus at the University of Illinois.

In 1997, the American Psychological Foundation awarded Cattell the prestigious Gold Medal Award for Life Achievement in Psychological Science. However, presentation of the award was postponed while a panel considered the controversial positions Cattell had taken on a number of social and political issues. Cattell requested that his name be withdrawn from consideration and it was.

Cattell died on February 2, 1998, at his home in Honolulu at the age of 92.

Hans J. Eysenck

Hans Jurgen Eysenck was born in Berlin on March 4, 1916. His father, Eduard, was a celebrated actor and singer, and his mother, Ruth (Werner) Eysenck acted in silent films using her stage name, Helga Molander. His parents divorced when he was 2 years old, and his father initially wanted Eysenck to carry on the family tradition in the theater. His acting career was short-lived, however. Eysenck recalled that at "the tender age of five or six" (1980, p. 154) he played a minor role in a film in which his mother starred, but he was not allowed to see his own performance in the adults-only feature (1990b, p. 6). In the film, he helped reconcile his estranged parents, but that role was not played out in his real life. His father remarried and remained in Berlin, and his mother moved to Paris to avoid Nazi persecution after marrying Max Glass, a Jewish filmmaker. Eysenck's father was Catholic and his mother was Protestant (Lutheran), however both were more deeply moved by the theater and theater life than by religion. Neither parent encouraged religious study by young Hans. After his parents' divorce, Ruth Glass left Hans to be raised by her mother in Berlin, and the grandmother had to promise him a new bicycle if he would study to be confirmed a Lutheran. He earned his bicycle, but religious training played no further role in Eysenck's development. For example, he stated that he "never had the slightest interest in religion, other than as a social and literary phenomenon" (Eysenck, 1990b, p. 10). Probably because of his mother's marriage to a Jew, one of Eysenck's college and graduate mentors later accused him of leading a Jewish conspiracy to take control of a psychiatric training facility. There is no evidence that he ever converted to Judaism, however.

Although young Eysenck believed that socialism could solve many of Germany's problems, he did not embrace Hitler's Nazi party, nor was he interested in joining the Communist party or various underground political movements. After being told that he could not attend college in Germany unless he joined the Nazi secret police, he left Germany permanently in the summer of 1934 to live in France with his mother and her husband. He studied literature and history for approximately one year at the University of Dijon and then moved to England where he took college prerequisite courses at Pitman College and then enrolled at the University of London.

Eysenck's early life experiences and his year in France convinced him that he did not want to pursue a career in the arts, and he went to London with the intention of studying physics. In his 1980 autobiographical essay, he recalled:

> I had, from the beginning of my conscious life, been quite decided that art was for fun, for emotional experiences, for enjoyment, and that my life's work would lie in science. By that I meant physics and astronomy. . . . I was told I could not study physics because I had taken the "wrong" subjects in my matric! I could not wait another year and retake the right subjects, so I asked if there was any scientific subject I could take. Yes, I was told, there was always psychology. "What on earth is that?" I inquired in my ignorance. "You'll like it," they said. And so I enrolled in a subject whose scientific status was perhaps a little more questionable than my advisers realized. (p. 156)

While at the university, Eysenck met and married Margaret Davies, a Canadian student who was conducting research in aesthetic responses to odors for her MA in psychology. Eysenck graduated in 1938 and immediately began his doctoral studies in psychology, which he completed in 1940 with a dissertation on aesthetics.

While his marriage to Margaret Davies was in its final stages, Eysenck was introduced to and began a romantic relationship with Sybil Rostal, a psychology student. Although the romance was potentially professionally damaging, Eysenck did not attempt to conceal his relationship with Rostal, and the incident passed without any negative effect on either of their careers. They were married in 1950 and gave birth to numerous research articles and books, as well as to three sons and a daughter.

During 1949 and 1950, Eysenck traveled to the United States where he held a visiting professorship at the University of Pennsylvania. During that visit, Eysenck studied training programs in clinical psychology and the roles of clinical psychologists in general. Upon his return to England, he campaigned for a more scientific psychological training for clinical psychologists, for more applications of scientific psychological principles in therapy, and for independence from psychiatrists. He became particularly dissatisfied with adherence to Freudian theory—both in psychiatry and clinical psychology—and began to develop a new approach in clinical training at Maudsley Hospital (a premier British psychiatric facility), an approach that focused on behavioral therapy. In 1952, he assessed the effectiveness of Freudian psychotherapy and published evidence that patients experiencing psychoanalytic therapy improved no more than patients who had received no therapy at all. He remained a severe critic of Freudian analysis as well as of projective testing methods (e.g., the Rorschach Ink Blot test) throughout his life.

Beginning with a review of L. L. Thurstone's work in factor analysis, published while he was still an undergraduate, Eysenck wrote 61 books and edited 10 others, and published more than 1,000 research articles, reviews, and book chapters. In a career that spanned more than 55 productive years, he also founded the graduate Department of Psychology in the Institute of Psychiatry at Maudsley Hospital and was its head for 30 years until his retirement in 1983 at age 65; founded and edited two psychological journals, *Behavior Research and Therapy* and *Personality and Individual Differences;* and gave numerous addresses at psychological conferences and lectured at numerous universities throughout the world. Eysenck continued to conduct research on personality and other topics until his death from cancer on September 4, 1997.

In 1991, both historians of psychology and departmental chairpersons rated Eysenck among the top 10 most important contemporary psychologists (Korn, Davis, & Davis, 1991). In 1988, he received the APA's Award for Distinguished Contribution to Science, and in 1994 he received the APA's Presidential Citation for Outstanding Contributions to Psychology. In 1996, the APA Division of Clinical Psychology, as part of the celebration of the 100th year of Clinical Psychology, presented Eysenck with a special Centennial Award. The citation read:

> We consider that you are one of the greatest contributors to the field of clinical psychology during its first century. Your 1952 article, "The Effects of Psychotherapy: An Evaluation," sent a necessary wake-up call to the field concerning the need for scientific evaluation of psychological interventions. Your role in the emergence of behavior therapy demonstrated that, indeed, treatments could be devised on the basis of well established psychological research findings, and tested stringently for their efficacy and effectiveness. Your contributions to the conceptualization and

measurement of personality dimensions such as extraversions and neuroticism have been highly influential. Your courageous and thought provoking stands on many issues have also stimulated much research by others. (Division 12 News, September 1996, p. 3)

Factor Analysis

Even the naive psychology student has heard something about Freud, Jung, or Skinner before reading this text. Few new students, if asked to name influential psychologists, would come up with the names of Cattell or Eysenck. It also seems fair to say that Cattell's and Eysenck's theories of personality have not become overwhelmingly popular among those studying personality. The lack of wide acceptance can be explained by two facts. First, the sheer bulk of these theorists' contributions has made it impossible for the "outsider" to digest. For example, Wiggins said in the 1968 edition of the *Annual Review of Psychology*:

> Cattell occupies such a unique position in the field of personality structure that his work demands separate consideration. In the three years under review (May 1964–May 1967) Cattell has published four books, 12 chapters and 40 articles, a total of almost four thousand pages that must somehow be summarized. In addition, he has found time to launch a new journal (*Multivariate Behavioral Research*) and edit a massive handbook (*Handbook of Multivariate Experimental Psychology*). This alone would warrant separate consideration but there is more. The appearance of so many major works and especially the publication of his *Collected Papers (Personality and Social Psychology)* has once again forced an evaluation of a body of literature so vast, uneven, and demanding that many American workers have simply tended to ignore it. (p. 313)

And, as we noted in the biographical sketch above, Eysenck's work was at least as extensive as Cattell's. It would be difficult for any scholar not devoted exclusively to mastering the works of Cattell or Eysenck to understand the breadth of their theoretical work and critique it effectively. All that one could reasonably do with either theory would be to sample parts of them and hope that the most important concepts are included in that sample. Such a sample is offered in this chapter.

Second, both theories rely on **factor analysis.** There is no doubt that the apparent complexities of this technique have caused many to overlook Cattell's and Eysenck's theories. We contend, however, that factor analysis is only *apparently* complex, and the logic behind it is simple and straightforward. Because, in most important ways, to understand factor analysis is to understand Cattell's, and to a lesser extent Eysenck's, theory of personality, we begin with a rudimentary discussion of factor analysis.

The cornerstone of factor analysis is the concept of **correlation.** When two variables vary together they are said to be correlated, that is, co-related. For example, a correlation exists between height and weight because when one increases, the other will also tend to increase. The stronger the tendency is for two variables to vary together, the stronger is the correlation between them. The strength of the relationship between two variables is expressed mathematically by a **correlation coefficient.**

A correlation coefficient can vary in magnitude from +1.00 to –1.00. A coefficient of +1.00 indicates a perfect **positive correlation** between two variables; that is, as measures on one variable increase, so will measures on the second variable. A coefficient of –1.00 indicates a perfect **negative correlation** between two variables; that is, as measures on one variable increase, measures on the other variable decrease. A correlation coefficient of +.80 indicates a strong positive correlation between two variables, but not a perfect one. That is, there is a tendency for the two variables to vary positively together. A coefficient of –.56 indicates a moderate negative correlation.

In general, factor analysis begins with a large number of measurements taken from a large sample of people, although one could also begin by taking those same measurements many times from one individual. The data may include many different types of dependent variables. For example, we might record biographical information (birth order, number of siblings, ages of parents, etc.), results of different tests and questionnaires (IQ scores, scores on various personality inventories, etc.), results of different experiments (scores from a learning experiment, reaction times in a decision-making task, etc.), and perhaps even physiological data such as heart rates or EEG recordings. The next step is to intercorrelate all of the data, creating a **correlation matrix.** To simplify matters, we assume the data we are analyzing consists of performance on five tests. A hypothetical outcome of such an analysis is shown in Table 8–1.

Next, the following assumptions are made:

1. Two tests that measure the same variable must give similar results. In other words, tests measuring the same ability will tend to be correlated.
2. The extent of agreement (correlation) between two tests will indicate the extent to which the two tests measure the same thing.

With these assumptions in mind, the correlation matrix is examined in order to find which tests are highly correlated with each other. In other words, clusters of correlations are sought. Such a search is called a **cluster analysis.** When a cluster of tests showing high correlation with one another is observed, the tests are considered to measure the same ability or characteristic. An ability discovered in such a way is called a **factor,** and in both Cattell's and Eysenck's theories the term factor can be equated with the **term trait.** For Cattell, factor analysis is a method used to discover traits that he regarded as the building blocks of personality. For Eysenck,

Table 8–1

Hypothetical Correlation Matrix Showing All Possible Intercorrelations among Five Tests

(Adopted from Cattell, 1965)

TESTS	A	B	C	D	E
A	—	1.00	1.00	.00	.00
B	1.00	—	1.00	.00	.00
C	1.00	1.00	—	.00	.00
D	.00	.00	.00	—	1.00
E	.00	.00	.00	1.00	—

*Note that each factor is bipolar. A high score on a particular factor indicates a tendency to possess the traits on the left of the diagram, and a low score indicates a tendency to possess the traits listed on the right side of the diagram.

factors themselves are subjected to additional analysis to discover what he calls **superfactors** or **types.**

The procedures of factor analysis can be summarized as follows:

1. Measure many people in a variety of ways.
2. Correlate performance on each measure with performance on every other measure. This creates a correlation matrix.
3. Determine how many factors (traits) need to be postulated in order to account for the various intercorrelations (clusters) found in the correlation matrix.

In the hypothetical correlation matrix depicted in Table 8-1, it is clear that Tests A, B, and C have a great deal in common with one another because they are perfectly correlated, but they have nothing in common with Tests D and E. Conversely, Tests D and E have a great deal in common because they are perfectly correlated with each other, but they have nothing in common with Tests A, B, and C. Under these circumstances our correlation matrix has detected two separate factors or traits. One is measured by Tests A, B, and C, and the other is measured by Tests D and E.

A sample of the ways in which three tests could be related to each other is shown in Figure 8–1. The upper left corner of the figure shows what would happen if the three tests measure separate factors. The upper right corner shows that Tests A and B tend to measure a common factor, but Test C measures a different factor. The lower left corner of the figure indicates that all three tests measure a common factor. The lower right corner of the figure shows Test A measures one factor, and Tests B and C measure another factor.

Factor analysis, then, is a technique, based on the methods of correlation, that attempts to account for the interrelationships found among numerous measures. The technique is certainly not confined to the study of personality. As mentioned earlier, Cattell's mentor, Charles Spearman, used factor analysis to study intelligence; and Cattell, in addition to using it to study personality, used factor analysis to study the characteristics of groups, institutions, and even nations.

Figure 8–1

Examples of how three tests can be related to each other. See text for explanation.

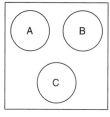
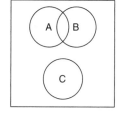
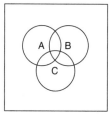
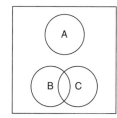

Cattell's Approach to Research

Cattell's early work is appropriately characterized as an example of **inductive reasoning** or inductive research. That is, he began without a specific guiding hypothesis, collected a large data set, and generated future hypotheses from patterns that emerged from the data. Cattell's procedure was to measure many persons in as many ways as possible. For example, he recorded the everyday behavior of various persons such as how many accidents they had, the number of organizations to which they belonged, and the number of social contacts they had. He called the information gathered by such observations **L-data,** the *L* for life record. He gave his subjects questionnaires on which they rated themselves on various characteristics. He called the information gathered by such a technique **Q-data,** the *Q* for questionnaire. Q-data includes performance on standard self-report inventories and various scales that measure attitudes, opinions, and interests. Cattell realized that Q-data has limitations. First, some persons may not know much about themselves and therefore their responses to questionnaires, inventories, and scales may not reflect their true personalities. Second, some subjects falsify or distort their responses to create a desirable image of themselves. For example, an aggressive person may believe his or her aggressiveness would be frowned upon and may respond in ways that make him or her look passive. To overcome the problems inherent in Q-data, Cattell used a third source of data that he called **T-data,** the *T* for test. T-data is gathered in situations in which examinees cannot know what aspect of their behavior is being evaluated. Examples include performance on word-association tests, the Rorschach inkblot test, or the thematic apperception test. Cattell referred to such tests as objective because they are resistant to faking. Cattell and Warburton (1967) listed more than 400 tests that appear to meet this criterion.

Cattell used factor analysis to search for clusters of measurements or factors, which occur in stable patterns across a number of situations or over long periods of time. He then attempted to determine the extent to which these factors are, in fact, fundamental personality traits. As we will see below, Cattell claimed to have identified 16 fundamental traits found in the normal personality.

Cattell (1965) provided a colorful summary of his approach to understanding personality that reflects his enthusiasm for factor analysis:

> The problem which baffled psychologists for many years was to find a method which would tease out . . . functionally unitary influences in the chaotic jungle of human behavior. But let us ask how in the literal tropical jungle, the hunter decides whether the dark blobs which he sees are two or three rotting logs or a single alligator? He watches for movement. If they move together—come and disappear together—he infers a single structure. (p. 56)

Eysenck's Approach to Research

Eysenck's approach was characterized by **hypothetico-deductive reasoning** (contrasted with Cattell's inductive reasoning). That is, he begins with an experimental hypothesis derived from an existing theory, logically deduces testable predictions from the hypothesis, and then gathers data to determine whether the predictions are accurate. When they are, the hypothesis is supported and subjected to additional tests. If the predictions are inaccurate, the hypothesis is refuted and must be either abandoned or modified.

Eysenck's procedure began much like Cattell's in that he gathered a large number of measurements and used factor analysis to identify fundamental personality traits, those traits that, as we will see, are assumed to have genetic and biological bases. While Cattell believed that these primary factors or traits are the appropriate focus for analysis of personality, Eysenck was more interested than Cattell in the intercorrelations among primary traits. He subjected this first set of factors to a second level of factor analysis, thus identifying clusters of primary traits called superfactors or types. Eysenck, therefore, focused on factors that are more general than those identified by Cattell.

It is important to note that Eysenck used factor analysis, for the most part, at the beginning of his research process. That is, he used the procedure to identify and verify the fundamental components of personality. Of factor analysis and his role as a factor analyst, he said:

> I'm the one who thinks least of it. I regard it as a useful adjunct, a technique that was invaluable under certain circumstances, but one which we must leave behind as soon as possible in order to get a proper causal type of understanding of the factors and to know what they mean. (quoted in Evans, 1976, p. 256)

Nomothetic versus Idiographic Techniques

Cattell's R- and P-Techniques

During the early 1940s, when Cattell was a lecturer at Harvard, he often had lunch with Gordon Allport. At the time, Cattell's interest was primarily to discover the basic traits that constitute personality and then determine how persons differ in the degree to which they possess those traits. As we have seen, Cattell's approach to discovering traits was to measure many persons in many ways and to factor-analyze the results. Allport expressed dismay that Cattell's approach stressed group performance (the nomothetic technique) and ignored the unique individual (the idiographic technique). As a result of Allport's influence, Cattell began to investigate how trait strengths differ in the same person from time to time. Cattell's early idiographic research was performed on his wife but was soon extended to other persons.

The type of factor analysis that we described, in which many subjects are measured on many variables and the scores intercorrelated, is called the **R-technique.** The type of factor analysis that traces the strength of several traits over a period of time for the same person is called the **P-technique.** Figure 8–2 shows the outcome of one P-technique study. This study measured the same individual 80 times on 8 traits over a 44-day period. The person being studied kept a diary during the experiment, and several of his major experiences are indicated along the baseline of Figure 8–2. For example, he had to rehearse for a play in which he was to play the lead role, he had a cold, the play for which he rehearsed was held, his father was in an accident, an aunt criticized him for not helping his family enough, and he was worried because

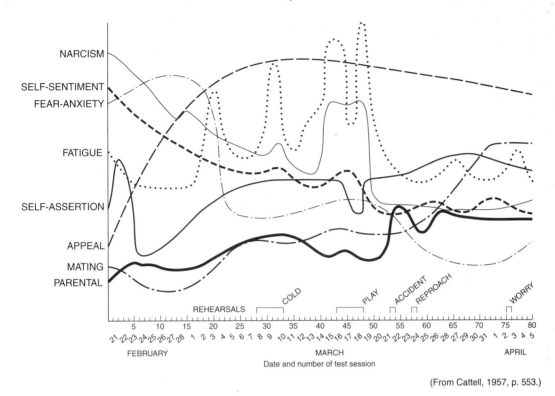

NARCISM
SELF-SENTIMENT
FEAR-ANXIETY

FATIGUE

SELF-ASSERTION

APPEAL
MATING
PARENTAL

REHEARSALS   COLD   PLAY   ACCIDENT REPROACH   WORRY

5 10 15 20 25 30 35 40 45 50 55 60 65 70 75 80

21 22 23 24 25 26 27 28 1 2 3 4 5 6 7 8 9 10 11 12 13 14 15 16 17 18 19 20 21 22 23 24 25 26 28 27 29 30 31 1 2 3 4 5

FEBRUARY   MARCH   APRIL

Date and number of test session

(From Cattell, 1957, p. 553.)

Figure 8–2 *An example of Cattell's P-technique in which certain traits that a person possesses are measured over time.*

his academic adviser was apparently hostile toward him. We can clearly see from Figure 8-2 that the various traits one possesses will manifest themselves with varying strength as one's life circumstances change.

Eysenck's Nomothetic–Idiographic Compromise

Eysenck viewed his approach to personality theory as a scientific compromise between a purely idiographic method, like the one advocated by Allport, and the nomothetic method used by most experimental psychologists. He believed that, in the extreme, the former, in which each individual is seen as unique, makes derivation of general scientific laws and principles impossible. The latter, which allows for the scientific derivation of general laws, ignores the unique characteristics of the individual. Eysenck and Eysenck (1985) wrote:

> One of the major arguments against the hypothesis that all organisms are unique, profoundly different from each other, and hence incapable of being studied by the ordinary methods of science appeals to the simple fact that the existence of differences implies the existence of similarities and that both differences and similarities must be along certain measurable dimensions. . . . We shall not pursue here the debate between ideographic [sic] and nomothetic psychologists. . . . From one point

of view the debate is a philosophical one and of little practical interest to psychologists. (pp. 5–7)

Taxonomy of Traits

Cattell's Analysis of Traits

As noted above, Cattell considered traits the building blocks of personality, and clearly the concept of trait is the most important concept in his theory. Most of his factor-analytic research was a search for personality traits, and that search has uncovered several categories of traits, which we review next.

Surface Traits and Source Traits.   The difference between surface traits and source traits was probably the most important distinction made in Cattell's theory. **Surface traits** are groups of observations that are correlated. For example, people with more formal education may go to the movies less than people with less formal education do. Such observations are superficial in that they explain nothing. They are simply a statement of what type of observed characteristics tend to be grouped together (correlated). Such characteristics can, and probably do, have many causes.

Source traits, conversely, are the causes of behavior. They constitute the most important part of a person's personality structure and are ultimately responsible for all of a person's consistent behavior. Thus every surface trait is caused by one or more source traits, and a source trait can influence several surface traits.

Another way to describe the difference between source traits and surface traits is to say that the latter are always manifestations of the former. The source traits can be considered the basic elements of personality, in that everything we do is influenced by them. Cattell concluded that all individuals possess the same source traits but do so in varying degrees. For example, all people possess intelligence (a source trait), but all people do not possess the same amount of intelligence. The strength of this source trait in a given individual will influence many things about that person, for example, what the person reads, who his or her friends are, and what he or she does for a living. All of these outward manifestations of the source trait of intelligence are surface traits. Our examples are somewhat misleading, however, because, as we have seen, hardly anything that a person does is caused by only one source trait.

Perhaps influenced by his background in chemistry, Cattell's goal was to establish a **personality sphere** that would provide the same function as the periodic table created by Mendeleev in 1869. Whereas the periodic table classifies the basic elements of the physical world, the personality sphere would describe the basic elements of personality. Unlike Mendeleev's effort, however, Cattell's goal has been elusive. The important question as to how many source traits exist is still unanswered. The search for source traits is complex and, at times, frustrating. For example, if a source trait exists, one might expect it to manifest itself in L-, Q-, and T-data, but this is not always the case. Although some source traits do appear when all three sources of data are factor-analyzed, others emerge from only one or two sources. Also, as Cattell's measures became more diverse and sophisticated, additional source traits were being discovered.

Cattell's early factor analysis of L- and Q-data yielded 16 source traits that characterize the normal personality (see Table 8–2). The first 12 factors listed were discovered by factor-analyzing L-data or by factor-analyzing L- and Q-data. The last four emerged only from the factor analysis of Q-data. Cattell (with Saunders and Stice) constructed his influential Sixteen Personality Factor Questionnaire (16 PF; 1950) around these 16 factors. In addition to assessing individual personalities, this questionnaire has been used to compare a wide variety of groups (for examples, see Figure 8–3). The performance of several groups on the 16 PF is also available for assessing the personality traits of various age groups, for example, ages 4–6, 6–8, 8–12, and 12–18. In agreement with Freud, these tests indicate that the major source traits characterizing adult personality appear at about the age of 4 (Coan, 1966).

Note, for comparison with Eysenck's analysis of traits, that Cattell (1979) recognized the intercorrelations between the 16 "first-order" traits that are identified by the 16 PF. Cattell's analysis of these intercorrelations yields 8 "second-order," or more general, traits. Unlike Eysenck, however, Cattell felt that the important level of analysis is at the level of the 16 primary traits rather than at the level of higher-order factors.

Table 8–2

Factors That Cattell Concluded Were the Building Blocks of the Personality*

(Apopted from Cattell, 1965)

FACTOR	HIGH SCORE INDICATES A TENDENCY TOWARD	LOW SCORE INDICATES A TENDENCY TOWARD
A	*Affectia*	*Sizia*
	Socially adjusted	Socially hostile
	Easygoing	Indifferent
	Warmhearted	Reserved
	Outgoing	
B	*Intelligence*	*Unintelligent*
	Alert	Dull
	Imaginative	Stupid
	Thoughtful	Unimaginative
	Wise	
C	*Ego Strength*	*Ego Weakness*
	Unworried	Anxious
	Mature	Infantile
	Stoic	Worried
	Patient	Impatient
E	*Domination*	*Subordination*
	Confident	Unsure
	Boastful	Modest
	Competitive	Accommodating
	Assertive	Humble
F	*Surgency*	*Desurgency*
	Talkative	Silent
	Genial	Serious
	Cheerful	Depressed
	Responsive	Seclusive
	Happy-go-lucky	
G	*Superego Strength*	*Superego Weakness*
	Conscientious	Unscrupulous
	Responsible	Frivolous
	Persevering	Irresolute
	Loyal	Undependable

(continued)

Table 8–2

(Continued)

FACTOR	HIGH SCORE INDICATES A TENDENCY TOWARD	LOW SCORE INDICATES A TENDENCY TOWARD
H	*Parmia*	*Threctia*
	Carefree	Careful
	Overtly interested in sex	Overtly disinterested in sex
	Venturesome	Shy
I	*Premisia*	*Harria*
	Introspective	Insensitive
	Sensitive	Practical
	Sentimental	Logical
	Intuitive	Self-sufficient
L	*Protension*	*Alaxia*
	Suspicious	Credulous
	Jealous	Trustful
	Skeptical	Unsuspecting
	Wary	Gullible
M	*Autia*	*Praxernia*
	Eccentric	Practical
	Imaginative	Conventional
	Complacent	Poised
	Self-absorbed	Earnest
N	*Shrewdness*	*Artlessness*
	Socially alert	Socially clumsy
	Insightful regarding others	Crude
	Expedient	Indifferent
	Calculating	Apathetic
O	*Guilt Proclivity*	*Guilt Rejection*
	Timid	Self-confident
	Worrisome	Cheerful
	Depressed	Without fear
	Moody	Self-sufficient
Q(1)	*Radicalism*	*Conservatism*
	Encourages change	Rejects change
	Rejects convention	Disgusted by foul language
	Freethinking	Traditional
Q(2)	*Self-Sufficiency*	*Group-Adherence*
	Temperamentally independent	Seeks social approval
	Prefers working with a few assistants rather than a committee	Group dependent
	Prefers reading to classes	Prefers to travel with others
	Prefers textbooks to novels	Joiner
Q(3)	*High self-sentiment strength*	*Low self-sentiment strength*
	Controlled	Careless
	Sensitive to uncertainty	Rapidly changing interests
	Does not make promise he cannot keep	Tries several approaches to the same problem
	Does not say things he later regrets	Does not persevere in the face of obstacles
Q(4)	*High ergic tension*	*Low ergic tension*
	Tense	Relaxed
	Unexpected lapses of memory	Composed
	Suffers frustration because of unsatisfied physiological needs	Few periods of depression Disinclined to worry

*Note that each factor is bipolar. A high score on a particular factor indicates a tendency to possess the traits on the left of the diagram, and a low score indicates a tendency to possess the traits listed on the right side of the diagram.

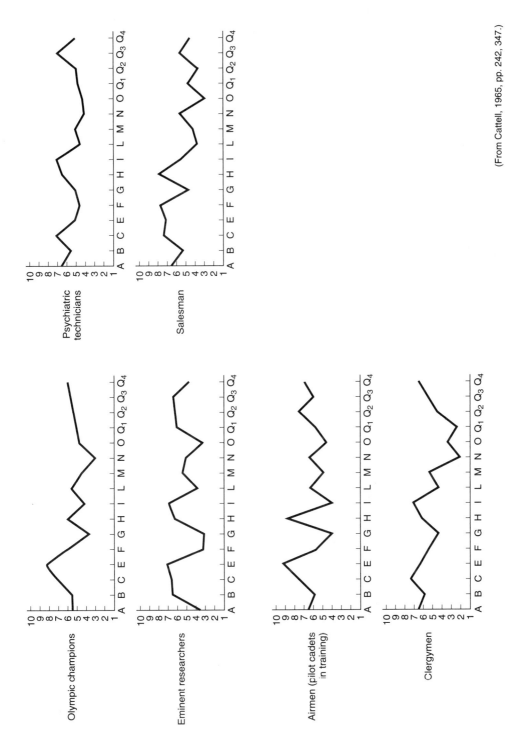

Figure 8–3 *A comparison of the performance of various groups on the Sixteen Personality Factor Questionnaire (16 PF).*

(From Cattell, 1965, pp. 242, 347.)

Constitutional and Environmental-Mold Traits.   Some source traits are genetically determined and are called **constitutional source traits;** others result from experience and are called **environmental-mold traits.**

> If source traits found by factorizing are pure, independent influences, as present evidence suggests, a source trait could not be due both to heredity and environment but must spring from one or the other. . . . Patterns thus springing from internal conditions or influences we may call constitutional source traits. . . . On the other hand, a pattern might be imprinted on the personality by something external to it. . . . Such source traits, appearing as factors, we may call environmental-mold traits, because they spring from the molding effect of social institutions and physical realities which constitute the cultural pattern. (Cattell, 1950, pp. 33–34)

Thus, for Cattell, some source traits are genetically determined and some are culturally determined.

Ability Traits.   Some source traits that a person possesses determine how effectively he or she works toward a desired goal; such traits are called **ability traits.** One of the most important ability traits is intelligence. Cattell distinguished between two types of intelligence, crystallized and fluid. He defined **fluid intelligence** as "that form of general intelligence which is largely innate and which adapts itself to all kinds of material regardless of previous experience with it" (1965, p. 369). Cattell defined **crystallized intelligence** as "a general factor, largely in a type of ability learned at school, representing the effect of past application of fluid intelligence, and amount and intensity of schooling; it appears in such tests as vocabulary and number ability measures" (p. 369).

Cattell believed that too often a person's intelligence is equated with crystallized intelligence, which most traditional IQ tests attempt to measure. To help remedy the situation, Cattell developed the **Culture Free Intelligence Test** (1944), designed to measure fluid intelligence.

Cattell's research led him to conclude that both fluid intelligence and crystallized intelligence are strongly influenced by heredity. This research indicates that fluid intelligence is 65 percent inherited and crystallized intelligence is 60 percent inherited (Cattell, 1980, p. 58). Thus, according to Cattell, not only is one's general intelligence (fluid intelligence) strongly influenced by heredity but so is one's ability to benefit from experience and to use what one has learned (crystallized intelligence).

Currently, in psychology, there is considerable debate concerning the relative contributions of genetics and experience to one's level of intelligence (a variation of the nature–nurture problem). Cattell's belief that intelligence is largely innate (genetically determined), and the implications of that belief, are among the issues that made Cattell a controversial figure.

Temperament Traits.   These are genetically determined characteristics that determine a person's general "style and tempo." **Temperament traits** determine the speed, energy, and emotion with which a person responds to a situation. They determine how mild-mannered, irritable, or persistent a person is. Temperament traits, therefore, are constitutional source traits that determine a person's emotionality. Of the source traits measured by the 16 PF, 15 are temperament traits and 1 (factor B, intelligence) is an ability trait.

Dynamic Traits.   Temperament traits determine a person's style of behaving; they determine how a person typically responds to situations. Ability traits determine a person's effectiveness in solving problems; they determine how well a person typically responds to situations. **Dynamic traits** determine why a person responds to situations. Dynamic traits set the person in motion toward some goal; they are the motivational elements of personality. Cattell elaborated two different dynamic or motivational traits: ergs and metaergs.

An **erg** is a dynamic, constitutional source trait. An erg is similar to what other theorists have called drives, needs, or instincts. Cattell chose the term erg (from the Greek ergon, meaning energy) because he thought the other motivational terms were too ambiguous. The ergs provide the energy for all behavior. Cattell defined erg as

> an innate psycho-physical disposition which permits its possessor to acquire reactivity (attention, recognition) to certain classes of objects more readily than others, to experience a specific emotion in regard to them, and to start on a course of action which ceases more completely at a certain specific goal activity than at any other. (1950, p. 199)

It can be seen from this definition that an erg has four aspects:

1. It causes selective perception; that is, it causes some things to be attended to more than others. For the hungry person, food-related events are attended to more than events unrelated to food.
2. It stimulates an emotional response to certain thoughts or objects. For example, the thought of eating is pleasant.
3. It stimulates goal-directed behavior. For example, the hungry person will do whatever is necessary to come into contact with food.
4. It results in some sort of consummatory response. That is, when one comes into contact with food, one will eat it.

Of course, ergs can vary in intensity. One can be hungry, sexually aroused, curious, or angry in varying degrees. The level at which an erg exists determines the amount of **ergic tension** present.

It is interesting to note that in claiming all human behavior is ultimately instinctual, Cattell essentially agreed with Freud. Cattell's list of instincts (ergs), however, was far more extensive than Freud's. Cattell's research has revealed 11 ergs, which are listed on the right side of Figure 8–4.

A **metaerg** is a dynamic source trait with an environmental origin. In other words, a metaerg is an environmental-mold, dynamic source trait. Thus a metaerg is the same as an erg except for its origin. Both ergs and metaergs cause motivational predispositions toward certain environmental objects, however, ergs are innate whereas metaergs are learned. Metaergs are divided into sentiments and attitudes. According to Cattell, **sentiments** are "major acquired dynamic trait structures which cause their possessors to pay attention to certain objects or classes of objects, and to feel and react in a certain way with regard to them" (1950, p. 161). Cattell believed sentiments are usually centered on such things as one's career or profession, sports, religion, one's parents, one's spouse or sweetheart, or oneself. The most powerful sentiment of all, according to Cattell, is the **self-sentiment,** which organizes the entire personality:

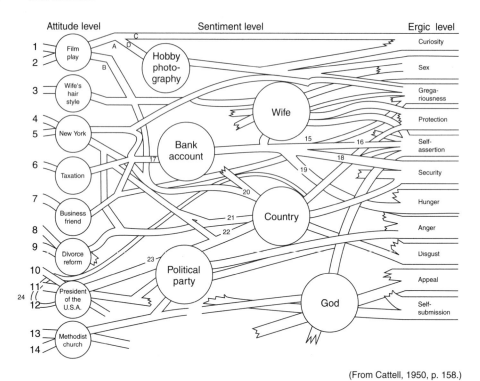

(From Cattell, 1950, p. 158.)

Figure 8–4 *A dynamic lattice showing the relationship among ergs, sentiments, and attitudes.*

In the first place, the preservation of the self as a physically healthy and intact going concern is obviously a prerequisite for the satisfaction of any sentiment or erg which the individual possesses! So also is the preservation of the social and ethical self as something which the community respects. . . . Dynamically, the sentiment towards maintaining the self correct by certain standards of conduct, satisfactory to community and super-ego, is therefore a necessary instrumentality to the satisfaction of most other of our life interests. . . . It contributes to all sentiment and ergic satisfactions, and this accounts also for its dynamic strength in controlling, as the "master sentiment," all other structures. (1965, pp. 272–273)

A sentiment is an acquired predisposition to respond to a class of objects or events in a certain way. An **attitude** is more specific but is derived from a sentiment, which, in turn, is derived from an erg. An attitude, according to Cattell, is a tendency to respond in a particular way in a particular situation to a particular object or event. Cattell (1957, p. 444) described the manifestation of an attitude:

In these circumstances	I	want so much	to do this	with that
(Stimulus situation)	(Organism)	(Interest-need of a certain intensity)	(Specific goal, course of action)	(Object concerned in action)

Thus an attitude is an interest, of a certain intensity, in doing something with something in a certain situation.

Cattell used the term **subsidiation** to describe the fact that sentiments are subsidiary to ergs (i.e., dependent on them) and attitudes are subsidiary to sentiments. Stated differently, attitudes are studied (factor-analyzed) to discover more basic sentiments, and sentiments are studied (factor-analyzed) to discover more basic ergs. The relationships among attitudes, sentiments, and ergs are diagramed in what Cattell called the **dynamic lattice,** shown in Figure 8–4.

It can be seen in Figure 8-4 that ergic desires are seldom satisfied directly. Instead, one usually goes about satisfying a basic need indirectly. For example, one may develop skills to get a job, get married, or satisfy one's sex drive. Cattell called this indirect satisfaction of an ergic impulse **long-circuiting.** Also, it can be seen that each sentiment is a function of, or subsidiary to, a number of ergs. For example, the sentiment toward wife reflects the ergs of sex, gregariousness, protection, and self-assertion. The most important point about the dynamic lattice is that it demonstrates the complexity of human motivation. Attitudes, sentiments, and ergs are constantly interacting and are constantly reflecting not only current circumstances but also an individual's future goals.

Eysenck's Analysis of Traits

Eysenck included the concept of intelligence in a general, informal discussion of personality, and he clearly acknowledged the genetic aspects of intelligence. The focus of his formal theory of personality, however, is **temperament,** defined as the emotional, motivational, and non-ability-related cognitive aspects of behavior. Eysenck did not include intelligence, cognitive ability, or other so-called ability traits in this definition (Eysenck, 1970; Eysenck & Eysenck, 1985), and he often used the terms "personality" and "temperament" interchangeably:

> The use of the term "personality" is often ambiguous; for some, such as R. B. Cattell, it includes intelligence, while for others it only refers to the non-cognitive aspects of behaviour. I will here continue the more usual habit of referring to non-cognitive aspects under the term "personality," and to the cognitive ones as "intelligence." (1990a, p. 193)

For Eysenck, the most important traits were those that Cattell would categorize as constitutional source traits. Thus, in Eysenck's theory, the important traits are those that are relatively permanent, have clear biological origins, and influence what he saw as the secondary behavioral patterns acquired through learning. Although he believed that the environment makes important contributions to overall patterns of behavior and personality, Eysenck's theory does not have a trait-concept akin to Cattell's environmental-mold trait. For Eysenck, types, and the traits they encompass, were genetically determined; they do not arise from learning.

Historical Roots of Eysenck's Theory

Jung's Hypothesis

As we saw in Chapter 3, Jung viewed the introvert as an individual who is reflective, basically withdrawn, and oriented toward subjective or internal reality while the extrovert is outgoing and oriented toward external events. Jung (1921) also speculated that, when introverts experience neurotic disorders, they exhibit internalized symptoms such as anxiety, sensitivity, fatigue, and exhaustion. Eysenck proposed the term **dysthymic** to refer to the severely disordered neurotic introvert. On the other hand, Jung proposed that the extrovert expresses neurotic disorders with hysteric symptoms or in other ways that are externalized and removed from the "inner" self. Eysenck used the term **hysteric** to refer to the disordered neurotic extrovert.

In his first book, *Dimensions of Personality* (1947), Eysenck reported that psychiatric patients (and personalities in general) were described by two major *independent* types or superfactors. These were **neuroticism** (vs. stability) (N) and **extroversion** (vs. introversion) (E). These superfactors appeared to separate highly neurotic soldiers into two groups. Indeed, the most severe cases seemed to be individuals who expressed either the introverted pattern of anxiety-related symptoms (dysthymia) or the extroverted pattern of hysteric disorders (hysteria), thus confirming the hypothesis suggested by Jung.

In the hierarchical structures shown in Figure 8–5, each higher-order type includes a number of correlated traits. Thus, an individual who is highly neurotic expresses this general factor through the traits of anxiety, depression, feelings of guilt, low self-esteem, and so on. Similarly, the figure shows that the individual who is highly extroverted tends to be sociable, lively, assertive, and sensation-seeking, to name only a few.

After identifying the first two general types, Eysenck constructed the Maudsley Medical Questionnaire, which could be administered to hospitalized, neurotic soldiers as well as to healthy individuals who were neither hospitalized nor complaining of psychological problems. (Questionnaires developed later included the Eysenck Personality Inventory [EPI], the Eysenck Personality Questionnaire [EPQ], and the revised Eysenck Personality Questionnaire [EPQ-R].) In his second book, *The Scientific Study of Personality* (1952), Eysenck paid considerable attention to differences between the hospitalized patients and healthy people. He concluded that a third superfactor, **psychoticism** (P), must be added to N and E to provide a complete description of personality. It should be noted that the final type, P, was included primarily to aid in making distinctions between those soldiers with neurotic disorders and those who would be diagnosed with psychotic disorders. Although psychoticism remains part of Eysenck's theoretical scheme, it has not played a major role in his research concerning the personality structures of normal, healthy people. In Figure 8–5, we see that the correlated traits under the superfactor of psychoticism include being aggressive, cold, egocentric, impulsive, and so forth. Despite the order in which these three superfactors were identified, Eysenck and others often use the acronym PEN (psychoticism, extraversion, neuroticism) to refer to the superfactor theory.

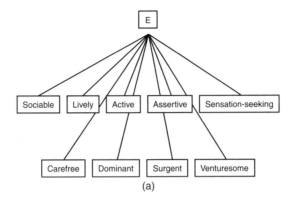

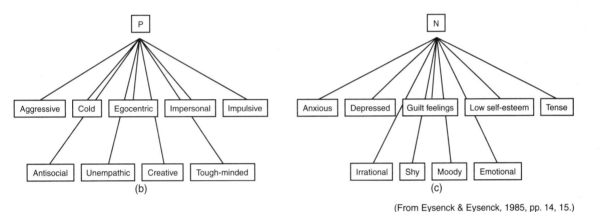

(From Eysenck & Eysenck, 1985, pp. 14, 15.)

Figure 8–5   *(a) Traits making up the type concept of extroversion. (b) Traits making up the type concept of psychoticism. (c) Traits making up the type concept of neuroticism.*

Additional Historical Influences

Although their approaches were not scientific by contemporary standards, Eysenck gave credit to Hippocrates (ca. 460–377 B.C.) and the Greek physician Galen (ca. 130–200) for their influence on his thinking about personality (Eysenck & Eysenck, 1985). Hippocrates believed that humans consisted of four elements: earth, air, fire, and water. Furthermore, he associated each element with a humor: earth with black bile; air with yellow bile; fire with blood; water with phlegm. It was Galen who extended Hippocrates's thinking to temperaments, thus creating an early theory of personality. If the dominant or excessive body humor is blood, the individual expresses a sanguine personality and is warm, optimistic, and easy-going. If black bile dominates, it produces a melancholic personality, and the individual is depressed and anxious. An excess of yellow bile produces a choleric personality, which is expressed by excitability, anger, and assertiveness. Finally, if there is excessive phlegm, the individual is phlegmatic and therefore slow, lazy or lethargic, and calm.

These embryonic ideas about personality were developed further by the influential philosopher Immanuel Kant (1724–1804) when he included a detailed discussion of temperament in his book *Anthropology From a Pragmatic Point of View* (1912). Like the analyses of Hippocrates and Galen, Kant's analysis of temperament did not allow for combinations of types. For example, one could not be a phlegmatic–melancholic, a person who is anxious and worried as well as reasonable and principled. It was Wilhelm Wundt (1832–1920), founder of the first experimental psychology laboratory, who developed the idea that personality was not a simple issue of categorical type. Wundt (1903) pointed out that the categories described by Kant were matters of degree, depending on one's position along the dimensions of *emotional strength* and *emotional changeability.* Choleric and melancholic types, for example, tend to experience intense emotions while sanguine and phlegmatic types tend to have less intense emotional experiences. In addition, choleric and sanguine types supposedly experience very rapid changes in their emotions while melancholic and phlegmatic types are described as more stable, experiencing slower emotional changes. Eysenck and Eysenck (1985) show the combination of Kant's analysis with Wundt's two dimensions of strength and changeability in Figure 8–6.

Eysenck's contribution to this analysis, shown in Figure 8-7, was recognizing that extroversion–introversion was equivalent to the dimension that Wundt called "emotional changeability" and that neuroticism (stability vs. instability) was identical to the dimension that Wundt labeled "emotional strength."

Figure 8–6

Diagrammatic representation of the classical theory of the four temperaments described by I. Kant and W. Wundt.

(From Eysenck & Eysenck, 1985, p. 45.)

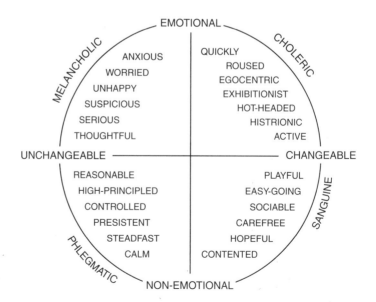

Figure 8–7

Relation between the four temperaments and the modern neuroticism-extroversion dimensional system.

(From Eysenck & Eysenck, 1985, p. 50.)

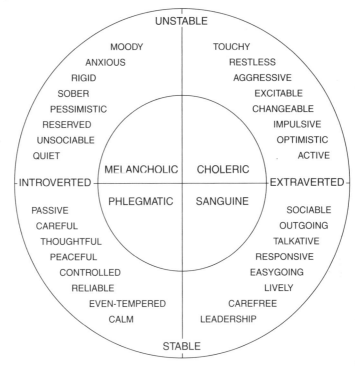

Biological Bases of Personality

For Eysenck, it was not enough to establish a measurement system and a taxonomy of personality types. His quest to interrelate test scores, behavior, and the underlying biological mechanisms with empirical data make his contribution to personality theory both unique and historically important.

Excitation and Inhibition

In his first attempt to develop a biological explanation of personality, Eysenck adopted ideas from the Russian researcher who discovered classical conditioning, Ivan Pavlov, and an American neobehaviorist, Clark L. Hull. (For further reading concerning both Pavlov and Hull, see Hergenhahn & Olson, 2001, 2005.) In early theorizing, Eysenck (1957) utilized concepts that were inferred from behavior rather than actually demonstrated in research. For example, Pavlov's explanation of classical conditioning relied heavily on his theoretical ideas about brain processes called excitation and inhibition. Noting that some dogs acquired conditioned responses more readily than others, Pavlov (1928) speculated that excitation dominated the nervous activity of some animals while inhibition dominated in others. Although Pavlov's studies were inconclusive, his ideas about excitatory versus inhibitory dominance captured Eysenck's attention. With respect to excitatory nervous activity, Eysenck borrowed from Pavlov's work and wrote in his typological postulate:

> Individuals in whom excitatory potential is generated slowly and in whom excitatory potentials so generated are relatively weak, are thereby predisposed to develop extraverted [sic] patterns of behavior . . . individuals in whom excitatory potential is generated quickly and in whom excitatory potentials so generated are strong, are thereby predisposed to develop introverted patterns of behavior. (1957, p. 114)

Eysenck's ideas about inhibition were greatly influenced by Hull's learning theory. Hull used the concept of *reactive inhibition* to explain phenomena like experimental extinction in which we observe decreased performance of a response. Basically, reactive inhibition is caused by fatigue—either muscular or neural—and acts to inhibit responding. Regarding the role of inhibition in personality, Eysenck (1957) continued in his typological postulate:

> Similarly, individuals in whom reactive inhibition is developed quickly, in whom strong reactive inhibitions are generated, and in whom reactive inhibition is dissipated slowly, are thereby predisposed to develop extraverted [sic] patterns of behavior . . . conversely, individuals in whom reactive inhibition is developed slowly, in whom weak reactive inhibitions are generated, and in whom reactive inhibition is dissipated quickly, are thereby predisposed to develop introverted patterns of behavior. (p. 114)

Cortical and Emotional Arousal

According to Jensen (2000), "Eysenck consistently rejected any theory, including his own, that was contradicted by empirical evidence" (p. 351). So, when Eysenck's efforts to explain personality in terms of excitation/inhibition proved disappointing he turned to arousal theory, which is based on well-documented brain processes. His use of **arousal theory** preserves the essential idea that the introvert's brain is characterized by higher levels of neural activity, and it improves on the earlier theory by providing an explanation for the neuroticism/stability (N) dimension of personality. The newer approach relies on two widely studied arousal systems in the brain. The first system, discovered by Moruzzi and Magoun (1949), is called the **ascending reticular activating system** (ARAS) and is responsible for patterns of excitation (and inhibition) of the cerebral cortex. The second system, referred to by Eysenck as the **visceral brain** (VB), is more often called the limbic system. It regulates emotional expression and controls autonomic responses (the symptoms of emotion) such as heartbeat, blood pressure, and sweating. Eysenck (1967) suggested that extroversion/introversion is controlled by the ARAS while emotional expression including neuroticism is independently mediated by the VB. As in the earlier theory summarized in the typological postulate, the introvert is characterized by higher levels of cortical excitation or arousal, mediated by the ARAS, than the extrovert. The neurotic is characterized by higher levels of autonomic activity (or reactivity), mediated by the VB, than the stable individual. Thus, the neurotic introvert, including Eysenck's dysthymic, has the highest overall arousal; both the ARAS and the VB are highly active. The individual that Eysenck called the "normal" extrovert experiences the lowest baseline arousal; both the ARAS and the VB are relatively inactive. The normal introvert and the neurotic extrovert are expected to fall between those extreme cases. Most recently, Eysenck (1990a) explored the relationships between psychoticism (P) and the activities of hormones such as testosterone and arousal-related enzymes such as monoamine oxidase (MAO). At this time, however, any links between hormones, enzymes, and psychoticism are only speculative.

Is Anatomy Destiny?

When posed for theorists like Freud or Horney, this question addresses the issue of gender. For Cattell and Eysenck, the question of anatomy and destiny takes on special meaning. Both theorists provide strong evidence for the **heritability** of key traits or types. Heritability is defined as the "proportion of the total variance in the phenotype which is due to the genotype" (Eysenck & Eysenck, 1985, p. 88), in other words, those differences in expression or appearance of a trait that are attributed to genetic influences rather than to environmental events. Thus, to the extent that genetic and biological factors are critical determinants of personality, the answer to the question, although not necessarily concerned with gender, must be "Yes!"

Cattell: Heredity versus Environment

No other personality theorist did more than Cattell to determine the relative contributions of heredity and environment to the development of each personality trait. To examine these contributions Cattell created a complicated statistical procedure called multiple abstract variance analysis (MAVA). In general, the method compares members of the same family raised together or raised apart, and unrelated persons raised either together or apart. Each person studied is given a test, or a series of tests, to assess a particular trait. More specifically, measurements are taken of identical twins raised together, identical twins raised apart, fraternal twins raised together, fraternal twins raised apart, siblings raised together, siblings raised apart, unrelated persons raised together, and unrelated persons raised apart (Cattell, 1982, p. 90). The number of genes in common is highest for identical twins, then fraternal twins and siblings, and is lowest for unrelated persons. The logic of such research is straightforward; if a trait is genetically determined, the degree to which it is possessed by two persons should be correlated with the degree to which they share the same genes. For example, if a trait is completely genetically determined, then identical twins should possess that trait whether they are raised together or apart.

On the basis of the type of research just described, Cattell concluded that heredity plays a significant role in the development of at least some traits. He confirmed his earlier observation that intelligence (fluid intelligence) is about 65 percent genetically determined. Also the tendency to have a zestful, active disposition versus a reflective, circumspective one was found to be about 70 percent genetically determined. Cattell, Schuerger, and Klein (1982) studied the heritability of three source traits: ego strength (factor C), superego strength (factor G), and self-sentiment (factor Q_3). In this particular study, a 10-hour battery of tests was administered to 94 identical twins reared together, 124 fraternal twins reared together, 470 brothers reared together, and 2,973 unrelated children reared apart. Using the MAVA procedure, the authors found that superego strength (factor G) is largely a function of environmental influences rather than heredity. However, ego strength (factor C) and self-sentiment (factor Q_3) were found to be strongly influenced by heredity. Cattell (1980, p. 58) reported the heritability of most of the other source traits. Several traits are found to have a genetic component of about 30% or more. When the overall contribution of heredity to personality is considered, Cattell essentially confirmed his earlier conclusion that personality is about two-thirds determined by environmental influences and about one-third by heredity (Hundleby, Pawlik, & Cattell, 1965).

Eysenck: The Biological Argument

Eysenck and Eysenck (1985) stated that, in order to demonstrate that P, E, and N have biological bases, four criteria must be met. These are: (1) data must demonstrate heritability or a genetic contribution to P, E, and N; (2) observations must confirm traits similar to P, E, and N in nonhuman animals; (3) evidence of P, E, and N must be found in many different cultures, and (4) P, E, and N must be found to be stable over time.

After reviewing a large body of data from twin studies, Eysenck and Eysenck (1985) summarized findings with respect to the heritability of personality traits:

> It is found that for practically all traits and dimensions of personality there is a considerable degree of genetic determination of individuals. . . . No serious worker in this field denies that genetic factors account for something like half the variance, and equally none would deny the importance of environmental variables. (p. 96)

The second criterion, the existence of personality in nonhuman animals, is an issue that must be approached carefully. We are often prone to anthropomorphize about our pets, attributing human moods and traits to their behavior. At the same time, we cannot deny that members of the same species often differ remarkably in *temperament.* In fact, the breeding of domesticated animals has focused on both physical and *temperamental* traits.

Research in the area of nonhuman temperament has generally been conducted by recording the activities of different individual animals in social groups. Researchers can avoid anthropomorphizing but still record whether an animal affiliates with others, is aggressive, actively avoids others, and so on. Using this method with rhesus monkeys, Chamove, Eysenck, and Harlow (1972) factor-analyzed their data and found that behaviors clustered in three independent clusters that corresponded roughly to P, E, and N. Chimpanzees also exhibit behaviors that are best described by three independent dimensions like those proposed by Eysenck (Van Hooff, 1971).

Although conducting cross-cultural personality assessment has its own difficulties, many attempts to gather trait and type data across cultures have confirmed widespread existence of P, E, and N. Again, summarizing a large data base, Eysenck and Eysenck (1985) wrote:

> Not wishing to paint the lily, we will refrain from commenting at too great length on the results, except to say that they are strongly in support of the view that *essentially the same dimensions of personality emerge from factor analytic studies of identical questionnaires in a large number of different countries* embracing not only European cultural groups but also many quite different types of nations. (p. 108)

And finally, many studies have demonstrated that Eysenck's superfactors, particularly E and N, are quite stable. They have been shown to be consistent over 12-year periods (Hindley & Giuganino, 1982), 15- to 20-year periods (Bronson, 1966,

1967), and even for more than 30 years (Conley, 1984; Leon, Gillenn, Gillenn, & Ganze, 1979; Mussen, Eichorn, Hanzik, Bieher, & Meredith, 1980). Even those theorists who have developed alternatives to Eysenck's theory and whose work will be discussed below have shown the long-term consistency of E and N (e.g., Costa & McCrae, 1980).

As we can see, the criteria that Eysenck identified as necessary in order to claim that a trait has a biological basis are satisfied. Most researchers working within the trait approach currently accept this conclusion to some degree, although the exact nature of the biological mechanisms underlying personality remain to be determined (Zuckerman, 1991, 1995).

Personality Development

Cattell's Multiple Influence Approach

Like most personality theorists, Cattell believed personality development is a function of both motivation and learning. Motivation is responsible for many changes in perceptual and behavioral capabilities.

Learning.   Learning allows changes in the way ergs are satisfied; that is, learning is responsible for the development of sentiments and attitudes. Cattell believed that there are three types of learning: classical conditioning, instrumental conditioning, and structured learning. He defined **classical conditioning** as a situation in which "a new stimulus gets attached to an old response by occurring a moment before the old stimulus" (1965, p. 266). **Instrumental conditioning** (also called reward learning or operant conditioning) is learning to perform a response that will produce a reward.

Cattell believed classical conditioning is important because it explains the learning of emotional responses toward people and objects. It also explains the development of phobias. Instrumental conditioning is important because it explains how specific acts are learned that satisfy specific needs. Most important, however, is **structured learning.** According to Cattell, when an element of the personality changes, it changes the entire configuration of traits. Although the ergs are innate, how ergic tensions are reduced is learned. For example, as we have seen, ergs manifest themselves in sentiments and attitudes. As these metaergs are learned, the entire structure of personality changes. The acquisition of a new trait, or the modification of an old one, is like throwing a pebble into a pond: The entire pond is influenced. One configuration of traits exists before learning; another exists after learning.

Importance of Early Experience.   Cattell believed that early experiences exert a strong influence on the development of certain personality traits. For example, he observed that adults displaying high *affectia* (see Table 8-2) typically come from a warm, loving home where the father was cheerful, the mother was calm, and the children were controlled through reasoning rather than punishment. The same is true for adults displaying a high level of ego strength (see Table 8-2). Proneness to dominance and guilt tends to characterize adults whose parents were authoritarian, used physical punishment, and were highly critical of their offspring. (For a further discussion of how various parental behaviors relate to the development of certain source traits, see Cattell, 1973, pp. 158–178).

Cattell (1973) also studied the Adlerian contention that birth order significantly impacts personality development. In general, he found that oldest children tend to be high in dominance, ego strength, and conservatism but low in self-sentiment strength. Only children tend also to be conservative but are high in self-sentiment strength. Children who are not the oldest tend to display surgency (see Table 8–2). Finally, Cattell found that ergic tension (trait Q 4) tends to increase as family size increases.

Syntality.   Cattell thought that because much of people's behavior is determined by their group affiliations, it is important to know as much as possible about the groups to which people belong. The term personality summarizes a person's traits whereas the term **syntality** summarizes a group's traits. Cattell studied groups such as families, various religions, schools, peer groups, and nations in the same way he studied people. For example, in one study (Cattell, Breul, & Hartman, 1952), 40 countries were evaluated on 72 variables. All measures were intercorrelated and factor-analyzed. It was found that the major differences between the countries could be explained using the following four factors:

Factor 1:   Enlightened Affluence versus Narrow Poverty

Factor 2:   Vigorous Order versus Unadapted Rigidity

Factor 3:   Cultural Pressure and Complexity versus Direct Ergic Expression

Factor 4:   Size

Thus the groups that influence people have traits too, and these traits can be uncovered by factor analysis, just as the traits characterizing people can be discovered using that technique. Once group or national traits have been discovered, a wide variety of comparisons can be made.

Eysenck and Heritable Traits

Eysenck's theory does not focus on development of traits during infancy and childhood, but, as we have seen, he did stress the genetic bases of P, E, and N. He did not claim, however, that types, traits, and the behaviors associated with them appear fully developed in human infants. A trait only provides a predisposition to behave in a certain way, and the behavior in question does not simply appear without appropriate environmental stimulation. Eysenck and Eysenck (1985) wrote:

> Usually the name of a given trait also implies the situation in which it can be demonstrated and measured, thus a trait theory directly implies a taxonomy of situations. . . . In other words, trait and situation form the two sides of a coin that cannot be separated from each other, and classical trait theories do not neglect situations; they directly imply them. (pp. 38–39)

Eysenck's position, like those of Allport and Cattell, exemplifies interactionism because it maintains that person variables (e.g., genetics and biological dispositions) and situation variables always interact to cause behavior. We will say more about interactionism when we discuss Bandura and Mischel's theory in Chapter 11.

Recent work by Jerome Kagan (1994) may help clarify the hereditarian position. Kagan's research demonstrates how a temperament-induced bias expresses itself both in infancy and in more fully developed adult behavior. Kagan and his colleagues note that some infants are more reactive than others to aversive stimuli. Furthermore, many of the extremely reactive infants grow, over the next few years, into what he calls *inhibited* children; and many of the extremely nonreactive children grow into what he calls *uninhibited* children (Kagan, 1994). Although Kagan does not refer directly to the similarities between inhibited children and introverts and between uninhibited children and extroverts, his research provides a glimpse of the early expression of these adult types. For example, inhibited children stay close to their mothers in novel situations, do not explore novel environments, and do not eagerly engage new people. That is, they behave in ways that Eysenck would call introverted. The uninhibited children, in contrast, leave their mothers' sides to explore new environments, play with new toys, and engage new people. They behave like Eysenck's classic extroverts.

For Eysenck, then, the development of personality is *directed* by genetically endowed traits but is tempered by environmental factors. Personality traits influence the kinds of situations that we find aversive and avoid as well as those that we enjoy and seek. Because they guide us toward some environments and turn us away from others, they influence the kinds of behaviors, experiences, and learning that we encounter and, therefore, indirectly shape the acquired, as opposed to the biological/genetic, aspects of our personalities.

Psychopathology

Cattell suggested two reasons for psychopathology. One is an abnormal imbalance of the normal personality traits; for example, those measured by the 16 PF. For instance, an excessive amount of factor A (affectia vs. sizia) could result in a manic-depressive disorder. The second reason for psychopathology is the possession of abnormal traits that are not found among normal individuals. Cattell and his colleagues isolated 12 abnormal traits that can be used to describe various types of neuroses and psychoses. Cattell (1975) devised the Clinical Analysis Questionnaire to assess those abnormal traits. The 12 abnormal traits Cattell discovered are listed in Table 8–3.

Table 8–3

Cattell's 12 Abnormal Source Traits

(Adopted from Cattell, , 1979, 1980)

FACTOR	LOW SCORE DESCRIPTION	HIGH SCORE DESCRIPTION
D_1	Low hypochondriasis	High hypochondriasis
D_2	Zestfulness	Suicidal disgust
D_3	Low brooding discontent	High brooding discontent
D_4	Low anxious depression	High anxious depression
D_5	High energy euphoria	Low energy depression
D_6	Low guilt and resentment	High guilt and resentment
D_7	Low bored depression	High bored depression
P_a	Low paranoia	High paranoia
P_p	Low psychopathic deviation	High psychopathic deviation
S_c	Low schizophrenia	High schizophrenia
A_s	Low psychasthenia	High psychasthenia
P_s	Low general psychosis	High general psychosis

Cattell concluded that abnormal persons are, first of all, like normal ones in that they possess all of the normal source traits. However, they may also possess pathological traits (Cattell, 1979, pp. 73–74). In Table 8-3, the first seven abnormal traits (symbolized by the letter D) are depressive traits. The last five traits are considered relatively more powerful and more serious.

Cattell, then, saw some individuals with serious psychopathology as *quantitatively* different from normal individuals while others were seen as *qualitatively* different. That is, they possess qualities—abnormal traits—not found in people who are not suffering from psychological disorders. Eysenck, on the other hand, saw the differences between normal individuals and those with psychopathologies only as quantitative. In other words, their personalities are described in terms of the same types, P, E, and N, as normals, but they have abnormally high scores on one or more superfactors, particularly on P and/or N.

It should be noted, however, that high scores on P or N do not necessarily guarantee psychopathology. As we saw above, traits require interaction with specific situations in order to attain full expression:

> There are many individuals whose psychoticism, neuroticism, and extraversion scores resemble those of the average manic-depressive or schizophrenic and yet who manage to lead relatively contented, symptom-free lives. Perhaps an individual's location within Eysenckian three-dimensional space can appropriately be regarded as a measure of his or her vulnerability to different kinds of mental illness. (Eysenck & Eysenck, 1985, p. 339)

Psychotherapy

Ideally for Cattell, psychotherapy should be preceded by a precise personality-factor assessment. Such a profile not only defines exactly what the problem is but also aids the clinician in determining the most effective treatment procedure. Furthermore, the P-technique should be used during treatment so that the changes occurring within the client, while he or she is in therapy, can be assessed. As far as therapeutic treatment is concerned, Cattell was an eclectic. He thought that the type of treatment should be dictated by the type of disorder that is revealed by precise personality assessment. Severe psychoses may be best treated by drugs or electric shock; certain neuroses may be best treated by dream analysis and the reliving of traumatic experiences; and for relatively minor problems some form of behavior therapy may be most effective (behavior therapy is discussed in the next chapter).

Eysenck also suggested that accurate personality testing leads to correct diagnoses and results in appropriate and more effective treatment. Wolpe and Plaud (1997) praise Eysenck for identifying E and N as biological influences that affect both acquisition of maladaptive behaviors and responsiveness to behavior therapies, such as systematic desensitization, used to treat those maladaptive behaviors.

While Cattell was eclectic in his approach to therapy, Eysenck, a long-time critic of psychoanalysis and proponent of behavior therapy, was far less accepting of therapies lacking empirical support. For Eysenck, therapy must be based on demonstrated psychological principles such as those derived from classical or operant conditioning. The ultimate test of a therapy lies not in its intent but in empirical evidence showing that patients receiving therapy actually improve more than no-treatment controls or patients receiving placebo treatments.

Contemporary Developments: The Big Five

A theory of personality called the "Big Five," or sometimes the "five-factor model," has generated considerable interest among trait theorists. This approach has a number of active advocates (Costa & McCrae, 1985; Costa & Widiger, 2002; DeRaad, 1998; Digman, 1989, 1990, 1996; Goldberg, 1990, 1993; McCrae & Costa, 1985, 1987, 1990, 1996, 1997) who challenge Cattell's and Eysenck's analyses and offer an alternative theory with five superfactors. Like Cattell and Eysenck, psychologists supporting the Big Five also use factor analysis as their primary analytical tool, and two of the five superfactors are virtually identical with two identified by Eysenck. And as we shall see, Cattell's research is often cited to support the contention that five factors are better than three or sixteen.

Specifically, the five superfactors include neuroticism and extroversion, defined in much the same way that Eysenck defined them. Also included are higher-order factors called openness (to experience), agreeableness, and conscientiousness. (Students may want to use the acronym OCEAN to remember the five factors.) Definitions of these factors are found in Table 8–4.

Although research on the Big Five has become popular in the last few years, the history of this approach can be traced back over 100 years to the work of Sir Francis Galton, and its history is grounded in what has become known as the **lexical**

Table 8–4

The Five-Factor Model of Personality

(Adopted: from Costa & McCrae, 1986c)

Neuroticism
Calm—Worrying
Even-tempered—Temperamental
Self-satisfied—Self-pitying
Comfortable—Self-conscious
Unemotional—emotional
Hardy—Vulnerable

Extraversion
Reserved—Affectionate
Loner—Joiner
Quiet—Talkative
Passive—Active
Sober—Fun-loving
Unfeeling—Passionate

Openness to experience
Down-to-earth—Imaginative
Uncreative—Creative
Conventional—Original
Prefer routine—Prefer variety
Uncurious—Curious
Conservative—Liberal

Aggreeableness
Ruthless—Soft-hearted
Suspicious—Trusting
Stingy—Generous
Antagonistic—Acquiescent
Critical—Lenient
Irritable—Good-natured

Conscientiousness
Negligent—Conscientious
Lazy—Hardworking
Disorganized—Well-organized
Late—Punctual
Aimless—Ambitious
Quitting—Persevering

hypothesis (Goldberg, 1981, 1993). The basic premise of the lexical hypothesis is that all we need to know about personality is contained in natural language (i.e., folk psychology). That is, the terms we commonly (and sometimes uncommonly) use to describe ourselves and each other contain all the information necessary to discern the fundamental dimensions of human personality.

Galton (1884), without the statistical power of factor analysis, collected terms from the dictionary that were descriptive of personality and noted that many of the words shared common meanings. Years later, L. L. Thurstone (1934), who was instrumental in the development of factor analysis, used an adjective checklist method in which he provided experimental participants with a list of 60 personality-descriptive adjectives. Participants were asked to think about some other person and to indicate whether each of the adjectives was descriptive of that person. Thurstone factor-analyzed the resulting data and concluded that the complexity of human personality could be described using as few as five major factors. He did not, however, suggest what those factors might be. Two years later, Allport and Odbert (1936), beginning with nearly 18,000 adjectives, developed a collection of approximately 4,500 personality-descriptive terms, 35 of which were used by Cattell (1943) in a factor-analytic study. As we saw previously, Cattell preferred to extract as many factors as possible in his data sets, and in his treatment of the 35 personality terms, he found at least 12 factors. Although Cattell did not become an advocate of the Big Five and did not deviate from his 16 PF approach, he is often credited with an early version of the lexical hypothesis when he insisted that "all aspects of human personality which are or have been of importance, interest, or utility have already become recorded in the substance of language." (Cattell, 1943, p. 483). Different researchers (Digman & Takemoto-Chock, 1981; Norman, 1963) and most notably Tupes and Christal (1961) reanalyzed Cattell's variables and concluded that only five of his factors could be replicated. Although some of the names have changed, those factors are the same as those that have been the basis of all subsequent work on the Big Five.

The researchers most often associated with the Big Five, Paul T. Costa and Robert R. McCrae, entered the trait debate with a three-factor theory derived from a personality questionnaire rather than from an adjective checklist. Their first set of superfactors consisted of neuroticism, extroversion, and openness, and the personality inventory that these authors developed is the NEO-PI (neuroticism, extroversion, openness—personality inventory). After attending two symposia held by Digman and Goldberg, two researchers from the lexical school described above, Costa and McCrae, were convinced that the two additional factors of agreeableness and conscientiousness should be added to their model. They further refined their personality questionnaire and arbitrarily developed six facets (lower-order traits) for each of the five superfactors in the Big Five. These are shown in Table 8–4.

Have the Big Five Displaced Cattell and Eysenck?

Despite the current popularity of the Big Five approach to personality, the two most prolific trait theorists, Cattell and Eysenck, refused to adopt it. Eysenck (1991) perhaps made the clearest argument against the position. Eysenck argued that agreeableness and conscientiousness are primary traits rather than superfactors. Eysenck concluded that advocates of the Big Five mix superfactors (e.g., neuroticism and extroversion) with primary traits (e.g., agreeableness and conscientiousness) in order to inflate the number of superfactors in their model from two to four. And what about openness? Eysenck suggested two possibilities. One (Eysenck & Eysenck, 1985) is that, like agreeableness and conscientiousness, openness is negatively related to P and is actually a primary trait rather than a superfactor. More recently, Eysenck (1991) indicated that several studies show openness to be correlated with intelligence and therefore a cognitive ability factor, not a temperament factor. Recall from our earlier discussion that Eysenck excluded ability factors from his formal analysis of personality. Draycott and Kline (1995) analyzed both Costa and McCrae's NEO-PI and the Eysenck Personality Questionnaire (Revised) (EPQ-R). They agree with Eysenck's earlier claim that the Big Five mixes lower-order with higher-order factors.

A direct attack on the Big Five comes from Block (1995), who retraces the history of the Big Five and suggests that the emergence of five factors is more a matter of research planning than it is a matter of empirical discovery. He suggests that the advocates of the Big Five have invested their research interests in validating the five factors rather than testing the theory. Even Costa and McCrae indicate that, beyond explicit identification of openness, agreeableness, and conscientiousness, the Big Five add little to the current body of data about personality. They note that the theory contains "few surprises; the basic ideas are familiar from many personality theories" (McCrae & Costa, 1996, p. 75). Thus, while the Big Five model enjoys a degree of popularity, it has not replaced Eysenck's PEN or Cattell's 16 PF. Block, for example, argues that the Big Five model is not at all what it claims to be:

> The Big Five are often called "the five-factor model of personality" and are referred to as providing an understanding of the "structure of personality." As the term "model" is used in conventional parlance among psychologists, it means a theoretically based, logically coherent, working representation or simulation that, in operation, attempts to generate psychological phenomena of interest. However, no identifiable hypotheses, theories, or models guided the emergence of or decision on this five-fold space. . . . Because the Big Five formulation was entirely atheoretical, usage of the term "model" may be premature. (p. 188)

Additional dissatisfaction with the Big Five has led Zuckerman (1991, 1995) to propose a biologically based "Alternative Five," which includes sociability (related to extroversion), neuroticism-anxiety, impulsive sensation seeking, aggression-hostility, and activity.

Thus, although it may be intuitively appealing that the complexity of human personality requires more than three superfactors, it may be inappropriate to proclaim the overthrow of Eysenck's three-factor model by the Big Five. In fact, it may turn out that something like Cattell's 16 personality factors may be necessary for a full description of personality. The matter is far from settled.

Evaluation

Cattell's and Eysenck's theories are unique among the theories presented so far in this text because of their substantial empirical support. Numerous studies have been discussed throughout this chapter and a few more are discussed below.

Cattell: Empirical Research

Cattell and Nesselroade (1967) used the 16 PF to determine the personality profiles of persons involved in a stable marriage and those involved in an unstable marriage. An unstable marriage was defined as one in which at least one step had been taken toward dissolution. Contrary to the old saying "opposites attract," it was found that stable marriages were characterized by similarities in traits among the couples, unstable marriages revealed dissimilar traits among the couples.

Cattell, Eber, and Tatsuoka (1970) used the 16 PF to study the personality profiles of men and women who had attempted suicide. The profiles for men and women were similar and both departed significantly from profiles generated by the general adult population. In general, those who had attempted suicide were more introverted, more anxious, and displayed lower superego strength when compared to the general adult population. The same study found that airline pilots and flight attendants had profiles nearly opposite to those who had attempted suicide. Compared to the general adult population, airline pilots and attendants were more extroverted, less anxious, and displayed more superego strength.

Predictive Science and Determinism.   Like Eysenck, Cattell believed a theory of personality is of little value unless it can predict behavior. In arriving at his predictions, Cattell was very much a determinist. That is, he believed behavior is a function of a finite number of variables, and if those variables are completely known, human behavior can be predicted with complete accuracy. Such a belief characterizes **determinism.** Cattell and other determinists realize that all of the variables influencing behavior can never be known, so the prediction of behavior will always be probabilistic. Realizing this, the determinist says that as more is known about the variables influencing human behavior, predictions of human behavior will become more accurate. According to Cattell, this is also true in the realm of personality research. The more we know about the various traits of a particular person, the better we will be able to predict his or her behavior.

What, then, is personality to Cattell? It is that which allows the accurate prediction of a person's behavior:

> Personality is that which permits a prediction of what a person will do in a given situation. The goal of psychological research in personality is thus to establish laws about what different people will do in all kinds of social and general environmental situations. . . . Personality is . . . concerned with all behavior of the individual, both overt and under the skin. (1950, pp. 2–3)

Eysenck: Empirical Research

Experimental and correlational studies spanning over 50 years have provided an impressive database to support Eysenck's beliefs concerning E and to a lesser extent N and P. These studies range from relatively straightforward confirmations concerning the behaviors of basic personality types to very complex attempts to reveal the brain functions assumed by the ARAS-VB arousal model.

Social Behavior.   Both male and female extroverts are more likely to have sexual intercourse at younger ages than introverts; they are more likely to have multiple sexual partners; and they are more likely to engage in different types of sexual activities (Eysenck, 1976; Giese & Schmidt, 1968). On the other hand, introverts in adolescence and adulthood tend to demonstrate superior academic achievement. This is found in both Western and non-Western cultures (Furneaux, 1957; Kline, 1966; Lynn, 1959). Finally, Eysenck (1967, 1977) reported that individuals with high E, high N, and high P scores are more likely to engage in criminal activity.

Perceptual Phenomena. Introverts, according to Eysenck, experience a high baseline arousal. They should, therefore, be more sensitive to high levels of environmental stimulation. Elliott (1971) and Ludvigh and Happ (1974) asked experimental participants to adjust auditory tones to levels that were just loud enough to be uncomfortable. In both experiments, extroverts adjusted tones to levels that were louder than those selected by introverts. Extroverts also have higher pain tolerance thresholds than do introverts. That is, they will tolerate strong electrical shock or painfully cold temperatures at more intense levels for longer periods of time before asking the experimenter to terminate the painful stimuli (Bartol & Costello, 1976; Shiomi, 1978).

Conditioning. Eyeblink conditioning is often used to demonstrate classical conditioning in humans, and Eysenck (1965) and Jones, Eysenck, Martin, and Levey (1981) reported that, in general, introverts demonstrate more rapid eyeblink conditioning than extroverts. Eysenck and Levey (1972) examined the variables involved in classical conditioning experiments and determined that introverts demonstrate superior conditioning under partial reinforcement schedules, with weak to moderately strong USs, and at short CS-US intervals, as might be predicted if they have higher cortical arousal. Conversely, extroverts acquire conditioned responses more rapidly under continuous reinforcement, with strong USs, and when the CS-US interval is relatively long. If needed, definitions of the symbols just used to denote the elements of classical conditioning can be found on page 266.

If introverts demonstrate superior conditioning because of higher levels of cortical arousal, then drugs that increase cortical arousal should also enhance conditioning. This phenomenon has, in fact, been demonstrated by administering a stimulant (dexamphetamine sulfate) prior to classical conditioning (Franks & Trouton, 1958). Also as expected, administration of sedative drugs that reduce arousal inhibit classical conditioning (Franks & Laverty, 1955; Franks & Trouton, 1958; Willet, 1960). Similarly, administration of stimulants enhances operant conditioning while depressants interfere with it (Gupta, 1973).

Drug Effects. An alternative method of testing the arousal model is called the sedation threshold method. In this approach, a sedative drug is given until a patient's behavior reflects a predetermined sedation criterion. The dependent variable in this experiment is the minimum amount of the drug necessary to produce this behavior. For example, we might determine the amount of drug necessary to produce slurred speech and compare the average dose needed to produce slurred speech in introverts with the amount needed to produce the same effect in extroverts. According to Eysenck's arousal theory, introverts have a higher baseline arousal level and should require more sedative drug to produce a given sedation effect. This prediction has been confirmed using barbiturates (Krishnamoorti & Shagass, 1963; Laverty, 1958; Shagass & Jones, 1958). Other studies have demonstrated that individuals with high levels of N and low E (introverts) require more sedative than other participants (Claridge, Donald, & Birchall, 1981; Claridge & Ross, 1973).

Electrophysiological Measures.   Numerous studies have attempted to detect differences between introverts and extroverts using electroencephalograms (EEGs) or a related technique called the event-related potential (ERP), which is an accumulated, averaged EEG elicited by a specific stimulus. Although results have been mixed, Eysenck (Eysenck, 1990a Eysenck & Eysenck, 1985;) reviewed the accumulated evidence and concluded that introverts show higher arousal, as measured in EEG recordings, in most cases and particularly in those instances where test conditions themselves are moderately arousing (Gale, 1973, 1983). Evidence from the ERP technique has been less supportive, although one experiment demonstrated ERPs of greater magnitude for introverts (Stelmack, Achorn, & Michaud, 1977). Although some critics claim that electrophysiological evidence clearly fails to confirm Eysenck's (1967) arousal hypothesis, the data from studies of conditioning, drug effects, and many other phenomena not discussed here reveal fundamental differences between extroverts and introverts that are not easily explained by theories that attribute personality differences primarily to socialization.

For a critical examination of Eysenck's main research endeavors, see Mogdil and Mogdil (1986).

Criticisms

Too Subjective.   As scientifically rigorous as Cattell's and Eysenck's theories appear to be, a number of critics claim that they still are characterized by too much subjectivity. One source of subjectivity, say the critics, is in determining what to study about people at the outset. What comes out of a factor analysis is totally dependent on what goes into it. Subjectivity is also involved in determining what will be accepted as evidence of a factor. That is, how many variables must be correlated and how high must the correlations be? Finally, how many factors need to be postulated to account for the data? The subjective nature of the many decisions involved in the factor-analytic approach to studying personality is reflected in the fact that, for example, others have not been able to replicate many of Cattell's findings. For example, Digman and Takemoto-Chock (1981) noted that many of Cattell's factors or source traits have not been found by other researchers. As we have seen, there is some disagreement concerning the number of factors required to adequately describe human personality.

Behavior Not as Consistent as Factor Theories Suggest.   Although Cattell and Eysenck did not ignore the influence of specific environmental situations on behavior, they still assumed a considerable amount of cross-situational consistency in behavior. Critics claim that such consistency simply does not exist (see, e.g., Mischel, 1968; Mischel & Peake, 1982). To the extent to which it is found that behavior is not at least moderately consistent across time and similar situations, theories such as those of Allport, Cattell, and Eysenck suffer.

Excessive Emphasis on Groups and Averages.   Although Cattell developed his P-technique partially to appease Allport, Allport was still dissatisfied with the way Cattell went about discovering traits to begin with. In a criticism that can be extended to Eysenck, Allport argued that Cattell's method yielded average traits that no person actually possessed:

An entire population (the larger the better) is put into the grinder, and the mixing is so expert that what comes through is a link of factors in which every individual has lost his identity. His dispositions are mixed with everyone else's dispositions. The factors thus obtained represent only average tendencies. Whether a factor is really an inorganic disposition in any one individual is not demonstrated. All one can say for certain is that a factor is an empirically derived component of the average personality, and that the average personality is a complete abstraction. This objection gains point when one reflects that seldom do the factors derived in this way resemble the dispositions and traits identified by clinical methods when the individual is studied intensively. (1937, p. 244)

Elsewhere Allport said that the traits produced by factor analysis "resemble sausage meat that has failed to pass the pure food and health inspection" (1958b, p. 251). Allport's point is valid only when one looks at how traits or superfactors are identified. Most of this research did involve large groups of people and dealt with averages. Once the 16 personality traits or three superfactors were isolated, however, they were used to understand the behavior of individual persons and to predict individual behavior. To say that Cattell and Eysenck were only interested in groups and in averages is incorrect.

Reification.   Reification occurs when it is assumed that a verbal label refers to something that exists physically. We saw in Chapter 7 that Allport believed traits were real psychophysical structures that determined behavior. Cattell and Eysenck, too, imply that the source traits and superfactors actually exist. If traits are considered convenient fictions postulated for scientific expediency, there is no problem. There is, however, little evidence suggesting that source traits and superfactors have material existence.

Contributions

Both Cattell and Eysenck are notable for their pioneering scientific efforts in a field that was, in its early forms, riddled with unbridled speculation and unsubstantiated, near-mystical beliefs. Because the use of scientific methodology in the study of personality is often characterized as the most significant contribution made by Cattell and Eysenck, we will elaborate their scientific orientations next.

Cattell: Beyondism.   Throughout his career, Cattell has combined scientific rigor with compassion for the human situation. These dual interests are exemplified in Cattell's books *A New Morality from Science: Beyondism* (1972) and *Beyondism: Religion from Science* (1987). Cattell (1987) defined **beyondism** as follows:

What, briefly, is Beyondism? It is a system for discovering and clarifying ethical goals from a basis of scientific knowledge and investigation, by the objective research procedures of scientific method. This does not deny it emotional richness, but in fact calls for the deepest, most genuine emotional satisfaction and loyalty, unaided and unbetrayed by myths and illusions. It believes that the difficult and honest thinking that has given us power, light, warmth, speed of travel, and worldwide instant communication by the physical sciences, and health and longevity by the medical sciences, is capable of giving us definiteness of values, true social progress, and peace of mind, in our individual, national, and international behavior. (p. 1)

Beyondism places great value on evolutionary principles such as fitness and natural selection (see Chapter 12). The relationship between biological and cultural evolution is extremely important for Cattell. The products of biological evolution (i.e., people) create culture, and culture, in turn, influences biological evolution. The optimal situation occurs when biological and cultural evolution are compatible. For example, it is best when a moral system is conducive to biological survival and advancement. Traditional moral systems were based on "revealed" knowledge and were taken on faith. By contrast, the religion of beyondism will be based on scientific facts whose effectiveness can be objectively evaluated:

> With good fortune we shall before long see the revealed religions fading out of the more advanced countries. The great cathedrals will become spiritual landmarks of the past. . . . Out of the superstition-ridden night of the past two thousand years will gradually dawn the light of science-based evolutionary religion. It is to this new structuring of life that the present believers in Beyondism must apply themselves. (Cattell, 1987, p. 256)

Needless to say, Cattell's proposal to replace the traditional religious foundation of morality with scientific objectivity was another reason he was surrounded by controversy.

Eysenck: Farewell to Mythical Psychology. As an advocate of the hypothetico-deductive method in scientific research, Eysenck attempted to develop a testable psychological theory in the natural science tradition. He challenged other psychologists to subject their own theories to the same scrutiny, and he rejected many theories—including many of those covered in this text—because of their scientific shortcomings:

> As an example, I would class among the inadmissable theories those of Freud, Adler, Jung, Binswanger, Horney, Sullivan, Fromm, Erikson, and Maslow. They fail essentially because for the most part they do not generate testable deductions; because where they do so the deductions have most frequently been falsified; and because they fail to include practically all the experimental and empirical studies which have been done over the last 50 years. Historically these theorists have had some influence, but their theorizing and their mode of working has not been in the tradition of natural science, and they have not been found responsive to adverse criticism or empirical disproof. (Eysenck, 1991, p. 774)

Why, then, are these theories popular? According to Eysenck, their popularity is largely explained by the common tendency of not letting the difficult, and often relatively uninteresting, scientific truth stand in the way of an unscientific good story.

Most people of course, whatever they may say, do not in fact, want a scientific account of human nature and personality at all—indeed, this is the last thing they really wish for. Hence they much prefer the great story-teller S. Freud, or the great myth-creator, C. G. Jung, to those who, like Cattell or Guilford, expect them to learn matrix algebra, study physiological details of the nervous system, and actually carry out experiments, rather than rely on interesting anecdotes, sex-ridden case histories, and ingenious speculation. After all, after-dinner conversation can easily encompass the Oedipus complex, or penis envy; it would be much more difficult to talk about a non-Gramian matrix, or the reticular formation! (Eysenck, 1972, p. 24)

According to Farley (2000), Eysenck's efforts to import the rigor of hard science into the "soft" area of personality were truly remarkable: "His identification and measurement of the most basic, pervasive, and reliable dimensions of personality stand as one of psychology's greatest achievements" (p. 674).

Applied Value. Personality tests devised by Cattell and Eysenck have been used for clinical diagnoses, personnel selection, vocational counseling, marital counseling, and to predict accident proneness, the possibility of heart attacks in men, rates of recovery from cancer, and scholastic performance. Versions of Cattell's evaluative devices, for example, have been translated into more than a dozen languages, and in each language they are used extensively for both research and practical applications.

Summary

Cattell and Eysenck begin the study of personality by measuring a large group of individuals in as many ways as possible. The measures then are intercorrelated and displayed in a correlation matrix. The measures that are moderately or highly correlated are thought to measure the same attribute. This procedure is called factor analysis, and the attributes it detects are called factors or traits. Cattell's theory emphasizes the source traits detected by factor analysis. Eysenck's theory emphasizes higher-order traits, derived from the intercorrelations between source traits, that are called superfactors or types.

Cattell described a number of different types of traits. His most important distinction was between surface traits and source traits. Surface traits are those that are actually measured and are, therefore, expressed in overt behavior of some kind. Source traits are those that are the underlying causes of overt behavior. Some source traits are genetically determined and are called constitutional traits. Other source traits are shaped by one's culture and are called environmental-mold traits. Cattell also distinguished between ability, temperament, and dynamic traits. The most important ability trait is intelligence, of which Cattell described two types. Fluid intelligence is general problem-solving ability and is thought to be largely genetically determined. Crystallized intelligence is the cumulated knowledge of the type learned in school and is thus gained through experience. Although crystallized intelligence is gained through experience, one's ability to effectively utilize such information is also largely genetically determined. Temperament traits are constitutional and determine a person's emotional makeup and style of behaving. Dynamic traits determine a person's motivational makeup. Cattell distinguished two categories of dynamic traits: ergs and metaergs. Ergs are roughly equivalent to instincts, biological needs, or primary drives. Metaergs are learned drives, divided into sentiments and attitudes. Sentiments are predispositions to act in certain ways to classes of objects or events. Attitudes are specific responses to specific objects or events. Because ergs are at the core of one's motivational patterns, sentiments are said to be subsidiary to ergs, and because attitudes depend on sentiments, attitudes are said to be subsidiary to sentiments. Cattell diagrammed the relationships among ergs, sentiments, and attitudes in what he called the dynamic lattice. The fact that humans almost inevitably take indirect routes to satisfy ergic tensions is referred to as long-circuiting.

Eysenck also believed that intelligence is, for the most part, genetically determined; but the focus of his theory of personality is temperament, a concept that, for Eysenck, did not include intelligence or ability. He argued that traits are genetically influenced rather than learned and are arranged hierarchically. Eysenck identified three superfactors that he believed are sufficient to describe human personality, all of which have biological bases. These include extroversion (vs. introversion), different levels of which are attributed to different levels of arousal of the cerebral cortex. Individuals with high extroversion are believed to have low levels of cortical arousal while individuals with high introversion are believed to have high levels of cortical arousal. The second major factor is neuroticism (vs. stability), and high levels of neuroticism are attributed to excessive activity of the autonomic nervous system. The third major factor, psychoticism, is used primarily to explain severe psychotic disorders and biological explanations are currently not well established.

To explain how personality develops, Cattell postulated three types of learning: classical and instrumental conditioning and structured learning. The latter is the most important type of learning because it involves a change in one's entire personality. Cattell has shown the relationship between various early home environments and the development of various personality traits. He also found support for Adler's assertion that birth order and family size significantly impact personality development. Using his MAVA, Cattell attempted to determine the relative contributions of heredity and environment to the development of various traits. He found that some traits have a very strong genetic component (e.g., intelligence), and some have practically none (e.g., superego strength). Overall Cattell concluded that about one-third of personality is determined by genetics and about two-thirds by environmental influence. Eysenck emphasized the genetic bases of traits and types and did not place great theoretical importance on developmental issues. He noted, however, that the situations in which traits and types manifest themselves always influence how they will be expressed.

Cattell believed that psychopathology can result from either an abnormal configuration of the normal source traits, or from the possession of one or more of the 12 abnormal traits. Eysenck attributed psychopathology only to abnormally high levels of the three superfactors that characterize all personality. He did not suggest the existence of separate, abnormal traits.

Cattell and Eysenck believed that trait analysis should precede psychotherapy because such an analysis will provide an accurate diagnosis of the problem and will suggest the most effective method of treatment. Also, trait evaluation should occur throughout therapy to determine how treatment is affecting the client's total personality. While Cattell was eclectic with respect to psychotherapy, Eysenck only advocated therapies, such as behavior therapy, that are derived from empirically demonstrated psychological principles and that have been shown to be effective. Both theories have been criticized for containing too many subjective elements, for assuming that human behavior is more consistent than it actually is, for concentrating too much on groups and group averages at the expense of the unique individual, and for implying that the source traits have actual physical existence.

Both theories have been praised for providing scientific rigor to the study of personality, an area that typically lacks such rigor, and providing tools that can be used in a large number of applied areas, for example, clinical diagnoses, vocational and marital counseling, and personnel selection.

Experiential Exercises

1. By referring to Table 8-2, administer Cattell's 16 PF questionnaire to yourself. Assume a 10 is the highest score you can attain on a factor and a 1 is the lowest. A score of 5 indicates you think you are about in the middle of the two extremes for any given factor. In other words, any score from 1 to 10 is possible for each of the 16 factors. Next, create a personality profile for yourself like those shown in Figure 8-3. Cattell has found that, at least in the case of married couples, the more similar the profiles of two persons, the more positive is their relationship. Have someone you are close to respond to the 16 PF questionnaire, and summarize his or her performance in a personality profile. Compare yours with his or hers. What conclusions do you draw from the comparison?

2. Look at the traits assumed under each of the superfactors illustrated in Figure 8-5. To simplify, assume that you either have a trait or that you don't. Using this all-or-nothing method, determine which of the traits under the P, E, and N types you possess. Do you have a majority of the traits under a particular type—enough to classify you as a "high P," "high E," or "high N"?

3. Assume the role of either Cattell or Eysenck. Approach the prediction of your behavior as one of these two theorists would. Assume the more you know about yourself and the situation you are in, the more accurate will be your prediction of your behavior in that situation. Take any situation that you will find yourself in shortly (e.g., a social event, a major test, going home for a visit with relatives) and list the types of information you would need to know about you and the situation to predict your behavior accurately. For this exercise you will need to use some of the information that you learned about yourself in exercise 1 (as Cattell) or exercise 2 (as Eysenck). What conclusion do you reach concerning the prediction of your behavior?

Discussion Questions

1. Describe the technique of factor analysis as it is used to study personality.
2. Summarize Eysenck's position concerning nomothetic versus idiographic research.

3. Discuss Eysenck's distinction between intelligence and personality. Why is his personality theory a theory of temperament?

Glossary

Ability trait.   Trait that determines how effectively a person works toward a desired goal. Intelligence is such a trait.

Arousal theory.   A general class of theories that assumes behavior is partly a function of the general state of arousal (excitation) or de-arousal (inhibition) of the cortex and/or other brain structures.

Ascending reticular activating system (ARAS).   A network of neurons in the reticular formation of the brain stem that is responsible for cortical arousal and de-arousal.

Attitude.   A learned tendency to respond in a particular way in a particular situation to a particular object or event. Attitudes derive from sentiments, which in turn derive from ergs. An attitude is one type of metaerg.

Beyondism.   Cattell's proposal that scientific facts be utilized to create moral systems rather than religious illusions or philosophical speculation.

Classical conditioning.   Type of learning in which a stimulus that did not originally elicit a response is made to do so. Cattell believed many emotional responses to persons, objects, or events are learned through classical conditioning.

Cluster analysis.   Systematic search of a correlation matrix in order to discover factors.

Constitutional trait.   Genetically determined trait.

Correlation.   Condition that exists when values on two variables vary together in some systematic way.

Correlation coefficient.   Mathematical expression indicating the extent to which two variables are correlated. Correlation coefficients can vary from +1.00, indicating a perfect positive correlation, to −1.00, indicating a perfect negative correlation.

Correlation matrix.   Display of the many correlation coefficients that result when many sources of information are intercorrelated.

Crystallized intelligence.   Type of intelligence that comes from formal education or from general experience. It is the type of intelligence that most intelligence tests attempt to measure.

Culture Free Intelligence Test.   Test designed by Cattell to measure fluid intelligence rather than crystallized intelligence.

Determinism.   Belief that behavior is a function of a finite number of variables, and if those variables were completely known, behavior could be predicted with complete accuracy.

Dynamic lattice.   Diagram showing the relationships among ergs, sentiments, and attitudes.

Dynamic trait.   Motivational trait that sets a person in motion toward a goal. Cattell postulated the existence of two types of dynamic traits: ergs and metaergs.

Dysthymic.   In Eysenck's theory, a diagnosis given to severely disordered, introverted neurotics whose symptoms include anxiety, sensitivity, fatigue, and exhaustion.

Environmental-mold trait.   Trait that is determined by experience rather than by heredity.

Erg.   Constitutional dynamic source trait that provides the energy for all behavior. Much the same as what other theorists call a primary drive. Hunger and thirst are examples of ergs.

Ergic tension.   Tension that varies as the intensity of an erg varies.

Extroversion.   The superfactor or type in Eysenck's theory that includes the traits of sociability, activity, assertiveness, and sensation-seeking, to name a few.

Factor.   Ability or characteristic that is thought to be responsible for consistent behavior. In Cattell's system, a factor is also called a trait.

Factor analysis.   Complex statistical technique based on the concept of correlation, which

Cattell and Eysenck used to discover and investigate personality traits.

Fluid intelligence. General problem-solving ability that is largely innate.

Heritability. The proportion of variability in the expression of a trait that is attributed to genetics, as opposed to environmental influences.

Hypothetico-deductive reasoning (or hypothetico-deductive research). A method (exemplified in Eysenck's research) that begins with a hypothesis that guides data collection.

Hysteric. In Eysenck's theory, a diagnosis given to severely disordered, neurotic extroverts whose symptoms may include hysterical conversion(s) such as non-neurological paralysis or blindness.

Inductive reasoning (or inductive research). A method (exemplified in Cattell's research) that begins with collection of data, which then leads to hypotheses.

Instrumental conditioning. Learning to make a response that will either make a reward available or remove an aversive stimulus.

L-data. Information about a person's everyday life. The *L* stands for life record.

Lexical hypothesis. The idea that all necessary information about personality is revealed in everyday language.

Long-circuiting. Indirect satisfaction of an erg. An example is a man developing athletic ability in order to be desirable to a woman who will satisfy his sexual desires.

Metaerg. Environmental-mold, dynamic source trait. Much the same as what other theorists called secondary or learned drives. *See also* Attitude and Sentiment.

Negative correlation. Condition that exists when, as values on one variable tend to increase, values on a second variable tend to decrease, and vice versa.

Neuroticism. The superfactor or type in Eysenck's theory that includes traits of anxiety, depression, guilt, low self-esteem, and shyness, to name a few.

Personality sphere. Universe of source traits in terms of which all humans can be compared. The number of source traits in this universe is as yet undetermined.

Positive correlation. Condition that exists when values on two variables tend to increase or decrease together.

Psychoticism. The superfactor or type in Eysenck's theory that includes traits of aggression, egocentricity, impulsiveness, and creativity, to name a few.

P-technique. Type of factor analysis that studies how a single individual's traits change over time.

Q-data. Information provided when people fill out a questionnaire on which they rate themselves on various characteristics. The *Q* stands for questionnaire.

R-technique. Type of factor analysis that studies many things about many people.

Self-sentiment. Concern for oneself that is a prerequisite to the pursuit of any goal in life.

Sentiment. Learned predisposition to respond to a class of objects or events in a certain way. A sentiment is one type of metaerg.

Source traits. Traits that constitute a person's personality structure and are thus the ultimate causes of behavior. Source traits are causally related to surface traits.

Structured learning. Type of learning that results in rearranging one's personality traits. According to Cattell, this is the most important type of learning.

Subsidiation. Sentiments depend on ergs, and attitudes depend on sentiments.

Superfactor (also called type). In Eysenck's theory, a higher-order factor that encompasses or explains a number of correlated traits or first-order factors.

Surface traits. Outward manifestations of source traits. These are the characteristics of a person that can be directly observed and measured.

Syntality. Description of the traits that characterize a group or a nation.

T-data. Information obtained about a person from performance on an objective test. The *T* stands for test.

Temperament. Composite factors that describe the emotional, motivational, and cognitive aspects of behavior. Temperament does not include intelligence or ability.

Temperament trait. Constitutional source trait that determines a person's emotionality and style of behaving.

Trait. Refers either to a group of interrelated overt behaviors (surface trait) or to the deeper determinant of such interrelated behavior (source traits). The main usefulness of surface traits is that they provide information about source traits.

Type. *See* Superfactor.

Visceral brain (VB). Eysenck's term for the limbic system, a subcortical brain system that influences the autonomic nervous system.

CHAPTER **9**

B. F. SKINNER

CHAPTER OUTLINE

Biographical Sketch
Skinner and Personality Theory
Respondent and Operant Behavior
Operant Conditioning
Chaining
Verbal Behavior
Reinforcement Schedules
Superstitious Behavior
Reinforcement Contingencies
Our Biggest Problem
Behavior Disorders and Behavior Therapy
Walden Two
Beyond Freedom and Dignity
Evaluation
Summary
Experiential Exercises
Discussion Questions
Glossary

It is ironic that B. F. Skinner's views are being considered in a text on personality theory because he denied both the concept of personality and the use of theories as research tools. With respect to personality, Skinner wrote:

> I do not believe that my life shows a type of personality à la Freud, an archetypal pattern à la Jung, or a schedule of development à la Erikson. There have been a few abiding themes, but they can be traced to environmental sources rather than to traits of character. They became a part of my life as I lived it; they were not there at the beginning to determine its course. (1983, p. 401)

As we see in the preceding quotation, Skinner rejected many of the core ideas of personality theories we have considered thus far. He adhered to an approach in psychology known as **radical behaviorism,** which we will describe shortly. Most importantly, many concepts found in other theories, concepts such as consciousness, the unconscious, anxiety, and even the idea of the "self"—real or ideal—are not considered.

Biographical Sketch

Burrhus Frederic Skinner was born on March 20, 1904, in Susquehanna, Pennsylvania. He was the first child of William Arthur and Grace Madge Skinner. A second son, Edward James, was born two and a half years later but died suddenly of a cerebral aneurism when Skinner was a freshman in college. Skinner considered his mother the dominant member of the family and was often reminded that she almost died bringing him into the world (Skinner, 1976, p. 23). The Presbyterian religion was a major theme in Skinner's early life. He attended bible classes and embraced a number of traditional religious beliefs. During adolescence, however, he abandoned his religious convictions and never returned to them. Skinner's father was a lawyer who wanted his son to follow in his footsteps, but that was not to be.

Skinner was raised according to strict standards but was physically punished only once:

> I was never physically punished by my father and only once by my mother. She washed my mouth out with soap and water because I had used a bad word. My father never missed an opportunity, however, to inform me of the punishments which were waiting if I turned out to have a criminal mind. He once took me through the county jail, and on a summer vacation I was taken to a lecture with colored slides describing life in Sing Sing. As a result I am afraid of the police and buy too many tickets to their annual dance. (1967, pp. 390–391)

Perhaps this unusually small amount of physical punishment influenced Skinner's later theoretical emphasis on the positive rather than on the negative (i.e., via punishment) control of behavior.

Skinner's aptitude for creative apparatus building, for which he became widely known, was evident in his childhood:

> I was always building things. I built roller-skate scooters, steerable wagons, sleds, and rafts to be poled about on shallow ponds. I made see-saws, merry-go-rounds, and slides. I made slingshots, bows and arrows, blow guns and water pistols from lengths of bamboo, and from a discarded water boiler a steam cannon with which I could shoot plugs of potato and carrot over the houses of our neighbors. . . . I worked for years on the design of a perpetual motion machine. (It did not work.) (1967, p. 388)

In high school, Skinner earned money by playing saxophone in a jazz band and with an orchestra. After Skinner graduated from high school, the Skinner family moved to Scranton, Pennsylvania, and soon thereafter Skinner enrolled in Hamilton College, a small liberal arts school in Clinton, New York. Skinner believed he never fit into the life of the college student because he was terrible at sports and was "pushed around" by unnecessary requirements such as daily chapel. He wrote highly critical articles about the faculty and administration in the school paper and disrupted the campus with a number of tricks. For example, he caused the campus and the local railroad station to be jammed with people by falsely announcing a lecture by Charlie Chaplin. The college president told Skinner to quit his antics, or he would not graduate. Skinner did graduate in 1926 with a Phi Beta Kappa Key and a BA degree in English literature. It is interesting to note that Skinner never took a course in psychology as an undergraduate.

Skinner left college with a burning desire to be a writer. Part of this desire is explained by the fact that the famous American poet Robert Frost had favorably reviewed three of Skinner's short stories. Skinner's first attempt at writing was in the attic of his parents' home. This attempt failed. His next attempt was in Greenwich Village, in New York City. This attempt also failed. Skinner referred to the period following his graduation from college as his "dark year." He became so depressed during this time that he pondered seeing a psychiatrist. However, his father believed doing so would be a waste of time and money and the idea was apparently abandoned (Skinner, 1976, p. 278). After 2 years of trying, Skinner concluded he "had nothing important to say" and gave up the idea of becoming a writer. He spent the next summer in Europe.

While in Greenwich Village, Skinner read the works of Ivan Pavlov, Bertrand Russell, and J. B. Watson, which greatly influenced him. Upon returning from Europe in 1928, he enrolled in the graduate program in psychology at Harvard. According to Elms (1981), enrollment in graduate school finally resolved the identity crisis that Skinner experienced following graduation from college. At Harvard, Skinner pursued his studies with extreme intensity.

> I would rise at six, study until breakfast, go to classes, laboratories, and libraries with no more than fifteen minutes unscheduled during the day, study until exactly nine o'clock at night and go to bed. I saw no movies or plays, seldom went to concerts, had scarcely any dates and read nothing but psychology and physiology. (1967, p. 398)

This high degree of self-discipline characterized Skinner's work habits throughout his life.

Skinner earned his MA in 2 years (1930), his PhD in 3 years (1931), and then remained at Harvard for the next 5 years as a postdoctoral fellow. He began his teaching career at the University of Minnesota in 1936 and remained there until 1945. During this time, Skinner established himself as a nationally prominent experimental psychologist by publishing his now famous book, *The Behavior of Organisms* (1938). It is interesting to note that although *The Behavior of Organisms* was instrumental in establishing Skinner's career as an experimental psychologist, it was received very poorly. Initially 800 copies were printed, and in the 4 years that followed only 80 copies were sold (Wiener, 1996, p. ix).

Shortly after moving to Minnesota, Skinner married Yvonne ("Eve") Blue, an English major at the University of Chicago. The marriage, although at times stormy and unconventional (Wiener, 1996, p. 58), lasted until Skinner's death. Skinner and his wife had two daughters: Julie, born in 1938, and Deborah (Debbie), born in 1944.

In 1945, Skinner moved to Indiana University as chairman of the psychology department where he remained until 1948 when he returned to Harvard. In 1974, Skinner became professor emeritus, and he remained affiliated with Harvard until his death in 1990.

Skinner was highly productive. In 1948, he published *Walden Two*, which describes a society that functions in accordance with his principles of learning. In 1953, he published *Science and Human Behavior,* which is perhaps the best overall presentation of his theory. *Verbal Behavior* was published in 1957, and in that same year he published (along with Charles B. Ferster) *Schedules of Reinforcement.* He wrote *Beyond Freedom and Dignity* in 1971, which garnered reactions from a wide variety of sources including an extremely negative one from then vice president of the United States, Spiro T. Agnew. Unlike the initial fate of *The Behavior of Organisms* (1938), *Walden Two* has sold over 3 million copies, *and Beyond Freedom and Dignity* was on the *New York Times* bestseller list for 20 weeks (Wiener, 1996).

Skinner was disturbed that his position had been misunderstood by so many (including many psychologists), so he wrote another book, *About Behaviorism* (1974), that attempted to clarify his position.

Skinner elaborated his brief autobiography (1967) with three more extensive volumes, *Particulars of My Life* (1976), *The Shaping of a Behaviorist* (1979), and *A Matter of Consequences* (1983).

Among Skinner's many honors were an honorary doctor of science degree from his alma mater, Hamilton College (Skinner subsequently received several additional degrees from leading colleges and universities in the United States and throughout the world); the American Psychological Association's Distinguished Contribution Award in 1958 and its Gold Medal Award in 1972; and the National Medal of Science Award for distinguished scientific achievement in 1968. On August 10, 1990, the American Psychological Association presented Skinner with an unprecedented Lifetime Contribution to Psychology Award. Skinner died of leukemia 8 days later on August 18, at the age of 86.

Skinner and Personality Theory

J. B. Watson (1878–1958), founder of the school of behaviorism, claimed that if psychology wanted to be truly scientific, it would require a subject matter that could be reliably and objectively studied. The subject matter on which Watson focused was overt behavior, and he insisted that the study of consciousness be abandoned completely. Likewise, Watson believed setting humans artificially apart from other animals made no sense. The behavior of both, he said, is governed by the same principles.

Watson insisted that, with the exception of a few basic emotions that are inherited, behavior patterns are acquired through experience. Therefore, if you can control a person's experiences, you can create any type of person you wish. Watson's following statement of this belief is one of the most famous (or infamous) statements ever made by a psychologist:

> Give me a dozen healthy infants, well-formed, and my own specified world to bring them up in and I'll guarantee to take any one at random and train him to become any type of specialist I might select—doctor, lawyer, artist, merchant, chief, and yes, even beggarman and thief, regardless of his talents, penchants, tendencies, abilities, vocations, and race of his ancestors. (1926, p. 10)

Although Watson's version of behaviorism is considered radical (as defined above), other forms of behaviorism that followed his were more moderate. That is, several subsequent forms of behaviorism were more willing to entertain inner, even cognitive, variables in their explanations of behavior. Dollard and Miller, considered in

John Broadus Watson

the next chapter, exemplify this more moderate form of behaviorism. However, Skinner, like Watson, was a radical behaviorist. Skinner even rejected the term personality itself because it suggests inner causation of behavior:

> It is often said that a science of behavior studies the human organism but neglects the person or self. What it neglects is a vestige of animism, a doctrine which in its crudest form held that the body was moved by one or more indwelling spirits. When the resulting behavior was disruptive, the spirit was probably a devil; when it was creative, it was a guiding genius or muse. Traces of the doctrine survive when we speak of personality, of an ego in ego psychology, of an I who says he knows what he is going to do and uses his body to do it, or of the role a person plays as a persona in a drama, wearing his body as a costume. (1974, p.167)

Hergenhahn and Olson (2005) note that Skinner not only refused to consider inner causes of behavior, he also considered the development of all theories to be "time-consuming and wasteful" (p. 109). Skinner did not even agree that theory was important for the generation of research:

> Research designed with respect to theory is also likely to be wasteful. That a theory generates research does not prove its value unless the research is valuable. Much useless experimentation results from theories, and much energy and skill are absorbed by them. Most theories are eventually overthrown, and the greater part of the associated research is discarded. This could be justified if it were true that productive research requires a theory—as is, of course, often claimed. It is argued that research would be aimless and disorganized without a theory to guide it. The view is supported by psychological texts which take their cue from the logicians rather than empirical science and describe thinking as necessarily involving stages of hy-

pothesis, deduction, experimental test, and confirmation. But this is not the way most scientists actually work. It is possible to design significant experiments for other reasons, and the possibility to be examined is that such research will lead more directly to the kind of information which a science usually accumulates. (1950, pp. 194–195)

Throughout his career, Skinner advocated a psychology that concentrates only on the relationship between environmental events and overt behavior. For this reason, Skinner's approach has been characterized as the "empty organism" approach. Skinner believed that no information is lost by making a **functional analysis** between measurable environmental events and measurable behavior and leaving out the intervening activities. In fact, he said, all of the problems inherent in a study of consciousness can be avoided:

> The mentalistic problem can be avoided by going directly to the prior physical causes while bypassing intermediate feelings or states of mind. The quickest way to do this is to confine oneself to what an early behaviorist, Max Meyer, called the "psychology of the other one": consider only those facts which can be objectively observed in the behavior of one person in its relation to his prior environmental history. If all linkages are lawful, nothing is lost by neglecting a supposed non-physical link. (1974, p. 13)

Thus, for Skinner, the phenomena that we might call "personality" include only overt behaviors, including language, that are emitted reliably in the presence of quantifiable stimuli. That is, personality is reduced to what people do under specified conditions. His contribution to this text is not in the formulation of a theory that describes the components of personality, the mentalistic forces—conscious or unconscious—that shape personality, or the stages through which personality ascends in its development. Rather, Skinner identified and described processes by which certain behaviors are acquired and expressed and by which other behaviors are eliminated. Skinner (1971) suggested a role for the environment in these acquisition and elimination processes parallel to the role that Darwinian evolutionary theory posits for environmental selection or elimination of physical traits:

> The environment is obviously important, but its role has remained obscure. It does not push or pull, it *selects,* and this function is difficult to discover and analyze. The role of natural selection in evolution was formulated only a little more than a hundred years ago, and the selective role of environment in shaping and maintaining the behavior of the individual is only beginning to be recognized and studied. As the interaction between organism and environment has come to be understood, however, effects once assigned to states of mind, feelings, and traits are beginning to be traced to accessible conditions, and a technology of behavior may therefore become available. It will not solve our problems, however, until it replaces traditional prescientific views, and these are strongly entrenched. (p. 25)

In the following section, we examine how, according to Skinner, the environment *selects* some behaviors and not others.

Respondent and Operant Behavior

Both John B. Watson and B. F. Skinner were radical behaviorists. However, there were important differences between the two because each emphasized a different type of behavior and postulated different principles to explain that behavior. Watson accepted the principles of learning developed by Ivan Pavlov as a model for his brand of behaviorism. Pavlov's work on learning contains the following ingredients:

> **Conditioned Stimulus.** (CS)—A stimulus that, at the beginning of training, does not elicit a predictable response from an organism.
>
> **Unconditioned Stimulus.** (US)—A stimulus that elicits an automatic, natural, and predictable response from an organism.
>
> **Unconditioned Response.** (UR)—The natural and automatic response elicited by the unconditioned stimulus.

Pavlov found that if the conditioned stimulus was paired several times with the unconditioned stimulus, it gradually developed the capacity to elicit a response similar to the unconditioned response; such a response is called a **conditioned response** (CR). Pavlovian or **classical conditioning** can be diagrammed as follows:

CS ⟶ US ⟶ UR   Original pairing

CS ⟶ CR   Demonstration of a Conditioned Response

Skinner referred to behavior elicited by a known stimulus as **respondent behavior,** and all conditioned and unconditioned responses are examples. He called Pavlovian or classical conditioning **type S conditioning,** to stress the importance of the stimulus. The important point to remember about respondent behavior is that a direct link exists between its occurrence and the stimulus that preceded it. In other words, a direct stimulus–response association occurs. All reflexes, such as pupillary constriction when light intensity is increased, or pupillary dilation when light intensity is decreased, are examples of respondent behavior.

Unlike Pavlov and Watson, Skinner did not emphasize respondent behavior in his theory. Rather, he emphasized behavior that is *not* linked to any known stimulus. He emphasized behavior that appears to be simply emitted by the organism rather than elicited by a known stimulus, which is labeled **operant behavior.** Skinner believed that operant behavior is indeed caused by stimulation, but that stimulation is not known, so that behavior *appears* to be emitted. Skinner also said that it is not important to know the origins of operant behavior. The most important characteristic of operant behavior is that it is under the control of its consequences. In other words, it is what happens *after* operant behavior is emitted that determines its fate. The name *operant* now might make more sense; operant behavior *operates* on the environment so as to change it in some way. The changes in the environment that it causes will determine the subsequent frequency with which the response is made. We have more to say about this concept in the next section, but for now suffice it to say that the conditioning of operant behavior is called **type R conditioning** to emphasize the importance of the response. Skinner's work was primarily in the area of operant conditioning.

Operant Conditioning

Operant conditioning has been used in psychotherapy, education, and childrearing, and has been proposed as a means of redesigning cultures. A technique this powerful must be complex and not easily comprehensible, right? Wrong! Operant conditioning is summarized in the following statement: "If the occurrence of an operant is followed by presentation of a reinforcing stimulus the strength is increased" (Skinner, 1938, p. 21). Putting this in slightly different form, we can say, if a response is followed by a reward, the response will be strengthened. This enormously powerful rule could not be more simple: *If you want to strengthen a certain response or behavior pattern, reward it!*

To modify behavior, two elements are necessary—behavior and a reinforcer. Having defined operant, or type R, conditioning, we look in more detail at its characteristics. It should be remembered as we go through these characteristics that, according to Skinner, personality is nothing more than consistent behavior patterns that have been strengthened through operant conditioning. As we look more carefully at the principles of operant conditioning, we are at the same time examining Skinner's theory of personality.

Acquisition

To demonstrate operant conditioning, Skinner invented a small experimental chamber for use with small animals, such as rats or pigeons, that has come to be called a Skinner box. Typically, the chamber contains a lever, a light, a food cup, and a grid floor. The apparatus is arranged so that when the lever is pressed, a feeder mechanism is activated that delivers a pellet of food into the food cup. In this box, the lever-press response is the operant response of interest, and the food pellet is the reinforcer. Even before the reinforcer is introduced into the situation, the animal will probably press the lever now and then just as part of its random activity. The frequency with which an operant response occurs before the introduction of a reinforcer is called the **operant level** of that response. When the response is followed by a reinforcer, the frequency with which it is made increases, which is what Skinner meant when he said a response has been strengthened. Operant conditioning is measured by the change in **rate of responding.** Under the conditions we have described, the rate with which the lever-press response is made will increase (relative to its operant level) and operant conditioning is said to have been demonstrated. Note that the origins of the initial lever-press responses are not known, nor do they need to be. The situation is arranged so that when a lever-press response is made, it is reinforced, and when it is reinforced, it is strengthened in that the frequency with which it is made increases.

So much for rats in Skinner boxes. Now, what about people? Remember, the radical behaviorist does not believe that one set of learning principles exists for humans and another set for nonhumans. It is assumed that the same principles apply to all living organisms. Such an assumption has not gone unchallenged. Greenspoon (1955) hypothesized that the therapist's "mmm-hmm" is reinforcing in a situation in which a client is talking quietly. To verify this notion, Greenspoon tested many subjects one at a time in a situation in which he uttered "mmm-hmm" each time a plural noun was spoken by the subject. This arrangement subsequently increased the frequency with which plural nouns were spoken, even though none of the subjects were aware that his or her verbal behavior was being modified.

Verplanck (1955) had his experimental class at Harvard condition a wide range of simple motor responses using points as the reinforcer:

> After finding a fellow student who was willing to be a subject, the experimenter instructed him as follows: "Your job is to work for points. You get a point every time I tap the table with my pencil. As soon as you get a point, record it on your sheet of paper. Keep track of your own points." With these instructions, it seemed likely that a tap, a "point," would prove to be a reinforcing stimulus. The method worked very well. Indeed, the experimenters were now able to condition a wide variety of simple motor behaviors, such as slapping the ankle, tapping the chin, raising an arm, picking up a fountain pen, and so on. They were further able to differentiate out, or shape, more complex parts of behavior, and then to manipulate them as responses. The data they obtained included the results of the manipulation of many of the variables whose effects were familiar in operant conditioning of rats and pigeons. Despite the fact that the experiments were carried out in a variety of situations, the experimenters were able to obtain graphical functions that could not be distinguished from functions obtained on the rat or the pigeon in a Skinner box. (pp. 598–599)

Verplanck and his students went on to condition the response of stating opinions (e.g., I think that or I believe that):

> The results of these experiments were unequivocal. In the first experiment, on opinion-statements, every one of 23 subjects showed a higher rate of giving opinion-statements during the 10-minute period when the experimenter reinforced each of them by agreeing with it, or by repeating it back to him in paraphrase, than he showed in the first 10-minute period when the experimenter did not reinforce. (1955, p. 600)

Verplanck, like Greenspoon, found that conditioning did not depend on the subject's awareness of what was happening. Most of Verplanck's subjects were totally unaware of the experimental conditions governing their behavior.

The Greenspoon and Verplanck studies represent only a sample of the hundreds of studies that have confirmed that operant principles apply to human as well as to nonhuman behavior. These two studies were chosen for this book because they show the ease with which operant principles are demonstrated.

Shaping

What do we do if the response we want to strengthen is not in the organism's response repertoire? The answer is that it is shaped into existence. Assume the lever-press response is one a rat would initially not make on its own in a Skinner box. Using the principles of operant conditioning already described, the lever-press response can be developed through a series of several steps. Using an external hand switch to trigger the feeder mechanism, the rat would be reinforced only for behavior that brings it closer and closer to making the response that is ultimately wanted, which, in this case, is the lever-press. We see that the shaping process has two components, **differential reinforcement,** which means that some responses are reinforced and some are not, and **successive approximations,** which means the responses that are reinforced are those that are increasingly close to the response ultimately desired. Hergenhahn (1974) lists the following steps as one way of **shaping** the bar-press response:

1. Reinforce the rat for being on the side of the test chamber containing the bar.
2. Reinforce him for moving in the direction of the bar.
3. Reinforce him for rising up in front of the bar.
4. Reinforce him for touching the bar.
5. Reinforce him for touching the bar with both paws.
6. Reinforce him for exerting pressure on the bar.
7. Reinforce him only for the bar-press response. (p. 361)

According to operant theory, the best way to teach a complex skill is to divide it into its basic components and gradually shape it into existence one small step at a time. According to this viewpoint, the shaping process is extremely important to education and to childrearing. For example, Skinner gave the following example of how a mother may unknowingly shape undesirable behavior in her child:

> The mother may unwillingly promote the very behavior she does not want. For example, when she is busy she is likely not to respond to a call or request made in a quiet tone of voice. She may answer the child only when [he or she] raises [his or her] voice. The average intensity of the child's vocal behavior therefore moves up to another level. . . . Eventually the mother gets used to this level and again reinforces only louder instances. This vicious circle brings about louder and louder behavior. . . . The mother behaves, in fact, as if she has been given the assignment of teaching the child to be annoying. (1951, p. 29)

Extinction

If operant behavior followed by a reinforcer is strengthened, it should follow that if the reinforcer is removed from the situation, the operant behavior will be weakened. This is exactly what happens. If, for example, after the lever-press response was conditioned, the feeder mechanism was disconnected, thus creating a situation in which a lever-press response is no longer followed by a food pellet, eventually that response would return to its operant level. In other words, when a reinforcer no longer follows a response, the frequency with which the response is made returns to the level it was at before the reinforcer was introduced into the situation, and we say that **extinction** has occurred.

Extinction can be regarded as the counterpart of acquisition, and the two processes together, according to Skinner, explain much of what we call personality. Briefly stated, rewarded behavior persists, and nonrewarded behavior extinguishes. For example, an infant emits the sounds contained in every language on earth. From these random babblings the child's language is shaped. Those sounds that resemble words of the parents' language are noticed or reinforced in some other way, and those utterances that are irrelevant to the parents' language are ignored. The reinforced verbal responses are strengthened and are shaped further, whereas the non-reinforced verbal responses are extinguished. So it is with all the behavior we refer to collectively as personality.

Extinction is important to the Skinnerian view of behavior modification. This view is quite simple: *Reinforce desired behavior and ignore undesirable behavior.* Skinner viewed extinction as the proper method of dealing with undesirable behavior, *not punishment*. He gave the following example:

> The most effective alternative process [to punishment] is probably extinction. This takes time but is much more rapid than allowing the response to be forgotten. The technique seems to be relatively free of objectionable by-products. We recommend it, for example, when we suggest that a parent "pay no attention" to objectionable behavior on the part of his child. If the child's behavior is strong only because it has been reinforced by "getting a rise out of" the parent, it will disappear when this consequence is no longer forthcoming. (1953, p. 192)

We will discuss the problems associated with punishment later in this chapter.

Discriminative Operants

A **discriminative operant** is an operant response made under one set of circumstances but not under others. The Skinner box typically contains a light, which is usually above the lever. The circuitry of the Skinner box can be arranged so a lever-press response is reinforced when the light is on but not reinforced when the light is off. Under these circumstances, the rate with which the lever is pressed is much higher when the light is on than it is when the light is off. We say that the light has become a **discriminative stimulus** (S^D) for the lever-press response. In other words, the light-on condition becomes the occasion for the lever-press response. With S^R symbolizing a reinforcing stimulus or simply a reinforcer, the situation can be diagrammed as follows:

S^D	R	S^R
Light on	Lever Press Response	Food Pellet

Everyday life is filled with discriminative operants. A few examples follow:

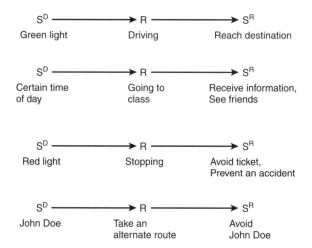

S^D	R	S^R
Green light	Driving	Reach destination
Certain time of day	Going to class	Receive information, See friends
Red light	Stopping	Avoid ticket, Prevent an accident
John Doe	Take an alternate route	Avoid John Doe

According to the principles of operant conditioning, any response that is consistently reinforced in a particular situation will be repeated when that situation recurs. However, there will also be a tendency to respond to similar situations in a like manner. This tendency to emit an operant response in situations similar to the one in which it was originally reinforced is called **stimulus generalization.** Stimulus generalization explains why we emit learned responses in situations other than those in which the learning actually occurred. Thus, learning to avoid John Doe will also create a tendency to avoid individuals resembling him. The closer the resemblance, the greater will be the tendency to avoid.

Secondary Reinforcement

At this point, we must distinguish between a **primary reinforcer** and a **secondary reinforcer.** Primary reinforcers are related to survival and include food, water, oxygen, elimination, and sexual activity. Primary reinforcers are not biologically neutral because if an organism (or in the case of sex, a species) goes long without any one of them, it will not survive. Food for a hungry animal is a natural, powerful, primary reinforcer, as is water for a thirsty animal. Secondary reinforcers are stimuli that are originally biologically neutral and thus not reinforcing but acquire their reinforcing properties through their association with a primary reinforcer. This principle can be stated as follows: Any neutral stimulus that is consistently paired with a primary reinforcer takes on reinforcing properties of its own.

It follows that every S^D that precedes a primary reinforcer, such as food, will become a secondary reinforcer. In our example in which a light was the occasion for a lever-press response to be reinforced by food, the light became a secondary reinforcer. Once a stimulus takes on reinforcing properties, it can be used to condition a new response or it can be used to maintain the response for which it was the occasion. The light in the example can be used to teach the animal a response other than the lever-press response, for instance, sticking its nose in a particular corner of the Skinner box. Likewise if the light followed the lever-press response during extinction, the animal would go on responding far beyond the point at which it would stop if the light did not follow the lever-press response.

According to Skinner, most human behavior is governed by secondary reinforcers. For example, because mothers are typically associated with the satisfaction of the child's basic needs, they become secondary reinforcers. Eventually the sight of the mother is enough to temporarily pacify a hungry or thirsty child. In fact, attention alone is a powerful secondary reinforcer because it must precede the satisfaction of almost all, if not all, basic needs. Besides attention, which is a secondary reinforcer for children and adults alike, other common secondary reinforcers include the following:

kind words	awards
bodily contact	recognition
glances	gifts
money	privileges
medals	points

Secondary reinforcers that do not depend on a particular motivational state are called **generalized reinforcers.** A mother, for example, is a generalized reinforcer because her presence is associated with several primary reinforcers. Her reinforcing properties do not depend on the child being hungry or thirsty. Money is another generalized reinforcer because, like a mother, it usually is associated with several primary reinforcers.

Chaining

For the Skinnerians, much complex behavior is explained using the concept of **chaining,** which involves the notion of secondary reinforcement. We mentioned that any S^D that is the occasion for primary reinforcement becomes a secondary reinforcer. It is also true that all stimuli that consistently and immediately precede primary reinforcement will take on secondary reinforcing properties. In turn, stimuli associated with those stimuli will take on reinforcing properties, and so forth. In this way, stimuli far removed from the primary reinforcement can become secondary reinforcers, and as such can influence behavior. These secondary reinforcers develop two functions: (1) They reinforce the response that preceded their appearance; and (2) they act as an S^D for the next response. The secondary reinforcers act as S^Ds that ultimately bring the organism into contact with the primary reinforcer. It is the primary reinforcer that holds this entire chain of events together. The process of chaining is diagramed in Figure 9–1.

Chained behavior also results when two people confront each other. Typically, what one person says acts as an S^D for a response from the second person, and the second person's response not only rewards the first person's response but also acts as an S^D for another response, and so forth. An example of this process is diagramed in Figure 9–2.

Skinner maintained that these principles also govern our behavior when we simply roam about or even when we free associate:

> A response may produce or alter some of the variables which control another response. The result is a "chain." It may have little or no organization. When we go for a walk, roaming the countryside or wandering idly through a museum or store, one episode in our behavior generates conditions responsible for another. We look to one side and are stimulated by an object which causes us to move in its direction. In the course of this movement, we receive aversive stimulation from which

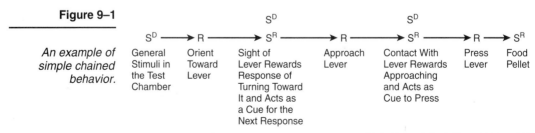

Figure 9–1

An example of simple chained behavior.

		S^D		S^D		
$S^D \longrightarrow$	R $\longrightarrow$	$S^R \longrightarrow$	R $\longrightarrow$	$S^R \longrightarrow$	R $\longrightarrow$	S^R
General Stimuli in the Test Chamber	Orient Toward Lever	Sight of Lever Rewards Response of Turning Toward It and Acts as a Cue for the Next Response	Approach Lever	Contact With Lever Rewards Approaching and Acts as Cue to Press	Press Lever	Food Pellet

(From Hergenhahn & Olson, 2005, p. 90.)

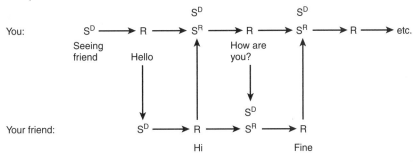

(From Hergenhahn & Olson, 2005, p. 91.)

Figure 9–2 *An example of chaining involving two people.*

we beat a hasty retreat. This generates a condition of satiation or fatigue in which, once free of aversion stimulation, we sit down to rest. And so on. Chaining need not be the result of movement in space. We wander or roam verbally, for example, in a casual conversation or when we "speak our thoughts" in free association. (1953, p. 224)

Anyone who plays a musical instrument has experienced a form of chained behavior. When into a musical piece, playing a note both reinforces the preceding response (S^R) and stimulates the next one (S^D).

Verbal Behavior

As indicated in Chapter 1, the nativism–empiricism controversy is an ancient one. The nativist maintains that important attributes such as intelligence, creativity, or even personality are mainly genetically determined. The empiricist, conversely, insists that such attributes are the product of experience and not of genes. As one might expect, both viewpoints are represented in the explanation of language.

Skinner falls squarely in the empiricist's camp. For him, language is simply verbal behavior that is governed by the same principles as any other behavior: Reinforced behavior persists; nonreinforced behavior extinguishes. Skinner (1957) did describe various categories of **verbal behavior** that are distinguished by what is being done to be reinforced. The mand is a verbal command that specifies its own reinforcer. For example, the **mand** "pass the salt" is reinforced when the salt is passed. A **tact** is the accurate naming of something. For example, if a child says "doll" while holding a doll, he or she will be reinforced. **Echoic behavior** is repeating something verbatim. For example, in the early stages of language training, a parent may point to her mouth and say "mouth"; if the child responds by saying "mouth," he or she will be reinforced.

We see then that Skinner's explanation of language is simply an extension of his general principles of learning. Skinner's most severe critic was Noam Chomsky (1959). Basically, Chomsky contended that language is simply too complex to be explained by learning. For example, it has been estimated that there are 10^{20} possible

20-word sentences in the English language, and it would take approximately 1,000 times the estimated age of the earth just to listen to them all (G. A. Miller, 1965). Thus, said Chomsky, a process other than learning must be operating. Chomsky's answer is that the brain is structured in a way that causes it to generate language. In other words, our verbal skills are genetically determined. Chomsky's nativistic explanation of language was diametrically opposed to Skinner's empirical explanation. At present, the issue is far from settled.

Reinforcement Schedules

So far we have talked as if modifying behavior necessitated reinforcing every desirable response that is made. That is, if we want to encourage children to read, they should be reinforced each time we observe them reading, or if we want a rat to continue to press a lever in a Skinner box, we should reinforce it with food each time it does so. If, indeed, each desirable response is followed by reinforcement, we say that the organism is on a 100 percent or **continuous reinforcement schedule.** Likewise, if a response that had been learned is now not followed by a reinforcement, we say that the organism is on a 0 percent reinforcement schedule, which leads to extinction.

A response that is sometimes followed by a reinforcer and sometimes not followed by a reinforcer is said to be on a **partial reinforcement schedule.** Many believe the research by Ferster and Skinner (1957) on schedules of reinforcement represents a major contribution to experimental psychology. Although Ferster and Skinner studied many schedules, the following four have become most representative of their work:

1. **Fixed interval reinforcement schedule (FI).** All interval schedules are based on time intervals. On the fixed interval schedule, the organism is reinforced for a response that is made following a specific period of time. For example, only the response made following a 30-second interval is reinforced. After an organism has been on this type of schedule for a while, its behavior quickens toward the end of the time interval and then slows down drastically after reinforcement has been obtained. Individuals working for a fixed weekly or monthly salary are on this type of schedule. Students preparing for a term paper also will often wait until the deadline approaches before starting and then "work like mad" to finish. Such behavior is typical of a FI schedule. Note that with this schedule, only one response is needed to obtain reinforcement if the response is made at just the right time.

2. **Fixed ratio reinforcement schedule (FR).** All ratio schedules are based on numbers of responses. On the fixed ratio schedule, the organism must make x number of responses before it is reinforced. For example, every fourth (FR4) response is reinforced. Such a schedule produces extremely high rates of responding and characterizes persons doing piecework or working for a commission. In both cases, the harder one works the more pay one receives because reinforcement is response-contingent instead of time-contingent.

3. **Variable interval reinforcement schedule (VI).** On this schedule, the organism is reinforced at the end of variable time intervals. In other words, rather than reinforcing the organism after a fixed interval of, say, 10 seconds, it is reinforced, *on average,* every 10 seconds. For example, it may be reinforced for a response made after 7 seconds, then after 20 seconds, then after 2 seconds. Bosses who believe their workers should be periodically rewarded place them on such a schedule. At various times as they were working, the boss reinforces them with a kind word, although they did nothing extra to deserve the kind word.
4. **Variable ratio reinforcement schedule (VR).** This, like the FR schedule, is response-contingent but, on this schedule, the organism is reinforced on the basis of an average number of responses. That is, instead of being reinforced for every fourth response, it is reinforced on the average of every fourth response. Thus reinforcements could be close together or fairly far apart. On this schedule, however, the faster the organism responds, the more reinforcement it will obtain. This schedule produces the highest rate of responding. Gambling behavior is under the control of a VR schedule, as is the behavior of salespersons. For example, the faster one pulls the handle of a slot machine, the more often one will receive a payoff (and the faster one will go broke). With salespersons, the more contacts they make, the more likely they will be to make a sale, although exactly when a sale will be made cannot be predicted.

Partial reinforcement schedules have two important effects on behavior: (1) They influence rate of responding. The VR schedule produces the highest rate of responding, followed by the FR schedule, then the VI schedule, and finally the FI schedule. (2) They increase resistance to extinction. All partial reinforcement schedules produce greater resistance to extinction than does a 100 percent or continuous schedule of reinforcement, and this fact is named the **partial reinforcement effect** (PRE). That is, a response followed by reinforcement only some of the time will persist much longer when reinforcement is discontinued than will a response followed by reinforcement each time it occurs. The PRE has implications for education and childrearing. For example, although a 100 percent schedule may be used in the early stages of training, a response should be switched to a partial reinforcement schedule as soon as possible. This will increase the perseverance of the response. In most cases, this will happen automatically because most behavior that occurs outside a laboratory is on some type of partial reinforcement schedule.

Superstitious Behavior

When a response is responsible for making a reinforcer available, we say that the reinforcer is contingent on the response. In our earlier example, a rat had to press the lever in a Skinner box in order to obtain a pellet of food. This is called **contingent reinforcement;** if the appropriate response is not made, the reinforcer will not become available.

Now let us imagine what would happen if a Skinner box were arranged so that the feeder mechanism would fire automatically, providing the animal with a pellet of food *regardless of what the animal was doing.* Let us imagine, for example, that the feeder mechanism is arranged so that it automatically provides a pellet of food on the average of every 15 seconds. According to the principles of operant conditioning, whatever the animal is doing when the feeder mechanism fires will be reinforced and thus tend to be repeated. As that response is being repeated, the feeder mechanism will again fire, further reinforcing the response. The end result will be that whatever the animal was "caught" doing when the feeder mechanism first fired will become a strong habit. Strange ritualistic behavior develops under these circumstances. For example, one animal may learn to turn in a circle, another may learn to bob its head, and still another may learn to sniff air holes on the top of the Skinner box. Such behavior is called **superstitious behavior** because it appears *as if* the animal believes its ritualistic response is responsible for producing the reinforcer, when in fact it is not. Reinforcement that occurs regardless of what the animal is doing is called **noncontingent reinforcement.** Superstitious behavior results from noncontingent reinforcement.

Numerous examples of superstitious behavior on the human level exist. A baseball player, for example, who adjusts his hat a certain way just before hitting a home run will have a strong tendency to adjust his hat that way again the next time he comes up to bat. A basketball player may insist on wearing the "lucky" socks she happened to wear during the last two winning games. Curiously, some people who buy lottery tickets always request the same series of lottery numbers, despite the observation that these lucky numbers have never produced a winning ticket.

Reinforcement Contingencies

Positive Reinforcement

As we have already seen, a **primary positive reinforcer** is related to survival. If a response produces a primary positive reinforcer, the rate with which that response is made increases. We have seen too that any biologically neutral stimulus paired with a primary positive reinforcer takes on positive reinforcing characteristics of its own, thus becoming a **secondary positive reinforcer.** As with primary reinforcement, if a secondary positive reinforcer follows a response, the rate with which that response is made will increase.

Negative Reinforcement

Positive reinforcement presents the organism with something it "wants" whereas **negative reinforcement** removes something the organism does not want. A **primary negative reinforcer** is a stimulus that is potentially harmful to the organism such as an extremely loud noise, a bright light, or an electric shock. Any response that removes or reduces one of these aversive stimuli will increase in frequency and is said to be negatively reinforced. This is labeled an **escape contingency** because the organism's response allows it to escape from an aversive situation. Any neutral stimulus consistently paired with a primary negative reinforcer becomes a **secondary negative reinforcer,** and an organism will work to escape from it just as it does from a primary negative reinforcer. Both primary and secondary negative reinforcement involve escaping from an aversive situation.

It is important to note that both positive and negative reinforcement result in an increase in response probability or in rate of responding. Both result in something desirable. In the case of positive reinforcement, a response produces something desirable. In the case of negative reinforcement, a response removes something undesirable.

Avoidance

An **avoidance contingency** exists when engaging in certain behavior prevents an aversive event from occurring. For example, opening an umbrella prevents getting wet, which is aversive. If a Skinner box is arranged so that a light precedes the onset of a shock, the animal will learn to respond to the light in such a way as to avoid the shock. With an avoidance contingency, the organism's behavior prevents it from experiencing a negative reinforcer. As with our earlier example with John Doe:

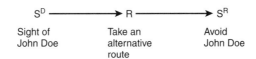

S^D ——————→ R ——————→ S^R

Sight of	Take an	Avoid
John Doe	alternative	John Doe
	route	

The sight of John Doe was a signal for an aversive encounter, and taking a route away from John Doe prevented or avoided that encounter. The reinforcement from negative reinforcement contingencies comes from escaping something aversive whereas the reinforcement from an avoidance contingency comes from *avoiding* an aversive experience.

Punishment

Punishment involves either removing a positive reinforcer or presenting a negative reinforcer. In other words, punishment either takes away something an organism wants or gives it something it does not want. A form of punishment that has become very popular among teachers and parents is called **time out from reinforcement.** With this technique, a child who has engaged in undesirable behavior is denied access, for a period of time, to positive reinforcers that are normally available in the situation. Kazdin (1989) gives the following example: "A child may be isolated from others in class for 10 minutes. During that time, he or she will not have access to peer interaction, activities, privileges, and other reinforcers that are usually available" (p. 149).

Consistently, Skinner emphasized his belief that behavior should be controlled using positive contingencies. He believed strongly that positive reinforcement and punishment are not opposite in their consequences. That is, although positive reinforcement strengthens behavior, punishment does not necessarily weaken it:

Punishment is designed to remove awkward, dangerous, or otherwise unwanted behavior from a repertoire on the assumption that a person who has been punished is less likely to behave in the same way. Unfortunately, the matter is not that simple. Reward and punishment do not differ merely in the direction of the changes they induce. A child who has been severely punished for sex play is not necessarily less inclined to continue; and a man who has been imprisoned for violent assault is not necessarily less inclined toward violence. Punished behavior is likely to reappear after the punitive contingencies are withdrawn. (1971, pp. 61–62)

Even if punishment effectively eliminates undesirable behavior, why use it if the same result can be accomplished with positive control? The use of punishment in controlling behavior appears to have several shortcomings. For example, it causes the punished person to become fearful; it indicates what the person should not do, instead of what he or she should do; it justifies inflicting pain on others; it often causes aggression; and it tends to replace one undesirable response with another, as when a child who is spanked for a wrongdoing now cries instead.

Skinner stressed positively reinforcing desirable behavior and ignoring undesirable behavior (extinction). This should be viewed as an ideal, however, because instances occur when punishing a child is strongly reinforcing to a parent. A child acting up in a supermarket may stop doing so immediately if spanked by a parent, and this will vastly increase the likelihood of the child being spanked again next time he or she acts up. Even parents are capable of learning. As Skinner said, there are always two organisms whose behavior is being modified in a learning situation, and sometimes it is difficult to know who is the experimenter and who is the subject. This point is made in the cartoon in Figure 9–3.

Although there is now considerable evidence that corporal punishment is ineffective in modifying a child's undesirable behavior, or that more effective methods of positive control are available (e.g., praise for desirable behavior), the widespread use of corporal punishment persists. A recent survey indicates that 80 percent of parents in the United States spank their children. Perhaps more surprising is the fact that 60 percent of psychologists spank their children when only 15 percent of those same psychologists believe in the effectiveness of corporal punishment (Murray, 1996a). Only five countries have outlawed the use of corporal punishment in childrearing (Austria, Cyprus, Finland, Norway, and Sweden). The remaining countries leave the choice as to whether to use corporal punishment up to the parents (Murray, 1996b).

Figure 9–3

"Boy, have I got this guy conditioned! Every time I press the bar down he drops in a piece of food."

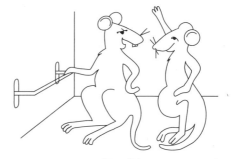

(From Skinner, 1959, p. 378.)

Our Biggest Problem

Malott, Ritterby, and Wolf (1973, pp. 2–4) stated our biggest problem as follows:

> MAN'S BIGGEST PROBLEM IS THAT
> HIS BEHAVIOR IS MORE EASILY
> INFLUENCED BY
> SMALL, BUT IMMEDIATE AND DEFINITE
> REINFORCERS
> THAN IT IS BY
> LARGE, BUT DISTANT AND UNCERTAIN
> REINFORCERS

It is the fact described in this quotation that explains why many people remain smokers when they "know" they should not and overeaters when they "know" that in the long run it will be harmful. The prospect of a long, healthy life is no contest for a small amount of nicotine or the immediate taste of food in one's mouth.

Contingency Contracting

So how do we solve our biggest problem? One solution is to make the future immediate, and one way to do that is through **contingency contracting.** Let us say you want to quit smoking but cannot seem to do it on your own. Let us assume further that $100 is a substantial amount of money for you. One plan is to make an agreement with another person in which you turn over $100 to that person with the stipulation that every week you go without smoking you will get back $10. If you have even one cigarette during the week, you will lose $10. Such an agreement is called a contingency contract, and many variations are possible. For example, the payoff could come on a daily basis instead of on a weekly basis, and the object of value could be such items as CDs or clothing instead of money. The major point is that by such an agreement you have rearranged the reinforcement contingencies in your environment so that they now encourage desirable behavior and discourage undesirable behavior. In the case of smoking, rather than waiting for old age for the effects of nonsmoking to become manifest, you need wait only a day or a week. Now your behavior is under the control of more immediate reinforcers instead of distant ones.

What happens when the contract expires? Perhaps other reinforcement contingencies will support the desired behavior. In other words, hopefully nonsmoking will be functional in producing reinforcement. Both smoking and nonsmoking produce reinforcers. The problem is switching from one source of reinforcement to another. For example, the reinforcers that support smoking include nicotine and perhaps a degree of social approval from other smokers. The reinforcers for not smoking include saving money, feeling better, not suffering the abuse from anticancer commercials, and social approval from other nonsmokers. Both smoking and nonsmoking are functional in producing reinforcement, and it is mainly a matter of switching from one source of reinforcement to another. Contingency contracting is one way of making the switch.

Since its early description as a behavior modification technique (e.g., Homme, Csanyi, Gonzales, & Rechs, 1969; Stuart & Lott, 1972), contingency contracting has been used to treat marital problems (Jacobson, 1978; Weiss, Birchler, & Vincent, 1974); study problems and other school-related behavior problems (Blechman, Taylor, & Schrader, 1981; Kelley & Stokes, 1982; Speltz, Shimamura, & McReynolds, 1982); self-control problems, such as drug abuse (Boudin, 1972; Frederiksen, Jenkins, & Carr, 1976); weight control problems (Aragona, Cassady, & Drabman, 1975; Mann, 1972); alcoholism (P. M. Miller, 1972); and heavy smoking (Paxton, 1980, 1981).

Behavior Disorders
and Behavior Therapy

Behavior Disorders

For the Skinnerians, inappropriate behavior is learned in the same way that appropriate behavior is learned. That is, both desirable and undesirable behavior are under the control of their consequences. In other words, so-called abnormal behavior is not viewed by the Skinnerians as resulting from some underlying neurophysiological disease, nor is it viewed as resulting from psychic conflicts such as those among the id, ego, and superego. As with normal behavior, the Skinnerian analysis of abnormal behavior stresses external, observable events, not inner causation. Skinner said, "A psychotic patient is psychotic because of his behavior. You don't institutionalize a person because of his feelings" (quoted in Evans, 1976, p. 89). Like appropriate behavior, inappropriate behavior persists because it is maintained by reinforcement. Thus, according to the Skinnerians, if you want to eliminate undesirable behavior, you must prevent its reinforcement. Furthermore, you should specify the behavior you want instead of the undesirable behavior and reinforce it when it occurs.

Behavior Therapy

Behavior therapy is a term that describes any approach to psychotherapy that is based on a learning theory; however, several learning theories exist. For example, behavior therapy may be based on Pavlovian learning theory, Bandura's observational learning theory (see Chapter 11), or on Skinnerian learning theory. The Skinnerian version of behavior therapy involves clearly specifying the undesirable behaviors that are to be extinguished, clearly specifying the desirable behaviors to be reinforced, and arranging reinforcement contingencies so they are responsive to the desirable behavior but not to the undesirable behavior. Because contingency contracting incorporates all of these procedures, it can be considered an example of Skinnerian behavior therapy.

The Skinnerian version of behavior therapy has been used successfully in treating a wide range of behavior disorders such as alcoholism, drug addiction, mental retardation, autism, juvenile delinquency, phobias, speech disorders, obesity, sexual disorders, and various neuroses and psychoses. (For reviews of the applications of behavior therapy, see, e.g., Craighead, Kazdin, & Mahoney, 1976; Kazdin & Hersen, 1980; Masters, Burish, Hollon, & Rimm, 1987).

Token Economies

An interesting example of the Skinnerian approach to therapy is **token economies.** In a token economy certain behaviors are deemed desirable, and other behaviors are deemed undesirable. When the participants in the economy act in desirable ways, they are given tokens (most often plastic disks like poker chips, but sometimes points or plastic cards are used). Because the tokens can subsequently be exchanged for items such as candy or cigarettes, they are secondary reinforcers. More specifically, the tokens are generalized reinforcers because they are paired with several primary reinforcers. Typically token economies are used in institutional settings such as schools or psychiatric hospitals. For a detailed description of the procedures, rules, and general considerations for such programs, see Ayllon and Azrin (1968); Schaefer and Martin (1969); Thompson and Grabowski (1972, 1977).

Token economies may sound contrived and unnatural, but perhaps it is the contingencies that exist within institutions without token economies that are unnatural. Masters et al. (1987) explain:

> Token economies are not really unnatural. Indeed, any national economy with a currency system is in every sense a token economy: any currency consists by definition of token or symbolic "reinforcers" that may be exchanged for items that constitute a more direct form of reinforcement. Whereas the individual in society works to earn tokens (money) with which he purchases his dwelling place, food, recreation, and so on, most institutions provide such comforts noncontingently and hence cease to encourage many adaptive behaviors that are appropriate and effective in the natural environment. (p. 222)

Ayllon and Azrin (1965, 1968) were among the first to use a token economy to treat maladaptive behavior. Working with psychotic patients in a mental institution, Ayllon and Azrin first spent 18 months teaching attendants which behavior to reinforce, how much to reinforce it, and when to reinforce it. By the time the behavior modification program started, they had created a standardized list of behaviors to be changed as well as a list showing how many tokens were to be given when the patients engaged in various activities. Typically, supply and demand determined how many tokens various activities earned. Jobs that were strenuous or tedious and took a long time tended to be worth more tokens than more attractive jobs. The program allowed for individualized treatment, however. For example, if, for whatever reason, the therapists wanted to encourage certain behaviors in a particular patient, then those behaviors, for that patient, would earn a relatively larger number of tokens. Examples of behaviors that would earn tokens included washing dishes; helping to serve meals to other patients; cleaning tables; keeping oneself or one's room clean; proceeding to the dining room in an orderly fashion at mealtime; and washing sheets, pillowcases, and towels in the laundry. The tokens earned could be subsequently exchanged for such items as candy, cigarettes, coffee, privacy, a 30-minute grounds pass, a private audience with the ward psychologist or a social worker, the exclusive use of a radio, or the choice of a television program.

In general, Ayllon and Azrin found that the frequency of desirable behavior increased significantly when it was reinforced by tokens. Furthermore, in another phase of the program, it was found that such behavior decreased in frequency when the tokens were withdrawn and increased again when the tokens were reinstated.

Criticisms and Shortcomings of Token Economies

Although token economies have tended to be successful, they have not gone uncriticized. One criticism directed at all forms of behavior therapy is that it treats only symptoms and not the causes of those symptoms. Admittedly, say the critics, getting a psychotic patient to groom him- or herself, or to choose a television program, is an improvement; however, the real problem, the psychosis itself, remains intact. Other critics complain that it may be unethical to deprive patients of goods and services to which they are legitimately entitled and then to provide those items selectively when the patients act in only appropriate ways.

A shortcoming of token economy programs is that the effects of the programs often do not generalize to extra treatment conditions such as the home, the community, or the place of employment (see, e.g., Kazdin, 1977; Kazdin & Bootzin, 1972). A study by Becker, Madsen, Arnold, and Thomas (1967) even suggested that behaviors learned in a token economy program during one part of the day do not generalize to other parts of the day. These and other studies indicate that people in fact learn desirable behavior when such behavior leads to reinforcement but will stop engaging in that behavior when the reinforcement is no longer forthcoming. Gagnon and Davison (1976) suggested that token economies actually do the participants a disservice because within the program certain behaviors are inevitably followed by reinforcement, whereas in the real world reinforcement is not nearly as predictable.

Finally, it seems that in some cases token economies simply do not work. For example, one token economy was designed to reduce the disruptive behavior of nine adolescent boys in a psychiatric hospital school. It turns out that disruptive behavior actually increased among the group when two of the boys realized the nature of the program. These two boys declared themselves "on strike" and labeled any boy willing to cooperate in the program "a fool" (Santogrossi, O'Leary, Romanczyk, & Kaufman, 1973).

Walden Two

The purposive manipulation of reinforcement contingencies so they encourage certain behaviors is called **contingency management.** We just saw how contingency management can be applied to the treatment of behavior disorders. Skinner believed it can be used on a far larger scale. In fact, he defined **culture** as a set of reinforcement contingencies that encourages certain behaviors and discourages others. It follows that cultures, like experiments, can be designed to produce certain effects:

> A culture is very much like the experimental space used in the analysis of behavior. Both are sets of contingencies of reinforcement. A child is born into a culture

as an organism is placed in an experimental space. Designing a culture is like designing an experiment; contingencies are arranged and effects noted. In an experiment we are interested in what happens, in designing a culture with whether it will work. (Skinner, 1971, p. 153)

When contingency management is used to design a culture, the effort is called **cultural engineering.** In 1948, Skinner published *Walden Two,* in which he described a utopian culture designed in accordance with the principles of operant conditioning.

Walden Two is a fictitious community of 1,000 people. A few of the community's characteristics follow: No private homes exist; rather, the inhabitants live in apartment complexes. Children do not live with their parents; they first live in a nursery and later in a dormitory, and they move to their own apartment when they are about 13 years old. No living quarters have cooking facilities; all meals are in community dining halls, which ensures a healthy diet and frees people from the drudgery of preparing meals. Women of Walden Two are not burdened by cooking, cleaning, or mothering and are thus able to realize their full potential along with men. Marriage and childbearing are encouraged in the mid-teens. Marriages tend to last because couples are matched by interests, money is no problem, and childrearing is no burden. As mentioned, children do not live with their parents; rather, they are raised by experts because average parents do not have the knowledge or the facilities to raise children properly. The goal is "to have every adult member of Walden Two regard all the children as his own and to have every child think of every adult as his parent" (Skinner, 1948, p. 142).

Education is individualized, in that every child progresses at his or her own pace. No "formal" education exists, and teachers act only as guides. Education is provided in the actual workshops and laboratories in the community. Even at the college level, students are merely "taught to think" and are left to learn anything else on their own. No grades or diplomas are given.

No prisons, taverns, unemployment, narcotics, mental institutions, wars, or crime exist. Is such an "ideal" society possible? Frazier, the hero of the novel, who to many represents Skinner himself, said:

> The one fact that I would cry from every housetop is this: the Good Life is waiting for us. . . . It does not depend on a change in government or on the machinations of world politics. It does not wait upon an improvement in human nature. At this very moment we have the necessary techniques, both material and psychological, to create a full and satisfying life for everyone. (1948, p. 193)

Skinner believed that using the ideas contained in *Walden Two* may actually solve several of our major problems:

> It is now widely recognized that great changes must be made in the American way of life. Not only can we not face the rest of the world while consuming and polluting as we do, we cannot for long face ourselves while acknowledging the violence and chaos in which we live. The choice is clear: Either we do nothing and allow a miserable and probably catastrophic future to overtake us, or we use our knowledge about human behavior to create a social environment in which we shall live productive and creative lives and do so without jeopardizing the chances that those

who follow us will be able to do the same. Something like a Walden Two would not be a bad start. (1978, p. 66)

Several experimental communities have been designed according to the suggestions found in *Walden Two*. One of these communities, in Virginia, publishes a newsletter that describes its progress (Twin Oaks; Louisa, VA 23093). The history of this particular project is summarized in a book by Kinkade (1973). In an article entitled "Easing Toward Perfection at Twin Oaks," Cordes (1984) gives a progress report on the Twin Oaks experiment after 17 years of existence.

Beyond Freedom and Dignity

Skinner believed that cultural engineering need not be fictional but before such engineering will be possible, we need to develop a technology of behavior:

> What we need is a technology of behavior. We could solve our problems quickly enough if we could adjust the growth of the world's population as precisely as we adjust the course of a spaceship, or improve agriculture and industry with some of the confidence with which we accelerate high-energy particles, or move toward a peaceful world with something like the steady progress with which physics has approached absolute zero (even though both remain presumably out of reach). But a behavioral technology comparable in power and precision to physical and biological technology is lacking, and those who do not find the very possibility ridiculous are more likely to be frightened by it than reassured. That is how far we are from "understanding human issues" in the sense in which physics and biology understand their fields, and how far we are from preventing the catastrophe toward which the world seems to be inexorably moving. (Skinner, 1971, p. 5)

What prevents the development of a technology of behavior? According to Skinner, the main barrier is the traditional view of human nature that depicts people as autonomous. Autonomous people are free to do as they choose, and therefore are worthy of praise and dignity when they accomplish something. If those same accomplishments could be ascribed to outside influences, they would lose their meaning: "We stand in awe of the inexplicable, and it is therefore not surprising that we are likely to admire behavior more as we understand it less" (Skinner, 1971, p. 53). Skinner elaborated:

> We recognize a person's dignity or worth when we give him credit for what he has done. The amount we give is inversely proportional to the conspicuousness of the causes of his behavior. If we do not know why a person acts as he does, we attribute his behavior to him. We try to gain additional credit for ourselves by concealing the reasons why we behave in given ways or by claiming to have acted for less powerful reasons. We avoid infringing on the credit due to others by controlling them inconspicuously. We admire people to the extent that we cannot explain what they do, and the word "admire" then means "marvel at." What we may call the literature of dignity is concerned with preserving due credit. It may oppose advances in technology, including a technology of behavior, because they destroy chances to be admired and a basic analysis because it offers an alternative explanation of behavior

for which the individual himself has previously been given credit. The literature thus stands in the way of further human achievements. (1971, pp. 58–59)

The trouble with the notion of autonomous people, according to Skinner, is that it explains nothing about human behavior; that is, in autonomous people the causes of behavior are mystical. As our knowledge about human behavior has increased, said Skinner, more of what once was attributed to autonomous people has been attributed to the environment. As we learn more, this trend will continue.

Evaluation

Empirical Research

Skinner's theory has no problem with empirical validation. Throughout this chapter, we have sampled research generated by Skinner's theory, and the studies we have mentioned indeed constitute only a sample. Because so many researchers follow Skinnerian principles, they have formed their own division of the American Psychological Association (Division 25, Experimental Analysis of Behavior). In addition, the Skinnerians have two journals in which to publish their research, the *Journal of Applied Behavior Analysis* and *Journal for the Experimental Analysis of Behavior*. With the possible exceptions of Cattell's and Eysenck's, no personality theory considered thus far is so intimately tied to experimental research as Skinner's.

Criticisms

Excessive Generalization from Nonhuman Animals to Humans. Skinnerians believe that much, if not all, of what is learned by studying nonhuman animals applies to humans as well. For example, they believe the behavior of all animals is controlled by its consequences. Therefore, if you can control consequences you can control behavior, whether the behavior in question is that of a rat, a pigeon, or a human. Many of the attributes thought to be uniquely human are essentially ignored in the Skinnerian analysis. For example, intentions, sense of self, thinking, reasoning, feeling, choosing, and reflecting have little or no place in Skinnerian theory. In fact, cognitive processes of any type are actively avoided by most Skinnerians. Skinner's relentless attack on cognitive psychology continued in the last article he wrote shortly before his death (Skinner, 1990). Judging from the facts that cognitive psychology is currently very popular, and the influence of Skinner's brand of behaviorism is declining, we can conclude that Skinner lost his battle with cognitive psychology. Whether this continues to be the case, only time will tell.

Other critics agree with Skinner that some of the principles of learning that apply to nonhuman animals can be generalized to humans. They believe he goes too far, however, when he uses those principles in social, religious, economic, cultural, and philosophical speculations.

Radical Environmentalism. The brand of determinism that Skinner embraced is called radical environmentalism because he assumed behavior is caused by reinforcement contingencies found in the environment. We have seen throughout this chapter that all Skinnerian efforts to modify behavior involved changing reinforcement contingencies. Critics say this view reduces humans to mindless automatons (or, say some critics, large white rats). Where in the Skinnerian analysis of behavior, ask the critics, is the explanation for such phenomena and experiences as suicide, depression, love, wonder, hope, purpose, and awe?

Who Controls the Controllers?   This reaction to Skinner's writings is more of a concern than a criticism. Skinner believed strongly that operant principles can be, and should be, applied in the area of cultural engineering. He believed an entire society could be arranged like a token economy. That is, desirable behavior would be defined and would be reinforced with such items as tokens, money, goods, or services. Because behavior is controlled by its consequences, members of this society would soon act as the dispensers of the reinforcers want them to act. Who, however, are the dispensers of the reinforcers? Who decides what behavior is desirable and what behavior is undesirable? Skinner argued that the people in the society could determine the answers to these questions and could institute methods for countercontrolling the controllers. Many critics are not convinced, however, and continue to believe that the possibility of serious abuse exists within Skinner's notion of cultural engineering. Skinner was aware of this possibility: "I think a science of behavior is just as dangerous as the atom bomb. It has the potential of being horribly misused" (quoted in Evans, 1981, p. 54).

Contributions

Applied Value.   Throughout this chapter we have seen how Skinnerian principles have been applied to education, childrearing, therapy, personal improvement, and societal problems. Increasingly, Skinner's ideas have also been used in prison reform, in which positive control was explored as an alternative to negative control (see, e.g., Boslough, 1972). A good theory explains, synthesizes large amounts of information, generates new information, and can be used as a guide in solving practical problems. Skinner's theory gets high marks in all of these categories. The criticisms that he generalizes too readily from the animal level to the human level and from the laboratory to the "real world" seem minor when compared to what has been accomplished using his theory as a guide.

Scientifically Rigorous Explanation of Human Behavior.   In an area such as personality theory, it is not uncommon to encounter terms, concepts, beliefs, and speculations that are difficult, if not impossible, to validate empirically. Skinner's theory (like Cattell's and Eysenck's) is an exception. All of the elements in Skinner's theory grew out of his laboratory research. The question concerning Skinner's theory is not whether or not it is correct. The question is not even whether it can be generalized to humans. The question is to what extent it can be employed to explain human behavior.

How popular is Skinner among psychologists? Davis, Thomas, and Weaver (1982) provided an answer to this question. They sent surveys to heads of departments with graduate programs in psychology. The professors were asked in 1966 and again in 1981 to first rank from 1 to 10 the greatest psychologists of all time and then rank only living psychologists. (A rank of 1 was the highest rating.) In 1966, Freud was ranked 1 on the all-time great list and Skinner ranked 9. In 1981, Freud still ranked 1, but Skinner was ranked 2. Among living psychologists Skinner ranked 1 in both 1966 and 1981. The authors also observe that the distance between Freud and Skinner on the all-time great list suggests that Skinner may soon replace Freud in the top position. In a more recent survey taken just prior to Skinner's death

(Korn et al., 1991), historians of psychology and chairpersons of graduate departments of psychology were asked to rank the 10 most eminent psychologists, both contemporary and all-time. The historians ranked Skinner eighth on the all-time list but first among contemporary psychologists. The chairpersons ranked Skinner first on both lists. In fact, weighted rankings of both the historians and chairpersons indicated that Skinner was substantially ahead of anyone else as the most eminent contemporary psychologist.

Summary

Skinner's position exemplifies radical behaviorism because it stressed the study of overt behavior and rejected internal mental or physiological causes of that behavior. He recognized two major categories of behavior: respondent behavior that is elicited by a known stimulus, and operant behavior that appears to be emitted rather than elicited. Respondent behavior is controlled by the events that precede it, and operant behavior is controlled by the events that follow it. Skinner's work was mainly on operant behavior. If an operant response is followed by reinforcement (either positive or negative) the rate at which it occurs will increase. If the desired response does not occur naturally, it can be shaped into existence using differential reinforcement and successive approximations. If the reinforcement for an operant response is discontinued, the rate eventually will return to its operant level, and extinction will have occurred. The situation can be arranged so that an operant response will be made under one set of circumstances but not under another set of circumstances. Such a response is called a discriminative operant. Any neutral stimulus consistently paired with a primary reinforcer becomes a secondary reinforcer, and thus all discriminative stimuli (S^Ds) become secondary reinforcers. A stimulus that is paired with more than one primary reinforcer becomes a generalized reinforcer.

Much complex behavior is explained using the concept of chaining. Chaining occurs when one response by an organism brings it into proximity with a reinforcer that both reinforces that response and triggers the next one. Chaining can also involve two people when the response of one triggers the response in the other. Verbal behavior or language is thought to be governed by the same principles as is any other behavior. Those utterances that are reinforced are repeated; those that are not reinforced are extinguished. Thus, Skinner was on the empiricism side of the nativism–empiricism debate. A response that is followed by a reinforcer on only some occasions is said to be on a partial reinforcement schedule. A response that is reinforced each time it occurs is said to be on a continuous or 100 percent reinforcement schedule. A response that has been on a partial reinforcement schedule takes much longer to extinguish than one that has been on a continuous schedule, which is called the partial reinforcement effect (PRE).

When a response makes a reinforcer available, the reinforcer is contingent on the response. When a reinforcer appears independent of any response, we refer to it as noncontingent reinforcement. The ritualistic responses labeled superstitious behavior result from noncontingent reinforcement. A primary positive reinforcer is something that contributes to survival. A secondary positive reinforcer is anything that has been consistently paired with a primary positive reinforcer. A primary negative reinforcer is anything that is physically harmful to the organism. A secondary negative reinforcer is anything that has been consistently paired with a primary negative reinforcer. Positive reinforcement occurs when a response adds a primary or secondary positive reinforcer to the situation. Negative reinforcement occurs when a response removes a primary or secondary negative reinforcer from the situation. Punishment occurs when a response adds a primary or secondary negative reinforcer to the situation or removes a primary or secondary positive reinforcer. A popular type of punishment among educators and parents is called time out from reinforcement. Skinner opposed the use of punishment in the control of behavior and stressed control through positive reinforcement.

A major problem for humans is that our behavior is controlled by small, immediate reinforcers instead of by larger, more distant reinforcers. One way to remedy this problem is to use contingency contracting that rearranges the reinforcement contingencies in the environment. According to Skinnerians, both appropriate and inappropriate behaviors are maintained by reinforcement. Their version of behavior therapy, then, involves arranging reinforcement contingencies so they strengthen appropriate behavior and weaken inappropriate behavior. Token economies exemplify the Skinnerian approach to behavior therapy. The Skinnerian belief that behavior can be directed by controlling reinforcement contingencies has special relevance to childrearing because parents have considerable control over their child's environment. Skinner wrote a utopian novel, entitled *Walden Two,* which describes a society designed in accordance with the principles of operant conditioning. Skinner believed, however, that cultural engineering need not be fictitious. We now have the knowledge that would allow us to develop a technology of behavior that could be used to solve many of our major problems. It is the traditional view of autonomous people with their freedom and dignity that is the major barrier to the development of such a technology of behavior.

Skinner's theory grew out of empirical research and has generated a massive amount of empirical research since its inception. His theory has been criticized for generalizing his findings too readily from the nonhuman to the human level, and for insisting that even complex human behavior can be explained in terms of reinforcement contingencies. His notion of cultural engineering has also raised questions concerning decisions as to which behaviors will be deemed desirable and which undesirable, and who will control the controllers. Among the contributions of Skinner's theory are its widespread applied value and scientifically rigorous attempts to understand personality.

Experiential Exercises

1. Assume that Skinner was correct in his assumption that frequently occurring behavior is maintained by reinforcement. First, note an activity that you engage in with considerable frequency, and then attempt to specify the reinforcers that maintain that activity.

2. According to the Skinnerians, you need only two elements to modify behavior: behavior and reinforcement. With this point in mind, attempt to modify someone's behavior. First, choose a behavior that occurs with some moderate frequency and is easy to measure. Examples are the utterance of

plural nouns, opinionated statements, various hand gestures, or laughter. When the person whose behavior you are attempting to modify engages in the behavior you have chosen, reinforce him or her with interest and attention. Arrange some type of a barrier between you and the person so you can note the frequency with which the behavior occurs initially and then as it is reinforced. Make tally marks on a sheet of paper each time the behavior occurs in 3-minute intervals. After 15 minutes discontinue the reinforcement but continue to count the occurrence of the behavior. Did the frequency of the response increase as a function of reinforcement? If it did, what conclusions do you reach about human behavior? If it did not, what conclusions do you reach?

3. Using the information in this chapter, work out a contingency contract with a friend to deal with some behavior thought by him or her to be undesirable. Describe the behavior, what will be used to reinforce abstaining from that behavior, and the conditions under which the reinforcers will be dispensed. For example, if your friend wants to quit smoking, what will be used to reinforce abstaining from smoking and how often will such nonsmoking behavior be reinforced? Describe in detail your contingency contract program and its effectiveness.

Discussion Questions

1. Describe the essential features of radical behaviorism.
2. Discuss the concept of secondary reinforcement. Indicate its importance in the control of human behavior. Include in your answer a definition of generalized reinforcers, and give a few examples of them.
3. Describe the various schedules of reinforcement. Describe the partial reinforcement effect and discuss its relevance to everyday life.

Glossary

Acquisition. That part of operant conditioning in which an operant response is followed by a reinforcer, thereby increasing the rate with which the response occurs.

Avoidance contingency. Situation in which the organism can avoid an aversive stimulus by engaging in appropriate activity.

Behavior therapy. Approach to treating behavior disorders that is based on any one of several learning theories.

Chaining. Situation in which one response brings the organism into contact with stimuli that (1) reinforce that response and (2) stimulate the next response. Chaining can also involve other people; for example, one person's response can both reinforce another person's response and determine the next course of action.

Classical conditioning. Type of conditioning studied by Ivan Pavlov and used by J. B. Watson as a model for his version of behaviorism.

Conditioned response (CR). Response similar to an unconditioned response that is elicited by a previously neutral stimulus (CS).

Conditioned stimulus (CS). Stimulus that, before classical conditioning principles are applied, is biologically neutral; that is, it does not elicit a natural reaction from an organism.

Contingency contracting. Agreement between two people that when one acts in an appropriate way, the other one gives him or her something of value.

Contingency management. Purposive manipulation of reinforcement contingencies so they encourage desirable behaviors.

Contingent reinforcement. Situation in which a certain response must be made before a reinforcer is obtained; that is, no response, no reinforcer.

Continuous reinforcement schedule (also called a 100 percent schedule of reinforcement). Schedule of reinforcement that reinforces a desired response each time it occurs.

Cultural engineering. Use of contingency management in designing a culture.

Culture. According to Skinner, a set of reinforcement contingencies.

Differential reinforcement. Situation in which some responses are reinforced and others are not.

Discriminative operant. Operant response that is made under one set of circumstances but not under others.

Discriminative stimulus (S^D). Cue indicating that if a certain response is made it will be followed by reinforcement.

Echoic behavior. Accurate repeating of what someone else had said.

Escape contingency. Situation in which an organism must respond in a certain way to escape from an aversive stimulus. All negative reinforcement involves an escape contingency.

Extinction. Weakening of an operant response by removing the reinforcer that had been following the response during acquisition. When a response returns to its operant level, it has been extinguished.

Fixed interval reinforcement schedule (FI). Reinforcement schedule that reinforces a response that is made only after a specified interval of time has passed.

Fixed ratio reinforcement schedule (FR). Reinforcement schedule that reinforces every nth response. For example, every fifth response the organism makes is reinforced (FR5).

Functional analysis. Skinner's approach to research that attempted to relate measurable environmental events to measurable behavior and bypass cognitive and physiological processes altogether.

Generalized reinforcers. Class of secondary reinforcers that have been paired with more than one primary reinforcer.

Mand. Verbal response that demands something and is reinforced when what is demanded is obtained.

Negative reinforcement. Type of reinforcement that occurs when a response removes a primary or secondary negative reinforcer.

Noncontingent reinforcement. Situation in which no relationship exists between an organism's behavior and the availability of reinforcement.

Operant behavior. Behavior that cannot be linked to any known stimulus and therefore appears to be emitted rather than elicited.

Operant conditioning(also called type R conditioning). Modification of response strength by manipulation of the consequences of the response. Responses that are followed by a reinforcer gain in strength; responses not followed by a reinforcer become weaker.

Operant level. Frequency with which an operant response is made before it is systematically reinforced.

Partial reinforcement effect (PRE). Fact that a partially or intermittently reinforced response will take longer to extinguish than a response on a continuous or 100 percent schedule of reinforcement.

Partial reinforcement schedule. Schedule of reinforcement that sometimes reinforces a desired response and sometimes does not. In other words, the response is maintained on a schedule of reinforcement somewhere between 100 percent and 0 percent.

Positive reinforcement. Type of reinforcement that occurs when a response makes available a primary or secondary positive reinforcer.

Primary negative reinforcer. Negative reinforcer that threatens an organism's survival—for example, pain or oxygen deprivation.

Primary positive reinforcer. Positive reinforcer that enhances an organism's survival—for example, food or water.

Primary reinforcer. Any stimulus that is positively or negatively related to an organism's survival.

Punishment. Either removing a positive reinforcer or presenting a negative reinforcer.

Radical behaviorism. The version of behaviorism proposed by J. B. Watson by which only directly observable events, such as stimuli and responses, should constitute the subject matter of psychology. Reference to all internal events can be, and should be, avoided. Skinner accepted this version of behaviorism.

Rate of responding. Used by Skinner to demonstrate operant conditioning. If a response is followed by a reinforcer, the rate or frequency with which it is made will increase; if a response is not followed by a reinforcer, its rate or frequency will stay the same (if it is at its operant level) or will decrease.

Respondent behavior. Behavior that is elicited by a known stimulus.

Respondent conditioning (also called type S conditioning). Another term for classical or Pavlovian conditioning.

Secondary negative reinforcer. Negative reinforcer that derives its reinforcing properties through its association with a primary negative reinforcer.

Secondary positive reinforcer. Positive reinforcer that derives its reinforcing properties through its association with a primary positive reinforcer.

Secondary reinforcer. Objects or events that acquire reinforcing properties through their association with primary reinforcers.

Shaping. Gradual development of a response that an organism does not normally make. Shaping requires differential reinforcement and successive approximations. *See also* Differential reinforcement and Successive approximations.

Skinner box. Small experimental chamber that Skinner invented to study operant conditioning.

Stimulus generalization. The tendency to emit operant responses in situations other than those in which the responses were learned. As the similarity between the original reinforcing situation and other situations increases, so does the probability of responding to them in a similar manner.

Successive approximations. Situation in which only those responses that are increasingly similar to the one ultimately desired are reinforced.

Superstitious behavior. Behavior that develops under noncontingent reinforcement in which the organism seems to believe that a relationship exists between its actions and reinforcement, when in fact no such relationship exists.

Tact. That part of verbal behavior that accurately names objects and events in the environment.

Time out from reinforcement. A form of punishment by which an organism is denied access to positive reinforcers that are normally available in the situation for a specified interval of time.

Token economies. Example of Skinnerian behavior therapy that usually occurs within an institutional setting such as a psychiatric hospital or a school. Within a token economy, desirable behavior is reinforced by tokens (or sometimes points or cards) that can subsequently be traded for desirable objects or events such as food, cigarettes, privacy, or a choice of a television program.

Type R conditioning (also called operant conditioning). Term Skinner used to describe the conditioning of operant or emitted behavior to emphasize the importance of the response (R) to such conditioning.

Type S conditioning (also called respondent conditioning). Term Skinner used to describe classical conditioning to emphasize the importance of the stimulus (S) to such conditioning.

Unconditioned response (UR). Natural, automatic response elicited by an unconditioned stimulus (US).

Unconditioned stimulus (US). Stimulus that elicits an automatic, natural response from an organism. Also called a primary reinforcer because conditioning ultimately depends on the presence of a US.

Variable interval reinforcement schedule (VI). Reinforcement schedule in which a certain average time interval must pass before a response will be reinforced. For example, the organism is reinforced on the average of every 30 seconds.

Variable ratio reinforcement schedule (VR). Reinforcement schedule in which a certain average number of responses need to be made before reinforcement is obtained. For example, the organism is reinforced on the average of every fifth response (VR5).

Verbal behavior. Skinner's term for language.

Walden Two. Novel written by Skinner to show how his learning principles could be applied to cultural engineering.

CHAPTER 10

JOHN DOLLARD
NEAL MILLER

CHAPTER OUTLINE

T he combined efforts of John Dollard and Neal E. Miller created a framework within which complex topics such as personality and psychotherapy could be understood more clearly than they had ever been before. As we shall see, they took two preexisting systems—namely, those of Sigmund Freud and neobehaviorist Clark L. Hull—and synthesized them, thus creating a more comprehensive and more useful theoretical structure than either Freud's theory or Hull's theory alone had been. Dollard and Miller dedicated their 1950 book, *Personality and Psychotherapy,* to "Freud, Pavlov and their students." The first paragraph of this book reads:

> This book is an attempt to aid in the creation of a psychological base for a general science of human behavior. Three great traditions, heretofore followed separately, are brought together. One of these is psychoanalysis, initiated by the genius of Freud and carried on by his many able students in the art of psychotherapy. Another stems from the work of Pavlov, Thorndike, Hull, and a host of other experimentalists. They have applied the exactness of natural-science method to the study of the principles of learning. Finally, modern social science is crucial because it describes the social conditions under which human beings learn. The ultimate goal is to combine the vitality of psychoanalysis, the rigor of the natural-science laboratory, and the facts of culture. We believe that a psychology of this kind should occupy a fundamental position in the social sciences and humanities—making it unnecessary for each of them to invent its own special assumptions about human nature and personality. (p. 3)

Biographical Sketches

John Dollard

John Dollard was born in Menasha, Wisconsin, on August 29, 1900. When Dollard was approaching college age, his father, a railroad engineer, was killed in a train wreck. Dollard's mother, a former school teacher, then moved the family to Madison so that the children could more easily attend the University of Wisconsin. After a short time in the Army, Dollard enrolled in the University of Wisconsin where he studied English and commerce. After obtaining his BA in 1922, Dollard remained at the university as a fundraiser for the Wisconsin Memorial Union. In his capacity as fundraiser Dollard met Max Mason who became a second father to him. When Mason became president of the University of Chicago, Dollard went with him and acted as his assistant from 1926 to 1929. In 1930, Dollard earned an MA in sociology from the University of Chicago and in 1931 his PhD, also in sociology. During the year 1931 to 1932 Dollard traveled to Germany as a research fellow and, while there, was psychoanalyzed by Hans Sachs, a colleague of Freud, at the Berlin Institute. Upon returning from Germany, Dollard took the position of assistant professor of anthropology at Yale University, and in 1933 he became an assistant professor of sociology in the newly formed Institute of Human Relations at Yale. In 1935, he became research associate at the institute, and in 1948 was appointed research associate and professor of psychology. Dollard was already at the Institute of Human

Relations when Neal E. Miller (whose biographical sketch is presented next) became affiliated there in 1936, and the two soon formed a close working relationship. Dollard remained at Yale, where he became professor emeritus in 1969. He died on October 8, 1980, at 80 years of age.

Dollard was truly a generalist. Besides teaching anthropology, sociology, and psychology, he also, as we have seen, was trained in psychoanalysis. He wrote *Caste and Class in a Southern Town* (1937), which is now considered a classic field study of the black person's social role in the South during the 1930s. Miller (1982) commented on the impact of Dollard's book *Caste and Class:*

> Today it is difficult to realize the courage that it took to make such a study and to write such a book. Southern whites, and some Northern white scholars as well, felt that it was despicable to describe such facts. The book was banned in South Africa and in Georgia. If conditions in this country are considerably better today, it is partly due to the long-term effects of the early insights provided by Dollard's classic study of Class and Caste. (p. 587)

A companion volume, *Children of Bondage* (1940) was coauthored with black social anthropologist Allison Davis, and was based on the study of black youths in New Orleans, Louisiana, and Natchez, Mississippi. During World War II, Dollard conducted a psychological analysis of military behavior that resulted in two books: *Victory over Fear* (1942) and *Fear in Battle* (1943). This list is only a sample of Dollard's publications.

In 1939, Dollard and Miller (along with Doob, Mowrer, and Sears) published a book entitled *Frustration and Aggression* that attempted to analyze frustration and its consequences in terms of learning principles. Shortly afterward, Miller and Dollard published *Social Learning and Imitation* (1941), which analyzed several complex behavior problems within the context of learning principles. In 1950, Dollard and Miller published *Personality and Psychotherapy: An Analysis in Terms of Learning, Thinking and Culture.* Much of this chapter is based on that book.

Neal Miller

Neal Elgar Miller was born in Milwaukee, Wisconsin, on August 3, 1909. His family moved to Bellingham, Washington, so Miller's father, an educational psychologist, could teach at Western Washington State College (now Western Washington University). Miller received his BS degree from the University of Washington in 1931. While at the University of Washington, he studied with the famous learning theorist Edwin Guthrie. He received his MA degree from Stanford in 1932 and his PhD degree from Yale in 1935. While at Yale he studied with another famous learning theorist, Clark L. Hull. As we shall see, Hull had a major influence on Miller's theory of personality. Miller undertook what Hull himself expressed an interest in doing but never did—that is, to explore the relationship between Hull's theory of learning and Freud's theory of personality.

Shortly after obtaining his PhD, Miller went to Europe as a Social Science Research Council Traveling Fellow. While in Europe, he was psychoanalyzed by Heinz Hartmann, a colleague of Freud, at the Vienna Institute of Psychoanalysis. Miller could not afford the $20-an-hour fee required to be analyzed by Freud himself (Moritz, 1974). From 1936 to 1941 he was an instructor, assistant professor, and associate professor at Yale's Institute of Human Relations. The Institute of Human Relations was founded in 1933 to explore the interdisciplinary relationships among psychology, psychiatry, sociology, anthropology, economics, and law. From 1942 to 1946 he directed psychological research for the Army Air Force. In 1946, he returned to Yale, and in 1952 he became the James Rowland Angell Professor of Psychology. In 1948, Miller married Marion Edwards and they subsequently had two children, York and Sara. Miller remained at Yale until 1966, and then moved to Rockefeller University to become professor of psychology and head of the laboratory of physiological psychology. Miller then became professor emeritus at Rockefeller University, and a research affiliate at Yale.

Through the years Miller was a courageous researcher who had been willing to apply the rigorous methods of science to the more subjective aspects of human experience, such as conflict, language, and unconscious mechanisms. This boldness continued with Miller's exploration of the conditions under which people can learn to control their own internal environment. His pioneer research in this area of **biofeedback** is but one area in which Miller has stimulated research and to which he has made significant contributions. Until the 1960s, it was believed that operant conditioning was possible for responses involving the voluntary or somatic nervous system but not for responses involving smooth involuntary or autonomic nervous system. Examples of the latter include heart rate, salivation, blood pressure, and skin temperature. Miller and his colleagues found that when a mechanical device, such as an auditory signal or flashing light, was used to display the status of the internal biological event of concern, individuals were often able to control them. The medical implications of biofeedback were immediately apparent. Heart patients could learn to control their cardiac abnormalities, epileptics could learn to suppress abnormal brain activity, and those suffering from migraine headaches could learn to control the dilation of blood vessels surrounding the brain. Furthermore, it was found that after using biofeedback for a period of time, patients became aware of their internal states and modified them as necessary. For example, patients could raise or lower their blood pressure, without the aid of biofeedback (for more details concerning the use of biofeedback and its current status, see Hergenhahn & Olson, 2005). More recently Miller had been concerned with the relatively new topic of behavioral medicine that, to a large extent, is an outgrowth of his research on biofeedback (see, e.g., Miller, 1983, 1984).

Among Miller's many honors are included the presidency of the American Psychological Association (1960–1961) and of the Society for Neuroscience (1971–1972); the Warren Medal from the Society of Experimental Psychologists in 1957; and the U.S. President's National Medal of Science in 1964. On August 16, 1991, the American Psychological Association presented Miller with an award for Outstanding Lifetime Contribution to Psychology (*American Psychologist,* 1992, p. 847). In his acceptance of this award, Miller (1992) emphasized the importance of basic scientific methodology and animal models to the understanding of such topics as social learning, psychopathology, and health. Miller argued that most significant advances in understanding human behavior, and, therefore, in the solution of social problems, have come from scientific research. For this reason, the teaching of science and scientific methodology should be a substantial part of even introductory psychology courses. According to Miller, the more people who understand science, the better off we all are. On November 4, 2000, the Association of Neuroscience Departments and Programs presented Miller its Millennial Award. Miller died in his sleep on March 23, 2002, at the age of 92.

Collaborative Goal

Dollard and Miller set as their goal combining Freudian insights with the rigors of scientific method as exemplified by the work of the learning theorists to better understand human behavior in a cultural setting.

Why the emphasis on learning principles? Miller and Dollard believed most human behavior is learned. In their earlier book, *Social Learning and Imitation* (1941), which was dedicated to the neobehavioristic learning theorist Clark L. Hull, they explained:

> Human behavior is learned; precisely that behavior which is widely felt to characterize man as a rational being, or as a member of a particular nation or social class, is acquired rather than innate. To understand thoroughly any item of human behavior—either in the social group or in the individual life—one must know the psychological principles involved in its learning and the social conditions under which this learning took place. It is not enough to know either principles or conditions of learning; in order to predict behavior both must be known. The field of psychology describes learning principles, while the various social science disciplines describe the conditions. (p. 1)

It is not just simple overt behavior that Dollard and Miller believed is learned, but also the complex processes such as language and the processes described by Freud such as repression, displacement, and conflict. Although Hull was a behaviorist, he was not a radical behaviorist. He postulated several biological, and a few mental, events in his effort to explain behavior (see Hergenhahn & Olson, 2005). Because Dollard and Miller embraced this moderate form of behaviorism as their model for explaining psychoanalytic phenomena, their work can be seen as representing the transition from the radical behaviorism of Watson and Skinner (see Chapter 9) to contemporary cognitive psychology.

Hull's Theory of Learning

In Chapter 9, we said that Skinner defined a reinforcer as anything that modified either the probability of a response or the rate of responding. Hull (1943) was more specific about the nature of **reinforcement.** He said that for a stimulus to be a reinforcer it must reduce a drive. Therefore Hull had a **drive reduction** theory of learning. A stimulus capable of reducing a drive is a **reinforcer,** and the actual drive reduction is the reinforcement.

The cornerstone of Hull's theory is the concept of **habit,** which he defined as an association between a stimulus and a response. If a stimulus (S) leads to a response (R), which, in turn, produces a reinforcer, the association between that stimulus (S) and that response (R) becomes stronger. We say that the *habit* of performing that response in the presence of that stimulus becomes stronger. Because habits describe relationships between stimuli and responses, Hull's theory is referred to as an S-R theory of learning.

In addition to the concepts of drive and habit, Dollard and Miller borrowed other concepts from Hull's theory of learning. Among them are the concepts of response hierarchies, stimulus generalization (which Hull borrowed from Pavlov), primary and secondary drives, primary and secondary reinforcers, anticipatory goal responses, and cue-producing responses.

A few of the Freudian concepts that Dollard and Miller attempted to explain or equate with learning principles are the pleasure principle; the relationship between frustration and aggression; the importance of early childhood experience to the formation of adult personality; conflict; repression; and the importance of the unconscious mind in the formation and maintenance of neurotic behavior. Dollard and Miller also attempted to explain many of the effective procedures in psychotherapy in terms of Hullian learning principles.

For the remainder of this chapter, we review certain aspects of Freudian theory and place them within the context of **Hull's theory of learning.**

Like Watson and Skinner, the Hullians, including Dollard and Miller, were nonapologetic about using lower animals, such as the rat, to study human behavior. In fact, Dollard and Miller believed that two of the best sources of information about the normal human personality are the rat and neurotic humans who seek professional help. They thought that studying rats is useful because their histories (both genetic and environmental) can be controlled; they are less complex than humans; and the simple behavioral "units" found in rats are also the ingredients of human behavior. Being a lifelong supporter of animal research, Miller has often defended such research against radical animal rights advocates (e.g., Coile & Miller, 1984; Miller, 1985, 1991).

Dollard and Miller thought that studying neurotics is useful because they seek help and therefore can be observed under controlled conditions; their behavior can be systematically studied during a fairly long period of time; they are more willing than normal people to speak openly about sensitive and highly personal aspects of their lives; and the same variables govern both neurotic and normal behavior, but the variables appear in exaggerated form in neurotics, making them easier to observe. Incidentally, Freud also believed that much could be learned about normal people by studying abnormal people: "Pathology has always done us the service of making discernable by isolation and exaggration conditions which would remain concealed in a normal state" (Freud, 1964b, p. 150). Dollard and Miller did caution, however, that any generalizations from rats or neurotics applied to normal humans should be checked empirically to test their validity. Dollard and Miller believed that a combination of psychotherapy and laboratory experimentation offers the best means of studying personality.

Drive, Cue, Response, and Reinforcement

Dollard and Miller's theory of personality relies heavily on four concepts that they borrowed from Hull's theory of learning. The four concepts are drive, cue, response, and reinforcement.

Drive

A **drive** is any strong stimulus that impels an organism to action and whose elimination or reduction is reinforcing. Drives may be internal, such as hunger or thirst, or they may be external, such as a loud noise or intense heat or cold. A drive may be primary, in that it is directly related to survival—for example, hunger, thirst, pain, sex, and elimination—or it may be secondary, or learned, such as fear, anxiety, or the need to be successful or attractive. Secondary drives are usually culturally determined whereas primary drives are not. It is important to note that primary drives are the building blocks of personality, and all acquired drives ultimately depend on them. This concept is similar to Freud's position that many of the everyday behaviors we observe in people are indirect manifestations of basic instincts such as sex or aggression.

Drive is the motivational concept in Miller and Dollard's theory; it is the energizer of personality. The stronger the stimulus, the stronger the drive and the greater the motivation:

> A drive is a strong stimulus which impels action. Any stimulus can become a drive if it is made strong enough. The stronger the stimulus, the more drive function it possesses. The faint murmur of distant music has but little primary drive function; the infernal blare of the neighbor's radio has considerably more. (Miller & Dollard, 1941, p. 18)

Cue

A **cue** is a stimulus that indicates the appropriate direction an activity should take. Drives energize behavior whereas cues guide behavior:

> The drive impels a person to respond. Cues determine when he will respond, where he will respond, and which response he will make. Simple examples of stimuli which function primarily as cues are the five o'clock whistle determining when the tired worker will stop, the restaurant sign determining where the hungry man will go, and the traffic light determining whether the driver will step on the brake or on the accelerator. (Dollard & Miller, 1950, p. 32)

Any stimulus can be thought of as having certain drive properties, depending on its strength, and certain cue properties, depending on its distinctiveness.

Response

Responses are elicited by the drive and cues present and are aimed at reducing or eliminating the drive. In other words, the hungry (drive) person seeing a restaurant (cue) must get into the restaurant (response) before the hunger drive can be reduced. In Dollard and Miller's theory (and in Hull's) a response can be overt—it can be directly instrumental in reducing a drive—or it can be internal, entailing the thinking, planning, and reasoning that will ultimately reduce a drive. Dollard and Miller refer to internal responses as cue-producing responses. We have more to say about such responses later in the chapter.

Some responses are more effective than others in reducing a drive and are the ones expected to occur when the next drive occurs. New responses must be learned to new situations, and old responses must be discouraged if they are no longer maximally effective. The rearrangement of response probabilities as new conditions emerge or as old conditions change is called **learning.** We say more about the circumstances under which response probabilities change in the next section.

Reinforcement

As we said earlier, reinforcement, according to Dollard and Miller, is equated with drive reduction: "Reward is impossible in the absence of drive" (Miller & Dollard, 1941, p. 29). Any stimulus that causes drive reduction is said to be a reinforcer. A reinforcer can be primary, in which case it satisfies a need related to survival, or it can be secondary. A secondary reinforcer, as in Skinner's theory, is a previously neutral stimulus that has been consistently paired with a primary reinforcer. A mother, for example, becomes a powerful secondary reinforcer because of her association with the reduction of primary drives.

If a cue leads to a response and the response leads to reinforcement, the association between the cue and the response will be strengthened. If this process is repeated, eventually the organism develops a strong habit.

As we have seen, Dollard and Miller's goal was to explain personality in terms of learning theory. Having discussed the concepts of drive, cue, response, and reinforcement, we are now in a position to understand what, according to Dollard and Miller, a learning theory is:

> What, then, is learning theory? In its simplest form, it is the study of circumstances under which a response and a cue stimulus become connected. After learning has been completed, response and cue are bound together in such a way that the appearance of the cue evokes the response. . . . Learning takes place according to definite psychological principles. Practice does not always make perfect. The connection between a cue and a response can be strengthened only under certain conditions. The learner must be driven to make the response and rewarded for having responded in the presence of the cue. This may be expressed in a homely way by saying that in order to learn one must want something, notice something, do something, and get something. Stated more exactly, these factors are drive, cue, response and reward. (Miller & Dollard, 1941, pp. 1–2)

The best summary of what the learning theorists call **reinforcement theory** is the preceding statement: "In order to learn one must want something, notice something, do something, and get something."

Response Hierarchies

Every cue elicits several responses simultaneously that vary in terms of their probability of occurrence. This group of responses elicited by a cue is what Hull called the **habit family hierarchy,** which can be diagrammed as follows:

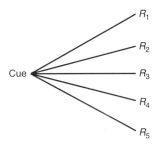

In the preceding diagram, R_1 is the most likely response to be made when the cue is encountered, R_2 is next likely, and so forth. If R_1 is prevented, R_2 will occur, and if R_1 and R_2 are blocked, R_3 will occur, and so on.

When a newborn child experiences an irritation, a set of responses is triggered, and because no learning is involved, it is called the **innate hierarchy of responses.** This hierarchy is a genetically determined set of responses that is triggered by certain drive conditions. The hungry infant first may become restless, then cry, and then kick and scream. Note that the innate hierarchy of responses exists for only a short period of time. As certain responses in the hierarchy are reinforced, they change their position in the hierarchy. The response most likely to occur at any given time is called the **dominant response** in the hierarchy and is the one that has been most successful in bringing about drive reduction.

Learning is constantly rearranging responses in the various habit family hierarchies. Prior to a learning experience, the arrangement of responses elicited by a cue is called the **initial hierarchy of responses.** After learning has occurred, the revised arrangement of responses is called the **resultant hierarchy of responses.** It should be noted that what is called the initial hierarchy of responses refers to either an innate hierarchy of responses or to a hierarchy that resulted from prior learning. In either case, it is the hierarchy that exists before a new learning experience that will rearrange the hierarchy, thus creating a resultant hierarchy of responses. The term initial refers to clusters of response probabilities that exist before a learning experience, whether those probabilities are determined by genetics or by prior learning experience.

It is also important to note that if the dominant response in a hierarchy always reduces the existing drive, no learning will occur. If, for example, the innate response of blinking always removes stray particles from one's eye, no need will exist to learn to rub the eye or roll it or wash it. According to Dollard and Miller, all learning, which we can now equate with the rearrangement of response hierarchies, depends on failure. This concept is labeled the **learning dilemma,** and has important implications for both education and childrearing:

In the absence of a dilemma, no new learning of either the trial-and-error or the thoughtful problem-solving type occurs. For example, a mother was worried because her child seemed to be retarded in learning to talk. Brief questioning revealed that she was adept at understanding the child's every want as expressed by its gestures. Having other successful means of responding, the child was not in a dilemma. He learned only his old habits of using gestures more thoroughly, and consequently he did not perform the type of random vocal behavior which would lead to speech. By gradually pretending to become more stupid at understanding gestures, the mother put the child in a dilemma and probably facilitated the learning of speech. At least, under these modified conditions, this child rapidly learned to talk.

The absence of a dilemma is one of the reasons why it is often difficult to teach successful people new things. Old, heavily rewarded habits must be interrupted before new learning can occur. When the accustomed rewards are withdrawn by unusual circumstances such as revolution, new responses may occur and, if rewarded, may be learned; Russian Counts can learn to drive taxicabs and Countesses to become cooks. (Dollard & Miller, 1950, pp. 45–46)

The Gradient of Reinforcement

Responses that are reinforced immediately after they are made are strengthened more than they would be if reinforcement was delayed. In other words, "Delayed reinforcements are less effective than immediate ones" (Dollard & Miller, 1950, p. 54). But there is another sense in which reinforcement can be delayed in a learning situation. Dollard and Miller observe that most learning involves a sequence of responses only the last of which is reinforced. In such a sequence, the last response made will be strengthened the most, then the second to the last, and so on. Dollard and Miller (1950) give the following example:

> When a hungry boy takes off his hat in the hall, dashes through the dining room into the kitchen, opens the icebox, and takes a bit to eat—the connections more remote from the reward are strengthened less than those closer to the reward. In this series, the connection between the sight of the hall closet and the response of hanging up the hat will be strengthened less than the connection between the sight of the icebox door and the response of opening it. (p. 54)

This **gradient of reinforcement** explains why activity quickens as a positive goal is approached: "A hungry man on his way to dinner has a tendency to quicken his pace in rounding the last corner on the way home" (p. 55). The gradient of reinforcement also explains why when two or more routes to a positive goal are available, the shorter route tends to be preferred.

Fear as an Acquired Drive

We have looked in detail at the complexities of Dollard and Miller's concepts of response and reinforcement. In this section, we focus on their concept of drive, and in the next section we discuss some additional properties of cues.

We mentioned earlier that two types of drives exist—primary and secondary. Primary drives are biologically determined, and secondary drives are learned or culturally determined. One of the most important secondary drives is fear, because it is so important to both adaptive and maladaptive human behavior (for our present purposes we will use the terms "fear" and "anxiety" as synonyms). Freud observed that anxiety serves as a warning of impending danger. Events that accompanied a painful experience, when reencountered, would cause fear or anxiety, thus warning the person to be careful. For example, a child burned by a hot stove would experience fear when next seeing a stove even though there was no pain in merely seeing the stove.

In 1948, Miller performed his now-famous experiment exploring the acquisition of fear (1948a). His apparatus consisted of an experimental chamber with black and white compartments. When a rat was allowed to roam freely, it showed no aversion to either the white or the black compartment. Next, Miller shocked the rat in the white compartment, and it was allowed to escape the shock by running through an open door into the black compartment. The rat quickly learned to escape the shock by leaving the white compartment. Later when the animal was placed in the white compartment without being shocked, it urinated, defecated, crouched, and ran into the black compartment. The animal had learned to fear the white compartment because it had been associated with shock.

Miller next arranged the experiment so the animal could escape the white compartment only by first turning a small wheel. The animal learned to do this, even though no additional shocks were given. Miller replaced the wheel with a lever and found the animal quickly extinguished the wheel-turning response, which was now ineffective, and learned the lever-pressing response, again with no further shocks. The animal had developed a **conditioned fear reaction** to the white chamber.

The most important point about Miller's experiment is that it demonstrates that fear itself becomes a drive that can be reduced, resulting in reinforcement. It was the reduction of fear, not pain, that caused the animal to learn the wheel-turning and the lever-pressing responses. Such behavior is highly resistant to extinction, because as long as fear is present, its reduction will be reinforcing. Note that, under these circumstances, the animal does not stay in the situation long enough to learn that it will not receive additional shocks and thereby extinguish its fear reaction. It continues to behave "as if" it will be shocked again if it lingers in the situation.

It is Dollard and Miller's contention that phobias and other irrational fears are produced by similar experiences on the human level. Such behavior appears irrational to the observer because the history of its development is not known as it is with the rat. It may be that because of harsh physical punishment for sexual behavior in early childhood, a person has an aversion to sexual activities and sexual thoughts. For this person, even approximating such activities or thoughts elicits fear that is reduced by escape or avoidance. Like the rat in Miller's experiment, this person never dwells long enough in the anxiety-provoking situation to learn that he or she will no longer be punished for such thoughts or activities. As with the rat, extinction of the fear reaction is extremely difficult. As we see later in this chapter, the main job of psychotherapy, as Dollard and Miller view it, is to provide a situation in which the client is encouraged to experience threatening thoughts without punishment and, in that way, to finally extinguish them. This goal is similar to what Freud attempted to do when he used free association and dream analysis to discover repressed thoughts.

Stimulus Generalization

As was mentioned in our coverage of Skinner's views on learning, if an association exists between S_1 and R_1, not only will S_1 elicit R_1, but so will various stimuli similar to S_1. The greater the similarity of a stimulus to S_1, the greater will be the tendency for it to elicit R_1. This is called **stimulus generalization.** In Miller's experiment on fear, we would expect not only the white compartment to elicit fear but also various shades of gray compartments to elicit fear. The lighter the shade of the compartment, however, the greater will be the fear response because it was the white compartment that was originally associated with pain.

All learned responses generalize to other stimuli. If a child learns to fear snakes, he or she probably will also, at least at first, fear rope. If an adolescent fears his or her father, he or she will also tend to fear men who resemble the father. A woman who is raped may shortly thereafter hate all men. With further experience, however, most normal humans learn to discriminate. **Discrimination** is the opposite of generalization. Thus the child learns that some snakes are to be feared but ropes are safe. The adolescent learns that the father perhaps should be feared under some circumstances but that men of similar appearance pose no threat, and the rape victim realizes that her attacker is not typical of all men. Therefore, generalization causes the initial tendency for learned responses to be elicited by a wide range of stimuli, but further experience allows the person to discriminate and thus respond selectively to stimuli. This is true, at least, of normal people. As we see later in this chapter, neurotics often lose their ability to discriminate and therefore tend to overgeneralize their anxieties.

Dollard and Miller distinguished two types of generalization: primary and secondary. **Primary generalization** is based on the physical similarity among stimuli. The closer two stimuli are in their physical attributes, the greater the probability is that they will elicit the same response. Primary generalization is innate and governed by a person's sensory apparatus. **Secondary generalization** is based on verbal labels, not on the physical similarity among stimuli. Thus one responds to all individuals labeled "friendly" in a similar way. Likewise the word *dangerous* equates many dangerous situations that tend to elicit similar types of responses. Secondary generalization is what Dollard and Miller called learned equivalence, which is mediated by language. It is important to realize that secondary generalization is not based on physical attributes; in fact, it can counteract primary generalization by labeling one event "good" and another event "bad," although the two events are physically similar.

Conflict

One of Freud's concepts that Miller studied intensively was that of **conflict.** Lewin (1935) had studied the concept earlier, and Miller borrowed from both Freud and Lewin. It was Miller, however, who experimentally analyzed in depth the concept of conflict. Freud had talked about the continuous conflict between libidinal desires and the demands of the ego and superego. To Freud, a person can be both attracted to an object and repelled by it at the same time. This was later called an approach–avoidance conflict and is one of four types of conflict studied by Miller. Each of the four is now described.

Approach–Approach Conflict

Here the conflict is between two positive goals that are equally attractive at the same time. Such a conflict can be diagrammed as follows:

An **approach–approach conflict** exists when two equally attractive people ask someone for a date on the same night or when one is both hungry and sleepy. Typically, this type of conflict is easily solved by attaining first one goal and then the other; for example, one could first eat and then go to bed. Dollard and Miller (1950) say, "Donkeys do not starve between two equally desirable stacks of hay, unless there are thorns, eliciting avoidance, concealed in the haystacks" (p. 366). If there were thorns, the hungry donkeys would have an approach–avoidance conflict, which, as we shall see, is a more difficult conflict to resolve.

Avoidance–Avoidance Conflict

Here the person must choose between two negative goals. For example, the child must eat her spinach or be spanked, the student must do his homework or get low grades, or a person must either go to a job he or she dislikes or lose the income. A person having such a conflict is "damned if he does and damned if he doesn't"; he or she can also be said to be "caught between the devil and the deep blue sea." Such a conflict can be diagrammed as follows:

Two types of behavior typically characterize an organism having an **avoidance–avoidance conflict:** (1) vacillation or indecision and (2) escape. Escape can be either actually leaving the conflict situation or it can be mental escape such as daydreaming or mental preoccupation with other thoughts.

Approach–Avoidance Conflict

Here the person is both attracted to and repelled by the same goal. A job may be attractive because of the money it generates but be unattractive because it is boring, or because it keeps the person from engaging in more enjoyable activities. A young woman may be attracted to an executive position because of the challenge, income, and responsibility involved but may have reservations because such a position might negatively impact her family life. Such a conflict can be diagrammed as follows:

Dollard and Miller (1950) listed the following as the most significant features of the **approach–avoidance** conflict:

1. The tendency to approach a goal is stronger the nearer the subject is to it. This will be called the gradient of approach.
2. The tendency to avoid a feared stimulus is stronger the nearer the subject is to it. This will be called the gradient of avoidance.
3. The strength of avoidance increases more rapidly with nearness than does that of approach. In other words, the gradient of avoidance is steeper than that of approach.

Figure 10–1

Diagram of an approach-avoidance conflict.

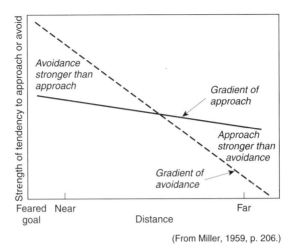

(From Miller, 1959, p. 206.)

4. The strength of tendencies to approach or avoid varies with the strength of the drive upon which they are based. In other words, an increase in drive raises the height of the entire gradient. (pp. 352–353)

It is on the approach–avoidance conflict that Miller did his most extensive research (e.g., 1944, 1959, and 1964). Figure 10–1 summarizes many of the characteristics of the approach–avoidance conflict.

Among the many deductions that can be made from Figure 10-1 is that as long as the approach gradient is higher than the avoidance gradient, the person will approach the goal. As soon as the avoidance gradient becomes higher, the person will avoid the goal. Therefore, because the approach gradient becomes higher the farther one is from the goal, a strong approach tendency will occur. As one approaches the goal, however, the avoidance tendency increases and eventually is stronger than the approach tendency. At that point, the person will retreat from the goal. Thus we would expect vacillation at the point at which two gradients cross. We all know couples who have doubts about their relationship and who are constantly separating and reconciling. While apart, the favorable aspects of their relationship are dominant, and therefore they are driven back together. Once reunited, however, they confront the negative aspects of their relationship and are once again driven apart. Approach–avoidance conflicts can be resolved either by increasing the strength of the approach tendency or by reducing the strength of the avoidance tendency. In the therapeutic situation, it is usually the latter that is attempted.

We have more to say about the approach–avoidance conflict in subsequent sections of this chapter.

Double Approach–Avoidance Conflict

Here the person has ambivalent feelings about two goal objects. Such a conflict can be diagrammed as follows:

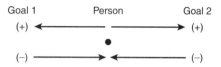

One example of a **double approach–avoidance conflict** comes from the female child's position relative to her parents in Freudian theory. She is attracted to her mother because the mother satisfies her biological needs but is repelled by the mother because she is thought responsible for denying the girl a penis. She is attracted to her father because he possesses the valued organ and yet is envious of him because he does. According to Freud, the female child has ambivalent feelings about both parents.

Dollard and Miller agree with Freud that most neurotic behavior involves conflict. For example, when neurotics begin to engage in activities or thoughts that will lead to the reduction of a strong drive such as sex, they are overwhelmed with anxiety. The closer they come to approaching a goal that will satisfy their need for sex, the stronger their anxiety will become, until eventually they retreat from the goal. Because their original need was not satisfied, however, they again approach sex-related goals, only to be eventually driven from them by anxiety, and on it goes. Only psychotherapy, or its equivalent, will rescue them from this vicious circle.

Displacement

Another Freudian concept that is explored thoroughly by Dollard and Miller is that of **displacement**. One of the most important aspects of Freud's theory was his contention that frustrated drives do not simply go away but rather surface in disguised form. In other words, if a need cannot be satisfied directly, it is displaced and satisfied indirectly. As we saw in Chapter 2, Freud's term for the displacement of the sex drive to more socially acceptable activities such as hard work, and creativity in general, is sublimation.

Miller's first step was to verify experimentally the phenomenon of displacement. To do this, Miller (1948b) placed two rats in an apparatus and shocked them until they started fighting, at which point the shock was turned off. In other words, the aggressive act of fighting was reinforced by escape from shock. Training continued in this manner until the animals began fighting immediately after the shock was turned on. At this point, a doll was placed in the apparatus, and the animals were shocked. Again, they fought with each other and ignored the doll. This is shown in Figure 10–2.

When only one animal was placed in the apparatus and shocked, however, it attacked the doll. This is shown in Figure 10–3. When the object of aggression was not available to the animal, it aggressed toward a substitute object—that is, the doll. Thus **displaced aggression** was demonstrated.

To show that displacement occurs is important, but it leaves unanswered questions as to what determines which objects are involved in displacement and why. For example, if an employee cannot aggress toward his or her boss after being refused a raise, toward what object or objects will he or she aggress? Miller (1959, pp. 218–219) reached the following conclusions about displacement:

Figure 10–2

The figure shows two rats that have been trained to fight each other to terminate an electric shock.

(From Miller, 1948b, p. 157.)

1. When it is impossible for an organism to respond to a desired stimulus, it will respond to a stimulus that is most similar to the desired stimulus. For example, if a woman is prevented from marrying the man she loved because of his death, she will tend to marry someday a man similar to him.
2. If a response to an original stimulus is prevented by conflict, displacement will occur to an intermediate stimulus. For example, if a girl leaves her boyfriend after a quarrel, her next boyfriend will tend to be similar to her original boyfriend in many ways and yet also different from him.
3. If there are strong avoidance tendencies to an original stimulus, displacement will tend to occur toward a dissimilar stimulus. For example, if a girl's original romance was extremely negative, her next boyfriend will tend to be much different from the first.

Figure 10–3

The figure shows the displacement of an aggressive response.

(From Miller, 1948b, p. 157.)

Figure 10–4

The figure shows that with a weak avoidance tendency, fear is not experienced until objects very near or very similar to the goal are encountered. When there is a strong avoidance tendency, however, fear is caused by objects more distant from and more dissimilar to the goal.

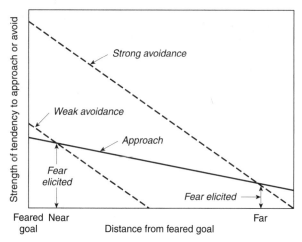

(From Miller, 1959, p. 208.)

If displacement occurs because of conflict, the strength of the conflicting responses will determine where displacement occurs. Figure 10–4 shows the nature of displacement when a weak conflicting response and a strong conflicting response occur.

We can see in Figure 10–4, for example, that if a desire to aggress toward a goal and a weak fear of punishment exist, a tendency to displace to an object similar to the original goal will occur. If a desire exists to aggress toward a goal and there is a strong fear of punishment, however, the aggression will probably be directed toward objects dissimilar to the original goal. In other words, increasing a person's fear will decrease the tendency to displace the response to similar objects, and decreasing a person's fear increases the tendency to displace the response to similar objects. For example, if an employee has no fear of her boss and her boss frustrates her, she will aggress directly toward the boss. If an employee has a mild fear of her boss and the boss frustrates her, she will not aggress toward the boss but will aggress toward someone similar to the boss—for instance, the vice president or manager. If an employee has a strong fear of her boss and the boss frustrates her, she will aggress toward objects dissimilar to the boss, such as other cars on the way home from work, her husband and children, or perhaps her pet.

We see, then, that if an object of choice is not available and no conflict exists, displacement is simply a matter of stimulus generalization. That is, an object most like the one not available will be chosen. If a conflict exists, however, displacement will be governed by the net of the approach and avoidance tendencies.

Frustration–Aggression Hypothesis

In 1939, Dollard and Miller (along with Doob, Mowrer, and Sears) published their first book together, *Frustration and Aggression.* They analyzed the contention, derived from Freudian theory, that frustration leads to aggression, better known as the **frustration–aggression hypothesis.** Dollard et al., made the following assumptions:

This study takes as its point of departure the assumption that aggression is always a consequence of frustration. More specifically, the proposition is that the occurrence of aggressive behavior always pre-supposes the existence of frustration and, contrariwise, that the existence of frustration always leads to some form of aggression. (1939, p. 1)

Frustration was defined as "that condition which exists when a goal-response suffers interference," and aggression was defined as "an act whose goal-response is injury to an organism (or organism-surrogate)" (1939, p. 11). It was assumed that the disruption of goal-directed behavior causes frustration, and frustration causes aggression toward the person or object acting as a barrier between the person and his or her goal.

Dollard et al. (1939, pp. 28–32) concluded that three main factors determine how much aggression will result from frustration:

1. ***Drive level associated with the frustrated response.*** The more intensely the person wants to attain a goal, the more frustrated he or she will be when the goal-directed activity is blocked, and thus the more aggressive that person will become.
2. ***Completeness of the frustration.*** Goal responses that are only partially blocked will lead to less frustration and therefore less aggression than produced by goal responses that are completely blocked.
3. ***Cumulative effect of minor frustrations.*** Minor frustrations or interferences will eventually add up to produce considerable frustration and therefore considerable aggression. If on the way to a restaurant to eat, for example, one first is interrupted by a friend who wants to chat, then by unusually heavy traffic, and then finds the restaurant closed, one is likely to become more frustrated than one would have been if one had gone directly to the restaurant and found it closed.

In all of these points, the message is always the same—the strength of aggression is a function of the magnitude of frustration.

In the last section we learned that as the threat of punishment for a direct act of aggression increases, the tendency for the act of aggression to be displaced to less threatening people or objects also increases. According to Dollard et al., "It follows that the *greater the degree of inhibition specific to a more direct act of aggression, the more probable will be the occurrence of less direct acts of aggression*" (1939, p. 40).

Through the years, the relationship between frustration and aggression has been found to be less direct than originally thought. For example, Miller and Dollard (1941) concluded that aggression is only one result of frustration. Other possible reactions to frustration include withdrawal or apathy, depression, regression, sublimation, creative problem solving, and fixation (stereotyped behavior). The aspect of the original frustration–aggression hypothesis that has been most often confirmed by subsequent research is that frustrated people act more aggressively than nonfrustrated people. However, research has indicated that, as just mentioned, a number of reactions other than aggression can result from frustration. Furthermore, it has been found that acting aggressively does not reduce the aggressive tendency, as Freud and Dollard et al. (1939) believed. A number of studies have shown that acting aggressively actually *increases* the aggressive tendency (e.g., Geen & Quanty,

1977; Geen, Stonner, & Shope, 1975). In order to account for the evidence that is inconsistent with its original formulation, Leonard Berkowitz (1989) has proposed that the frustration–aggression hypothesis be reformulated. Berkowitz finds that if the aversiveness or unpleasantness of an event is emphasized, instead of its capacity to frustrate, many of the current findings are more comprehensible.

Most researchers still believe, however, that aggression is one of the most common and important reactions to frustration and that the relationship between the two has many implications for penal reform, childrearing, and behavior modification in general.

Importance of Language

Earlier in the chapter, we listed "response" as one of the four essential ingredients in Dollard and Miller's theory. The other three are drive, cue, and reinforcement. Two types of responding were mentioned, instrumental or overt and internal or thinking. Both types of responses were considered important by Dollard and Miller, which is a major distinction between their theory and Skinner's. Although Skinner did not avoid the topic of language, to him, language was simply verbal behavior that was governed by the same laws as any other behavior. Dollard and Miller were more willing to speculate on the nature of internal thought processes and their relationship to language than Skinner was. Furthermore, Dollard and Miller analyzed Freudian notions of repression and neurosis in terms of internal response mechanisms. Dollard and Miller thought that people's ability to use language accounts for their higher mental processes, which are part of both neurotic and normal functioning.

Many years ago, Pavlov referred to physical stimuli that precede biologically significant events as the **first signal system.** Such stimuli allow an organism to anticipate biologically significant events and thus deal with them effectively when they occur. For example, we avoid hot stoves, and we salivate when we are hungry and see food. Pavlov called the first signal system "the first signals of reality." In addition to learning anticipatory responses to physical stimuli, however, humans also learn to respond to symbols of reality. For example, we become fearful when we hear words like "fire," "danger," or "enemy." Likewise, we feel good when we hear the name of a loved one or hear such words as "love," "peace," or "friend." Pavlov called the words that symbolize reality "signals of signals," or the **second signal system.**

Dollard and Miller followed Pavlov in believing that language becomes a symbolic representation of reality. As this set of symbols develops, one can "think through" experiences without actually having them. Thinking, then, is a kind of talking to oneself about several behavioral possibilities. Dollard and Miller called images, perceptions, and words **cue-producing responses** because they generally determine the next responses in a sequence. Counting, for example, is a series of cue-producing responses because response "one" triggers response "two," and so forth. Thoughts constitute responses but they also act as cues in eliciting further responses.

Two of the most useful functions of cue-producing responses are **reasoning** and **planning.** Reasoning replaces overt behavior trial and error with cognitive trial

Figure 10–5

An example of how reasoning replaces behavioral trial and error in a problem-solving situation.

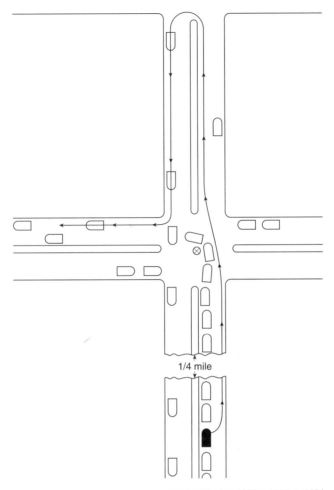

(From Dollard and Miller, 1950, p. 112.)

and error. The latter is far more efficient because mentally a problem can be approached from various viewpoints and no set sequence needs to be followed.

Figure 10–5 shows the advantage of reasoning in problem solving. In this example of reasoning, the driver in the black car is blocked from making a left turn by the traffic jam in the left lane. In the distance, he sees the cars in the lighter traffic coming from the opposite direction making the right turn easily on to the road he wants to take. He thinks, "If I were only going the other way." This stimulates him to think of how he could be going the other way. He pulls out into the right lane, passes the cars ahead, turns around, comes back the other way, and makes a right turn onto the highway. (The small circle at the center intersection indicates a traffic light.)

When cue-producing responses are part of solving an immediate problem, the process is called reasoning. When the cue-producing responses are directed at the solution of a future problem, the process is called planning.

Unconscious Mind

Like Freud, Dollard and Miller considered unconscious processes to be extremely important in determining behavior. They described two major categories of unconscious material: (1) experiences that were never verbally labeled and (2) experiences that have been repressed.

Experiences That Were Never Verbalized

Learning that occurs before language is developed is not labeled or recorded in a way that allows it to be recalled, and therefore, such learning becomes part of the unconscious:

> According to our hypothesis, drives, cues, and responses that have never been labeled will necessarily be unconscious. One large category of this kind will be experiences that occurred before the child learned to talk effectively. Since the effective use of speech develops gradually and may not be established for certain categories until long after the child has learned to say "Mamma," the period during which major parts of social learning are unconscious extends over a considerable number of years and has no set boundaries. (Dollard & Miller, 1950, p. 198)

At the time in life thought by Freud to be critical to adult personality development, experiences are unlabeled and thus cannot be recalled. These early experiences have a profound effect on one's later conscious life, and yet they themselves remain unconscious:

> The young child does not notice or label the experiences which it is having at this time. It cannot give a description of character traits acquired during the first year of life nor yet of its hardships, fears, or deep satisfactions. What was not verbalized at the time cannot well be reported later. An important piece of history is lost and cannot be elicited by questionnaire or interview. Nevertheless, the behavioral record survives. The responses learned occur and may indeed recur in analogous situations throughout life. They are elicited by unlabeled cues and are mutely interwoven into the fabric of conscious life. (Dollard & Miller, 1950, p. 136)

Repressed Experiences

Some thoughts are uncomfortable because they cause anxiety. A few examples are: thinking about an automobile accident in which a loved one was killed or injured; thinking about sex after learning how evil some believe such thoughts are; thinking about how you would like to steal something from a store; thinking about how you would like to caress your teacher or minister. Anxiety is a negative drive, just as pain, hunger, and thirst are, and therefore anything that reduces anxiety is reinforcing. In other words, anything that terminates an anxiety-provoking thought will be learned as a habit.

If suddenly during a conversation you find yourself pondering sexual activity with your best friend's boyfriend, you may find such a thought anxiety-provoking because of your early moral training. If so, you may respond by consciously "putting the thought out of your mind." Such a conscious and deliberate effort to stop an anxiety-provoking thought is called **suppression.** Suppression is learned just like any other response; that is, because it is followed by drive reduction (in this case, anxiety is reduced) it gains in strength. Suppression is a common way of stopping thoughts that cause anxiety.

Eventually the suppression of anxiety-provoking thoughts becomes anticipatory in that such thoughts are terminated automatically before they can cause anxiety. When a potentially painful thought is aborted before it enters consciousness, the process is called **repression.** Repression is the learned response of not thinking thoughts that are unpleasant. In repression, early thoughts act as signals that, if a line of thought is continued, it will result in the experience of anxiety. Therefore the line of thought is terminated before it can become painful. For this reason, repression is said to be anticipatory, and because it prevents the experience of anxiety, it is said to be a conditioned avoidance response. Suppression allows escape from anxiety-provoking thoughts whereas repression allows avoidance of them. In other words, repression is triggered when unacceptable material starts to emerge from the unconscious, and suppression is triggered when such material is already conscious. Both processes are learned responses that are maintained by the elimination, reduction, or prevention of anxiety.

It may appear that a process such as repression is beneficial because it allows a person to avoid many painful thoughts, and this certainly is true. Repression also has a negative side. A thought that is repressed cannot be treated rationally because it does not enter consciousness. As we saw in the preceding section, it is conscious mechanisms that are part of the problem-solving processes of reasoning and planning. If a category of experience is repressed, it cannot be considered logically, and the activities related to it will be irrational. Furthermore, any attempt to bring repressed material into consciousness is typically met with great resistance, which is the case during psychoanalysis.

As you may have deduced by now, Dollard and Miller (as did Freud) thought the mechanism of repression was causally related to most neurotic behavior. The goal of psychotherapy is to free certain thoughts from repression so they may be treated logically and realistically.

Neurosis and Symptom Formation

Neurosis

As we have seen, Dollard and Miller followed Freud in assuming conflict is at the heart of neurotic behavior, and that this conflict is unconscious and usually learned in childhood:

> An intense emotional conflict is the necessary basis for neurotic behavior. The conflict must further be unconscious. As a usual thing, such conflicts are created only in childhood. How can it be that neurotic conflicts are engendered when there is no deliberate plan to do so? Society must force children to grow up, but it does not idealize neurosis and makes no formal provision in its system of training for the production of neurotic children. Indeed we deplore the neurotic and recognize him as

a burden to himself and others. How then does it happen? Our answer is that neurotic conflicts are taught by parents and learned by children. (Dollard & Miller, 1950, p. 127)

Although the term **neurosis** is hard to define precisely, it is clear the neurotic is miserable, unwise about certain aspects of his or her own existence, and often develops physical symptoms that are manifestations of a repressed conflict.

If children are severely punished for sexual activities, they will learn to repress sexual behaviors and thoughts as adults. They will therefore need to live with a sex drive that strongly impels them to engage in sexual activities but with a strong fear of punishment if they do so. As we saw in the last section, thoughts of sexual activity will be repressed under these circumstances and, as a result, this strong approach–avoidance conflict will remain unconscious, so that language cannot be used to describe and analyze it:

> Without language and adequate labeling, the higher mental processes cannot function. When these processes are knocked out by repression, the person cannot guide himself by mental means to a resolution of his conflict. Since the neurotic cannot help himself, he must have the help of others if he is to be helped at all—though millions today live out their lives in strong neurotic pain and never get help. The neurotic, therefore, is, or appears to be, stupid because he is unable to use his mind in dealing with certain of his problems. He feels that someone should help him, but he does not know how to ask for help since he does not know what his problem is. He may feel aggrieved that he is suffering, but he cannot explain his case. (Dollard & Miller, 1950, p. 15)

The neurotic, therefore, is caught in an unbearable conflict between frustrated drives, on the one hand, and the fear connected with the approach responses that would bring about their satisfaction, on the other.

Symptom Formation

Neurotics often develop symptoms such as phobias, inhibitions, avoidances, compulsions, and physical disorders such as paralysis or nervous tics. Although it is common for neurotics to think their symptoms constitute their problem, they do not. Neurotic symptoms are manifestations of repressed conflicts. As an example, Dollard and Miller (1950) cited the case of Mrs. A., who was an orphan, born of unknown parents in a southern city. She was raised by foster parents who gave her very repressive sex training. Although she had strong sexual appetites, sex became a dirty, loathsome activity about which it was painful for her to talk or think. Eventually she developed several phobias and a preoccupation with her heartbeat. In analysis, it was learned that her preoccupation with her heartbeat was used as a means of preventing sex-related thoughts. Dollard and Miller summarized the case of Mrs. A. as follows:

> When on the streets alone, her fear of sex temptation was increased. Someone might speak to her, wink at her, make an approach to her. Such an approach would increase her sex desire and make her more vulnerable to seduction. Increased sex desire, however, touched off both anxiety and guilt, and this intensified her conflict when she was on the street. . . . When sexy thoughts came to mind or other sex

stimuli tended to occur, these stimuli elicited anxiety. . . . Since [heartbeat] counting is a highly preoccupying kind of response, no other thoughts could enter her
mind during this time. While counting, the sexy thoughts which excited fear
dropped out. Mrs. A. "felt better" immediately when she started counting, and the
counting habit was reinforced by the drop in anxiety. (p. 21)

Neurotic symptoms are learned because they reduce fear or anxiety. Such
symptoms do not solve the basic problem any more than repression does but they
make life temporarily more bearable:

The symptoms do not solve the basic conflict in which the neurotic person is
plunged, but they mitigate it. They are responses which tend to reduce the conflict,
and in part they succeed. When a successful symptom occurs it is reinforced because it reduces neurotic misery. The symptom is thus learned as a habit. One very
common function of symptoms is to keep the neurotic person away from those
stimuli which would activate and intensify his neurotic conflict. Thus, the combat
pilot with a harrowing military disaster behind him may walk away from the sight
of any airplane. As he walks towards the plane his anxiety goes up; as he walks
away it goes down. Walking away is thus reinforced. It is this phobic walking away
which constitutes his symptom. If the whole situation is not understood, such behavior seems bizarre to the casual witness. (Dollard & Miller, 1950, pp. 15–16)

Psychotherapy

The major assumption that Dollard and Miller made about neurosis is that it is
learned, and because it is learned, it can be unlearned. **Psychotherapy** provides a situation in which neurosis can be unlearned:

If neurotic behavior is learned, it should be unlearned by some combination of the
same principles by which it was taught. We believe this to be the case. Psychotherapy establishes a set of conditions by which neurotic habits may be unlearned and nonneurotic habits learned. Therefore, we view the therapist as a kind
of teacher and the patient as a learner. In the same way and by the same principles
that bad tennis habits can be corrected by a good coach, so bad mental and emotional habits can be corrected by a good psychotherapist. There is this difference,
however. Whereas only a few people want to play tennis, all the world wants a
clear, free, efficient mind. (Dollard & Miller, 1950, pp. 7–8)

As we have seen, the only way for a learned response to be extinguished is for
it to occur and not be followed by reinforcement. For unrealistic fears to be extinguished, they must occur and then not be followed by the type of events that produced the fears in the first place. As previously mentioned, however, the person has
learned to repress such fears, thus preventing their expression and therefore their
subsequent extinction. Psychotherapy can be regarded as a situation in which the expression of repressed thoughts is encouraged. If the patient can be made to express
these painful thoughts, the therapist is extremely careful to be encouraging, positive,
and not punitive. Dollard and Miller (1950) explained:

In addition to permitting free speech, the therapist commands the patient to say everything that comes to mind. By the free-association technique the therapist sets the patient free from the restraint of logic. The therapist avoids arousing additional anxiety by not cross-questioning. By encouraging the patient to talk and consistently failing to punish him, the therapist creates a social situation that is the exact opposite of the one originally responsible for attaching strong fears to talking and thinking. The patient talks about frightening topics. Since he is not punished, his fears are extinguished. This extinction generalizes and weakens the motivation to repress other related topics that were originally too frightening for the patient to discuss or even to contemplate. Where the patient cannot say things for himself, the therapist helps by attaching a verbal label to the emotions that are being felt and expressed mutely in the transference situation. (p. 230)

To persuade the patient to express a repressed thought is no easy matter, however, and typically a procedure similar to successive approximations is used. Let us imagine that a patient, for whatever reason, has learned to fear his mother to the point at which he cannot talk about her or anything directly related to her. The therapist using Dollard and Miller's theory would not confront the patient directly with a conversation about his mother. Rather, the therapist would begin the discussion with events only indirectly related to the patient's mother. How indirect this needs to be depends on the magnitude of the avoidance the patient has toward his mother. As the therapist and patient discuss events only remotely related to the mother in a nonthreatening environment, a small amount of the avoidance of the mother is extinguished, or what Freud called catharsis occurs. With the avoidance response somewhat reduced, the therapist can steer the conversation a bit closer to the mother but still stay a safe distance away. When doing so, the avoidance response is further reduced, and the therapist can move still closer to the ultimate target, the mother. Gradually, usually over several sessions, the therapist moves closer and closer to a discussion of the mother and then, when the avoidance response is sufficiently reduced, to a discussion of the mother herself. Now with the avoidance reduced, the patient can talk about his mother phobia openly and rationally.

Psychotherapy, as viewed by Dollard and Miller (and also by Freud), is a process of gradual extinction that depends on generalization, because the events discussed must be related in some way to the object, person, or event of ultimate concern. It also can be said that avoidance is displaced onto objects similar to the one that is avoided the most, so that not only will the patient avoid his mother, he will also avoid people who look like her (primary generalization) or all mothers (secondary generalization); he may even be mildly apprehensive of women in general. Thus conflict, extinction, generalization, and displacement are part of the therapeutic process.

Psychotherapy usually does not end when repressions have been released. Because the patient has spent such a large amount of his or her life with repressed thoughts, and because it is impossible to deal effectively with repressed material, there will be significant gaps in the person's life even after successful therapy. For example, a person who is suddenly able to ponder her sex drive at the age of 35 will need some guidance as to how best to adjust to the relative absence of inhibition. Such guidance also is considered by Dollard and Miller to be essential to the therapeutic process.

Four Critical Training Situations of Childhood

As we have seen throughout this chapter, Dollard and Miller agreed with Freud that most neuroses originate in early childhood. This is an especially vulnerable time because children have no verbal labels for their feelings and experiences and are not aware of time; for example, they do not know that "in a little while" their hunger, thirst, or pain will be reduced. Their lives vacillate from extreme discomfort to bliss and back again. In fact, Dollard and Miller (1950) referred to early childhood as a period of "transitory psychosis" (p. 130). Also, infants, because of their helplessness, are completely at the mercy of their parents for the satisfaction of their needs, and how the parents go about satisfying their infants' needs will make the difference between a normal, healthy adult and a neurotic one. Dollard and Miller (pp. 132–156) described four critical training situations they believed have a profound influence on adult personality:

1. **Feeding situation.** (occurs primarily during the Freudian oral stage). The conditions under which the hunger drive is satisfied will be learned and generalized into personality attributes. If, for example, children are fed when active, they may become active people; if they are fed while quiet and passive, they may become passive or apathetic individuals. If their hunger drives are satisfied in an unpredictable manner, they may grow up believing the world is an unpredictable place. If children are left alone for long periods when they are hungry, they may develop a fear of being alone. If the mother is harsh and punitive during the feeding situation, the child may grow up disliking other people and avoid them at all costs. If, however, the mother is kind, warm, and positive during the feeding situation, the child may grow up with a positive attitude toward other people and seek them out as friends.
2. **Cleanliness training.** (occurs primarily during the Freudian anal stage). Dollard and Miller, like Freud, believed the events surrounding toilet training are extremely important to personality development. If the parents respond negatively to children's inability to control their bladder or bowels, the children may not be able to distinguish between parental disapproval of what they have done and disapproval of themselves:

   > The child may not be able to discriminate between parental loathing for its excreta and loathing for the whole child himself. If the child learns to adopt these reactions, feelings of unworthiness, insignificance, and hopeless sinfulness will be created—feelings which sometimes so mysteriously reappear in the psychotic manifestations of guilt. (Dollard & Miller, 1950, pp. 139–140)

   Although it is necessary to toilet train a child, how it is done may have a profound influence on the child's emerging personality.
3. **Early sex training.** (occurs primarily during the Freudian phallic stage). The first sex training a child normally receives in our culture is related to the child's early efforts to masturbate. Often, such behavior elicits physical punishment or such terms as "nasty" and "dirty." So it may be

with most sexually oriented activities in which the child engages. There are probably more taboos in our culture related to sexual matters than there are for any other type of activity, and these taboos are all part of our childrearing practices. No wonder sexual conflict is such a common theme in the analyst's office. The sex drive is innate, but the fear of sexual thoughts and activities is learned in childhood.

4. **Anger–anxiety conflicts.** (this training is not specific to any Freudian stage of development). Frustration is inevitable in childhood (and at any other age), and as we learned earlier, the most common reaction to frustration is aggression. However, aggressive behavior on the part of children in our culture is often met with parental disapproval or punishment. Children are placed in still another approach–avoidance conflict; that is, they want to be aggressive but inhibit this impulse because of fear of punishment. This may result in being too passive to compete successfully in modern society:

> After this learning has occurred, the first cues produced by angry emotions may set off anxiety responses which "outcompete" the angry emotional responses themselves. The person can thus be made helpless to use his anger even in those situations where culture does permit it. He is viewed as abnormally meek or long-suffering. Robbing a person of his anger completely may be a dangerous thing since some capacity for anger seems to be needed in the affirmative personality. (Dollard & Miller, 1950, p. 149)

Dollard and Miller (1950) described the types of childhood experiences they believed lead to adult neuroses and their message was change these childhood conditions and neuroses can be eliminated:

> As a learning theorist sees it, the existence of neuroses is an automatic criticism of our culture of child rearing. Misery-producing, neurotic habits which the therapist must painfully unteach have been as painfully taught in the confused situation of childhood. A system of child training built on the laws of learning might have the same powerful effect on the neurotic misery of our time as Pasteur's work had on infectious diseases. (p. 8)

Evaluation

Empirical Research

Dollard and Miller's theory is firmly grounded in empirical research. Almost without exception, when a concept is used in their theory, several experiments are cited that empirically verify that concept. Dollard and Miller's theory is, to a large extent, an extension of Hullian learning theory, which itself is one of the most scientifically rigorous theories in psychology's history. Throughout this chapter, we have reviewed experiments that Dollard, Miller, and their colleagues ran to verify or test their theoretical concepts. For example, research was cited showing how fear is acquired; how fear and other tendencies generalize; how various conflicts impact behavior;

how fear and other tendencies are displaced; how frustration and aggression are related; how physical symptoms partially reduce neurotic conflict; and how learning principles operate in the therapeutic process.

Dollard and Miller's theory earns marks as high as the theories of Cattell, Eysenck, and Skinner in its effort to empirically validate the terms, principles, and concepts that it contains.

Criticisms

Unsuccessful Synthesis of Hullian Learning Theory and Psychoanalysis. Prominent members of both camps have complained that Dollard and Miller's attempt to synthesize Hullian learning theory and psychoanalysis did not work. Learning theorists such as Bandura (whose theory we review in the next chapter) and Skinner complained that no need exists to use nebulous, subjective psychoanalytic terminology to explain personality. Bandura and Skinner (and others) claimed that learning principles alone can do the job. As we saw in the last chapter, Skinner went so far as to say that "personality" can be understood without reference to mental events of any type.

Skinner believed that even Dollard and Miller's use of such "hypothetical fictions" as cues, drives, conflicts, and cue-producing responses was not only unnecessary but may, in fact, interfere with a true understanding of personality. In the next chapter, we see that Bandura's analysis does allow, even emphasizes, mental events, but those events are not the unconscious variety stressed by the psychoanalysts.

Many psychoanalysts were equally unimpressed by the efforts of Dollard and Miller. Their argument was that the dynamics of the human mind are far more complicated than Dollard and Miller's analysis suggests. To them phenomena such as displacement, repression, conflict, and neuroses are too complex to be understood in terms of a few principles of learning. Furthermore, they say, it is foolish to suggest that the processes occurring during psychotherapy (especially psychoanalysis) can be demonstrated by a rat in an experimental chamber.

Overgeneralization from Nonhuman Animals to Humans. Like Skinner, Dollard and Miller have been criticized for assuming that the principles observed in nonhuman animals also apply to humans. What good, ask the critics, are all of the carefully controlled laboratory experiments on nonhuman animals if a tenuous assumption concerning the generalizability of the findings must be made? Insofar as humans are different from rats and pigeons, the findings from such research is irrelevant. In fairness to Dollard and Miller, however, it must be noted that they stressed that any such generalizations should be carefully investigated; they did do a considerable amount of research on humans as well as nonhuman animals.

Overly Simplistic Approach. Some critics say that a theory such as Dollard and Miller's that stresses environmental stimuli, a few mental events, and overt responses misses the richness and complexity of human personality. Love, despair, the importance of the future, meaning of life, and the experience of the self are just a few of the human experiences that are not addressed by such a theory. In addition, to suggest that dysfunctional mental or emotional habits can be corrected by a therapist in much the same way that a good coach corrects bad tennis habits is just too simplistic say the critics.

Contributions

Synthesis of Hullian Learning Theory and Psychoanalysis.   As so often happens, what some find to be a weakness in a theory, others view as a strength. For many, Dollard and Miller's synthesis of Hullian learning theory and psychoanalysis was a milestone in the history of psychology. The synthesis achieved two goals: It broadened the application of an otherwise limited theory of learning to a wide array of human phenomena; and it made several psychoanalytic concepts more testable than they had been. Until Dollard and Miller's efforts, the gulf between the research laboratory and the clinical consulting room was enormous. Their work provided a bridge across that gulf, and ideas have been flowing back and forth ever since. In fact, Dollard and Miller were the first theorists to explore the role of learning in personality development specifically, a role now accepted by most theorists as substantial.

Scientifically Respectable Approach to the Study of Personality.   In the area of personality in which the early theories were difficult to test empirically, a scientifically rigorous theory is welcomed. Most of the terms and concepts in Dollard and Miller's theory are defined precisely enough to allow them to be empirically verified. In terms of testability, Dollard and Miller's theory ranks high along with the theories of Cattell, Eysenck, and Skinner.

Clear Description of Therapeutic Process.   By describing traditional psychotherapeutic procedures in terms of learning principles, Dollard and Miller were able to account for successful therapy and to make sound recommendations for the improvement of the therapeutic process. It is now widely accepted that at least some forms of anxiety are learned, and once learned, thoughts and events that elicit such anxiety are avoided. It is, according to Dollard and Miller, this avoidance that causes anxiety-provoking thoughts to persist. Effective therapy creates a situation in which such thoughts can be expressed without experiencing the unpleasant consequences originally associated with them. As this change occurs, extinction gradually takes place, and the thoughts that were once too anxiety-provoking to entertain can now be dealt with rationally. All of these elements of the therapeutic process were discussed by Freud but restating them using the terminology of learning theory makes them clearer and more testable. What has become known as behavior therapy was given a tremendous boost by the work of Dollard and Miller.

Dollard and Miller provided information that is certainly helpful in treating neuroses, and that information may also someday be responsible for a reduction in their frequency of occurrence. If this is true, one can forgive them for favoring animal research and for having a deterministic model of human nature. Every theory must be judged by its ultimate effectiveness, not by origins or by its assumptions.

Summary

Dollard and Miller's goal was to combine Hullian learning theory with Freud's theory of personality. Hull's theory of learning equated reinforcement with drive reduction and defined a habit as a strong association between a stimulus (cue) and a response. Central to Dollard and Miller's theory were the concepts of drive, cue, response, and reinforcement. Drive impels an organism to action, cue directs its behavior, response is what the organism does either overtly or internally, and reinforcement occurs when the motivational drive is either reduced or terminated. In other words, in order to learn, the organism must want something, notice something, do something, and get something it wants.

Every cue elicits several responses arranged in accordance with their probability of occurrence. This set of responses is called the habit family hierarchy. Shortly after birth, before learning has occurred, this is called the innate hierarchy of responses. The hierarchy that exists before new learning occurs is called the initial hierarchy of responses. The hierarchy that exists after learning has occurred is called the resultant hierarchy of responses. The most likely response to any situation is called the dominant response. The learning dilemma refers to the fact that previously learned responses or innate responses must fail to solve a problem before learning can take place. Thus all learning depends on failure. The gradient of reinforcement refers to the fact that when a series of responses ultimately results in reinforcement, the last response in the series is strengthened the most, then the second to the last, and so on.

Dollard and Miller demonstrated that events associated with the experience of pain themselves will become feared, and an organism will learn responses that will allow it to escape from those fear-producing cues. Stimulus generalization refers to the fact that a learned response will be elicited not only by the cue in the actual learning, but by a variety of similar stimuli as well. The more similar a cue is to the one actually used in training, the greater the probability that it will elicit the same response. Primary generalization is determined by the physical properties of stimuli. Secondary generalization is caused by using the same verbal label to describe events. For example, one responds to all events labeled "dangerous" in a similar fashion. Discrimination is the opposite of generalization.

Dollard and Miller studied four types of conflict: approach–approach conflicts, in which the organism is attracted to two goals at the same time; avoidance–avoidance conflicts, in which the organism is repelled by two goals at the same time; approach–avoidance conflicts, in which the organism is attracted to and repelled by the same goal; and double approach–avoidance conflicts, in which the organism is both attracted to and repelled by two goals at the same time. Dollard and Miller did most of their research on approach–avoidance conflict and found that at great distances from the goal the approach tendency is strongest, but as one approaches the goal, the avoidance tendency becomes stronger. This causes vacillation at the point that the two tendencies have about equal strength.

If the goal of choice is not available, the organism will choose a substitute goal object, which is called displacement. If one cannot aggress toward the object, event, or person that caused frustration, one will aggress toward a substitute object; this is called displaced aggression. If one is fearful of aggressing toward an object, event, or person causing frustration, displacement will be toward dissimilar objects, events, or people. If little fear exists, displacement will be to more similar things.

The frustration–aggression hypothesis originally stated that aggression followed from frustration and that frustration always resulted in aggression. This was later modified, however, to state that aggression was just one result of frustration, instead of the only one. Furthermore, recent research has indicated that aggression does not necessarily result in a reduction of the aggressive tendency, as Freud and Dollard et al. (1939) had believed. Leonard Berkowitz has proposed that the frustration–aggression hypothesis be reformulated to account for the disparate predictions resulting from its original formulation.

Language is important to Dollard and Miller's theory. Thinking is essentially talking to oneself. Thinking allows for cognitive trial and error to replace behavioral trial and error. Dollard and Miller called images, perceptions, and words cue-producing responses because they determine what the next response in a series will be. Thinking consists of a series of cue-producing responses. Two important types of thinking are reasoning, which is directed at solving a current problem, and planning, which is directed at solving a future problem.

The unconscious mind, according to Dollard and Miller, consists of experiences that were never verbalized and experiences that have been repressed. Repression is considered a response of not thinking, which is reinforced because it prevents an anxiety-provoking thought from becoming conscious. Suppression is the act of driving an anxiety-provoking thought out of consciousness. Repressed thoughts are practically immune to extinction because they are not experienced consciously long enough for the person to realize that they are no longer followed by negative consequences.

Most neurotic conflicts are learned in childhood and therefore are not verbally labeled. Neurotics are miserable and unwise about matters related to their repressions. Neurotics often develop symptoms that stem from their repressed conflict. Symptoms such as phobias, compulsions, or physical disorders temporarily relieve neurotics' distress because they act as a barrier between neurotics and anxiety-provoking situations. For example, by becoming obese, a person can decrease the likelihood of confronting sexual situations. Thus, for the person with a repressed sexual conflict, obesity is reinforcing. The desire for sex does not go away, however, so the conflict continues to manifest itself in harmful ways. Both repression and neurotic symptoms are learned for the same reason; they temporarily reduce or prevent anxiety.

Psychotherapy is a situation in which patients are encouraged to label their conflicts verbally and to confront them gradually. The therapist is encouraging and nonthreatening, so that if and when repressed material emerges, it can be extinguished. Therapy usually starts by discussing objects, people, or events that are only indirectly related to those causing strong anxiety. As distant, but related, events are discussed, a certain amount of anxiety is extinguished, and gradually the person can talk directly about events that previously were too anxiety-provoking. Psychotherapy, as Dollard and Miller view it, treats conflict and repression using the processes of generalization, displacement, and extinction.

Dollard and Miller believed neurotic conflicts are learned in childhood. The difference between a mentally healthy, normal adult and a neurotic adult is thought to be fairly well determined by how parents handle the four critical training periods of childhood, namely, the feeding situation, cleanliness training, sex training, and anger–anxiety training.

Dollard and Miller's theory is firmly grounded in empirical research but has been criticized for failing to synthesize Hullian learning theory and psychoanalysis successfully; generalizing too freely from nonhuman animals to humans; and being too simplistic in its account of personality and of the therapeutic process. Their theory has been praised for combining Hullian learning theory and psychoanalytic theory, thereby making both more useful; clarifying the processes that are actually involved in effective psychotherapy; and being scientifically rigorous.

Experiential Exercises

1. Give at least one example of an approach–approach, avoidance–avoidance, and approach–avoidance conflict that you have experienced and state how you resolved each conflict. In the case of the approach–avoidance conflict, did your experiences conform to Miller's description? That is, did you experience a great deal of vacillation and indecision as the goal was approached?
2. Give an example of displaced aggression in your life. That is, describe a situation in which you could not aggress directly toward a source of frustration and therefore aggressed, in some way, toward a person or an object other than the one that actually frustrated you. Explain, in terms of Dollard and Miller's theory, why you chose that object or person.
3. Privately ponder an idea or topic that you cannot openly discuss without experiencing considerable anxiety. Review how Dollard and Miller suggest such anxiety-provoking thoughts should be approached and resolved. Do you believe that by following their procedure of systematic extinction your anxiety-provoking thought will become increasingly more tolerable? Why or why not?

Discussion Questions

1. Dollard and Miller's theory is often called a blending of Hullian learning theory and Freudian psychoanalytic theory. Explain why their theory is identified this way. Give several examples of such a blend.
2. Discuss the concepts of drive, cue, response, and reinforcement. Give both the formal definition and an example of each.
3. What did Dollard and Miller mean by the term learning dilemma? Discuss the implications of this concept for education and childrearing.

Glossary

Acquired drive. Drive that is learned, not innate. Fear is an example of an acquired drive.

Anger–anxiety conflicts. One of the four training situations in childhood that, if not handled properly, could result in neurotic conflict.

Approach–approach conflict. Situation that exists when a person must choose between two equally attractive goals.

Approach–avoidance conflict. Situation that exists when a person is both attracted to and repelled by the same goal.

Avoidance–avoidance conflict. Situation that exists when a person must choose between two equally aversive goals.

Biofeedback. The use of some mechanical device, such as an auditory signal or flashing light, to provide individuals with information about the functioning of one or more of their internal biological processes.

Cleanliness training.   One of the four critical training situations in childhood that, if not handled properly, could lead to neurotic conflict.

Conditioned fear reaction.   Learning to fear something that was not previously feared.

Conflict.   Situation in which two or more incompatible response tendencies exist simultaneously.

Cue.   Stimulus that indicates the appropriate direction an activity should take.

Cue-producing responses.   Images, perceptions, and words, the main functions of which are to determine subsequent behavior. Thinking is an example of a cue-producing response.

Discrimination.   Opposite of generalization. That is, stimuli similar to the stimulus in the learning process do not elicit a learned response.

Displaced aggression.   Aggressing toward a substitute person or object when the actual object of aggression is either not available or is feared.

Displacement.   Act of substituting one goal for another when the primary goal is not available or feared.

Dominant response.   That response in a habit family hierarchy that has the greatest probability of occurrence.

Double approach–avoidance conflict.   Situation that exists when a person has both positive and negative feelings about two goals.

Drive.   Any strong stimulus that impels an organism to action and whose elimination or reduction is reinforcing.

Drive reduction.   Constitutes reinforcement in Hull's theory of learning.

Early sex training.   One of the four critical training situations in childhood that, if not handled properly, could result in neurotic conflict.

Feeding situation.   One of the four critical training situations in childhood that, if not handled properly, could result in neurotic conflict.

First signal system.   According to Pavlov, physical stimuli that precede biologically significant events allowing their anticipation and thus appropriate responses to them.

Frustration–aggression hypothesis.   Originally the contention that frustration always leads to aggression and aggression results only from frustration. Later modified to state that aggression is only one of several possible reactions to frustration.

Gradient of reinforcement.   The observation that if a series of responses leads to reinforcement, the last response in the series will be strengthened the most, then the second to the last, etc.

Habit.   Association between a stimulus and a response.

Habit family hierarchy.   Group of responses elicited by a single stimulus that are arranged in accordance with their probability of occurrence.

Hull's theory of learning.   Theory of learning that Dollard and Miller synthesized with Freud's theory. Hull's theory equates reinforcement with drive reduction. In other words, for learning to take place, the organism must engage in an activity that leads to the elimination or reduction of a need.

Initial hierarchy of responses.   Hierarchy of responses elicited by a cue before new learning occurs.

Innate hierarchy of responses.   Habit family hierarchy that is genetically determined.

Learning.   According to Dollard and Miller, the rearrangement of response probabilities that results when certain responses are reinforced and others are not.

Learning dilemma.   Contention that for learning to occur, both innate responses and previously learned responses must be ineffective in solving a problem. Therefore, learning is said to depend on failure.

Neurosis.   Condition that causes a person to function at less than maximal efficiency, which typically results from unconscious conflict that originated in early childhood.

Planning.   Use of cue-producing responses (thinking) in attempting to solve some future problem.

Primary generalization.   Generalization that is determined by the physical properties of stimuli.

Psychotherapy.   For Dollard and Miller, a situation in which repressed conflicts can be unlearned, that is, extinguished.

Reasoning.   Attempted solution of an immediate problem through the use of cue-producing responses (thinking) rather than through overt trial and error.

Reinforcement.   In Hull's theory of learning, drive reduction constitutes reinforcement.

Reinforcement theory.   Any theory of learning that states that reinforcement must occur before learning can take place.

Reinforcer. In Hull's theory, a stimulus capable of reducing a drive.

Repression. Learned response of "not thinking" an anxiety-provoking thought. The reinforcement for this response comes from the avoidance of anxiety.

Response. Any overt or internal action elicited by a stimulus.

Resultant hierarchy of responses. Hierarchy of responses elicited by a cue after learning has taken place.

Second signal system. According to Pavlov, the verbal labels that symbolize environmental events.

Secondary generalization. Generalization that is based on verbal labels (words), not on the physical similarity among stimuli.

Stimulus generalization. Tendency for stimuli other than the stimulus present in the learning process to elicit a learned response. The more similar these stimuli are to the one actually used in the learning process, the greater the probability is that they will elicit a learned response.

Suppression. Actively putting an anxiety-provoking thought out of one's mind. Suppression is reinforced by the escape from anxiety.

Symptom formation. Neurotic's tendency to develop such things as phobias, compulsions, or physical disorders because they reduce anxiety temporarily.

<table>
<tr>
<td>

CHAPTER **11**

</td>
<td>

ALBERT BANDURA
AND
WALTER MISCHEL

CHAPTER OUTLINE

</td>
</tr>
</table>

Although Bandura and Mischel have not collaborated on major books, as did Dollard and Miller, their viewpoints are so similar that we consider them together. The position of Bandura and Mischel is referred to as **social-cognitive theory.** Bandura (1986) explains the reasons for the name: "The social portion of the terminology acknowledges the social origins of much human thought and action; the cognitive portion recognizes the influential causal contribution of thought processes to human motivation, affect, and action" (p. xii). Social-cognitive theory views the interaction between the person and the environment as highly complex and individualistic.

Each individual brings to each situation the remnants of previous experience, which are used to deal with the present situation. The outcome of negotiations with the present situation, in turn, influences how similar situations are dealt with in the future. At the heart of social-cognitive theory is the notion of observational learning. The most important fact about observational learning is that it requires no reinforcement. According to Bandura and Mischel, humans learn what they attend to, and therefore, for them, learning is a perceptual process. Thus social-cognitive theory contrasts sharply with the theories of Skinner (see Chapter 9) and Dollard and Miller (see Chapter 10), which rely heavily on the concept of direct reinforcement.

Biographical Sketches

Albert Bandura

Albert Bandura was born on December 4, 1925, in Mundare, a small town in the province of Alberta, Canada. His parents were wheat farmers of Polish heritage. The high school he attended had only 20 students and 2 teachers. Following graduation from high school, Bandura spent the summer working on the Alaskan highway. Many of the men with whom he worked had fled to Alaska to escape "creditors, alimony, and probation officers." Working with such characters instilled in Bandura "a keen appreciation for the psychopathology of everyday life" (*American Psychologist,* 1981). Bandura entered the University of British Columbia in 1946 and obtained his BA in 1949, with a major in psychology. He then went to the University of Iowa where he obtained his MA in 1951 and his PhD in 1952. It was at the University of Iowa that Bandura met his future wife, Virginia (Ginny) Varns, who was teaching in the school of nursing there. Bandura and his wife eventually had two daughters, Mary and Carol. After a year's clinical internship at the Wichita, Kansas, Guidance Center, he moved to Stanford University, where he has been ever since.

After arriving at Stanford, Bandura began working on the familial causes of aggression with his first graduate student, Richard Walters (1918–1967). It was during this work that Bandura became aware of the importance of modeling and observational learning for personality development. A section on observational learning appears later in this chapter. Bandura's first book (coauthored with Richard Walters) was *Adolescent Aggression* (1959). His second book (also written with Richard Walters) was *Social Learning and Personality Development* (1963). Subsequent books were *Principles of Behavior Modification* (1969), *Aggression: A Social-Learning Analysis* (1973), *Social Learning Theory* (1977), *Social Foundations of Thought and Action: A Social Cognitive Theory* (1986), *Self-Efficacy in Changing Societies* (1995) of which he was editor; and *Self-Efficacy: The Exercise of Control* (1997). In addition to his books, Bandura has written many influential articles.

Included among Bandura's many honors are Fellow of the Center for Advanced Study in the Behavioral Sciences, 1969–1970; a Guggenheim fellowship, 1972; a Distinguished Scientist Award from Division 12 (Clinical Psychology) of the American Psychological Association (APA), 1972; a Distinguished Scientific Achievement Award from the California Psychological Association, 1973; president of the

APA, 1974; David Starr Jordan Professor of Social Science in Psychology, Stanford University, 1974; the James McKeen Cattell Award, 1977; honorary Doctor of Science degree from the University of British Columbia, 1979; fellow of the American Academy of Arts and Sciences, 1980; a Distinguished Contribution Award from the International Society for Research on Aggression, 1980; presidency of the Western Psychological Association, 1980; the Distinguished Contribution Award from the APA, 1980; member of the Institute of Medicine of the National Academy of Sciences, 1989; the James McKeen Cattell Fellow Award from the American Psychological Society, 2003–2004; and the APA's highest honor, the Lifetime Contribution to Psychology Award, 2004.

Walter Mischel

Walter Mischel, the second son of upper-middle-class parents, was born on February 22, 1930, in Vienna, Austria, within walking distance of Freud's house. In 1938, when Mischel was 9 years old, the Nazis invaded Austria, and his family moved to the United States. After living in various parts of the country, the family settled in Brooklyn, New York, in 1940. There, Mischel attended primary and secondary school and earned a college scholarship, but because his father became ill he was forced to work. He worked as a stock boy, elevator operator, and assistant in a garment factory before he was finally able to attend New York University, where he pursued his interests in painting, sculpture, and psychology.

In college, Mischel was disenchanted by behavioristic psychology but was attracted to psychoanalysis. At the same time, he strengthened his humanistic inclinations by reading existential philosophy and poetry. After graduation from college Mischel entered the MA program in clinical psychology at City College of New York. While working on his degree Mischel became a social worker working primarily with juvenile delinquents in the Lower East Side slums of New York. It was this work that caused Mischel to doubt the usefulness of psychoanalytic theory.

Between 1953 and 1956 Mischel worked on his PhD at Ohio State University where he came under the influence of George Kelly and Julian Rotter. Rotter's work emphasized the importance of expectancies in human behavior, and Kelly stressed the importance of the formulation of mental concepts (personal constructs) in dealing with the world. Both Rotter and Kelly emphasized cognitive events in dealing with the current situations and deemphasized the importance of traits and early developmental experience. The influence of both men is seen in Mischel's work. George Kelly's theory is covered in Chapter 13.

From 1956 to 1958, Mischel lived in a Trinidad village in the Caribbean studying religious cults that practiced spirit possession. It was at this time that Mischel observed that some people have the ability to reject small, immediate rewards in favor of larger, but delayed rewards. Mischel also observed that people with this ability to delay gratification had higher needs for achievement and showed more social responsibility (1958, 1961a, 1961b). As we will see later in this chapter, studying delayed gratification became one of Mischel's lifelong passions.

Mischel next taught for 2 years at the University of Colorado before joining the Department of Social Relations at Harvard. While at Harvard his interests in personality theory and assessment were furthered by discussions with Gordon Allport. It was also at Harvard that Mischel met his future wife, Harriet Nerlove, who was a graduate student in cognitive psychology. The Mischels eventually had three daughters and have collaborated on several studies. In 1962, Mischel moved to Stanford where he became a colleague of Bandura. In 1983, after more than 20 years at Stanford, Mischel returned to New York City, where he joined the faculty at Columbia University. There, Mischel continues to pursue his long-standing interests in delayed gratification, self-control, and the cognitive processes utilized by individuals in their interactions with the world as the Robert Johnson Niven Professor of Humane Letters in Psychology.

In 1978, Mischel received a Distinguished Scientist Award from the clinical division of the American Psychological Association, and its Distinguished Scientific Contribution Award in 1982. His books include *Personality and Assessment* (1968) and *Introduction to Personality,* first published in 1971 and revised in 1976, 1981, 1986, and 1993. In 2004, he was elected to the National Academy of Sciences.

Consistency of Human Behavior

Through the years, most personality theorists have assumed that a person's behavior is fairly consistent over time and across similar situations. That is, it was assumed that how people act at one time in their lives will be more or less how they act at other times, and that they will tend to respond to similar situations in similar ways. For example, if a person was outgoing in one social situation, it was assumed he or she would be outgoing in other situations and will continue to respond in that characteristic way throughout most of his or her life. It was also assumed that scores on various personality tests and questionnaires would correlate significantly with actual behavior. That is, if a person scored high on a scale intended to measure introversion, he or she would tend to be introverted in social situations. The question was not whether behavior was consistent; rather, theorists attempted to account for the consistency they assumed existed. Psychoanalytic theory attempted to account for it by postulating repressed experiences, complexes, fixations, or internalized values. Within psychoanalytic theory, however, the conclusion of consistency can sometimes only be reached by a trained psychoanalyst because it is assumed that sometimes extreme aggression really means passivity, love sometimes really means hate, and repulsion sometimes really means attraction, to give but a few examples. Trait theory postulated enduring traits to explain why, for example, a neat person tended to be neat in a wide variety of situations. Learning theory emphasized the role of reinforcement. That is, behavior that was reinforced tended to persist and to transfer to situations similar to the one in which the reinforcement had occurred.

Traditionally, personality theory has attempted to account for individual differences among people, but it was always assumed that although people differ from one another, the behavior of any given individual tended to be consistent across similar situations and over time. In the early 1960s, Mischel was given the task of predicting the success of Peace Corps volunteers. In this effort, he found that standardized personality tests designed to measure traits were weak predictors of behavior (Mischel, 1965). He found that people are better predictors of their own behavior than the best available personality tests. It was this work that led to Mischel's highly influential book *Personality and Assessment* (1968). In this book,

Mischel reviewed many studies designed to measure consistency of behavior across situations or to measure the relationship between performance on personality questionnaires and actual behavior. He found the typical correlation to be about 0.30. Mischel called this weak correlation the **personality coefficient,** and he argued that the weakness of the coefficient was not due to problems in measuring such characteristics as traits or behavior but, rather, to the fact that human behavior is simply not very consistent.

Thus, according to Mischel, although traits and various other inner states have been used to describe behavior for a long time, they are of limited use in actually predicting behavior. The use of traits to describe and explain behavior, says Mischel, often indicates what the theorist thinks should be the case rather than what actually *is* the case. Mischel (1990) uses the term **consistency paradox** to describe the fact that both laypersons and professional psychologists persist in believing that people's behavior is consistent when evidence indicates that it is not (e.g., Carlson & Mulaik, 1993; Hayden & Mischel, 1976). Chapman and Chapman (1969) coined the term *illusory correlation* to describe the belief or perception that variables are correlated when, in fact, they are not. According to Mischel, the belief that traits and behavior are highly correlated is an example. Mischel ended *Personality and Assessment* (1968) with the plea to abandon the trait approach to understanding personality, "This conceptualization of man, besides being philosophically unappetizing, is contradicted by massive experimental data" (p. 301).

Since 1968, Mischel and many others have performed research that confirms the inconsistency of human behavior. For example, in a much cited study, Mischel and Peake (1982) examined the consistency of college students on two "traits"—conscientiousness and friendliness. While common sense, and many psychologists, would predict that students would behave consistently across situations according to the degree to which they possess the traits in question, the prediction was not confirmed. There was essentially no intersituational consistency ($r = .13$).

In the years since 1968, Mischel has moderated his attack on trait theory (1979, 1984, 1990). He no longer denies the value of describing people in terms of such traits as intelligence, friendliness, and aggressiveness. He does say, however, that it is practically impossible to predict how these, and other, traits will manifest themselves in a person's behavior in any given situation. Thus, Mischel no longer wishes to purge psychology of the concept of trait. Rather, he seeks to clarify how the traits that an individual may possess actually contribute to that person's behavior. For example, he wants to be able to make conditional statements such as "person A, in situation x, tends to do y" (Wright & Mischel, 1987). In other words, Mischel remains opposed to making generalized predictions about people based on the traits that they supposedly possess. Whatever consistency a person may demonstrate can only be discovered by observing how he or she responds to specific situations. Cantor and Mischel (1979) say, "Consistency of personality may be demonstrable only when theorists abandon their search for distinctive nomothetic traits and instead look for more idiographic patterns of person–environment interactions" (p. 43).

Although Mischel's observation that human behavior is not as consistent as was traditionally believed caused quite a stir among personality theorists, he believes their concern was misguided. Mischel believes that the degree of consistency previously thought to exist may actually be maladaptive.

Personologists have long searched for behavioral consistencies from situation to situation as if such consistency were the essence of personality. Perhaps that form of consistency will prove to be more characteristic of rigid, maladaptive, incompetent social functioning than of the integrated individual. (1984, p. 360)

Mischel's major criticism of traditional personality theories is that they emphasize **person variables** and deemphasize **situation variables.** Person variables are those aspects of a person, like traits, habits, and repressed experiences, that are assumed to cause the person to act consistently in a variety of similar situations. According to those theories emphasizing person variables, behavior is consistent because internal variables are enduring and thus continue to generate the same behavior patterns. Situation variables consist of the environmental circumstances in which the person finds him- or herself.

Although Mischel believes situation variables have been deemphasized by most personality theories, he believes they have been overemphasized by certain behavioristic theories—for instance, Skinner's. According to Mischel, Skinner's attempt to explain behavior entirely in terms of environmental conditions overlooks the significant contributions made by the person to his or her own behavior. What is needed, says Mischel, is a theory that considers the contributions of both the person and the situation.

Reciprocal Determinism

The position taken by the social-cognitive theorist is called **reciprocal determinism,** which means person variables, situation variables, and behavior continuously interact with one another. Situation variables provide the setting in which a person behaves, person variables determine how a situation is analyzed and which behaviors are chosen, and behavior both provides information concerning the person's analysis of the situation and modifies the environment. Bandura (1986, p. 24) diagrams reciprocal determinism as follows, where P is the person, E is the environment, and B is the person's behavior:

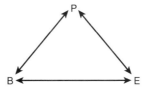

One implication of reciprocal determinism is that people's beliefs about themselves and the world will influence both how they behave and the environments in which they place themselves. In turn, feedback from behavior and environmental experience will confirm or disconfirm people's beliefs. For example, a gregarious person believing that people are generally friendly will tend to respond warmly to strangers. Such positive responses tend to create an environment that encourages positive human interactions. Thus the person's gregarious tendency is confirmed and strengthened. In contrast, a shy, withdrawn person will dread interpersonal inter-actions and therefore avoid or minimize them. Such reactions create social envi-ronments that are negative and encourage the person to remain shy and withdrawn. However, beliefs are not the only aspect of a person that influence his or her envi-ronment. Person variables also include a person's gender, social position, size, and physical attractiveness. Bandura (1978) says, "People activate different environ-mental reactions, apart from their behavior, by their physical characteristics (e.g., size, physiognomy, race, sex, attractiveness) and socially conferred attributes, roles, and status" (p. 346).

Social-cognitive theory, then, does not exclude person variables. In fact, they are considered extremely important. The person variables postulated, however, are not the traditional types such as traits, habits, and repressed experiences. Rather, they are beliefs, values, and information-processing strategies. Furthermore, they are im-portant only insofar as they manifest themselves in the present.

Cognitive Social Person Variables

How a given individual will interact with a situation is determined by what Mischel calls **cognitive social person variables** (1993, p. 403). It is these variables that de-termine which of the myriad stimuli confronted by a person are perceived, se-lected, interpreted, and used. Unlike the traditional person variables, the person variables in social-cognitive theory are active cognitive processes that operate in the present. These variables provide dynamic, reciprocal relationships among the per-son, the person's behavior, and the environment. Mischel (1993, pp. 403–411) de-scribes five cognitive social learning person variables.

1. **Encoding strategies: How we see things.** People not only select different aspects of the environment to attend to, but they also assign different meanings to the stimuli selected. Mischel (1993) says:

   > People differ greatly in how they encode (represent, symbolize) and group information from stimulus inputs. The same "hot weather" that upsets one person may be a joy for another who views it as a chance to go to the beach. The same stranger in the elevator who is perceived as "dangerous" by one person may be seen as "attractive" by another. (p. 404)

   To understand a person it is necessary to know the categories with which he or she embraces the world. Here we see the influence of George Kelly (see Chapter 13) on Mischel. Kelly suggested that any given event can be construed (interpreted) in any number of ways and that people are free to choose the constructs (concepts, categories, symbols, or words) with which they interpret their experiences. This means that in the same physical situation, people will encode it, construe it, and respond to it dif-ferently. Furthermore, because person variables are dynamic, no reason exists to assume that even for a given person the same situation will be construed the same way twice. It is a person's **encoding strategies** that provide some consistency in behavior, but the fact that those strategies can be changed by the individual at any time at least partially accounts for the fact that cross-situational behavior is not very consistent. Encoding strategies determine what aspects of the world are attended to and how they are interpreted.

2. **Expectancies: What we think will happen.** The person variable of encoding strategies determines how one categorizes experience. At some point, however, people must actually act on the environment. The most important variable for actual performance is a person's expectations. For example, in a given situation, the person hypothesizes, If I act in this way, it will have the following result. This is called a **behavior–outcome expectancy.** In the absence of any information about a specific situation, one tends to create **expectancies** based on past experience with similar situations. If specific information is available, however, one's expectations change accordingly. In preparation for a job interview, for example, if one hears that the job interviewer is especially impressed by assertiveness, one might expect that acting assertively would increase the probability of getting the job, and then would act on this newly formed expectancy.

Mischel refers to a second type of hypothesis we formulate in dealing with our experience as a **stimulus–outcome expectancy.** We learn that if event 1 occurs, event 2 is likely to follow. For example, if we hear a siren, we expect a speeding emergency vehicle will soon be seen; or, noting that it is six o'clock, we expect that dinner will soon be available.

A third type of hypothesis we use in dealing with the world is called a **self-efficacy expectancy.** It is one thing to know what behavior would be effective in a given situation and another to be able to perform that behavior. One's ability to perform the behaviors required in a particular situation is called self-efficacy. Because what one can actually do often differs from what one thinks he or she is capable of doing, social-cognitive theory places great stress on **perceived self-efficacy,** which is what a person thinks he or she is capable of doing in various situations. We return to a discussion of self-efficacy later in the chapter.

In general, the person variable of expectancies answers the questions, What should I expect if I act in a certain way? If I see one thing, what should I expect to see next? and Am I capable of doing what I think needs to be done?

3. **Subjective values: What is worth having or doing?** Even if a person has a strong behavior outcome expectancy and a strong self-efficacy expectancy, he or she may decide not to translate those expectancies into behavior because what would be gained simply is not seen as worth the effort. For example, a student may know exactly what needs to be done to write an outstanding term paper, and may believe he or she has the ability to do what is necessary but may decide that getting an A on a term paper is not worth the time and effort. Another student in the same situation may value an A more, and thus expend the time and energy and engage in the behaviors necessary to obtain it. Likewise, a given student

may, at one time, under certain conditions, decide an A is worth pursuing and at another time, under different circumstances, decide that it is not. One's values will to a large extent determine whether or not the other person variables will be translated into performance. The **subjective values** of a person determine what is worth having or doing.

4. **Self-regulatory systems and plans: How do we attain our goals?** According to social-cognitive theory, human behavior is largely self-regulated. Performance standards are established, and when actual performance meets or exceeds those standards, one feels good; when it does not, one feels bad. Behavior, then, is influenced more by **intrinsic** (internal) **reinforcement** and punishment than it is by **extrinsic** (external) **reinforcement** and punishment.

   Humans also set future goals and then plan the events in their lives so that they are compatible with those goals. Typically, a major future goal is approached by first reaching a sequence of lesser short-term goals. For example, the goal of obtaining a college degree is met by doing well in high school, graduating from high school, applying for admission into a college, surviving the first term in college, and so on. Thus social-cognitive theory views much human behavior as teleological, that is, purposive. **Self-regulatory systems and plans** make it possible to attain those goals deemed important. We say more about self-regulated behavior later in this chapter.

5. **Competencies: What we are capable of doing.** Through observational learning, which is discussed shortly, the person acquires information about the physical and social worlds and his or her relationship to them. The person develops skills, concepts, and problem-solving strategies that are actively used in dealing with the environment. Mischel stresses the fact that these **competencies** are not static memories that are mechanically activated by environmental stimuli. Rather, they are active processes that can be used by the person to generate a wide variety of creative constructions or responses to any given situation. Competencies, then, are seen as tools available to the individual in doing commerce with the environment. Like any tools, what can be done with them is limited only by the imagination of those using them. Competencies refer to what a person knows and what he or she is capable of doing.

It is not only one's competencies that are learned from observational learning but also one's encoding strategies, expectancies, values, and self-regulatory systems and plans. It is to the important topic of observational learning that we turn next.

Observational Learning

Although within social-cognitive theory reinforcement is not believed to influence learning, it is believed to be importantly related to *performance* and to perceptual processes. In other words, reinforcement is thought to influence what is attended to, and thus learned and, more importantly, it is thought to determine which aspect of what has been learned is translated into behavior.

The distinction between learning and performance is illustrated in a famous study performed by Bandura (1965). In this experiment, a 5-minute film was shown of a **model** aggressing toward a large Bobo doll. In social-cognitive theory, a model is anything that conveys information—for instance, a person, television, a book, a film, a demonstration, or instructions. In this experiment, the model was an adult human.

The film began with a scene in which a model walked up to an adult-sized plastic Bobo doll and ordered him to clear the way. After glaring for a moment at the non-compliant antagonist the model exhibited four novel aggressive responses each accompanied by a distinctive verbalization.

First, the model laid the Bobo doll on its side, sat on it, and punched it in the nose while remarking, "Pow, right on the nose, boom, boom." The model then raised the doll and pommelled it on the head with a mallet. Each response was followed by the verbalization, "Sockeroo . . . stay down." Following the mallet aggression, the model kicked the doll about the room, and these responses were interspersed with the comment, "Fly away." Finally, the model threw rubber balls at the Bobo doll, each strike punctuated with "Bang." This sequence of physically and verbally aggressive behavior was repeated twice. (Bandura, 1965, pp. 590–591)

Following presentation of the film, one group of children was shown a second film in which a second adult was shown praising the model for his aggressive behavior and rewarding him with pop and candy. A second group of children saw a film in which a second adult punished the model for his aggressive behavior. In this group, the model was called a coward and a bully, spanked with a rolled-up newspaper, and threatened with a beating if he was caught being aggressive again. A third group of children, the control group, saw only the first 5-minute film. The children were then exposed to a doll similar to that in the film, and their aggressiveness toward it was measured. Results indicated that the group who saw the model being reinforced for aggressiveness was most aggressive; the group who saw the model punished for aggressiveness was least aggressive; and the control group was between the other two groups in aggressiveness.

This portion of Bandura's study demonstrated that children performed on the basis of what they had seen happen to someone else. That is, rather than performing on the basis of direct reinforcement and punishment, they were responding to **vicarious reinforcement** and **vicarious punishment.** To put this in terms of the person variables described earlier, it was as if the children had formulated behavior–outcome expectancies on the basis of what they had seen in the film. The children who saw the model's aggressiveness reinforced appeared to develop the hypothesis that if they acted aggressively, they, too, could expect reinforcement. Those children who saw the model punished for aggressiveness expected similar behavior on their part would yield similar results.

The first phase of Bandura's study seemed to indicate that reinforcement was still important for learning, but that it could be vicariously experienced and need not be contingent on one's own behavior. This finding alone was in contradiction to the theories of Skinner and Dollard and Miller, which state that for reinforcement to be effective, it must be contingent on one's own behavior. In their view, seeing someone else's behavior being reinforced or punished should have no effect on one's own behavior.

The results of the second phase of Bandura's study were even more surprising. In this phase, all the children were offered attractive incentives (stickers and juice) to act as the model had acted in the film. Remember that in the first film the model was shown aggressing toward the doll, but the consequences of the model's aggression varied according to what group the children were in. When offered the incentive to replicate the model's behavior, the children in all three groups did so. This means that all the children had learned what they had observed—that is, the model being aggressive—but they had translated what had been learned into the type of behavior they expected would be either reinforced or at least not punished. Bandura's experiment shows that indeed what is observed is learned, and that how what is learned is translated into performance depends on the learner's behavior–outcome expectancies. The behavior–outcome expectancies in this case came vicariously from observing the consequences of a model's behavior. Bandura indicates that the research just discussed made the Bobo doll famous in psychology, "When I'm introduced at invited lectures at other universities the students place a Bobo doll by the lectern. From time to time I have been asked to autograph one. The Bobo doll has achieved stardom in psychological circles" (quoted in Evans, 1989, p. 23).

Research has shown that emotional responses can also be learned vicariously (e.g., Bandura & Rosenthal, 1966; Berger, 1962; Craig & Weinstein, 1965). Berger (1962) found that when a model was shown reacting with pain, presumably in response to extreme electric shock, following the sound of a tone, the observer, too, would develop an emotional response to the tone. Physiological measures indicated that after observing a model experience what appeared to be a tone–shock relationship, the observer responded emotionally when the tone sounded even when the model was no longer present. Thus a conditioned emotional response was developed on the basis of what appeared to be happening to another person.

Bandura (1986) notes that the ability to learn by observing the consequences of other people's behavior not only enhances survival but also makes life less tedious:

> If human behavior depended solely on personally experienced consequences, most people would not survive the hazards of early development. Of those who managed to outlive their mistakes, each would have to rediscover, through tiresome trial and error, what works and what fails in everyday transactions with their environment. Fortunately, people are spared many hazards and much tedium by their capacity to benefit from the experiences of others. (p. 283)

Elsewhere, Bandura says, "One would not teach military recruits how to lob grenades through trial and error. This mode of learning would create a situation of, 'Look, sergeant, no arms.' It would give new meaning to the wartime movie, 'A Farewell to Arms'" (quoted in Evans, 1989, p. 8).

We do, of course, learn by observing the consequences of our own behavior but, according to Bandura, whatever can be learned by direct experience can also be learned by vicarious experience. Bandura (1986) says, "Virtually all learning phenomena resulting from direct experience, can occur vicariously by observing other people's behavior and its consequences for them" (p. 19).

News and Entertainment Media as Models

Because, according to social-cognitive theory, we learn from what we observe, it follows that newspapers, television, and films can act as influential models. Bandura (1986) makes the following observations about fictional television:

> Analyses of televised programs reveal that violent conduct is portrayed, for the most part, as permissible, successful, and relatively clean. . . . Witnesses to the violence in the dramatic presentations are more likely to approve of such behavior or to join in the assaults rather than to seek alternative solutions. Violence not only is shown to pay off but is readily used by superheroes, who dispose of their adversaries in a quick, perfunctory way as though slaying human beings was of no great concern. (p. 292)

Since Bandura's early work on modeled aggression, numerous studies have examined the relationship between television violence and aggression and other forms of antisocial behavior. Typically these studies confirm a positive relationship between the two (e.g., Geen & Thomas, 1986; Huesmann & Malamuth, 1986; Turner, Hesse, & Peterson-Lewis, 1986). Recent research has indicated that despite considerable current societal concern, 58 percent of television programs still contain violence and that 78 percent of that violence is depicted as at least unremorseful, if not actually glamorized. Furthermore, evidence indicates that the use of warning labels has not prevented children from watching violent programs (Seppa, 1997). It has also been found that violent rock videos can create, in some men, violent attitudes toward women (Peterson & Pfost, 1989).

Clearly, not everyone exposed to violence becomes violent nor does everyone exposed to sexually explicit literature or movies become sexually deviant. For some, however, such modeling provides learning experiences that promote antisocial behavior. Nor are the news and entertainment media the only places in society where violence is modeled; for example, parents who employ corporal punishment in their childrearing practices are modeling aggression. Bandura (1973) observes that children whose parents employ considerable corporal punishment often become highly aggressive. Such children also tend to be less obedient (Power & Chapleski, 1986). Bandura supports neither the extensive use of corporal punishment nor "unconditional love." He believes that unconditional love is self-defeating because it eliminates the informative relationship between performance and reward. In the absence of this relationship children are directionless.

> Some child-rearing authorities have popularized the view that healthy personality development is built on "unconditional love." If this principle were, in fact, unfailingly applied, parents would respond affectionately regardless of how their children behaved—whether or not they mistreated others, stole whatever they wanted, disregarded the wishes and rights of others, or demanded instant gratification. Unconditional love, were it possible, would make children directionless and quite unlovable. Most readers are undoubtedly acquainted with families where parents who attempted to approximate this condition succeeded in producing "self-actualized" tyrants. (Bandura, 1977, p. 102)

In any case, news and entertainment media are among society's influential models and "humane living requires reducing social influences that promote cruelty and destructiveness [and] . . . society has the right to regulate obscene materials that can cause harm" (Bandura, 1986, p. 296). However, Bandura recognizes that controlling such material is complex. First, there is disagreement over what is harmful. Second, the suppression of material considered harmful may conflict with the basic right of free expression.

Although it is accurate to say that, according to social-cognitive theory, what is observed is learned, certain processes influence what is attended to, what is retained, how what is learned is translated into behavior, and why it is translated into behavior. Bandura (1986) describes four such processes.

Attentional Processes

These processes include aspects of the environment that influence attention, such as the complexity, distinctiveness, and prevalence of the stimulation. For example, screeching brakes attract almost everyone's attention. Certain characteristics of models determine the extent to which they are observed. For instance, it has been found that models are attended to more if they are seen as similar to oneself, are respected, are considered powerful, or are attractive. Related to the concept of power, it has been found that adults who control resources, that is, have the ability to dispense rewards, are more powerful models for children than adults who do not control resources (Bandura, Ross, & Ross, 1963; Grusec & Mischel, 1966). **Attentional processes** also include observer characteristics such as sensory capacities. Blind and deaf people, for example, do not respond to the same stimuli as people with normal sight and hearing.

Also, the consequences of past behavior can create a perceptual set in the observer. For example, if attending to certain stimuli in the past resulted in positive consequences, a tendency will exist to attend to similar stimuli in similar situations.

Retentional Processes

What is learned by observation is of no value unless it is retained. We saw earlier that how information is encoded and construed varies from person to person but, in general, Bandura (1986) says that experiences are stored either imaginally or verbally. That is, we either retain an actual cognitive picture of what was experienced or we retain the words that describe the experience. These memories make **delayed modeling** possible. Delayed modeling refers to the fact that often information gained by observational learning is first translated into behavior long after the time that it had been learned.

Motor Reproduction Processes

To translate learning into performance, one needs to have the necessary motor apparatus. Also, even if one has the necessary motor apparatus, one can be temporarily prevented from performing because of injury, fatigue, or illness. Even with the necessary motor system available and functioning well, complex skills cannot simply be observed and immediately translated into performance. First, with complex skills, many observations may be required before all of the relevant information can be attended to and remembered. Second, if all the relevant information is learned, many rehearsals that attempt to match performance with what had been learned and retained may be necessary. According to Bandura (1986), it is the observer's conceptualization of modeled behavior that provides the frame of reference necessary for skill improvement:

> The conceptual representation provides the internal model for response production and the standard for response correction. Behavioral production primarily involves a conception-matching process in which the incoming sensory feedback from enactments is compared to the conception. The behavior is then modified on the basis of the comparative information to achieve progressively closer correspondence between conception and action. (p. 64)

Motivational Processes

No matter how much one has learned, and no matter what one's capabilities are, learning will not be translated into performance unless there is an incentive to do so. Observational learning may create potentially effective behavior–outcome expectations, but unless the person believes that behavior will yield something valued, no behavior will occur. According to social-cognitive theory, **reinforcement,** either direct or vicarious, provides the information necessary for the development of effective behavior–outcome expectancies. Even with direct reinforcement, however, it is assumed that learning is observational and not an automatic, unconscious strengthening of response tendencies, as Skinner and Dollard and Miller had assumed. According to social-cognitive theory, a person learns from observing the consequences of either his or her own behavior (direct reinforcement) or from observing the consequences of other people's behavior (vicarious reinforcement). In either case, information is provided about what behaviors lead to what consequences.

In addition to providing information concerning what behaviors lead to what consequences, reinforcement provides an incentive for action. Within social-cognitive theory, reinforcement is equated with something of value to the person under existing circumstances. People, then, are motivated to act in ways that provide things they value and that allow them to avoid things considered aversive. Bandura's views on observational learning and the translation of that learning into behavior can be summarized as follows: A person must observe something; remember what was observed; be able to perform the behaviors necessary to reproduce what was observed; and want to reproduce those behaviors.

Self-Regulated Behavior

Social-cognitive theory maintains that most human behavior is **self-regulated.** Through cumulative direct and vicarious experience, people develop **performance standards** that they use to evaluate their own behavior. Almost constantly, the person compares what he or she does in a situation with some performance standard. If performance meets or exceeds the standard, the person experiences intrinsic reinforcement. If a performance falls short of a standard, the person experiences intrinsic punishment.

Modeling has been found to influence the formulation of one's performance standards. Bandura and Kupers (1964), for example, found that children exposed to models who set high performance standards reinforced themselves only for superior performance, whereas children exposed to models accepting minimal performance standards reinforced themselves for minimal performance. It would be expected, then, that relevant people in a child's life—for instance, parents, siblings, and peers—would have a profound influence on the development of a child's performance standards.

Goals and plans extend self-directed behavior over long periods of time. Once a future goal has been established, one organizes his or her experiences so they increase the probability of goal attainment. Bandura (1991) says, "People form beliefs about what they can do, they anticipate the likely consequences of prospective actions, they set goals for themselves, and they otherwise plan courses of action that are likely to produce desired outcomes" (p. 248). Experiences that keep the person on track toward the goal result in self-reinforcement; those that are incompatible with the goal cause self-punishment. As mentioned earlier, major goals are seldom accomplished all at once. Rather, a series of subgoals are established, and as they are attained, one approximates the major goal. Personal frustration and depression can occur if goals are either too distant or too difficult. Goals must be related to one's capabilities and must be attainable through the achievement of reasonable subgoals that are of moderate difficulty relative to a person's competencies. Performance standards, too, must be realistic. If they are too lenient, they will be too easily met, and little, if any, self-reinforcement will result from performing in accordance with them. If they are too stringent, one will experience frustration or worse. Bandura (1986) says, "In its more extreme forms, harsh standards for self-evaluation give rise to depressive reactions, chronic discouragement, feelings of worthlessness, and lack of purposefulness" (p. 358). Bandura (1991) finds that people prone to depression generally judge themselves more harshly than people not prone to depression, "Compared to nondepressed persons, those who are prone to depression react less self-rewardingly for similar successes but more self-critically for similar failures" (pp. 274–275).

The situation is best if one's performance standards are modified as a function of one's accomplishments and failures. Bandura (1986) notes:

> One's previous behavior is continuously used as a reference against which ongoing performance is judged. In this referential process, self-comparison supplies the measure of adequacy. Past attainments affect self-appraisal mainly through their effects on standard setting. . . . After a given level of performance has been attained, it is no longer challenging, and people seek new self-satisfactions by means of progressive improvement. Hence, people tend to raise their performance standards after success and to lower them to more realistic levels after repeated failure. (pp. 347–348)

Self-Efficacy

In his recent writings about social-cognitive theory, Bandura (2001, 2002a, 2002b) emphasizes **human agency,** the conscious planning and intentional execution of actions that influence future events. In his words, "people are not just onlooking hosts of internal mechanisms orchestrated by environmental events. They are agents of experience rather than simply undergoers of experiences" (Bandura, 2001, p. 4). Bandura observes, "Efficacy beliefs are the foundation of human agency" (p. 10). **Self-efficacy** refers to what a person is actually capable of doing. More important, however, is **perceived self-efficacy,** that which a person *believes* he or she is capable of doing. Perceived self-efficacy is influenced by several factors—for example, personal accomplishments and failures, seeing models perceived as similar to oneself succeed or fail at various tasks, and verbal persuasion. Through verbal persuasion, people can often be encouraged to try to achieve goals they would otherwise avoid; an example is when a coach "fires up" the team before a game. The effects of verbal persuasion are short-lived, however, if the resulting perceived self-efficacy is not manifested in real performance. It has also been found that people tend to judge their self-efficacy in a potentially threatening situation in terms of their emotional arousal. Because high arousal typically inhibits performance, strong emotion is usually correlated with feelings of perceived self-inefficacy. Conversely, being relaxed in such a situation facilitates perceived self-efficacy.

Research performed by Bandura and others (for a summary of this research, see Bandura, 1986, 1989, 1995; Bandura & Locke, 2003) has demonstrated that compared to individuals with low perceived self-efficacy, individuals with high perceived self-efficacy have the following characteristics:

They set more challenging goals and performance standards.

They persist longer in the pursuit of goals.

They are more venturesome in their behavior.

They recover more quickly from setbacks and frustrations.

They experience less fear, anxiety, stress, and depression.

As with goals and performance standards, the situation is best when one's perceived self-efficacy is in line with one's true capabilities. Thinking one can do more than one can actually do results in frustration. Thinking that one is not capable of doing something that one is actually capable of doing inhibits personal growth. Both distortions of one's self-efficacy result in dysfunctional (erroneous) self-expectancies, which, if severe enough, can cause a person to seek psychotherapy.

Bandura's concept of perceived self-efficacy has become one of the most popular research topics in the realm of personality theory. What follows represents only a sample of that research. Perceived self-efficacy has been found to be related to reduction of guilt and fear (Covert Tangney, Maddux, & Heleno, 2003); the effectiveness of weight loss programs (Mitchell & Stuart, 1984; Weinberg, Hughes, Critelli, England, & Jackson, 1984); the effectiveness of programs designed to help people quit smoking (Baer, Holt, & Lichtenstein, 1986; Garcia, Schmitz, & Doerfler, 1990; Wojcik, 1988); the effectiveness of alcohol treatment programs (Annis, 1990); AIDS prevention (Bandura, 1990b; O'Leary, 1992); academic performance (Multon, Brown, & Lent, 1991; Tuckman, 1990); depression (Bandura, 1989; Bandura, Adams, Hardy, & Howells, 1980; Davis-Berman, 1990); job burnout (Meier, 1983); maternal competence (Teti & Gelfand, 1991); occupational choice (Betz & Hackett, 1981; Bonett, 1994; Bores-Rangel, Church, Szendre, & Reeves, 1990); athletic performance (Gould,

Hodge, Peterson, & Giannini, 1989); managerial decision making (Bandura & Jourden, 1991; Bandura & Wood, 1989; Wood & Bandura, 1989; Wood, Bandura, & Bailey, 1990); gender differences (Lent, Brown, & Larkin, 1986; Nevill & Schlecker, 1988; Poole & Evans, 1989); developmental experiences (Holden, Moncher, Schinke, & Barker, 1990; Skinner, Chapman, & Baltes, 1988); physiological reactions (Bandura, Reese, & Adams, 1982; Bandura, Taylor, Williams, Mefford, & Barchas, 1985); immune system functioning (Bandura, Cioffi, Taylor, & Brouillard, 1988; Bandura, O'Leary, Taylor, Gauthier, & Gossard, 1987; Wiedenfeld et al., 1990); coping ability (Ozer & Bandura, 1990); and job satisfaction and performance (Saks, 1995).

Later in this chapter we will also see that the concept of perceived self-efficacy is central to Bandura's approach to, and understanding of, psychotherapy.

Moral Conduct

Standards of right and wrong are also highly personal and are also derived from one's direct and vicarious experience. As with performance standards, moral principles are usually modeled by a child's parents and are eventually internalized. Once internalized, these moral principles determine which behaviors and thoughts are self-sanctioned and which result in self-contempt. Thus moral behavior comes to be self-regulated and is maintained independently of, and in many cases despite, environmental consequences. Bandura (1977) says, "The anticipation of self-reproach for conduct that violates one's standards provides a source of motivation to keep behavior in line with standards in the face of opposing inducements. There is no more devastating punishment than self-contempt" (p. 154).

Certain cognitive mechanisms, however, allow a person to act contrary to his or her moral principles without experiencing self-contempt. These **self-exonerating mechanisms** (Bandura, 1986, pp. 375–385) are summarized here:

1. **Moral justification.** One's otherwise reprehensible behavior becomes a means to a higher purpose and therefore is justifiable. "I committed the crime so I could provide food for my family." Bandura (1986) says, "Over the years, much destructive and reprehensible conduct has been perpetrated by decent people in the name of religious principles, righteous ideologies, and nationalistic imperatives" (p. 377).

2. **Euphemistic labeling.** By calling an otherwise reprehensible act something other than what it really is, one can engage in an act without self-contempt. For example, nonaggressive individuals are far more likely to aggress toward another person when doing so is called a game.

   Through the power of hygienic words, even killing a human being loses much of its repugnancy. Soldiers "waste" people rather than kill them, CIA operatives "terminate (them) with extreme prejudice." When mercenaries speak of "fulfilling a contract," murder is transformed by admirable words into the honorable discharge of duty. (Bandura, 1986, p. 378).

3. **Advantageous comparison.** By comparing one's self-deplored acts with even more heinous acts, it makes one's own reprehensible acts look trifling by comparison: "Sure I did that, but look at what he did."

Promoters of the Vietnamese war and their supporters, for example, minimized the slaying of countless people as a way of checking massive communist enslavement. Given the trifling comparison, perpetrators of warfare remained unperturbed by the fact that the intended beneficiaries were being killed at an alarming rate. Domestic protesters, on the other hand, characterized their own violence against educational and political institutions as trifling, or even laudable, by comparing it with the carnage perpetrated by their country's military forces in foreign lands (Bandura, 1986, p. 379).

4. **Displacement of responsibility.** Some people can readily depart from their moral principles if they believe a recognized authority sanctions their behavior and takes responsibility for it: "I did it because I was ordered to do so."

   Nazi prison commandants and their staffs felt little personal responsibility for their unprecedented inhumanities. They were simply carrying out orders. Impersonal obedience to horrific orders was similarly evident in military atrocities, such as the My Lai massacre (Bandura, 1986, p. 379).

   Bandura (1990a) observes that terrorists who have taken hostages often "warn officials of targeted nations that if they take retaliatory action they will be held accountable for the lives of the hostages" (p. 175).

5. **Diffusion of responsibility.** A decision to act in an otherwise reprehensible manner that is made by a group is easier to live with than an individual decision. Where everyone is responsible, no single individual feels responsible: "I couldn't be the only one saying no."

6. **Disregard or distortion of consequences.** Here people ignore or distort the harm caused by their conduct and therefore there is no need to experience self-contempt. The farther people remove themselves from the ill effects of their immoral behavior the less pressure there is to censure it: "I just let the bombs go and they disappeared in the clouds."

7. **Dehumanization.** If some individuals are looked upon as subhuman, they can be treated inhumanly without experiencing self-contempt. Once a person or a group has been dehumanized, they no longer possess feelings, hopes, and concerns, and they can be mistreated without risking self-condemnation: "Why not take their land, they are nothing but savages without souls."

> Once dehumanized, [individuals] are no longer viewed as persons with feelings, hopes, and concerns but as subhuman objects demeaningly stereotyped as "gooks," "fags," or "niggers." Subhumans are presumably insensitive to maltreatment and influenceable only through more primitive methods. If dispossessing disfavored people of their humanness does not blunt self-reproof, it can be fully eliminated by attributing bestial qualities to them. They become "degenerates," "pigs," and other bestial creatures. Over the years slaves, women, manual laborers, and religious and racial minorities have been treated as chattel or as subhuman objects. (Bandura, 1986, p. 382)

8. **Attribution of blame.** One can always choose something that a victim said or did and claim that it caused one to act in a reprehensible way.

> Rapists and males who acknowledge a proclivity to rape subscribe to myths about rape embodying the various mechanisms by which moral self-censure can be disengaged. . . . These beliefs hold rape victims responsible for their own victimization because they have supposedly invited rape by sexually provocative appearance and behavior and by resisting a sexual assault weakly. (Bandura, 1986, pp. 384–385)

The self-exonerating mechanisms provide another reason why human behavior tends to be inconsistent. Even if a person's moral principles were known with certainty, employing one or more of these mechanisms would make the person's moral behavior unpredictable to the outside observer. Such behavior would undoubtedly seem consistent and logical to the person him- or herself, however.

Delay of Gratification

In a series of experiments that began soon after he received his PhD from Ohio State University in 1956, Mischel and his colleagues have extensively explored the variables related to the ability to delay gratification. In one early study, Mischel and Metzner (1962) found that the ability to delay gratification increased with age, intelligence, and with shorter intervals of delay. Later, Mischel and his colleagues began their influential research on 4- and 5-year-old children attending the Bing nursery school at Stanford University (Mischel & Ebbesen, 1970; Mischel, Ebbesen, & Zeiss, 1972). In these studies, children were given a choice between a small reward given immediately (e.g., one marshmallow or pretzel) or a larger reward given after a delay (e.g., two marshmallows or pretzels). There were four experimental conditions: (1) both the immediate and delayed rewards were visible; (2) neither the immediate nor the delayed rewards were visible; (3) only the immediate reward was visible; and (4) only the delayed reward was visible. The researchers predicted that being able to see the rewards would enhance the ability to delay. The opposite was true: Children waited the longest when no rewards were visible. It turned out that when rewards were visible it caused the children to think about them, and thinking about them reduced their ability to delay gratification. It was also found that children who could delay the longest employed a number of self-distraction strategies in order to make the aversive delay period more pleasant. These children talked to themselves, sang, invented games to be played with their hands and feet, and even tried to fall asleep (one child was successful). Mischel and Moore (1973) found that instructing children to think of pictures of rewards instead of actual rewards increased their ability to delay gratification. Other studies showed that instructing children to think of otherwise desirable rewards in undesirable ways (e.g., to think of pretzels as little brown logs or of marshmallows as round white clouds or as balls of cotton) increased their ability to delay (Mischel & Baker, 1975; Mischel & Moore, 1980; Moore, Mischel, & Zeiss, 1976). From the experiments just described, Mischel (1993) concludes, "What is in the children's heads—not what is physically in front of them—determines their ability to delay [and] if you can make the waiting easier for yourself, you are more likely to wait successfully" (pp. 457, 458). Numerous studies have confirmed the contention that imposed or self-created distractions facilitate the ability to delay gratification (Mischel, Shoda, & Rodriguez, 1989).

In the more than 40 years of research on **delay of gratification,** one of the most dramatic findings is the relationship between the ability to delay gratification as a preschool child and a number of positive adolescent personality characteristics. Mischel and his colleagues followed up their research on the Stanford preschool children 10 years after the original research (Mischel et al., 1988, 1989; Shoda, Mischel, & Peake, 1990). Of special interest were the children who were able to delay even when rewards were visible and who were not given strategies to facilitate delay. It was assumed that such children were capable of generating their own self-distracting strategies, and that this capability would continue to exist later in life. These assumptions were clearly supported. Preschool children who could delay gratification with rewards visible and without imposed distractions were rated positively by their parents on a variety of social and academic skills when they were high school students. Table 11–1 summarizes the attributes these parents saw in these adolescents.

In addition to positive parental ratings, it was found that both verbal and quantitative scholastic aptitude test (SAT) scores were significantly related to the preschool ability to delay gratification in the condition in which rewards were visible and no strategies for distraction were supplied to the child. In contrast, preschool delay behavior when rewards were not visible or when distraction strategies were provided did not reliably predict either positive parental ratings or SAT scores. Mischel (1993, p. 460) notes evidence that people with the ability to self-distract can also deal more effectively with pain, stress, and severe life crises.

What determines the extent to which one possesses such an important personality attribute? As with other factors influencing self-regulated behavior, it has been found that the willingness to delay gratification can be learned by observing models (Bandura & Mischel, 1965; Mischel & Liebert, 1966; Stumphauzer, 1972). The fact that the ability to delay gratification can be taught to young children, and that the ability is clearly advantageous later in life, suggests that such teaching be incorporated into early education and in childrearing practices. In any case, it is vital that we understand the kind of **self-control** necessary to delay gratification because,

Table 11–1	More likely to . . .
	Exhibit self-control when frustrated
As adolescents, children who delayed gratification longer in preschool were described by parents as:	Cope with important problems
	Do well academically when motivated
	Pursue goals when motivated
	Display intelligence
	Maintain friendships and get along with peers
	Less likely to . . .
	Be sidetracked by minor setbacks
	Yield to temptations
	Be distracted while trying to concentrate
	Settle for an immediate but less desirable goal
	Lose self-control when frustrated

Summarized from Mischel, 1993, p. 459

according to Mischel (1993), without it humans are as impulsive as nonhuman animals, and the goal-oriented behavior necessary for civilized living is impossible.

Dysfunctional Expectancies and Psychotherapy

According to social-cognitive theory, psychological problems result from **dysfunctional expectancies** (i.e., erroneous, nonfunctional, or faulty expectancies), and any type of therapy that corrects them—that is, brings them in line with reality—will be, by definition, effective.

If, for example, one believes that developing a close relationship with a member of the opposite sex will bring pain and frustration, one will avoid such relationships. Such expectancies are usually based on real experiences, but they can be overgeneralized and, when they are, prevent the person from having the types of experiences that would disconfirm them. The defensive behavior based on a dysfunctional expectancy is therefore often difficult to remedy.

Some dogs do bite, some airplanes do crash, some intimate relationships do result in pain and frustration, some members of minorities do commit crimes, and some men and some women are insensitive. To generalize on the basis of a few cases to all possible experiences, however, does not accurately represent reality. People forming strong expectancies on the basis of limited experiences need to have further experiences with the same types of objects, events, or people without those experiences being negative. Bandura (1986) observes, "What such individuals need in order to relinquish their erroneous beliefs are powerful disconfirming experiences, which verbal assurances alone do not provide" (p. 190). Providing powerful disconfirming experiences is a key ingredient of the kind of therapy promoted by social-cognitive theory.

Another type of dysfunctional expectancy concerns perceived self-efficacy. As we have seen, if people believe they are incapable of doing something, they will not try to do it. If one believes he or she cannot touch dogs, cats, snakes, children, or members of the opposite sex, that person will not do so regardless of his or her true capabilities. Likewise, a person who believes he or she is incapable of handling success will avoid success. Thus, according to social-cognitive theory, a major goal of **psychotherapy** is to change the client's perceived self-efficacy. The assumption is that if a person's perceived self-efficacy becomes more realistic, behavior will become more adaptive. Bandura summarizes how he believes perceived self-efficacy is most effectively changed during psychotherapy as follows: "Treatments that are most effective are built on an empowerment model. If you really want to help people, you provide them with . . . competencies, build [in them] a strong self-belief, and create opportunities for them to exercise these competencies" (quoted in Evans, 1989, p. 16).

The assumption that perceived self-efficacy relates directly to behavior was tested by Bandura, Adams, and Beyer (1977). Seven men and 26 women who suffered a chronic snake phobia were recruited through newspaper advertisements. Before treatment, each person was given a Behavioral Avoidance Test that consisted of 29 performance tasks requiring increasingly close interactions with a red-tailed boa constrictor. Self-efficacy expectancies were also measured before treatment. Each person was given a list describing various interactions with a snake and was asked to indicate which ones he or she would be able to perform. Subjects were also asked to indicate the certainty with which they believed they could or could not engage in various interactions with the snake.

After pretesting, Bandura et al. (1977) randomly assigned subjects to one of three treatment groups. The first was the **participant modeling** condition in which first a live model handled a boa constrictor in a series of interactions ranging from mildly threatening to extremely threatening. Then subjects were asked to perform these same interactions. The time required for these interactions ranged from 40 minutes to 7 hours, with the average time being 1½ hours. In some cases, the fear of a subject was so intense that a baby boa had to be used initially. The second group was called the *modeling condition* where subjects observed a model engage in a series of interactions with the snake, but the observer did not actually come into contact with the snake him- or herself. In the *control condition,* the pretreatment measures were made but no treatment was given.

After the various treatments, subjects were again given the Behavior Avoidance Test, the final step of which was to let the boa constrictor crawl on the subject's lap while his or her hands were held passively to the side. Results indicated that both the participant modeling and the modeling conditions significantly reduced avoidance behavior, but the participant modeling condition was the more effective of the two treatments.

Efficacy expectations were measured again after conclusion of treatment. It was found that the participant modeling condition and the modeling condition significantly changed the self-efficacy expectations of being able to handle a snake. Again, although both techniques were effective, the participant modeling technique was most effective in changing self-efficacy expectations. Most important, however, was the finding that self-efficacy expectations were accurate predictors of behavior. Those subjects who indicated they now believed they could handle a snake actually did so. The relationship between perceived self-efficacy and actual performance existed for subjects in all groups. In almost every case, the type of interactions a person believed he or she could engage in were those in which he or she actually engaged. Maximal efficacy expectations, however, did not always result from maximal interactions with the snake; that is, some of the individuals in the participant modeling group who were able to perform the most threatening interactions with the snake during treatment did not form the expectation that they would be able to interact that way with a snake on subsequent occasions, and they were correct. The formation of efficacy expectations, then, is based on more than one's experience with successful performance, although successful performance has a powerful influence on the formation of efficacy expectations.

Further measures indicated that the reduction of avoidance caused by the treatments generalized to other snakes, that the results of the experiment persisted over time, and that the results generalized positively into other aspects of the subjects' lives. For instance, in some cases, improvement was reported in dealing effectively with other animal and social threats. Bandura et al. (1982) performed a similar experiment on people with spider phobias with essentially the same results as those just described.

In another study, Bandura, Blanchard, and Ritter (1969) tested the effectiveness of various techniques in dealing with a snake phobia. In this experiment, adults and adolescents were divided into four groups: symbolic modeling in which subjects were shown a film showing models interacting with a snake; live modeling with participation in which subjects interacted with a snake along with the model; **systematic desensitization,** in which subjects were asked to imagine interactions with a snake ranging from low-anxiety-producing interactions to those producing high anxiety. Subjects, starting with imagining low-anxiety scenes, continued to imagine each scene until it no longer caused anxiety, and continued in this manner until the scenes that previously caused the greatest amount of anxiety no longer did so. The last group was the control condition in which subjects received no treatment. The ability to interact with a snake was measured for all subjects before and after the experiments. Results are shown in Figure 11–1.

It can be seen that again live modeling with participation was most effective, followed by **symbolic modeling** and then desensitization. Subjects in the control condition showed little or no improvement in their ability to interact with a snake. Follow-up research again indicated that the effects of the experiment endured and generalized positively into other areas that had produced fear prior to the experiment. Many other experiments have shown the effectiveness of modeling in dealing with a wide variety of dysfunctional expectancies. In all of this research, the emphasis is on the person's current perceptions and expectancies. There is no mention of traits,

Figure 11–1
_____

The ability to interact with a snake before and after various types of therapeutic treatments.

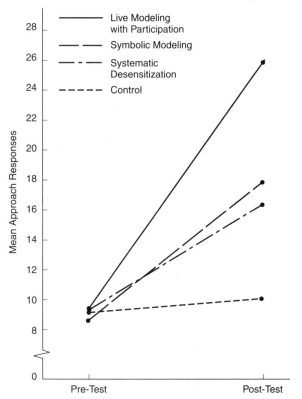

From Bandura, Blanchard, & Ritter, 1969, p. 183. Copyright 1969 by The American Psychological Association. Reprinted by permission.

reinforcement histories, or internal conflicts. In fact, Bandura (1986) believes those therapists looking for such things tell us more about themselves than they tell us about the source of their client's problems:

> Advocates of differing theoretical orientations repeatedly discover their chosen motivators at work but rarely find evidence for the motivators emphasized by the proponents of competing viewpoints. . . . Hence, one can predict better the types of insights and unconscious motivators that persons are apt to discover in themselves in the course of psychodynamic analysis from knowledge of the therapists' conceptual belief system than from the clients' actual psychological status. (p. 5)

Social-Cognitive Theory View of Human Nature

Freedom versus Determinism

Social-cognitive theory portrays human nature as complex and rational but is that the same as saying humans possess a free will? Bandura rejects the notion that humans are autonomous, that is, free to act independently of the environmental and personal influences impinging on them. He also rejects the notion that humans respond mechanistically to those influences. Rather, as we have seen, Bandura accepts reciprocal determinism in which people can influence both their behavior and their environment. People can even produce unique thoughts and actions "through their capacity to manipulate symbols and to engage in reflective thought, people can generate novel ideas and innovative actions that transcend their past experiences" (Bandura, 1989, p. 1182). However, says Bandura, "self-generated influences operate deterministically on behavior the same way as external sources of influence do" (1989, p. 1182). Thus, according to Bandura, humans are rational but they do not possess an autonomous free will.

William James (1956) distinguished between hard and soft determinism. Hard determinism is the belief that the causes of human behavior function in an automatic, mechanistic manner, thus rendering the idea of personal responsibility meaningless. Hergenhahn (2001) describes soft determinism:

> With soft determinism . . . cognitive processes such as intentions, motives, beliefs, and values intervene between experience and behavior. The soft determinist sees human behavior as resulting from thoughtful deliberation of the options available in a given situation. Because rational processes manifest themselves prior to actions, the person bears responsibility for those actions. Although soft determinism is still determinism, it is a version that allows uniquely human cognitive processes into the configuration of the causes of human behavior. Soft determinism, then, offers a compromise between hard determinism and free will—a compromise that allows for human responsibility. (pp. 13–14)

Bandura is a soft determinist. This conception allows human behavior to be viewed as teleological, or goal-oriented: "By representing foreseeable outcomes symbolically, people can convert future consequences into current motivators and regulators of foresightful behavior" (Bandura, 1986, p. 19). It also allows people to be viewed as at least partially responsible for their own behavior, "[People can] serve as a causal contributor to their own life course by selecting, influencing, and constructing their own circumstances" (Bandura, 1986, p. 38). Elsewhere, Bandura (1989) says, "the capacity to exercise control over one's own thought processes, motivation, and action is a distinctively human characteristic. Because judgment and actions are partly self-determined, people can effect change in themselves and their situations through their own efforts" (p. 1175). And finally, demonstrating that soft determinism is still determinism, Bandura says, "self-generated influences operate deterministically on behavior the same way as external sources of influence do" (p. 1182).

Freedom as Options

Within the context of social-cognitive theory, **freedom** is defined as "the number of options available to people and their right to exercise them. The more behavioral alternatives and prerogatives people have, the greater is their freedom of action" (Bandura, 1986, p. 42). Bandura (1989) elaborates:

> Given the same environmental conditions, persons who have developed skills for accomplishing many options and are adept at regulating their own motivation and behavior are more successful in their pursuits than those who have limited means of personal agency. It is because self-influence operates deterministically on action that some measure of self-directedness and freedom is possible. (p. 1182)

Anything that reduces a person's options, then, limits his or her freedom. According to Bandura (1986, pp. 42–43), the factors that can limit personal freedom include the following:

Deficiencies in knowledge and skills

Perceptions of self-inefficacy

Internal standards that are too stringent

Social sanctions that limit a person's opportunities because of his or her skin color, sexual orientation, gender, religion, ethnic background, or social class

Chance Encounters and Life Paths

Bandura (1982) defines a **chance encounter** as an "unintended meeting of persons unfamiliar to each other" (p. 748). Such encounters can also be called fortuitous because of their unplanned, accidental nature. Bandura observes that chance encounters can significantly impact one's life and provide another reason for the unpredictability of human behavior.

> Some chance encounters touch people only lightly, others leave more lasting effects, and still others branch people into new trajectories of life. Psychology cannot foretell the occurrence of fortuitous encounters, however sophisticated its knowledge of human behavior becomes. This factor introduces a measure of unpredictability about the direction of the flow of human lives. Patterns of change can therefore

vary widely in different individuals. They may display basic continuities throughout their life spans, continuities in some aspects of life but discontinuities in others, or a base discontinuity at any point along the way affecting virtually all domains of functioning. (p. 749)

As an example of the latter, Bandura describes how Nancy Davis met her future husband, Ronald Reagan:

> While pursuing her acting career, she began to receive in the mail announcements of communist meetings intended for another person bearing the same name, who appeared on a Hollywood list of communist sympathizers. Fearing that her career might be jeopardized by mistaken identity, she voiced concern to her film director, who arranged a meeting with Ronald Reagan, then president of the Screen Actors Guild. Before long they were wed. In this instance a coincidental likeness of names and a postal mix-up altered the course of lives. (1982, p. 749)

Reciprocal determinism is not violated by noting the importance of fortuitous experience. Such experience indicates an additional way in which the environment can influence people and their subsequent behavior.

Mind–Body Relationship

Although social-cognitive theory gives cognitive events a prominent role as causative agents, it does not accept psychophysiological dualism. Bandura (1989) states, "Thoughts are higher brain processes rather than psychic entities that exist separately from brain activities. Ideational and neural terminology are simply different ways of representing the same cerebral processes" (p. 1181). However, at least at the present time, psychological laws cannot be derived from neurophysiological laws:

> One must distinguish between biological laws governing the mechanics of cerebral systems and psychological laws of how cerebral systems can be orchestrated to serve different purposes. Psychological knowledge of how best to structure influences to create belief systems and personal competencies is not derivable from knowledge of the neurophysical mechanisms that subserve such changes. Thus, understanding the brain circuits involved in learning does not tell one much about how best to present and organize instructional contents, how to code them for memory representation, and how to motivate learners to attend to, cognitively process, and rehearse what they are learning. Nor does understanding of how the brain works furnish rules on how to create social conditions that cultivate the skills needed to become a successful parent, teacher, or executive. The optimal conditions must be specified by psychological principles. (Bandura, 1989, p. 1182)

Thus while it is true psychological laws cannot violate the laws of the neurophysiological systems that subserve them, attempting to reduce psychology to biology serves no useful purpose:

Were one to embark on the road to reductionism, psychology would be reduced to biology, biology to chemistry, and chemistry to physics, with the final stop in atomic particles. Neither atomic particles, chemistry, nor biology will provide the psychological laws of human behavior. (Bandura, 1989, p. 1182)

Evaluation

Empirical Research

Like the theories of Cattell, Eysenck, Skinner, and Dollard and Miller, the theories of Bandura and Mischel are well grounded in empirical research. Throughout this chapter we have sampled numerous experimental studies that Bandura and Mischel and their colleagues have run to test their concepts. Social-cognitive theory continues to generate an enormous amount of research. Also, Mischel's book, *Personality and Assessment* (1968), triggered a debate among personality theorists concerning the consistency of human behavior that has lasted to the present time. This debate has stimulated research programs designed to answer the question, Is human behavior consistent? If so, to what extent, and in what areas? (For an extensive review of this research, see Zuckerman, 1991.) It now appears that whether behavior consistency is found or not depends on what is meant by consistency and how the research is performed. For example, if average behavior is measured, it pools those behaviors that are consistent with those that are not. The result tends to support the notion that behavior is inconsistent. Bowers (1973) and Bem and Allen (1974) argue that research on consistency should be correlational rather than experimental because the correlational method preserves individual differences. Bem and Allen tested the hypothesis that "individuals who identify themselves as consistent on a particular trait dimension will in fact be more consistent cross-situationally than those who identify themselves as highly variable" (p. 512). The hypothesis was supported, indicating that some people are consistent on some traits and others are not; further, people themselves know whether or not they are consistent.

After reviewing the literature and the arguments on consistency versus inconsistency, Pervin (1984) reached the following conclusion:

> Perhaps the conclusion that makes most sense is that most people are consistent in their behavior some of the time and variable in their behavior the rest of the time. . . . In other words, each person can be expected to be consistent in ways that are salient or meaningful for him or her. The areas of consistency differ with different individuals. Thus, for example, for some individuals it may be important to be always honest while for others it may be important to be always dominant. Each individual may have many or few such areas in which there exists cross-situational consistency. Sampling of a large group of individuals on any one characteristic might suggest little cross-situational consistency since it is unlikely that more than a small proportion of the total sample will be consistent in that particular area. The consistency of a subgroup in the population can be masked by the situational specificity of the larger group: this is true for every personality characteristic that is assessed. The conclusion might then be that behavior is situationally specific rather

than that behavior is stable in some ways for some individuals and in other ways for other individuals. What appears to be needed is a more differentiated picture of consistency and of the relationship between person and situational determinants. (p. 17)

The information just summarized refutes the position of neither the social-cognitive theorist nor the trait theorist. Although the position that Mischel took in 1968 tended toward situationalism, by claiming that the probability of reward or punishment in any situation is the most powerful determinant of behavior, he never said that behavior was entirely inconsistent; if it were, he said, memory would have no value (1977, p. 333). In any case, regardless of Mischel's early position, he is, as we have seen, now an **interactionist** who stresses the importance of both person and situation variables. Just as showing consistency of behavior is no longer a valid argument against social-cognitive theory, finding inconsistency in behavior is not necessarily an argument against trait theory. We saw in Chapter 7 that Allport believed the possession of personality traits did not cause a person's behavior to be fixed and stable. Rather, Allport viewed traits as representing ranges of possible behavior. He believed differing situations determined which behavior, in the possible range of behaviors, occurred. Thus Allport's theory was in fact similar to the interactionism of social-cognitive theory. The major differences are in Allport's use of the term *trait* and his belief that a person's behavior must occur within a specified range of possibilities. Also, we saw in Chapter 8 that Cattell and Eysenck believed traits interact with situational variables to produce behavior in any given situation. Thus Allport, Cattell, and Eysenck did not believe that behavior was entirely consistent nor that it could be predicted on the basis of personality traits alone.

Criticisms

Behavior Is More Consistent Than Social-Cognitive Theory Claims.   A great deal of criticism was triggered by Mischel's early book (1968) that seemed to emphasize situation variables almost to the exclusion of person variables and in which he suggested that little consistency exists in human behavior. Since that time, however, Mischel has accepted an interactionist position in which both the person and the environment are considered important. Also, Mischel claims that his earlier statements about the consistency of behavior were misunderstood. He notes that he never said no consistency existed; rather, he argued that the amount of consistency predicted by trait and psychoanalytic theories did not exist.

Mental Events Cannot Cause Behavior.   Radical behaviorists, such as Skinner, take issue with any theory that contains mentalistic concepts. They believe that mental events are irrelevant to understanding human behavior. Terms like *perceived self-efficacy* and *functional* and *dysfunctional expectancies,* say the radical behaviorists, confuse the study of human behavior rather than clarify it. Also, say the Skinnerians, *observational learning* is probably just a special case of operant conditioning in which acts of imitation sometimes lead to reinforcement and are thus repeated. Therefore, observational learning is under the control of reinforcement not independent of it as the social-cognitive theorists claim (see, e.g., Gewirtz, 1971).

Unfair to Psychoanalytic Theory.   The social-cognitive theorists have been harshly critical of both traditional psychoanalytic theory and Dollard and Miller's attempt to synthesize psychoanalytic theory and Hullian learning theory. Social-cognitive theorists claim that no need exists to employ the nebulous language of psychoanalytic theory because the clearly defined terms from social-cognitive theory work as well, if not better. Psychoanalytic theorists believe this position is naive and misses the complex interplay between the conscious and unconscious mind. It is because social-cognitive theory does not understand the workings of the human mind, say these critics, that it can only deal with relatively simple psychological problems such as phobias, and with nothing more complex.

Important Aspects of Personality Neglected.   Psychoanalysts criticize social-cognitive theory because it does not recognize the importance of unconscious motivation. Another important area neglected by social-cognitive theory is development. Other theorists have found that maturational factors are important in determining the emotions people experience and how they process information. Little is said in social-cognitive theory about the biological, hormonal, or maturational influences on personality development. Other topics neglected or minimized by social-cognitive theory include motivation and conflict. Motivation appears to be covered by social-cognitive theorists mainly in relationship to goal formulation and in the formulation of plans to reach goals. Also, the concept of conflict, so important to so many personality theorists (e.g., Freud and Dollard and Miller), does not appear in the index of Bandura's most comprehensive book (1986).

Social-Cognitive Theory Is Not Unified.   Social-cognitive theory has been criticized for being neither systematic nor unified. Several important topics have been studied extensively (e.g., the variables governing observational learning, perceived self-efficacy, and the self-regulation of behavior) but how these topics are related to each other is not clear. The same is true for Mischel's cognitive social learning person variables; they are simply listed and described but little discussion occurs on how they relate to each other, let alone to social-cognitive theory in general.

Contributions

Emphasis on Human Empirical Research.   One reason that social-cognitive theory is currently so popular among personality psychologists is because its terms are defined precisely enough to be verified empirically. Bandura and Mischel, and their colleagues, have always been associated with active research programs. Furthermore, Bandura and Mischel have avoided the touchy problem of generalizing research on nonhumans to humans by performing all of their research on humans. Likewise, they have avoided the problem of generalizing from simple behavior to complex behavior by doing research on complex behavior originally. By concentrating on human subjects and on complex behavior, social-cognitive theory avoids many of the criticisms of Skinner's and Dollard and Miller's theories.

Applied Value.   Social-cognitive theory has been extremely heuristic. It has provided information about topics of vital importance in today's world: aggression, moral behavior, delay of gratification, the influence of models (e.g., parents, television, and films) on behavior, dysfunctional expectancies and how to correct them, self-regulation of behavior, and the importance of perceived self-efficacy.

For many, the social-cognitive theory view of humans as thinking, planning, reasoning, expecting, and reflecting organisms is more realistic than the mechanistic, simplistic view of humans derived from animal research. Social-cognitive theory recognizes the importance of language, symbols, and cognitive information-processing mechanisms; the research it generates is usually directed at something relevant; it views humans optimistically; and it emphasizes the importance of the present or the future, rather than the past.

Summary

The major spokespersons for social-cognitive theory are Albert Bandura and Walter Mischel. Social-cognitive theory stresses cognitive factors in learning and in performing, and emphasizes that behavior in any given situation is a function of both the characteristics of the person and the situation. Early in his career, Mischel took both trait and psychoanalytic theories to task because he found that human behavior was not nearly as consistent as it should be if it was determined by factors thought to exist within the person, such as traits or repressed experiences. Although in 1968 Mischel was basically a situationalist, in that he believed the probability of reward or punishment was the strongest determinant of behavior in any given situation, he later became an interactionist who saw the importance of both person and situation variables and their interaction. Bandura labeled the interactionist's position reciprocal determinism, which states that the person, the person's behavior, and the environment influence each other. Mischel replaced the traditional person variables such as traits and internal conflicts with what he called cognitive social person variables: encoding strategies, or how experiences are retained and categorized; expectancies, or what a person believes will happen if he or she behaves in a certain way or sees a certain event; subjective values, or what a person believes is worth having or doing; self-regulatory systems and plans, which determine what people will reward and punish themselves for, and how they will organize their lives to attain future goals; and competencies, or the various skills a person possesses.

According to social-cognitive theory, we learn what we observe. We learn by either observing the consequences of our own behavior or by observing the consequences of other people's behavior. That is, we learn from either direct or vicarious reinforcement and punishment. Although learning is an almost continuous process, we only translate what we have learned into performance when there is an incentive to do so. Because they believe humans learn through observation, the content of television programs and films are of special interest to social-cognitive theorists.

According to Bandura, observational learning is influenced by four variables: attentional processes, which determine what we can and do attend to; retentional processes, which determine how experience is encoded in memory; motor reproduction processes, which determine what behaviors can be performed; and motivational processes, which determine the circumstances under which learning is translated into performance.

Most human behavior is, according to social-cognitive theory, self-regulated. Performance standards are established, and if one's behavior meets or exceeds those standards, one experiences self-reinforcement; if they are not, one experiences self-punishment. Humans also formulate future goals and then plan their lives so as to increase the probability of attaining those goals. Usually, future goals are approached by first attaining a series of smaller, immediate subgoals. A great deal of self-regulated behavior is influenced by one's perceived self-efficacy or one's own view of what one is capable of doing. Those people with high perceived self-efficacy try more, do more, persist longer, and are less anxious than those with low perceived self-efficacy. Moral conduct is governed by internalized moral principles that, if violated, cause a person to experience self-contempt. Self-contempt can be escaped, however, by using one of the self-exonerating mechanisms. The ability to tolerate delay of gratification has been shown to develop early in life for some individuals, and having done so, has a positive influence on later personality characteristics. Like the other variables involved in self-regulated behavior, the ability to delay gratification has been shown to be influenced by modeling.

Psychological and behavioral problems result from dysfunctional expectancies. Such erroneous or ineffective expectancies can result from the overgeneralization of a single or small number of negative personal experiences or from modeling. Within social-cognitive theory, psychotherapy is seen as a means of changing self-efficacy expectations. If a person does not believe he or she can handle a snake, for example, a film of a model interacting with a snake can be shown (symbolic modeling), a live model can be shown interacting with a snake (live modeling), or a model and the client can interact with a snake together (live modeling with participation). Although all forms of modeling have been found effective in treating many types of phobias, live modeling with participation is usually found to be the most effective. It has been shown that modeling changes a person's perceived self-efficacy, which, in turn, changes behavior.

Social-cognitive theory views humans as thoughtful problem solvers who are dealing with the present but are also planning for the future. Bandura rejects the notions that humans are autonomous or respond mechanically to external or internal events (hard determinism). Reciprocal determinism portrays humans as capable of reflective, imaginative thought. These rational processes, in turn, determine a person's behavior (soft determinism). In this view, the level of personal freedom is determined by the number of options available to a person and his or her right to exercise them. Social-cognitive theory also recognizes fortuitous experience as a major determinant of human behavior. Although psychological laws cannot violate the neurophysiological laws that subserve them, social-cognitive theory contends that psychological laws must be studied independently of neurophysiological laws.

Social-cognitive theory is firmly grounded in empirical research but has been criticized for claiming human behavior is more inconsistent than it actually is; suggesting that mental events can cause behavior; being too critical of psychoanalytic theory and thus missing the importance of unconscious motivation; neglecting important aspects of personality such as development, motivation, and conflict; and not being a systematic, unified theory. Social-cognitive theory has been praised for emphasizing empirical research using human subjects; performing research on complex, socially relevant topics; and for recognizing the many cognitive processes that differentiate humans from nonhuman animals.

Experiential Exercises

1. According to social-cognitive theory, most human behavior is self-regulated. For example, it is claimed that much of our behavior is guided by internalized performance and moral standards. If performance meets or exceeds these standards we feel good about ourselves, and if it does not we feel bad. Give an example of how such standards guide your behavior. Do you agree with the social-cognitive contention that intrinsic reinforcement has more of an impact on behavior than extrinsic reinforcement? Explain. Also, attempt to account for the origins of your moral and performance standards.

2. A key concept within social-cognitive theory is perceived self-efficacy. Discuss how your perceptions of your abilities influence your behavior. That is, how do they influence what you try, how long you persist, and what you avoid doing? Discuss how you think your perceived self-efficacy originated and the circumstances under which you think it can be changed. Do you agree with the contention of the social-cognitive theorists that changing dysfunctional expectancies is largely a matter of changing perceived self-efficacy? Explain.

3. An important concept within social-cognitive theory is that of modeling. Describe a person who has acted as an influential model in your life. What important values did you learn from this person? Discuss the topic of observational learning as it applies to this modeling experience.

Discussion Questions

1. What was Mischel's basic argument with trait and psychoanalytic theories?
2. Define and give an example of each of the following: behavior–outcome expectancy, stimulus–outcome expectancy, and self-efficacy expectancy.
3. Why, according to social-cognitive theory, should we be concerned about the content of television programs and films?

Glossary

Attentional processes. Processes that determine what is attended to and therefore what is learned through observation.

Behavior–outcome expectancy. Belief that acting a certain way in a certain situation will have a certain consequence.

Chance encounter. An unintended, or fortuitous, meeting of persons that has the potential to significantly alter the lives of those involved.

Cognitive social person variables. Those variables thought by Mischel to determine how a person selects, perceives, interprets, and uses the stimuli confronting him or her. *See* *also* Competencies; Encoding strategies; Expectancies; Subjective values; Self-regulatory systems and plans.

Competencies. Cognitive social person variable that describes what a person knows and what he or she is capable of doing.

Consistency paradox. According to Mischel, the persistent belief that human behavior is more consistent than is indicated by experimental evidence.

Delay of gratification. Postponement of a small, immediate reinforcer in order to obtain a larger, more distant reinforcer.

Delayed modeling.   Refers to the fact that there is often a long delay between when something is learned observationally and when that learning is translated into behavior.

Dysfunctional expectancies.   Expectancies that do not result in effective interactions with the environment. Such expectancies can result from inaccurate modeling, from overgeneralization of nonrepresentational personal experience, or from distorted perceived self-efficacy.

Encoding strategies.   Cognitive social person variable that determines which aspects of the environment are selected for attention and how those aspects are interpreted by the individual.

Expectancies.   Cognitive social person variable that determines how individuals anticipate events in their lives. *See also* Behavior–outcome expectancy, Self-efficacy expectancy, and Stimulus–outcome expectancy.

Extrinsic reinforcement.   Reinforcement that results from sources outside of the person.

Freedom.   Within social-cognitive theory, freedom is determined by the number of options available to people and their right to exercise them.

Human agency.   Conscious planning and intentional execution of actions that influence future events.

Interactionist.   Any theorist who contends it is the interaction of person variables and situation variables that determines behavior at any given moment.

Intrinsic reinforcement.   Self-reinforcement.

Model.   Anything that conveys information to an observer.

Moral conduct.   Behavior that is in accordance with internalized moral principles. When a person acts in accordance with internalized moral principles, he or she experiences self-praise. If not, the person experiences self-contempt.

Motivational processes.   Those processes that determine the circumstances under which learning is translated into behavior. Such a translation will not occur unless the person has an adequate incentive.

Motor reproduction processes.   Those processes that determine what behavior a person is physically capable of performing.

Observational learning.   Learning that results from attending to something. Such learning is said to occur independently of reinforcement.

Participant modeling.   Type of modeling that requires the observer to participate in the modeling experience. Typically, both the model and the observer engage in activities together that are anxiety-provoking to the observer. This type of modeling is generally found to be the most effective.

Perceived self-efficacy.   What a person believes he or she is capable of doing.

Performance standards.   Those standards that must be met or exceeded before one experiences self-reinforcement. If a person's performance does not meet or exceed a performance standard, he or she experiences self-punishment.

Person variables.   Variables contained within the person that determine how he or she responds to a situation.

Personality coefficient.   Mischel's quantification of the amount of consistency found in human behavior. He found that the correlation of behavior across time, across similar situations, and between personality questionnaires and behavior was about 0.30. This weak correlation suggested that human behavior was not nearly as consistent as it had been widely assumed to be.

Psychotherapy.   Within social-cognitive theory, any procedure that corrects dysfunctional expectancies. Typically, the procedure used is some type of modeling.

Reciprocal determinism.   Contention that person variables, situation variables, and behavior constantly interact with one another. For example, the person influences the environment, the environment influences the person, and the consequences of one's behavior change both the person and the environment.

Reinforcement.   Within social-cognitive theory, reinforcement (either direct or vicarious) provides information concerning what behavior will be effective in a given situation. Also, reinforcement provides an incentive for translating learning into performance. *See also* Vicarious reinforcement.

Retentional processes.   Those processes that determine how experiences are encoded into memory for possible future use.

Self-control.   Ability to tolerate a delay in gratification.

Self-efficacy.   What a person is actually capable of doing.

Self-efficacy expectancy.   Expectancy one has concerning one's ability to engage in effective behavior. *See also* Perceived self-efficacy and Self-efficacy.

Self-exonerating mechanisms. Cognitive mechanisms a person can employ to escape the self-contempt that ordinarily results when a person acts contrary to an internalized moral principle.

Self-regulated behavior. Behavior governed by intrinsic reinforcement and punishment. Self-regulated behavior is often directed at some major future goal that is approached through a series of subgoals. Once goals are set, an individual organizes his or her life so as to increase the probability of their attainment. Also, much of a person's self-directed behavior is determined by his or her perceived self-efficacy. *See also* Delay of gratification and Moral conduct.

Self-regulatory systems and plans. Cognitive social learning person variable that determines the circumstances under which an individual experiences self-reinforcement and self-punishment. This variable also determines the setting of future goals and the formulation of plans (strategies) used in attaining those goals.

Situation variables. Variables in the environment that provide the setting in which person variables manifest themselves.

Social-cognitive theory. Name given to Bandura and Mischel's theory because of its emphasis on the social and cognitive origins of human behavior.

Stimulus–outcome expectancy. Belief that one environmental event will be followed by another specific event that has been consistently associated with the first event in the past.

Subjective values. Cognitive social person variable that determines under what circumstances a person will translate what has been learned into behavior. Subjective values determine what is worth having or aspiring for, and what is not.

Symbolic modeling. Modeling involving something other than a live human, for instance, a film, television, instructions, reading material, or a demonstration.

Systematic desensitization. Therapeutic procedure whereby a client is asked to imagine a series of interrelated anxiety-provoking scenes until they no longer cause anxiety.

Vicarious punishment. Punishment that comes from observing the negative consequences of another person's behavior.

Vicarious reinforcement. Reinforcement that comes from observing the positive consequences of another person's behavior.

CHAPTER **12**

DAVID M. BUSS

CHAPTER OUTLINE

In 1975, Edward O. Wilson published *Sociobiology: The New Synthesis,* which marked the formal beginning of **sociobiology,** a discipline seeking to unite fields such as anthropology, psychology, and sociology under the unifying assumptions of Darwinian evolutionary theory. The major contention of sociobiologists was that certain human *social* behaviors were selected by evolution because they contributed to the biological fitness of those who engaged in them. In other words, just as various bodily structures and physiological processes are the products of the natural selection that occurred in our evolutionary past, so too are patterns of social behavior. In the years since the publication of this important book, **evolutionary psychology** has emerged as an influential force in our discipline. It shares several Darwinian assumptions with sociobiology, but, as we will see, some evolutionary psychologists differ with sociobiologists and want to make clear the distinctions between the two approaches. David M. Buss has been one of the more prolific and articulate psychologists to develop and differentiate the field, and we have chosen to focus this chapter primarily on his contributions.

Biographical Sketch

David Buss was born in Indianapolis, Indiana, in April 1953. His father was (and still is) a professor of psychology, and his mother held a master's degree in special education. Despite his academically rich home environment, Buss was not initially interested in education. He dropped out of high school to work at a truck stop where his duties included "pumping gas, bumping tires to make sure they were not flat, cleaning windshields, and dealing with an assortment of odd characters who came through" (personal communication, 2004). He eventually left the truck stop, earned his diploma at night school, and decided to attend college.

He enrolled at the University of Texas at Austin, where he did not declare a major for several years. He considered astronomy and geology as possible majors, but he finally chose psychology after concluding "that the human mind was the most complex and mysterious entity in the known universe" (personal communication, 2004). After completing his undergraduate degree, he entered the doctoral program in psychology at the University of California at Berkeley in the area of personality psychology. (Note that he is the only theorist presented in this text who was actually trained in personality theory.) He worked with many influential professors at Berkeley, including Ken Craik, Jack Block, Harrison Gough, and Richard Lazarus, but none of them had interests in evolutionary theory. Reflecting on theories of personality, Buss (personal communication, 2004) writes

> Although I found elements of each theory to be interesting and some to be intuitively on target, all seemed "arbitrary" in the sense that they were not anchored in any fundamental set of principles. It seemed as though there was no way of deciding which theory was correct. I sought a theory of personality that could be based on a fundamental and nonarbitrary set of principles. I was drawn to evolutionary theory as potentially providing that foundation. There is no reason to think that humans have somehow been exempt from the fundamental causal forces that have fashioned all other species—particularly evolution by natural selection.

After completing his graduate training in 1981, he went to Harvard University as an assistant professor. There he met then graduate students Leda Cosmides, a cognitive psychologist, and her husband John Tooby, a biological anthropologist, who further stimulated his interests in the theory of evolution; and the core of what was to become evolutionary psychology was formed. Cosmides and Tooby currently are co-directors of the Center for Evolutionary Psychology at the University of California at Santa Barbara.

Buss joined the faculty at the University of Michigan as associate professor in 1985 and was promoted to full professor in 1991. In 1996 he joined the faculty at the University of Texas at Austin, where he continues to teach and conduct research in evolutionary psychology. Buss has published over 150 research articles and seven books exploring evolutionary influences on mating strategies, love, jealousy, and related topics. He has served on the editorial boards of numerous journals including *American Psychologist, Journal of Personality and Social Psychology, Psychology,* and *Journal of Personality, Evolution, and Human Behavior.* In 2003 Buss was named on the Intercollegiate Studies Institute list of 250 Most Highly Cited Psychologists. Among other honors, he has been awarded the APA Distinguished

Scientific Award for Early Career Contribution to Psychology (1988), the Distinguished Faculty Recognition Award at the University of Michigan (1989), the G. Stanley Hall Award of the APA (1990), the President's Associates Teaching Excellence Award at the University of Texas (2001); and he was president-elect of the Human Behavior and Evolution Society from 2003 until 2005 and assumes the presidency from 2005 until 2007.

Darwin's Theory of Evolution

Because evolutionary psychology applies Darwinian evolutionary theory to the explanation of human behavior, we spend a moment reviewing that theory.

Darwin (1859) observed that all species of living organisms are capable of producing more offspring than environmental resources can support. When this happens a **"struggle for existence"** occurs. Traits necessary for existence—for survival—vary among members of a species, and only those members possessing traits allowing **adaptation** (successful adjustment) to the environment survive and reproduce. If the traits that allow adaptation to a particular environment are at least partially heritable, the offspring of parents who survived in that environment will also tend to possess traits conducive to survival. This tendency will continue to be true as long as the environment does not radically change. The term **natural selection** refers to the fact that environmental demands determine or select which organisms will survive and reproduce. Organisms that possess adaptive traits are more likely to succeed in their environment, and their traits are more likely to appear in subsequent generations.

Darwin observed several characteristics of animals that he believed could not have resulted from natural selection. As examples he gave bird songs and colorful plumage, the tendency of males to engage in physical combat with other males, and the physical attributes that increase the likelihood of victory (e.g., the horns of a stag). To explain these and other characteristics, Darwin proposed his theory of **sexual selection.** Sexual selection results from the competition among members of the same species for mates. This competition is usually, but not always, among males.

Darwin's theory of sexual selection can be summarized as follows: (1) members of a species with adaptations that lead to a mating advantage will reproduce more, thus passing their characteristics into future generations; and (2) to the extent that certain characteristics of one sex are preferred, on average, by members of the other sex, those characteristics will be passed to future generations.

The term **survival of the fittest** refers to the fact that only those members of a species who are best adapted to their environment survive and reproduce. **Fitness,** then, is measured in terms of differential reproduction and nothing else. Crawford (1987) cautions us not to confuse fitness with social standing: "It is essential to distinguish biological fitness from social standing. Michelangelo, Isaac Newton, and Leonardo da Vinci had zero reproductive fitness since they apparently did not leave offspring. However, their social standing is beyond question" (p. 16). Fitness is sometimes mistakenly equated with such factors as physical size, strength, or aggressiveness. As we shall see, however, the tendencies to love children and to cooperate with fellow humans can be fitness enhancing, but they do not involve aggression.

Inclusive Fitness

Individuals do not have to produce offspring to perpetuate copies of their genes into subsequent generations. They may also do so by helping relatives, who share their genes, survive and reproduce. This expanded notion of gene reproduction is called **inclusive fitness.** The concept of inclusive fitness, although suggested by others earlier, including Darwin himself (1859, pp. 250–257), was most fully developed in two highly influential papers by W. D. Hamilton (1964). The notion of inclusive fitness is used to explain various social phenomena and we return to it often throughout this chapter.

Evolutionary Psychology Is Not Sociobiology

Sociobiology and Perpetuation of the Genes

According to sociobiologists, whether we know it or not, our primary goal in life is to perpetuate copies of our genes into the next generation, and this was, of course, also true of our ancestors. It is because of the natural selection of genes that we now possess the types of brains, minds, bodies, and behavioral tendencies we do. Although the perpetuation of our genes is the master motive in life, it controls much of what we do without our being aware of that control. "Genes need not know what they are doing in order to function effectively and—here is the painful part—neither need we. We can spend a whole lifetime serving their purposes without ever knowing it" (Barash, 1979, p. 25). This assumption underlies all of sociobiology: *We live to pass copies of our genes into the next generation.* Everything we do serves this goal or, if not, is deleterious to us.

Evolutionary Psychology and Problems of Adaptation

Some authors, including E. O. Wilson (1998, p. 150), equate evolutionary psychology and sociobiology. Buss and other evolutionary psychologists, however, insist on a clear distinction between the two disciplines. For example, with respect to sociobiology's contention that our primary goal in life is the perpetuation of genes, Buss says

> I have labeled this view the *sociobiological fallacy* . . . because it conflates a theory of the origins of mechanisms (inclusive-fitness theory) with a theory of the nature of those mechanisms. If men had as a goal of maximization of fitness, then why aren't they all lined up to give donations to sperm banks, and why do some individuals decide to forgo reproduction entirely? . . . The nature of mechanisms as end products should not be confused with the causal process that created them. The sociobiological fallacy has led to some dubious speculating about how, if one really looks closely enough, one will see that person X really is maximizing fitness, even though the behavior seems anomalous with respect to this goal (e.g., suicidal, schizophrenic, dysfunctional). (Buss, 1995, p. 10)

Put simply, some behaviors are adaptive because they solve problems—not because they perpetuate genes. Their goals exist in the short run, relative to evolutionary time, and they are confined to specific environmental challenges. The view that these behaviors are guided by a master motive to perpetuate genes is incorrect for a number of reasons (Buss, 1995, 1999, 2004). First, it takes many generations to determine whether a behavior has contributed to evolutionary fitness. Analysis of a specific behavior for a specific individual at a specific point in time makes no sense in an evolutionary context. Second, a general-purpose fitness-maximization motive is not likely to exist given that a specified behavior cannot be adaptive for all environments, for all sexes, at all ages, or for all species. Finally, sociobiological explanations do not address the *psychological* mechanisms and processes that underlie development of a new strategic behavior or maintenance of a previously successful strategic behavior. That is, sociobiological explanations are often not psychological explanations. Buss concludes:

> Humans are collections of mechanisms, each one of which was forged over evolutionary time by the process of selection. The products of this process tend to be problem specific—keep warm, avoid predators, get food, find a mate, have sex, socialize children, help kin in need, and so on. The product of the evolutionary process is not, and cannot be, the goal of maximal gene propagation. (1999, p. 22)

What is Selected by Natural Selection?

If we are, as Buss claims, "collections of mechanisms," where do these mechanisms exist and how is it that natural selection operates on them? Cosmides and Tooby (1997) identify five principles of evolutionary psychology that provide answers to these questions. First, they note that it is the brain, a physical system—not an abstract motive, idea, behavior, or strategy—that is acted on by natural selection. In a simplified view, the brain is a system of input and output circuits. Some circuits may lend an adaptive advantage, others may not. It is those physical systems that we euphemistically call "circuits" that are acted on by natural selection.

Second, Cosmides and Tooby note that the neural circuits we currently possess were selected because they solved *adaptive* problems faced during the evolution of the species. Adaptive problems are challenges that tended to occur frequently for our species and that had effects on reproduction. Thus, we have inherited sex-typical circuits for attracting mates because finding mates recurred generation after generation and because mate-finding clearly affected reproductive success for our ancestors.

Third, Cosmides and Tooby remind us that the brain circuitry underlying any behavior is far more complex than we might imagine. Most importantly, those aspects of any behavior of which we are conscious constitute only a small fraction of the neural activity in question. In their words, "Consciousness is just the tip of the iceberg" (1997, p. 7).

Fourth, Cosmides and Tooby reiterate Buss's reminder that our evolved neural circuits are specialized for specific problems in specific contexts. Thus we have specialized circuits for face recognition, for detecting a potential rival for our mate's affections, and for learning which foods tend to make us ill—all of which may vary with age or between the sexes.

Finally, although we feel like modern and contemporary humans, our brains and their circuitry evolved over thousands of generations as hunter-gatherers. As Buss (1995) puts it, "Humans are living fossils—collections of mechanisms produced by prior selection pressures operating on a long and unbroken line of ancestors" (p. 10). The circuits that enable our behavior were very successful for

Leda Cosmides and John Tooby.

hunter-gatherers. It remains to be seen whether they will be successful in an environment that differs so radically from that of our evolutionary ancestors.

Personality Theory and Human Nature

Buss writes:

> I view personality psychology as the broadest of all the psychological disciplines, one that attempts to understand both human nature and the ways in which individuals differ. Historically, theories of personality from Freud on have been concerned with human nature (e.g., humans have sexual and aggressive "instincts" in Freud's theory), yet most research in personality psychology focuses on individual differences. I believe that the meta-theory of evolutionary psychology provides a way to bridge this gulf. (personal communication, 2004)

While, as Buss says, most research in personality theory is concerned with how and why individuals differ from each other, evolutionary psychology sets as its primary goal a description of human nature. A theory of human nature attempts to describe what it means to be human—how we are like every other human being. Theories of human nature are extremely important within the realm of personality theory because every theory of personality accepts a theory of human nature either explicitly or implicitly. Buss (2004) explains:

Humans also have a nature—qualities that define us as a unique species—and all psychological theories imply its existence. For Sigmund Freud human nature consisted of raging sexual and aggressive impulses. For William James human nature consisted of dozens or hundreds of instincts. Even the most ardently environmentalist theories, such as B.F. Skinner's theory of radical behaviorism, assume that humans have a nature—in this case consisting of a few highly general learning mechanisms. All psychological theories require as their core a specification of, or fundamental premises about, human nature. (p. 49)

Next, we discuss two theories of human nature. The first is sometimes called the **empirical theory** or the **social science model** (Tooby & Cosmides, 1997). The second is the **evolutionary psychological theory of human nature.**

The Social Science Model

The empirical or social science model of personality maintains that what characterizes a person at any given time is a function of what that person has experienced in his or her lifetime. Although John Locke (1631–1704) was not the first to offer an empirical view of human nature, his was among the most clearly articulated. According to Locke, except for a few innate faculties such as the ability to reflect upon experience, the mind is essentially a *tabula rasa* (a blank tablet) at birth, and experience writes on that tablet. For Locke, what you become as a person depends on what you experience. According to this view of human nature, the environment, including cultural environment, is all-important in determining personality. Other than a general (or *context-independent*) capacity to become whatever you experience, a concept of human nature does not exist. We come equipped with *no* inherited predispositions. According to this approach, "Human nature is formless, shapeless, and vague. And it remains that way until the cultural symbols, social scripts, social roles, or external contingencies of reinforcement supply structure, roles are assigned, and agents of the culture impress their indelible stamp" (Buss, 2001, p. 960).

Evolutionary Psychological Theory of Human Nature

Evolutionary psychologists disagree strongly with the *tabula rasa* explanation of human nature. They assume that the human mind has been shaped by evolution and is predisposed to act in some ways and avoid acting in others. For evolutionary psychologists, the principal task of personality theory is to document and describe these perceptual/behavioral tendencies.

The evolutionary psychological rejection of the social science model is not merely a convenient theoretical assumption. Evidence against the *tabula rasa* is accumulating rapidly. Rather than coming into the world equipped with only a general-purpose ability to learn, infants exhibit many predisposed abilities. They demonstrate a preference for looking at human faces only minutes after birth (Johnson & Morton, 1991); they appear to have a rudimentary understanding of the solidity of objects at only a few months of age (Baillargeon, Graber, DeVois, & Black, 1990; Keen, 2003); and as toddlers they seem able to infer intentions of others without verbal cues (Baron-Cohen, 1995). Cosmides and Tooby (1997) write that there "is now evidence for the existence of circuits that are specialized for reasoning about objects, physical causality, number, the biological world, the beliefs and motivations of other individuals, and social interactions" (p. 11), all of which develop without formal instruction and without extensive external reinforcement.

Nature or Nurture?

Contemporary evolutionary psychologists reject the nature versus nurture dichotomy as artificial; similarly, they reject questions concerning "how much nature" or "how much nurture." Like other interactionist theorists who show that personality is the result of both internal (or person) variables and environmental variables (see, e.g., Chapters 7, 8, and 11), evolutionary psychologists remind us that evolutionary adaptations require appropriate environments if they are to be manifested. Furthermore, different environments may induce different degrees of expression of an adaptation. Thus it is not a question of "nature or nurture" but a question of "nature *with* nurture." Buss (2004) says that "evolutionary theory in fact represents a truly interactionist framework. Human behavior cannot occur without two ingredients: (1) evolved adaptations and (2) environmental input that triggers the development and activation of these adaptations." He adds that "notions of genetic determinism—behaviors caused by genes without influence from the environment—are simply false" (p. 19). Stated more dramatically, "If you drop a human zygote (a fertilized human egg) into liquid nitrogen, it will not develop into an infant" (Cosmides & Tooby, 1997, p. 17). (Do not try this experiment at home.)

Culture

A claim often made by advocates of the social science model is that the vast array of cultures is strong evidence against the notion of a universal human nature. The supposition of cultural *plasticity*—the idea that culture can assume any shape—was based on anthropological reports of cultures in which sex roles were reversed (relative to the Western European norm), in which there was no violence or homicide, in which there was no jealousy, and so on. Unfortunately, many of these idyllic anthropological reports lacked empirical support, and others appeared to be outright hoaxes (see, e.g., Freeman, 1983, 1999).

Evolutionary psychology does not claim that all cultures are identical; however, there is substantial evidence that universal human behaviors are expressed in most—if not all—cultures and that these behaviors occur in different degrees depending on variations in environmental conditions. These cultural universals include

> incest avoidance, facial expressions, favoritism toward in-group members, favoritism toward kin members over non-kin members, collective identities, fear of snakes, division of labor by sex, revenge and retaliation, self distinguished from others, sanctions for crimes against the collectivity, reciprocity in relationships, envy, sexual jealousy, and the emotion of love. (Buss, 2001, p. 966)

It is important to caution that, while characteristics such as those listed above appear in a wide variety of cultures, they are not expected to be uniformly true of every individual in every culture. Thus, while it is characteristic, *on average,* for people to favor their kin or to engage in revenge-taking, not all people in all cultures do so, nor do those who engage in these behaviors do so to the same degree. What is important is that these behaviors appear to some degree in diverse cultures around the world. In the sections that follow, we examine the accumulated evidence for universally predisposed behaviors and begin to see how they come together to comprise personality.

Sex Differences: Mating Strategies

As an aspect of personality, **sex differences** are so pervasive that, ironically, they are sometimes overlooked in the study of personality. We often recognize that an individual is male or female long before we discern their levels of neuroticism, extroversion, or other well-studied personality characteristics. Evolutionary psychology is particularly concerned with femaleness and maleness as universal phenomena, and a substantial amount of Buss's work focuses on sex differences. In the following section, we present the evolutionary perspective concerning differences in strategies employed by men and women who are seeking and attempting to attract mates.

What is a Strategy?

Evolutionary psychologists use various terms to describe the processes we inherit from our evolutionary past with which we confront current problems. For example, the terms "mechanisms," "circuits," and "adaptations" have been used. The important commonality among these is that they all refer to inherited predispositions to confront immediate, contemporary problems in ways shaped by our evolutionary past. The word "predisposition" is important because it indicates that these behavioral tendencies are not hard-wired by evolution; they always interact with environmental conditions and cultural influences to solve specific problems.

In Cosmides and Tooby's (1997) five principles of evolutionary psychology, "circuits" is used to describe the physical systems that take in information and generate behavior. Buss often uses "evolved psychological mechanism" or, more simply, **"strategy"** to refer to these physical systems, and we will use "strategy" in future references. This term is, perhaps, more useful because it indicates the complexity of the neural mechanisms we are trying to describe. A strategy is more than a simple input–output reflex. It is an evolutionarily selected neural system developed to solve a specific problem. We have strategies for finding food, for getting warm, for finding mates, and so on. Clearly, we do not apply our food-finding strategy when we need shelter, nor do we apply our mating strategy when we need food. The sensory systems corresponding to strategies are finely tuned to environmental (or internal) signals, and they are comparably tuned to detect appropriate goals to satisfy our needs. Hunger pangs and a rumbling stomach tell us we need food. In response, we become increasingly aware of road signs informing us of restaurants at the next interstate exit and less aware of how many miles lie between us and our final destination. Our strategies often involve numerous and appropriate options for behavior. We rarely, if ever, gobble a spoonful of sand or make flirtatious eye contact with a potential mate in response to signals of hunger. There are a number of behaviors from which to choose when we are hungry; and selection of a behavior depends on many factors including intensity of need, availability and variety of food, and resources we possess in order to obtain food. Finally, although the output of a strategy is directed toward solving the problem at hand, it may not always result in overt behavior. We may choose to eat whatever is available, we may defer eating until later and continue to experience the physiological symptoms of hunger, or we may decide that fasting makes us a better person. By calling a mechanism a *strategy,* we in no way suggest that its inputs, targets, decisions, and outputs are consciously planned, rehearsed, and executed. It is called a strategy because it is a multifaceted solution to an adaptive problem.

Long-Term Mating Strategies: Women's Preferences

Long-term mating for the purpose of reproduction has surely been a target of evolutionary selection pressures. Few adaptive problems have such direct implications for evolutionary fitness. Furthermore, we expect to observe sex differences in mate selection strategies because the tasks of successful reproduction are much different for women and men. The explanation for sex differences in mating strategies rests on fundamental Darwinian sexual selection theory, discussed previously, and the related **theory of parental investment** (Trivers, 1972).

Females of a species are often more biologically valuable than males and this differential-value principle is extremely important in mammals. The value principle begins with differences between ova and sperm. A woman has a finite number of ova. They are a limited, complex, and biologically expensive resource, and she will usually exhaust her supply during her lifetime. Men generate large numbers of sperm, and the ability to produce them can last well into old age—sometimes with surprising consequences. In addition, female mammals must carry a fetus, devote precious resources during pregnancy, give birth, and, until only recently in human history, feed and protect the child for a period that may last several years. As agents of reproduction, women are invaluable. Males, although necessary, may be relatively uninvolved after fertilization. The result is that females are more selective than males. She guards her sexual resources and remains resistant to mating until she encounters a male who displays preferred characteristics. If women are more selective than men, it follows that they will apply different criteria when selecting a long-term mate.

Consider the following scenario:

> A woman finds herself attracted to a "bad boy"—an irresponsible man who is carefree, coarse, and often violent. He carouses with pals, drinks to excess, and has no concern for the welfare of the woman or any children who result from their union. He has few, if any, resources to devote to the woman or children; extra income is spent on his vintage car and his escalating fascination with recreational drugs. He has no plans to better himself or to acquire the resources that may secure his family's future. In fact, he finds such ideas constraining and annoying, and they are the source of heated arguments.

Mating with such a man could be disastrous. The woman's safety as well as that of her children may be jeopardized; she and her children might not survive the relationship. Women who selected mates like him during our evolutionary past are not likely to have been our ancestors. On the other hand, if she is careful to select a male who has resources and is willing to share them, who is kind and nurturing, and who will provide care and safety for her and her children, she increases chances for her own survival as well as that of her children. We are much more likely to be descended from women who made these more prudent choices.

Buss and Schmitt's (1993) **sexual strategies theory (SST)** adds an additional twist to the complex dynamics of mating. According to SST, what we desire and what we do to make ourselves desirable differs between males and females and can change depending on whether we are looking for a long-term mate or a short-term mate.

Based on this analysis, evolutionary psychology predicts that selection pressures have sculpted women's long-term mating strategies to detect qualities in men like those described in the latter case above and to find those characteristics desirable. In other words, women should desire males who not only can produce viable offspring, but can and do provide resources, commitment, and safety for the woman and her children. Buss (2003) writes "Evolution has favored women who prefer men who possess attributes that confer benefits and who dislike men who possess attributes that impose costs" (p. 21).

Buss and his colleagues (e.g., 1989, 1994, 1998, 2000, 2003; Buss & Schmitt, 1993) report survey results from more than 10,000 male and female participants in 37 different cultures. It was consistently found that both men and women seek mates who are loving, kind, understanding, and intelligent. It does no good for either women or men to select mates who are abusive, indifferent, and slow-witted. Beyond these basic criteria, however, it was found that men and women differ in what they are attracted to in a mate. As predicted, women seeking long-term mates tend to value men with resources and the ability to attain them more than men value those same characteristics in potential mates. Interestingly, this preference for men with resources is observed to an even greater degree among women who already possess resources and status themselves (Buss, 1989; Wiederman & Allgeier, 1992). It has been found that women tend to prefer men who are slightly older than themselves, given that mature men are more likely to have attained positions of status and to have access to resources, and they also tend to prefer men who are athletic, tall, and strong—signals of the potential to produce viable offspring and provide security and protection (Buss & Schmitt, 1993). Not surprisingly, men who demonstrate affection toward children are viewed as more attractive than men who do not (La Cerra, 1994).

Preference for men with resources and status is observed in many cultures, from Western, information-technology cultures to small, nontechnological tribal societies. In the United States, it is not uncommon to see aged actors, rock stars, or businessmen in romantic relationships with highly desirable, younger women—matches that seem incomprehensible unless we consider the prestige and wealth of the men involved. In the Tiwi (Northern Australia), Yanomamö (Venezuela), Ache (Paraguay), and !Kung (Botswana) cultures, men of high status and prestige have considerable control of resources and are more desirable mates. As a benefit, their children also have greater status and access to resources and are therefore more likely to thrive (Buss, 2003).

Buss (1987) reviewed seven studies of mate selection criteria that occurred during a period of more than 40 years. These studies and their major findings are summarized in Table 12–1. The data clearly support the contention that females,

				FEMALES VALUE MORE	MALES VALUE MORE
Table 12–1					
Summary of Seven Studies on Sex Differences in Mate Selection Criteria Done over a Period of More Than 40 Years	AUTHORS	YEAR	SAMPLE SIZE	METHOD	
	Hill	1945	600	Ratings	Ambition & industrious: good financial prospect	Good looking
	Langhorne & Secord	1955	5000	Nominations	Getting ahead; ambitious; enjoys work; high-status profession; good provider; wealth	Physical attractiveness
	McGinnis	1958	120	Ratings	Ambition & industrious; favorable social status; good financial prospect	Good looks
	Hudson & Henze	1969	566	Ratings	Ambition & industrious; favorable social status; good financial prospect	Good looks
	Buss	1985	162	Rankings	Good earning capacity	Physical attractiveness
	Buss & Barnes*	1986	186	Ratings	Good earning capacity; ambitious & career oriented	Good looking; Physically attractive
	Buss & Barnes	1986	100	Rankings	Good earning capacity	Physically attractive

*This sample was composed of married couples between the ages of 20 and 42. (From Buss, 1987, p. 345.)

more so than males, tend to value mates with qualities directly or indirectly related to resources.

Long-Term Mating Strategies: Men's Preferences

An overly simplified analysis of men's strategies suggests that, because they do not expend great resources in reproduction and because they have a seemingly unlimited supply of sperm, men should simply have sex with as many partners as is possible, thus relying on shear numbers of offspring to attain evolutionary success. Buss (1994, 2004) notes, however, that it was evolutionarily advantageous for men to engage in long-term mating because (1) women's strategies favor men who signal long-term commitment, (2) men willing to commit are more likely to attract higher quality mates, (3) paternity of offspring is more likely to be assured in monogamous long-term relationships, and (4) chances that offspring survive increases with committed partnership. Given the benefits of long-term mating, what qualities do men find attractive and desirable when they seek long-term mates?

According to Buss (1994), "Men evolved mechanisms to sense cues to a woman's underlying reproductive value. These clues involve observable features of females. Two obvious cues are youth and health" (p. 50). Clearly, a prepubertal girl has no reproductive value, nor does a post-menopausal woman. Early studies of mate preference (Symons, 1979; Williams, 1975) suggest that young men of marriageable age (21 years) prefer women, on average, who are 18.5 years of age. Although the exact age may vary across cultures, there appears to be a universal preference by men for women who are younger and whose ages fall within a few years of the figure cited above. The predictable exception to this rule applies to younger, teen-aged boys who express desire for *older* women—women closer to the ideal reproductive age of 18.5 years (Kenrick, Keefe, Gabrielidis, & Cornelius, 1996).

A woman is not guaranteed to be desirable simply because she is at the ideal reproductive age. Consider, again, the condition of our evolutionary ancestors. Women who were strong and healthy were more likely to be our ancestral mothers than were women who were, for whatever reasons, weakened and unhealthy. Male strategies developed, therefore, to detect signs of good health—lustrous hair, smooth skin free of sores and infection, clear and bright eyes, good muscle tone, and so on—and to find those characteristics desirable. Buss (2004) says, "Men who failed to prefer qualities that signal high fertility or reproductive value—men who preferred to marry gray-haired women with rough skin and poor muscle tone—would have had fewer offspring, and their line would eventually have died out" (p. 143). Note that these standards of female beauty transcend Western cultural norms and appear in a wide variety of societies all around the world. Nowhere have researchers found people whose cultural standards for attractiveness for women (or men, for that matter) include patchy hair, ulcerated skin, dull and opaque eyes, and deteriorated muscle tone.

In addition, Singh (1993, 2000; Singh & Young, 1995) has discovered that, although standards for ideal weight vary across cultures, there appears to be an ideal waist-to-hip ratio (WHR) for women. Women who are healthy and in reproductive prime tend to have WHR between .67 and .80. That is, their waist circumference is roughly 67 to 80 percent of the circumference of their hips. Prepubertal girls—like young boys—tend to have WHR that is closer to 1.00, and in individuals who are obese, and who are thus more susceptible to diabetes, cardiovascular diseases, and stroke, the WHR exceeds 1.00. Men tend to rate female figures with WHR of .70 as more attractive than figures with WHR of .80 or greater, regardless of cultural standards of ideal weight. Initial studies show that these preferences are replicated across different cultures (Singh & Luis, 1995).

Beyond observable physical characteristics, there are female behavioral patterns that are desirable to men. Unless our ancestral man could assure his mate's virginity at marriage and completely isolate her from potential suitors after marriage, he could never be 100 percent positive that any children born in their mating were his. Obviously, there were no DNA testing labs in our ancestral past. It would not be adaptive for a man to commit resources to a child that was not his own, nor to commit resources to a woman who was sexually active outside a mating arrangement. It follows, therefore, that women who showed signs of fidelity and commitment were more desirable than those who exhibited promiscuity, thus signaling the possibility of future promiscuity. Buss and Schmitt (1993) found that "faithfulness" and "sexual loyalty" are among the traits most highly valued by men seeking long-term relationships, and lack of previous sexual experience in a woman—a possible signal that she may not be promiscuous in the future—is also seen as highly desirable. Buss (2004) writes

> The trend for men to value chastity more than women holds up worldwide, but it varies tremendously among cultures. At one extreme, people in China, India, Indonesia, Iran, Taiwan, and the Palestinian Arab areas of Israel attach a high value to chastity in a potential mate. At the opposite extreme, people in Sweden, Norway, Finland, the Netherlands, West Germany, and France believe that virginity is largely irrelevant. (p. 152)

Long-Term Strategies: Females Attracting Males

Mating involves more than desiring certain characteristics in a prospective partner. When we discover someone who has everything we are looking for, there remains the problem of making ourselves desirable to him or her.

According to sexual selection theory, "mate preferences of one sex influence the form and content of . . . competition exhibited by the other sex" (Schmitt & Buss, 1996, p. 1186). Thus, if males desire females who are young and healthy, and who signal fidelity and commitment, it is reasonable to expect that women have evolved strategies to capitalize on those preferences. Schmitt and Buss (1996) write:

> There are two fundamental avenues for increasing romantic attractiveness. . . . The first avenue is to embody, or at least appear to embody, the characteristics preferred by the opposite sex. This form of mate competition . . . involves tactics of *self-promotion.* The second major avenue is to reduce the perceived mate value of same sex competitors. Convincing the opposite sex that one's competitor does not possess the attributes they desire enhances one's relative standing. This form of mate competition involves tactics of *competitor derogation.* (p. 1187)

In other words, a woman interested in a long-term relationship should engage in behavior that emphasizes or exaggerates her youth, vitality, and potential as a faithful mate. In a similar vein, a woman who detects a rival in competition for a desirable man will attempt to sabotage the rival's ability to communicate those same characteristics.

With respect to the strategy (or tactic) of **self-promotion,** consider the multibillion dollar businesses of cosmetics, beauty, and youth. Buss (2003) says, "Women do not compete to communicate accurate information to men. Rather, they compete to activate men's evolved psychological standards of beauty, keyed to youth and health" (p. 110). Young, healthy women have naturally full lips, clear skin, flushed cheeks, and firm muscle tone. Skillful application of makeup can reproduce many of these effects and maintain them well past sexual prime. Cosmetic surgery can remove wrinkles from aging skin and restore youthful characteristics to fading body parts. Regular attendance at health clubs provides additional benefits by restoring or maintaining muscle tone and a healthy, athletic appearance.

As we have seen, visible cues related to reproductive value are not the only female characteristics that are desired in a long-term mate. Buss (2003) suggests that

> displays of fidelity should in evolutionary terms be paramount in women's tactics of attraction. These tactics would signal that the woman is pursuing a long-term

rather than a short-term sexual goal and that she is pursuing it without deception and exclusively with one man. (p. 114)

A woman who is not sexually promiscuous and who appears selective and hard-to-get signals her future faithfulness to a prospective long-term mate, thus ensuring that she will bear his children rather than those of another man.

With respect to the tactic of **competitor derogation,** the direction is clear. A woman who wants to eliminate a rival can undermine either the competitor's attempts to display her youth and beauty or her potential fidelity, or both. Buss (2003) writes that women can shape men's perceptions of other women by pointing out their imperfections.

Women can draw attention to flaws that are otherwise unobserved or not salient, such as heavy thighs, a long nose, short fingers, and an asymmetrical face, and make them salient. . . . Knowledge that others find a woman unattractive causes a downward shift in our view of that woman's appearance. (p. 112)

Similarly, women can undermine a competitor's value as a committed and faithful mate. Effective derogation tactics include suggesting that a competitor can't be loyal, that she is already in a committed relationship, that she is bisexual, or that she is sleazy and has slept with many other men (Schmitt & Buss, 1996).

Long-Term Strategies: Males Attracting Females

Men seeking long-term relationships tend to emphasize their access to resources. Thus they may exaggerate their career potential, ambition and upward mobility, and the prestige of their college or graduate school. On the other hand, men seeking long-term mates tend not to offer *immediate* access to their wealth or resources (Buss, 2003). In order to signal their good genetic potential, strength, and the ability to provide security, men may talk about their successes in sports or casually mention that they lift weights or practice martial arts. The critical tasks for men, however, are displays of commitment. Whereas a male suitor can reveal resource potential or athletic prowess relatively quickly, it takes an investment of time to display behaviors that signal commitment. Effective long-term tactics include showing understanding of a woman's problems, remaining faithful to her, finding common interests, and showing loving devotion (Schmitt & Buss, 1996)—none of which can be accomplished during one evening at a bar.

Competitor derogation tactics follow logically. Buss (2003) says that men "counteract the attraction tactics of other men by derogating a rival's resource potential. Typically men tell women that their rivals are poor, have no money, lack ambition, and drive cheap cars" (p. 100). They may derogate a rival by making fun of his (lack of) athletic prowess, suggesting that he is clumsy, or even challenging him to an athletic contest—including the old-fashioned fistfight, thus undermining the rival's attempt to display his physical worth as a potential father and provider of security and safety. And finally, men may subvert a rival's attempt to signal commitment and fidelity. Highly effective tactics include telling a woman that the rival already has a girlfriend or wife, that he uses women, that he is bisexual, or that he is abusive toward women (Schmitt & Buss, 1996).

Short-Term Strategies, Strategic Interference, and Deception

Most students reading this text will agree that we sometimes attempt to attract others for reasons other than long-term mating and raising families. It may be the case that we merely want companionship, a date for the big event on campus, or a partner for casual sex. Buss and Schmitt's (1993) sexual strategies theory asserts that when we are seeking short-term mating arrangements, rather than long-term commitment, men's strategies will differ from women's and both will differ from typical long-term mating strategies.

If the focus is on a short-term relationship, the loyalty, fidelity, and commitment that were valuable in long-term mating are not important. In fact, a man or a woman seeking a casual sexual encounter may be dissuaded if the prospective mate shows strong signals of commitment. Although a woman who plays hard-to-get suggests future fidelity and loyalty in a long-term relationship, she may discourage a short-term suitor. Similarly, a man who wants to demonstrate devotion and long-term interest may deter a woman seeking a short-term affair. If we dispose of the loyalty, fidelity, and commitment factors, what characteristics are desirable?

Women Seeking Short-Term Mates

Sexual selection theory suggests that women will be less inclined than men to engage in short-term mating strategies. Nonetheless, there are occasions when women do seek short-term relationships, including those for purposes of casual sex. If there are fewer women than men looking for short-term mates, it follows that they can be even more selective than when in search of a long-term mate. Women who engage in short-term mating place great importance on physical attractiveness and want men who are also attractive to other women (Buss & Schmitt, 1993).

Short-term mating can be costly for women—particularly for women who are already in relationships. A number of hypotheses have been generated and supported to account for this potentially dangerous behavior. Greiling and Buss (2000) report that the goals of terminating an ongoing relationship or finding a mate who is superior to a current mate can motivate short-term mating. Gangestad and Thornhill (1997) suggest that women have short-term relationships with men who are attractive and physically symmetrical, thus suggesting that a man's "good genes" play a role in women's preferences for casual affairs. Women who seek short-term relationships appear to be more interested in quality rather than quantity of short-term matings.

Given that short-term relationships are often of a sexual nature, it follows that women will use self-promotion tactics that are highly sexualized. Women who wear sexy or revealing clothes are sometimes signaling sexual availability, and such displays are judged by men to be desirable in a short-term mate but not in a potential marriage partner (Hill, Nocks, & Gardner, 1987). In an older study of behavior in singles bars, the only female behaviors that men found more attractive than wearing sexy clothes were overtly sexual acts such as requesting sex, or, in some other manner, making a sexual advance (Allan & Fishel, 1979).

Competitor derogation tactics should undermine displays of sexuality in rivals. For example, a woman might inform a desirable man that her rival is only a tease and therefore lacks potential as a casual sex partner. Some of the most effective derogation tactics for women include suggesting that the rival has a sexually transmitted disease, that she is gay or bisexual, that she never showers, or that she is frigid (Schmitt & Buss, 1996).

Men Seeking Short-Term Mates

Men's strategies for short-term mating may be fairly easy to analyze. From a reproductive perspective, it does a woman little good to have multiple sexual partners. If she is impregnated, her sexual resources are committed for at least nine months. Sex with multiple partners cannot increase her evolutionary fitness. Men's fitness, on the other hand, may actually benefit from multiple matings. Among men who pursue short-term strategies, there is strong preference for relationships with numerous partners who consent to sex after a relatively short courtship period (Buss & Schmitt, 1993). Furthermore, data indicate that men are universally predisposed to engage in sexually oriented short-term relationships. For example, men engage in more sexual fantasy than do women and their fantasies often include sexual encounters with strangers (Ellis & Symons, 1990). When college-aged students are asked how many sexual partners they would like to have during the next month, next year, or over their lifetimes, men consistently desire more partners than do women (McBurney, Zapp, & Streeter, 2005), and they are more willing than women to have sexual intercourse after knowing a potential partner for a short period of time (Buss & Schmitt, 1993). These male–female differences in desire for sexual variety have been confirmed in surveys conducted with more than 16,000 respondents in 10 major world regions, including Africa, the Middle East, and Asia, and findings are consistent whether the respondents are married or single, heterosexual, homosexual, or bisexual (Schmitt, 2003).

In addition, males of many mammalian species are physiologically "wired" for sexual encounters with different partners. Consider the **Coolidge effect.** The term Coolidge effect was derived from a popular anecdote concerning President Coolidge and his wife.

> One day the President and Mrs. Coolidge were visiting a government farm. Soon after their arrival they were taken off on separate tours. When Mrs. Coolidge passed the chicken pens, she paused to ask the man in charge if the rooster copulates more than once each day. "Dozens of times," was the reply. "Please tell that to the President," Mrs. Coolidge requested. When the President passed the pens and was told about the rooster, he asked "Same hen every time?" "Oh, no, Mr. President, a different one each time." The President nodded slowly, then said, "Tell that to Mrs. Coolidge." (Kenrick, 1989, pp. 7–8)

Males of most species experience a *post-ejaculatory refractory period* after copulation. That is, they are incapable of engaging in sex with the same female immediately following ejaculation and require time to recover full sexual function. Technically, the Coolidge effect refers to reduction or elimination of this post-ejaculatory refractory period *when a new female partner is available.* Haselton and Buss (2001) have discovered an emotional/perceptual effect that accompanies the physiological component of the Coolidge effect. Men who engage in frequent, casual sexual encounters tend to experience a decline in attraction to their partner immediately after sexual intercourse. This phenomenon is not observed in women or in men who do not have frequent casual sex.

Given that men are evolutionarily predisposed for the sexual variety that can be found in short-term mating, what attracts them to potential mates? Because there are

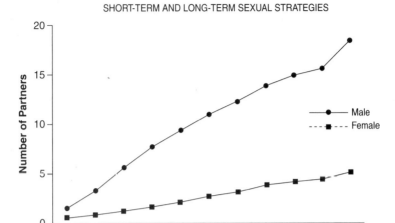

SHORT-TERM AND LONG-TERM SEXUAL STRATEGIES

Figure 12–1   *Number of sexual partners desired. (Subjects recorded in blank spaces provided how many sexual partners they would ideally like to have for each specified time interval.)*

typically more men than women seeking short-term relationships, men will frequently reduce their standards, relative to those criteria desired in a long-term mate. Here the story is not a pretty one. Buss (2003) writes, "For brief encounters, men require a lower level of such assets as charm, athleticism, education, generosity, honesty, independence, kindness, intellectuality, loyalty, sense of humor, sociability, wealth, responsibility, spontaneity, cooperativeness, and emotional stability" (p. 78). It may be the case that men seeking casual sexual relationships select partners based less on positive characteristics they possess but on their *lack* of important aversive characteristics. The characteristics that men seem to find particularly unattractive in short-term mates are "low sex drive, physical unattractiveness, need for commitment and hairiness" (p. 79).

Self-promotion tactics in short-term strategies have evolved to meet the high standards that women maintain when looking for a casual relationship. Thus, a man will exaggerate his success and confidence and engage in an immediate presentation of wealth. In the context of short-term mating, "immediate display of wealth, such as flashing money, buying a woman gifts, or taking her out to an expensive restaurant on the first date, proves more effective for attracting casual sex partners than long-term mates" (Buss, 2003, p.100).

Competitor derogation tactics typically focus on the sexual worth of a competitor. Highly rated tactics include suggesting that a rival might be gay or bisexual, that he has a sexually transmitted disease, or that he is in a serious relationship and is thus not "on the market" for a short-term relationship (Schmitt & Buss, 1996).

Strategic Interference

We have examined long-term strategies, short-term strategies, self-promotion tactics, and competitor derogation tactics. With all of these adaptive strategies afoot, there are many occasions for confusion. What happens when a man who is seeking a short-term mate is attracted to a woman who wants long-term commitment? The result is an evolutionary conflict that Buss calls **strategic interference.** Strategic interference occurs when "a person employs a particular strategy to achieve a goal and another person blocks or prevents the successful enactment of that strategy or the fulfillment of the desire" (Buss, 2004, p. 312).

Women, more often than men, desire commitment and long-term relationships. Because men, more often than women, look for short-term matings or casual sex, their purposes are often at odds with the strategies of the women they pursue. The result is that men want to accelerate the sexual aspect of a relationship, while women delay sex and look for signals of commitment. Thus, male strategies interfere with female strategies, and vice versa. Of course, the opposite may be true. A woman seeking a short-term, sexually casual fling might encounter a desirable man who is looking for love. Once again, the result will be strategic interference.

An interesting offshoot of the theory of strategic interference concerns our attempts to derogate competitors. Consider a scenario in which a man seeks a casual encounter. One woman, attracted to him as a potential long-term mate, senses that another woman is a rival for his affection and attention. She attempts to derogate her rival by pointing out that the rival is "easy" and that she is sexually adventurous. While such derogation tactics would be quite successful *if* the man was seeking a mother for his children, in this case the man can only feel overwhelmed by his good fortune.

Deception

"Some men are cads. . . . Other men are dads. . . ." (Buss, 2003, p. 23). It is a woman's problem to discriminate between the two. The most likely conflict between sexes is between a man who is looking for a casual sexual encounter and a woman who is looking for commitment. It is in this area that men are likely to adopt deception as a tactic. Buss (2003) writes that men "deceive women by feigning an interest in commitment to achieve a quick sexual gain. Men also feign confidence, status, kindness, and resources that they lack for the goal of brief encounters" (p. 121). It is costly for women to be deceived by such tactics if they are looking for long-term mates. Buss notes that women have evolved strategies to detect deception. Typically, a woman looking for a long-term relationship will impose "courtship costs" (p. 155) on a potential mate. She will take longer to assess his characteristics, evaluate his levels of commitment and loyalty, and judge his intentions before consenting to sex. Men looking only for a casual encounter are not likely to pay these costs.

While men deceive about commitment, women deceive about sexual availability. Buss (2003) cites the results of a survey of college women:

> When 104 college women were asked how often they flirted with a man to get something they wanted . . . knowing that they did not want to have sex with him, they gave it on average a frequency of 3 on a 4-point scale, where 3 signified "sometimes" and 4 signified "often". . . . Women gave similar responses to questions about using sexual hints to gain favors and attention, yet admitted they had no intention of having sex with the targets of these hints. Women admit to being sexual deceivers part of the time. (p. 154)

Given that it is costly for women or men to fall for deception, evolutionary psychologists propose that we have evolved a mechanism to detect cheating and deception, a topic to which we will return shortly. Buss (2003) concludes

The modern generation is merely one more cycle in the endless spiral of an evolutionary arms race between deception perpetrated by one sex and detection accomplished by the other. As the deceptive tactics get more subtle, the ability to penetrate deception becomes more refined. (p. 155)

Love and Jealousy

Let's assume the best: A man and woman have navigated strategic interference and traps of deception. They are enjoying what may be a long-term relationship.

> Tremendous benefits flow to couples who remain committed. From this unique alliance comes . . . a division of labor, a sharing of resources, a unified front against mutual enemies, a stable home environment for rearing children, and a more extended kin network. To reap these benefits, people must be able to retain the mates they have won. (Buss, 2003, p. 123)

Retaining a mate is not an easy task. According to the National Center for Health Statistics (2002), 40 percent of marriages in the United States end in divorce. (Statistics on long-term relationships not involving traditional marriage are not kept in systematic ways, but failure rates are most likely comparable.) It should be noted that although 60 percent of married couples in the United States remain married, that does not necessarily mean that those 60 percent maintain a satisfactory long-term relationship or continue living together. There are many reasons why couples may choose to maintain an unsatisfactory marriage, for example, concern for children, pressure from friends and relatives, and religious convictions.

Although divorce rates vary considerably across cultures, provisions for divorce and its occurrence appear to be universal. Unfortunately, reasons for failure of long-term relationships are not stated in evolutionary psychological terms. For example, most marital failures in the United States are recorded as vague "irreconcilable differences." Hidden in those irreconcilable differences are many conflicts: Couples may disagree about fundamental values, family decision making, childrearing, financial matters, and sex. Certainly, a number of relationships fail because one or both partners have sexual and/or emotional encounters with others; they cheat. With all the possibilities for the collapse of relationships, what mechanisms have evolved to hold them together?

One solution is **love.** Given that love and kindness are primary characteristics desired in a long-term mate, it only makes sense that one rekindles behaviors signaling love and kindness when a valued relationship begins to dissolve. Buss (1988) reports that both men and women use increased displays of love and kindness in order to keep a mate, although this tactic is more effective when performed by men than by women. Love, however, presents a quandary for evolutionary psychology. Buss (2000) writes:

> More than in any other domain . . . we expect evolution to produce supremely rational mechanisms of mate choice, rational in the sense that they lead to wise decisions rather than impetuous mistakes. How could a blind passion like love—a form of dementia that consumes the mind, crowds out all other thoughts, creates emotional dependency, and produces delusional idealization of a partner—possibly evolve to solve a problem that might be better solved by cool rationality? (p. 10)

The answer seems to be that irrational love is superior to a rational alternative. First, consider the quality of relationships we might have if "cool" rationality dictated mating behavior. A woman might keep an unconscious spreadsheet on which she records important characteristics of her mate. For example, a man with good resources, athletic prowess, and strong commitment gets high marks; but what happens as he ages, becomes less athletic, reaches his career peak, and loses earning potential? Worse yet, what happens if the woman checks her spreadsheet and notes that the best man at her wedding is truly the best man? Buss (2000) argues that the blind irrationality of love facilitates commitment and prevents the kind of mate-switching that might occur if mating and business accounting followed similar practices. He says that

> if the person is blinded by an uncontrollable love that cannot be helped and cannot be chosen, a love for only you and no other, then commitment will not waver when you are in sickness rather than in health, when you are poorer rather than richer. Love overrides rationality. (p. 11)

Unfortunately, love, being irrational, is not stable. Most, if not all, of those individuals in the 40 percent of couples who married but then divorced would claim that they were in love when they became engaged, took their wedding vows, and began their honeymoons. No doubt, some significant number of those individuals felt nothing like love as divorce proceedings concluded. For the 60 percent who remained married, most, if not all, would agree that love changed over time, that it was not the same dementia it was at its outset. Something other than irrational "blind passion" must be at work to maintain those relationships.

According to Buss (2000), and contrary to conventional thinking, **jealousy** is an evolutionary adaptation that protects long-term relationships. Jealousy is often condemned, in clichéd terms, as the "green-eyed monster," an immature sense of possession, or a form of psychopathology. Buss recognizes that there are occasions when jealousy motivates abuse, violence, or even murder, but he contends that jealousy evolved as a means of protecting a long-term mating arrangement.

In support of this argument, Buss and his colleagues begin with a decision analysis, called signal detection theory, which is applied to a number of perceptual and diagnostic problems (see, e.g., Swets, Dawes, & Monahan, 2000; Tanner & Swets, 1954). Consider the following signal detection problem: You are in your apartment and smell smoke. It could be the case that the building is on fire, or it could be that a neighbor has (harmlessly) burned dinner. You have two choices: You can run from the building into the cold rain, or you can ignore the smoke and stay inside. If you run from your apartment, and it turns out that the building is indeed burning, your life is spared. If you flee and it turns out that the smoke is only a ruined dinner, you are only inconvenienced. Consider the outcomes if you stay in your apartment and ignore the smoke. If the smoke is only a burned dinner, you get to stay comfortably inside, but you actually gain nothing. On the other hand, if you ignore the smoke and the building is ablaze, costs could include serious injury or death.

Formal signal detection theory analyzes factors that make you run outside (whether or not the building is actually ablaze), and it focuses on the trade-offs between running outside and saving your life (a correct positive response) and mistakenly running out and only experiencing inconvenience (a false-positive response). In a subtle shift, **error management theory (EMT)** (Haselton & Buss, 2000; Haselton, Buss, &

DeKay, 1998) focuses primarily on errors in judgment. Specifically, it examines error costs in the case where there is a fire that you mistakenly ignore (false-negative response) versus error costs when there is no fire and you mistakenly run out into the cold rain (false-positive response). Clearly, the costs can be great if we make the former error, but they are often inconsequential in the second. Ancient men and women who responded to smoke by fleeing were more likely to be our ancestors than those who ignored it. Thus, according to EMT, we have evolved strategies to minimize error costs.

In the context of jealousy, there are numerous clues that might signal a mate's infidelity. For example, your mate might start dressing more attractively, join a health club to lose a few pounds, get a fashionable new hairstyle, or take tango lessons at the community center. These signals are the "smoke" in the air. It could be the case that these behaviors are meaningless diversions, and your relationship is sound—perhaps soon to improve. Alternatively, they could be signals that your mate is thinking of cheating or is already having an affair. Now, consider the costs of decision errors. On one hand, if you err with jealousy, but your mate is only engaged in meaningless diversions, the costs are low. Your jealousy might even signal that you are concerned, loyal, and committed. On the other hand, if you ignore these signals, and your mate is drifting away, the costs could be substantial. Better to make the error with fewer costs. Thus, jealousy can be an adaptive, preemptive strategy that preserves the benefits of long-term mating.

As he did with mating strategies, Buss (2000; Buss, Larsen, Westen, & Semmelroth, 1992), examines sex differences in jealousy. He dismisses, however, the common stereotype that men are simply more jealous than women. From an evolutionary psychology perspective, there is no reason to predict global sex differences in the occurrence of overall jealousy. Buunk and Hupka (1987), for example, reported that men and women from a variety of cultures, including Mexico, Ireland, Russia, and the United States, show comparable levels of jealousy. Rather, sex differences are expected with respect to the kinds of events that induce jealousy.

Men should be more jealous if his mate's reproductive resources are at stake; women should be more jealous if her mate's material (or emotional-supportive) resources are at stake. If a woman cheats on her loyal mate, a child she bears may not be his. The man loses in an evolutionary sense because (1) he has not reproduced and (2) he expends his emotional and material resources helping to perpetuate another man's genes. If a man is cheating on his loyal mate, a child his mate bears will, obviously, be hers; but if her mate is channeling supportive assets elsewhere, she and her child may lose those resources. Thus, men should be more jealous when a mate has a sexual affair. Women, on the other hand, should be more jealous when a mate devotes resources outside the primary relationship.

When asked to chose which kind of cheating would cause greater distress, twice as many women as men reported emotional infidelity to be more upsetting while approximately three times as many men as women found sexual infidelity to be more disturbing (Buss et al., 1992). Using this forced-choice method, these sex differences have been replicated in Germany, the Netherlands, Korea, and Japan (Buss, Larsen, & Westen, 1996; Buss et al., 1999). Other experiments have challenged these findings, suggesting that they result from the use of the forced-choice procedure, but the challenges do not resolve the issue. C. R. Harris (2000), for example, found that men and women, both heterosexual and homosexual, are most distressed about *emotional* infidelity when they recalled actual incidents of cheating by mates.

DeSteno, Bartlett, Braverman, and Salovey (2002) report that both men and women are most distressed about *sexual* infidelity when they imagine cheating by mates. The most consistent results, however, replicate and extend the sex differences in jealousy found by Buss and his colleagues (e.g., Pietrzak, Laird, Stevens, & Thompson, 2002; Schützwohl, 2004, 2005; Schützwohl & Koch, 2004).

Altruism, Inclusive Fitness, and Social Groups

In the play *No Exit,* by Jean Paul Sartre, a character called Garcin declares that "Hell is other people" (*"l'enfer, c'est les autres"*). Indeed, other people request unreasonable favors, make promises they fail to keep, play music too loudly late at night, and ignore our discomfort. Despite these annoyances, however, we seem to seek the company of others, even when we should know better. Baumeister and Leary (1995) suggest that, because groups rather than solitary individuals were often more successful in hunting, foraging, and defense, the tendency to seek and belong to a group is a fundamental evolutionary adaptation. They say:

> The likely result of this evolutionary selection would be a set of internal mechanisms that guide individual human beings into social groups and lasting relationships. These mechanisms would presumably include a tendency to orient toward other members of the species, a tendency to feel affective distress when deprived of social contact or relationships, and a tendency to feel pleasure of positive affect from social contact and relatedness. (p. 499)

As we have seen, and will see again, other personality theorists recognize the importance of the human tendency toward belongingness (e.g., Erikson, Chapter 6; Maslow, Chapter 15). In the following, however, we explore the evolutionary psychology perspective on social behavior, which emphasizes the conflict between the individual's struggle for survival and coexistence with larger social groups.

Parenting as Altruism

Of particular interest to evolutionary psychologists is the phenomenon of **altruism.** In general, altruism is defined as behavior that risks our resources, including our own physical safety, to benefit others. Of course, altruistic behavior varies in both quality and quantity. A firefighter who runs into a burning building to save a stranger may be behaving altruistically. A wealthy individual who donates food to a homeless shelter might also be described as altruistic. Both behaviors risk personal resources to benefit others, but they differ in the immediacy of their effects, in level of resource-risk, and in numerous other ways. For evolutionary psychology the question is why a person would extend any benefits whatsoever to another individual.

Tiger (1979) noted that being a parent entails sacrificing time and resources in "a set of radically unselfish and often incomprehensibly inconvenient activities" (p. 96). From a simple Darwinian perspective, survival and reproduction are the basics of evolutionary success. Sharing *my* food, water, and shelter puts me at risk, even if I am sharing it with members of my family. In 2000, the USDA estimated that the cost of raising one child to the age of 17 was more than $160,000, and that cost is not expected to decrease in the future. This represents an "altruistic" contribution to one child that is between two and four times the median family income (for a family of four), depending on your state of residence. Note that estimates like these do not include the emotional costs of caring for a sick child, stresses incurred while explaining human sexuality or teaching your child how to drive, nor contributions to college tuition. Why should a person expend extensive amounts and types of resources on offspring—even after they have reached an age at which they can struggle to survive on their own?

One part of the answer is found in the neo-Darwinian principle of inclusive fitness (evolutionary fitness involves perpetuating our own genes either by reproduction or by helping those to whom we are biologically related). Helping those who share our genes is called **kin selection** (or **kin altruism**). **Hamilton's rule** (Hamilton, 1964) tells us that we will risk or sacrifice resources for another based on a genetic **cost–benefit analysis.** First, we should risk our resources only when the genetic benefit is greater than the cost of our risky action. Second, we consider benefit on the basis of genes that the altruistic actor and the recipient of the altruistic act have in common. Specifically, the rule says that we will share or risk resources when

$$rB > C \text{ AND:}$$
$$B = \text{THE } \textit{BENEFIT} \text{ GAINED BY THE RECIPIENT OF THE ACT}$$
$$C = \text{THE } \textit{COST} \text{ INCURRED BY THE ACTOR}$$
$$r = \text{THE } \textit{PROPORTION} \text{ OF GENES SHARED BY THE ACTOR AND THE}$$
$$\text{RECIPIENT OF THE ALTRUISTIC ACT}$$

In the most simple and selfish case, consider an act that one does for one's own good. Because the actor and recipient are the same person, $r = 1.00$. That is, genetic correspondence between actor and recipient is 100 percent. Hamilton's rule suggests that we are likely to act on our own behalf even when the benefit of the act is barely greater than the cost. Thus, the probability of acting selfishly is always quite high. A child has one-half of the genes of its parent, so $r = .50$. This means that the benefit of sacrificing for a child must be more than twice the cost to the parent. We are therefore less likely to act for our children than for ourselves, and Hamilton's rule suggests that, unless the benefit-to-cost ratio is large, we will not extend an unselfish parental act. Thus, parents sacrifice resources for their child's health, safety, and education, but they are less likely to do so to promote their child's popularity with peers. If we consider other relatives in the equation, we begin to see the sense of Hamilton's rule. Our brothers, sisters, and parents also share 50 percent of our genes, but nieces, nephews, uncles, aunts, and grandparents share only 25 percent of our genes. For these latter individuals, the rule suggests that the benefit of an act must be more than four times the cost if we are to risk our resources on their behalf. Thus, we are most likely to act for ourselves, next for our offspring and immediate family, next for more distant relatives, and last for individuals with whom we are not biologically related. The fewer genes we share with another individual, the less likely we are to put ourselves or resources at risk, and the logic of Hamilton's rule tells us that the likelihood of an altruistic act for an unrelated individual is, for all practical purposes, zero. Spouses often sacrifice resources for each other, but, in the best case, they do not share a significant number of genes. Thus, Hamilton's rule falls short of explaining all altruistic behavior. Altruism between individuals who are not biologically related is addressed shortly.

Sex Differences

In order for people to engage in kin selection, there must be mechanisms by which they can recognize relatives, including their children, as carriers of their genes. Sex differences in parenting are believed to arise partly because men and women must rely on different kinds of cues to solve the problem of parental uncertainty. Buss (1998) notes that, in the evolution of modern humans, women could be very sure that a child she bore was her own (pp. 415–416). It is only recently, however, with the availability of DNA testing, that a man can be sure of his paternity. Because a woman has carried and delivered a child, she knows it is hers (except in the case of "surrogate mothers"). Therefore it should be the case that, on average, she is more likely than a man to sacrifice time, energy, and resources in parental behaviors. This does not mean that men cannot and do not sacrifice for their children. It does suggest, however, that they tend to rely on other cues of shared genes, such as physical appearance, that are less compelling than those utilized by a mother (Krebs, 1998). One strategy to resolve the uncertainty faced by the father, and thus to increase the likelihood that he will devote resources to an infant, is for the mother (and her relatives) to point out physical similarities between him and the new baby and to comment less on the resemblance between the mother and the baby. Studies with both Canadian (Daly & Wilson, 1982) and Mexican (Regalski & Gaulin, 1993) samples have documented this phenomenon. Father–child resemblance, whether real or imagined, may well increase a father's involvement in parental behavior. For example, Apicella and Marlowe (2004) report that fathers are willing to invest more in children when perceived resemblance is high and when they believe their wives have been faithful. Although they are less willing to invest resources if divorced or separated, fathers are still willing to invest more in those children who resemble them than in those who do not. Furthermore, although they can and do serve as good fathers for children that are not biologically related to them, studies from the United States, South Africa, and Tanzania suggest that men are more likely to devote money, instruction, and play time to (purported) biological children than to stepchildren (Anderson, Kaplan, Lam, & Lancaster, 1999; Anderson, Kaplan, & Lancaster, 1999; Marlow, 1999). As we will see, serious problems can arise when families include children that are not biologically related to parents.

Reciprocal Altruism

Xenophobia is the fear or distrust of strangers (or foreigners), and its evolutionary explanation is straightforward. Unless ancient humans had abundant food, water, and shelter, it was likely that outsiders were competitors for those resources. In most cases, those who readily gave up foraging and hunting grounds and other resources to others did not thrive and were not our ancestors. From this perspective, an inclination to be distrustful of those who are different from us is predisposed by our evolutionary heritage. Here again, care must be taken when discussing inherited predispositions. Hergenhahn and Olson (2005) write:

> In xenophobia one may see a natural inclination toward prejudice. Two important cautions are necessary here. First, according to evolutionary psychologists, to observe that a tendency is natural (has a biological origin) does not mean that the tendency is necessarily good. To assume that what is natural is good is to commit the

naturalistic fallacy. Second, the evolutionary psychologists do not say that humans are "hard wired" to act in certain ways. (p. 439)

Many of us are victims of the naturalistic fallacy: Advertisers may tell us that a new breakfast cereal "is *organic,* is natural, and therefore good." On the other hand, arsenic, rabies, and hurricanes are natural but not necessarily good. Fear of strangers or territorial defense that erupt into warfare might be natural as evolved adaptations, but there are many instances when such tendencies would be immediately maladaptive. Also, as we have seen, humans may have a natural inclination toward prejudice but, in most cases, such an inclination is seen as undesirable (see Allport's insightful discussion of prejudice in Chapter 7). Fortunately, our behavior is not simply reflexive or instinctive. Even strongly predisposed behaviors can be modified by prevailing environmental conditions (e.g., availability of resources) and by what one has been taught about sharing.

When we extend resources to risk our safety for others to whom we are not biologically related, including strangers, it is called **reciprocal altruism** (Axelrod & Hamilton, 1981; Trivers, 1971; Williams, 1966). The key here is "reciprocity," and once again we see an intuitive, cost–benefit analysis. Cosmides and Tooby (1997) refer to this as the "I'll scratch your back if you scratch mine" principle. Buss (1995) notes that

> tremendous benefits can accrue to individuals who form cooperative reciprocal relationships. . . . Costs are incurred that provide a larger benefit to someone else; at some later time, the recipient of the initial benefit bestows a benefit on the initial giver. Both individuals can gain by this process above and beyond what they could have gained by acting alone. Indeed, humans seem to have reached something of a pinnacle of reciprocal alliance formation. . . . (p. 17)

This principle helps—at least in part—to explain altruism between spouses. Shared reciprocities can be an important bonding factor in a mating relationship, given that mates must work together to survive and to raise children, and they share few, if any, genes. Note, however, that spouses may also extend resources to each other in what evolutionary psychologists call "mating effort." That is, reciprocal altruism aside, they may still exchange favors in the process of securing their mate's attention, sexual contact, and fidelity.

Darwin was well aware of the fact that individuals can and often do participate in group activities to enhance their survival. In *The Descent of Man,* Darwin (1871) wrote:

> There can be no doubt that a tribe including many members who, from possessing in a high degree the spirit of patriotism, fidelity, obedience, courage and sympathy, were always ready to aid one another, and to sacrifice themselves for the common good, would be victorious over most other tribes; and this would be natural selection. (p. 203)

Cooperative behavior is common in both work and casual organizations, but it raises an interesting problem.

Imagine that we have an informal student lounge. It includes a dispenser that provides coffee, hot cocoa, hot water, and so on; and everything operates on the "honor" system. There is no established price for coffee or hot chocolate, but users are encouraged to "feed the kitty," to contribute a little money each week to maintain the operation. Given that there is no formal supervision of the lounge, it is possible that one or more individuals may cheat. **Cheating** in this context involves consuming more than one's share of benefits, paying less than one's share of costs, or both. It is even possible for one or more members to drink as much as they want and *never* make a contribution. Obviously, it is to the individual's advantage to cheat, but if everyone cheats, the entire system will fail. In the same sense, among our hunter-gatherer ancestors, it may have been individually advantageous to cheat—perhaps to eat heartily at communal meals but contribute little or nothing in hunting and gathering efforts. As in our coffee lounge example, the spread of cheating in our hunter-gatherer band would mean its failure. Given the potential catastrophic effects of cheating, we anticipate a number of adaptations to prevent its occurrence.

The problem of actually *detecting* cheaters is a central issue in Cosmides and Tooby's (1992) *Social Contract Theory*. They suggest that humans have evolved a number of cognitive abilities, including abilities to understand costs, benefits, and exchanges, and to detect individuals who violate rules of reciprocity. Furthermore, these abilities operate readily in the domain of social reciprocity, but they are strained and awkward when removed from their "natural" context. For example, many psychology students have seen some version of the following problem, paraphrased from Wason (1966):

> There are four cards in front of you, each with a letter on one side and a single digit on the other, but, for now, you can only see one side of each card. You are told that the "rule" about these cards is:
> *If a card has a vowel on one side, then there is an even number on the other side.*
>   The card "faces" you see are
>   **A, B, 4,** and **7.**
> Your task is to turn only the cards you would need to turn to determine if the rule stated above is true.

Most people choose the A and the 4, believing that, if there is an even number on the other side of the A and a vowel on the other side of the 4, the rule is true (or that violations of either of these proves it false). The correct solution, unfortunately, is to turn the A and the 7: If there is an even number opposite the A, the rule is true (otherwise false); and, if there is a vowel opposite the 7, the rule is false. The other cards, B and 4, actually provide no relevant information concerning the hypothetical rule.

In numerous studies (e.g., Cosmides, 1985, 1989; Cosmides & Tooby, 1989, 1992), people readily solve this kind of problem if it is posed in terms of cheating rather than as an abstract reasoning problem. From our coffee lounge above, our rule can be "If you drink coffee, cocoa, etc. (vowel), then you have paid your weekly contribution (even number). The people we encounter in the lounge are either drinking coffee (vowel) or not (consonant). They have either paid their share (even number) or not (odd number). Now, who do you question to determine if the drink-if-you-pay rule is followed? If you are like most people, you examine the coffee drinkers (vowel) and the non-payers (odd number). Suddenly the card-turning task is simplified. These cheater-detection abilities are observed in other cultures (Cosmides & Tooby, 1997; Sugiyama, Tooby, & Cosmides, 1995), and they are conspicuously absent in individuals with specific types of brain damage (Stone, Cosmides, Tooby, Kroll, &

Knight, 2002), even when these brain-injured patients can perform other types of reasoning tasks. Cosmides and Tooby (1992) conclude that "human reasoning is well designed for detecting violations of conditional rules when these can be interpreted as cheating on a social contract" (p. 205).

Dysfunctional Behavior

Many of the theories we have presented place great importance on anxiety, neuroses, and dysfunctional behavior. So far, in our treatment of evolutionary psychology, we have seen that people seek mates and sometimes find them, secure mates and sometimes lose them, sacrifice to raise children, and give of themselves to help others—pretty much the behavior of normal, everyday life. Evolutionary psychologists recognize that we also engage in self-destructive behaviors, kill each other both individually and in large groups, and suffer from debilitating and sometimes fatal cognitive and emotional disorders. From an evolutionary psychological perspective, dysfunctional behavior occurs because evolved psychological mechanisms fail to activate appropriately. In the sections that follow, we examine evolutionary psychological perspectives on less frequent and sometimes darker sides of human behavior, with particular attention to a mechanism dysfunction that Buss (2004, p. 400) calls **context failure.** This term refers to activation of an evolved mechanism by stimuli or situations other than those for which it evolved. The result is that behavior is not suited to the environment or context in which it is expressed and may therefore be socially inappropriate, dangerous, or self-destructive.

Suicide

There is no behavior that more effectively terminates individual evolutionary fitness than suicide. One would expect that, over many generations, any heritable tendency toward suicide would be eliminated from the gene pool. Yet, according to the World Health Organization, suicide rates are robust from Albania to Zimbabwe (data on the Middle East and North Africa are incomplete), with men leading the way by more than a three-to-one margin.

Serious psychiatric disorders often precede suicidal ideation and behavior (e.g., Gili-Planas, Roca-Bennasar, Ferrer-Perez, Bernardo, & Arroyo, 2001; Harkavy-Friedman, Nelson, Venarde, & Mann, 2004), but this is not always the case. De Catanzaro (1987), for example, offers an explanation for suicide based on principles of inclusive fitness. His account may explain why an individual who is *not* suffering major depression, for example, attempts or commits suicide. De Catanzaro proposes a cost–benefit approach in which an individual's potential reproductive (and inclusive fitness) benefits, relative to costs that he or she imposes on kin, are extremely important. Simply, if one provides no benefits and incurs great costs from (related) others, suicide may indirectly assist those kin by relieving them of their obligation. De Catanzaro writes:

> In fact, to the extent that postreproductive or nonreproductive individuals consumed resources that otherwise would be available to potential reproducing kin,

their self-preservation could actually have adverse effects upon their inclusive fitnesses. . . . Wherever the continued existence of one individual impedes the reproduction of close kin . . . more than it enhances the reproduction of the individual himself, self-destructiveness is at least theoretically possible. (p. 317)

Logically, this hypothesis excludes those who have not yet reached reproductive age, and De Catanzaro points out that suicide is rare in children under the age of 14. Similarly, it excludes those who may still reproduce, and he notes that individuals in healthy marriages are less likely to commit suicide than are social isolates or individuals that are divorced or widowed.

One of the best predictors of true suicidal intent are feelings of hopelessness and desperation. In a follow-up to De Catanzaro's (1987) analysis, Brown, Dahlen, Mills, Rick, and Biblarz (1999) report that one's perceived failure to benefit relatives is the best predictor of feelings of hopelessness and depressed mood, and is thereby linked to suicidal behavior. Of course, a number of other variables moderate suicidal ideation. For example, we may be less likely to feel hopeless and, in turn, suicidal if our condition does not threaten inclusive fitness, for example, when kin upon whom we rely are themselves incapable of reproducing.

Murder

No psychological theory completely explains why one person kills another, with the possible exception of killing in the context of war. The evolutionary perspective, however, does help to explain some of the consistent patterns in murder. First, evolutionary psychologists reject the idea that homicide represents either psychopathology or failure of some psychological control mechanism that, under normal circumstances, prevents violent behavior. Daly and Wilson (1997) write that violence "cannot in general be explained as a maladaptive byproduct of such failures since people and other animals possess complex psychophysiological machinery that is clearly designed *for* the production and regulation of violence" (p. 57). Second, these authors point out that violence, including violent behavior resulting in homicide, is context specific. That is, it is most often provoked by threats to resources or sexual reproduction. (Perhaps because this is the typical context for murder, seemingly random murders provide both horror and fascination in novels and films.) If competition for resources or reproduction is an important contextual factor in homicide, we would expect that homicides will be committed more often during late adolescence and young adulthood, the years during which competition for mates peaks. This pattern is exactly what Wilson and Daly (1994) found in samples from Chicago, Canada, England, and Wales. Third, there are dramatic sex differences in the expression of violence. Noting that murder is typically between same-sex acquaintances or mere strangers (rather than family members), Daly and Wilson (1997) add that "men kill unrelated men at rates vastly higher than women kill unrelated women, everywhere" (p. 69). These sex differences are observed whether we examine murder rates in Botswana, Chicago, India, Scotland, or Uganda.

The propensity for male violence is, no doubt, influenced by enculturation, hormones, and many other variables. One factor that has interested evolutionary psychologists is related to sexual selection (females tend to choose males rather than vice versa) and subsequent influences on risk-taking and competitive behavior. Because females are courted and males are chosen, females are likely to reproduce, but their reproduction rate is limited. In women, reproductive rate is, on average, one child per year for a limited number of years, and this is true of all women. Some men (the "duds") will court and never succeed, thus their reproductive rate will be zero. Other men (the "dads") will have children with one mate only and will thus match her low reproductive rate. Still others (the "cads") will have several children each with a number of different women. This disparity between the nonreproducing and the multiply reproducing males is called **reproductive variance.** Daly and Wilson (2001) say that high reproductive variance "generally entails both a bigger prize for winning and a greater likelihood of failure, both of which may exacerbate competitive effort and risk acceptance" (p. 8). **Effective polygyny** refers to greater reproductive variability in males than in females. In other mammals and primates, effective polygyny leads to fierce competition among males—including a propensity to engage in risky behaviors—in order to gain access to mates and mate-attracting resources. Therefore, one factor contributing to the sex differences in homicide may be evolutionarily predisposed male tendencies to compete with other males and to take extreme risks. In this view, the potential for male violence may be an adaptation that was useful and even celebrated in our ancestral history but that is inappropriate in contemporary life.

Homicide within Families

The evolutionary psychological perspective tells us who is most likely to commit homicide, and it also tells us who is most likely to be the victim. The benevolent side of inclusive fitness is kin altruism; and, as mentioned above, victims of male-on-male or female-on-female murder are most likely to be acquaintances or strangers rather than family members. (See Figure 12–3.)

The principles of inclusive fitness, therefore, suggest a measure of security for our kin. Daly and Wilson found that murder is more than twenty times more likely to be committed against a spouse (usually a nongenetic relative) or an unrelated individual than against one's child, parents, or other genetic relatives. Summarizing data from a variety of cultures, they write,

> Close genetic relationships are far more prevalent among collaborators in violence than among victim and killer. . . . Even in patrilineal social systems, in which brothers are one another's principal rivals for familial lands and titles, there is evidence that close genealogical relationship softens otherwise equivalent conflicts and reduces the incidence of violence. . . . Familial solidarity cannot be reduced to a mere consequence of proximity and familiarity. (1998, p. 440)

A troubling implication of inclusive fitness and Hamilton's rule concerns the relationships between stepparents and their children. Pinker (1997) writes, "The stepparent has shopped for a spouse, not a child; the child is a cost that comes as part of the deal" (p. 433). Daly and Wilson (1998) pose the problem in the following way:

> It is adaptive and normal for genetic parents to accept nontrivial risks to their own lives in caring for their young, but selection presumably favors much lower thresholds of tolerable cost in stepparenting. . . . Little wonder, then, that the exploitation and mistreatment of stepchildren is a thematic staple of folk tales all around the world. (p. 441)

Figure 12–2

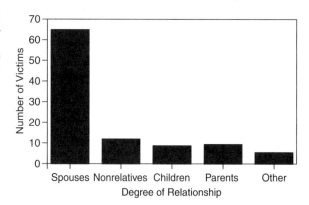

Homicide among cohabitants in Detroit, 1972. Summarized from Daly & Wilson (1982).

But are these only folktales? Are stepchildren really more likely than genetic children to be selected as targets of violence? The answer is "yes." In studies of homicides in Canada between 1974 and 1990, Daly and Wilson (1988, 1994) found that children, particularly those between birth and five years of age, were between 50 and 100 times more likely to be killed by a stepparent than by a genetic parent. Similarly, Buss notes that "Child abuse is 40 times greater among preschoolers in step families than in 'intact' families in which there are two genetic parents" (p. 8).

Psychological Disorders

Addiction

Humans ingest a dizzying array of mood-altering substances. We smoke the leaves or flowers of plants, sniff the aerosols of paints and glues, snort or inject numerous processed chemicals, and drink any number of fermented or distilled beverages. Some of these substances, such as soft drinks containing caffeine, are relatively harmless; others, like methamphetamine or heroin, are potentially deadly. Many people experiment with legal (tobacco and alcohol) or illegal (marijuana, cocaine, etc.) substances without developing patterns of habitual use. For others, however, experimentation leads to frequent use, and eventually to addiction. Here the issue becomes extraordinarily complex. Professionals who study addiction disagree on definitions of terms like "drug abuse," "drug dependence," and "drug addiction." To further complicate the problem, there are addictions to gambling, sex, and thrill seeking, none of which necessarily involve drugs or alcohol but any of which can be as disruptive as addiction to chemical substances (Shaffer, 2005). The literature on addiction and its treatments is too large to be addressed here. Rather, we attempt to develop an evolutionary perspective on addiction to substances, rather than to activities like sex or gambling, in light of current theory and research.

Our hominid ancestors did not have access to distilled alcohol, crack cocaine, or cigarettes. What they did have, however, was an evolving midbrain system that served an important biological function. Specifically, most mammals, including humans, have a set of brain circuits specialized to stimulate feelings of need (craving) and behavioral striving for biologically significant substances. This neural circuitry does not mediate pleasure sensations associated with food, water, or sex as was once thought; but it does match specific substances with specific need-states and underlies drives to attain those substances (Berridge & Robinson, 1995; Robinson & Berridge, 2000, 2003; Salamone & Correa, 2002). This system evolved to signal the vital importance of biological reinforcers, things that were, and still are, imperative for our survival. Nesse (2002) says that substances like cocaine "arouse reward mechanisms artificially, thus stimulating the circuits that are normally fired by an event that provides a huge gain in fitness; but they provide no fitness gain, they simply create an illusion" (p. 470). Indeed, what all addictive substances seem to have in common is that they have gained counterfeit access to the circuitry of our reward-craving system (Leshner & Koob, 1999; Nestler & Malenka, 2004).

A relatively recent hypothesis suggests that ethanol (alcohol resulting from yeast-fermentation of fruit sugars) is the original, evolutionary, "gateway" drug. Natural fermentation occurs in ripe fruit, which has more nutritional value than unripe fruit. Dudley (2000, 2002) points out that the aroma of alcohol thereby provides cues to the best fruit nutrition sources. Second, alcohol acts to stimulate appetite, thus increasing food consumption and nutritional intake. Finally, there are additional calories in ethanol itself, once again promoting nutrition. (Keep in mind that our ancient ancestors did not worry about losing a few pounds to look good at the beach.) Dudley tentatively suggests that modern humans are predisposed to consume alcohol because our ancestors developed feeding strategies attuned to the nutritional cues of ethanol. Because alcohol was associated with natural reinforcers, which had legitimate access to our reward-craving circuits, it also arouses those circuits. Thus, addiction to alcohol may be an unfortunate byproduct of a valuable, nutrition-related adaptation.

Dudley's ethanol hypothesis does not attempt to explain how we acquired addictions to nicotine, opium, amphetamines, or the myriad substances that humans use and abuse. We may never know the full evolutionary history of addiction; but by the Neolithic period (8500–4000 BC), humans were well beyond a naive fascination with ripening fruit. Many cultures had refined the skills necessary to make wine and Babylonian and Egyptian cultures were brewing numerous varieties of beer. Since that time, we have gained considerable expertise in deceiving our biological, reward-craving circuitry with substances that provide no fitness benefits whatsoever.

Anorexia Nervosa

Anorexia nervosa (AN) is a puzzle. Virtually all species have mechanisms that drive them to eat when they are hungry and to produce strong motives to avoid starvation. By definition, patients (90 percent of whom are female) suffering from AN have lost 15 percent of their body weight, yet they avoid eating and do not seem to experience normal hunger. With a mortality rate of 10 percent, AN is now our most deadly psychiatric disorder (American Psychiatric Association, 2000). It would be inaccurate, however, to think of AN simply as self-imposed starvation affecting contemporary teen-aged girls. Evidence of the disorder appeared in the Middle Ages (Bell, 1985), and Freud wrote about AN (1954). It has been approached by psychodynamic, social, and biomedical theorists; but Guisinger (2003) points out that no single approach provides sufficient explanation for the cause(s) of AN, nor does any single approach lead to particularly effective treatment.

When otherwise healthy people starve, adaptive mechanisms are activated to conserve energy and find food: Metabolic rate decreases and food-seeking increases.

If starvation continues, individuals become lethargic and depressed (G. H. Anderson & Kennedy, 1992; Prentice et al., 1992). In contrast, many patients with AN are energetic and restless, and they may exercise excessively. They avoid food and may even find it aversive. They often have distorted images of their own bodies, believing that they are fat despite dramatic weight loss and emaciation. Although they currently lack a recommendation for treatment, evolutionary hypotheses (J. L. Anderson & Crawford, 1992; Guisinger, 2003; Nesse, 1984) may help us understand the anomalies presented by patients with AN.

Early evolutionary approaches (J. L. Anderson & Crawford, 1992) suggest that AN evolved as an adaptive, *reproductive* response to harsh conditions or resource shortages. Because women who suffer from AN often experience hormonal imbalances and cessation of ovulation and menstruation, they cannot reproduce. AN, in this view, is a strategy to delay or permanently prevent pregnancy. Thus, this hypothesis suggests that AN is a means by which a woman protects potential offspring from dangers of a hazardous environment.

A more recent hypothesis (Guisinger, 2003) posits that AN is an adaptive, *migratory* response to resource shortages. Guisinger (2003) suggests that our ancient hunter-gatherer ancestors were prone to extracting all possible resources from a particular foraging territory. When resources were depleted, starvation ensued, and it became necessary to migrate to another territory. Migration would be hindered by "normal" starvation symptoms such as incessant food craving, lethargy, and depression, but it would have been facilitated by symptoms of AN—decreased interest in food, increased energy, and inattention to or distortion of body image. In support of this hypothesis, Guisinger points out that AN occurs most frequently in groups that, in evolutionary time, were most recently migrating foragers (Native Americans, Hispanics, and Caucasians) and least frequently in groups that evolved away from migrational foraging long ago (Asians and Africans).

These hypotheses are interesting, but they do not, at this time, explain why either reproductive adaptations or migratory adaptations are triggered in the midst of relative abundance. The resource depletion that would instigate either a reproductive or migratory starvation strategy typically does not exist in the United States and Western Europe, where we see the greatest increases in AN. Thus, viewed as a context failure, AN is an adaptive starvation strategy that is somehow mistakenly activated in the midst of plentiful foods and nutritional supplements.

Anxiety Disorders

A little fear at the right time is a good thing. In our ancestral past it helped us avoid predators and powerful enemies. "Without fear, few would survive long under natural conditions" (Marks, 1987, p. 3). It continues to facilitate our survival today, although we have an entirely unnatural buffet of new things to fear. For example, a good, healthy fear may help some students prepare for the examination on this chapter. Too often, healthy and adaptive fears become **phobias,** which Buss (2004) defines as "fears that are wildly out of proportion to the realistic danger, are typically beyond voluntary control, and lead to the avoidance of the feared situation" (p. 91). Phobias have long interested evolutionary thinkers because our most common phobias pertain to events that, in our evolutionary past, *should* have been feared. Lumsden and Wilson (1981) say,

> It is a remarkable fact that the phenomena that evoke these reactions consistently (closed spaces, heights, thunderstorms, running water, snakes, and spiders) include some of the greatest dangers present in mankind's ancient environment, while guns, knives, automobiles, electric sockets, and other far more dangerous perils of technologically advanced societies are rarely effective. It is reasonable to conclude that phobias are the extreme cases of irrational fear reactions that gave an extra margin needed to ensure survival. . . . Better to crawl away from a cliff, nauseated with fear, than to casually walk its edge. (pp. 84–85)

Öhman and Mineka (2001, 2003) argue that some phobias are acquired rapidly because they are mediated by evolved mechanisms that predispose "automatic" and adaptive learning of certain fears. These authors show that fear of snakes, for example, occurs in other mammals and is prevalent among other primates; and it can even develop in lab-raised monkeys that watch videotaped wild monkeys exhibiting fear of real (or toy) snakes (Cook & Mineka, 1990). Consistent with our general description of a mechanism or strategy, there is a sensory component: Snakes and spiders easily capture our attention (Öhman, Flykt, & Esteves, 2001). And there are multiple response components that include the "symptoms" of fear, including sweating, increased heart rate, and so on, as well as overt behavioral components including avoidance of situations or fleeing. More importantly, they present data from studies with human participants indicating that fear of snakes or spiders may not require conscious perception of these stimuli (see Hergenhahn & Olson, 2005, for a discussion of these studies). Öhman and Mineka suggest, therefore, that as part of our evolutionary heritage, we share with other animals a neural mechanism that provides an automatic predisposition to rapidly learn fear responses to evolutionary significant stimuli. These stimuli capture our attention, and we can learn to fear them without conscious information processing. This does not mean that all humans are naturally fearful of snakes, spiders, snarling dogs, and so on. It does suggest, however, that these kinds of stimuli are naturally salient for our species and that we are naturally prepared to learn snake or spider phobias. The curious problem is, of course, that most modern humans with snake or spider phobias have never been attacked by spiders or snakes, nor do they live in environments where such fears might be adaptive. And once again, we see in phobias Buss's (2004) notion of context failure.

Evaluation

Evolutionary psychology is still a newcomer in the psychological sciences. It has made considerable scientific progress in recent years, moving smoothly from naturalistic observation to controlled experimentation. It should not be surprising that this relatively new area is still examining basic assumptions and developing testable hypotheses. Keeping in mind our basic premises that no theory completely captures the entirety of human personality and that every viable theory contributes an important piece to this complex puzzle, we now explore criticisms and contributions of this expanding field.

Criticisms

Evolutionary Psychology Engages in Adaptationism.   Several critics (Gould, 1997; Gould & Lewontin, 1979; Panksepp & Panksepp, 2000) argue that evolutionary psychology engages in adaptationism—technically panadaptationism. This term refers to the assumption that virtually everything humans or nonhumans do is the result of an evolutionary adaptation. Panadaptationism suggests that almost any current behavior is both heritable and, in effect, beneficial because it has—or had—adaptive significance. For example, panadaptationistic reasoning would suggest that, because a modern teenager is fascinated with video games, selection pressures must have shaped cognitive mechanisms that could be captured by bright colors and animated motion. According to this assumption, these mechanisms would not exist if they were not adaptive, and there is, no doubt, some yet-to-be discovered fitness benefit that accrues from such behavior. Taken to an extreme, consider the benefits that accrue from adaptations that allow one to play a video game while simultaneously driving an automobile and talking on a cell phone.

Evolutionary psychologists are well aware of the limitations of panadaptationism. Buss, Haselton, Shackelford, Bleske, and Wakefield (1998) provide two examples. **Exaptations** occur when an ancient adaptation manifests itself in distinctly different ways in contemporary organisms. For example, a bird's feathers first evolved as a mechanism for regulating a bird's body temperature but were later used for flying. **Spandrels** occur when an original adaptation has several unforeseen side effects in contemporary organisms. For example, the increased capacity of the human brain provided many adaptive benefits such as improved problem-solving skills, superior tool making, increased memory for the location of food, water, predators, and so on. However, the side effects of a larger brain might have included the development of language, music, art, and a wide range of complex societal rules and regulations. Thus, generalizing from ancient adaptations to the behavior of contemporary organisms must be done with caution and evolutionary psychologists know this.

Evolutionary psychologists contend that, while one of their primary goals is to discover and study adaptations, they are not panadaptationists. Following a model first developed by Cronbach and Meehl (1955), evolutionary psychologists only hypothesize that a psychological behavior is an adaptation if it satisfies the restrictions of a **nomological network** (Schmitt & Pilcher, 2004). A nomological network interrelates (1) the theoretical framework for a psychological construct, (2) an empirical framework for how the construct is measured, and (3) empirical relationships among and between these two frameworks. Thus, a nomological network interrelates a hypothetical psychological adaptation (e.g., reciprocal altruism) with several different sources of empirical data (e.g., psychology, medicine, physiology, genetics, anthropology and so on). In addition, the network may link one psychological construct, such as reciprocal altruism, with a related construct, such as kin altruism. It may also relate one type of data—surveys, for example—and another type of data, such as actual helping behavior. Only those psychological constructs that are developed within a nomological network are considered to be valid, and, in the end, relatively few human behaviors qualify as adaptations. As we have seen, mating strategies, mate-keeping strategies, kin and reciprocal altruism, and detection of social reciprocity violators are a few examples that meet these criteria. Preoccupation with video games, playing music loudly enough to vibrate the windows in your car, and chewing gum, to name only a few behaviors, do not.

Evolutionary Psychology Invents Stories about Our Ancient Ancestors. Gould (1997) criticized evolutionary psychologists for making up scenarios—"just-so" stories—so that ancient adaptive problems seem perfectly suited to shape mechanisms underlying our contemporary behavior. He and others (e.g., Panksepp & Panksepp, 2000; Rose & Rose, 2000) question the value of reconstructing the lives of our Pleistocene ancestors. According to this criticism, we have only current humans or nonhumans as databases because "we have no time machine that can promote a reasonably credible analysis of specific phases of our ancestral past" (Panksepp & Panksepp, 2000, p. 112).

Cosmides and Tooby (1997) assert that reasoning about our ancestors is not an act of wild imagination, nor does it fabricate "just-so" scenarios:

> Our ancestors nursed, had two sexes, hunted, gathered, chose mates, used tools, had color vision, bled when wounded, were predated upon, were subject to viral infections, were incapacitated from injuries, had deleterious recessives and so were subject to inbreeding depression if they mated with siblings, fought with each other, lived in a biotic environment with felids, snakes, and plant toxins, etc. (p. 5)

Granted, we have managed to drive some predators into extinction and to decimate the populations of others. We have conquered a few deadly viruses and managed others; but, except for lack of modern conveniences, our ancestors' adaptive problems were not too different from those of modern humans. Thus, it is not unreasonable to hypothesize that we use mechanisms to solve contemporary problems that are comparable to those used by our ancestors to solve similar problems.

Evolutionary Psychology Justifies the Status Quo (That is, Is Sexist or Racist). Critics claim that because evolutionary psychologists attempt to explain phenomena in which there are sexual differences (e.g., mating strategies) or the tendency to avoid or fear people unlike ourselves (xenophobia), the field uses scientific means to justify sexism or racism in society. This is equivalent to claiming that, because Bandura's social-cognitive theory attempts to explain observationally learned aggression, his theory justifies aggression. We have spent the better part of the last century attempting to explain depression and schizophrenia, yet no critics arose to claim that psychological investigators want to justify and maintain depression and schizophrenia. Evolutionary psychology, like other areas in psychology, attempts to explain human behavior as it exists, rather than how it should be, and to test explanatory hypotheses in scientific ways. Basic scientific research does not have and should not have an agenda to advance social causes or to right the wrongs of society. It does, however, have an agenda to describe and explain psychological phenomena, including those that are sexist, racist, or otherwise undesirable. That is exactly what evolutionary psychology attempts to do. Attribution of certain behaviors to selection pressures and adaptation does not mean that those behaviors are necessarily good for society, as we saw in the preceding discussions of murder and addiction.

Furthermore, as we have seen, evolutionary psychologists believe that behavior always results from the interaction between inherited predispositions and cultural influences. Thus, even when there are genetic tendencies to engage in socially unacceptable ways (e.g., xenophobia), those tendencies can be modified by the culture in which they occur.

Evolutionary Psychology Ignores Important Research in the Neurosciences. Some critics (e.g., Panksepp & Panksepp, 2000) claim that evolutionary psychology's context-specific, "modular" approach to mechanisms or strategies has no basis in contemporary neuroscience and is therefore incorrect. Recall that hypotheses about circuits, mechanisms, or strategies are guided by the assumption that there are separate neural mechanisms for mating, for aggression, for feeding, and so on. While Panksepp and Panksepp (2000) agree that older, subcortical mechanisms for feeding or sex, for example, are well studied and relatively well understood, they also argue that neural mechanisms for higher functions, such as jealousy or altruism, are not documented. Although this is true, it must be remembered that evolutionary psychologists use the terms "circuit" or "mechanism" as metaphors for extremely complex neural events that include interactions among sensory, emotional, cognitive, and behavioral brain processes. Nowhere is it suggested that there is a place in the brain where a jealousy module or an altruism module has been identified. Rather, when evolutionary psychologists refer to a jealousy circuit, they allude to a multifaceted set of functions, all of which must logically have their bases in brain activity. As a mosaic, the mechanism for jealousy must be quite different from an equally complex mechanism for altruism because the cues to which we are attuned, the emotions we experience, the decisions we make, and the actions we take are distinctly different when we are jealous, on one hand, or altruistic, on the other. In this sense, they are separate modules, but there is no claim that these modules are currently known in the way that brain areas mediating language, for example, are known. Context-specific circuits, mechanisms, or strategies are hypothetical structures, posited in opposition to the idea of a global, general-purpose, fitness-maximizing brain mechanism. They are constantly subjected to empirical scrutiny and potential falsification, as any scientific hypothesis should be. Cosmides and Tooby (1997) make this point explicitly:

> It may certainly turn out, for example, that we are wrong in our heterodox view that the faculty of human reasoning includes a large and heterogeneous set of evolved, functionally specialized circuits (for cooperation, threat, hazard avoidance, etc.). But the point is that modern evolutionary functionalism led to a series of predictions about human reasoning that no one would otherwise have thought to make or to test, and so to discoveries that would otherwise not have been made. (p. 5)

Contributions

Evolutionary Psychology Connects with Other Theories. Buss (2004) is quick to point out that Freud was influenced by Darwin's theory and that the earliest version of Freud's instinctual theory posited "preservative" and "sexual" instincts, shaped by natural selection and sexual selection. Thus, both Freudian and evolutionary explanations of personality are tied to evolutionary processes. In addition, although they do so in different ways, both Freudian theory and evolutionary psychology deal with unconscious events. For Freud, the id and its unconscious wishes were central. For evolutionary psychologists, unlearned predispositions to act according to evolved adaptations are central. A man seeking a mate does not say, "Tonight I think I'll desire a woman who is reproductively fit, is loyal, and has ideal waist-to-hip ratio." Rather, he is predisposed to respond positively to these features in a way that may be described as unconscious, although he may well become cognizant of his intentions once he sees such a woman and he begins to solve the problem of impressing her. Of course, both theories address sex, a centerpiece of evolutionary theory, but they also deal with aggression, which we treated only briefly in this chapter. As the reader may recall, Freud claimed that aggression stems from the death instinct, which, if instigated, strives for expression. This "drive–discharge" model suggests that aggression, once provoked, has to be expressed in direct, displaced, or sublimated form. Although evolutionary psychologists recognize that humans have the potential to act aggressively, they hypothesize that aggressive behavior is expressed only if its benefits—acquisition or defense of territorial or sexual resources, for example—outweigh its costs, which may include injury or even death. From this perspective, aggression "is based on evolved psychological mechanisms but is not rigid or invariant and does not get 'pushed out' regardless of circumstances" (Buss, 2004, p. 285). Thus, according to evolutionary psychology, and unlike Freud's drive–discharge explanation, humans may or may not act aggressively in a given situation depending on the outcome of a cost–benefit analysis.

Evolutionary psychology also makes connections with more recent personality theories. As we noted previously, studies of altruism and group cooperation address some of the same social-belongingness concerns covered by Erikson (Chapter 6) and Maslow (Chapter 15). In addition, Buss and others (Buss & Greiling, 1999; Ellis, Simpson, & Campbell, 2002) make connections between current trait theories such as the Big Five (see Chapter 8) and evolutionary theory, suggesting that we may have evolved mechanisms to detect individuals high in traits of Agreeableness and Conscientiousness, along with predispositions to behave cooperatively and expect reciprocal exchange with those individuals. On the other hand, it would be advantageous to detect and be cautious of individuals who are high in Neuroticism.

Evolutionary Psychology is Heuristic. In Chapter 1, we discussed both the synthesizing and heuristic functions of theories, and we emphasized that the value of a scientific theory lies partially in its ability to generate new research. The explosion of research in evolutionary psychology in the last few years gives testimony to the heuristic function of evolutionary theory. Recall from Cosmides and Tooby (1997) that evolutionary psychology has generated research questions that were not asked previously and has led to discovery of new phenomena. Symons (1987) adds:

> Darwinism can aid our understanding of the mind: It guides research, prevents certain kinds of errors, inspires new questions, and calls attention to aspects of the mind that are normally too mundane or uniform to be noticed. . . . Even such a modest contribution to the formidable task of understanding the most complex thing in the known universe, the human brain/mind, surely will be welcomed. (pp. 143–144)

Evolutionary Psychology Eliminates False Dichotomies. As we have seen, evolutionary psychologists do not entertain the nature–nurture debate. They emphasize that those aspects of human behavior typically attributed to "nurture," such as learning, are sometimes facilitated and sometimes restricted by evolved human nature. Similarly, they reject a distinction between "proximate" causes of behavior, those things that currently characterize an organism and its immediate environment, and "ultimate" causes, those things that could be attributed to evolutionary predispositions. Alcock (2000) reminds us of the fundamental biological principle that

> proximate and evolutionary levels of explanation are complementary rather than competitive. True, the genetic, developmental, hormonal, and other physiological

mechanisms that individuals possess provide immediate or proximate explanations for their behavior. Evolutionary biologists, however, can still ask why species possess their particular proximate mechanisms and how these mechanisms spread after they once appeared in the species, questions that require an understanding of the history of the species—the evolutionary side of the equation. . . . In reality, scientists interested in proximate causes often identify mechanisms worth investigating by considering the evolutionary level of explanation. (pp. 2–3)

Evolutionary Psychology is Grounded in Scientific Principles.   Finally, we return to Buss's (personal communication, 2004) observation that, while the theories of personality he encountered during his graduate training were all intuitively "on target," they were not grounded in fundamental and nonarbitrary principles. For example, we have seen that Freud defined the unconscious in a specific way and placed great import on its role. Other theories have freely redefined the nature and role of the unconscious or even eliminated it as a determinant of human behavior. In contrast, evolutionary psychology adheres to established principles of evolutionary theory that also guide contemporary research in biology, physiology, and medicine. According to Buss (2004), evolutionary theory provides "the only known scientific theory that has the power to account for the origins and structure of complex adaptive mechanisms—from callous producing mechanisms to oversized brains—that comprise human nature" (p. 38). Furthermore, noting that the discipline of psychology currently exists as a number of separate, highly specialized areas (social psychology, cognitive neuroscience, developmental psychology, decision sciences, etc.) that do not necessarily share fundamental assumptions or principles, Buss writes that evolutionary psychology "provides the conceptual tools for emerging from the fragmented state of current psychological science and linking psychology with the rest of the life sciences in a move toward larger scientific integration" (p. 411).

Summary

Evolutionary psychologists develop and test research hypotheses generated by Darwin's theories of natural and sexual selection. In addition, they rely on more recently developed theories derived from Darwinian principles (e.g., Hamilton's [1964] inclusive fitness theory and Trivers's [1972] parental investment theory.)

Contrary to Locke's idea that the human mind is at birth a *tabula rasa* and is subsequently shaped by experience, evolutionary psychologists assume that there is an innate, fundamental human nature that has been shaped by natural and sexual selection. The primary task of evolutionary psychology is to discover and study the behavioral and cognitive adaptations that contributed to survival and reproduction of our ancestors, and to show how those adaptations manifest themselves in the behavior of modern humans. Evolutionary psychologists emphasize that evolution acted on the brain to produce circuits or strategies that facilitate the solving of adaptive problems that have recurred throughout human history and still challenge us today. These problems include attracting and keeping mates, raising children, finding and protecting resources, forming cooperative alliances with others, and so on.

However, evolutionary psychologists contend that we are only *predisposed* to act in certain ways under specific conditions and that we are by no means mere instinctive creatures. Culture, learning, and the immediate environment can facilitate, modify, or inhibit the expression of our evolved predispositions.

Much of David Buss's work focuses on sex differences because, with respect to mating behaviors, selection pressures were different for males and females. Studies of cultures around the world show that both men and women prefer long-term mates who are kind and intelligent, however, women show a higher preference for mates who have access to resources and are willing to share them while men show a higher preference for mates who are reproductively fit. Both men and women capitalize on the mate-preferences of the other sex and try to attract mates through self-promotion and competitor derogation. When seeking long-term mates, women tend to exaggerate their cues of youth, health, and fidelity; they may undermine attempts of their competitors to display those characteristics. Men seeking long-term mates tend to exaggerate their cues of prestige, resources, and physical superiority; they may undercut attempts by rivals to display those qualities. When women seek short-term mates, they become highly selective for men with excellent physical characteristics and may use displays of sexuality to attract them. Men seeking short-term mates tend to reduce their standards for mates and may use immediate displays of wealth to attract them.

Strategic interference occurs when one person's strategy conflicts with that of another, for example, when a woman seeking a long-term mate is pursued by a man seeking a short-term sexual relationship. Both men and women may use deception to overcome strategic interference, but centuries of selection pressures have also shaped strategies to contend with deception.

Buss sees love as an irrational but necessary adaptation that helps to maintain mating relationships when rational analyses might otherwise end them. He also sees jealousy as an evolved response to signals of potential infidelity, an additional tool to maintain long-term relationships. Men are more likely to exhibit jealousy over sexual infidelity; women are more likely to exhibit jealousy when resources are threatened by a rival.

Although other people may be competitors for resources, there are many occasions when we must engage in cooperative behavior. Altruism is the term used to describe behavior in which one individual extends resources to another or when members of a group sacrifice individually so that the entire group benefits. Kin altruism is helping behavior extended to those who share our genes, and we tend to extend resources to those individuals in proportion to the numbers of genes that we have in common (Hamilton's rule). Reciprocal altruism is helping behavior that we extend to others who are not our genetic relatives. According to evolutionary psychologists, we extend helping behavior based on an intuitive cost–benefit analysis and will only risk our resources when the expected benefit outweighs the costs of the action. Furthermore, humans seem to have evolved abilities to understand the dynamics of reciprocal social cooperation and to detect violations of the implicit rules of social reciprocity.

One recent direction in evolutionary psychology is the study of dysfunctional behavior. For evolutionary psychologists, dysfunctional behavior is attributed to failure of evolved mechanisms. Context failure involves the activation of an adaptive mechanism in response to stimuli or contexts other than those for which it was (or is) adaptive. Evolutionary psychologists have studied phenomena such as suicide, murder, addiction, anorexia nervosa, and anxiety disorders; and they have argued that at least some of these behaviors may be due to activation of evolved mechanisms in inappropriate contexts.

Evolutionary psychology has been criticized for engaging in panadaptationism, for inventing imaginary, evolutionary scenarios to account for contemporary behavior, for justifying sexist and racist status quo, and for ignoring important research in the neurosciences. We make the case that it has weathered these criticisms well and that some of these criticisms are unfounded. The evolutionary perspective has made important contributions to personality theory by connecting with other established theories, by posing new research questions and leading to new discoveries, by eliminating false dichotomies (e.g., the nature-versus-nurture debate), and by basing its premises on established scientific principles of Darwinian and neo-Darwinian evolutionary theory.

Experiential Exercises

1. Make one list describing characteristics of your ideal husband or wife, the "love of your life." Make a second list describing characteristics of the perfect "summer fling." Do these lists differ in the ways predicted by evolutionary psychologists?
2. Think about romantic relationships that you have had in the past or that you currently have. What sorts of things have made you jealous? According to evolutionary psychologists, men and women experience jealousy for different reasons.

Have your experiences of jealousy been in accordance with evolutionary theory?
3. List 10 people for whom you would be most willing to make a sacrifice. According to evolutionary psychology, your list should be dominated by persons with whom you are either genetically related or with whom you have bonded through sexual intimacy. How does your list compare with the one predicted by evolutionary psychology?

Discussion Questions

1. Explain why applying evolutionary principles to the study of human behavior might be disturbing to some people.
2. Briefly define the following terms: struggle for survival, adaptation, survival of

the fittest, fitness, inclusive fitness, natural selection.
3. Explain how *love* and *jealousy* can be viewed as evolutionary adaptations.

Glossary

Adaptation. Any physiological structure, trait, or behavioral pattern that facilitates survival and reproduction.

Altruism. Behavior that risks resources of the actor in order to benefit a recipient. *See also* Kin selection and Reciprocal altruism.

Cheating. Occurs in an altruistic system when one accepts help from another but does not reciprocate or when one accepts more help than one gives.

Competitor derogation. A mating tactic in which one provides negative information about a rival.

Context failure. Activation of an evolved mechanism or strategy by inappropriate stimuli or in an inappropriate context.

Coolidge effect. In most male mammals, a reduction or elimination of the post-ejaculatory refractory period when a novel female is introduced.

Cost–benefit analysis. In evolutionary psychology, an intuitive or unconscious evaluation of the trade-off between costs of a behavior and the benefits that the behavior might accrue.

Effective polygyny. Increased reproductive variability observed in males, rather than females, of a species. *See also* Reproductive variance.

Empirical theory. As a theory of human nature, claims that the mind is blank at birth, without inherited dispositions, and that experience, rather than innate factors, shapes the mind and its characteristics. *See also* Social science model.

Error management theory (EMT). A proposal that humans are predisposed to make those types of errors for which costs are minimized.

Evolutionary psychology. Uses Darwinian and neo-Darwinian evolutionary principles to generate hypotheses and explanations of psychological phenomena.

Evolutionary psychology's theory of human nature. Claims that some aspects of the mind have been shaped by natural selection and that certain behaviors are predisposed.

Exaptations. Use of an adaptation for purposes other than those for which it originally evolved. *See also* Adaptation.

Fitness. According to Darwin, the ability to produce viable offspring.

Hamilton's rule. We extend help and resources in proportion to genes shared with the recipient of our actions.

Inclusive fitness. Evolutionary fitness can be increased by reproducing, by contributing to the fitness of those with whom we share genes, or both. *See also* Hamilton's rule.

Jealousy. The emotion experienced by males when they know, or suspect, that their mate is sexually unfaithful and by females when they know, or suspect, that the resources provided to her and her offspring by her mate are threatened by a rival.

Kin selection (or Kin altruism). Helping behavior extended to those to whom we are genetically related. *See also* Hamilton's rule and Inclusive fitness.

Love. According to Buss, an irrational but necessary emotion that evolved to maintain long-term mating relationships.

Natural selection. According to Darwin, only organisms that possess adaptive traits in a given environment survive and reproduce.

Naturalistic fallacy. Mistaken belief that what naturally "is" is also what "ought" to be.

Nomological network. In development of a psychological construct, a relationship between (1) the theoretical framework for the construct, (2) an empirical framework for how the construct is measured, and (3) empirical relationships between these two frameworks.

Panadaptationism. Attribution of all contemporary behaviors to evolved adaptations.

Phobias. Defined by Buss as fears that are wildly out of proportion to the realistic danger, are typically beyond voluntary control, and lead to avoidance of the feared situation.

Reciprocal altruism. Helping behavior extended to individuals genetically unrelated to us with the explicit or implicit expectation that the favor will be repaid or returned

Reproductive variance. A measure of how frequently a person can potentially reproduce: low variance (between zero and once per year) for women; high variance (between zero and potentially many times per year) for men. *See also* Effective polygyny.

Self-promotion. Attempting to attract a mate by displaying or exaggerating the characteristics desired by that mate.

Sex differences. Differences between males and females attributed to biological rather than social factors.

Sexual selection. Darwin's proposal that, typically, females, but sometimes males, within a species will select mates with certain physical and behavioral characteristics, thereby perpetuating those characteristics into future generations.

Sexual strategies theory (SST). Buss and Schmitt's proposal that mating strategies differ due to sex and whether a short-term or long-term relationship is sought.

Social science model. As a theory of human nature, claims that experience, rather than innate factors, shapes the mind and its characteristics. *See also* Empirical theory.

Sociobiology. A predecessor of evolutionary psychology, the systematic study of the biological basis of social behavior, including that of humans.

Spandrels. Unexpected byproducts or side effects of an adaptation.

Strategic interference. According to Buss, this occurs when a person employs a particular strategy to achieve a goal and another person interferes with successful enactment of that strategy.

Strategy. An evolved, multifaceted solution to a recurring adaptive problem, also called a mechanism or circuit.

Struggle for existence. According to Darwin, this occurs when living organisms produce more offspring than environmental resources can support.

Survival of the fittest. Refers to the fact that only those members of a species who are best adapted to their environment survive and reproduce.

Theory of parental investment. Trivers's proposal that the sex with greater investment in reproduction (females) will be more selective in choosing a mate while the sex with less investment in reproduction (males) will be more competitive.

Xenophobia. Fear of strangers or of people who are different from us.

GEORGE KELLY

CHAPTER OUTLINE

Compared to the other theorists covered in this book, Kelly wrote relatively little. The major presentation of his theory is found in his two-volume work, *The Psychology of Personal Constructs* (1955). In the preface to Volume 1 of this work, Kelly gave his readers fair warning about what they were about to read. We reproduce Kelly's warning here to give the flavor of his writing style, to show his iconoclastic approach to psychology, and to provide an overview of his theory of personality:

> It is only fair to warn the reader about what may be in store for him. In the first place, he is likely to find missing most of the familiar landmarks of psychology books. For example, the *learning,* so honorably embedded in most psychological texts, scarcely appears at all. That is wholly intentional; we are for throwing it overboard altogether. There is no *ego,* no *emotion,* no *motivation,* no *reinforcement,* no *drive,* no *unconscious,* no *need.* There are some words with brand-new psychological definitions, words like *foci of convenience, preemption, propositionality, fixed-role therapy, creativity cycle, transitive diagnosis,* and *the credulous approach.* Anxiety is defined in a special systematic way. *Role, guilt,* and *hostility* carry definitions altogether unexpected by many; and to make heresy complete, there is no extensive bibliography. Unfortunately, all this will make for periods of strange, and perhaps uncomfortable, reading. Yet, inevitably, a different approach

calls for a different lexicon; and, under its influence, many old terms are unhitched from their familiar meanings.

To whom are we speaking? In general, we think the reader who takes us seriously will be an adventuresome soul who is not one bit afraid of thinking unorthodox thoughts about people, who dares peer out at the world through the eyes of strangers, who has not invested beyond his means in either ideas or vocabulary, and who is looking for an ad interim, rather than an ultimate, set of psychological insights. (pp. x–xi)

Biographical Sketch

George Alexander Kelly was born on a farm near Perth, Kansas, on April 28, 1905. He was an only child. Kelly's father had been a Presbyterian minister but because of poor health he gave up the ministry and turned to farming. In 1909, Kelly's father converted a lumber wagon into a covered wagon and used it to move his family to Colorado, where they staked a claim to a plot of land offered free to settlers. They returned to their farm in Kansas, however, when they were unable to find water on their claim. Kelly never lost the pioneer spirit derived from his early experiences. He remained a practical person throughout his life; his overriding concern with an idea or a device was whether it worked—if it did not, he had no time for it. Furthermore, Kelly was strongly influenced by his parents' deep religious convictions and remained an active member of the church.

Kelly's early education consisted of attending a one-room schoolhouse and being tutored by his parents. When he was 13, he was sent to Wichita, where he eventually attended four high schools. After the age of 13, Kelly seldom lived at home again. Upon graduation from high school, he enrolled in the Friends University in Wichita, a Quaker school. After 3 years he moved to Park College in Parkville, Missouri, where he earned his BA degree in physics and mathematics in 1926. Kelly remembered his first psychology class as totally unimpressive. For the first few weeks he waited in vain for something interesting to be said. One day the instructor began to discuss stimulus–response psychology and placed "S -> R" on the blackboard. Finally, Kelly thought, they were getting to the crux of the matter. Kelly (1969) recalled his disappointment:

> Although I listened intently for several sessions, after that the most I could make of it was that the "S" was what you had to have in order to account for the "R" and the "R" was put there so the "S" would have something to account for. I never did find out what that arrow stood for—not to this day—and I have pretty well given up trying to figure it out. (p. 47)

Kelly had originally planned on a career as an engineer but decided such a career would not allow him to deal with social problems, with which he was becoming increasingly concerned. As a result, he enrolled in the MA program at the University of Kansas, with a major in educational sociology and a minor in labor relations. For his master's thesis, he studied how workers in Kansas City spent their leisure time. He was awarded an MA degree in 1928. It was during his graduate training at the University of Kansas that Kelly decided it was time for him to become acquainted with the writings of Freud. Kelly was about as impressed by Freud's theory as he was by S → R psychology: "I don't remember which one of Freud's books I was trying to read, but I do remember the mounting feeling of incredulity that anyone could write such nonsense, much less publish it" (1969, p. 47).

The next year was a busy one for Kelly. He taught part time in a labor college in Minneapolis, speech classes for the American Bankers Association, and an Americanization class to immigrants wishing to become citizens. Finally, in the winter of 1928, he joined the faculty at a junior college in Sheldon, Iowa, where he met his future wife, Gladys Thompson. Among his other duties, he coached dramatics and that, as we shall see, may have influenced Kelly's later theorizing.

In 1929, Kelly was awarded an exchange scholarship, which enabled him to spend a year at the University of Edinburgh, in Scotland, where he worked closely with Sir Godfrey Thomson, who was largely responsible for Kelly developing an interest in psychology. In 1930, Kelly earned a degree in education from the University of Edinburgh. His thesis, under the supervision of Thomson, was on predicting teaching success.

Upon returning to the United States in 1930, Kelly enrolled in a psychology program at the State University of Iowa where he earned his PhD in 1931. His dissertation was on the common factors in speech and reading disabilities. Two days after graduation, he married Gladys Thompson, and they eventually had two children. By the time Kelly obtained his PhD in psychology at the age of 26, he had already studied physics, mathematics, sociology, education, labor relations, economics, speech pathology, cultural anthropology, and biometrics.

Kelly's academic career began at Fort Hays Kansas State College, in the midst of the Great Depression. He soon learned that his interest in physiological psychology that he had pursued at the State University of Iowa would do him little good under his present circumstances. He noted that the people with whom he had contact simply did not know what to do with their lives—they were confused. Kelly, therefore, switched his interests to clinical psychology for which there was a great need. It turns out that Kelly had a great advantage at this point, in that he was not formally trained in any particular clinical technique. This, along with his practical nature, gave him great latitude in trying a variety of approaches in treating emotional problems. What worked was salvaged; what did not work was discarded.

During his 13-year (1931–1943) stay at Fort Hays, Kelly developed traveling clinics, which serviced the state's public school system and which made Kelly an early school psychologist (Guydish, Jackson, Markley, & Zelhart, 1985). This service allowed Kelly and his students to experience a wide range of psychological problems and to experiment with ways of treating them. Initially, Kelly returned to the Freudian notions that, as a student, he found to be untenable, and he found them to be effective: "Through my Freudian interpretations, judiciously offered at those moments when clients seemed ready for them, a good many unfortunate persons seemed to be profoundly helped" (Kelly, 1963, p. 51). However, Kelly was haunted by the feeling that Freudian therapy worked only because his clients believed it should. It was at this time that Kelly made two observations that were to have a profound influence on his later theory. First, he found that even if he made up a radical explanation for a client's problem, the client would accept it and usually improve. In other words, Kelly noted that anything that caused clients to look at themselves or their problems differently caused improvement in the situation. Logic, or "correctness," seemed to have little to do with it. Kelly described his experiment with psychotherapy as follows:

> I began fabricating "insights." I deliberately offered "preposterous interpretations" to my clients. Some of them were about as un-Freudian as I could make them—first proposed somewhat cautiously, of course, and then, as I began to see what was happening, more boldly. My only criteria were that the explanation account for the crucial facts as the client saw them, and that it carry implications for approaching the future in a different way. (1969, p. 52)

Second, Kelly noted that a teacher's complaint about a student often said more about the teacher than it did about the student. It was the way the teacher was seeing things that determined the nature of the problem rather than some objective event that everyone could experience. It was observations like these that stimulated Kelly to develop perhaps one of the boldest theories of personality since Freud's theory.

At the beginning of World War II, Kelly was in charge of a local civilian pilot-training program. Eventually he joined the navy as a psychologist in the Bureau of Medicine and Surgery and was stationed in Washington, D.C. While in the service, he did much to improve the quality and effectiveness of clinical psychology in the armed forces. Kelly remained active in a number of government programs related to clinical psychology until his death.

In 1945, when the war ended, Kelly was appointed associate professor at the University of Maryland, where he remained for 1 year. In 1946, he became professor of psychology and director of clinical psychology at Ohio State University. Although the department was extremely small, Kelly, along with Julian B. Rotter, also destined to become a prominent psychologist, developed a clinical psychology program that many considered to be the best in the country. It was during his 19 years at Ohio State that Kelly refined and tested his theory of personality. As we mentioned in the previous chapter, Walter Mischel was a student of Rotter's and Kelly's and their influence is clearly evident in social-cognitive theory.

During 1960 to 1961, Kelly and his wife received a grant from the Human Ecology Fund that allowed them to travel around the world lecturing on the relationship between Kelly's theory and various international problems. Their journey carried them to Madrid, London, Oslo, Louvain, Copenhagen, Prague, Warsaw, Moscow, the Caribbean area, and South America. It was quite an adventure for someone who claimed never to have gotten all the Kansas mud off his shoes. In 1965, Kelly left Ohio State to accept an appointment as an endowed chair at Brandeis University. Kelly died on March 6, 1967, at the age of 62.

Among Kelly's honors were the presidencies of both the clinical and counseling divisions of the American Psychological Association. He also played a major role in formulating the American Board of Examiners in Professional Psychology, an organization whose purpose is to upgrade the quality of professional psychologists. He served as president of the Board of Examiners from 1951 through 1953.

Kelly was remembered by his students and colleagues as a warm, accepting person. George Thompson, a former colleague of Kelly's, shared the following reflections on the occasion of Kelly's death:

At the 1963 Convention of the American Psychological Association, some 40 former students of George Kelly attended a dinner to pay tribute to their good teacher and warm friend. These professors, scientists, and therapists came from all parts of the United States. All of them knew that here was a man who helped them find their ways to more productive lives. Many others who could not attend wrote letters of appreciation for his wise counsel and guidance. (1968, pp. 22–23)

And then there was the occasion during the summer of 1965 when Kelly's colleagues at Ohio State gathered to congratulate him for having been awarded an endowed chair at Brandeis University. Papers were read by three of Kelly's former doctoral students and by a prominent colleague from England. At the end of the presentations, Kelly rose to invite the entire gathering to his house for dinner. Nearly 100 individuals accepted the offer. Thompson (1968) says of this occasion, "There was good food for all and a characteristic abundance of warm fellowship. The dinner [reflected] in modest measure the affectionate humanity of George Alexander Kelly—scholar, teacher, and warm friend" (pp. 22–23).

Categorization of Kelly's Theory

As already mentioned, Kelly started as a clinical psychologist with no formal clinical training. In other words, he was not indoctrinated in any particular school of thought. Kelly was confronted by people with problems and, because he had no clinical skills, had to improvise his own techniques. He had no mentor to guide him, he came from no department with a particular philosophical leaning, and he was not surrounded by clinical colleagues who steered him in a certain direction. He therefore "played it by ear." Thus, if Kelly's theory resembles anyone else's, it is coincidental. As we shall see, Kelly believed that a person's present personality need not be tied to his or her past. He believed the same to be true of personality theories; that is, to be valid, a theory need not grow out of those theories already in existence. Kelly's theory of personality is probably as independent of other theoretical positions as a theory can be. Similarities between his and other theories have been noted mainly by other people; Kelly did not care much about them.

Kelly's theory, however, can be classified in certain ways. First, Kelly was a **phenomenologist** (see, e.g., Walker, 1990). Phenomenologists believe that intact conscious experience should be psychology's focus of attention. It should not matter where such experiences originate; the important thing to study, the phenomenologists believe, is a person's individual conscious experiences, without breaking them down into component parts or attempting to determine their origin. Although Kelly can be labeled a phenomenologist because he studied intact conscious experience, it should be noted that he was only interested in such experience in relationship to objective reality. That is, unlike some phenomenologists, Kelly was interested in how thought processes were used while interacting with the environment.

Kelly's theory can also be labeled cognitive (see, e.g., Cantor & Zirkel, 1990) because it emphasizes mental events. It is not a behavioral theory because the emphasis is not on behavior and its causal relationships to the environment; it is not a psychoanalytic theory because it does not stress unconscious mechanisms or early experience in the determination of adult personality; and it is not a trait theory because it does not attempt to categorize people in terms of their traits. It is a **cognitive theory** because it stresses how people view and think about reality.

Kelly's theory can also be considered an **existential theory** because it emphasizes the present and the future rather than the past, and because it assumes that humans are free to choose their own destinies. In general, existentialism assumes that humans are free and future oriented, that their subjective feelings and personal experience are extremely important, and that they are concerned with the meaning of life. The existentialists also believe that because humans are free, they are also responsible for their own destinies. Generally, existentialists examine the problems of human existence. The statement that man "is what he wills to be," by the famous existential philosopher Jean-Paul Sartre (1956, p. 291), fairly well summarizes both Kelly's and the existentialist's position.

Last, Kelly's theory can be considered a **humanistic theory** (see, e.g., Epting & Leitner, 1992) because it stresses the human capacity for improvement. Kelly urged each person to continue to explore new possibilities for living, possibilities that may turn out to be more effective than those already tried. Both Kelly and the humanists believed humans sought, and were capable of, better personal, sociological, and international conditions.

It should be emphasized that all of these labels for Kelly's theory were provided by individuals other than Kelly. Kelly believed that his theory was "too fluid to be pinned down by verbal labels" (1966, p. 15).

Basic Postulate—People as Scientists

Kelly took the scientist as the model for describing all humans. He noted that scientists constantly seek clarity and understanding in their lives by developing theories that will allow them to predict future events; in other words, the scientist's main goal is to reduce uncertainty. Kelly believed that, like scientists, all humans are attempting to clarify their lives by reducing uncertainty, and therefore the distinction between the scientist and the nonscientist is not a valid one:

> It is as though the psychologist were saying to himself, "I, being a *psychologist,* and therefore a *scientist,* am performing this experiment in order to improve the prediction and control of certain human phenomena; but my subject, being merely a human organism, is obviously propelled by inexorable drives welling up within him, or else he is in gluttonous pursuit of sustenance and shelter." (Kelly, 1955, p. 5)

According to Kelly, all humans are like scientists in that they are interested in the future and use the present only to test a theory's ability to anticipate events. "Anticipation is not merely carried on for its own sake; it is carried on so that future reality may be better represented. It is the future which tantalizes man, not the past. Always he reaches out to the future through the window of the present" (Kelly, 1955, p. 49).

The major tool a person uses in anticipating events is the **personal construct.** Personal constructs are used by individuals to **construe** or interpret, explain, give meaning to, or predict experiences. A construct is an idea that a person uses when attempting to interpret his or her own personal experiences. A construct is like a miniscientific theory, in that it makes predictions about reality. If the predictions generated by a construct are confirmed by experience, it is useful; if the predictions are not confirmed, the construct must be revised or abandoned. "Man looks at his world through transparent patterns or templets which he creates and then attempts to fit over the realities of which the world is composed. . . . Let us give the name *constructs* to these patterns that are tentatively tried on for size. They are ways of construing the world" (Kelly, 1955, pp. 8–9).

We have more to say about constructs in the next section, but it is important to note they are usually verbal labels that a person applies to environmental events and then tests with subsequent experience with those events. For example, upon meeting a person for the first time, one might construe that person with the construct of "friendly." If the person's subsequent behavior is in accordance with the construct of friendly, then the construct will be useful in anticipating that person's behavior. If the new acquaintance acts in an unfriendly manner, he or she will need to be construed either with different constructs or by using the other pole (see "Dichotomy Corollary" in the next section) of the friendly–unfriendly construct. The point is that constructs are used to anticipate the future so they must fit reality. Arriving at a **construct system** that corresponds fairly closely to reality is largely a matter of trial and error. According to Kelly, a person's **personality** refers to the collection of constructs that constitute his or her construct system at any given time.

Kelly emphasized the fact that each person creates his or her own constructs for dealing with the world. He believed that, although all people have the goal of reducing future uncertainty, they are free to construe reality any way they wish. He called this belief **constructive alternativism,** which he described as follows: "We take the stand that there are always some alternative constructions available to choose among in dealing with the world. No one needs to paint himself into a corner; no one needs to be completely hemmed in by circumstances; no one needs to be the victim of his biography" (1955, p. 15).

Although it is true that no one needs to "paint himself into a corner," it does not mean people do not do so. Here we have an interesting distinction between freedom and determinism. Kelly believed individuals are free to create their own construct systems, but he also believed they are controlled by them after they are created.

Kelly noted that some of the construct systems created by people were more effective than others. Some individuals arrive at inflexible convictions about the world and become slaves to them. The lives of such individuals are dominated by rules and regulations, and they live within a narrow range of highly predictable events. Others have a broader perspective. They live their lives in accordance with flexible principles rather than rigid rules. Such individuals live a richer life because of their openness to experience:

> Ultimately a man sets the measure of his own freedom and his own bondage by the level at which he chooses to establish his convictions. The man who orders his life in terms of many special and inflexible convictions about temporary matters makes himself the victim of circumstances. Each little prior conviction that is not open to review is a hostage he gives to fortune; it determines whether the events of tomorrow will bring happiness or misery. The man whose prior convictions encompass

a broad perspective, and are cast in terms of principles rather than rules, has a much better chance of discovering alternatives which will lead eventually to his emancipation. (Kelly, 1955, pp. 21–22)

Thus, according to Kelly, whether one lives an open, creative life or a restrictive one is largely a matter of personal choice. Likewise, some people can look at a situation positively, and others can look at the same situation negatively. Again, it is a matter of personal choice. This brings us to the fundamental postulate in Kelly's theory: "*A person's processes are psychologically channelized by the ways in which he anticipates events*" (1955, p. 46). In other words, an individual's activities (behavior and thoughts) are guided in certain directions by the personal constructs used to predict future events.

Kelly, Vaihinger, and Adler

In our coverage of Adler's theory in Chapter 4, we discussed Vaihinger's philosophy of "as if" in which it was claimed that ideas can be simultaneously fictitious and useful. That is, although an idea has no counterpart in reality, it can still provide a useful tool for dealing with reality. Although there are important differences between Vaihinger's philosophy and Kelly's theory (see Hermans, Kempen, &, Van Loon, 1992), both stressed the importance of propositional thinking, that is, experimenting with ideas to see where they lead. Kelly noted the similarity between his position and Vaihinger's:

> Toward the end of the last century a German philosopher, Hans Vaihinger, began to develop a system of philosophy he called the "philosophy of 'as if'." In it he offered a system of thought in which God and reality might best be represented as [propositions]. This was not to say that either God or reality was any less certain than anything else in the realm of man's awareness, but only that all matters confronting man might best be regarded in hypothetical ways. In some measure, I suppose, I am suggesting that Vaihinger's position has particular value for psychology. At least, let us pursue the topic—which is probably just the way Vaihinger would have proposed that we go at it. (1964, p. 139)

In addition to sharing with Vaihinger and Adler the belief in the importance of propositional thinking, Kelly also shared with them the belief that the interpretation of events is more important than the events themselves (see, e.g., Neimeyer & Mahoney, 1995). In other words, they all believed that subjective reality was a more important determinant of behavior than objective reality.

The Eleven Corollaries

Kelly embellished his basic postulate by adding 11 corollaries.

1. **Construction Corollary.** "A person anticipates events by construing their replications" (Kelly, 1955, p. 50).

    Events in one's life occur with some regularity; for example, a friendly person will tend to remain friendly; day follows night; it tends to be cold in winter; and the physical objects in one's environment will tend to remain in place—for instance, the refrigerator probably will still be in the kitchen tomorrow. Although no two events are exactly the same ("No man ever steps into the same river twice"), nonetheless, themes running through events bind them together. It is on the basis of these themes that constructs are formed and that predictions about the future are made. In other words, if the events in our lives did not occur with some regularity, it would be impossible to form constructs that represent them.

2. **Individuality Corollary.** "Persons differ from each other in their construction of events" (Kelly, 1955, p. 55).

This corollary cannot be stressed too much; it is the essence of Kelly's theory. According to Kelly, not only is beauty in the eye of the beholder, so is everything else. Reality is what we perceive it to be. This, of course, is a restatement of Kelly's notion of constructive alternativism, which says that we are free to construe events as we wish. This freedom is thought to apply not only to our interpretation of external reality but to ourselves as well.

> On occasion I may say of myself . . . "I am an introvert." "I," the subject, "am an introvert," the predicate. The language form of the statement clearly places the onus of being an introvert on the subject—me. What I actually am, the words say, is an introvert.
>
> The proper interpretation of my statement is that I *construe* myself to be an introvert, or, if I am merely being coy or devious, I am inveigling my *listener into construing me* in terms of introversion. The point that gets lost in the shuffle of words is the psychological fact that I have identified myself in terms of a personal construct—"introversion." (Kelly, 1958, p. 38)

3. **Organization Corollary.** "Each person characteristically evolves, for his convenience in anticipating events, a construction system embracing ordinal relationships between constructs" (Kelly, 1955, p. 56).

Not only do individuals differ in the constructs they use to construe events but they also differ in how they organize their constructs. According to Kelly, personal constructs are arranged in a hierarchy, some being more comprehensive than others. For example, the construct extrovert–introvert subsumes such constructs as likes people–dislikes people and likes parties–dislikes parties. A construct that subsumes other constructs within it is called a **superordinate construct,** and the constructs that are subsumed under it are called **subordinate constructs.**

Neimeyer (1985b) discusses a female patient who viewed herself as "businesslike" as opposed to "emotional." When asked why she chose to be viewed as businesslike, she said that she regarded it as a "mature approach to life" as opposed to an "unstable" one. When asked her definition of maturity she said that it meant "being in control" as opposed to "being controlled by others." When asked why it was important to be in control, she answered that her very "survival" depended on it and the opposite of survival was viewed as "just death." Figure 13–1 summarizes

Figure 13–1

Shows the super-ordinate and sub-ordinate constructs used by a female patient to describe herself. The p indicates the pole of the construct with which the patient aligned herself.

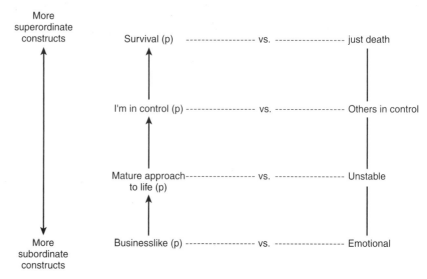

More superordinate constructs

Survival (p) ----------------- vs. ----------------- just death

I'm in control (p) ----------------- vs. ----------------- Others in control

Mature approach----------------- vs. ----------------- Unstable
to life (p)

More subordinate constructs

Businesslike (p) ----------------- vs. ----------------- Emotional

(From Neimeyer, 1985a, p. 281.)

the constructs the patient used to describe herself and shows that some of those constructs were superordinate and some were subordinate.

Kelly believed that without this hierarchical arrangement of constructs, one would experience contradictions and would make inaccurate predictions of events. Because this is undesirable, a person organizes constructs in a way that reduces contradictions and increases predictive efficiency.

4. **Dichotomy Corollary.** "A person's construction system is composed of a finite number of dichotomous constructs" (Kelly, 1955, p. 59).

According to Kelly, all constructs are bipolar or dichotomous. He believed that for a construct to be significant, it must indicate at least two elements that are similar to each other and a third element that is different from those two. One might say, for example, that males and females are similar in that they are both humans. This, in turn, implies that some organisms are not humans, for example, apes. Also, after observing a person who provides help to his aging parents and another who donates substantially to charity, one may conclude that both individuals are "good" or "generous." This implies that people who do not engage in such activities are perhaps "bad" or "stingy" or "insensitive." It is important to note, however, that for Kelly not only is the choice of the constructs used to construe reality a personal matter but so is the choice of the poles of a construct. The dichotomous poles of a construct are not determined by logic or convention; they are whatever a person views them to be. For example, for one person, one pole of a construct may be beautiful and the contrasting pole may be insensitive. For another person, beautiful might be contrasted with ugly. For still another person, beautiful might be contrasted with unsexy. Because a person uses these personally defined constructs to construe his or her world, if one is ever going to know another person, one must know his or her construct system. For Kelly, then, a construct is a personal way of construing certain experiences as being alike and yet different from other experiences.

It has been observed that under stress people sometimes abruptly switch from construing events with one pole of an important construct to construing them using the opposite pole. For example, people previously construed as friendly may now be construed as unfriendly. Winter (1993) argues that the conversion of law-abiding police officers to law breakers can be explained by such an abrupt change in the way events are construed. The Kellians refer to such pole shifts as **slot movements.** Because therapy can be stressful, it is not uncommon for slot movements to occur during the therapeutic process (Landfield & Epting, 1987).

5. **Choice Corollary.** "A person chooses for himself that alternative in a dichotomized construct through which he anticipates the greater possibility for extension and definition of his system" (Kelly, 1955, p. 64).

Here the person can either be safe or take a risk. If one applies previously effective constructs to new but similar experiences, one is merely seeking further validation of one's construct system. Kelly referred to this relatively safe path as **definition** because such experiences further define or validate a construct system. Conversely, one can use the occasion to try new constructs that, if validated, would further expand one's construct system, thereby making it better able to assimilate experiences that previously were foreign to it. Kelly referred to this as **extension.** The danger in extension, as opposed to definition, is the possibility of failure. When choosing a construct, one is torn between security and adventure. One can make safe predictions or one can attempt to expand one's construct system, thereby making an ever-increasing number of experiences understandable. In Kelly's words, "One may anticipate events by trying to become more and more certain about fewer and fewer things [definition] or by trying to become vaguely aware of more and more things on the misty horizon [extension]" (1955, p. 67). According to Kelly, too much emphasis on definition may result in too much certainty and in a very restricted view of life. Conversely, emphasis on extension may result in too much uncertainty and confusion. A middle ground is best.

6. **Range Corollary.** "A construct is convenient for the anticipation of a finite range of events only" (Kelly, 1955, p. 68).

A construct such as hot versus cold cannot be applied to a situation that requires a good versus bad judgment. Each construct has a **range of convenience** that includes all of the events to which the construct is relevant:

> Suppose, for example, A and B are men, C is a woman, and O is the time of day. We abstract an aspect of A, B, and C which we may call sex. Sex, then is our z. Sex is not applicable to O, the time of day; at least most of us would not so abstract it. The time of day, O, does not fall

within the range of convenience of sex, z. Now, with respect to sex, z, the two men, A and B, are alike and in contrast to the woman, C. (Kelly, 1955, p. 60)

The events within the range of convenience for which a construct is maximally pertinent define the construct's **focus of convenience.** For example, if one is menaced by a stray dog, the construct of danger–safe may be a useful one to employ in construing the situation. Certainly the event of being charged by the dog would fall within the range of convenience of the danger–safe construct. Furthermore, the notion of very dangerous would seem especially appropriate within that construct. In this situation, the construct of danger–safe would be employed, and the notion of very dangerous would be the focus of convenience within that construct's range of convenience. Constructs such as nice weather–bad weather or politically liberal–politically conservative would seem irrelevant to the situation. In other words, the range of convenience of the latter constructs would not include the situation at hand.

7. **Experience Corollary.** "A person's construction system varies as he successively construes the replications of events" (Kelly, 1955, p. 72).

Experience alone was unimportant to Kelly; what was important was the construing of experience:

> Experience is made up of the successive construing of events. It is not constituted merely by the succession of events themselves. A person can be a witness to a tremendous parade of episodes and yet, if he fails to keep making something out of them, or if he waits until they have all occurred before he attempts to reconstrue them, he gains little in the way of experience from having been around when they happened. It is not what happens around him that makes a man experienced; it is the successive construing and reconstruing of what happens, as it happens, that enriches the experience of life. . . . The person who merely stands agog at each emerging event may experience a series of interesting surprises, but if he makes no attempt to discover the recurrent themes, his experience does not amount to much. It is when man begins to see the orderliness in a sequence of events that he begins to experience them. (1955, pp. 73–74)

Thus, for Kelly, experience alone is not the best teacher but the active construing of experience is. With his characteristic wit, Kelly (1963) recalled a school administrator who "had one year of experience—repeated thirteen times" (p. 171).

8. **Modulation Corollary.** "The variation in a person's construction system is limited by the permeability of the constructs within whose range of convenience the variants lie" (Kelly, 1955, p. 77).

Some constructs are more **permeable**—that is, open to experience—than are others. "A construct is permeable if it will admit to its range of convenience new elements which are not yet construed within its framework" (Kelly, 1955, p. 79).

For example, a person's construct nice people–awful people might be defined in terms of certain individuals, nice people consisting of a circle of close friends and awful people consisting of everyone else. Such a person is not open to experience because one pole of the construct nice people–awful people is not permeable. Thus, even if the individual encountered a person with several admirable characteristics, that person could not be assimilated into the individual's construct system because of its lack of permeability.

A person who has several permeable constructs will be in a better position to extend his or her construct system than a person who has an abundance of impermeable constructs will. The former person can be characterized as open-minded and the latter as close-minded.

9. **Fragmentation Corollary.** "A person may successively employ a variety of construction subsystems which are inferentially incompatible with each other" (Kelly, 1955, p. 83).

   Kelly said that a person's construct system is in a state of continual flux. Different constructs are constantly being tested, and new elements are constantly entering into one's more permeable constructs. Likewise, one is constantly reorganizing one's construct system so the most reliable predictions are made. This experimentation with one's construct system creates the possibility for inconsistent behavior. One may not respond in a consistent way to the same event each time that it is encountered. For example, the interaction with one's boss on the job and in a local bar may be totally different. One may act differently because the situation has changed, one's constructs have changed, or the organization of one's constructs has changed. Kelly believed a certain number of inconsistencies were inevitable because construct systems "are in flux," but he believed even with minor inconsistencies the overall outcome was still consistent. "We can say that while a person's bets on the turn of minor events may not appear to add up, his wagers on the outcome of life do tend to add up" (Kelly, 1955, p. 88).

10. **Commonality Corollary.** "To the extent that one person employs a construction of experience which is similar to that employed by another, his psychological processes are similar to the other person" (Kelly, 1955, p. 90).

    With this corollary, Kelly emphasized the point that it is not common experiences that make people similar but the fact that they construe their experiences in a similar way. Two people can have the same physical experiences but construe them differently. Likewise, it is conceivable that two similar construct systems can result from distinctly differrent sets of physical experiences.

11. **Sociality Corollary.** "To the extent that one person construes the construction processes of another, he may play a role in a social process involving the other person" (Kelly, 1955, p. 95).

    The concept of **role** was important to Kelly's theory but he did not use the concept in the traditional way. Kelly defined role as "an ongoing pattern of behavior that follows from a person's understanding of how the others who are associated with him in the task think" (1955, pp. 97–98).

In other words, playing a role is acting in accordance with the expectations of others. To play a role one must understand another person's construct system. For example, if a man wants to play the role of husband to his wife, he must first understand her expectations for the construct husband and then act accordingly. Kelly called our understanding of another person's outlook and expectations a **role construct;** how we act in light of this understanding is called a role. "A role is a psychological process based upon the role player's construction of aspects of the construction systems of those with whom he attempts to join in a social enterprise" (Kelly, 1955, p. 97).

This corollary was Kelly's major statement on social behavior. He said that if we want to engage in constructive interactions with other people, we must first determine how other people see things and then take their perceptions into consideration when dealing with them. The deepest social interaction occurs when this role playing is reciprocal.

CPC Cycle

According to Kelly, the **CPC cycle** characterizes the actions of a person confronted with a novel situation. The initials CPC symbolize the three phases of the cycle: circumspection, preemption, and control. Let us use the example of being in a minor traffic accident. Upon realizing that we have collided with the car in front of us, we enter the **circumspection phase** of the CPC cycle by pondering several constructs that seem to be pertinent to the situation, for example, my fault–other driver's fault, vehicle damage–no damage, injury–no injury, and so on. In the **preemption phase,** we choose from the constructs pondered in the preceding phase. Let us say that we decide on the construct "my fault or the other driver's." In the **control phase,** we choose that pole of the chosen construct that seems most useful under the circumstances and will then act on it. Let us say that we choose to accept responsibility: We exchange insurance information, check on the well-being of the other driver, and apologize for following too closely. The whole idea is to control the situation. If the course of action is successful, the construct "my fault–other driver's fault" will be validated and will thus tend to dominate our thinking if we are, at some later time, in another traffic accident. To summarize, the CPC cycle consists of:

Circumspection Phase

In this phase, the person ponders several **propositional constructs** that could possibly be used to interpret the situation. The thinking during this phase is hypothetical and tentative, and might be labeled cognitive trial and error.

Preemption Phase

In this phase, the person chooses from all the constructs pondered in the preceding phase the one construct that seems especially relevant to the situation. In other words, a person cannot go on pondering the situation forever; he or she must choose a strategy for dealing with the experience.

Control Phase

During the preemption phase, a choice is made concerning which construct would be used to construe the situation. In the **control phase,** the person decides which pole of the dichotomous construct chosen during the preemption phase is most relevant to the situation.

Thus the CPC cycle involves pondering several possible constructs with which to construe a situation, deciding on one of those constructs, and then deciding which pole of that construct seems best for construing the situation. Once the final choice is made, subsequent experience will validate or invalidate the person's predictions.

Creativity Cycle

The **creativity cycle** is employed when a person seeks innovative solutions to problems or a fresh way of construing experiences. The creativity cycle, like the CPC cycle, involves three phases.

Loosened Construction Phase

According to Kelly, creative thinking involves a loosening of one's construct system. A loosened construct system allows varying alignments of elements and constructs. Thus bananas can be thought of as blue, loud, or intelligent. A teacher can be thought of as a paintbrush, a door stopper, or a hat. A loosened construct system allows for cognitive experimentation. Kelly (1955) said, "Creativity always arises out of preposterous thinking" (p. 529).

Tightened Construction Phase

The whole idea of the preceding stage is to discover solutions to problems or interpretations of situations that may not be obvious. For a loosened construct system to be useful, however, it must eventually be tightened. That is, a construct system is loosened to explore new ideas, but once an idea that may be useful is discovered, the cognitive experimentation must stop and the idea must be evaluated. Kelly (1955) said:

> Just as a person who uses tight constructions exclusively cannot be creative, so a person who uses loose constructions exclusively cannot be creative either. He would never get out of the stage of mumbling to himself. He would never get around to setting up a hypothesis for crucial testing. The creative person must have the important capacity to move from loosening to tightening. (p. 529)

Test Phase

The creative idea discovered in the loosened construction phase is submitted to a test and if validated by subsequent experience, it is retained as part of one's construct system. If not, it is discarded and the creativity cycle is repeated.

Kelly's Interpretation of Traditional Psychological Concepts

As we have seen, in the preface of Volume 1 of his 1955 book, Kelly warned the reader that he has ignored many traditional concepts, has redefined others, and has invented several new ones. In this section, we review a sample of the traditional psychological concepts that Kelly redefined in accordance with his personal construct theory.

Motivation

Kelly disagreed with most of the traditional views of **motivation.** He thought they looked on humans as naturally inert and therefore in need of being set in motion by something. In other words, traditional theories of motivation claimed that humans needed a drive, a need, a goal, or a stimulus to set them in motion. Kelly thought this was nonsense. He believed that humans are born motivated, and nothing more needs to be said. Every person, according to Kelly, is motivated "for no other reason than that he is alive" (1958, p. 49):

> Motivational theories can be divided into two types, push theories, and pull theories. Under push theories we find such terms as drive, motive, or even stimulus. Pull theories use such constructs as purpose, value, or need. In terms of a well-known metaphor, these are the pitchfork theories on the one hand and the carrot theories on the other. But our theory is neither of these. Since we prefer to look to the nature of the animal himself, ours is probably best called a jackass theory. (p. 50)

Examples of what Kelly called **push theories of motivation** include those of Freud, Skinner, and Dollard and Miller. Examples of what Kelly called **pull theories of motivation** include those of Jung and Adler. Other jackass theories include those of Rogers, Maslow, and May, to which we turn in the next three chapters. Concerning motivation, social-cognitive theory is also more like a **jackass theory of motivation** (because motivation is viewed as inherent) than it is a push or pull theory.

Anxiety

Kelly defined **anxiety** as *"the recognition that the events with which one is confronted lie outside the range of convenience of one's construct system"* (1955, p. 495).

As we have seen, the ability to predict the future accurately is everyone's goal. The extent to which our predictions are invalid is the extent to which we experience anxiety.

Because the primary function of a construct system is to accurately anticipate events, anxiety is evidence of a failed construct system and, therefore, one requiring modification. According to Kelly (1955), the necessary modifications to one's construct system may be large or small:

> From the standpoint of the psychology of personal constructs, anxiety . . . represents the awareness that one's construction system does not apply to the events at hand. It is, therefore, a preconsideration for making revisions. . . . Our definition of anxiety . . . covers the little confusions and puzzles of everyday living. The sum of a

column of numbers does not check. Anxiety! We add it up again, it still does not check. More anxiety! We add it up another way. Good adjustment. Ah, there was our error! (pp. 498–499)

In the extreme, life can become so unpredictable that the only certain thing one can imagine is death. For some this may stimulate suicide. "For the man of constricted outlook whose world begins to crumble, death may appear to provide the only immediate certainty which he can lay his hands on" (Kelly, 1955, p. 64). Anxiety is caused by the uncertainty that results when one's construct system does not permit the accurate construing of life's experiences. In some extreme cases, the certainty of death may be preferred to the uncertainty of the future.

It should be pointed out that some construct systems may require modification even if anxiety is not experienced. Again displaying his sense of humor, Kelly (1963) gave an example:

A friend of mine, while driving her car, customarily closes her eyes when she gets in a tight spot. This is an anticipatory act; she suspects something may happen that she would prefer not to see. So far, it hasn't happened though it's hard to understand why. (p. 26)

Hostility

Kelly defined **hostility** as the *"continued effort to extort validational evidence in favor of a type of social prediction which has already proven itself a failure"* (1955, p. 510).

Hostility is related to anxiety. Anxiety is experienced when one's predictions are incorrect. When it is clear that one's construct system has failed to construe the situation properly (i.e., when anxiety is inevitable), one may refuse to accept this fact and attempt to demand validation from the environment. Such demands characterize hostility. Bannister and Fransella (1971) said:

There are times when, if his construct system is to be preserved, a person simply cannot afford to be wrong. If he acknowledges that some of his expectations are ill-founded, this might involve the modification or abandonment of the constructions on which those expectations were based. If, in turn, these constructions are central to the whole of his system, he might well be faced with chaos, having no alternative way of viewing his situation. In such a position the person is likely to become hostile, to extort evidence, to bully people into behaving in ways which confirm his predictions, to cook the books, to refuse to recognize the ultimate significance of what is happening. (p. 35)

Leitner and Pfenninger (1994) give the example of a man who became violent with his wife when she asked him for a divorce, an idea he could not tolerate.

Aggression

Kelly (1955) defined **aggression** as *"the active elaboration of one's perceptual field"* (p. 508). Thus, according to Kelly, the aggressive individual opts to extend his construct system rather than define it (see the choice corollary). He or she seeks adventure rather than security. He or she seeks to expand his or her construct system so that it includes an increasing range of events. Aggression, then, in Kelly's theory, is the opposite of hostility. Bannister and Fransella (1971) put it as follows:

> It is interesting to note that Kelly is here attempting to define aggression (and similarly attempts to define hostility) in terms of what is going on within the individual rather than in terms of other people's reaction to him. Thus, a person is being aggressive when he actively experiments to check the validity of his construing; when he extends the range of his constructions (and thereby his activities) in new directions; when he is exploring. Obviously from the point of view of the people around and about such a person, this can be a very uncomfortable process and they may well see it as an attack upon them and handle it as such. But in terms of the aggressive person's construction system it is essentially an extending and elaborating process and thereby the opposite of hostility. (pp. 37–38)

To Kelly, hostility was the unwillingness to give up an ineffective construct system, and aggression is an attempt to expand one's construct system to an ever-increasing range of events.

Guilt

Kelly defined **guilt** as the "*perception of one's apparent dislodgement from his core role structure*" (1955, p. 502). The term **core role structure** refers to the roles we play while interacting with the relevant individuals and groups in our lives. According to Kelly, "Guilt arises when the individual becomes aware that he is alienated from the roles by which he maintains his most important relationships to other persons" (1963, p. 228). Thus if a man construes his relationship with his wife as loving, reliable, and caring, he will feel guilty if he acts in an unloving, unreliable, and uncaring way toward her.

In Kelly's view, the experience of guilt has nothing to do with good versus evil or right versus wrong. It has to do with the consistency or inconsistency with which one interacts with significant people or groups in one's life. It is inconsistency in these relationships that causes guilt. Even as Kelly defined it, however, guilt can be devastating:

> If you find yourself doing, in important respects, those things you would not have expected to do if you are the kind of person you always thought you were, then you suffer from guilt. . . . To live in a world where you cannot understand and predict others can be terrifying—how much more terrifying is it to find that one cannot understand and predict oneself. (Bannister & Fransella, 1971, p. 36)

Threat

Kelly defined **threat** as the "*awareness of imminent comprehensive change in one's core structures*" (1955, p. 489).

Just as we have a core role structure that governs our significant interpersonal relationships, we have other constructs for predicting external events on which we rely heavily. These **core structures** are used to make sense out of life. They become the heart of what others may call our belief system. When these basic core constructs suddenly seem no longer validated by experience, we feel threatened. To challenge our core constructs is to challenge our very existence, and that could be dangerous.

For Kelly, guilt is experienced when the constructs we use to predict our significant interpersonal relationships are not validated, and we feel threatened when previously validated constructs for dealing with external events lose their validity. For example, a person who spent most of his life avoiding alcohol would feel guilty if he accepted a drink at a party; if a person looked out her window in the middle of summer and saw snow, she would feel threatened. Threat can also be caused by the anticipation of one's death (Moore & Neimeyer, 1991; Neimeyer, Moore, & Bagley, 1988).

It should be clear that because people have different core structures, they will find different situations threatening. Furthermore, threat is not only caused by negative events. Kelly (1955) gave an example: "A prisoner of twenty years, while eager, is nevertheless threatened on the last day by the imminence of his release" (p. 490).

Fear

Fear, according to Kelly, is similar to threat but less severe. Fear results when a peripheral element of one's construct system is invalidated rather than one's core constructs. *"Fear is like threat, except that, in this case, it is a new incidental construct, rather than a comprehensive construct, that seems about to take over"* (Kelly, 1955, p. 494). A person may experience fear if a previously friendly dog growls at him. The change this experience necessitates in one's construct system is a minor one; for instance, a friendly dog now becomes a friendly dog that sometimes growls.

Unconscious

Kelly believed constructs could be described in terms of their cognitive awareness. Constructs with low cognitive awareness are considered more or less as **unconscious.** According to Kelly, there are three types of constructs with low cognitive awareness: preverbal, submerged, and suspended.

Preverbal Constructs. Kelly defined a preverbal construct as "one which continues to be used even though it has no consistent word symbol" (1955, p. 459). Preverbal constructs typically are formed early in life, before language is available. Although words are not available to infants, they still describe and anticipate events in terms of nebulous, nonverbal constructs such as feelings of warmth and security. Because verbally labeling a construct makes it easier to use, preverbal constructs are less definite than those that are verbally labeled.

Submergence. As stated earlier, every construct has two poles. Sometimes a person will act as if only one of the two poles exists, however: for example, believing that all people are good or everything is living. Emphasizing one pole of a construct and ignoring the other pole is what Kelly called submergence. "There is the *likeness* and the *contrast* end. Sometimes one of these two ends is less available than the other. When this is markedly true we may refer to the less available end as the *submerged* end" (Kelly, 1955, p. 467). A person may choose not to entertain one pole of a construct because doing so challenges his or her construct system. Kelly's notion of submergence is somewhat similar to Freud's notion of repression.

Suspension. Another way by which an element of experience can have low cognitive awareness is through **suspension.** An experience is suspended when it cannot be used constructively in one's construct system. It is as if an experience is kept in a holding pattern until a construct system that can assimilate it is created:

Our theory does not place the emphasis upon remembering what is pleasant or for-getting what is unpleasant; rather, it emphasizes that one remembers what is struc-tured and forgets what is unstructured. In contrast with some notions of repression, suspension implies that the idea or element of experience is forgotten simply because the person can, at the moment, tolerate no structure within which the idea would have meaning. Once he can entertain such a structure the idea may become available within it. (Kelly, 1955, p. 473)

Experiences that cannot be construed by one's construct system have no mean-ing. Therefore, such experiences must be suspended until a construct system devel-ops that can assimilate them. What can be understood by a person is always determined by his or her construct system. In Chapter 4, we noted that Adler be-lieved experiences incompatible with a person's worldview, guiding fiction, and lifestyle cannot be pondered consciously and therefore cannot be understood. Al-though they employed different terminology, Adler and Kelly agreed that only those experiences capable of assimilation into one's personality structure can be experi-enced consciously. In their own ways, Adler and Kelly viewed the unconscious as the "not understood." Here we have another of the several points of agreement be-tween Adler and Kelly.

Learning

Learning, for Kelly, was the constant alteration of one's construct system with the goal of increasing its predictive efficiency. Any change in one's construct system exemplifies learning. When Kelly considered the value of classical conditioning, so popular at the time, Pavlov faired no better than Freud had:

Salivation . . . takes place in a manner that suggests the anticipation of food, or perhaps hunger—I am not sure which. Perhaps what is anticipated is an activity we call eating. Whatever it indicates, Pavlov seems to have demonstrated it and there is no reason we should not be grateful even though we are not quite sure what it was he demonstrated. (1980, p. 29)

Reinforcement

Kelly replaced what others call reinforcement or reward with the concept of **validation.** According to Kelly, people do not seek reinforcement or the avoidance of pain. Peo-ple seek validation of their construct systems. If a person predicts that something un-pleasant will occur and it does, his or her construct system will have been validated even though the experience was a negative one. Again, according to Kelly, the pri-mary goal in one's life is to reduce uncertainty by accurately predicting future events: "Confirmation and disconfirmation of one's predictions [have] greater psychological significance than rewards, punishments, or . . . drive reduction" (1970, p. 11).

Psychotherapy

According to Kelly, neurotic people are like bad scientists; they keep making the same predictions in the absence of validating experiences. "From the standpoint of the psychology of personal constructs, we may define a disorder as any personal construction which is used repeatedly in spite of consistent invalidation" (Kelly, 1955, p. 831). In other words, a neurotic's construct system does not adequately predict future events, and therefore anxiety is inescapable. What the neurotic person needs is a more effective construct system, and psychotherapy is a procedure designed to help that person develop one. For Kelly, **psychotherapy** provides a person with an opportunity to examine and reformulate his or her construct system. In other words, psychotherapy trains people to be better scientists.

Role Construct Repertory Test

Because psychotherapy must deal with a client's constructs, the therapist must first discover what those constructs are. Kelly devised the **Role Construct Repertory Test** to identify the constructs a client uses to construe the relevant people in his or her life. This test has come to be called the Rep test. A typical form used in administering the Rep test is shown in Figure 13–2.

The first step in administering the Rep test is to ask the client to fill in the grid portion of the form, numbered 1 to 22, with the names of 22 persons relevant to his or her life. The client taking the test usually is asked to place the names of the following people in the blanks above the numbers on the test sheet (see Figure 13–2):

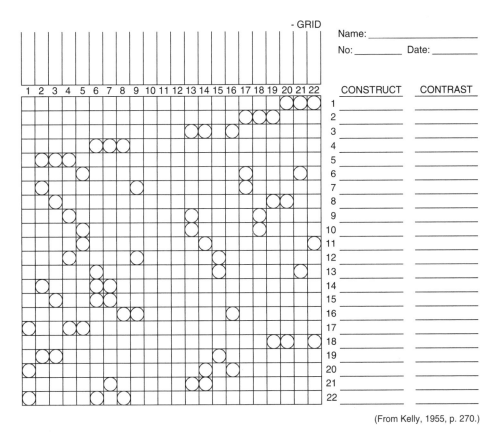

(From Kelly, 1955, p. 270.)

Figure 13–2 *A typical form used for Kelly's Role Construct Repertory (Rep) Test.*

1. The name of the client taking the test.
2. Mother's first name (or the person who acted as your mother).
3. Father's name (or the person who acted as your father).
4. Brother nearest to you in age, or if no brother, a boy near your age most like a brother.
5. Sister nearest to you in age, or if no sister, a girl near your age most like a sister.
6. Your wife or husband, or if not married, your closest friend of the opposite sex.
7. Closest friend of the opposite sex after the person listed in item 6.
8. Closest friend of your own sex.
9. A person who was once a close friend but no longer is.
10. A religious leader, for example, a minister, priest, or rabbi to whom you would be willing to discuss your feelings about religion.
11. Your medical doctor.
12. The neighbor you know best.
13. A person you now know who dislikes you.
14. A person for whom you feel sorry and would like to help.
15. The person with whom you feel most uncomfortable.
16. A recent acquaintance you would like to know better.
17. Your most influential teacher when you were in your teens.
18. The teacher with whom you disagreed the most.
19. An employer or supervisor for whom you worked while you were experiencing stress.
20. The most successful person you know personally.
21. The happiest person you know personally.
22. The most ethical person you know personally.

When the names have been furnished, the client is asked to compare them in groups of three. The three names that are to be compared are indicated by circles on the test sheet. For example, the first comparison is of the individuals whose names appear in blanks 20, 21, and 22. The second comparison is of the individuals whose names appear in blanks 17, 18, and 19, and so on. For each triad the client is asked to choose a word or phrase that describes how two of the three individuals are alike and a word or phrase that describes how the third person is different from the other two. The way in which the two people are the same is listed under construct, and the way in which the third person is different is listed under contrast. An X is placed in the circles of the two people who are alike, and the circle of the person thought to be different is left blank. A partially completed Rep test is shown in Figure 13–3.

It can be seen in Figure 13–3 that the client construed individuals 20 and 22 as highly motivated but individual 21 as lazy; individuals 18 and 19 were thought to be mean whereas individual 17 was thought to be understanding, and so forth.

By analyzing the client's performance on the Rep test, the psychotherapist can answer a number of questions about a client's construct system. For example, which constructs are used? What aspects of people do they emphasize, for example, physical characteristics and social characteristics? Which people are seen as most like or different from the client? Does the client have many constructs available or only a few? What poles does a client use to define the ranges of the constructs?

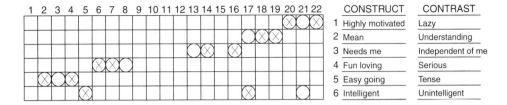

	1	2	3	4	5	6	7	8	9	10	11	12	13	14	15	16	17	18	19	20	21	22	CONSTRUCT	CONTRAST
1																				⊗	⊗	⊗	Highly motivated	Lazy
2																			⊗	⊗	⊗		Mean	Understanding
3															⊗	⊗		⊗					Needs me	Independent of me
4								⊗	⊗	⊗													Fun loving	Serious
5	⊗	⊗	⊗																				Easy going	Tense
6				⊗												⊗					◯		Intelligent	Unintelligent

Figure 13–3 *An example of a partially completed Rep test. Typically the client is asked to make 22 comparisons instead of the 6 indicated in the figure.*

The Rep test was only one tool that Kelly used to learn about his clients' construct systems. Another tool was simply to ask the clients about themselves. Kelly adopted what he called a **credulous attitude** toward his clients. In other words, he believed that the information they furnished about themselves should be trusted. *"If you don't know what's wrong with a client, ask him; he may tell you"* (Kelly, 1955, p. 201). What a client reports may not be true in an objective sense, but what a client believes to be true is true in at least a subjective sense. Because these personal beliefs or perceptions determine the client's behavior, they must be understood by the therapist:

> A person may misrepresent a real phenomenon, such as his income or his ills, and yet his misrepresentation will itself be entirely real. This applies even to the badly deluded patient: What he perceives may not exist, but his perception does. (Kelly, 1955, p. 8)

Like Allport's theory (see Chapter 7), Kelly's theory is idiographic and values the narrative accounts people provide of their lives (Harvey, 1989; Neimeyer, 1994). In fact, Allport's classic idiographic study, *Letters From Jenny* (1965), has been reinterpreted from a personal construct perspective (Feixas & Villegas, 1991). Although Kelly did not dwell on a client's past, he did acknowledge the usefulness of case histories (a kind of narrative). According to Kelly (1955), the events contained within a case history provide

> the validational evidence against which [the client] won and lost his wagers, against which he tested his personal constructs. They are the checkpoints he had to use in charting the course of his life. To understand what they actually were is to get some notion of the ranges of convenience of the client's constructs, what the system was designed to deal with, one way or another. Moreover, many of these events will have to be given some stabilizing interpretation in the new construct system produced under therapeutic intervention. (p. 688)

In keeping with his credulous attitude, Kelly often had his clients write a **self-characterization:**

> I want you to write a character sketch of Harry Brown (i.e., client's name), just as if he were the principal character in a play. Write it as it might be written by a friend who knew him very *intimately* and *very sympathetically,* perhaps better than anyone ever really could know him. Be sure to write it in the third person. For example, start out by saying, "Harry Brown is . . ." (1955, p. 323).

Again, as with the Rep test, the purpose of this sketch was to help the therapist see how clients construed themselves and their interactions with the world and with other people.

Fixed-Role Therapy

Kelly believed that one way to cause clients to explore different ways of construing is to have them pretend they are different people. In **fixed-role therapy**, the therapist presents the client with a personality sketch and asks the client to act it out, just as an actor would play a part in a play. To enhance the development of new constructs, the personality of the person the client is asked to play is markedly different from the client's own personality. Kelly asked the client to try on a new personality as one would try on a new set of clothes. Under these circumstances, the therapist becomes a supporting actor. Kelly said the therapist must "play in strong support of an actor—the client—who is continually fumbling his lines and contaminating his role" (1955, p. 399).

The client plays his role for about 2 weeks during which time he lives "as if" he were the person in the role he is playing. The therapist, during this time, responds to the client "as if" he were the person in the part and offers encouragement and validating experiences for the new constructs with which the client is experimenting. The therapist must give the client enough courage to overcome the threat involved in giving up his core constructs and developing new ones:

> What I am saying is that it is not so much what man is that counts as it is what he ventures to make of himself. To make the leap he must do more than disclose himself; he must risk a certain amount of confusion. Then, as soon as he does catch a glimpse of a different kind of life, he needs to find some way of overcoming the paralyzing moment of threat, for this is the instant when he wonders what he really is—whether he is what he just was or is what he is about to be. (Kelly, 1964, p. 147)
>
> By providing validating data in the form of responses to a wide variety of constructions on the part of the client, some of them quite loose, fanciful, or naughty, the clinician gives the client an opportunity to validate constructs, an opportunity which is not normally available to him. (Kelly, 1955, p. 165)

We see, then, that Kelly maintained his cognitive viewpoint even in psychotherapy. Emotional problems are *perceptual* problems. To resolve a perceptual problem, one must be made to *look* at experiences differently. Psychotherapy is a process by which a client is encouraged to look at experiences differently, while the therapist attempts to minimize the anxiety or threat in doing so.

Kelly suggested that neurotics have lost their ability to make-believe, and the therapist tries to help them regain it. Healthy people make-believe all the time. In fact, in Kelly's opinion, brilliant novelists and brilliant scientists do much the same thing; that is, they make-believe:

> Both [the novelist and the scientist] employ . . . human tactics. The fact that the scientist is ashamed to admit his phantasy probably accomplishes little more than to make it appear that he fits a popular notion of the way scientists think. And the fact that a novelist does not continue his project to the point of collecting data in support of his portrayals and generalizations suggests only that he hopes that the

experiences of man will, in the end, prove him right without anyone's resorting to formal proof.

But the brilliant scientist and the brilliant writer are pretty likely to end up saying the same thing—given, of course, a lot of time to converge upon each other. The poor scientist and the poor writer, moreover, fail in much the same way—neither of them is able to transcend the obvious. Both fail in their make-believe. (1964, p. 140)

The principles contained in personal construct theory have been used to study and treat a wide variety of disorders. Examples include *schizophrenia* (Bannister, Adams-Webber, Penn, & Radley, 1975; Bannister & Fransella, 1966; Pierce, Sewell, & Cromwell, 1992); *anxiety disorders* (McPherson & Gray, 1976); *phobias* (Huber & Altmaier, 1983); *eating disorders* (Button, 1985a; Fransella & Crisp, 1979; Neimeyer & Khouzam, 1985); *stress* (Talbot, Cooper, & Ellis, 1991); *depression among the elderly* (Viney, Benjamin, & Preston, 1989); and in *helping HIV and AIDS patients cope with their condition* (Viney, Allwood, Stillson, & Walmsley, 1992).

Being Oneself

Kelly took issue with the advice that encourages people to be themselves. In fact, his advice is quite the opposite:

> A good deal is said these days about being oneself. It is supposed to be healthy to be oneself. While it is a little hard for me to understand how one could be anything else, I suppose what is meant is that one should not strive to become anything other than what he is. This strikes me as a very dull way of living; in fact, I would be inclined to argue that all of us would be better off if we set out to be something other than what we are. Well, I'm not so sure we would all be *better* off—perhaps it would be more accurate to say life would be a lot more *interesting*. (1964, p. 147)

Construct Systems and Paradigms

In many ways, Kelly's view of personality is similar to Kuhn's view of science. Kelly maintained that the way in which an individual construes reality is only one of many possible ways, but for that particular individual his or her construct system is reality, and it is sometimes difficult for him or her to imagine other constructions. For Kuhn, as we saw in Chapter 1, a paradigm is a way of looking at a subject matter, and scientists doing research while following a paradigm are said to be doing normal science. Such scientists, according to Kuhn, are often blinded to other, perhaps more effective, ways of looking at a body of information.

Perhaps the most important similarity between Kelly and Kuhn is that they both emphasized *perceptual mechanisms*. For Kelly, a construct system is a set of personal constructs that result in a person construing the world in a certain way. Likewise, Kuhn's paradigm is a perceptual habit shared by several scientists that causes them to view their subject matter in a similar way.

Both Kelly and Kuhn insisted there are many equally valid interpretations of reality, not just one. Whereas Kelly took this view of an individual's adjustment to the world and Kuhn took this view of science, we take the same view of personality theory. One of the main functions of this book is to offer the various personality theories, not as *truths* but as *ways of viewing* personality. In other words, we believe that, like reality in general, personality can be construed in several equally valid ways. It is hoped that your construct for personality is permeable enough to allow various viewpoints to enter it.

We end our coverage of Kelly's theory with the following quotation that seems to summarize Kelly's philosophy of the individual, Kuhn's philosophy of science, and this book's approach to personality theory: "Whatever nature may be, or howsoever the quest for truth will turn out in the end, the events we face today are subject to as great a variety of constructions as our wits will enable us to contrive" (Kelly, 1970, p. 1).

Evaluation

Current Status

A relatively small but highly productive group of Kellians currently exists (Jankowicz, 1987). A clearinghouse for research generated by Kelly's theory is at the University of Nebraska, Lincoln, headed by Al Landfield. The clearinghouse issues a newsletter and publishes bibliographies of recent research on personal construct theory. Similar clearinghouses are scattered throughout the world. Worldwide membership in these clearinghouses has risen from 112 in 1970 to over 500 currently.

Although interest in Kelly's theory is increasing in the United States, the theory is most popular in England. A major reason for the theory's popularity in England is that Kelly's former student and prominent clinical psychologist, Donald Bannister, effectively promoted it there for many years. The London-based Centre for Personal Construct Psychology, under the direction of Fay Fransella, is also influential in disseminating Kelly's ideas in England. So popular is Kelly's theory there that exposure to it is required in most clinical programs approved by the British Psychological Society (Jankowicz, 1987, p. 483).

A major reason why Kelly's theory did not become more popular in the United States was that it was extremely critical of the other approaches to psychology that were so popular at the time—for example, behaviorism and psychoanalysis. Because Kelly actively avoided forming links between his theory and those of others, they, in turn, avoided forming links to his. As psychology in the United States has become increasingly cognitive in nature, however, Kelly's theory has become more popular. In fact, for many, Kelly is viewed as having been ahead of his time.

Empirical Research

Almost every aspect of Kelly's theory has received some research attention but most of that attention has involved the Rep test. An early research project using the Rep test was conducted by James Bieri, one of Kelly's students. Using the Rep test, Bieri (1955) was able to distinguish between a **cognitively complex person** and a **cognitively simple person.** A cognitively complex person has many highly differentiated constructs available to him or her. As a result, such a person can cast other people into many categories and can perceive much variety among them. Conversely, a cognitively simple person has a limited, poorly differentiated construct system. As a result, such a person casts all of humanity into a few categories such as good–bad.

Bieri was able to substantiate Kelly's assumption that the more constructs one has available, the better one will be at predicting future events. Bieri found that cognitively complex people are far better at predicting the behavior of others than cognitively simple ones. Other variables related to cognitive complexity include *age* (Signell, 1966; Vacc & Greenleaf, 1975); *adaptive flexibility* (Stein, 1994); *vocational choice* (Bodden, 1970; Harren, Kass, Tinsley, & Moreland, 1979; Neimeyer, 1988, 1992a, 1992b); *decisions of Supreme Court justices* (Gruenfeld, 1995); *the ability to cope with stress* (Dixon & Baumeister, 1991; Linville, 1985; Niedenthal, Setterlund, & Wherry, 1992; Smith & Cohen, 1993); and *gender differences* (Engelhard, 1990; Pratt, Pancer, Hunsberger, & Manchester, 1990).

The Rep test has been found useful in industrial-organizational psychology. Bannister and Fransella (1971) pointed out that the Rep test need not only be used to evaluate the set of fixed role titles that Kelly had suggested. In addition, it could be used to evaluate how individuals construe most anything. A recent nonclinical application of the Rep test is in the area of market research. Because consumer behavior is largely determined by consumer perceptions, it makes sense to use the Rep test to determine how consumers perceive (construe) various products. Stewart and Stewart (1982) gave several examples of how the Rep test is applied to the world of business. For example, one study explored the constructs used by a panel of home testers to describe a range of cosmetics and perfumes. Knowing the constructs that consumers use in evaluating and comparing products is important because it is on the basis of those constructs that consumers make purchasing decisions; it is to those constructs that advertisers must appeal. Jankowicz (1987) gives several examples of how personal construct theory is being used by industrial-organizational psychologists, management development specialists, and occupational counselors. Jankowicz concludes that, "In all these fields of psychology, finding out what the other person thinks, as a guide to discovering why he or she acts, is a central undertaking" (p. 481).

In addition to the areas already discussed, the Rep test has been found useful in studying the *decision-making processes of managers and school psychologists* (Jankowicz, 1987; Salmon & Lehrer, 1989); *marital satisfaction* (G. J. Neimeyer, 1984; Neimeyer & Hall, 1988; Neimeyer & Hudson, 1984, 1985); *friendship formation* (Duck, 1979); *values and beliefs* (Horley, 1991); *gender roles* (Baldwin, Critelli, Stevens, & Russell, 1986); and *recidivism rates of psychiatric patients* (Smith, Stefan, Kovaleski, & Johnson, 1991). For further examples of how the Rep test has been used as a research tool, see Bannister and Mair (1968); Landfield and Leitner (1980); and Mancuso and Adams-Webber (1982).

With a device as complex as the Rep test, inevitably computers would become involved in its administration and scoring. For examples of such efforts, see Bringmann, 1992; Ford and Adams-Webber, 1991; and Sewell, Adams-Webber, Mitterer, and Cromwell, 1992.

We see then that Kellian psychology has a substantial base of empirical research. Furthermore, this empirical base appears to be growing. Neimeyer and Jackson (1997) first describe a worldwide network of research centers that disseminate information on personal construct theory and then conclude:

> The outpouring of nearly 3000 conceptual, clinical, and empirical publications generated by this international community (the majority in the last decade) demonstrates that interest in personal construct theory continues to burgeon; there is no

indication that interest in the theory has peaked or entered a period of decline across its 35-year history. (p. 370)

Criticisms

Limited Empirical Research. Although Kelly's theory has generated a considerable amount of empirical research, most of it has involved the Rep test. Little research has been designed to test the theory of personal constructs on which the Rep test is based. Because little has been done to extend the theory, it remains more or less as Kelly originally proposed it in 1955.

Important Aspects of Personality Neglected or Denied. In his effort to create a new way of viewing personality, Kelly may have gone too far in his rejection of other theoretical approaches. In his rather flippant rejection of learning, motivation, and the developmental aspects of personality, Kelly may have discarded information vital to a comprehensive understanding of personality. Others think that his treatment of the unconscious mind and of human emotions was superficial, at best. For example, Jerome Bruner (1956) referred to Kelly's theory as "a genuine new departure and spirited contribution to the psychology of personality" (p. 356). However, he went on to say that the theory's greatest failure was its inability to deal with the human passions (e.g., love). In this, according to Bruner, Freud did a much better job.

It should be noted that several theorists have attempted to revise or expand Kelly's theory so that it will more adequately address the emotions (e.g., Fisher, 1990; Katz, 1984; McCoy, 1977; Miall, 1989).

Difficulty in Predicting Behavior. For Kelly, construing was a private, creative process. Furthermore, construct systems are constantly being tested and revised. These features of Kelly's theory make it practically impossible to predict what a person will do in a particular situation. In fact, Kelly insisted that unpredictability is an important characteristic of a healthy person. For many, this violates the scientific definition of understanding. That is, if something is truly understood its behavior can be predicted and controlled. Kelly focused his attention on the unique person almost as much as Allport did. When one seeks to understand an individual, one does not seek the general laws that govern human behavior. Thus, for many, a focus on individual behavior violates the tenets of science.

Many Unanswered Questions. Kelly left unanswered such basic questions as, Why do some people have more constructs available to them than others? Why do some people opt for the definition of their construct systems and others opt for extension? What is the origin of a personal construct? What causes people to construe the same situation differently? Is the model of humans as scientists really an accurate one? That is, do people really spend that much time trying to accurately predict future events?

Contributions

Emphasis on Cognition. Just as Kelly has been criticized for emphasizing the cognitive aspects of humans, others have praised him for doing just that. Both the psychoanalysts and the behaviorists (for different reasons) played down the type of rational thought that Kelly made the cornerstone of his theory. As other personality theorists were attempting to explain human behavior in terms of repressed memories, stimuli and responses, reinforcement, habits, ego-defense mechanisms, or the built-in tendency toward self-actualization, Kelly was attempting to explain it in terms of cognitive hypotheses testing. It is a tribute to Kelly that the newer theories (e.g., information-processing psychology) are more like his own than those he opposed. His theory is compatible with the popular interactionist position because it stressed both person variables (e.g., constructs and construct systems) and situation variables (those events people construe). One with the other would have been meaningless to Kelly. In fact, as we have seen, Kelly rejected pure phenomenology because it was concerned only with subjective reality, and he rejected behaviorism because it was concerned only with objective reality. Kelly's concern was with the relationship between subjective and objective reality and that concern is now in vogue.

Applied Value. Beyond furnishing a new theory with which to explore human personality and new methods for treating disturbed people, Kelly's ideas have been applied to a number of different areas. As we have seen, his ideas are now widely used in industrial-organizational settings. Other areas in which Kelly's ideas are either applied or researched or both include friendship formation, developmental psychology, person perception, education, political science, and environmental psychology (Adams-Webber, 1979; Mancuso & Adams-Webber, 1982).

Examples of clinical areas to which construct theory has been applied include *suicide* (R. A. Neimeyer, 1984; Parker, 1981); *obsessive–compulsive disorder* (Rigdon & Epting, 1983); *drug abuse* (Dawes, 1985; Rivers & Landfield, 1985); *childhood disorders* (Agnew, 1985); *physical illness* (Robinson & Wood, 1984; Viney, 1983, 1984); *couples in conflict* (Neimeyer & Hudson, 1984); and other *relationship disorders* (Leitner, 1984; Neimeyer & Neimeyer, 1985).

Starting with practically no formal training in clinical psychology, Kelly developed a unique theory of personality and therapeutic procedures that were both innovative and effective. Kelly's belief that truth is mainly a way of looking at things freed him from the dogma of the past and gave him latitude to experiment with his theorizing. We agree with Pervin's eloquent evaluation of Kelly's theory:

> George Kelly, then, was a person who refused to accept things as black or white, right or wrong. He was a person who liked to test new experiences; a person who dismissed truth in any absolute sense and, therefore, felt free to reconstrue or reinterpret phenomena; a man who challenged the concept of "objective" reality and felt free to play in the world of "make-believe"; a person who perceived events as occurring to individuals and, therefore, was interested in the interpretations of these events by individuals; a person who viewed his own theory as only a tentative formulation and who, consequently, was free to challenge views that others accepted as fact; a man who experienced the frustration and challenge, the threat and joy, of exploring the unknown. (1989, p. 235)

The criticisms of Kelly's theory should not disturb those who find it enlightening. No personality theory—indeed, no theory of any type—is without valid criticism. As Kelly would have said, every theory, like any construct, has a range of convenience and a focus of convenience, and that includes his own theory as well.

As we have seen, many aspects of Kelly's theory are found in social-cognitive theory that is popular today. Kelly's theory also has much in common with the popular existential–humanistic theories to which we turn in the next three chapters.

Summary

Kelly was born in the Midwest and raised by educated, religious parents. From his early pioneering experiences with his parents came a practical, flexible outlook that characterized Kelly all of his life. Kelly's theory can be categorized as phenomenological because it studied intact, conscious experiences; cognitive because it studied mental events; existential because it emphasized the present and future and people's freedom to choose their own destinies; and humanistic because it emphasized people's creative powers and was optimistic about people's ability to solve their problems.

Kelly's major premise was that all humans act like scientists in that they attempt to reduce uncertainty by developing theories (construct systems) that allow them to anticipate future events accurately. People construe—that is, interpret, explain, or predict—the events in their lives by utilizing constructs. A construct is a category of thought that describes how events are similar to one another and yet different from other events. All individuals are free to create whatever constructs they choose in their attempts to give meaning to their experiences. This freedom to choose constructs is called constructive alternativism. People are free to choose constructs but are more or less bound to them once they have been selected. Vaihinger, Adler, and Kelly all valued propositional thinking and all believed subjective reality to be a more important determinant of behavior than objective reality.

Kelly elaborated his theory through 11 corollaries. The construction corollary states that constructs are formed on the basis of the common themes in our experiences. The individuality corollary states that all individuals construe their experiences in their own unique way. The organization corollary states that some constructs are subsumed under other constructs. The dichotomy corollary states that each construct must describe how certain events are similar and also how those events are contrasted with other events. Under stress, people sometimes display slot movement. That is, they switch abruptly from construing with one pole of a construct to construing with its other pole. The choice corollary states that those constructs are chosen that have the best chance of either defining (validating) or extending (generalizing) one's construct system. The range corollary states that each construct has a range of convenience consisting of the events to which the construct is relevant and a focus of convenience to which the construct is maximally relevant. The experience corollary states that it is not physical experience that is important but the active construing of physical experiences. It is construing that provides for the testing and revision of one's construct system. The modulation corollary states that some constructs are more permeable—that is, more open to experience—than other constructs. The fragmentation corollary states that while trying new constructs people may at times be inconsistent, but if the larger picture is viewed, people tend to be consistent. The commonality corollary states that in order for two individuals to be considered similar they must construe their experiences in a similar manner. The sociality corollary states that in order to play a role, one must first determine what another person's expectations are and then act in accordance with those expectations.

When individuals are confronted with a novel situation, they apply the CPC cycle. In the circumspection phase of the cycle, people ponder a number of constructs they believe may be appropriate to the situation. In the preemption phase, they choose that construct that seems to be the most relevant. In the control phase, they choose the pole of the dichotomous construct chosen during the preemption phase and act on it. The creativity cycle is used when an innovative idea is sought, and it too involves three phases: loosening of the construct system to experiment with new ideas; tightening of the construct system so that the cognitive experimentation of the previous phases comes to an end; and testing the innovative idea arrived at in the first phase.

Kelly redefined several traditional psychological concepts in terms of his theory. The concept of motivation was thought unnecessary because humans are born motivated. Anxiety was defined as the feeling one gets when it is recognized that what is being experienced lies outside one's construct system. In Kelly's view, anxiety indicates that a construct system has failed and must be modified. Hostility was defined as an attempt to force the validation of one's construct system when it is clear that it is generating inaccurate predictions. Aggression was defined as the attempt to expand one's construct system. Guilt, according to Kelly, is experienced when one's core role structure is threatened; in other words, when one acts contrary to the role he or she typically plays in relation to a significant person or group in his or her life. Threat was defined as the feeling one experiences when one's core structures are invalidated. Fear was defined as the feeling one has when constructs other than core constructs are invalidated. The unconscious, to Kelly, was explained in terms of preverbal constructs; submergence, in which one pole of a construct is emphasized; and suspension, in which certain experiences are ignored until they can be assimilated into one's construct system. Learning was defined as any change in one's construct system.

Kelly compared a neurotic person to a bad scientist because he or she continues to make inaccurate predictions in the absence of validating experiences. Psychotherapy, to Kelly, was a process in which a client could try out different, potentially more effective, construct systems. In order to discover what constructs a client used in dealing with experiences, Kelly devised the Role Construct Repertory Test, better known as the Rep test. Kelly maintained a credulous attitude toward his clients, believing that they could provide a great deal of valid information about themselves. For example, he often had his clients write a self-characterization in which they described themselves in the third person. Kelly used fixed-role therapy in which he had clients act "as if" they were different people and in which the therapist was much like a supporting actor. Such a procedure allowed clients to test an alternative construct system while the therapist provided encouragement and validating experiences.

Kelly's theory was compared to Kuhn's notion of scientific paradigms, in that both emphasize that reality can be viewed in several equally valid ways.

Currently Kelly's theory has a relatively small but highly productive group of supporters scattered throughout the world. The empirical research generated by Kelly's theory has concentrated on the Rep test but almost all aspects of Kelly's theory have generated some research. Currently there is a rather widespread application of Kelly's ideas to industrial-organizational psychology, management development, and occupational counseling.

Kelly's theory has been criticized for generating a limited amount of empirical research, neglecting or denying important aspects of personality, having difficulty in predicting behavior, and leaving too many important questions unanswered. Kelly's theory has been praised for refocusing the study of personality back on the rational, intellectual aspects of human behavior; and for having considerable applied value. Because many aspects of Kelly's theory are found in both social-cognitive theory and in existential–humanistic theory, it promises to remain influential.

Experiential Exercises

1. Choose an issue in your life about which you feel strongly. Write down the issue and how you feel about it. Possibilities include abortion, capital punishment, the existence of God, the rights of women and gay people, and so on. Next, try taking a stand that is diametrically opposed to your own. Try to think about the issue as would those with views contrary to your thinking. Can you "see" their viewpoint? Is one viewpoint concerning this issue clearly correct and others clearly incorrect? With regard to this exercise, comment on Kelly's contention that "truth" is largely a viewpoint.

2. Take the Role Construct Repertory Test found earlier in this chapter yourself. Carefully note the number and the variety of the constructs that you use in construing other people. Also note what you listed as the two poles of your constructs. What does the Rep test tell you about your construct system? Next, administer the Rep test to someone you are very close to and compare responses. Summarize your observations.

3. To experience what fixed-role therapy is like, write a self-characterization of yourself in the third person. Next, write a description of a person very much unlike yourself. For the next few days, keep this fictitious description in mind. As you have various experiences, note not only how you interpret and respond to them but try to imagine how the fictitious person might construe and respond. Remember, Kelly's clients were instructed to actually construe and respond as if they were the fictitious person. Do you think it would be easy to try on a new personality as one would try on a new set of clothes? Explain.

Discussion Questions

1. Explain how Kelly used the model of the scientist to explain the psychological processes of all humans.
2. Define the term construct as Kelly used it. List the various characteristics of constructs.
3. Discuss each of the following terms from Kelly's point of view: motivation, anxiety, hostility, aggression, guilt, threat, fear, learning, and reinforcement.

Glossary

Aggression. Effort to expand one's construct system so it is capable of assimilating a greater range of experiences.

Anxiety. Feeling one has when one realizes that an experience lies outside one's construct system.

Choice corollary. States that people will choose a construct that will either further define or extend their construct system. *See also* Definition of a construct system and Extension of a construct system.

Circumspection phase. That phase of the CPC cycle in which a person ponders several constructs that might be useful in construing a novel situation.

Cognitive theory. Any theory that focuses on the study of mental events.

Cognitively complex person. Person with many well-differentiated constructs in his or her construct system.

Cognitively simple person. Person with only a few poorly differentiated constructs in his or her construct system.

Commonality corollary. States that people can be considered similar not because of similar physical experiences but because they construe their experiences in a similar fashion.

Construct. *See* Personal construct.

Construct system. Collection of constructs used by a person at any given time to construe the events in his or her life.

Construction corollary. States that constructs are formed on the basis of the recurring themes in one's experience.

Constructive alternativism. Term that reflects Kelly's belief that there are numerous ways of construing one's experience and therefore one is free to choose from a number of construct systems.

Construe. One's active effort to interpret, explain, and give meaning to experiences.

Control phase. That phase of the CPC cycle in which people choose a pole of the construct chosen in the preemptive phase of the cycle and act in accordance with that pole.

Core role structure. Roles we play while interacting with the important people and groups in our lives.

Core structures. Those constructs on which we rely most heavily when construing experience—that is, those that have been most consistently validated.

CPC cycle. Series of activities engaged in by a person confronted with a novel situation. *See also* Circumspection phase, Control phase, and Preemption phase.

Creativity cycle. Three-phase cycle in which innovative ideas are sought. Phase 1 involves loosening one's construct system to allow realignments of elements and constructs. Phase 2 involves retightening one's construct system after an innovative idea has been found. Phase 3 involves testing the idea and retaining it if it is found useful and discarding it if not.

Credulous attitude. Assumption that the information provided by clients about themselves can be trusted as accurate and valid.

Definition of a construct system. Choice of a construct in construing a situation that has already been successful in construing similar situations. Such a choice has the effect of further validating one's construct system.

Dichotomy corollary. States that each construct has two poles, one of which describes what characteristics the events to which the construct is relevant have in common, the other of which describes events without those characteristics. For example, if one pole of a construct describes beautiful things, the other pole may describe things without beauty, or ugly things.

Existential theory. Any theory that focuses on the nature of, or the problems related to, human existence.

Experience corollary. States that mere passive experience is unimportant. It is the active construing of experience that ultimately results in a more effective construct system.

Extension of a construct system. Choice of a construct, in construing a situation, that has never been tried. Such a choice has the potential effect of extending one's construct system so that it is capable of assimilating a greater range of experience.

Fear. Feeling one has when a relatively unimportant construct is about to be invalidated, thus requiring a minor change in one's construct system.

Fixed-role therapy. Clinical technique that asks clients to act as if they were other people. Thus clients become actors, and the therapist becomes a supporting actor. The idea is to have the clients try different ways of construing their experiences in a non-threatening situation as the therapist provides validating information about their new construct systems.

Focus of convenience.   Events within the range of convenience of a construct to which that construct is maximally significant.

Fragmentation corollary.   States that as a construct system is being tested, revised, or extended, certain inconsistencies in behavior may result.

Guilt.   Feeling one has when one acts contrary to a role one has assumed while interacting with a significant person or group in one's life.

Hostility.   Attempt to force the validation of a prediction that has already proved to be erroneous.

Humanistic theory.   Any theory that assumes that humans are basically good and rational and their behavior is purposive.

Individuality corollary.   States that each person is unique in his or her manner of construing experience.

Jackass theory of motivation.   Kelly's description of his own theory because it claimed that motivation is inherent to human nature. Therefore, there is no need to postulate events that push or pull humans into action.

Learning.   Any change in one's construct system.

Modulation corollary.   States that a construct system is more likely to change if the constructs contained in it are permeable. *See also* Permeable construct.

Motivation.   For Kelly, a synonym for life.

Organization corollary.   States that constructs are arranged in a hierarchy from most general to most specific. *See also* Subordinate construct and Superordinate construct.

Permeable construct.   Construct that easily assimilates new experiences.

Personal construct.   Idea or thought that a person uses when construing personal experience. Sometimes simply called a construct.

Personality.   For Kelly, the term personality refers to a person's construct system.

Phenomenologist.   One who studies intact, conscious experience.

Preemption phase.   That phase of the CPC cycle in which people decide which construct to use to construe a novel situation.

Preverbal construct.   Construct formulated early in one's life, before language was adequately developed. Although such a construct cannot be labeled verbally it can still be used to construe one's experiences.

Propositional construct.   Construct that is cognitively tested as one that might be useful in construing a situation.

Psychotherapy.   Because Kelly equated people suffering emotional problems with bad scientists, therapy was regarded as a setting in which the client could learn to be a better scientist—that is, learn to develop a more effective construct system.

Pull theories of motivation.   Those theories that emphasize terms such as purpose, value, or need. Kelly also called these carrot theories.

Push theories of motivation.   Those theories that emphasize terms such as drive, motive, and stimulus. Kelly also called these pitchfork theories.

Range corollary.   States that a construct is relevant to only a finite range of events. *See also* Focus of convenience and Range of convenience.

Range of convenience.   Finite range of events to which a particular construct is relevant.

Role.   For Kelly, a role is acting in accordance with another person's expectations of how one will act.

Role construct.   Awareness of another person's expectations. In a sense, a role construct involves seeing the world through someone else's eyes.

Role Construct Repertory Test (Rep test).   Test developed by Kelly to identify the constructs clients use to construe the relevant people in their lives.

Self-characterization.   Sketch that Kelly sometimes had his clients write about themselves (in the third person) in order to learn what constructs they used to construe themselves and other people.

Slot movements.   The abrupt shifting from the use of one pole of a construct to its opposite that is often precipitated by stress.

Sociality corollary.   States that to engage in constructive social interaction with another person, one must first understand how that person construes his or her experiences. Only then can one play a role in that person's life. *See also* Role.

Submergence.   Situation in which one pole of a construct is used, but the other pole tends not to be. The unused pole is said to be submerged or unconscious.

Subordinate constructs. Constructs that are subsumed under a more general construct.

Superordinate construct. General construct that subsumes other constructs.

Suspension. Situation in which an experience has low cognitive awareness because it is incompatible with one's current construct system. If one's construct system is changed so it can assimilate the experience, it (the experience) will enter full awareness; that is, it will no longer be suspended.

Threat. Awareness that one or more important constructs will be invalidated, thus requiring a major change in one's construct system. *See also* Core structures.

Unconscious. Constructs with low cognitive awareness. *See also* Submergence and Suspension.

Validation. Results when a construct or a construct system successfully anticipates an experience.

CHAPTER **14**

CARL ROGERS

According to Carl Rogers, all humans, as well as all other living organisms, have an innate need to survive, grow, and enhance themselves. This "forward thrust of life" continues despite many obstacles. For example, children first learning to walk stumble frequently, but, despite the pain, press on with their attempts to walk. There are numerous examples of humans who, while living under dire circumstances, not only survive but continue to enhance their lives.

Rogers's view of human nature is essentially the opposite of the view suggested by Freud. Freud viewed humans as having the same needs, drives, and motives as any other animal. Therefore, human tendencies toward uninhibited sex and aggression must be controlled by society. In contrast, Rogers believed that humans are basically good and therefore need no controlling. In fact, he believed it is the attempt to control humans that makes them act badly. Rogers's view of human nature clearly placed him in the humanistic camp:

> I have little sympathy with the rather prevalent concept that man is basically irrational, and that his impulses, if not controlled, will lead to the destruction of others and self. Man's behavior is exquisitely rational, moving with subtle and ordered complexity toward the goals his organism is endeavoring to achieve. (1961, pp. 194–195)

I am inclined to believe that fully to be a human being is to enter into the complex process of being one of the most widely sensitive, responsive, creative, and adaptive creatures on this planet.

So when a Freudian such as Karl Menninger tells me (as he has, in a discussion of this issue) that he perceives man as "innately evil" or more precisely, "innately destructive," I can only shake my head in wonderment. (quoted in Kirschenbaum, 1979, p. 250)

Biographical Sketch

Carl Ranson Rogers was born to Walter and Julia Cushing Rogers on January 8, 1902, in Oak Park (a Chicago suburb), and he was the fourth of six children. Because his father was a successful civil engineer and contractor, there were no economic problems in Rogers's early life. Rogers described himself as "the middle child in a large, close knit family, where hard work and a highly conservative (almost fundamentalist) Protestant Christianity were about equally revered" (1959, p. 186). Rogers (1961) commented on the religious and ethical atmosphere that characterized his childhood home: "I have a hard time convincing my children that even carbonated beverages had a faintly sinful aroma, and I remember my slight feeling of wickedness when I had my first bottle of 'pop'" (p. 5). Rogers's parents discouraged the development of friendships outside their home because, it was argued, nonfamily members engaged in questionable activities. Rogers commented:

> I think the attitudes toward persons outside our large family can be summed up schematically in this way: Other persons behave in dubious ways which we do not approve in our family. Many of them play cards, go to movies, smoke, drink, and engage in other activities—some unmentionable. So the best thing to do is to be tolerant of them, since they may not know better, and to keep away from any close communication with them and live your life within the family. (1973, p. 3)

As a result of the attitude toward "outsiders" he described, Rogers spent a great deal of time by himself, reading everything he could get his hands on, including encyclopedias and a dictionary. In Oak Park, the Rogers family lived in an upper middle-class neighborhood where young Carl attended Holmes elementary school. His classmates included Ernest Hemingway (who was two years older than Carl) and the children of Frank Lloyd Wright, the famous American architect.

When he was 12 years old, Rogers and his family moved to a farm about 30 miles from Chicago. Moving to a farm, however, did not require that the Rogers family give up their middle-class lifestyle: "It is widely known that Carl Rogers grew up on a farm, but not so widely known that the farm house had a slate roof, tile floors, eight bedrooms and five baths, and a clay tennis court behind the house" (Kirschenbaum, 1979, p. 10). On this farm, Rogers first developed an interest in science. Because his father insisted the farm be run scientifically, Rogers read about many agricultural experiments. From his reading, he developed an interest in a species of moth that he captured, raised, and bred. This interest in science is something that never left Rogers, although he worked in one of the more subjective areas of psychology all of his professional life.

Rogers's tendency toward solitude lasted throughout high school, during which time he only had two dates. He was an excellent student and obtained almost straight As. His main interests were English and science.

In 1919, Rogers enrolled at the University of Wisconsin, which both parents, two brothers, and a sister had attended, and chose to study agriculture. Rogers was very active in church work through his early years in college. In 1922, he was one of 10 college students selected to attend the World Student Christian Federation Conference in Peking, China. This 6-month trip had a profound effect on Rogers. Having experienced, firsthand, people of different cultures with different religions, Rogers (1961) reflected on an insight that he had aboard ship on his return from China: "It struck me one night in my cabin that perhaps Jesus was a man like other men—not divine! As this idea formed and took root, it became obvious to me that I could never in any emotional sense return home. This proved to be true" (p. 351). Rogers wrote to his parents declaring his independence from their conservative religious viewpoint. Rogers found his declaration of independence intellectually refreshing, but it seems he had to pay an emotional price for his newfound freedom. Shortly after he returned from the Orient, he was increasingly troubled by abdominal pains that were diagnosed as a duodenal ulcer. Rogers was hospitalized for several weeks and received intensive treatment for 6 months. Rogers was not the only child in the family to develop ulcers: "Something of the gently suppressive family atmosphere is perhaps indicated by the fact that three of six children developed ulcers at some period during their lives. I had the dubious distinction of acquiring mine at the earliest age" (1967, p. 353). Upon returning to the University of Wisconsin, he changed his major from agriculture to history. Rogers received his BA degree in 1924.

After graduation, Rogers married (despite strong parental disapproval) his childhood sweetheart, Helen Elliott, and they later had two children (David, born in 1926, and Natalie, born in 1928). It is interesting to note that when David was born Rogers was inclined to raise him according to the principles of Watsonian behaviorism. He notes, however, that his wife "had enough common sense to make a good mother in spite of all this damaging psychological 'knowledge'" (1967, p. 356). Rogers said observing his children grow up taught him "far more about individuals, their development, and their relationships than I could ever have learned professionally" (1961, p. 12). Following his graduation from the University of Wisconsin, Rogers enrolled in the liberal Union Theological Seminary in New York. Although by now Rogers was interested in helping people with problems, he was increasingly doubtful that the best vehicle for help was to be found in religious doctrine. After 2 years at the seminary, Rogers transferred to Columbia University to study clinical and educational psychology. He received his MA in 1928 and his PhD in 1931. His dissertation was on the measurement of personality adjustment in children.

Upon receiving his PhD, Rogers accepted a position as psychologist in the Child Study Department of the Society for the Prevention of Cruelty to Children in Rochester, New York, where he had worked as an intern while pursuing his PhD. It was here that Rogers had a number of experiences that greatly influenced his later theory of personality and his approach to psychotherapy. First, he learned that the psychoanalytic approach to therapy, which dominated the department, was often ineffective. Second, because of the vastly different approaches to therapy he had studied at Columbia and in the Child Study Department, he learned that so-called authorities could not agree on what constituted the best treatment for a troubled person. Third, he learned that looking for an "insight" into a problem is often met with frustration. Rogers described one situation in which he believed a mother's rejection of her son was the cause of his delinquent behavior. He tried his best to share this "insight" with the mother but failed:

> Finally I gave up. I told her that it seemed we had both tried, but we had failed. . . . She agreed. So we concluded the interview, shook hands, and she walked to the door of the office. Then she turned and asked, "Do you ever take adults for counseling here?" When I replied in the affirmative, she said, "Well then, I would like some help." She came to the chair she had left, and began to pour out her despair about her marriage, her troubled relationship with her husband, her sense of failure and confusion, all very different from the sterile "case history" she had given before. Real therapy began then. . . .
>
> This incident was one of a number which helped me to experience that fact—only fully realized later—that it is the client who knows what hurts, what directions to go, what problems are crucial, what experiences have been deeply buried. It began to occur to me that unless I had a need to demonstrate my own cleverness and learning, I would do better to rely upon the client for the direction of movement in the process. (1961, pp. 11–12)

It was also about this time that Rogers was influenced by Alfred Adler:

> I had the privilege of meeting, listening to, and observing Dr. Alfred Adler. This was the winter of 1927–28, when I was an intern. . . . Accustomed as I was to the rather rigid Freudian approach of the Institute [where he was interning]—seventy-five-page case histories, and exhaustive batteries of tests before even thinking of "treating" a child—I was shocked by Dr. Adler's very direct and deceptively simple manner of relating to the child and the parent. It took me some time to realize how much I learned from him. (quoted in Ansbacher, 1990, p. 47)

From Adler, Rogers learned that lengthy case histories are cold, mechanical, and unnecessary. He also learned that a therapist need not spend time probing the past of a patient. Rather, a therapist could learn more by determining how the patient relates to the here and now.

Rogers wrote his first book, *The Clinical Treatment of the Problem Child* (1939), while at the Child Study Department. In 1940, Rogers moved from a clinical setting to an academic setting by accepting a faculty position in clinical psychology at Ohio State University. It was here that Rogers began to formulate and test his own approach to psychotherapy. In 1942, Rogers published his now-famous book, *Counseling and Psychotherapy: Newer Concepts in Practice* that described the first major alternative to psychoanalysis (for a discussion of how revolutionary Rogers's ideas were, see Hergenhahn, 2004). The publisher was reluctant to publish, believing the book would not sell 2,000 copies, the number necessary to break even. By 1961 it had sold more than 70,000 copies, and it is still going strong.

In 1944, as part of the war effort, Rogers left Ohio State and moved back to New York as Director of Counseling Services for the United Service Organization (USO). After a year, he moved to the University of Chicago as professor of psychology and director of counseling. It was during his stay at the University of Chicago that Rogers published what many consider to be his major work: *Client-Centered Therapy: Its Current Practice, Implications, and Theory* (1951).

In 1957, Rogers left the University of Chicago to return to the University of Wisconsin, where he held the dual position of professor of psychology and professor of psychiatry. At Wisconsin, Rogers found the atmosphere to be overly competitive and nonsupportive. He was primarily concerned with what he perceived as the inhumane treatment of graduate students (Kirschenbaum, 1979, pp. 291–292). Failing in his attempt to improve the situation, he resigned his positions at the University of Wisconsin to become a member of the Western Behavioral Sciences Institute (WBSI) in La Jolla, California. In 1968, Rogers, and several of the more humanistically oriented members of WBSI, left the organization to form the Center for the Studies of the Person, also in La Jolla.

Many of Rogers's moves were coupled with a shift in his interests, techniques, or philosophy. His last move stressed his interest in the individual as he or she experiences the world. Rogers explained, "We are deeply interested in persons but are rather 'turned-off' by the older methods of studying them as 'objects' for research" (1972b, p. 67). In his later years, Rogers worked with encounter groups and taught sensitivity training. He was mainly interested in discovering the conditions under which a person can fully develop his or her potentialities. Also toward the end of his life, Rogers became interested in promoting world peace. He organized the Vienna Peace Project that brought leaders of 13 countries together in 1985, and conducted peace workshops in Moscow in 1986. Rogers continued to work on these and other projects until his death on February 4, 1987, from cardiac arrest following surgery for a broken hip. He was 85 years old.

Rogers received many honors. He served as president of the American Association for Applied Psychology (1944–1945), of the American Psychological Association (APA) (1946–1947), and of the APA's Division of Clinical and Abnormal Psychology (1949–1950); and he was the first president of the newly formed American Academy of Psychotherapists (1956). Also, in 1956, he received the first Distinguished Scientific Contribution Award (along with two other prominent psychologists, Kenneth W. Spence and Wolfgang Köhler) presented by the APA. The latter award moved Rogers to tears because he had believed his colleagues viewed his efforts as nonscientific. In 1972, Rogers received the first Distinguished Professional Contribution Award from the APA, making him the first psychologist in that organization's history to receive both the Distinguished Scientific and Professional Contribution Awards. In 1964, he was named "Humanist of the Year" by the American Humanist Association. In 1986, he was presented a Lifetime Achievement Award by the American Association of Counseling and Development (AACD). On the day of his death, a letter arrived informing Rogers that he had been nominated for the Nobel Peace Prize (Dreher, 1995).

Through the years Rogers maintained that the most important resource people have is their actualizing tendencies, and it is to a discussion of that tendency that we turn next.

Actualizing Tendency

Rogers postulated one master motive that he called *self-actualization*, "The organism has one basic tendency and striving—to actualize, maintain, and enhance the experiencing organism" (1951, p. 487). Rogers further postulated that there is one central source of energy in the human organism; that is a function of the whole organism rather than some portion of it; and that it is perhaps best conceptualized as a tendency toward fulfillment, toward actualization, toward the maintenance and enhancement of the organism. (1963, p. 6)

Rogers was aware that people sometimes act negatively. But, he claimed, such actions are not in accordance with human nature. Such actions result from fear and defensiveness:

> I do not have a Pollyanna view of human nature. I am quite aware that out of defensiveness and inner fear individuals can and do behave in ways which are incredibly cruel, horribly destructive, immature, regressive, anti-social, and hurtful. Yet one of the most refreshing and invigorating parts of my experience is to work with such individuals and to discover the strongly positive directional tendencies which exist in them, as in all of us, at the deepest levels. (1961, p. 27)

The **actualizing tendency**, which is the driving force in everyone's life, causes the person to become more differentiated (complex), more independent, and more socially responsible. We say more about the actualizing tendency when we describe the fully functioning person later in this chapter.

Organismic Valuing Process

All of the organism's experiences can be evaluated using the actualizing tendency as a frame of reference. Rogers called this method of evaluation of one's experiences the **organismic valuing process.** Those experiences that are in accordance with the actualizing tendency are satisfying and therefore are approached and maintained. Those experiences that are contrary to the actualizing tendency are unsatisfying and therefore are avoided or terminated. The organismic valuing process, therefore, creates a feedback system that allows the organism to coordinate its experiences with its tendency toward self-actualization. This means that people can trust their *feelings.* Rogers believed that even infants, if given the opportunity, will choose what is best for them:

> The simplest example is the infant who at one moment values food, and when satiated, is disgusted with it; at one moment values stimulation, and soon after, values only rest; who finds satisfying the diet which in the long run most enhances his development. (1959, p. 210)

In his own life, Rogers learned the value of acting on his own feelings:

> One of the basic things which I was a long time in realizing, and which I am still learning, is that when an activity feels as though it is valuable or worth doing, it is

worth doing. Put another way, I have learned that my total organismic sensing of a situation is more trustworthy than my intellect.

> All of my professional life I have been going in directions which others thought were foolish, and about which I have had many doubts myself. But I have never regretted moving in directions which "felt right," even though I have often felt lonely or foolish at the time. . . . *Experience is, for me, the highest authority.* . . . Neither the Bible nor the prophets—neither Freud nor research—neither the revelations of God nor man—can take precedence over my own experience. (1961, pp. 22–24)

Valuing feelings (emotions) over the intellect and believing in the inherent goodness of humans places Rogers in the philosophical tradition of romanticism (Hergenhahn, 2004). There is a close correspondence between romanticism and humanistic psychology.

Phenomenological Field

The following quotation identifies Rogers as a phenomenologist and shows a kinship between his position and Kelly's:

> The only reality I can possibly know is the world as I perceive and experience it at this moment. The only reality you can possibly know is the world as you perceive and experience it at the moment. And the only certainty is that those perceived realities are different. There are as many "real worlds" as there are people! (Rogers, 1980, p. 102)

According to Rogers, all people live in a subjective world, which can be known, in any complete sense, only to themselves. It is this **phenomenological reality,** rather than the physical world, that determines people's behavior. In other words, how people interpret things is, for them, the only reality. This private reality will correspond in varying degrees to objective reality depending on the individual. It is this subjective, phenomenological reality that the therapist, according to Rogers, must attempt to understand. Again, a great deal of similarity exists on this point between Rogers's theory and Kelly's. Both stressed the individual's singular, subjective interpretation of experience, and that is why they both are labeled phenomenologists. The major difference between Rogers and Kelly is in the actualizing tendency. Kelly's major point was that people continue to try new constructs in order to find the set that best anticipates the future. There was, for Kelly, no innately determined condition toward which all humans were evolving. Rather, each individual, in a sense, invents his or her personality rather than having its major features genetically determined. The view of the social-cognitive theorist (see Chapter 11) is similar to Kelly's.

Rogers differentiated between **experience** and **awareness.** Experience is all that is going on within the organism's environment at any given moment that is potentially available to awareness. When these potential experiences become *symbolized,* they enter awareness and become part of the person's **phenomenological field.** The symbols that act as vehicles for experiences to enter awareness are usually words but they need not be. Rogers believed that symbols also could be visual and auditory images. The distinction between experience and awareness was important to Rogers because, as we shall see, certain conditions cause people to deny or distort certain experiences, thereby preventing them from entering their awareness.

Emergence of the Self

At first, infants do not distinguish between events in their phenomenological field; the events all blend together in a single configuration. Gradually, however, through experiences with verbal labels such as "me" and "I," a portion of their phenomenological field becomes differentiated as the **self.** At this point, a person can reflect on him- or herself as a distinct object of which he or she is aware.

The development of the self is a major manifestation of the actualizing tendency, which, as stated earlier, inclines the organism toward greater differentiation and complexity. The actualizing tendency that, prior to the development of the self, characterized the organism as a whole, now characterizes the self as well. In other words, those experiences viewed as enhancing one's self-concept are positively valued; those viewed as detrimental to the self-concept are negatively valued.

Need for Positive Regard

With the emergence of the self comes the **need for positive regard** that Rogers believed was universal although not necessarily innate (whether it was learned or innate was unimportant to Rogers). Positive regard means receiving warmth, love, sympathy, care, respect, and acceptance from the relevant people in one's life. In other words, it is the feeling of being prized by those people who are most important to us.

As a typical part of the socialization process, children learn there are things they can and cannot do. Most often parents will make positive regard contingent on desirable behavior on the part of their children. That is, if the children do certain things, they will receive positive regard; if they do other things, they will not. This creates what Rogers called **conditions of worth** that specify the circumstances under which children will receive positive regard. Through repeated experiences with these conditions of worth, children internalize them, making them part of their self-structure. Once internalized, they become a conscience, or superego, guiding the children's behavior even when the parents are not present.

From the need for positive regard comes the **need for self-regard.** That is, children develop the need to view themselves positively. In other words, children first want others to feel good about them and then they want to feel good about themselves. The conditions that make relevant people in their lives regard them positively are introjected into their self-structure and thereafter they must act in accordance with those conditions in order to regard themselves positively. The children are now said to have acquired conditions of worth. Unfortunately, when conditions of worth have been established, the only way children can view themselves positively is by acting in accordance with someone else's values that they have internalized. Now children's behavior is no longer guided by their organismic valuing process but by the conditions in their environment that are related to positive regard.

Whenever there are conditions of worth in children's lives, they may be forced to deny their own evaluations of their experiences in favor of someone else's evaluation, and this causes an alienation between people's experiences and their self. This alienation creates a condition of incongruence that we discuss in the next section.

The only way not to interfere with children's actualizing tendencies is to give them **unconditional positive regard** that allows them to experience positive regard no matter what they do:

> If an individual should *experience only unconditional positive regard,* then no *conditions of worth* would develop, *self-regard* would be unconditional, the needs for *positive regard* and *self-regard* would never be at variance with *organismic evaluation,* and the individual would continue to be *psychologically adjusted,* and would be fully functioning. (Rogers, 1959, p. 224)

This does not mean that Rogers believed children should be allowed to do whatever they please. He believed a rational, democratic approach to dealing with behavior problems is best. Because, according to Rogers, conditions of worth are at the heart of all human adjustment problems, they should be avoided at all costs. Rogers suggested the following strategy for dealing with a misbehaving child:

> If the infant always felt prized, if his own feelings were always accepted even though some behaviors were inhibited, then no conditions of worth would develop. This could at least theoretically be achieved if the parental attitude was genuinely of this sort: "I can understand how satisfying it feels to you to hit your baby brother (or to defecate when and where you please or to destroy things) and I love you and am quite willing for you to have those feelings. But I am quite willing for me to have my feelings, too, and I feel very distressed when your brother is hurt, . . . and so I do not let you hit him. Both your feelings and my feelings are important, and each of us can freely have his own." (1959, p. 225)

In other words, Rogers believed the following message should be conveyed to the child: We love you deeply as you are but what you are doing is upsetting and therefore we would be happier if you would stop. The child should always be loved, but some of his or her behaviors may not be.

Incongruent Person

Incongruency exists when people no longer use their organismic valuing process as a means of determining if their experiences are in accordance with their actualizing tendency. If people do not use their own valuing process for evaluating their experiences, then they must be using someone's **introjected values** in doing so. That is, conditions of worth have replaced their organismic valuing process as the frame of reference for evaluating their experiences. This results in an alienation between the self and experience because, under these circumstances, what may truly be satisfying to the person may be denied awareness because it is not in accordance with the person's introjected conditions of worth.

Rogers looked on incongruence as the cause of all human adjustment problems. It follows, then, that eliminating incongruence will solve those problems:

> This, as we see it, is the basic estrangement of man. He has not been true to himself, to his own natural organismic valuing of experience, but for the sake of preserving the positive regard of others has now come to falsify some of the values he experiences and to perceive them only in terms based upon their value to others. Yet this has not been an obvious choice, but a natural—and tragic—development in infancy. The path of development toward psychological maturity . . . is the undoing of this estrangement in man's functioning . . . the achievement of a self which is congruent with experience, and the restoration of a unified organismic valuing process as the regulator of behavior. (Rogers, 1959, pp. 226–227)

When an incongruency exists between self and experience the person is, by definition, maladjusted and is vulnerable to anxiety and **threat** and therefore is defensive.

Anxiety results when people *subceive* an experience as being incompatible with their self-structure and its introjected conditions of worth. In other words, anxiety is experienced when an event is encountered that *threatens* the existing self-structure. Note that Rogers said that the event is *subceived* rather than *perceived*. **Subception** is the detection of an experience before it enters full awareness. This way a potentially threatening event can be denied or distorted before it causes anxiety. According to Rogers, the process of **defense** consists of editing experiences, using the mechanisms of **denial** and **distortion,** to keep them in accordance with the self-structure. It is important to note that an experience, according to Rogers, is not denied **symbolization** because it is "sinful" or "naughty" or contrary to cultural mores, as Freud believed. It is denied symbolization because it is contrary to the self-structure. For example, if a person's introjected conditions of worth include being a poor student, then receiving a good grade on a test would be threatening, and the experience would tend to be distorted or denied. The person may say, for example, that he or she was just lucky or that the teacher made a mistake.

According to Rogers, almost all individuals experience incongruency and therefore defend against symbolization of certain experiences into awareness. It is only when the incongruency is severe that adjustment problems occur.

Psychotherapy

Like Kelly, Rogers's notion of personality came from his therapeutic practice. **Psychotherapy** was paramount to Rogers; his personality theory developed only as he tried to become more effective as a therapist, and as he tried to comprehend the principles that operated during the therapeutic process.

> The gradually formed and tested hypothesis [was] that the individual has within himself vast resources for self-understanding, for altering his self-concept, his attitudes, and his self-directed behavior—and that these resources can be tapped if only a definable climate of facilitative psychological attitudes can be provided. (1974, p. 116)

Through the years, Rogers's description of the therapeutic process changed (Holdstock & Rogers, 1977). First, he referred to his approach to therapy as **nondirective therapy** that emphasized clients' ability to solve their own problems if they were given the proper atmosphere for doing so. Next, Rogers labeled his technique **client-centered therapy.** Now therapy was regarded as a joint venture deeply involving both client and therapist. Instead of simply providing an atmosphere in which clients could gradually comprehend the nature of their problems, as was the case in the earlier stage, the therapist's job now was to attempt actively to understand the client's phenomenological field or **internal frame of reference.** The next stage was called the **experiential stage.** During this stage in the evolution of Rogers's thinking, the therapist became as free as the client. Now the deep, personal feelings of both therapist and client were equally important, and the therapeutic process was regarded as a struggle to put these feelings into words.

The last stage in Rogers's thinking was labeled the **person-centered stage.** During this stage, Rogers's theory was extended to many areas beyond the therapeutic process. A sample of the areas to which his theory has been applied includes education, marriage and the family, encounter groups, problems of minority groups, and international relations. Rogers believed, however, that it is not the greater applicability that is most important to this stage of development; rather, it is the emphasis on the *total* person instead of looking at an individual in terms of some specific role:

> The shift in emphasis to person-centered points out more than the widespread applicability of the theory. It attempts to emphasize that it is as person; as I am, as being, and not just in terms of some role identity as client, student, teacher, or therapist that the individual is the unit of all interactions. The name change conveys the full complexity of each person; it indicates that each individual is more than the sum of the parts that make the person. (Holdstock & Rogers, 1977, p. 129)

In 1980, Rogers described his person-centered approach as follows:

> I am no longer talking simply about psychotherapy, but about a point of view, a philosophy, an approach to life, a way of being, which fits any situation in which *growth*—of a person, a group, or a community—is part of the goal. (p. ix)

With the many changes in Rogers's thinking through the years, however, certain basic components of his theory have remained unchanged. These are the importance of the actualizing tendency, the importance of the organismic valuing process as a frame of reference in living one's life, and the importance of unconditional positive regard in allowing a person to live a rich, full life.

Rogers (1959, p. 213) summarized the six conditions he thought were necessary for effective therapy as follows:

1. The client and the therapist must be in psychological contact; that is, both must make a difference in the phenomenological field of the other.
2. The client must be in a state of incongruence and therefore vulnerable or anxious.
3. The therapist must be in a state of congruency in relation to the client.
4. The therapist must give the client unconditional positive regard.

5. The therapist must seek an empathic understanding of the client's internal frame of reference.
6. The client must perceive the fact that the therapist is giving him or her unconditional positive regard and is attempting to understand empathetically his or her internal frame of reference.

If the above conditions necessary for effective therapy have been met, then, according to Rogers (1959, p. 216), the following changes in the client will be observed:

1. Clients express their feelings with increased freedom.
2. Clients become more accurate in their description of their experiences and of the events around them.
3. Clients begin to detect the incongruity between their concept of self and certain experiences.
4. Clients feel threatened as incongruity is experienced, but the unconditional positive regard of the therapist allows them to go on experiencing incongruent experiences without the necessity of distorting or denying them.
5. Clients eventually are able to symbolize accurately, and thus be aware of, feelings which in the past had been denied or distorted.
6. Clients' concepts of self become reorganized and thus are able to include those experiences which had previously been denied awareness.
7. As therapy continues, clients' concepts of self become increasingly congruent with their experience; that is, they now include many experiences which were previously threatening. As clients feel less threatened by experience, they become less defensive.
8. Clients become increasingly able to experience, without feeling threatened, the therapist's unconditional positive regard.
9. Clients feel an increasing amount of unconditional positive self-regard.
10. Therapy is successful if, in the end, clients' experiences are evaluated in terms of their organismic valuing process and not in terms of conditions of worth.

Rogers shared the reactions of one of his clients after several therapeutic sessions:

I find that many individuals have formed themselves by trying to please others, but again, when they are free, they move away from being this person. So one professional man, looking back at some of the process he has been through, writes, toward the end of therapy: "I finally felt that I simply had to begin doing what I wanted to do, not what I thought I should do, and regardless of what other people feel I should do. This is a complete reversal of my whole life. I've always felt I had to do things because they were expected of me, or more important, to make people like me. The hell with it! I think from now on I'm going to just be me—rich or poor, good or bad, rational or irrational, logical or illogical, famous or infamous. So thanks for your part in helping to rediscover Shakespeare's 'To Thine Own Self be True.'" (1961, p. 170)

Therapy, then, is designed to eliminate incongruity between experience and the self. When the person is living in accordance with his or her organismic valuing process, rather than conditions of worth, the defenses of denial and distortion are no longer necessary and the individual is referred to as a **fully functioning person.**

Fully Functioning Person

In many ways, the fully functioning person is like a young infant because he or she lives in accordance with his or her own organismic valuing process rather than conditions of worth. Rogers equated "being true to oneself" with the good life. Happiness is not the tranquility that comes when all of one's biological needs are satisfied or when one attains a sought-after goal, such as a house, a large amount of money, or a college degree. Happiness comes from the active participation in the actualizing tendency that is a continuous process. It is important to note that Rogers stressed the actualizing tendency, and not the *state* of self-actualization.

We have seen that to use one's organismic valuing process as a guide for living one's life, it is necessary to exist in an unconditional environment. Rogers believed unconditional positive regard was an essential ingredient of psychotherapy but one need not undergo psychotherapy in order to experience unconditional positive regard. A few people experience it in their home, in their marriage, or with close friends.

In 1980, Rogers extended the conditions that he believed must be present in any human relationship if growth is to occur:

> There are three conditions that must be present in order for a climate to be growth promoting. These conditions apply whether we are speaking of the relationship between therapist and client, parent and child, leader and group, teacher and student, or administrator and staff. The conditions apply, in fact, in any situation in which the development of the person is a goal. . . . The first element could be called *genuineness,* realness, or congruence. . . . The second attitude of importance in creating a climate for change is acceptance, or caring, or prizing—what I have called *"unconditional positive regard."* . . . The third facilitative aspect of the relationship is *empathic understanding.* . . . This kind of sensitive, active listening is exceedingly rare in our lives. We think we listen, but very rarely do we listen with real understanding, true empathy. Yet listening, of this very special kind, is one of the most potent forces for change that I know. (pp. 115–116, emphasis added)

For Rogers, it was important not to confuse empathy with passive listening or with sympathy. Empathy, he said, "Means temporarily living in the other's life, moving about in it delicately without making judgments" (1980, p. 142). In an article published after his death, Rogers explained further:

> To be really empathetic is one of the most active experiences I know. You have to really understand what it feels like to this person in this situation. . . . To really let oneself go into the inner world of this other person is one of the most active, difficult, and demanding things I know. (1987, p. 45)

If people are fortunate enough to have a generous portion of the three types of experiences just described, they will be free to act in accordance with their feelings—that is, in accordance with their organismic valuing process. Such people will be fully functioning and, according to Rogers (1959, pp. 234–235), they will have at least the following characteristics:

1. They will be **open to experience**—that is, they will exhibit no defensiveness. Therefore, their experiences will be accurately symbolized and thus available to awareness.
2. Their self-structures will be congruent with their experiences and will be capable of changing so as to assimilate new experiences.
3. They will perceive themselves as the locus of evaluation of their experiences. In other words, their organismic valuing process is used to evaluate their experiences instead of conditions of worth.
4. They will experience unconditional self-regard.
5. They will meet each situation with behavior that is a unique and creative adaptation to the newness of that moment. In other words, they meet each new experience with honest spontaneity instead of with preconception of what those experiences should mean. In 1961, Rogers referred to this characteristic of a fully functioning person as "existential living," which he described as follows: "What I will be in the next moment, and what I will do, grows out of that moment, and cannot be predicted in advance either by me or by others" (p. 188).
6. They will live in harmony with others because of the rewarding nature of reciprocal unconditional positive regard.

In 1961, Rogers added two characteristics to his description of fully functioning persons. One was the experience of subjective freedom:

He is *free*—to become himself or to hide behind a facade; to move forward or to retrogress; to behave in ways which are destructive of self and others, or in ways which are enhancing; quite literally free to live or die, in both the physiological and psychological meaning of those terms. (p. 192)

The other was creativity:

With his sensitive openness to his world, his trust of his own ability to form new relationships with his environment, he would be the type of person from whom creative products and creative living emerge. He would not necessarily be "adjusted" to his culture, and he would almost certainly not be a conformist. (p. 193)

Q-Sort Technique

One of the more interesting aspects of Rogers's theory is that he stressed the importance of the completely subjective phenomenological field of the individual, on the one hand, and the importance of scientific methodology, on the other:

Therapy is the experience in which I can let myself go subjectively. Research is the experience in which I can stand off and try to view this rich subjective experience with objectivity, applying all the elegant methods of science to determine whether I have been deceiving myself. The conviction grows in me that we shall discover laws of personality and behavior which are as significant for human progress or human understanding as the law of gravity or the laws of thermodynamics. (1961, p. 14)

As a therapist with an inclination toward science, Rogers could not accept on faith the changes that were *supposed* to occur during therapy, or the changes that *appeared* to take place. Like any good scientist, Rogers had to find a way to *quantify* the extent to which a client changed as a function of therapy. The technique that Rogers found most useful was one developed by William Stephenson, a colleague of Rogers at the University of Chicago (Stephenson, 1953). The method was called the **Q-sort technique.**

The Q-sort technique can be administered in a number of different ways, but all of them use the same basic concepts and assumptions. First, it is assumed that the client can describe him- or herself accurately, and this is called the **real self.** Second, it is assumed that a person can describe those attributes that he or she would like to possess but currently does not; this is called the **ideal self.** Typically, when therapy begins there is a discrepancy between a person's real self (what he or she is) and the ideal self (what he or she would like to be).

The procedures used in administering the Q-sort are as follows:

1. The client is given 100 cards, each containing a statement such as the following:

   I have a warm, emotional relationship with others.

   I put on a false front.

   I am intelligent.

   I have a feeling of hopelessness.

   I despise myself.

   I have a positive attitude toward myself.

   I often feel humiliated.

   I can usually make up my mind and stick to it.

   I express my emotions freely.

   I am fearful of sex.

2. The client is asked to choose those statements that best describe the way he or she is. This creates the **self-sort.** To facilitate the statistical analysis of the results of the various Q-sorts, the client is asked to select cards in a manner that approximates a normal distribution. This is done by asking the client to place the cards in nine piles. The piles are arranged to reflect those statements that are most like the client, on one extreme, to the statements least like the client, on the other. Statements placed in the middle pile are those for which the client cannot decide whether the trait listed is like him or her or not; that is, they are neutral. The number of piles and the number of cards the client is asked to place in each pile are shown in Table 14–1.

3. Next, the client is asked to sort the cards again but this time in such a way that they describe the person he or she would most like to be. This creates the **ideal-sort.**

Table 14–1		LEAST LIKE ME			UNDECIDED			MOST LIKE ME		
A typical Q-sort arrangement.	Pile No.	0	1	2	3	4	5	6	7	8
	No. of Cards (Total: 100)	1	4	11	21	26	21	11	4	1

These procedures allow the therapist to examine several features of the therapeutic process. Most importantly, the therapist can examine the relationship between the person's real self and his or her ideal self at the beginning, during, and at the end of therapy. The most common way of quantifying these changes is by using the correlation coefficient. When two sets of scores are perfectly correlated in a positive direction, the correlation coefficient is +1.00. When there is a perfect negative or inverse relationship, the correlation coefficient is −1.00. When there is no relationship, the correlation coefficient is .00. The stronger the tendency is for two sets of measures to be positively related, the higher the positive correlation coefficients will be. For example, +.95, +.89, and +.75 all represent high, positive correlations. The stronger the tendency is for two sets of measures to be inversely related, the higher the negative correlation coefficient will be. For example, −.97, −.85, and −.78 all represent high, negative correlations.

Rogers (1954a) reported the following correlation coefficients between a self-sort for a client, known as Mrs. Oak, before therapy and a self-sort for that client at the following points during the therapeutic process:

After seventh session	.50
After twenty-fifth session	.42
After therapy	.39
Twelve months after therapy	.30

The correlation coefficients just listed indicate the self-concept of the client became increasingly *unlike* the self-concept the client had when she started therapy. Rogers also correlated the ideal-sort *after therapy* with the self-sort at various stages of therapy and obtained the following coefficients:

Before therapy	.36
After seventh session	.39
After twenty-fifth session	.41
After therapy	.67
Twelve months after therapy	.79

The foregoing correlation coefficients indicate that the self-concept became increasingly like the ideal self-concept as therapy progressed, with the tendency continuing after therapy had terminated. In other words, the client became more like the person he or she had described as ideal. It seems that in this case, based on the aforementioned data, therapy was accomplishing exactly what Rogers had hoped it would.

We will examine additional Q-sort research when we evaluate Rogers's theory later in this chapter.

In addition to being the first therapist actually to measure the effectiveness (or ineffectiveness) of therapy, Rogers was also the first to record and film therapy sessions. He did this, with the client's permission, so that the therapist would not need to rely on his or her memory (perhaps selective) of what happened in order to evaluate the session. In addition, recording and filming allows the careful analysis of aspects of behavior such as speech mannerisms and physical gestures as possible indicators of the extent to which the client was experiencing stress or anxiety.

Again, it is somewhat paradoxical that the theorist who insisted the only way to know a person is to attempt to understand his or her private, unique, subjective world was also the therapist who did the most to stimulate the scientific evaluation of the therapeutic process.

Rogers–Skinner Debate

On September 4, 1955, members of the American Psychological Association held their breath as two of the world's most influential psychologists climbed on stage at the association's annual meeting in Chicago to engage in debate. What psychologist could ask for more? In one corner was Carl Rogers, representing the phenomenological, subjective approach to understanding humans, who claimed the master motive behind human action is the actualizing tendency. Rogers also represented the belief in the innate goodness of the individual whose freedom comes from within. In the other corner was B. F. Skinner, representing the behavioristic, objective approach to understanding humans. Skinner also represented the belief that what a person becomes is explained in terms of environmental reinforcement contingencies, not of a built-in actualizing tendency. The stage was set for an intense philosophical confrontation. What actually happened was less than a battle; in fact, there was about as much agreement between the two men as there was disagreement.

Both Rogers and Skinner agreed that humans have always attempted to understand, predict, and control human behavior; that the behavioral sciences have made vast progress in developing the ability to predict and control human behavior; and both stated their commitment to the further development of the behavioral sciences.

The most important difference between Rogers and Skinner was over the idea of cultural engineering. Skinner believed behavioral principles should be used in designing a culture that more efficiently satisfied human needs. To Rogers that notion raised the following important questions: "Who will be controlled? Who will exercise control? What type of control will be exercised? Most important of all, toward what end or what purpose, or in the pursuit of what value, will control be exercised?" (1956c, p. 1060).

Rogers proposed a model of humans that emphasizes their actualizing tendency and creative powers. Rather than controlling human behavior from the outside, Rogers suggested that principles developed in the behavioral sciences be applied to the creation of conditions that would release and facilitate humans' inner strengths.

Another major difference between Rogers and Skinner was over the issue of whether human behavior is free or determined. Skinner maintained that human behavior is determined by reinforcement contingencies. Rogers, however, maintained that the existence of choice cannot be denied. He agreed that science must assume determinism, but believed this did not conflict with the existence of responsible choice on the individual level:

> Behavior, when it is examined scientifically, is surely best understood as determined by prior causation. This is one great fact of science. But responsible personal choice, which is the most essential element in being a person, which is the core experience in psychotherapy, which exists prior to any scientific endeavor, is an equally prominent fact in our lives. To deny the experience of responsible choice is, to me, as restricted a view as to deny the possibility of a behavioral science. That these two important elements of our experience appear to be in contradiction has perhaps the same significance as the contradiction between the wave theory and the corpuscular theory of light, both of which can be shown to be true, even though incompatible. We cannot profitably deny our subjective life, any more than we can deny the objective description of that life. (Rogers, 1956c, p. 1064)

> My experience in therapy and in groups makes it impossible for me to deny the reality and significance of human choice. To me it is not an illusion that man is to some degree the architect of himself . . . for me the humanistic approach is the only possible one. It is for each person, however, to follow the pathway—behavioristic or humanistic—that he finds most congenial. (Rogers, 1974, p. 118)

Skinner maintained that his major argument with Rogers was over method, because they both wanted to see approximately the same type of person in the future:

> The whole thing is a question of method. That's the crux of my argument with Carl Rogers; I'd like people to be approximately as Rogers wants them to be. I want independent people, and by that I mean people who don't have to be told when to act or who don't do things just because they've been told they're the right things to do. . . . We agree on our goals; we each want people to be free of the control exercised by others—free of the education they have had, so that they profit by it but are not bound by it, and so on. (quoted in Evans, 1968, pp. 67–68)

As already mentioned, Rogers agreed with Skinner that the behavioral sciences are, and should be, advancing but to have such knowledge is not necessarily to know how to use it. Rogers contended that, depending on how this information is used, we will experience great positive growth or destruction:

> So I conclude that knowledge in the science of psychology will in the near future be used and exploited as fully as knowledge in the physical sciences is used today. The challenge for educators is unreal only if we are looking a year or two ahead. From the long view I know of no problem holding greater potentiality of growth and of destruction than the question of how to live with the increasing power the behavioral sciences will place in our hands and the hands of our children. (1956b, p. 322)

Freedom to Learn

We have already seen that Rogers was very disturbed by the cold, mechanical way that graduate students were trained when he was a faculty member at the University of Wisconsin (see, e.g., Rogers, 1968). However, Rogers was also highly critical of the

American educational system in general and suspected that the worst would happen unless our educational system was changed radically.

> I have days when I think that educational institutions at all levels are doomed, and perhaps we would be well advised to bid them farewell—state-required curricula, compulsory attendance, tenured professors, hours of lectures, grades, degrees, and all that—and let true learning begin to blossom outside the stifling hallowed walls. Suppose every educational institution, from kindergarten through the most prestigious Ph.D. program, were to close tomorrow. What a delightful situation that would be! Parents and children and adolescents and young people—even a few faculty members, perhaps—would begin to devise situations in which they could *learn*! Can you imagine anything more uplifting to the spirit of all our people? (1980, pp. 268–269)

What Rogers was calling for was nothing short of a revolution: "We should recognize that the transformation to a truly humanistic, person-centered education constitutes a full-scale revolution. It is not a way of tinkering with conventional education. Rather, it entails turning the politics of education upside down" (1980, pp. 307–308).

Rogers believed education in the United States was based on faulty assumptions about the learner. For example, it is widely believed that students must have information given to them and digested for them while they remain passive in the process. Instead of basing education on these and other faulty assumptions, Rogers believed education would be improved if it took into consideration the following facts about the learning process (Rogers, 1969, pp. 157–163):

1. Humans have a natural potential for learning.
2. Learning is best when the student sees relevance in what is being learned.
3. Some learning may require a change in the learner's self-structure, and such learning may be resisted.
4. Learning that necessitates a change in the learner's self-structure occurs more easily in a situation in which external threats are at a minimum.
5. When threats to the learner's self-concept are small, experience can be perceived in great detail, and learning will be optimal.
6. Much learning takes place by doing.
7. Learning proceeds best when the student participates responsibly in the learning process.
8. Self-initiated learning, which involves the whole person, that is, both intellectually and emotionally, is the most long-lasting learning.
9. Independence and creativity are facilitated when self-criticism and self-evaluation are of primary importance, and evaluation by others is of secondary importance.
10. The most useful type of learning is the learning to learn that results in a continuing openness to experiences and a tolerance of change.

In general, Rogers (1968, 1969, 1983) believed that it was wrong to assume that students cannot be trusted to pursue their own educational goals, that creative people develop from passive learners, and that evaluation is the same as education.

Rogers (1968) observed with dismay that "examinations have become the beginning and end of education" (p. 691).

Rogers thought the term **teacher** was unfortunate because it suggests a person who dispenses information to students. Instead, Rogers suggested the term facilitator, to emphasize the fact that the person is there to create an atmosphere conducive to learning. A **facilitator of education** acts on the principles of learning we have listed, and thereby treats each student as a unique person with feelings of his or her own rather than as an object to be taught something.

We see that Rogers's approach to education was not unlike his approach to psychotherapy. In both cases, he insisted it must be recognized that each person is unique, each person has feelings, and each person has an actualizing tendency that functions best when experiencing unconditional positive regard and freedom.

Modern Marriage

Statistics indicate that the institution of marriage in our culture is in trouble and, according to Rogers, this is because marriages are too often based on outdated, simplistic, fallacious, or selfish assumptions. For example, couples frequently believe that simply being in love or being committed to each other is enough to sustain a marriage. Rogers (1972a) gathered statements that he believed signaled these dangerous assumptions:

> "I love you"; "We love each other." . . . "I commit myself wholly to you and your welfare" . . . "I am more concerned for you than I am for myself." . . . "We will work hard on our marriage." . . . "We hold the institution of marriage sacred, and it will be sacred for us." . . . "We pledge ourselves to each other until death do us part." . . . "We are destined for each other." (pp. 199–200)

According to Rogers, all of the preceding statements miss the important point that for marriage to work it must be egalitarian, enriching, and satisfying for *both* partners. Marriage should be a dynamic process within which both partners continually grow. The only pledge that made any sense to Rogers is, "We each commit ourselves to working together on the changing process of our present relationship, because that relationship is currently enriching our love and our life and we wish it to grow" (1972a, p. 201). A good marriage is one that is *mutually beneficial* to the partners involved.

Rogers observed themes running through the apparently successful marriages of couples who had learned the person-centered philosophy from discussion groups, encounter groups, or individual therapy. Rogers summarized those themes:

> Difficulties already present in the partnership are brought into the open. . . . Communication becomes more open, more real, with more mutual listening. . . . The partners come to recognize the value of separateness. . . . The woman's growing independence is recognized as valuable in the relationship. . . . There is increasing recognition of the importance of feelings, as well as reason, of emotions as well as intellect. . . . There is a thrust toward the experiencing of greater mutual trust, personal growth, and shared interests. . . . Roles, and role expectations, tend to drop

away and are replaced by the person choosing her own way of behaving. . . . There is a more realistic appraisal of the needs each can meet in the other. . . . So-called satellite relationships may be formed by either partner, and this often causes pain as well as enriching growth. (1977, pp. 45–52)

Rogers (1977) elaborated on the point concerning **satellite relationships:**

Satellite relationship means a close secondary relationship outside the marriage which may or may not involve sexual intercourse, but which is valued for itself. . . . When two persons in a partnership learn to look upon each other as separate persons, with separate as well as mutual interests and needs, they are likely to discover that outside relationships are one of those needs. (pp. 52–53)

The notion of satellite relationships brings jealousy to mind. For Rogers, however, jealousy suggested possessiveness:

To the extent that jealousy is made up of a sense of possessiveness, any alteration in that feeling makes a profound difference in the politics of the marriage relationship. To the degree that each partner becomes truly a free agent, then the relationship only has permanence if the partners are committed to each other, are in good communication with each other, accept themselves as separate persons, and live together as persons, not roles. This is a new and mature kind of relationship toward which many couples are striving. (1977, p. 55)

Rogers (1977) described a married couple that apparently had overcome possessiveness and its related feeling of jealousy:

Fred and Trish endeavored to make their marriage a relationship in which primary value is placed on each of them as persons. They have tried to share in decision-making, the desires of each having equal weight. Each seems to have avoided, to an unusual degree, any need to possess or control the other. They have developed a partnership in which their lives are both separate and together. They have each developed relationships outside of marriage, and these intimate interactions have often been sexual in nature. They have communicated openly about these relationships and appear to have accepted them as a natural and rewarding part of their individual lives and of their marriage. They like their life-style. Theirs is a marriage both person-centered and far from conventional. (p. 205)

Permitting an intimate satellite relationship within a marriage is apparently easier to accept intellectually than it is emotionally because so many of the couples that have tried one or more of them have ended in divorce. For it to work, according to Rogers, the idea must be acceptable to both marital partners on both intellectual and emotional levels.

Person of Tomorrow

On June 7, 1969, Rogers was at Sonoma State College to deliver the commencement address. He began by saying:

As an undergraduate student I majored in medieval history. I have enormous respect for the scholars of the Middle Ages and their contributions to learning. But I want to speak to you as Carl Rogers, in 1969, not as a medieval symbol. So I hope I will not offend you if I remove these medieval trappings—this nonfunctional cap, this handsome but useless hood, and this robe, designed to keep one warm even in the rigors of a European winter. (quoted in Kirschenbaum, 1979, p. 395)

After removing the garments, the 67-year-old Rogers began discussing "the person of tomorrow." Rogers believed that a "new person" is emerging who has many of the characteristics of a fully functioning person. Such a person is humanistically oriented rather than technologically oriented. It was because of the emergence of such a person that Rogers was optimistic about the future:

> In all candor I must say that I believe that the humanistic view will in the long run take precedence. I believe that we are, as a people, beginning to refuse to allow technology to dominate our lives. Our culture, increasingly based on the conquest of nature and the control of man, is in decline. Emerging through the ruins is the new person, highly aware, self-directing, an explorer of inner, perhaps more than outer, space, scornful of the conformity of institutions and the dogma of authority. He does not believe in being behaviorally shaped, or in shaping the behavior of others. He is most assuredly humanistic rather than technological. In my judgment he has a high probability of survival. (1974, p. 119)

Rogers (1980, pp. 350–352) enumerated 12 characteristics he thought persons of tomorrow will possess. As you can see, the person of tomorrow shares many characteristics with the fully functioning individual described earlier.

1. An openness to both inner and outer experience.
2. A rejection of hypocrisy, deceit, and double talk. In other words, a desire for authenticity.
3. A skepticism toward the kind of science and technology that has as its goal the conquest of nature or the control of people.
4. A desire for wholeness. For example, equal recognition and expression of the intellect and the emotions.
5. A wish for shared purpose in life or intimacy.
6. A tendency to embrace change and risk-taking with enthusiasm.
7. A gentle, subtle, nonmoralistic, nonjudgmental caring.
8. A feeling of closeness to, and a caring for, nature.
9. Antipathy for any highly structured, inflexible, bureaucratic institution. They believe that institutions should exist for the people, not the other way around.
10. A tendency to follow the authority of their own organismic valuing process.
11. An indifference toward material comforts and rewards.
12. A desire to seek a meaning in life that is greater than the individual. Rogers referred to this characteristic as "a yearning for the spiritual."

Rogers believed the emergence of the humanistic person of the future will not go unopposed. He summarized what he considered to be the sources of opposition to such a person in the form of slogans:

> 1. "The State above all." . . . 2. "Tradition above all." . . . 3. "The intellect above all." . . . 4. "Human beings should be shaped." . . . 5. "The status quo forever." . . . 6. "Our truth is the truth." (1980, pp. 353–355)

Rogers was confident that person-centered individuals will prevail, however, and the result will be a more humane world.

Evaluation

Empirical Research

Among Rogers's accomplishments is the fact that he, more than any other therapist, exposed the psychotherapeutic process to scientific examination. Using techniques such as the Q-sort, Rogers and his colleagues were able to examine a client's tendency toward congruency as a function of therapy. We have already seen examples of how the Q-sort has been used to measure therapeutic effectiveness. Further evidence that the Q-sort can be used to measure therapeutic success is provided by Butler and Haigh (1954). These researchers found that the average correlation between real self and ideal self for 25 clients before therapy was −.01, indicating essentially no relationship. Following therapy, the average correlation between real self and ideal self rose to +.34, indicating significant movement toward the clients' ideal selves. A control group consisting of 16 people not undergoing therapy did the Q-sort at the same time as the 25 clients undergoing therapy. For the control group, the first Q-sort showed an average correlation between the real and ideal selves was +.58 and the second Q-sort yielded an average correlation of +.59. The latter correlations showed that the people not involved in therapy showed less of a discrepancy between their real and ideal selves than the clients involved in therapy and that this small discrepancy persisted over time.

Rogers was also responsible for creating encounter groups (sometimes called sensitivity groups or T-groups), and there have been several studies designed to determine their effectiveness. For example, Dunnette (1969) observed that people were found to be more empathetic following an encounter group experience, and Diamond and Shapiro (1973) observed that encounter group participants subsequently felt more in control of their own lives.

The Q-sort has also been widely used as a research tool outside of the therapeutic situation. Turner and Vanderlippe (1958) studied the relationships among the discrepancy between the real self and the ideal self, general effectiveness, and degree of satisfaction for 175 college students. These investigations found that the students for whom the discrepancy between the real and ideal selves was small were active, sociable, emotionally stable, and had higher scholastic averages, as compared to students displaying a wider discrepancy between their real and ideal selves. Rosenberg (1962) found that small discrepancies between the real and the ideal selves related to a variety of measures of successful living. Mahoney and Harnett (1973) found that a measure of self-actualization correlated with degree of congruence. That is, as the discrepancy between the real and ideal selves became smaller, the tendency to display the characteristics of a self-actualizing person became greater.

A great deal of research has been performed in an effort to validate Rogers's claim that empathy, unconditional positive regard, and genuineness are the necessary ingredients for personal growth. Aspy and Roebuck (1974) tested the Rogerian hypothesis in the realm of education. These researchers recorded over 3,500 hours of student–teacher interactions involving 550 primary and secondary school teachers in various parts of this country and abroad. They found that the most important variable in producing favorable educational outcomes was teacher empathy, or the effort to understand the meaning of the school experience from the student's viewpoint. Unconditional positive regard and genuineness were also found to be important. Taken together, empathy, unconditional positive regard, and genuineness produced the most powerful effect. The presence of these three conditions correlated highly with academic achievement, positive self-concepts in the students, decreased discipline problems, decreased truancy, and higher student morale, creativity, and problem-solving ability. In the realm of psychotherapy, Truax and Mitchell (1971) found that the extent to which genuineness, unconditional positive regard, and empathy characterized the therapeutic process, it was successful. Likewise, Gurman (1977) reviewed 22 studies in which clients' perceptions of their therapists were obtained. It was found that those clients who perceived their therapist as displaying empathy, unconditional positive regard, and genuineness tended also to be the clients who perceived their therapy as effective. Because empathy is an important characteristic of effective therapy and other forms of helping relationships, it is important to know if it is something that can be learned or if it is something one is born with. Research strongly suggests that it can be learned (Aspy, 1972; Aspy & Roebuck, 1974; Goldstein & Michaels, 1985). Thus, numerous studies have supported Rogers's contention that empathy, unconditional positive regard, and genuineness are necessary for effective therapy to occur. However, other studies suggest that these ingredients are not sufficient for effective therapy (Sexton & Whiston, 1994). It appears that the personality characteristics of clients interact with the extent to which therapists display empathy, unconditional positive regard, and genuineness produce varying results. In other words, some clients benefit more from "the big three" attributes of therapists than others. In 1967, Truax and Carkhuff reached a similar conclusion: "The therapeutic triad may or may not be 'necessary' but it is clearly not 'sufficient'" (p. 114).

Many studies have also been performed to investigate the Rogerian hypotheses that incongruent individuals must defend themselves by denying or distorting certain experiences. For example, using male undergraduates as subjects, Chodorkoff (1954) tested the hypotheses that congruent people will display less perceptual defense and will be better socially adjusted than incongruent individuals. Both hypotheses were confirmed. Incongruent subjects took significantly longer to identify emotional words (e.g., whore, bitch, or penis) than they did to identify neutral words (e.g., tree, house, or book). For congruent subjects, there was no difference in time of recognition. Also, using clinically experienced judges and a variety of measures, it was found that the congruent people were better socially adjusted than incongruent people. Cartwright (1956) and Suinn, Osborne, and Winfree (1962) also supported the Rogerian contention that congruent individuals tend to be open to experience whereas incongruent individuals tend to be less open to experience.

Rogers (1954b) suggested that adult creativity could be enhanced if a child's early home environment is characterized by openness to experience, if a child is encouraged to have an internal locus of evaluation, and if playing with ideas is encouraged. Harrington, Block, and Block (1987) tested and confirmed Rogers's speculations concerning creativity.

Criticisms

Overly Simplistic and Optimistic Approach. Many believe Rogers's assumption that humans are basically good and born with a tendency toward self-actualization is nothing more than wishful thinking. Carl Rogers has even been compared to Fred Rogers, the kind, sensitive neighbor on children's television (Palmer & Carr, 1991). Real people, say some critics, experience hate as much as love and are often motivated by intense sexual desires. Moreover, except for subception, the importance of unconscious motivation is denied by Rogers. For those who experience bizarre dreams, intense conflict, deep depression, anger, or psychosomatic illness, the Rogerian view of humans does not ring true. Also considered simplistic is Rogers's heavy reliance on self-reports that others have found to be notoriously unreliable. Many have criticized Rogers for a simplicity that is opposite to the simplicity of which Kelly was accused. Rogers emphasized the emotional aspect of personality by saying that what truly feels good is the best guide for action. For Rogers, emotions were more important than the intellect; for Kelly, the opposite was true.

Failure to Credit Those Who Have Influenced His Theory. Many elements are similar in Rogers's and Adler's theories. Both emphasized the whole individual, conscious experience, and an innate drive toward harmonious relationships with fellow humans. A strong relationship also exists between Rogers's theory and Horney's. The crux of Horney's theory was that psychological problems begin when the healthy real self is displaced by the unhealthy idealized self and with its associated tyranny of the should. For Horney, the way to make unhealthy people healthy is to bring them back in touch with their real selves so that the real self, instead of the externally imposed idealized self, would be used as a guide for living. Except for slight differences in terminology, Rogers and Horney were saying about the same thing. There is also considerable similarity between Rogers's theory and that of Allport. For example, both describe the characteristics of psychologically healthy individuals, emphasize the innate goodness of humans, and emphasize conscious rather than unconscious motivation. Although Rogers did acknowledge the influence of Adler on his early thinking about the therapeutic process, he said essentially nothing about the influence of Horney or Allport.

Important Aspects of Personality Ignored or Denied. We have seen that Rogers essentially dismissed the darker side of human nature (e.g., aggressive, hostile, selfish, and sexual motives). He also said very little about the development of personality. Except for the fact that for some the organismic valuing process is displaced by conditions of worth, Rogers said little about the developmental experiences that are conducive to healthy growth.

Contributions

Alternative, Positive View of Humans. Rogers helped illuminate a facet of human nature that was previously obscure. He contributed to the development of a "third force" in psychology that successfully challenged psychology's other two dominant forces, behaviorism and psychoanalysis. This third force within psychology has been named humanistic psychology because of its emphasis on the goodness of human nature and its concern with the conditions that allow humans to reach their full potential. These concerns run through every aspect of Rogers's writings.

New Form of Therapy.   No one since Freud has had more influence on psychotherapy than Rogers. His positive, humanistic approach to counseling and therapy have become extremely popular. Three reasons for its popularity are (1) it is effective; (2) the approach does not require the long, tedious training that psychoanalysis does; and (3) it is positive and optimistic about human nature. Not only did Rogers create a new form of therapy, but he created methods for evaluating the effectiveness of therapy as well. By recording therapeutic sessions, making recordings and transcripts available to other professionals, and developing objective measures of personality change as a function of the therapeutic experience, Rogers, for the first time, made research on psychotherapy scientifically legitimate.

Applied Value.   Again, no one since Freud has had more of an impact on both psychology and on other disciplines. Rogers's person-centered psychology has been applied in such diverse areas as religion, nursing, dentistry, medicine, law enforcement, social work, race and cultural relations, industry, politics, and organizational development (for the various applications of person-centered psychology, see, e.g., Levant & Schlien, 1984). In an interesting paper, Rogers and Ryback (1984) showed how person-centered psychology might be used on the global level to reduce or avoid international conflict, and to reduce conflict within nations among warring factions (see also McGaw, Rice, & Rogers, 1973). Toward these ends, Rogers, in the last years of his life, led workshops in such countries as Brazil, England, Germany, Hungary, Ireland, Japan, South Africa, the former Soviet Union, and Switzerland (Gendlin, 1988; Heppner, Rogers, & Lee, 1984). Lastly, Rogers (1969, 1983) showed how his person-centered principles might be used to improve education at all levels.

In his 1973 address to the American Psychological Association upon receipt of that organization's first Distinguished Professional Contribution Award, Rogers assessed the impact of his work:

> It turned the field of counseling upside down. It opened psychotherapy to public scrutiny and research investigation. It has made possible the empirical study of highly subjective phenomena. It has helped to bring some change in the methods of education at every level. It has been one of the factors bringing change in concepts of industrial (even military) leadership, of social work practice, of nursing practice, and of religious work. It has been responsible for one of the major trends in the encounter group movement. It has, in small ways at least, affected the philosophy of science. It is beginning to have some influence in interracial and intercultural relationships. It has even influenced students of theology and philosophy. (1974, p. 115)

So who was Carl Rogers? Rogers himself offered an answer:

> So, who am I? I am a psychologist whose primary interest, for many years, has been in psychotherapy. . . . I rejoice at the privilege of being a midwife to a new personality—as I stand by with awe at the emergence of a self, a person, as I see a birth process in which I have had an important and facilitating part. (1961, pp. 4–5)

Rosalind Dymond Cartwright, a former colleague of Rogers at the University of Chicago, said of him:

Carl provided a role model for a couple of generations of therapists, clinical psychologists, counseling people and others . . . he is a living example of the theory. He is a man who has continued to grow, to discover himself, to test himself, to be genuine, to review his experiences, to learn from it, and to fight the good fight, which means to stand up and be counted, to stand for something, to live honestly, fully, in the best human sense. (quoted in Kirschenbaum, 1979, p. 394)

In his comments on the occasion of Rogers's death, Gendlin (1988) succinctly described the type of person Rogers was: "He cared about each person—but not about institutions. He did not care about appearances, roles, class, credentials, or positions, and he doubted every authority including his own" (p. 127).

Summary

Rogers was born into a financially successful, religious family. He spent his adolescent years on a farm, where he first became interested in science. A trip to the Far East while in college was highly influential, in that it introduced Rogers to several different cultures, with their own religions and philosophies.

The main premise of Rogers's theory is that all people are born with an actualizing tendency, which causes them to seek those experiences that will maintain and enhance their lives. This tendency drives individuals toward greater complexity, independence, creativity, and social responsibility. Ideally, all individuals evaluate their experiences using the organismic valuing process that indicates if experiences are in tune with the actualizing tendency. Those experiences that cause satisfaction are sought; those experiences that are unsatisfying are avoided. Healthy people use their organismic valuing processes as guides in living their lives.

All people live in their own subjective reality, called their phenomenological field. People act in accordance with their phenomenological field rather than objective reality, that is, physical reality. Experience was defined as all of those events occurring around people of which they could be aware. However, only a small portion of those events is symbolized, thus, entering awareness. Gradually, a portion of the phenomenological field becomes differentiated as the self. The self-concept emerges as a result of repeated experiences involving such terms as I, me, and mine.

With the emergence of the self comes the need for positive regard, which is receiving warmth, love, sympathy, and respect from the relevant people in one's life. The need for positive regard expands into the need for self-regard. This means that now, in addition to children needing relevant individuals to respond to them positively, they also need to respond positively to themselves. Typically, adults do not give children positive regard no matter what they do. Rather, they respond selectively according to what children are doing. In other words, children experience positive regard after certain behaviors but not after other behaviors. This creates conditions of worth that specify how children must behave or feel in order to be positively regarded. These conditions of worth are introjected into children's self-concept and thereby control their self-regard. Now, even in the absence of adults, children must act in accordance with these conditions of worth in order to feel good about themselves. The only way to escape imposing conditions of worth on children is to give them unconditional positive regard.

Conditions of worth create an incongruent person because they force the person to live in accordance with introjected values rather than his or her own organismic valuing process. The incongruent person is vulnerable because he or she must constantly guard against experiences or feelings that violate conditions of worth. Such experiences threaten the self-structure and therefore cause anxiety. When an experience is perceived or subceived as threatening, it is either distorted or denied symbolization. Thus incongruent people, because they are not living in accordance with their true feelings, are more likely to experience anxiety and to perceive experiences selectively.

According to Rogers, the goal of psychotherapy is help the incongruent person become congruent. His approach to therapy, which was originally called nondirective, then client-centered, then experiential, and finally person-centered, emphasized unconditional positive regard that presumably will reduce threat, eliminate conditions of worth, and align the person with his or her own organismic valuing process, thereby becoming a fully functioning person who is open to experience, not defensive, capable of living with others in maximum harmony, experiences subjective freedom, and is creative. Rogers concluded that in addition to unconditional positive regard, genuineness and empathy must characterize any human relationship in which positive growth is sought.

Rogers had two major interests in his professional life: one was to encourage the phenomenological person-centered approach in psychology, and the other was to study scientifically the changes that occur in a person as a function of therapy. His most frequently used method for accomplishing the latter goal was the Q-sort technique. Using this technique, the client is asked to sort 100 cards containing trait descriptions into nine piles. Into which pile a card is placed depends on the extent to which the trait on the card is thought, by the client, to be like or unlike him or her. First, the client is asked to sort the cards in a way that describes how he or she is at the moment; this creates a self-sort. Next, the client is asked to sort the cards so they describe the type of person he or she would like to become; this creates an ideal-sort. These two sorts allow the therapist to make many comparisons; for example, real self-concept before therapy versus real self-concept after therapy, or real self-concept after therapy versus ideal self-concept after therapy. Many other comparisons are possible. Research has indicated that Rogerian therapy can effectively change a client's self-concept in a positive direction.

In 1955, Rogers debated with B. F. Skinner, the world's leading behaviorist. Both men agreed that the behavioral sciences had been growing exponentially, and that such growth was beneficial. However, the two parted company when they discussed how the principles generated by the behavioral sciences should be used. Skinner maintained they should be used as a guide in creating an environment that would encourage desirable behavior and satisfy human needs. His approach emphasized control of behavior from the outside. Rogers maintained that the principles should be used to avoid control from the outside; rather, they should be used to create an environment that gives humans maximal freedom so their actualizing tendencies can function without interference. Skinner suggested that both he and Rogers wanted to see the same type of people but differed in the methods they would employ in producing them.

Rogers believed our educational system is in poor shape. It treats the student as an object to be taught and the teacher as an authority figure who dispenses information in a highly structured environment. Rogers believed such an educational system is based on faulty assumptions about human nature. He believed that it would be more constructive if we assumed that each human wants to learn and that each human will learn if placed in a nonthreatening learning environment characterized by unconditional positive regard. Also, learning will occur much faster and will be retained better if the material to be learned has personal relevance to the learner. Rogers opposed the term teacher and believed that the term facilitator of education was better.

Rogers thought that many marriages fail because they are based on outdated, superficial, or selfish assumptions. He thought that for a marriage to work it must be viewed as a dynamic, mutually satisfying relationship by both partners. Because in such a relationship both partners must remain free, autonomous individuals, one or both may choose to develop a satellite relationship, a close relationship with someone other than one's marital partner.

Rogers envisioned a person of tomorrow emerging that would display many of the characteristics of a fully functioning person. Such a person rejects hypocrisy, has a respect for nature and other people, and resists any attempts to control his or her thoughts or behavior externally. The emergence of such a person, according to Rogers, will be resisted by those who want to maintain the status quo, maintain tradition, emphasize the intellect over emotions, or believe they possess the one truth with which everyone else should act in accordance.

A considerable amount of empirical research has been generated by Rogers's theory and most of it has been supportive. Rogers's theory has been criticized for portraying an overly simplistic and optimistic view of humans; not giving proper credit to other theories on which his is based; and ignoring important aspects of personality. His theory has been praised for promoting a positive view of humans, as opposed to the more negative views of behaviorism and psychoanalysis; creating a new form of therapy as well as methods that can be used to test its effectiveness; and creating a heuristic theory of personality.

Experiential Exercises

1. Rogers thought any relationship characterized by unconditional positive regard, empathy, and genuineness is conducive to positive growth. On the other hand, relationships characterized by conditions of worth stifle positive growth. First, describe a relationship within which you receive unconditional positive regard, empathy, and genuineness and another one in which conditions of worth are placed on you. Do you agree with Rogers that the former is more conducive to your positive growth than the latter? Next, describe what you feel you give in an important relationship. Ask the person involved in this relationship with you if he or she agrees with your assessment. What was his or her response?

2. Explain why you agree or disagree with Rogers's assertion that humans are basically good and if left alone to live in accordance with their organismic valuing process, would live in peace and harmony

with their fellow humans. Include in your response how you think Rogers would explain the fact that some humans engage in criminal activities. What, in your opinion, would Rogers recommend as the most effective way of dealing with criminals? In other words, what would likely reduce the probability of them again committing a criminal act?

3. Make a list of at least 15 statements that you believe accurately describe you as you really are. Some possibilities include:
   I am basically lazy.
   I am overly sensitive.
   I am very moody.
   I am optimistic.
   I am intelligent.
   I am able to express my feelings openly.
   I feel others control me too much.
   I am reliable.

I am pessimistic.
I make new friends easily.
I often feel phony.
I am confused about my future.
I understand myself quite well.
I frequently feel guilty.
I am too critical of myself.

Next, make a list of at least 15 statements that describe the type of person you would ideally like to become. Carefully examine the two lists. If the two lists have many characteristics in common, Rogers would say you are a congruent person. If the lists are quite different, he would say you are an incongruent person. Which are you? In either case, does Rogers's description of the congruent or the incongruent person (whichever applies to you) accurately describe you? Explain.

Discussion Questions

1. First define the actualizing tendency and then discuss its importance to Rogers's theory. Include in your answer a discussion of the organismic valuing process.
2. Explain why Rogers's theory is labeled humanistic and existential. Could it also be labeled cognitive? Explain.
3. Indicate why Rogers was so critical of the American educational system and what he proposed to improve the situation.

Glossary

Actualizing tendency. Innate tendency in all humans to maintain and enhance themselves.

Anxiety. Results when a person perceives or subceives an experience as being incompatible with his or her self-structure and its introjected conditions of worth.

Awareness. Characterizes the events in one's experience that have been symbolized and therefore have entered consciousness.

Client-centered therapy. Description of Rogers's second approach to therapy in which the therapist makes an active effort to understand the client's subjective reality.

Conditions of worth. Conditions under which an incongruent person will experience positive regard.

Defense. Effort to change a threatening experience through distortion or denial.

Denial. Refusal to allow threatening experiences to enter awareness.

Distortion. Modification of a threatening experience so it is no longer threatening.

Experience. All the events of which a person could be aware at any given moment.

Experiential stage. Third stage in the evolution of Rogers's approach to therapy in which the feelings of the therapist become as important as the feelings of the client.

Facilitator of education. Term that Rogers thought was better than teacher because it suggests someone who is helpful and uncritical and who will provide the freedom that is necessary for learning to take place.

Fully functioning person. Person whose locus of evaluation is his or her own organismic valuing process rather than internalized conditions of worth.

Ideal self. Client's description of how he or she would like to be.

Ideal-sort. Statements chosen by a client as best describing the person he or she would most like to be. Part of the Q-sort technique.

Incongruency. Exists when a person is no longer using the organismic valuing process as a means of evaluating experiences. The person, under these conditions, is no longer acting honestly toward his or her self-experiences.

Internal frame of reference. Subjective reality, or phenomenological field, according to which a person lives his or her life.

Introjected values. Conditions of worth that are internalized and become the basis for one's self-regard.

Need for positive regard. Need to receive warmth, sympathy, care, respect, and acceptance from the relevant people in one's life.

Need for self-regard. Need a person develops to feel positively about him- or herself.

Nondirective therapy. Description of Rogers's first approach to therapy in which the emphasis was on the client's ability to solve his or her problems.

Openness to experience. One of the chief characteristics of a fully functioning person.

Organismic valuing process. Frame of reference that allows an individual to know if his or her experiences are in accordance with his or her actualizing tendency. Those experiences that maintain or enhance the person are in accordance with this process; other experiences are not.

Person-centered stage. Final stage in Rogers's thinking in which the emphasis was on understanding the total person, not on understanding the person merely as a client.

Phenomenological field. That portion of experience of which an individual is aware. It is this subjective reality, rather than physical reality, that directs a person's behavior.

Phenomenological reality. Person's private, subjective perception or interpretation of objective reality.

Psychotherapy. To Rogers, an experience designed to help an incongruent person become congruent.

Q-sort technique. Method Rogers used to determine how a client's self-image changed as a function of therapy. *See also* Ideal-sort and Self-sort.

Real self. Client's description of how he or she currently views him- or herself.

Rogers–Skinner debate. Debate held in 1955 between Rogers and Skinner over how best to use the principles discovered by the behavioral sciences.

Satellite relationships. Close relationship with individuals other than one's spouse.

Self. That portion of the phenomenological field that becomes differentiated because of experiences involving terms such as I, me, and mine.

Self-sort. Statements chosen by a client as best describing the person as he or she actually is at the moment. Part of the Q-sort technique.

Subception. Detection of an experience before it enters full awareness.

Symbolization. Process by which an event enters an individual's awareness.

Teacher. Term that Rogers believed was unfortunate because it connotes an authoritarian figure who dispenses information to passive students.

Threat. Anything that is thought to be incompatible with one's self-structure.

Unconditional positive regard. Experience of positive regard without conditions of worth. In other words, positive regard is not contingent on certain acts or thoughts.

ABRAHAM MASLOW

CHAPTER OUTLINE

Like Rogers's theory, the humanistic personality theory developed by Abraham Maslow focuses on human growth and potential. Unlike Rogers, however, Maslow's primary focus was on outstanding individuals who had significant impact in politics, history, medicine, or other fields. Stimulated by the tragedy of World War II, Maslow explained:

> I gave up everything I was fascinated with in a selfish way around 1941. I felt I must try to save the world and to prevent these horrible wars and this awful hatred and prejudice.
>
> It happened very suddenly, you know. One day just after Pearl Harbor I was driving home and my car was stopped by a poor, pathetic parade. Boy Scouts and fat people and old uniforms and a flag and someone playing a flute off-key. . . . As I watched, tears began to run down my face. I felt we didn't understand—not Hitler, nor the Germans, nor Stalin, nor the communists. We didn't understand any of them. I felt that if we could understand, then we could make progress. I had a vision of a peace table, with people sitting around it, talking about human nature and hatred and war and peace and brotherhood.
>
> I was too old to go into the army. It was at that moment that I realized that the rest of my life must be devoted to discovering a psychology for the peace table.
>
> That moment changed my whole life and determined what I have done since. . . . I wanted to prove that human beings are capable of something grander than war and prejudice and hatred. I wanted to make science consider all the problems that nonscientists have been handling—religion, poetry, values, philosophy, art.
>
> I went about it by trying to understand great people, the best specimens of mankind I could find. (quoted in Hall, 1968, pp. 54–55)

Although a number of personality theorists fall into the humanistic camp (for instance Allport and Rogers), it was Maslow who emerged as the spokesperson for humanistic psychology. It was Maslow who took the development of humanistic psychology on as a cause, and he did so with a religious fervor.

Biographical Sketch

Abraham Harold Maslow was born on April 1, 1908, in Brooklyn, New York. He was the first of seven children. His parents were poor, uneducated Jewish immigrants from Russia. Being the only Jewish boy in his neighborhood, he was alone and unhappy much of the time. Like Rogers, Maslow took refuge in books. Maslow described his childhood as follows: "With my childhood, it's a wonder I'm not psychotic. I was a little Jewish boy in the non-Jewish neighborhood. It was a little like being the first Negro enrolled in the all-white school. I was isolated and unhappy. I grew up in libraries and among books, without friends" (quoted in Hall, 1968, p. 37).

Unfortunately, not all of Maslow's problems were outside of his home. Maslow recalled his father as loving whiskey, women, and fighting (Wilson, 1972, p. 131) and thinking of his son (Maslow) as ugly and stupid. Once, at a large family gathering, his father, Samuel, asked, "Isn't Abe the ugliest kid you've ever seen?" Hoffman (1988) describes the impact of such remarks on young Maslow: "Such thoughtless remarks affected the boy's self-image so much that for a time he sought out empty cars when riding the subway, 'to spare others the sight' of him, as though he were horribly disfigured" (p. 6).

If anything, Maslow's mother, Rose, was worse than his father:

[Maslow] grew to maturity with an unrelieved hatred for her and never achieved the slightest reconciliation. He even refused to attend her funeral. He characterized Rose Maslow as a cruel, ignorant, and hostile figure, one so unloving as to nearly induce madness in her children. In all of Maslow's references to his mother—some uttered publicly while she was still alive—there is not one that expresses any warmth or affection. (Hoffman, 1988, p. 7)

One reason for Maslow's bitterness toward his mother was the miserly way in which she ran her household:

[Maslow] recalled bitterly that she kept a bolted lock on the refrigerator, although her husband was making a good living. Only when she was in the mood to serve food would she remove the lock and permit her children to take something to eat. Whenever the young Maslow had a friend over to the house, she was especially careful to keep the refrigerator bolted. (Hoffman, 1988, p. 7)

And then there was the episode with the cats:

As a youngster, [Maslow] was walking alone one day, when he discovered two abandoned baby kittens on the street. He decided to take them home and care for them. Quietly he carried them into the house and down into the basement. That evening, Rose came home and heard the kittens' meows. She descended to the basement and found her son feeding the kittens from a dish of milk. Doubly enraged that he had brought stray cats into her house and then used her dishes to feed them, she seized the kittens. Before his horrified eyes, Rose smashed each one's head against the basement wall until it was dead. (Hoffman, 1988, p. 8)

It is ironic that one so closely associated with humanistic psychology found the motivation for his life's work in his hatred of his mother. In 1969, shortly before his death, Maslow entered the following comments in his personal journal:

> What I had reacted against and totally hated and rejected was not only [my mother's] physical appearance, but also her values and world view, her stinginess, her total selfishness, her lack of love for anyone else in the world, even her own husband and children . . . her assumption that anyone was wrong who disagreed with her, her lack of concern for her grandchildren, her lack of friends, her sloppiness and dirtiness, her lack of family feeling for her own parents and siblings. . . . I've always wondered where my Utopianism, ethical stress, humanism, stress on kindness, love, friendship, and all the rest came from. I knew certainly of the direct consequences of having no mother-love. But the whole thrust of my life-philosophy and all my research and theorizing also has its roots in a hatred for and revulsion against everything she stood for. (Lowry, 1979, p. 958)

Maslow eventually made peace with his father and often spoke of him kindly. Not so, however, with his mother.

In 1925, Maslow enrolled at the City College of New York (CCNY) at the age of 17. In 1926, while still a student at CCNY, Maslow, in an effort to please his father, enrolled in an evening program at the Brooklyn Law School. After only 2 weeks, however, he decided his interests were elsewhere and he abandoned law school. In 1927, Maslow transferred to Cornell University in Ithaca, New York. At Cornell, Maslow took an introductory psychology course from the illustrious Edward B. Titchener who lectured wearing full academic robes. Maslow found Titchener's "scientific introspection" cold and boring, and it caused Maslow to lose interest in psychology temporarily. After only one semester at Cornell, Maslow returned to New York City and re-enrolled at CCNY. In 1928, Maslow transferred to the University of Wisconsin, where he received his BA in 1930, his MA in 1931, and his PhD in 1934.

Shortly after moving to Wisconsin in 1928, Maslow married Bertha Goodman (his first cousin and childhood sweetheart), and they eventually had two children. Maslow claimed that his life really did not start until he married. He was 20 years old at the time, and Bertha was 19. They remained happily married until Maslow's death.

As strange as it now seems, Maslow decided to study psychology when, while a student at CCNY, he discovered the behaviorism of J. B. Watson. He described his excitement over his discovery:

> I had discovered J. B. Watson and I was sold on behaviorism. It was an explosion of excitement for me. . . . Bertha came to pick me up and I was dancing down Fifth Avenue with exuberance; I embarrassed her, but I was so excited about Watson's program. It was beautiful. I was confident that here was a real road to travel, solving one puzzle after another and changing the world. (Hall, 1968, p. 37)

This infatuation with behaviorism ended when Maslow and his wife had their first child:

Our first baby changed me as a psychologist. It made the behaviorism I had been
so enthusiastic about look so foolish I could not stomach it anymore. That was the
thunderclap that settled things. . . . I was stunned by the mystery and by the sense
of not really being in control. I felt small and weak and feeble before all this. I'd say
anyone who had a baby couldn't be a behaviorist. (Hall, 1968, p. 55)

While at the University of Wisconsin, Maslow became the first doctoral student
of Harry Harlow, the famous experimental psychologist, who was just in the process
of developing a primate laboratory to study the behavior of monkeys. Maslow's dissertation was on the establishment of dominance in a colony of monkeys. He noted
that dominance appeared to result from a type of inner confidence or dominance-
feeling rather than through physical strength or aggression. Maslow also observed
that sexual behavior within a primate colony was determined by a member's dominance or subservience, and he wondered if the same was true for humans. He would
soon explore that possibility.

After receiving his PhD in 1934, Maslow continued to teach at the University
of Wisconsin for a short time and even enrolled in medical school there. He found
that medical school, like law school, reflected a dispassionate and negative view of
people and he soon dropped out. In 1935, he moved to Columbia University as a
Carnegie fellow where he worked for 18 months with the eminent learning theorist
Edward L. Thorndike. Thorndike administered one of his intelligence tests to Maslow
and it revealed an IQ of 195, the second highest ever recorded by the test. When
Maslow expressed his interest in pursuing the relationship between dominance and
sexuality, Thorndike expressed his dismay but gave his permission, saying:

I dislike your work [on dominance and sexuality], I wish you wouldn't do it, but
if I don't have faith in my intelligence tests, who will? And I'll assume that if I give
you [permission], it'll be the best for you and me—and for the world. (quoted in
Hoffman, 1988, p. 74)

With this freedom Maslow began his research on human sexuality in late 1935.
He began by interviewing both males and females to determine their feelings of dominance or subservience and their sexual preferences. He soon abandoned males,
however, because they were evasive and "tended to lie, exaggerate, or distort their
sexual experiences" (Hoffman, 1988, p. 77). Maslow devised a standard interview
consisting of such questions as, "What are your physical preferences during lovemaking?", "How often do you masturbate?", "What particular fantasies do you experience while masturbating?" (Hoffman, 1988, p. 78). Based on the answers to these
and other questions, Maslow published several articles on female sexuality between
1937 and 1942. In general he found that when compared to subservient females,
dominant females tended to be unconventional, less religious, less tolerant of female stereotypes, extroverted, more sexually adventuresome, and less anxious, jealous, and neurotic. Maslow also found that the high-dominance female was attracted
to the high-dominance male, who was described as "highly masculine, self-confident,
fairly aggressive, sure of what he wants and able to get it, generally superior in most
things" (quoted in Lowry, 1973, p. 126). In the realm of sex, high-dominance women
expressed preference for:

Straightforward, unsentimental, rather violent, animal, pagan, passionate, even sometimes brutal lovemaking. It must come quickly, rather than after a long period of wooing. She wishes to be suddenly swept off her feet, not courted. She wishes her favors to be taken, rather than asked for. In other words she must be dominated, must be forced into subordinate status. (quoted in Lowry, 1973, p. 127)

Low-dominance women, conversely, were attracted to men who were kind, friendly, gentle, faithful, and showed a love for children. It is interesting to note that Maslow's work on human sexuality appeared several years before Kinsey's famous research appeared in the mid-1940s.

In 1937, Maslow moved to Brooklyn College where he remained until 1951. At Brooklyn College, Maslow taught a full load, continued his research on human sexuality, and advised students. Maslow became so popular as a teacher that the college newspaper referred to him as the Frank Sinatra of Brooklyn College. In 1947, an illness, later diagnosed as a heart attack, forced Maslow to take a medical leave. The Maslows, with their two daughters, moved to Pleasanton, California, where Maslow temporarily managed a branch of the Maslow Cooperage Corporation, and read biographies of illustrious historical figures. In 1949, he returned to Brooklyn College.

We have seen that Maslow's early work was concerned with the healthy, exceptional, dominant specimen. It was but a minor step from these early interests to a concern for the most outstanding human beings.

Maslow was in New York in the late 1930s and early 1940s, when the best minds in Europe were arriving in the United States to escape Nazi Germany. Among those individuals Maslow sought out and learned from were Alfred Adler, Max Wertheimer, Karen Horney, and Erich Fromm.

Also among those having a strong influence on Maslow at this time was the American anthropologist Ruth Benedict. In fact, it was Maslow's deep admiration for Max Wertheimer, a founder of the school of Gestalt psychology, and Ruth Benedict that finally stimulated his interest in self-actualizing people. Maslow described how his efforts to understand these two individuals evolved into what became his life's work:

My investigations on self-actualization were not planned to be research and did not start out as research. They started out as the effort of a young intellectual to try to understand two of his teachers whom he loved, adored, and admired, and who were very, very wonderful people. It was a kind of high-IQ devotion. I could not be content simply to adore, but sought to understand why these two people were so different from the run-of-the-mill people in the world. These two people were Ruth Benedict . . . and Max Wertheimer. They were my teachers after I came with a Ph.D. from the West to New York City, and they were most remarkable human beings. My training in psychology equipped me not at all for understanding them. It was as if they were not quite people but something more than people. My own investigation began as a prescientific or nonscientific activity. I made descriptions and notes on Max Wertheimer, and I made notes on Ruth Benedict. When I tried to understand them, think about them, and write about them in my journal and my notes, I realized in one wonderful moment that their two patterns could be generalized. I was talking about a kind of person, not about two noncomparable individuals. There was wonderful excitement in that. I tried to see whether this pattern could be found elsewhere, and I did find it elsewhere, in one person after another.

By ordinary standards of laboratory research, i.e., of rigorous and controlled research, this simply was not research at all. (1971, pp. 40–41)

The deep admiration Maslow had for Wertheimer and Benedict was only an extension of the admiration he generally had for highly esteemed individuals. He referred to his college professors and illustrious historical figures as his angels because they were always there when he needed help. Maslow idealized his angels and was shocked whenever he learned they were merely human. For example, Maslow once found himself in a washroom with his philosophy professor at an adjoining urinal. About this experience Maslow said, "It stunned me so that it took hours, even weeks, for me to assimilate the fact that a professor was a human being and constructed with the plumbing that everyone else had" (quoted in Wilson, 1972, p. 138). Throughout his professional career Maslow's angels were always there when he needed them.

> I have worked out a lot of tricks for fending off professional attacks. . . . I have a secret. I talk over the heads of the people in front of me to my own private audience. I talk to people I love and respect. To Socrates and Aristotle and Spinoza and Thomas Jefferson and Abraham Lincoln. And when I write, I write for them. This cuts out a lot of crap. (quoted in Hall, 1968, p. 56)

In 1951, Maslow moved to the then new Brandeis University in Waltham, Massachusetts, as chairman of the psychology department. During his early years at Brandeis, administrative duties and personal problems kept Maslow from pursuing his theoretical goals. At this time, he underwent psychoanalysis because of his persistent hostility toward his mother and of the remnants of his childhood experience with anti-Semitism (Hoffman, 1988, p. 203). Before long, however, Maslow was able to resume his study of psychologically healthy humans, and he soon emerged as the leader of third-force psychology (to be discussed shortly). His highly influential book *Motivation and Personality* was published in 1954. Following several highly productive years, however, Maslow's academic life became increasingly turbulent.

In the mid-1960s, there was widespread social unrest in the United States, and a growing counterculture was seeking leadership. Although Maslow appeared to be a likely candidate, Hoffman (1988, pp. 287–312) discusses the reasons why Maslow was a poor choice. Those in the counterculture movement wanted to emphasize feelings, intuition, and spontaneity at the expense of objective inquiry into human nature. Maslow's position was always that the higher aspects of human nature can be, and should be, studied objectively. He refused to totally condemn the American presence in Indochina. He resigned from the American Civil Liberties Union because he believed it was becoming too soft on criminals. He criticized as simplistic the passivism and other political views of his younger daughter, Ellen, and the former Brandeis psychology major, Abbie Hoffman. He openly disagreed with Timothy Leary's advice to "tune in, turn on [with drugs], and drop out." More generally, he further alienated himself from the academic community by criticizing universities in the United States for not contributing to the solution of world problems, and by criticizing faculty members for clinging to medieval guild privileges such as tenure. Furthermore, he concluded that colleges and universities were among the country's most poorly managed organizations. In the midst of all this dissention, Maslow was stunned to learn on July 8, 1966, that he was elected president of the American Psychological Association (Hoffman, 1988, p. 294).

During these turbulent times Maslow viewed his students as self-indulgent and intellectually undisciplined. In one case, Maslow's students wanted to take over a class and teach themselves. Maslow initially resisted but finally conceded. Hoffman (1988) describes what followed:

> Matters improved after he let the malcontents form their own class. He now believed that they had craved fellowship so intensely that they had simply been unable to participate in serious intellectual dialogue. They were merely confused adolescents, not deliberately hurtful. He realized, too, that his own theory of human nature cogently explained their behavior: the need for belongingness is more pressing than the need for self-actualization. But he considered it a pity, and a waste of his intellect, that these young adults were still struggling to satisfy basic needs that should have been met when they were children. (p. 314)

The student takeover of the library and administration building at Columbia University, and failing health, finally convinced Maslow it was time to quit teaching.

Escape from the academic world came when, in late 1968, Maslow was offered a fellowship by the Saga Administrative Corporation, which would provide him with unlimited free time for writing and scholarly work. Maslow accepted the offer and enjoyed his freedom immensely. Unfortunately this ideal situation did not last long. On June 8, 1970, Maslow suffered a fatal heart attack while jogging. He was 62 years old.

Among Maslow's many honors are included presidencies of the American Psychological Association's Division of Personality and Social Psychology (1955–1956) and Division of Esthetics (1960–1961), the Massachusetts Psychological Association (1960–1961), the New England Psychological Association (1962–1963), and the American Psychological Association (1967–1968). He was the recipient of the American Psychological Foundation's Gold Medal Award (1971).

Third-Force Psychology

As noted earlier, Maslow believed his training in psychology did not equip him to understand the positive qualities of people he considered remarkable. By viewing humans as victims of animal instincts and of the conflicts caused by culture, the psychoanalytic camp told only part of the story. Likewise, the behaviorists, who viewed humans as creatures whose behavior is molded by the environment, shed only limited light on the mysteries of human existence. In fact, Maslow believed all of psychology had concentrated on the dark, negative, sick, and animalistic aspects of humans. It was hoped by Maslow that **humanistic psychology** would attend to humans' positive aspects and thus provide information that could be used in formulating a comprehensive theory of human motivation, a theory that would include both the positive and the negative aspects of human nature. For Maslow it was clear that if we wanted to discover the best in humans we had to study exceptional humans.

It was to the study of exceptional people that Maslow dedicated most of his professional life. Maslow believed the typical **reductive-*analytic approach to* science,** which reduces human beings to a collection of habits or conflicts, overlooks the essence of human nature. The **holistic-analytic approach to science,** which studies the person as a thinking, feeling totality, is more likely to yield valid results. If, said Maslow, the standard scientific techniques cannot be applied to the study of the whole person, throw them out and develop techniques that can be used: It is the understanding of humans that is important, and if traditional scientific procedures do not aid in gaining that understanding, so much the worse for them. Maslow even suggested that some scientists are preoccupied with the reductive-analytic approach because it serves as a defense against knowing their own nature. In other words, some scientists in the name of scientific rigor cut themselves off from the poetic, romantic, tender, and spiritual aspects of themselves and other people. Maslow said that such scientists **desacralize** people by making them less marvelous, beautiful, and awesome than they really are.

Maslow's goal was to round out psychology by making it focus on a subject that it had ignored through the years, that is, the healthy, fully functioning human being. This effort was to become psychology's **third force,** with psychoanalysis and behaviorism constituting the other two forces. Maslow (1968) said, "Freud supplied to us the sick half of psychology and we must now fill it out with the healthy half" (p. 5). Maslow was impressed with behaviorism's scientific objectivity but not with its relevance to the real world: "Behaviorism's fatal flaw is that it's good for the lab and in the lab, but you put it on and take it off like a lab coat. It's useless at home with your kids and wife and friends" (quoted in Lowry, 1973, p. 5).

In 1962, Maslow, along with several other humanistically oriented psychologists (including Gordon Allport, George Kelly, Carl Rogers, and Rollo May) established the American Association of Humanistic Psychology, which operated in accordance with the following principles:

1. The primary study of psychology should be the experiencing person.
2. Choice, creativity, and self-realization, rather than mechanistic reductionism, are the concern of the humanistic psychologist.
3. Only personally and socially significant problems should be studied—significance, not objectivity, is the watchword.
4. The major concern of psychology should be the dignity and enhancement of people.

A humanistic science of psychology would consider these principles, and the result would be *less* external prediction and control of human behavior, but greater self-knowledge:

> If humanistic science may be said to have any goals beyond sheer fascination with the human mystery and enjoyment of it, these would be to release the person from external controls and to make him less predictable to the observer (to make him freer, more creative, more inner determined) even though perhaps more predictable to himself. (Maslow, 1966, p. 40)

Maslow was not antiscience. What he opposed was science that excluded important aspects of human nature. Maslow always viewed himself as an objective scientist:

It may sound peculiar in view of [my humanistic psychology work], but I still feel the same love and admiration for objective research. I have not repudiated it nor will I attack it as such. All that happened is that I was forced to realize its limitation, its failure to generate a true and useful image of man. (quoted in Hoffman, 1988, p. 40)

Hierarchy of Needs

The cornerstone of Maslow's position is his theory of motivation that he first proposed in two articles published in 1943 when he was at Brooklyn College (1943a, 1943b). Maslow centered his theory of motivation on the **hierarchy of human needs.** He contended that humans have a number of needs that are **instinctoid,** that is, innate. Maslow chose the term *instinctoid* instead of *instinctive* to demonstrate the difference between our biological heritage and that of nonhuman animals:

> This inner core, even though it is biologically based and "instinctoid," is weak in certain senses rather than strong. It is easily overcome, suppressed or repressed. It may even be killed off permanently. Humans no longer have instincts in the animal sense, powerful, unmistakable inner voices which tell them unequivocally what to do, when, where, how and with whom. All that we have left are instinct-remnants. And furthermore, these are weak, subtle and delicate, very easily drowned out by learning, by cultural expectations, by fear, by disapproval, etc. (1968, p. 191)

Maslow also assumed our needs are arranged in a hierarchy in terms of their potency. Although all needs are instinctoid, some are more powerful than others. The lower the need is in the hierarchy, the more powerful it is. The higher the need is in the hierarchy, the weaker and the more distinctly human it is. The lower, or basic, needs in the hierarchy are similar to those possessed by nonhuman animals, but only humans possess the higher needs.

Physiological Needs

These are the needs directly related to survival that we share with other animals. Included here are the needs for food, water, sex, elimination, and sleep. If one of the **physiological needs** is not met, it will completely dominate the individual's life:

> For our chronically and extremely hungry person, Utopia can be defined simply as a place where there is plenty of food. He or she tends to think that, if only guaranteed food for the rest of life, he or she will be perfectly happy and will never want anything more. Life itself tends to be defined in terms of eating. Anything else will be defined as unimportant. Freedom, love, community feeling, respect, philosophy, may all be waved aside as fripperies that are useless, since they fail to fill the stomach. Such a person may fairly be said to live by bread alone. (Maslow, 1987, p. 17)

Obviously, such needs are extremely important and must be satisfied. But, according to Maslow, psychology has overemphasized the importance of such needs in determining the behavior of humans in a modern society. For most humans, these needs are easily satisfied. The real question, to Maslow, was what happens *after* the physiological needs are satisfied. "It is quite true that humans live by bread alone—when there is no bread. But what happens to their desires when there *is* plenty of bread and when their bellies are chronically filled?" (Maslow, 1987, p. 17). Maslow's answer was that the individual is then dominated by the next level or cluster of needs. It is important to note that Maslow did not believe one set of needs had to be completely satisfied before the individual was released to deal with the next level. Rather, he believed one set of needs had to be consistently and substantially satisfied. In other words, a person can be periodically hungry or thirsty and still be able to deal with higher needs but the person's life cannot be *dominated* by hunger or thirst.

Safety Needs

When the physiological needs are satisfactorily met, the **safety needs** emerge as dominant motives. Included here are the needs for structure, order, security, and predictability. The person operating at this level is very Kellian, in that the primary goal is to reduce uncertainty in his or her life. These needs are most clearly seen operating in children, who typically show great fear when confronted with novel (unpredictable) events. The satisfaction of the safety needs assures individuals they are living in an environment free from danger, fear, and chaos.

Belongingness and Love Needs

With the physiological and safety needs essentially satisfied, the person now is driven by the need for affiliation. Included here are the needs for friends and companions, a supportive family, identification with a group, and an intimate relationship. If these needs are not met, the person will feel alone and empty. Maslow believed the failure to satisfy needs at this level is a major problem in the United States, and this explains why so many people are seeking psychotherapy and joining support groups.

Esteem Needs

If one has been fortunate enough to satisfy one's physiological, safety, and **belongingness and love needs,** the need for esteem will begin to dominate one's life. This group of needs requires both recognition from other people that results in feelings of prestige, acceptance, and status, and self-esteem that results in feelings of adequacy, competence, and confidence. Both types of feelings usually result from engaging in activities considered to be socially useful. Lack of satisfaction of the **esteem needs** results in discouragement and feelings of inferiority.

Self-Actualization

If all the lower needs have been adequately satisfied, the person is in a position to become one of the rare people who experiences **self-actualization:**

> So far as motivational status is concerned, healthy people have sufficiently gratified their basic needs for safety, belongingness, love, respect, and self-esteem so that

Figure 15–1

*Maslow's Hierarchy of
Needs.*

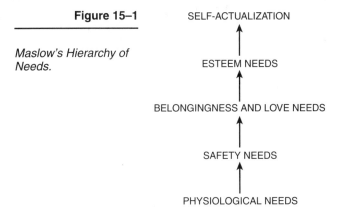

SELF-ACTUALIZATION

↑

ESTEEM NEEDS

↑

BELONGINGNESS AND LOVE NEEDS

↑

SAFETY NEEDS

↑

PHYSIOLOGICAL NEEDS

they are motivated primarily by trends to self-actualization [defined as ongoing actualization of potentials, capacities, and talents, as fulfillment of mission (or call, fate, destiny, or vocation), as a fuller knowledge of, and acceptance of, the person's own intrinsic nature, as an unceasing trend toward unity, integration, or synergy within the person]. (Maslow, 1968, p. 25)

Musicians must make music, artists must paint, poets must write if they are to be ultimately at peace with themselves. What humans can be, they must be. They must be true to their own nature. This need we may call self-actualization. (Maslow, 1987, p. 22)

We have more to say about the characteristics of self-actualized people later in this chapter. Maslow's hierarchy of needs is diagrammed in Figure 15–1.

Exceptions in the Hierarchy of Needs

Maslow believed that most people progress through the hierarchy of needs in the order shown in Figure 15-1. Exceptions occur, however. For example, some people have gone so long with their physiological needs only partially satisfied that they lose all desire to ever progress beyond them. For the rest of their lives, these people may be satisfied if only they can get enough food to eat. Something similar may happen with the need for love. If a person is starved for love in his or her early childhood, the desire for and the ability to give affection may be lost forever. Both of these cases are reminiscent of a Freudian fixation. In the first case, the person is "fixated" on the physiological level of the hierarchy, and in the second case, on the belongingness and love level. Maslow (1987, p. 26) also suggested that the creativity of some innately talented people does not seem to require the satisfaction of the pre-self-actualization needs. Rather, their creativity seems to occur despite such satisfaction.

Degrees of Satisfaction

We saw earlier that one set of needs does not require complete satisfaction before the next higher set is reached. It is also true that no matter what set of needs in the hierarchy a person is concentrating on, he or she is also addressing other sets of needs at the same time. Maslow (1987) explained:

So far, our theoretical discussion may have given the impression that these five sets of needs—physiological, safety, belongingness, esteem, and self-actualization—are somehow in such terms as the following: If one need is satisfied, then another emerges. This statement might give the false impression that a need must be satisfied 100 percent before the next need emerges. In actual fact, most members of our society who are normal are partially satisfied in all their basic needs and partially unsatisfied in all their basic needs at the same time. A more realistic description of the hierarchy would be in terms of decreasing percentages of satisfaction as we go up the hierarchy of prepotency. For instance, to assign arbitrary figures for the sake of illustration, it is as if the average citizen is satisfied perhaps 85 percent in physiological needs, 70 percent in safety needs, 50 percent in love needs, 40 percent in self-esteem needs, and 10 percent in self-actualization needs.

As for the concept of emergence of a new need after satisfaction of the prepotent need, this emergence is not a sudden, saltatory phenomenon, but rather a gradual emergence by slow degrees from nothingness. For instance, if prepotent need A is satisfied only 10 percent, then need B may not be visible at all. However, as this need A becomes satisfied 25 percent need B may emerge 5 percent, as need A becomes satisfied 75 percent need B may emerge 50 percent, and so on. (pp. 27–28)

It should also be noted that no matter how far one has progressed up the hierarchy, if lower needs are frustrated for a considerable length of time, the person will regress to the level of the hierarchy corresponding to those needs and will remain there until those needs are satisfied. Thus, no matter what one has accomplished in life, if the need for food is suddenly unsatisfied, that need will again dominate one's life. Maslow said, "For the man who is extremely and dangerously hungry, no other interests exist but food" (quoted in Lowry, 1973, p. 156). Elsewhere he said, "Respect is a dispensable luxury when compared with food or safety" (1987, p. 57).

Desire to Know and Understand

Maslow believed the **desire to know and understand** was related to the satisfaction of the basic needs. In other words, knowing and understanding were thought to be tools used in solving problems and overcoming obstacles, thereby allowing the satisfaction of the basic needs:

If we remember that the cognitive capacities (perceptual, intellectual, learning) are a set of adjustive tools, which have among other functions that of satisfaction of our basic needs, then it is clear that any danger to them, any deprivation or blocking of their free use, must also be indirectly threatening to the basic needs themselves. Such a statement is a partial solution of the general problems of curiosity, the search for knowledge, truth, and wisdom, and the ever-persistent urge to solve the cosmic mysteries. Secrecy, censorship, dishonesty, and blocking of communication threaten *all* the basic needs. (Maslow, 1987, p. 23)

Thus the needs to know and understand exist at all motivational levels but will be directed at the satisfaction of different needs depending on a person's position in the hierarchy. To progress upward in the hierarchy, the needs to know and understand must be unencumbered.

The Aesthetic Needs

The **aesthetic needs** are for order, symmetry, closure, structure, and for completion of actions, which are seen in some adults and almost universally in children. Maslow believed that evidence exists for such needs in every culture as far back as the cavepeople.

Although the physiological, safety, love and belongingness, and esteem needs and the need for self-actualization form a hierarchy, and the needs to know and understand are functionally related to their satisfaction, it is not clear how the aesthetic needs relate to other needs. Two things are clear, however. First, Maslow believed the aesthetic needs are instinctoid, and second, they are given their fullest expression in self-actualizing individuals.

Being Motivation

What happens to an individual when all of the basic needs have been met to a satisfactory degree, and he or she enters the realm of self-actualization? Maslow's answer was that, in a sense, the person becomes qualitatively different from those who are still attempting to meet their basic needs. The self-actualizing person's life is governed by **being values** (B-values) that Maslow also labeled **metamotives**. "Self-actualizing people are not primarily motivated (i.e., by basic needs); they are primarily metamotivated (i.e., by metaneeds = B-values)" (Maslow, 1971, p. 311). Because **being motivation** affects personal inner growth, it is also called **growth motivation.** Examples of B-values are beauty, truth, and justice.

The lives of nonactualizing people are governed by **deficiency motives (D-motives)**; in other words, they are influenced by the absence of such things as food, love, or esteem. The perception of a nonactualizing person is influenced by his or her deficiencies and is therefore called **need-directed perception** (also called **D-perception** or **D-cognition**). "Need-directed perception is a highly focused searchlight darting here and there, seeking the objects which will satisfy needs, ignoring everything irrelevant to the need" (Jourard, 1974, p. 68).

Being cognition (B-cognition), on the other hand, is qualitatively different from need-directed perception. "Being-cognition . . . refers to a more passive mode of perceiving. It involves letting oneself be reached, touched, or affected by what is there so that the perception is richer" (Jourard, 1974, p. 68).

As an example of the difference between D-motivation and B-motivation, Maslow used the concept of love. He differentiated between D-love and B-love. **D-love** is motivated by the lack of fulfillment of the need for love and belongingness. A person in such a need-state craves love as a hungry person craves food. Such love is selfish because, when obtained, it satisfies a personal deficiency. In contrast to D-love, Maslow (1968, pp. 42–43) listed some of the characteristics of **B-love:**

1. B-love is nonpossessive.
2. B-love is insatiable, it can be enjoyed without end. It usually grows stronger rather than disappearing. D-love, however, can be satiated.
3. The B-love experience is often described as having the same effect as an aesthetic or mystic experience.

4. B-love has a profound and widespread therapeutic effect.
5. B-love is a richer, higher, and more valuable experience than D-love.
6. There is a minimum of anxiety and hostility in B-love.
7. B-lovers are more independent of each other, less jealous, less needful, more interested, and more autonomous than D-lovers. Also, they are more eager to help the other toward self-actualization and are genuinely proud of the other's triumphs.
8. B-love makes the truest, most penetrating perception of the other possible.
9. B-love, in a sense, creates the partner. It offers self-acceptance and a feeling of love-worthiness, both of which permit the partner to grow. Perhaps full human development cannot occur without the experience of B-love.

The list of 15 B-values that Maslow believed dominated the lives of self-actualizing people is shown in Table 15–1.

Although B-values are metaneeds, they are still needs and, as such, they must be satisfied if a person is to experience full psychological health. Failure to satisfy a metaneed (B-value) causes what Maslow called a **metapathology.** A description of the metapathologies caused by the failure to satisfy the various B-values is shown in Table 15–1.

Moments of intense B-cognition cause feelings of ecstasy or rapture. Maslow called these mystic or oceanic feelings **peak experiences,** and we have more to say about them in the next section as we consider the characteristics of self-actualizing people.

Table 15–1

B-Values, Condition That Exists if a B-Value Is Not Satisfied (Pathogenic Deprivation), and the Effect That Not Satisfying a B-Value Has in One's Life (Specific Metapathologies).

B-VALUES AND SPECIFIC METAPATHOLOGIES

B Values	Pathogenic Deprivation	Specific Metapathologies
1. Truth	Dishonesty	Disbelief; mistrust; cynicism; skepticism; suspicion
2. Goodness	Evil	Utter selfishness; hatred; repulsion; disgust; reliance only on self and for self; nihilism; cynicism
3. Beauty	Ugliness	Vulgarity; specific unhappiness, restlessness, loss of taste, tension, fatigue; philisitinism; bleakness
4. Unity; wholeness	Chaos, atomism, loss of connectedness	Disintegration; "the world is falling apart"; arbitrariness
4A. Dichotomy-Transcendence	Black-and-white dichotomies; loss of gradations, of degree; forced polarization; forced choices	Black-and-white thinking, either/or thinking; seeing everything as a duel or war, or a conflict; low synergy; simplistic view of life
5. Aliveness; process	Deadness; mechanization of life	Deadness; robotizing; feeling oneself to be totally determined; loss of emotion; boredom (?); loss of zest in life; experiential emptiness

		B-VALUES AND SPECIFIC METAPATHOLOGIES	

Table 15–1

(continued)

B Values	Pathogenic Deprivation	Specific Metapathologies
6. Uniqueness	Sameness; uniformity; interchangeability	Loss of feeling of self and of individuality; feeling oneself to be interchangeable, anonymous, not really needed
7. Perfection	Imperfection; sloppiness; poor workmanship, shoddiness	Discouragement (?); hopelessness; nothing to work for
7A. Necessity	Accident; occasionalism; inconsistency	Chaos, unpredictability; loss of safety; vigilance
8. Completion; finality	Incompleteness	Feelings of incompleteness with perseveration; hopelessness; cessation of striving and coping; no use trying
9. Justice	Injustice	Insecurity; anger; cynicism; mistrust; lawlessness; jungle worldview; total selfishness
9A. Order	Lawlessness; chaos; breakdown of authority	Insecurity; wariness; loss of safety, of predictability; necessity for vigilance, alertness, tension, being on guard
10. Simplicity	Confusing complexity; disconnectedness; disintegration	Overcomplexity; confusion, bewilderment, conflict, loss of orientation
11. Richness; totality; comprehensiveness	Poverty; coarctation	Depression; uneasiness; loss of interest in world
12. Effortlessness	Effortfulness	Fatigue, strain, striving, clumsiness, awkwardness, gracelessness, stiffness
13. Playfulness	Humorlessness	Grimness; depression; paranoid humorlessness; loss of zest in life; cheerlessness; loss of ability to enjoy
14. Self-sufficiency	Contingency; accident; occasionalism	Dependence on (?) the perceiver (?); it becomes his responsibility
15. Meaningfulness	Meaninglessness	Meaninglessness; despair; senselessness of life

(From Maslow, 1971, pp. 308–309.)

Characteristics of Self-Actualizing People

As noted earlier, Maslow's interest in self-actualizing people began with his great admiration for Ruth Benedict and Max Wertheimer. After discovering that these two people had much in common, he began to search for others with the same qualities. He searched for people who seemed to be operating at full capacity, that is, doing the best they were capable of doing. Such people were found among his students, his personal acquaintances, and historical figures. They were found, but they were not found very often. Of the 3,000 college students Maslow screened for his study, he found only one useful subject and a few others that showed promise as future subjects (Maslow, 1987, p. 126). The general population fared only slightly better. Maslow estimated that only 1% of the entire human population becomes self-actualized. The group he finally isolated for more detailed study consisted of 23 persons: 9 highly probable actualizers, 9 fairly sure actualizers, and 5 partial actualizers. Among the public or historical figures listed as highly probable actualizers were Albert Einstein, Eleanor Roosevelt, Jane Addams, William James, Albert Schweitzer, Aldous Huxley, and Benedict Spinoza (Maslow, 1987, p. 128).

Maslow realized fully that his research on self-actualizers was not scientific and could be criticized on several levels, but he was so startled by what he found that he felt obliged to share his observations with others:

> [This] study . . . is unusual in various ways. It was not planned as ordinary research; it was not a social venture but a private one, motivated by my own curiosity and pointed toward the solution of various personal, moral, ethical, and scientific problems. I sought only to convince and to teach myself rather than to prove or demonstrate to others.
>
> Quite unexpectedly, however, these studies have proved to be so enlightening to me, and so laden with exciting implications, that it seems fair that some sort of report should be made to others in spite of its methodological shortcomings. (Maslow, 1987, p. 125)

Maslow compared his method of gathering data on his self-actualizing individuals to the gradual development of a global impression of a friend or acquaintance. In other words, the impression came from a large number of informal observations, under a wide variety of circumstances, rather than from controlled observations under laboratory conditions. This, along with the fact that his conclusions were based on such a small sample, has stimulated much criticism of Maslow's work.

From his informal research, Maslow concluded that self-actualizing people exhibit the following characteristics:

1. **They perceive reality accurately and fully.** Their perceptions are not colored by specific needs or defenses. In other words, their perception of the world is characterized by B-cognition rather than by D-cognition. They also have "an unusual ability to detect the spurious, the fake, and the dishonest in personality, and in general to judge people correctly and efficiently" (1987, p. 128).

2. **They demonstrate a greater acceptance of themselves, others, and of nature in general.** Self-actualizers accept themselves as they are. They lack defensiveness, phoniness, and are not burdened by undue guilt, anxiety, or shame.

> Self-actualizing people tend to be good animals, hearty in their appetites and enjoying themselves without regret or shame or apology. They seem to have a uniformly good appetite for food; they seem to sleep well; they seem to enjoy their sexual lives without unnecessary inhibition and so on for all the relatively physiological impulses. (Maslow, 1987, p. 131)

Similarly, they accept others and have no need to instruct, inform, or convert them. Not only can they tolerate weakness in others, but they are not threatened by their strengths. Nature is also accepted as it is.

3. ***They exhibit spontaneity, simplicity, and naturalness.*** Self-actualizers tend to be true to their feelings; what they really feel they tend to say or experience. They do not hide behind a mask and do not act in accordance with social roles. They are true to themselves.

4. ***They tend to be concerned with problems rather than with themselves.*** Self-actualizers are typically committed to some task, cause, or mission toward which they can direct most of their energies. This is contrasted with the preoccupation with oneself often found in nonactualizers.

5. ***They have a quality of detachment and a need for privacy.*** Because self-actualizing individuals depend on their own values and feelings to guide their lives, they do not need constant contact with other people:

> It is often possible for them to remain above the battle, to remain unruffled, undisturbed by that which produces turmoil in others. They find it easy to be aloof, reserved, and also calm and serene; thus it becomes possible for them to take personal misfortunes without reacting violently as the ordinary person does. They seem to be able to retain their dignity even in undignified surroundings and situations. Perhaps this comes in part from their tendency to stick by their own interpretation of a situation rather than to rely upon what other people feel or think about the matter. This reserve may shade over into austerity and remoteness. (Maslow, 1987, p. 134)

6. ***They are autonomous.*** Because self-actualizers are B-motivated rather than D-motivated, they are more dependent on their inner world than on the outer world:

> Deficiency-motivated people must have other people available, since most of their main need gratifications (love, safety, respect, prestige, belongingness) can come only from other human beings. But growth-motivated [B-motivated] people may actually be hampered by others. The determinants of satisfaction and of the good life are for them now inner-individual and not social. They have become strong enough to be independent of the good opinion of other people, or even of their affection. The honors, the status, the rewards, the popularity, the prestige, and the love they can bestow must have become less important than self-development and inner growth. (Maslow, 1987, p. 136)

7. ***They exhibit a continued freshness of appreciation.*** Self-actualizers continue to experience the events of their lives with awe, wonder, and pleasure. Every baby or sunset is as beautiful and exciting as the first they had seen. Marriage is as exciting after 40 years as it was in the beginning. Sex, too, can have special meaning to self-actualizers: "For several of my subjects the sexual pleasures and particularly the orgasm provided not pleasure alone, but some kind of basic strengthening and revivifying that some people derive from music or nature" (1987, p. 137).

Generally such individuals derive great inspiration and ecstasy from the basic experiences of everyday life.

8. ***They have periodic mystic or peak experiences.*** Maslow believed that all humans had the potential for peak experiences, but only self-actualizers could have them full-blown, because such people were not threatened by them and therefore would not inhibit or defend against them in any way. Generally, peak experiences are the embracing of B-values:

> Feelings of limitless horizons opening up to the vision, the feeling of being simultaneously more powerful and also more helpless than one ever was before, the feeling of great ecstasy and wonder and awe, the loss of placing in time and space with, finally, the conviction that something extremely important and valuable had happened, so that the subject is to some extent transformed and strengthened even in his daily life by such experiences. (Maslow, 1987, p. 137)

One of Maslow's own peak experiences involved his "angels." He imagined that he was part of the greatest commencement exercise of all time:

> I was in a faculty procession here at Brandeis. I saw the line stretching off into a dim future. At its head was Socrates. And in the line were the ones I love most. Thomas Jefferson was there. And Spinoza. And Alfred North Whitehead. I was in that same line. Behind me that infinite line melted into the dimness. (quoted in Hall, 1968, p. 35)

Maslow concluded that some self-actualizers peak more often than others. The *nonpeakers* (low frequency of peak experiences) tend to be practical, effective people. *Peakers* (relatively high frequency of peak experiences) tend to be more poetic, aesthetically oriented, transcendent, and mystical.

We will have more to say about peak experiences when we consider the empirical research supporting Maslow's theory later in this chapter.

9. ***They tend to identify with all of humankind.*** The concerns that self-actualizers have for other people do not extend only to their friends and family but to all people in all cultures throughout the world. This feeling of fellowship extends also to individuals who are aggressive, inconsiderate, or otherwise foolish. Self-actualizers have a genuine desire to help humanity.

10. ***They develop deep friendships with only a few individuals.*** Self-actualizers tend to seek out other self-actualizers as their close friends. Such friendships are few in number but are deep and rich.

11. ***They tend to accept democratic values.*** Self-actualizers do not respond to individuals on the basis of race, status, or religion. "They can be and are friendly with anyone of suitable character regardless of class, education, political belief, race, or color. As a matter of fact it often seems as if they are not even aware of these differences, which are for the average person so obvious and so important." (Maslow, 1987, p. 139)

12. ***They have a strong ethical sense.*** Although their notions of right and wrong are often unconventional, self-actualizers, nonetheless, almost always know the ethical implications of their actions. The ethical issues with which self-actualizers become involved are substantial. They avoid trivial issues such as the morality of "card playing, dancing, wearing short dresses, exposing the head (in some churches) or not exposing the head (in others), drinking wine, or eating some meats and not others, or eating them on some days but not on others" (1987, p. 147).

13. ***They have a well-developed, unhostile sense of humor.*** Self-actualizers tend not to find humor in things that injure or degrade other humans. Rather, they are more likely to laugh at themselves or at human beings in general.

14. ***They are creative.*** Maslow found this trait in all of the self-actualizers:

> This is a universal characteristic of all the people studied or observed. . . . There is no exception. . . . This creativeness appears in some of our subjects not in the usual forms of writing books, composing music or producing artistic objects, but rather may be much more humble. It is as if this special type of creativeness, being an expression of healthy personality, is projected out upon the world or touches whatever activity the person is engaged in. In this sense there can be creative shoemakers or carpenters or clerks. (1987, pp. 142–143)

This creativity comes from the fact that self-actualizers are more open to experience and more spontaneous in their feelings. It is directly related to B-motivation.

15. ***They resist enculturation.*** Self-actualizers tend to be nonconformists because they are inner-directed people. If a cultural norm is contrary to their personal values, they simply will not adhere to it.

Negative Characteristics of Self-Actualizing People

Most people would describe these 15 characteristics as positive, but Maslow wanted to make it clear that self-actualizing people are far from perfect:

> Our subjects show many of the lesser human failings. They too are equipped with silly, wasteful, or thoughtless habits. They can be boring, stubborn, irritating. They are by no means free from a rather superficial vanity, pride, partiality to their own productions, family, friends, and children. Temper outbursts are not rare.
>
> Our subjects are occasionally capable of an extraordinary and unexpected ruthlessness. It must be remembered that they are very strong people. This makes it possible for them to display a surgical coldness when this is called for, beyond the power of the average man. The man who found that a long-trusted acquaintance was dishonest cut himself off from this friendship sharply and abruptly and without any observable pangs whatsoever. Another woman who was married to someone she did not love, when she decided on divorce, did it with a decisiveness that looked almost like ruthlessness. Some of them recover so quickly from the death of people close to them as to seem heartless. (1987, p. 146)

Maslow concluded that as healthy, creative, democratic, and spontaneous as his self-actualizers were, *"there are no perfect human beings!"* (1987, p. 146)

Why Self-Actualization Is Not Universal

Why, if the tendency toward self-actualization is innate, is not every mature adult self-actualized, instead of Maslow's estimate that only 1% of them are? Maslow suggested four basic explanations for this fact:

1. Because self-actualization is at the top of the hierarchy, it is the weakest of all the needs and therefore easily impeded. "This inner nature is not strong and overpowering and unmistakable like the instincts of animals. It is weak and delicate and subtle and easily overcome by habit, cultural pressure, and wrong attitudes toward it" (1968, p. 4).
2. Most people fear the kind of knowledge about themselves that self-actualization requires. Such knowledge requires giving up the known and entering a state of uncertainty:

> More than any other kind of knowledge we fear knowledge of ourselves, knowledge that might transform our self-esteem and our self-image. . . . While human beings love knowledge and seek it—they are curious—they also fear it. The closer to the personal it is, the more they fear it. (Maslow, 1966, p. 16)

Related to the fear of self-knowledge is the **Jonah complex,** which Maslow (1971) defined as "fear of one's own greatness . . . evasion of one's destiny . . . running away from one's best talents" (p. 34). The complex is named after the biblical Jonah, who tried, in vain, to escape the responsibilities of becoming a prophet. Thus, according to Maslow, not only do we fear our weaknesses but we fear our strengths as well:

> We fear our highest possibilities (as well as our lowest ones). We are generally afraid to become that which we can glimpse in our most perfect moments, under the most perfect conditions, under conditions of greatest courage. We enjoy and even thrill to the godlike possibilities we see in ourselves in such peak moments. And yet we simultaneously shiver with weakness, awe, and fear before these very same possibilities. (1971, p. 34)

The Jonah complex explains why peak experiences are brief and transitory: *"We are just not strong enough to endure more!"* (1971, pp. 36–37).

Not only does the Jonah complex explain the aversion to our own potential greatness, it also explains why we often resent greatness in others:

> Not only are we ambivalent about our own highest possibilities, we are also in a perpetual and I think universal—perhaps even *necessary*—conflict and ambivalence over these same highest possibilities in other

people, and in human nature in general. Certainly we love and admire good men, saints, honest, virtuous, clean men. But could anybody who has looked into the depths of human nature fail to be aware of our mixed and often hostile feelings toward saintly men? Or toward very beautiful women or men? Or toward great creators? Or toward intellectual geniuses? (1971, p. 35)

3. The cultural environment can stifle one's tendency toward actualization by imposing certain norms on segments of the population. For example, the way our culture defines *manly* tends to prevent the male child from developing such traits as sympathy, kindness, and tenderness, all of which characterize the self-actualized individual.

4. As indicated in item 2, in order to become self-actualized one must choose growth over safety. Maslow observed that children from warm, secure, friendly homes are more likely to choose experiences that lead to personal growth than children from insecure homes. Thus childhood conditions influence the probability of a person becoming self-actualized. Maslow characterized what he believed was the optimal set of circumstances for a child as **freedom within limits.** He believed too much permissiveness was as harmful as too much control. What is needed, he thought, was a proper mixture of the two.

Conditions Necessary for Self-Actualization

In addition to satisfying the physiological needs, the safety needs, and the love and belongingness needs, an environment must have several other characteristics before self-actualization can occur. These characteristics, according to Maslow, include freedom of speech, freedom to do what one wants to do as long as it harms no one else, freedom of inquiry, freedom to defend oneself, order, justice, fairness, and honesty. Later Maslow added "challenge" (proper stimulation) as a characteristic of an environment conducive to self-actualization.

With these environmental prerequisites in mind, along with the four reasons why more people are not self-actualized cited earlier, it becomes easier to understand why only about 1% of the population becomes self-actualized. Most of the rest of us live out our days somewhere between the love and belongingness and self-esteem needs.

Self-Actualization and Gender

Generalizing from his early work with primates, Maslow believed that human male and female psychology had different instinctual foundations. Although Maslow's work was embraced by the feminist movement of the 1960s (see, e.g., Friedan, 1963), he was uneasy about the egalitarian tenor of that movement (Nicholson, 2001, p. 88). Maslow never waivered in his belief that important personality characteristics are gender specific. For example, although he didn't stress that point publicly, privately he believed that the process of self-actualization is different for males and females. In his personal journal, Maslow wrote:

Self-actualization for women does not mean a dichotomy between home & career, forcing an either–or choice. Home & family, etc. are far more basic & important &

prepotent, & must remain the base on which higher developments rest. If they're taken away . . . then the so-called "higher" things, the career, etc. become empty & meaningless. . . . True self-actualization for the female . . . accepts the primacy of the family. (Lowry, 1979, Vol. 2, p. 1139)

So like Freud, and Horney early in her career, Maslow accepted a version of the contention that "anatomy is destiny." For more about how Maslow's thoughts on masculinity and femininity influenced his life and work, see Nicholson, 2001.

Eupsychia

Because Maslow believed all human needs, including the need for self-actualization, were instinctoid, it must be the environment (society, culture) that determines the highest level of attainment in the hierarchy of needs one will reach. Maslow rejected the Freudian notion that humans and society had to be engaged in constant conflict. Rather, he believed society could be designed to maximize the probability of self-actualization. Because Maslow believed people's needs are good rather than bad (as the Freudians believed) their satisfaction should be encouraged rather than discouraged.

Maslow speculated on the type of utopia that would be developed if 1,000 healthy families moved to a deserted island where they could determine their own destiny. He called this potential utopia **Eupsychia** (pronounced Yew-sigh-key-a), which can be broken down as follows: Eu = good, psych = mind, and ia = country. In Eupsychia, there would be complete **synergy,** a concept he borrowed from Ruth Benedict: syn = together, and ergy = working. Thus, in Maslow's utopia, there would be complete cooperation, or working together. What other features would characterize Eupsychia?

> What kind of education would they choose? Economic system? Sexuality? Religion?
> I am very uncertain of some things—economics in particular. But of other things I am very sure. One of them is that this would almost surely be a (philosophically) anarchistic group, a Taoistic [nature-oriented] but loving culture, in which people (young people too) would have much more free choice than we are used to, and in which basic needs and metaneeds would be respected much more than they are in our society. People would not bother each other so much as we do, would be much less prone to press opinions or religions or philosophies or tastes in clothes or food or art on their neighbors. In a word, the inhabitants of Eupsychia would tend to be more Taoistic, nonintrusive, and basic need-gratifying (whenever possible), would frustrate only under certain conditions that I have not attempted to describe, would be more honest with each other than we are, and would permit people to make free choices wherever possible. They would be far less controlling, violent, contemptuous, or overbearing than we are. Under such conditions, the deepest layers of human nature could show themselves with greater ease. (Maslow, 1987, pp. 121–122)

In 1962, Maslow went to Non-linear Systems, Inc. as a visiting fellow. His experiences at this voltmeter factory resulted in his book **Eupsychian Management**

(1965). The basic message in the book was that if industrial management was more aware of human needs and what is required to satisfy those needs, both the worker and the industry would be far healthier. "Eupsychian . . . conditions of work are often good not only for personal fulfillment, but also for the health and prosperity of the organization, as well as for the quantity and quality of the products or services turned out by the organization" (Maslow, 1971, p. 227). Eupsychian management, then, is an attempt to create a working situation conducive to satisfying human needs as Maslow described them.

Ashrams—Places for Personal Growth

For hundreds of years, India has had **ashrams,** or retreats, where people could escape the anxieties associated with everyday life. The pace of living in the ashram is radically slowed down, so that individuals can meditate and reflect on the meaning of their lives. Each ashram is led by a **guru** (spiritual teacher) who acts as a guide for those seeking inner peace. People stay in the ashram for a day, a week, months, or, in some cases, years. Others, however, visit the ashram for a few hours, and then return to their regular, routine lives.

In 1963, Michael Murphy and Richard Price developed the first U.S. equivalent to the Indian ashram in Big Sur, California. The philosophy of the ashram was directly in accordance with Maslow's views that psychology should concentrate more on healthy people than on unhealthy ones. Ashrams were places where non-neurotic individuals could go and search themselves and reflect on their own values and thus become even more effective in their daily lives. Whereas psychotherapy is available to the emotionally disturbed, ashrams are places where the already healthy person can become healthier. It is not surprising, then, that Maslow was among the first to conduct seminars at this newly founded ashram, which was named the **Esalen Institute,** after the Esalen Indians, who once inhabited the Big Sur region.

The Western version of the Indian ashram has come to be called a **growth center.**

Although the Esalen Institute and its participants embraced Maslow's humanistic psychology enthusiastically, they provided Maslow with one of the most unpleasant experiences of his life. While on sabbatical leave from Brandeis in 1966, Maslow agreed to conduct a workshop at Esalen. The approximately 25 people in the workshop included Fritz Perls, the renowned and irascible psychotherapist. When Maslow began the workshop in the academic style of questions and answers, the group was confused and irritated. They sought (as Maslow's students at Brandeis did later) a more personal sharing of experiences. Perls exclaimed, "This is just like school. . . . Here is the teacher, and there is the pupil, giving the right answer" (Hoffman, 1988, p. 290). Perls became increasingly bored and "began crawling toward an attractive woman across the room chanting 'you are my mother; I want my mother; you are my mother'" (Maslow, 1987, p. xi). The situation became increasingly tense but neither Maslow nor the Esalen leaders did anything about it. The next day the climax came when, during Maslow's presentation, Perls "dropped to the floor and began to make whining, infantlike sounds before the astonished gathering as he slowly wrapped himself around Maslow's knees. . . . The meeting broke up in confusion" (Hoffman, 1988, p. 291).

Maslow finally had enough and the next day he gave the leaders of Esalen and its participants a scolding. He said they valued spontaneous feelings over rationality and objective research. They wanted to be childlike, he said, not to engage in the difficult work necessary for understanding human nature. "If you don't just want to be a selfish person contemplating your navel . . . you put your shoulder to the wheel. . . . If you don't use your brain, you're not fulfilling your potential" (quoted in Hoffman, 1988, pp. 292–293).

After the Esalen fiasco, Maslow and his wife Bertha gladly returned home. They spent the remainder of his sabbatical traveling through the southern and eastern United States. They were unaware that soon an experience similar to that at Esalen would be repeated at Brandeis.

Transpersonal Psychology

Toward the end of his life, Maslow began to realize that even humanistic psychology could not adequately explain certain aspects of humans. For example, various mystical, ecstatic, or spiritual states were viewed by Maslow as experiences beyond self-actualization. They were experiences that transcended the customary limits of personal identity and experience. Maslow believed the study of such phenomena should constitute a fourth force in psychology, which he called **transpersonal psychology.** In the preface of his book *Toward a Psychology of Being* (1968), he summarized his views on transpersonal psychology:

> I consider Humanistic, Third Force Psychology to be transitional, a preparation for a still "higher" Fourth Psychology, transpersonal, transhuman, centered in the cosmos rather than in human needs and interest, going beyond humanness, identity, self-actualization, and the like. . . . These new developments may very well offer a tangible, usable, effective satisfaction of the "frustrated idealism" of many quietly desperate people, especially young people. These psychologies give promise of developing into the life-philosophy, the religion-surrogate, the value-system, the life-program that these people have been missing. Without the transcendent and the transpersonal, we get sick, violent, and nihilistic, or else hopeless and apathetic. We need something "bigger than we are" to be awed by and to commit ourselves to in a new, naturalistic, empirical, nonchurchly sense. (pp. iii–iv)

Maslow lived to see the founding of the *Journal of Transpersonal Psychology* in 1969. This journal was organized by Anthony Sutich, the same person who founded the *Journal of Humanistic Psychology.* Following is Sutich's statement of the purpose of the *Journal of Transpersonal Psychology,* a statement that was enthusiastically endorsed by Maslow:

> The emerging Transpersonal Psychology ("Fourth Force") is concerned specifically with the empirical, scientific study of, and responsible implementation of the findings relevant to, becoming, individual and species-wide meta-needs, ultimate values, unitive consciousness, peak experiences, B-values, ecstasy, mystical experience, awe, being, self-actualization, essence, bliss, wonder, ultimate mean-

ing, transcendence of the self, spirit, oneness, cosmic awareness, individual and species-wide synergy, maximal interpersonal encounter, sacralization of everyday life, transcendental phenomena, cosmic self humor and playfulness, maximal sensory awareness, responsiveness and expression, and related concepts, experiences, and activities. (1976, pp. 13–14)

Maslow's "The Farther Reaches of Human Nature" was the lead article in the first issue of the new journal. By 1985, there were 1,200 members in the Association for Transpersonal Psychology, and the International Transpersonal Association has sponsored conferences on transpersonal psychology throughout the world.

With the emergence of transpersonal psychology in the United States came an appreciation for non-Western psychologies, philosophies, and religions. It was realized that such views have offered ways of inducing and understanding the "higher" states of consciousness for centuries, for example, through intense meditation.

Evaluation

Empirical Research

A major criticism of Maslow's theory has concerned the subjective way he and his colleagues described and studied self-actualizing people. One response to this criticism has been the development of the Personal Orientation Inventory (POI) by Everett Shostrom (1963, 1964, 1974; Shostrom, Knapp, & Knapp, 1976). The POI consists of 150 self-administered items. Each item consists of two statements and the respondent simply chooses the statement that most consistently applies to him or her. For example, the choices corresponding to one item may be "my ethical standards are dictated by society" and "my ethical standards are self-determined." For another item, the choices may be "I find some people to be uninteresting," and "I never find people to be uninteresting." The test yields two overall scores. One is for *inner-directed support,* or the degree to which a person is his or her own source of support. The other is *time competence,* or the degree to which a person lives in the present. In addition to the two overall scores, 10 subscales measure values important to the development of a self-actualizing person: self-actualizing values, existentiality, feeling reactivity, spontaneity, self-regard, self-acceptance, nature of humans, synergy, acceptance of aggression, and capacity for intimate contact.

The POI has proved to be a reliable measure of the extent to which an individual is self-actualized, as Maslow had defined the term (Ilardi & May, 1968; Klavetter & Mogar, 1967; Shostrom, 1966). The POI has also proven to be a valuable research tool. For example, Dosamantes-Alperson and Merrill (1980) administered the POI to groups of people before and after they participated in several group therapy sessions. Control groups (those waiting for therapy but not yet participating in the program) were also given the POI at the same times as the groups receiving group therapy. Results indicated that those receiving therapy became more inner directed, spontaneous, and self-accepting—that is, they became more self-actualizing. POI scores have also been found to be positively correlated with academic achievement (LeMay & Damm, 1968; Stewart, 1968), teaching effectiveness (Dandes, 1966), and the effectiveness of psychotherapists (Foulds, 1969). Additional research involving measures of self-actualization has found that those having relatively high scores tend to be more creative (Buckmaster & Davis, 1985; Runco, Ebersole, & Mraz, 1991; Yonge, 1975); more assertive (Ramanaiah, Heerboth, & Jinkerson, 1985); more capable of sexual enjoyment (McCann & Biaggio, 1989); less influenced by social pressure (Bordages, 1989); and less likely to become bored (McLeod & Vodanovich, 1991).

Graham and Balloun (1973) found support for Maslow's concept of the hierarchy of needs. Thirty-seven participants were asked to describe the most important things in their lives. Judges rated these responses on a scale ranging from "very high" to "little or no" desire expressed for physiological, safety, love and belongingness, and self-actualization needs. Results supported Maslow's hypothesis that individuals at different levels of the hierarchy show greater satisfaction of the needs below their level than of the needs above it. Lester, Hvezda, Sullivan, and Plourde (1983), using their Need Satisfaction Inventory, found a significant, positive relationship between the satisfaction of the basic needs and psychological health. Maslow's concept of the hierarchy of needs has also received considerable attention in the area of industrial-organizational psychology. For example, Marrow, Bowers, and Seashore (1967) found that providing conditions that gratify higher needs produces improvement in both employee production and morale (see also Alderfer, 1972; Buttle, 1989; Massarik, 1992). Williams and Page (1989) developed the Maslowian Assessment Survey (MAS) to determine a person's position in the hierarchy of needs. Using college students as research participants, it was found that among them esteem needs were the most salient, with love and belongingness needs a close second. There was little concern for physiological and safety and security needs. Also, there was little concern for the self-actualizing needs. With this population the results were as Maslow would have predicted. Finally, researchers have found Maslow's concept of the hierarchy of needs to be valid across cultures (Davis-Sharts, 1986).

Maslow's notion of peak experiences has been studied rather extensively. For example, Panzarella (1980) found that artistically and musically oriented people claim that peak experiences have deepened their appreciation of music or art and that such mystical moments provide them with a sense of renewal and an urge to be creative. Ravizza (1977) had 20 athletes in 12 different sports describe their "greatest moments" as athletes. Their descriptions had much in common with Maslow's description of peak experiences. During their greatest moments the athletes felt no fear; were totally immersed in their activity; had a God-like feeling of control; felt a sense of self-validation; felt a unity with the experience and with the universe; viewed themselves as passive and their activity as effortless; and described their activity in terms of awe, ecstasy, and wonder. Mathes, Zevon, Roter, and Joerger (1982) developed the Peak Scale to measure the tendency to have peak experiences. Several studies using the Peak Scale yielded results consistent with Maslow's theorizing. For example, those scoring high on the scale tended to have experiences of a mystical nature as well as feelings of intense happiness. High scorers also reported living in terms of B-values (e.g., truth, beauty, and justice) instead of D-values. Keutzer (1978) found that, among college students, observing the beauties of nature, moments of quiet reflection, and listening to music were the events most likely to trigger peak experiences. Yeagle, Privette, and Dunham (1989) found that both artists and college students have peak experiences but for the college students they were most often associated with interpersonal relationships whereas for the artists they were most often associated with observations of beauty. Gordon (1985) found that peak experiences were characterized by feelings of loving acceptance, open-minded insight, spontaneity, pleasant fear, absorption, and self-detachment. However, there were gender differences. The peak experiences for women were more likely to be characterized by loving acceptance and spontaneity than those of men. Contrary to what Maslow suggested, several researchers have found that peak experiences can be negative as well as positive (e.g., Blanchard, 1969; Wilson & Spencer, 1990). Influenced by Maslow's concept of peak experience, Csikszentmihalyi (1975, 1990, 1996) has studied people from different cultures and vocations to explore what he calls "flow" or "optimal experience." Among other things, he found that people experiencing flow are oblivious to time and sense of self. Privette and Bundrick (1991) found that such experiences are often related to playful activities and significant interpersonal relationships.

Criticisms

Too Many Exceptions.   Too many people seem to be highly productive and creative even though their basic needs do not seem to have been satisfied. Although Maslow noted such exceptions to his theory, he did little to account for them. Also, there are people who appear to have satisfied all their deficiency needs but do not become self-actualized. Maslow was struggling with this problem shortly before his death (see his interview with Frick, 1989) but he never solved it.

Unscientific Approach.   Maslow has been accused of using uncontrolled and unreliable research techniques, basing his conclusions about self-actualizing people on a small sample of people; accepting as valid the conscious self-reports of his subjects, using his own intuitive criteria as to what constitutes a self-actualizing person; and of using ambiguous terms in his theory such as metaneed, metapathology, love, beauty, and peak experience. To be fair, we must realize that Maslow was aware the higher aspects of humans had not previously been investigated objectively. However, he desperately wanted psychology to expand its domain so these aspects could be studied scientifically. Several psychologists have followed the leads of Allport, Rogers, Maslow, and others and have attempted to develop a scientifically rigorous humanistic psychology (e.g., Giorgi, 1992; Polkinghorne, 1992; Rychlak, 1988, 1991, 1997).

Recently, a field called **positive psychology** has developed, which agrees with a number of the tenants of humanistic psychology. However, according to Seligman and Csikszentmihalyi (2000), positive psychology will be more sciently rigorous and less self-centered than was humanistic psychology.

> Unfortunately, humanistic psychology did not attract much of a cumulative empirical base, and it spawned myriad therapeutic self-help movements. In some of its incarnations, it emphasized the self and encouraged a self-centeredness that played down concerns for collective well-being. Future debate will determine whether this came about because Maslow and Rogers were ahead of their times, because these flaws were inherent in their original vision, or because of overly enthusiastic followers. However, one legacy of the humanism of the 1960s is prominently displayed in any large bookstore: The "psychology" section contains at least 10 shelves on crystal healing, aromatherapy, and reaching the inner child for every shelf of books that tries to uphold some scholarly standard. (p. 7)

In their statement on the purpose of positive psychology, Seligman and Csikszentmihalyi (2000) indicate what it has in common with humanistic psychology and what makes it different:

> [The purpose of positive psychology] is to remind our field that psychology is not just the study of pathology, weakness, and damage; it is also the study of strength and virtue. Treatment is not just fixing what is broken; it is nurturing what is best. Psychology is not just a branch of medicine concerned with illness or health; it is much larger. It is about work, education, insight, love, growth, and play. And in this quest for what is best, positive psychology does not rely on wishful thinking, faith, self-deception, fads, or hand waving; it tries to adapt what is best in the scientific method to the unique problems that human behavior presents to those who wish to understand it in all its complexity. (p. 7)

Overly Optimistic View of Human Nature.   Like Rogers, Maslow has been criticized for assuming humans have an innate tendency toward self-actualization. Critics say that many humans are too violent, insensitive, and inhumane to justify such an assumption. To these critics, theories such as those of Freud, Jung, and the evolutionary psychologists present a more realistic picture of humans, and the theories of Rogers and Maslow represent wishful thinking rather than fact.

Several Unanswered Questions.   For example, who can become self-actualized? Most, if not all, of Maslow's subjects were highly intelligent and financially successful. What about less intelligent and financially successful persons? Can they also become self-actualized? Are feeble-minded persons capable of using their full potential to become self-actualized? Also, can people intentionally become self-actualized or is it something that must occur naturally? That is, if one knows the criteria for self-actualization, can one adopt those characteristics and thus be self-actualized? Finally, as we have seen, Maslow was vague about how much satisfaction must be achieved at a given level of the hierarchy before the next higher needs become prominent in a person's life.

Concepts Biased Toward Western Culture.   Maslow's description of optimal psychological health emphasized personal achievement, autonomy, and self-esteem. This emphasis on the individual is contrary to the concept of "fulfillment" in a number of non-Western cultures. For example, in Japan and China, people are taught to value autonomy less than cooperation and not to demonstrate superiority over other people (Kitayama & Markus, 1992; Markus & Kitayama, 1991). Kitayama and Markus (1992) found that Japanese college students associated positive emotions with interpersonal relationships whereas American college students associated them with personal accomplishments. Furthermore, the conception of enlightenment offered by Buddhism emphasizes mental discipline as a means of overcoming the suffering, craving, and disappointment that would otherwise dominate one's life (Das, 1989). This conception of optimal psychological health is distinctly different than Maslow's. Similarly, Daniels (1988) criticizes Maslow's conception of psychological health for neglecting the hard work and pain involved in growth and development.

It has also been suggested that Maslow's description of optimal psychological health reflects male values (e.g., personal accomplishment) rather than female values (e.g., interpersonal relationships) (Josephs, Markus, & Tafarodi, 1992).

Contributions

Vastly Increased Psychology's Domain. Maslow took a position essentially opposite Freud's. In discussing Freud, we pondered a view of humans as animals in conflict with a society that imposes restrictions on their animal impulses. When we considered Maslow, we pondered a view of humans as basically good, nonaggressive seekers of truth, beauty, and perfection. For Freud, given complete freedom, humans would become sexually promiscuous and aggressive. For Maslow, given complete freedom, humans would create Eupsychia, a loving, harmonious, and nonaggressive society. The views of human nature held by Freud and Maslow are about as different as two views of human nature can be.

There is no doubt Maslow's contention that psychology had traditionally focused on the darker side of human nature was valid. Of course, there have been theorists whose works have been exceptions to this; for example, Adler, Allport, Bandura, Mischel, Kelly, and Rogers. In general, however, psychology has been preoccupied with either the importance of the physiological drives in determining behavior or the conditions under which neuroses and psychoses develop. Maslow did about as much as one person could have done to extend the domain of psychology to the study of healthy humans. His efforts, along with those of other theorists such as Rogers, have indeed created a viable third force in psychology.

Applied Value. In addition to its impact on psychology, Maslow's theory has been highly influential in the areas of education, business, religion, and childrearing.

We conclude this chapter with the last entry that Maslow made in his diary a month before he died. The entry, dated May 7, 1970, attempts to explain why he was willing to take so many unpopular positions and what he was attempting to accomplish in his life:

> Somebody asked me the question . . . How did a timid youngster get transformed into a (seemingly) "courageous" leader and spokesman? How come I was willing to talk up, to take unpopular positions, while most others didn't? My immediate tendency was to say: "Intelligence—just realistic seeing of the facts," but I held that answer back because—alone—it's wrong. "Good will, compassion *and* intelligence," I finally answered. I think I added that I'd simply *learned* a lot from my self-actualizing subjects and from their way of life and from their metamotivations, which have now become *mine.* So I respond emotionally to the injustice, the meanness, the lies, the untruths, the hatred and violence, the simplistic answers. . . . So I feel cheap and guilty and unmanly when I *don't* talk up. So then, in a sense, I *have* to.
>
> What the kids *and* the intellectuals—and everybody else too—need is an ethos, a scientific value system and way of life and humanistic politics, *with* the theory, the facts, etc., all set forth soberly. . . . So *again* I must say to myself: to work! (Lowry, 1979, Vol. 2, p. 1309)

Summary

Maslow survived the many negative experiences of his early years by taking refuge in books. He claimed his life did not really begin until he married shortly after moving to the University of Wisconsin.

Maslow's early research on dominance in monkeys led to research on dominance in humans and then finally to an interest in "the good specimen" or actualizing humans. His interest in the latter was stimulated by his efforts to understand two individuals he admired very much, Ruth Benedict and Max Wertheimer. He was distressed that his training in psychology had not equipped him to understand truly healthy, well-adjusted individuals. He concluded the reason for this was that psychology had been preoccupied with either the study of lower animals, children, or maladjusted adults. Psychology also had borrowed the reductive-analytic approach from the natural sciences. This approach attempts to understand humans as a collection of habits or conflicts. This technique is desacralizing because it denies or distorts many positive human qualities. Instead, Maslow suggested a holistic-analytic approach that studies the total person. Such an approach is humanistic because it emphasizes the positive qualities of humans. Humanistic psychology is also called third-force psychology because it is an alternative to the psychoanalytic and behavioristic models of humans. Maslow had no argument with the psychoanalysts or the behaviorists; he simply believed they did not tell the whole story. He thought humans had several positive attributes that had been ignored by psychology.

Human nature, according to Maslow, consists of a number of instinctoidal (innate but weak) needs that are arranged in a hierarchy according to their potency. The nature of these needs is such that as one group of needs is satisfied, the next group in the hierarchy comes to dominate a person's life until they too are satisfied, at which time the next group becomes dominant, and so on. The needs from the most basic to the least basic are physiological needs, safety needs, belongingness and love needs, esteem needs, and the need for self-actualization.

Self-actualizing people are no longer motivated by deficiencies (D-motivation); they are motivated by being values (B-motivation). B-values include such things as truth, goodness, beauty, justice, and perfection. B-values are also called metamotives. D-motivated people search for specific need-related events in their environment; this is called D-perception (or D-cognition) because it is need-motivated. B-motivated people perceive their environments most fully because they are not looking for anything in particular; this is called B-perception (or B-cognition). Failure to give expression to a B-value results in a metapathology.

Maslow attempted to correct the fact that psychology had concentrated too much on unhealthy humans by studying the characteristics of the healthiest individuals he could find. Some of these people were his friends, some were famous living people, and some were famous historical figures. He found that self-actualizing people tended to have in common the following characteristics: They perceive reality accurately; show great acceptance of themselves, others, and nature; are spontaneous; are problem-oriented rather than self-oriented; tend to be detached and private; are autonomous; exhibit continued freshness of appreciation; have peak experiences; identify with all of humanity; have only a few deep friendships; accept democratic values; have a strong ethical sense; have a well-developed sense of humor that is not hostile; are creative; and tend to be nonconformists. In addition to these positive qualities, self-actualizers also show some negative qualities such as vanity, pride, partiality, silliness, temper outbursts, and a coldness toward death.

Although the tendency toward self-actualization was thought by Maslow to be innate, it is not universally experienced because the need is so weak that it is easily impeded; it takes considerable courage to be self-actualized (the fear of one's own potential greatness is called the Jonah complex); cultural norms are often incompatible with the self-actualizing process; and early childhood experiences must instill adequate security in the child so he or she is willing to grow rather than constantly seek safety, but such childhood experiences are uncommon. Maslow believed that although women can become self-actualized, their ultimate concern with home and family cannot be abandoned or minimized in the process.

Maslow described a utopian society that he speculated a group of healthy people might design. He called this society Eupsychia. He thought there would be complete synergy, or working together, in Eupsychia because all human needs would be recognized, respected, and gratified. When an industry attempts to consider human needs, as Maslow defined them, the process is known as Eupsychian management.

Maslow's humanistic psychology was enthusiastically embraced by an ashram in California that came to be called the Esalen Institute. An ashram is a place where already healthy individuals can fully explore themselves and thus revitalize their lives. Maslow had a confrontation with the leaders of the Esalen Institute and its participants because they wanted to simply share spontaneous feelings, whereas he wanted to explore those feelings objectively. There are now several hundred of these centers for personal growth in the Western world.

Later in his life, Maslow became interested in transpersonal or fourth-force psychology. Such psychology examines the human relationship to the cosmos and the various emotional experiences that an awareness of such a relationship creates.

The Personal Orientation Inventory has been used successfully to determine the extent to which individuals are self-actualized. Other research has supported Maslow's notion of the hierarchy of needs and of peak experiences. Maslow's theory has been criticized for having too many exceptions to its predictions, being unscientific, being overly optimistic about human nature, leaving many important questions unanswered and for being biased toward Western (and also perhaps male) values. His theory has been praised for vastly increasing psychology's domain and having substantial applied value.

Experiential Exercises

1. At what level of Maslow's hierarchy of needs do you think you are currently operating? Justify your answer.
2. Evaluate your personality in terms of the 15 characteristics of the self-actualizing person. Indicate which of the 15 characteristics you possess to some degree and which you do not. What conclusions do you draw from your observations?
3. As part of his research on peak experiences, Maslow (1968) gave 190 college students the following instructions:

   I would like you to think of the most wonderful experience or experiences of your life; happiest moments, ecstatic moments, moments of rapture, perhaps from being in love, or from listening to music or suddenly "being hit" by a book or a painting, or from some great creative moment. First list these. And then try to tell me how you feel in such acute moments, how you feel differently from the way you feel at other times, how you are at the moment a different person in some ways. (p. 71)

   Respond to Maslow's instructions.

Discussion Questions

1. What is third-force psychology? Why did Maslow feel that his third force was needed? Include in your answer the difference between the reductive-analytic approach to science and the holistic-analytic approach. Also discuss the term desacralization.

2. Discuss the hierarchy of needs. Which needs are included and how are they related to one another?

3. If the tendency toward self-actualization is innate, why is it that self-actualization is not universal?

Glossary

Acceptance of democratic values. Characterizes the self-actualizing person.

Acceptance of self, others, and nature. Characterizes the self-actualizing person.

Accurate and full perception of reality. Characterizes the self-actualizing person.

Aesthetic needs. Innate need for such qualities as symmetry, closure, and order, observed most clearly in children and in self-actualizing adults.

Ashrams. Retreats in India where ordinary citizens can go for various periods of time to escape everyday anxieties and reflect on the meaning of their lives.

B-cognition. *See* Being cognition.

Being cognition (also called B-perception or B-cognition). Thinking or perceiving that is governed by B-values rather than by D-motives. Such cognition is richer and fuller than D-cognition.

Being motivation (also called growth motivation). Motivation governed by the pursuit of B-values instead of by the satisfaction of basic deficiencies. *See also* Being values.

Being values (B-values) (also called metamotives). Those higher aspects of life pursued by self-actualizing individuals. Included are such values as truth, goodness, beauty, justice, and perfection.

Belongingness and love needs. Third cluster of needs in the hierarchy of needs. Included are the needs for affiliation with others and for the feeling of being loved.

B-love. Deep, nonpossessive, insatiable, emotional relationship that is not aimed at satisfying any particular need. Such love contrasts with D-love.

B-perception. *See* Being cognition.

Continued freshness of appreciation. Characterizes the self-actualizing person.

Creativity. Characterizes the self-actualizing person.

D-cognition. *See* Need-directed perception.

D-love. Motivated by the need for love and belongingness. Such love is selfish because it satisfies a personal deficiency. Such love contrasts with B-love.

Deep friendships with only a few people. Characterizes the self-actualizing person.

Deficiency motivation (D-motivation). Motivation governed by the basic needs. Characterizes the lives of individuals who are not self-actualizing.

Deficiency motive (D-motive). Needs or deficiencies that exist in the hierarchy of needs prior to the level of self-actualization.

Desacralization. Any process that distorts human nature and depicts it as less marvelous and dignified than it is.

Desire to know and understand. Innate curiosity that Maslow believed was functionally related to the ability to satisfy all human needs.

Detachment and a need for privacy. Characterizes the self-actualizing person.

D-perception. *See* Need-directed perception.

Esalen Institute. Institute in California modeled after the Indian ashram where non-neurotic, healthy people can further develop their inner resources.

Esteem needs. Fourth cluster of needs in the hierarchy of needs. Included are the needs for status, prestige, competence, and confidence.

Eupsychia. Maslow's name for the utopia that he believed a community of healthy adults could create.

Eupsychian management. Industrial or societal management that attempts to consider the basic human needs as Maslow viewed them.

Fourth-force psychology. *See* Transpersonal psychology.

Freedom within limits. Maslow's description of what he considered the optimal psychological atmosphere for a child to experience.

Growth center. Western equivalent of the Indian ashram. A place where healthy individuals can expand their potentialities. *See also* Esalen Institute.

Growth motivation. *See* Being motivation.

Guru. Spiritual leader of an ashram.

Hierarchy of human needs. Arrangement of the needs from lowest to highest in terms of their potency.

Holistic-analytic approach to science. Strategy of studying an object of interest as a totality rather than attempting to reduce it to its component parts.

Humanistic psychology (also called third-force psychology). Approach to psychology that emphasizes the experiencing person, creativity, the study of socially and personally significant problems, and the dignity and enhancement of people.

Identification with all of humanity. Characterizes the self-actualizing person.

Independence from the environment and culture. Characterizes the self-actualizing person.

Instinctoid. Term Maslow used to describe the nature of the human needs. An instinctoid need is innate but weak and is easily modified by environmental conditions.

Jonah complex. The fear of one's own potential greatness and the ambivalent feelings toward greatness in others.

Metamotives. *See* Being values.

Metapathology. Psychological disorder that results when a being motive is not allowed proper expression.

Need-directed perception (also called D-perception or D-cognition). Perception motivated by a search for objects or events that will satisfy a basic need; for example, a hungry person looks for food.

Nonconformity. Characterizes the self-actualizing person.

Peak experiences. Mystical, oceanic experiences that are accompanied by a feeling of ecstasy or rapture. Such experiences were thought by Maslow to reach their full magnitude as B-values are fully embraced.

Physiological needs. Most basic cluster of needs in the hierarchy of needs. Included are the needs for water, food, oxygen, sleep, elimination, and sex.

Positive psychology. Field in contemporary psychology that explores the higher aspects of humans but does so in a way that is more scientifically rigorous and less self-centered than was humanistic psychology.

Problem-oriented rather than self-oriented. Characterizes the self-actualizing person.

Reductive-analytic approach to science. Strategy of reducing an object of interest to its component parts in order to study and understand it.

Safety needs. Second cluster of needs in the hierarchy of needs. Included is the need for order, security, and predictability.

Self-actualization. Highest level in the hierarchy of needs, which can be reached only if the preceding need levels have been adequately satisfied. The self-actualizing individual operates at full capacity and is B-motivated rather than D-motivated.

Sense of humor that is unhostile. Characterizes the self-actualizing person.

Spontaneity, simplicity, and naturalness. Characterize the self-actualizing person.

Strong ethical sense. Characterizes the self-actualizing person.

Synergy. Working together. Individuals in a community characterized by synergy work in harmony and are not in conflict with their society.

Third-force psychology. Humanistic psychology, which was viewed by Maslow and others as an alternative to psychoanalysis and behaviorism.

Transpersonal psychology (also called fourth-force psychology). Psychology that examines the human relationship to the cosmos or to something "bigger than we are" and the mystical, spiritual, or peak experiences that the realization of such a relationship produces.

CHAPTER 16

ROLLO REESE MAY

CHAPTER OUTLINE

Biographical Sketch
Existentialism
Human Dilemma
Anxiety and Guilt
Importance of Values
Nature of Love
Psychotherapy
Importance of Myth
New Science of Humans
Evaluation
Summary
Experiential Exercises
Discussion Questions
Glossary

The theories of Adler, Allport, Kelly, Rogers, and Maslow have a clear existential orientation, in that they are concerned with the meaning of human life. However, it is May's theory that is most compatible with existential philosophy. In fact, May was as responsible as anyone for incorporating European existential philosophy into American psychology. Although humanistic and existential psychology have much in common, there are important differences between the two. For example, humanistic psychologists assume humans are inherently good whereas existential psychologists view human nature as neutral. That is, for the existentialists, whether a person becomes good or evil is essentially a matter of personal choice. (For other differences between humanistic and existential psychology, see, e.g., DeCarvalho, 1990a; Hergenhahn, 2004.)

Biographical Sketch

Rollo Reese May was born to Earl Tittle and Matie Boughton May in Ada, Ohio, on April 21, 1909, and grew up in Marine City, Michigan. He was the first son, and the second child, in a family of six children. Neither of his parents were well educated and there was little intellectual stimulation in his home. When his older sister became schizophrenic, May's father blamed it on too much education. May was not close to either parent but he especially disliked his mother whom he described as a "bitch-kitty on wheels." May believed his mother's erratic behavior and his older sister's schizophrenia contributed to his own two failed marriages later in his life (Rabinowitz, Good, & Cozad, 1989). May's first marriage, to Florence DeFrees, lasted from 1938 to 1968 and produced three children: Robert Rollo, who is Director of Counseling at Amherst College, and twins Carolyn Jane, a social worker-therapist and artist, and Allegra Anne, a documentary film writer and single mother of two adopted multiracial children (Bugental, 1996, p. 418). After about 10 years, it became clear to May that his marriage to Florence was unsuccessful but he persisted in it for an additional 20 years for the sake of the children (Rabinowitz et al., 1989, pp. 438–439). His second marriage to Ingrid Scholl from 1971 to 1978 was also unsuccessful and ended in divorce. His third marriage to Georgia Miller Johnson, a Jungian analyst, was successful and lasted from 1988 until May's death in 1994.

May first attended college at Michigan State University where he majored in English but was asked to leave when he became editor of a radical student magazine. He transferred to Oberlin College in Ohio where he obtained his BA in 1930.

Following graduation, May pursued his interest in art by roaming through Europe with a group of artists. He remained in Europe from 1930 to 1933, and during that time, in addition to studying art, he taught at an American college in Greece and took summer school seminars from Alfred Adler in Vienna. During his second year in Europe, May began questioning the meaning in his life and finally had a "nervous breakdown."

> Finally, in the spring of that second year I had what is called euphemistically a nervous breakdown. *Which meant simply that the rules, principles, values by which I used to work and live simply did not suffice anymore.* I got so completely fatigued that I had to go to bed for two weeks to get enough energy to continue my teaching. I had learned enough psychology at college to know that these symptoms meant that something was wrong with my whole way of life. I had to find some new goals and purposes for my living and to relinquish my moralistic, somewhat rigid way of existence. (1985, p. 8)

In 1932, while still in Europe, May had an important insight while sketching a field of poppies:

> I realized that I had not listened to my inner voice, which had tried to talk to me about beauty. I had been too hard-working, too "principled" to spend time merely looking at flowers! It seems it had taken a collapse of my whole former way of life for this voice to make itself heard. (1985, p. 13)

In addition to learning to listen to his inner voice, May learned from this experience that psychological health often required challenging one's old values and replacing them with new ones. Incidentally, the impressive sketch of the poppies that May was making as he had the insights just described is reproduced on page 13 of May's book *My Quest for Beauty* (1985).

In 1934, May returned to the United States and enrolled in the Union Theological Seminary—not, May said, to become a preacher but to study the basic questions related to human existence. It was at this time that May met Paul Tillich, the eminent Protestant theologian and existential philosopher, who was a recent refugee from Germany and a faculty member at the seminary. Tillich became May's lifelong friend, and in 1973 May *wrote Paulus: Reminiscences of a Friendship* as a tribute to Tillich, who died in 1965. It was through Tillich that May was exposed to existential thought, although he had already concluded, after his exposure to Adler's thinking, that he could never accept a mechanistic, deterministic view of humans. May, then, was ready for the existential view of humans, and he embraced that view enthusiastically. After a year at Union Seminary, May learned that his parents divorced and his father left the home. May returned to Michigan to provide for what remained of his family (his mother, a younger sister, and a brother). During this time (1934–1936) he was employed by Michigan State College as a student advisor and counselor. In 1936, May returned to Union Seminary and he received his BD cum laude from Union Theological Seminary in 1938, and served as a minister for 2 years in Montclair, New Jersey.

May's first book, written during his senior year at Union Seminary, was *The Art of Counseling* (1939), and his second was *The Springs of Creative Living: A Study of Human Nature and God* (1940). Both books were religiously oriented, but neither endorsed blind obedience to religious dogma. May considered religions that required blind acceptance of dogma to be unsound and unhealthy. Contrasted with unhealthy religion, true, healthy religion is defined as follows: "Call it confidence in the universe, trust in God, belief in one's fellow-men, or what not, the essence of religion is the belief that something matters—the *presupposition that life has meaning*" (1940, pp. 19–20). So the religious person is one who has found meaning in life, and an *atheist* is one who cannot, or has not, found it.

In the 1940s, May studied psychoanalysis at the William Alanson White Institute of Psychiatry, Psychoanalysis, and Psychology in New York, where he was influenced by such illustrious individuals as Harry Stack Sullivan and Erich Fromm. May remained affiliated with the institute in a variety of capacities for many years. May became a practicing psychoanalyst in 1946, and shortly thereafter enrolled in the Clinical Psychology Program at Teacher's College, Columbia University. It was about this time that he contracted tuberculosis and lived for 18 months in a sanitorium in upstate New York. His close brush with death had a profound influence on his thinking and brought him still closer to existential philosophy.

During his illness, May read both Kierkegaard's and Freud's analyses of anxiety. Søren Kierkegaard (1813–1855) was a Danish theologian and philosopher who rejected the attempts of other philosophers to view humans as totally rational and logical. He viewed humans as largely emotional and free to choose their own destinies. Although May agreed with Freud on many points, he agreed most with Kierkegaard's conclusion that anxiety results from a threat to one's existence. This definition of anxiety has become a focal point in May's theory and therefore is elaborated later in this chapter. May's analysis of anxiety was submitted to Columbia University as his PhD dissertation and was published as *The Meaning of Anxiety* (1950). In 1949, May was granted the first PhD in clinical psychology ever awarded by Columbia University. The degree was granted *summa cum laude.*

In 1975, May moved to Tiburon, California, where he resumed his private practice and served in various capacities at the Saybrook Institute, a graduate school and research center in San Francisco, and at the California School of Professional Psychology. He also continued to elaborate his version of existential psychology. In poor health the last 2 years of his life, May died of multiple causes in his home on October 22, 1994 (Bugental, 1996, p. 418).

In his long career, May was visiting professor at Harvard and Princeton, and lectured at Yale, Columbia, Dartmouth, Oberlin, Cornell, Vassar, and the New School for Social Research. His honors included the American Psychological Association's (APA) Award for Distinguished Contribution to the Science and Profession of Clinical Psychology (1971); the Distinguished Contributions Award of New York University (1971); the Dr. Martin Luther King, Jr., Award of the New York Society of Clinical Psychologists (1974); the Distinguished Graduate's Award of Columbia Teacher's College (1975); and the American Psychological Foundation's Gold Medal Award for Lifetime Contribution to Psychology (1987). May also received at least 10 honorary doctorates, including those from Oberlin, Columbia, and Ohio Northern University in his birth city of Ada, Ohio.

In 1987, the Saybrook Institute established a Rollo May Center consisting of a library and a program designed to encourage research and publication in the spirit of May. The Saybrook Institute also granted an honorary doctorate to May accompanied by the following citation:

[To Rollo May] a man of mythic vision and dedication, who has explored the borderlands of our art and science of psychology. . . . You have devoted your long, productive, and courageous life to the study of the human soul . . . [through examining] love, will, courage, anxiety, innocence, beauty, and existence. . . . You are [William] James's worthy successor in the breadth of your vision, the articulateness of your descriptions, and the productiveness of your conceptions. (Bugental, 1996, p. 419)

In addition to those already mentioned, May's books include:

Man's Search for Himself (1953)

Existence: A New Dimension in Psychiatry and Psychology (coedited with Ernest Angel and Henri Ellenberger) (1958)

Existential Psychology (Ed.) (1961)

Psychology and the Human Dilemma (1967)

Love and Will (1969)—winner of the Ralph Waldo Emerson award for Humane Scholarship given by Phi Beta Kappa

Power and Innocence: A Search for the Sources of Violence (1972)

The Courage to Create (1975)

Freedom and Destiny (1981)

The Discovery of Being: Writings in Existential Psychology (1983)

My Quest for Beauty (1985)

Politics and Innocence (1986)

The Cry for Myth (1991)

Existentialism

Although elements of existential philosophy were in several of the theories we have reviewed, May's theory has the most in common with existential philosophy. Therefore, to review the major concepts of **existentialism** is also to review much of May's theory of personality. The concepts and terms that follow have come from various sources including the writings of such existential thinkers as Kierkegaard, Nietzsche, Heidegger, Binswanger, Boss, Jaspers, Sartre, Camus, Frankl, and Tillich.

Dasein

Dasein literally means to be there (Da = there; sein = to be). The term indicates that the focus of interest for the existentialist is a particular person experiencing and interpreting the world at a particular time in a particular place. It is the study of a person as a being-in-the-world. The world and the person exist simultaneously and cannot be separated. To say that a human being exists at a certain time and in a certain place is not the same as saying a physical object exists there. Guignon (1984) discusses the complex nature of Dasein:

> To be human, as [Heidegger's] term Dasein suggests, is to be "there," caught up [in the world], taking a stand on one's life, active and engaged in ordinary situations, with some overview of what is at stake in living. What characterizes human life in its most natural ways of being is not a relationship between mind and body but a concrete "existing" in a world. Our most natural experience of ourselves is described as "Being-in-the-world," where "world" refers not to the universe studied by physics, but rather to a life-world in the sense in which we speak of "the academic world" or the "world of the theater." To be "in" such a world is not like a pencil's being "in" a drawer; it is more like being engaged or involved in something. (p. 231)

For humans then, existence is a complex, dynamic process. By choosing, valuing, accepting, and rejecting, humans are constantly **becoming** something different than they were.

Three Modes of Existence

Many existential writers divide human existence into three categories: the **Umwelt,** the physical aspects of the internal and external environments; the **Mitwelt,** the realm of interpersonal relationships; and the **Eigenwelt,** a person's consciousness. Each person is thought to live in all three worlds simultaneously, and only the three worlds taken together give a full account of human existence.

Alienation

Alienation refers to a person's estrangement from some aspect of his or her nature. Alienation results in feelings of loneliness, emptiness, and despair. Because there are three modes of existence, one can become alienated from nature (Umwelt), from other people (Mitwelt), or from oneself (Eigenwelt).

Freedom

The most important human attribute, and the attribute that makes humans unique, is freedom of choice. **Freedom** exists only as a potentiality, however, and can be underdeveloped in some people, or even denied. One increases freedom by expanding consciousness. It is through freedom of choice that the person can transcend his or her immediate circumstances, so no human needs to be a victim of environment, genetics, early experiences, or anything else. In the words of Sartre, "Man is nothing else but what he makes of himself. Such is the first principle of existentialism" (1957, p. 15).

Responsibility

Because we have the freedom to become whatever type of person we choose, we must assume full **responsibility** for what we become. No other person(s), circumstances, or fate can be praised or blamed for the nature of our existence; we alone are responsible. Freedom and responsibility are inseparable.

Ontology

In philosophy, **ontology** is the study of existence, or what it means to be. An ontological analysis of such concepts as time, knowledge, or love attempts to determine what all instances of each concept have in common. For example, such an analysis seeks to determine the essential ingredients of the experience of love. The existentialists are concerned with two ontological questions: (1) What is the essence of human nature, or what does it mean to be human? and (2) What does it mean to be a particular human, or what makes a person the way he or she is? In other words, the existentialist is interested in discovering the essence of people in general and of particular individuals.

Phenomenology

The existentialists use the person's consciousness as their subject matter. Awareness of all types is analyzed—for instance, awareness of the external world, awareness of bodily events, and awareness of awareness. It is generally assumed by the existentialists that humans are the only animals that are aware and know they are aware. Furthermore, consciousness is studied as an intact, meaningful, phenomenon, and is not divided or compartmentalized for further study. Phenomenon means that which is given, and **phenomenology** is the study of that which is given in human consciousness.

Authenticity

If a person exercises his or her free will to expand consciousness further, to establish values that minimize anxiety and provide positive relationships with fellow humans, and to create the challenges necessary for further personal growth, then he or she is living an authentic life. If, however, a person lives in accordance with someone else's values and does not exercise his or her free will to enhance personal growth and effective living, the person is said to be living an inauthentic life. Living an authentic life necessarily involves risk, and therefore such a life takes **courage**—thus the title of Paul Tillich's book *The Courage to Be* (1952).

Death

Most existentialists emphasize the importance of the fact that humans are aware they must someday die. **Death** represents nothingness or nonbeing and is the polar opposite of the rich, full, creative life. It therefore represents the opposite of what most existentialists are urging people to become. No one can escape this dichotomy: We seek a full life but at the same time we are aware we must die. The knowledge of our mortality causes anxiety but this anxiety need not be negative; it can be (and should be) used to motivate people to get as much out of life as they can in the time available to them. May (1983) said, "To grasp what it means to exist, one needs to grasp the fact that he might not exist" (p. 105). Furthermore, death is not viewed as an all-or-nothing phenomenon. People die symbolically, by degrees, each time one of their established values is threatened. Such a threat is perceived as an attack on one's existence and therefore it too causes anxiety. Living an authentic life necessarily involves dealing with both literal and symbolic death and, therefore, **authenticity** and anxiety are inseparable.

Thrownness

Thrownness (also called facticity and ground of existence) refers to the facts that characterize a person's existence over which he or she has no control. The facts that one is born and ultimately must die are two examples. Other examples include natural events such as earthquakes, volcanoes, and hurricanes; genetic factors, such as the color of one's skin, one's gender, and the possession of exceptional talents (e.g., artistic, musical, or mathematical abilities); cultural factors, such as familial and societal factors into which one is born (e.g., being rich or poor, American or Russian, or being born during peacetime or wartime). It is these natural, familial, historical, and cultural conditions that, to a large extent, constitute the da of Dasein. It is thrownness that determines the conditions under which we exercise our personal freedom. That is, some facts characterizing our existence are impossible for us to control; how we interpret, value, and act on those facts, however, is a matter of personal choice.

What other existentialists call thrownness, facticity, or ground of existence, May called **destiny,** which he defined as the "pattern of limits and talents that constitutes the 'givens' in life" (1981, p. 89). According to May, these personal limitations in our existence give meaning to our personal freedom. It is true that the givens in one's life are determined by circumstances beyond one's control, but the meaning assigned to those givens is freely chosen. Thus, determinism and freedom are closely related.

> *Freedom and determinism give birth to each other. Every advance in freedom gives birth to new determinism, and every advance in determinism gives birth to a new freedom.* Freedom is a circle within a larger circle of determinism, which is, in turn, surrounded by a larger circle of freedom. And so on, ad infinitum. (May, 1981, p. 84)

All of the foregoing terms and concepts are found in May's theory of personality. Next, we turn to some of May's specific applications of existential philosophy to psychology.

Human Dilemma

May (1967) stated that the **human dilemma** is the fact that humans are capable of viewing themselves as both subject and object at the same time. May described the **object–subject dichotomy** in various ways, which have not always been consistent (see Reeves, 1977, pp. 198–201). In general, however, May said that humans are capable of seeing themselves as an object to which things happen. For example, as people, we are influenced by the physical environment, the presence or absence of other people, genetics (we are tall, short, male, female, light-skinned, dark-skinned, etc.), and by social or cultural variables. In other words, we are influenced by our destiny.

These objective events are those variables that deterministically oriented theories stress as the causes of behavior. That is, because we are stimulated in certain ways, we respond in certain ways. As subjects, however, we are aware of the fact that these things are happening to us. We perceive, ponder, and act on this information. We determine which experiences are valuable and which are not, and then act according to these personal formulations.

May said that **self-relatedness** is what distinguishes humans from the rest of nature. It is "man's capacity to stand outside himself, to know he is the subject as well as the object of experience, to see himself as the entity who is acting in the world of objects" (1967, p. 75). As humans, we view the world, and we can view ourselves viewing. It is this self-relatedness, or consciousness of self, that allows humans to escape determinism and personally influence what they do. "Consciousness of self gives us the power to stand outside the rigid chain of stimulus and response, to pause, and by this pause to throw some weight on either side, to cast some decision about what the response will be" (May, 1953, p. 161).

Here we have the concept of *Dasein* in May's theory. "Being there" is to be understood as a being who is there. The "there" is whatever deterministic forces are present in a given situation, whereas the being (the person) brings to bear on these forces his or her own freedom, values, interpretations, and so forth. For May, then, both ends of the dichotomy need to be taken into consideration to reach a full understanding of a person—that is, both one's physical circumstances (the objective part) and how one subjectively structures and values those circumstances (the subjective part).

May believed it is a mistake to stress one pole of the object–subject dichotomy at the expense of the other pole. "Curiously enough, both these alternatives—being purely free and purely determined—amount to the same kind of playing God in the respect that we arrogantly refuse to accept the dilemma which is our fate and our great potentiality as humans" (May, 1967, p. 9).

May thought that Skinner and Rogers represented two psychologists who emphasized one side of the dilemma at the expense of the other. Skinner avoided subjective experience, but May asked, "Is it not a fact that people do react to an inner experience of their environment, do see their environment in terms of their past experiences, and do interpret it in terms of their own symbols, hopes and fears?" (May, 1967, p. 15).

May criticized Rogers for both his emphasis on subjectivity and for omitting from his analysis the negative components of human existence such as the emotions of anger, aggression, hostility, and rage. In an open letter to Rogers, May (1982) said we must "actively confront the issues of evil and good in ourselves, our society, and our world" (p. 19). Elsewhere, May said, "We need, therefore, to put the question, Does not Rogers' emphasis on rationality, and his belief that the individual will simply choose what is *rational* for him, leave out a large section of the spectrum of human experience, namely, all the irrational feelings?" (1967, p. 18).

As we see when we discuss the daimonic later in this chapter, May believed the potential for evil is part of human nature and must be taken into consideration in fully understanding humans.

Intentionality

In *Love and Will* (1969), May spoke of **intentionality** as the means by which the dichotomy between subject and object is partially overcome. Although mental acts are purely subjective, they always intend, or relate to, events outside of themselves. Love, for example, is a subjective experience but one must love someone or something. Likewise, perception is a subjective experience but one must perceive something. So it is with all mental and emotional experiences; they must intend, or relate to, objects or events outside of themselves. In the object–subject dichotomy, the object pole is given, but it is the individual who determines which aspects of objective reality are valued positively or negatively, attended to or ignored, or approached or avoided. Intentionality, then, is the human capacity to perceive selectively and to assign meaning to objects and events in the world; it describes the relationship between the thinking person and the outside world. Thus the same environmental event will be responded to differently depending on what meaning the person assigns to it. For example, the same house in the mountains will have different meaning depending on whether it is perceived as a possible temporary vacation home, a possible permanent residence, the home of friends, the home of enemies, or as an object to be sketched (May, 1969, pp. 224–225).

For May, then, intentionality elaborates an important aspect of Dasein. As beings-in-the-world, our interactions with the physical world are highly personal and dynamic. Each person responds to the world in terms of his or her personal structure of meaning (e.g., beliefs, values, and expectations). We see here considerable similarity between May's version of existential theory and Kelly's constructive alternativism (see Chapter 13).

Will and wish are closely related to intentionality. May defined **will** as "the capacity to organize oneself so that movement in a certain direction or toward a certain goal may take place" (1969, p. 218). He defined **wish** as "the imaginative playing with the possibility of some act or state occurring" (1969, p. 218). Thus, given a person's structure of meaning, he or she will use his or her imagination to ponder several possible future courses of action. It is this wishing that provides vitality, imagination, and innovation to the personality. From the many possible courses of action, the person chooses those that are possible and most meaningful, and organizes his or her life so that the chosen goals can be attained (will).

Intentionality, wish, and will are three of the most important concepts in May's theory because they relate to several other human attributes. Reeves (1977) says, "It is, then, asserts May, in intentionality and will, in the broad reach of human orientation toward meaning, decision, and act, in the weighing, deciding, and acting on possibilities sensed, that the individual person experiences his identity, exercises his freedom, and senses his being" (p. 158).

Anxiety and Guilt

Most existential thinkers assume that the experience of **anxiety** is part of the human condition, and May was no exception. As mentioned earlier, May studied the theories of anxiety proposed by Kierkegaard (e.g., *The Concept of Anxiety*, 1944) and Freud while he was in a sanitorium because of his tuberculosis. He rejected Freud's interpretation of anxiety as resulting from a conflict between one's biological needs and the demands of society. For May, Freud's analysis of anxiety was too biological and compartmentalized. That is, for Freud, anxiety was viewed as resulting from the conflicts among the id, ego, and superego.

Instead of accepting Freud's complex and ultimately biological explanation of anxiety, May accepted Kierkegaard's existential definition. For Kierkegaard, human freedom and anxiety go hand in hand. When freedom is threatened, as it always is, anxiety results:

> The distinctive quality of human anxiety arises from the fact that man is the valuing animal, the being who interprets his life and world in terms of symbols and meanings, and identifies these with his existence as a self. . . . It is the threat to these values that causes anxiety. Indeed, I define anxiety as *the apprehension cued off by a threat to some value which the individual holds essential to his existence as a self.* The threat may be to physical life itself, i.e., death; or to psychological life, i.e., loss of freedom. Or it may be to some value the person identifies with his existence as a self: patriotism, the love of a special person, prestige among one's peers, devotion to scientific truth or to religious belief. (May, 1967, p. 72)

May pointed out it is a uniquely human characteristic that we sometimes prefer death to the abandonment of a cherished value:

> Death is the most obvious threat cueing off anxiety, for unless one holds beliefs in immortality, which is not common for our culture, death stands for the ultimate blotting out of one's existence as a self. But immediately we note a very curious fact: some people *prefer to die rather than to surrender some other value.* The taking away of psychological and spiritual freedom was not infrequently a greater threat than death itself to persons under the dictatorships of Europe. "Give me liberty or give me death" is not necessarily histrionic or evidence of a neurotic attitude. Indeed, there is a reason for believing . . . that it may represent the most mature form of *distinctively* human behavior. (1967, p. 73)

Normal Anxiety

To grow as a person, one must constantly challenge one's structure of meaning, which is the core of one's existence, and this necessarily causes anxiety. Thus to be human is to have the urge to expand one's awareness, but to do so causes anxiety.

Such anxiety is not only inescapable; it is normal and healthy. "All growth consists of the anxiety-created surrender of past values as one transforms them into broader ones. Growth, and with it normal anxiety, consists of the giving up of immediate security for the sake of more extensive goals" (May, 1967, pp. 80–81). The authentic person recognizes the hazards of exploring uncharted territory and does so nonetheless. The anxiety associated with moving forward into the unknown is an unfortunate concomitant of exercising one's freedom.

Normal anxiety, then, is viewed as part of the growth process, and no attempt should ever be made to eliminate it from a person's experience. May strongly disagreed with those psychotherapists who have as their goal the elimination of anxiety.

Neurotic Anxiety

A certain amount of anxiety is normal, but nonetheless it is still anxiety, and some people attempt to escape from it. People who decide to conform to values arrived at by others, for example, give up their own personal freedom and the possibility for personal growth by seeking "security" in conformity. Such attempts to escape normal anxiety, which is healthy, result in **neurotic anxiety,** which is unhealthy. It is neurotic anxiety that must be addressed by a psychotherapist. May (1967) distinguished between normal and neurotic anxiety:

> *Normal anxiety* is anxiety which is proportionate to the threat, does not involve repression, and can be confronted constructively on the conscious level. . . . Neurotic anxiety, on the other hand, is a reaction which is disproportionate to the threat, involves repression and other forms of intrapsychic conflict, and is managed by various kinds of blocking-off of activity and awareness. The anxiety connected with the "loneliness at the top" and the "loneliness of the long distance runner" which the movies tell us about can be seen as *normal* anxiety. The anxiety that comes from conforming, to escape this loneliness, is the neurotic transformation of the original, normal anxiety.
>
> Actually, neurotic anxiety develops when a person has been unable to meet normal anxiety at the time of the actual crisis in his growth and the threat to his values. Neurotic anxiety is the end result of previously unmet normal anxiety. (p. 80)

To summarize, normal anxiety is experienced when one attempts to expand one's consciousness or when new values displace old ones because of changing circumstances. Normal anxiety is an integral part of healthy growth: "All growth consists of the anxiety-creating surrender of past values" (May, 1967, p. 80). Neurotic anxiety is experienced when consciousness is restricted, old values are clung to at all costs, or when one attempts to escape normal anxiety by accepting dogma. "Dogma, whether of the religious or scientific variety, is a temporary security bought at the price of surrendering one's opportunity for fresh learning and new growth. Dogma leads to neurotic anxiety" (May, 1967, p. 80). Neurotic anxiety leads to psychological stagnation and to intense feelings of guilt.

Normal and Neurotic Guilt

If one does not live up to his or her potentiality as a human, one feels guilty; therefore, all humans experience a certain amount of **guilt.** May referred to guilt as ontological because it, like anxiety, is part of the human condition. Guilt, according to

May, does not result from violating a generally accepted moral code; rather, it results from not approaching or striving toward one's full potential as a human. "Ontological guilt does not consist of I-am-guilty-because-I-violated-parental-prohibitions, but arises from the fact that I can see myself as the one who can choose or fail to choose. Every developed human being would have this ontological guilt" (May, Angel, & Ellenberger, 1958, p. 55).

Normal guilt is part of a healthy existence and can be used constructively. Guilt, however, if not recognized and dealt with, can, like anxiety, become neurotic and debilitating. There is a close relationship between the experience of anxiety and guilt. The more one takes risks to expand consciousness the more one experiences normal anxiety, but this very risk taking reduces normal guilt. On the other hand, avoiding such risk taking results in neurotic anxiety, which, in turn, results in **neurotic guilt.** Furthermore, because there are three modes of existence, there are three major sources of anxiety and guilt. Various levels of anxiety and guilt result from how we embrace the Umwelt, the Mitwelt, and the Eigenwelt.

Importance of Values

Values summarize in symbolic form those classes of experience we deem especially important. Valuing some experiences more than others cannot be avoided because the valuing process is part of human nature. A person's value system determines how much meaning an experience will have, how much emotionality it elicits, and what is worth aspiring to in the future. To a large extent, how much anxiety a person experiences will be determined by the adequacy of his or her value system. "A person can meet anxiety to the extent that his values are stronger than the threat" (May, 1967, p. 51).

According to May, a developmental pattern in the formation of values exists. Following birth, love, care, and nourishment provided by the mother are valued most. Any threat to these causes the infant to experience anxiety. As the child matures, typically such matters as approval, success, and status among peers are valued. Mature values, however, are not viewed as outgrowths of previously held values. Rather, they reflect basic human nature by emphasizing freedom, the future, and the betterment of the human condition:

> The criteria for mature values follows from the distinctive characteristics of the human being . . . mature values are those which transcend the immediate situation in time and encompass past and future. Mature values transcend also the immediate in-group, and extend outward toward the good of the community, ideally and ultimately embracing humanity as a whole. . . . The more mature a man's values are, the less it matters to him whether his values are literally satisfied or not. The satisfaction and security lie in the holding of values. To the genuine scientist or religious person or artist, security and confidence arise from his awareness of his devotion to the search for truth and beauty rather than the finding of it. (May, 1967, p. 82)

For May, the **Oedipus conflict** is not an attraction toward one parent and a feeling of hostility toward the other, as Freud had proposed. Rather, it is a struggle between dependence and independence. That is, as young children our needs for food, shelter, and safety are satisfied by our parents. We have a tendency to continue to depend on them, or others, for need satisfaction even when it is no longer necessary to do so. To approximate our potential as humans, we must give up the dependence that we valued in our early years. This is not easy to do, and yet it is a prerequisite for positive growth.

When conditions remain stable for a long period of time, it is possible for people to develop values that are effective in dealing with the world and also in manifesting themselves as human beings. It is even possible for many people to hold more or less the same values. This was the case for the pioneers in the United States, when individualism and pragmatism were widely accepted. In our modern world, however, conditions have changed so rapidly we have not had time to evolve values that are adequate for coping with modern life. "In a period of transition, when old values are empty and traditional mores no longer viable, the individual experiences a particular difficulty in finding himself in his world" (May, 1967, p. 25).

When we do not have adequate values, we feel alienated from the world and we lose our sense of identity, worth, and significance. May believed it was the breakdown of traditional values that caused a widespread identity crisis in the United States in the 1950s. However, he observed that this identity crisis developed into an even more serious problem:

> Persons of all sorts these days, especially younger people, diagnose their trouble when they come to a counselor or therapist as an "identity crisis"—and the fact that the phrase has become trite should not lead us to overlook the fact that it may also be importantly true. . . . My thesis is that the problem of identity in the 1950's has now become, more specifically, the crisis of the loss of the sense of significance. . . . The feeling tends to be, "Even if I did know who I am, I couldn't make any difference as an individual anyway." (1967, p. 26)

According to May, people today are confronted with "mass" everything—for example, mass communication and mass education. The emphasis is on sameness not individuality. Yet we were brought up believing in the power and worth of the individual. Thus the values we learned as children do not fit the modern world, and therefore we feel insignificant, alone, and anxious. Without functional values, one has nothing to be committed to and one feels helpless. Without a strong value system, it is difficult, if not impossible, for a person to choose a course of action or a way of life. According to May, then, the major problem of our time is that "the younger generation . . . do not have viable values available in the culture on the basis of which they can relate to their world" (1967, p. 42).

Without an adequate system of values, people tend to be outer directed. That is, people with inadequate values depend on things outside of themselves to indicate their significance—for instance, social mores, peer evaluation, church dogma, teachers' opinions, and grades. Those people with strong values know they are significant independently of these external events and are therefore able to experience these things in a much different perspective. Peer approval may be valued, for example, but it is not depended on for a sense of worth.

For May, as well as many other existential thinkers, values and **commitment** go hand in hand. Mature values allow a person not only to deal effectively with present events but to consider the feelings and values of others and therefore to form deep, meaningful interpersonal relationships. Also, mature values allow one to become future oriented. Such values give a person hope and therefore a reason to commit him- or herself to a course of action. A person without an adequate value system has no good reason to be committed to anything. For this reason, the existentialists include commitment as an ontological human characteristic; that is, commitment characterizes every normal, healthy, mature human being.

A person's values determine how he or she acts, and because values are consciously and freely chosen, one is fully responsible for one's actions:

> It is in the act of valuing that consciousness and behavior become united. One can take over rote values . . . from the church, or the therapist, school, American Legion, or any other group in the culture. But the act of valuing, in contrast, involves a commitment on the part of the individual which goes beyond the "rote" or automatic situation. This, in turn, implies some conscious choice and responsibility. (May, 1967, p. 220)

Nature of Love

In his book *Love and Will* (1969), May described four types of **love** and stated that authentic love is a blending of the four. The four types of love are sex, eros, philia, and agapé.

Sex

Sex is one of our biological drives, and it can be satisfied by engaging in sexual intercourse, just as eating a meal can satisfy the hunger drive. Both sexual intercourse and eating can be almost automatic activities triggered by a need and the availability of an object that will satisfy that need. "Sex can be defined fairly adequately in physiological terms as consisting of the building up of bodily tensions and their release" (May, 1969, p. 73). Many in the modern world have equated sex with love and, according to May, this is most unfortunate.

Eros

Eros is the desire for union with another person. With sex the goal is termination, gratification, and relaxation. In contrast, we seek to continue the experience of eros. Eros causes us to seek a tender, creative relationship within the context of sexual experience. In addition, eros is responsible for humans seeking such a relationship with the world and with people in general. Eros is the human drive to seek wholeness or interrelatedness among all of our experiences. Seeking such feelings in a sexual relationship is but one manifestation of eros.

Although it may appear eros must always be experienced positively, that is not the case because eros exemplifies the daimonic forces within us. May (1969) defined the **daimonic** as

> any natural function which has the power to take over the whole person. Sex and eros, anger and rage, and the craving for power are examples. The daimonic can be

either creative or destructive and is normally both. . . . The daimonic is the urge in every being to affirm itself, assert itself, perpetuate and increase itself. The daimonic becomes evil when it usurps the total personality without regard to the integration of that self, or to the unique forms and desires of others and their need for integration. It then appears as excessive aggression, hostility, cruelty—the things about ourselves which horrify us most, and which we repress whenever we can, or more likely, project on others. But these are the reverse side of the same assertion which empowers our creativity. All life is a flux between these two aspects of the daimonic. (p. 123)

The term *daimonic* comes from the Greek word meaning both divine and diabolic. Thus we have forces within us that in moderation lead to personal growth and creativity, but when allowed to dominate become negative and destructive. So it is with eros. One must be assertive to have a loving union with another person but when assertiveness dominates, one is in danger of exploiting one's partner.

The existence of daimonic forces within humans provides the continuing potential for cruel, irrational, and inhumane behavior. It is impossible for humans to rid themselves of these forces, and it is not necessary for them to do so. What is important is to keep daimonic urges under control and to use them productively rather than to harm. May viewed the tension between the positive and negative forces within each human as the greatest source of the creativity shown in art, drama, literature, and even science.

As we have just observed, the daimonic must be experienced in moderation if eros is going to contribute positively to a loving relationship. But there is another danger associated with eros. Merging with another person can be viewed as a form of death; the death of the person who existed before the merger took place. By entering into a loving relationship one is exposed to the possibilities of grief, sorrow, and disappointment as well as to the many delights such a relationship can bring. It is a major gamble.

> For death is always in the shadow of the delight of love. In faint adumbration, there is present the dread[ed], haunting question, Will this new relationship destroy us? When we love, we give up the center of ourselves. We are thrown from our previous state of existence into a void; and though we hope to attain a new world, a new existence, we can never be sure. . . . This experience of annihilation is an inward one and, as the myth [of eros] rightly puts it, is essentially what eros does to us. To love completely carries with it the threat of annihilation of everything. This intensity of consciousness has something in common with the ecstasy of the mystic in his union with God: just as he can never be sure God is there, so love carries us to that intensity of consciousness in which we no longer have any guarantee of security. (May, 1969, p. 101)

Philia

The third type of love is **philia,** which is ordinarily defined as friendship or brotherly love. According to May, eros cannot last for long without philia because the tension of continuous attraction and passion would be too great. May (1969) explained philia further:

> Philia is the relaxation in the presence of the beloved which accepts the other's being as being; it is simply liking to be with the other, liking to rest with the other, liking the rhythm of the walk, the voice, the whole being of the other. This gives a width to eros, it gives it time to grow; time to sink its roots down deeper. Philia does not require that we do anything for the beloved except accept him, and enjoy him. It is friendship in the simplest, most direct terms. (p. 317)

For May, then, for a deep, loving relationship to exist, the partners must truly like each other as persons in addition to seeking a creative union with them. To be able to say honestly, "I like you" to one partner is an important part of authentic love.

Agapé

The fourth type of love is **agapé**, which May (1969) defined as follows:

> Esteem for the other, the concern for the other's welfare beyond any gain that one can get out of it; disinterested love, typically, the love of God for man. It is an analogy—though not an identity—with the biological aspect of nature which makes the mother cat defend to her death her kittens, and the human being love his own baby with a built-in mechanism without regard for what that baby can do for him. (p. 310)

Agapé is an unselfish giving of one's self to another; a giving of one's self without any concern of what one will get in return. May's concept of agapé is similar to what Rogers called unconditional positive regard. In both cases, the love offered to another has no conditions placed on it.

May believed that in modern times many have had an unfortunate tendency to equate love with sex. For May, however, authentic love must involve a blending of sex, the biological component of love; eros, the seeking of a creative union with another human, the sharing and combining of two selves; philia, friendship, a simple liking of one's partner even when sex and eros are not involved; and agapé, the unselfish concern for one's partner, the aspect of love that is unconditional.

Psychotherapy

For May, the goal of **psychotherapy** is not to eliminate anxiety or guilt but rather to convert neurotic anxiety or guilt to normal anxiety or guilt, which, as we have seen, are part of being human and are necessary for personal growth:

> Our chief concern in therapy is with the potentiality of the human being. The goal of therapy is to help the patient actualize his potentialities. . . . The goal of therapy is not the absence of anxiety, but rather the changing of neurotic anxiety into normal anxiety, and the development of the capacity to live with and use normal anxiety. The patient after therapy may well bear more anxiety than he had before, but it will be conscious anxiety and he will be able to use it constructively. Nor is the goal the absence of guilt feeling, but rather the transformation of neurotic guilt into normal guilt, together with the development of the capacity to use this normal guilt creatively. (May, 1967, p. 109)

May used the term **unconscious** to describe cognitive experiences that are denied awareness because a person is not living an authentic life. May's treatment of the unconscious is similar to Kelly's. Kelly said that certain experiences are suspended because they do not fit into a person's construct system. For May, certain experiences are denied because they would cause too much anxiety if experienced. For both Kelly and May, repression in the Freudian sense is not involved because the person is at least partially aware of these experiences but they are denied full conscious expression. For May, then, the unconscious is not a reservoir of unacceptable impulses, thoughts, and wishes. Rather, it consists of "*those potentialities for knowing and experiencing which the individual cannot or will not actualize*" (1983, pp. 17–18).

According to May, effective therapy cannot occur if the therapist views the client as an object and attempts to explain his or her problem in terms of various causes—for example, past experiences. Rather, the therapist must try to determine what the client is attempting to express via his or her "problem":

> From the ontological approach . . . we see that *sickness is precisely the method that the individual uses to preserve his being.* We cannot assume in the usual oversimplified way that the patient automatically wants to get well; we must assume, rather, that he cannot permit himself to give up his neurosis, to get well, until other conditions in his existence and his relation to his world are changed. (May, 1967, p. 95)

In a manner reminiscent of Adler and Kelly, the existential therapist encourages clients to view the events into which they have been thrown, that is, their destiny, differently. In this sense, the goal of therapy is to help clients find meaning in circumstances they otherwise find meaningless or hopeless. In his classic book *Man's Search for Meaning* (1984), Viktor Frankl (1905–1997) argued that meaning can be found in even the most dire circumstances:

> We must never forget that we may also find meaning in life even when confronted with a hopeless situation, when facing a fate that cannot be changed. For what then matters is to bear witness to the uniquely human potential at its best, which is to transform a personal tragedy into a triumph, to turn one's predicament into a human achievement. When we are no longer able to change a situation—just think of an incurable disease such as inoperable cancer—we are challenged to change ourselves. . . . In some way, suffering ceases to be suffering at the moment it finds a meaning. (p. 135)

May used the term **encounter** to describe the therapeutic process. By encounter May meant two selves coming together and sharing aspects of their existence:

> Encounter is what really happens; it is something much more than a relationship. In this encounter I have to be able, to some extent, to experience what the patient is experiencing. My job as a therapist is to be open to his world. He brings his world with him and therein we live for fifty minutes. . . . In addition, the therapeutic encounter requires that we ourselves be human beings in the broadest sense of the word. This brings us to a point where we can no longer talk about it merely psychologically, in any kind of detached way, but must "throw" ourselves into the therapeutic encounter. In this it helps to realize that we also have gone through

similar experiences, and though perhaps not involved in them now, we know what they mean. (1967, p. 108)

We see, then, that both Rogers and May viewed empathetic understanding as a key ingredient in effective therapy.

May's approach to psychotherapy includes all the terms and concepts of his theory of personality. Humans, he believes, have the potential to be free and to live authentic lives but many factors can inhibit this freedom and authenticity. People who have adequate values can see their normal anxiety and guilt constructively and creatively. People without adequate values must block out various categories of experience, and healthy anxiety and guilt become neurotic. Such people cannot reach their full potential as human beings. The job of the therapist is to help the client approximate his or her full potential. The therapist's job, according to May, is to help the client to live an authentic life. What May meant by authenticity is much the same as what Rogers called congruency and what Maslow called self-actualization.

Importance of Myth

In the same spirit as Jung's contention that archetypes guide human existence through symbolization and myths, Vaihinger's philosophy of "as if," Adler's guiding fictions, sociobiology's claim that myth supports communal cohesion, and Kelly's concept of constructive alternativism, May believed "myth is a way of making sense in a senseless world. Myths are narrative patterns that give significance to our existence" (1991, p. 15). According to May, many of the problems in our society such as cults, drug addiction, suicide, and depression can be traced to the lack of myths that provide individuals with a sense of inner security. About people seeking psychological help, May (1991) said, "As a practicing psychoanalyst I find that contemporary therapy is almost entirely concerned, when all is surveyed, with the problems of the individual's search for myths" (p. 9).

May's contention that effective living depends on effective myths is supported by a recent development in clinical psychology called *narrative therapy*. Narrative therapy stresses the importance of the stories by which people live and understanding their lives and the functional, or dysfunctional, significance of these stories (see, e.g., McLeod, 1997; White & Epston, 1990).

In close agreement with Jung, May (1991) believed "myths are archetypal patterns in human consciousness [and therefore] where there is consciousness, there will be myth" (p. 37). Also like Jung, May believed myths reflect the core of human nature: "Individual myths will generally be a variation on some central theme of the classical myths" (p. 33). The universal themes of which individual myths are usually some variation include birth; death; love and marriage; the Oedipal complex, which May viewed as the struggle for independence; and the conflict between good and evil, which May explained as the manifestation of the daimonic. Finally, May made the following statement that could easily have been made by Jung: "In the moments when eternity breaks into time, there we find myth. Myth partakes of both dimensions: it is of the earth in our day-to-day experiences, and is a reaching beyond our mundane existence" (p. 297). May also demonstrated his agreement with Adler by noting that we forget most of our early experiences but a few are remembered. These "first memories" whether they are accurate or not become the main ingredients of our "guiding fictions" or the myths according to which we live our lives. Thus "memory and myth are inseparable" (p. 70).

To illustrate how myths give expression to the universal truths of human nature, May (1991) analyzed the myths portrayed in such classics as the Bible, Homer's *Odyssey*, Sophocles's *Oedipus Rex* and *Oedipus in Colonus*, Sartre's *The Flies*, Dante's *Divine Comedy*, Ibsen's *Peer Gynt*, Grimm's *Briar Rose* (later renamed *Sleeping Beauty*), Melville's *Moby Dick*, Goethe's *Faust*, Fitzgerald's *The Great Gatsby*, Poe's *The Raven*, and Shakespeare's *Hamlet, King Lear*, and *Macbeth*. In all of these, and other works, May showed how important aspects of human nature are given expression, allowing the reader to experience catharsis. May noted that one of the most common themes in classical literature is the portrayal of the conflict between the positive and negative aspects of human nature. For May, this eternal conflict between good and evil (e.g., between God and Satan) is the greatest source of creativity. As we have seen, May had little patience with those who portray humans as only good or only bad. For May, we are both, and therein lies the primary drama of human existence.

According to May, myths serve four primary functions in our lives: They give us a sense of personal identity; they give us a sense of community; they support our moral values; and they allow us to deal with the mysteries of creation. Above all the "hunger for myth is a hunger for community. . . . To be a member of one's community is to share in its myths" (1991, p. 45). However, different communities (societies, cultures) are bound together by different myths and therein lies possible friction among people. Xenophobia may be explained by the fact that an outsider may not share one's myths and is therefore to be feared: "The outsider, the foreigner, the stranger is the one who does not share our myths, the one who steers by different stars, worships different gods" (1991, p. 45). Thus, like other aspects of human nature, the same characteristic that can bind people together has the potential to drive them apart.

Are some myths better than others? May's answer was yes. Some myths are undesirable because they do not encourage a sense of kinship among humans. According to May, many of the current problems in the United States stem from the myth of the rugged individualist attempting to live in isolation from other people. This myth has resulted in the Age of Narcissism and thus loneliness and violence. According to May, true happiness can result only from positive interpersonal relationships and, therefore, only myths that bind people are conducive to psychological health. Survival itself depends on caring for our fellow humans—all of them. May (1991) offered the type of myth that he believed we now need to embrace:

> We awake after a sleep of many centuries to find ourselves in a new and irrefutable sense in the myth of humankind. We find ourselves in a new world community; we cannot destroy the parts without destroying the whole. In this bright loveliness we know now that we are truly sisters and brothers, at last in the same family. (p. 302)

In the preceding, we see agreement with Adler (Chapter 4) who used social interest to index mental health. We also see agreement with Allport (Chapter 7) who argued that friction among humans could be substantially reduced by adopting a one-world perspective, that is, by each individual identifying with all humankind.

New Science of Humans

Unlike many existential thinkers, May was not antiscience. What is needed, according to May, is an approach to the study of humans that does not reduce us to collections of habits, brain functions, genetically determined traits, early experiences, or environmental events. We need a science of humans based on the ontological characteristics of humans. That is, we need a science that takes into consideration human freedom; the importance of phenomenological experience; the use of symbols and myths; the ability to consider the past, present, and future in making decisions; and the valuing process. Such a science would emphasize the wholeness and uniqueness of each individual. A science of humans based on existential philosophy would differ from what is now called scientific psychology. Animal research would be irrelevant, and elementism of any type would be avoided. May (1967) summarized his views on this **new science of humans** as follows:

> The outlines of a science of man we suggest will deal with man as the symbol-maker, the reasoner, the historical mammal who can participate in his community and who possesses the potentiality of freedom and ethical action. The pursuit of this science will take no less rigorous thought and wholehearted discipline than the pursuit of experimental and natural science at their best, but it will place the scientific enterprise in a broader context. Perhaps it will again be possible to study man scientifically and still see him whole. (p. 199)

Schneider (1998) elaborates the kind of science envisioned by May and discusses its relevance for contemporary psychology.

Evaluation

Empirical Research

Most existential theorists are unconcerned with the empirical validation of their concepts. They believe the place to validate their concepts is in the arena of everyday life, or in the therapeutic situation, and not with systematic laboratory or field investigations. Van Kaam (1966), an existential psychologist, summarized this viewpoint: "Experiences such as responsibility, dread, anxiety, despair, freedom, love, wonder or decision cannot be measured or experimented with. . . . They are simply there and can only be explicated in their givenness" (p. 187).

Some have made efforts to validate existential concepts empirically, however. Gendlin and Tomlinson (1967) created the Experiencing Scale, designed to measure the extent to which a person is in touch with his or her true feelings. Because a major goal of psychotherapy is to encourage persons to recognize, accept, and live in accordance with their feelings, the scale can be used to measure the extent to which therapy is effective (Gendlin, Beebe, Cassens, Klein, & Oberlander, 1968). Crumbaugh (1968) devised the Purpose-in-Life Test to measure the extent to which a person's life is meaningful. It was found that persons scoring low on the test tended to have worldviews that were negative and lacking purpose. Also, the test was found to positively correlate with a scale of depression. That is, people who scored high on the Purpose-in-Life Test displayed little depression whereas people scoring low displayed considerable depression. Thorne and Pishkin (1973) developed the Existential Study, which consists of seven scales: self-status, self-actualization, existential morale, existential vacuum, humanistic identification, existence and destiny, and suicidal tendency. Thus the scales are designed to quantify several terms and concepts from existential theory.

Although a few have made attempts to quantify existential concepts, most existentialists believe that attempting to study and understand humans by using the traditional methods of science is misguided. May (1967) described what might eventually happen to psychologists who attempt to study humans using the traditional scientific methodology of such disciplines as physics and physiology. In other words, to psychologists who overlook those qualities that are truly important about humans and instead study simple, meaningless behavior because it can be more easily measured:

> A psychologist—any psychologist, or all of us—arrives at the heavenly gates at the end of his long and productive life. He is brought up before St. Peter for the customary accounting. . . . An angel assistant in a white jacket drops a manila folder on the table which St. Peter opens and looks at, frowning. Despite the awesome visage of the judge, the psychologist clutches his briefcase and steps up with commendable courage. But St. Peter's frown deepens. He drums with his fingers on the table and grunts a few nondirective "uhm-uhm"s as he fixes the candidate with his Mosaic eyes.
>
> The silence is discomfiting. Finally the psychologist opens his briefcase and cries, "Here! The reprints of my hundred and thirty-two papers."
>
> St. Peter slowly shakes his head.
>
> Burrowing deeper into the briefcase the psychologist offers, "Let me submit the medals I received for my scientific achievement."
>
> St. Peter's frown is unabated as he silently continues to stare into the psychologist's face.
>
> At last St. Peter speaks. "I'm aware, my good man, how industrious you were. It's not sloth you're accused of. Nor is it unscientific behavior." . . .
>
> Now St. Peter slaps his hand resoundingly down on the table, and his tone is like Moses breaking the news of the ten commandments: "You are charged with *nimis simplicandum* [oversimplification]!
>
> "You have spent your life making molehills out of mountains—that's what you're guilty of. When man was tragic you made him trivial. . . . When he suffered passively, you described him as simpering; and when he drummed up enough courage to act, you called it stimulus and response. . . . You made man over into the image of your childhood Erector Set or Sunday School maxims—both equally horrendous.
>
> "In short, we sent you to earth for seventy-two years to a Dantean circus, and you spent your days and nights at sideshows!" (pp. 3–4)

Criticisms

Philosophy Not Psychology. Historically, concepts such as values, responsibility, and commitment have been studied by philosophers and theologians, not by psychologists. Many critics of existential psychology would like this historical trend to continue.

Unscientific Approach.   As we have seen, most existential psychologists reject traditional scientific methodology as a valid way of studying humans. Such methodology, say the existentialists, treats humans as passive objects not as authors of their own existence. Furthermore, the existentialists reject the assumption of determinism made by traditional science. Human behavior, the existentialists say, is freely chosen, not determined. Critics say that the rejection of scientific methodology and the assumption of determinism represent a throwback to psychology's prescientific past—a throwback to the time when psychology, philosophy, and religion were indistinguishable. Existential psychology, then, say the critics, is jeopardizing the scientific respectability that psychology has gained since its prescientific era.

Nebulous Terminology.   It is difficult to define precisely terms such as freedom, responsibility, commitment, guilt, intentionality, love, and courage. Often the meanings of these and other terms change from one existential theorist to another, and sometimes for the same theorist at different times. This lack of precision makes understanding difficult and quantification practically impossible.

Contributions

Call for Human Science.   Like Maslow, May did not reject the idea of objectively studying humans; it is only that traditional scientific methodology is not appropriate for doing so. What is needed is an approach that studies humans as whole, unique, complex beings. Many welcome May's idea of developing a science more appropriate to the study of humans—one not based on the assumptions and techniques of the natural sciences.

Important, New Way of Conceptualizing Personality.   For many, the existential description of humans rings true: We do seek meaning in our lives and seem lost without it; some humans do seem to grow constantly by exercising their choices whereas others seem to escape from their freedom; most humans are aware of and disturbed by our finitude; and humans do differ in the experiences they seek and in their interpretations of those experiences. Many believe the existential view of humans has breathed new life into psychology.

Summary

Under the influence of Freud, Kierkegaard, and Tillich, and with a special interest in the nature and causes of anxiety, May developed a theory of personality based on existential philosophy. From existential philosophy, May accepted the following: (1) the term Dasein, which is the study of a particular person in the world at a particular time and existing under a particular set of circumstances; (2) a description of three modes of human existence: the Umwelt, or our interactions with the physical world; the Mitwelt, or our interactions with other humans; and the Eigenwelt, which is one's interactions with oneself; (3) alienation, the fact that a person can become separated from one or more of the modes of existence; (4) the belief that each person is free to choose the meaning of his or her own existence; (5) responsibility, which goes hand in hand with freedom; (6) ontology, which attempts to determine the essential features of human nature in general or of a particular human; (7) the importance of phenomenology, or the study of intact, meaningful conscious experience without dividing it or reducing it for study or analysis; (8) authenticity, or the effort to live one's life in accordance with freely chosen values rather than having values imposed on one from the outside; (9) the importance of death in the ontology of humans (e.g., death is the ultimate state of nonbeing, and to ponder the inevitability of one's death is a source of great anxiety); and (10) thrownness, referring to the circumstances of our lives over which we have no control. What other existentialists referred to as thrownness, facticity, or ground of existence, May called destiny.

May described the human dilemma as our ability to view ourselves as both an object in the world to which things happen and as a subject who acts on things by interpreting them, valuing them, projecting them into the future, and thus transforming them. May believed that to develop a complete understanding of humans, both aspects, humans as objects and as subjects, must be studied. May believed that a theory like Skinner's stresses the objective side of humans too much, whereas a theory like Rogers's stresses the subjective side too much. Also, Rogers, according to May, ignored the irrational, evil aspects of human existence.

Intentionality refers to the fact that mental events are directed toward objects outside of themselves. It is through intentionality that we interact with the objective world and, therefore, it is the means by which the object–subject dichotomy is bridged.

Will is the commitment to action. After a structure of meaning has been developed and intentions formulated, we must act on those intentions. Will is directly related to action. Wish is the imaginative playing with possible courses of action before actually committing ourselves to one.

According to May, to be human is to experience anxiety and guilt. Normal anxiety results when we ponder death or when our values are threatened. Because humans are mortal, and because to grow psychologically our values must constantly be challenged, normal anxiety cannot be avoided. Likewise, when we become aware we are not living up to our full potential, we experience guilt, and because no human ever lives up to his or her full potential, normal guilt is unavoidable. Some people, instead of using normal anxiety and guilt for personal growth, attempt to escape them by conforming to external values or by refusing to acknowledge that such anxiety and guilt exist. When normal anxiety and guilt are not dealt with in a conscious, constructive manner, they become neurotic. Neurotic anxiety and guilt cause a person to deny important areas of personal experience and therefore stifle personal growth. It is neurotic anxiety and guilt that typically cause a person to seek psychotherapy.

Our values summarize those experiences that we have deemed to be most valuable. Mature values seek a harmony among people and are future oriented. Because each person can freely choose his or her values, each person is responsible for the actions derived from them. Values require a commitment to action and it is the person who is responsible for his or her value structure and the actions that they necessitate. For some people, some values are so important that they would rather die than abandon them. The amount of anxiety that one experiences is directly related to one's values. If one's value structure is adequate, one will experience normal anxiety. Value structures must be dynamic, however, because an unwillingness to change values stifles personal growth and results in excessive guilt. The healthy human is constantly becoming more than he or she had been.

May described four types of love. Sex is the attraction toward a member of the opposite sex based solely on biology. Eros seeks a union and a sharing of one's self with one's lover. Philia, which is the friendship that holds two people together even when sex and eros are not involved, means liking as well as loving the other person. Agapé means caring for the other person even when one gets nothing in return. Authentic love, according to May, involves a blending of all four types of love. One must be aware of the daimonic, however, which has the power to destroy our relationships with other humans. The daimonic is any human function that has the power to dominate a person. If sex dominates a relationship, for example, authentic love is lost because one's lover is nothing more than an object used to satisfy one's biological sex drive. Likewise, if eros is allowed to dominate one's seeking of a union, the partner's individuality is ignored, and the union is at the expense of one's partner. It is the daimonic that provides the potential for evil in human existence. According to May, entering a loving relationship is risky because there is no guarantee that the personal sacrifices required will benefit those involved.

For May, effective psychotherapy cannot occur if the client is viewed as a collection of habits, past experiences, genetically determined dispositions, test scores, or as representing a diagnostic category. Rather, it must result from an encounter between two humans. The therapist must attempt to understand what the client is trying to do or say through an emotional problem. In other words, the therapist must try to see experiences as the client does. When this is done, the therapist attempts to help the client convert neurotic anxiety or guilt into normal anxiety or guilt and begin to live an authentic life. Another goal of existential therapy is to help clients find meaning in circumstances that appear to them as meaningless or hopeless.

For May, the unconscious is not a storehouse of repressed memories. Rather, it consists of several potential experiences that must be denied because of various defenses a person has used to avoid normal anxiety, or because the person is using a very restrictive value structure. When those barriers are overcome, the person becomes open to experience, becomes aware of previously denied possibilities, and in general, becomes freer as a human being.

May contended that it is through myth the basic components of human nature are given expression. Myths that give people a sense of community are conducive to mental health. Myths that encourage individualism isolate people and result in feelings of loneliness and despair.

May believed that psychology needs a new model for a science of humans. The old one, based on mechanistic determinism, had as its primary goals the seeking of the objective causes of behavior, and the prediction and control of behavior. Within this model, humans are viewed as the objects of the physical forces acting on them. For May, a better model would be one based on existential philosophy, a model that addresses the human capacities for freedom, valuing, and loving.

A few attempts have been made to verify existential concepts empirically but most existential psychologists believe the place to verify their concepts is in the arena of everyday life or in the therapeutic situation. May's theory has been criticized for representing philosophy (or perhaps religion) instead of psychology, being unscientific, and containing nebulous terminology. May's theory has been praised for calling for the development of a human science and offering a new way of conceptualizing personality.

Experiential Exercises

1. May defined an atheist as a person with little or no meaning in his or her life. According to May's definition, are you an atheist? Explain.
2. Analyze a loving relationship that you have, or have had, in terms of May's four-part definition of love. Indicate if you agree or disagree with May's description of love.

3. Using the existentialists' definitions of anxiety and guilt, describe the circumstances under which you have experienced these two emotions. Have you ever experienced what the existentialists call neurotic anxiety or neurotic guilt? Explain.

Discussion Questions

1. Briefly describe the following terms from existential philosophy: Dasein, Umwelt, Mitwelt, Eigenwelt, alienation, ontology, phenomenology, responsibility, and thrownness.

2. What, according to May and other existentialists, is an authentic life?
3. What, according to May, is the human dilemma? Give an example.

Glossary

Agapé. Unselfish giving of one's self in a loving relationship. One loves but expects nothing in return.

Alienation. Separation from nature, other people, or oneself that results in feelings of loneliness, emptiness, or despair.

Anxiety. To be human is to experience anxiety. Anxiety is the experience we have when our existence as an individual is threatened. To ponder one's inevitable death causes anxiety, as does the threat to one's values. To grow, one's values must be threatened. Therefore, anxiety is an unavoidable component of a normal, healthy life. *See also* Neurotic anxiety and Normal anxiety.

Authenticity. If people live their lives in accordance with values that are freely chosen, they are living authentic lives. If, however, people conform to values established by others, they have not exercised their personal freedom and are therefore living inauthentic lives. Inauthenticity is causally related to neurotic anxiety and guilt and the feelings of loneliness, ineffectiveness, self-alienation, and despair.

Becoming. Contention that through their active involvement with their life's circumstances, authentic people are constantly changing.

Commitment. One must exist in the world and therefore act on it. Values are meaningless unless they are manifested in behavior. The formulation of values, therefore, also commits people to a course of action. Behavioral commitment to self-formulated, future-oriented, human values characterizes the authentic life.

Courage. An authentic life involves creating for oneself a structure of meaning that will guide one's thoughts and actions. Such a life requires courage because it means that often one's beliefs and actions may be contrary to those that are widely accepted.

Daimonic. Potential for evil or harm that is part of human nature. The daimonic occurs when any natural function that in moderation is positive, dominates the individual—for example, when assertiveness becomes aggression or hostility or when eros causes one to dominate one's lover and thereby destroy his or her individuality.

Dasein. Study of the individual as a being in the world. The emphasis is on an individual's existence at a certain time under certain circumstances. The conditions a person finds him- or herself in can never be separated from the person him- or herself. The two must be viewed as a whole. The individual as an object and as a subject can never be separated.

Death. Because humans are mortal, and because death is the ultimate state of nonbeing, awareness of one's inevitable death causes anxiety. This source of anxiety is part of human existence and cannot be avoided. The awareness of death, however, can add vitality to life by motivating a person to get as much out of life as possible in the limited time available.

Destiny. According to May, the givens in one's life that are creatively interpreted, and are thus provided meaning. For example, it is a given that all humans will die, but whether this fact is a source of vitality or despair is a personal choice. *See also* Thrownness.

Eigenwelt. The intrapersonal world. An individual's self-awareness.

Encounter. The meeting of two selves. Seeing things as the other sees them and vice versa. An honest sharing of one's self with another person. For May, an encounter is a necessary component of successful psychotherapy. The client must be understood as a total human being, not as a collection of test scores or repressed experiences or as an object that fits into some diagnostic category.

Eros. Desire to form a union with or to feel at one with one's partner in love. Through the sharing of two selves, both experience new things and both expand their consciousness. With sex, the goal is satisfaction and termination; with eros, the goal is to prolong the loving experience as long as possible.

Existentialism. Philosophy that studies the essence of human nature. The emphasis is on freedom, individuality, and phenomenological experience.

Freedom. Not the absence of negative conditions, but the potential to set future-oriented goals and then to act in accordance with them. According to the existential philosopher Sartre, "We are our choices," or, "We are what we choose to be." Freedom exists only as a potential and must be attained over time by increasing one's self-awareness. Because freedom necessarily involves anxiety and responsibility, many people deny, minimize, or escape from their personal freedom.

Guilt. Feeling we have when we realize we are not living up to our full potential. *See also* Neurotic guilt and Normal guilt.

Human dilemma. Capacity of humans to see themselves as objects to which things happen, and as subjects who act on their experiences and thereby give them meaning.

Intentionality. The fact that mental events are directed toward objects outside of themselves. For example, perception always involves the perception of something. It is through intentionality that a relationship between objective and subjective reality is formed.

Love. True or authentic love involves a harmonious blending of sex, eros, philia, and agapé. *See also* Agapé, Eros, Philia, and Sex.

Mitwelt. World of human interactions.

Neurotic anxiety. Anxiety that results from not being able to deal adequately with normal anxiety. For example, if a person conforms or develops inflexible values to avoid normal anxiety, the normal anxiety is converted into neurotic anxiety, which causes a person to live life within narrow limits and inhibit various experiences that are necessary for healthy growth. The person experiencing neurotic anxiety is shut off from many of his or her potentialities. *See also* Anxiety and Normal anxiety.

Neurotic guilt. If normal guilt is not recognized and dealt with constructively, it can overwhelm a person, causing him or her to block out the very experiences conducive to personal growth.

New science of humans. Rather than a science of humans based on determinism and elementism and one that has as its goal the prediction and control of behavior, May proposed a science of humans based on existential philosophy. Such a science would take into consideration the human use of symbols, the human sense of time, the importance of values, the uniqueness of each human, and the importance of freedom.

Normal anxiety. Anxiety that results from the revisions of one's value system and from the awareness of one's inevitable death. To grow as a person requires taking risks, which causes normal anxiety.

Normal guilt. Feeling experienced when one recognizes the difference between what one is and what one could be. Because we can always be more than we are, normal guilt is unavoidable. *See also* Guilt and Neurotic guilt.

Object–subject dichotomy.   The fact that as humans we are both the objects of experience and the interpreters, transformers, and originators of experience. *See also* Human dilemma.

Oedipus conflict.   Rather than interpreting the Oedipus conflict as an attraction toward one parent and hostility toward the other, as Freud did, May interpreted the conflict as a struggle between dependence and independence.

Ontology.   Study of being. Within existentialism, ontological analysis is directed at understanding the essence of humans in general and of individuals in particular.

Phenomenology.   Study of conscious experience as it exists for the person without any attempt to reduce, divide, or compartmentalize it in any way.

Philia.   Experience of friendship or companionship with one's loved one even when sex and eros are not involved. Simply liking to be with your loved one.

Psychotherapy.   For May, effective psychotherapy can only result from an encounter between two humans. The therapist must attempt to understand things as the client does and try to understand how the client is using a "problem" to maintain his or her identity as a person. The goal of therapy is to free the client from neurotic anxiety and guilt, so that the person will be freer to actualize his or her potential. *See also* Encounter.

Responsibility.   Because we are free to choose our own existence, we are also entirely responsible for that existence. We can praise or blame no one but ourselves for whatever we become as people.

Self-relatedness.   To be aware of one's existence as a being in the world who both has

experiences and transforms them. To be conscious of the fact that one is both the object and subject of experience.

Sex.   Biological aspect of love. To satisfy the sexual aspect of love requires only sexual activity with a partner. In such cases, the partner becomes the object by which the need for sex is satisfied.

Throwness (also called facticity, destiny, and ground of existence).   Those facts that characterize a person's life over which he or she has no control. Such facts include the biological, historical, and cultural events that characterize his or her life.

Umwelt.   Physical, objective world. The world that is studied by the physical and biological sciences.

Unconscious.   For May, the unconscious is not a "cellar" in which repressed experiences reside, as it was for Freud. Rather, it consists of the experiences denied awareness because of inflexible values or because of the restrictive influence of neurotic anxiety and guilt. When values become flexible and neurotic anxiety and guilt are overcome, the person is again open to experience, and nothing needs to be denied awareness.

Values.   Those categories of experience that are deemed most important to the person. Typically, values early in life involve the love, security, and nourishment provided by one's mother; later values include status and success. Mature values are future oriented, are arrived at independently, and are concerned with other humans.

Will.   Commitment to action.

Wish.   Cognitive exploration of possible courses of action before actually committing oneself to one particular course.

A FINAL WORD

After our review of the major theories of personality in the preceding chapters, the following four conclusions seem warranted:

1. Personality theories often reflect the biographies of their authors.
2. Much about personality remains unknown.
3. The best available explanation of personality comes from a composite of all the major theories (rather than from any single theory or paradigm).
4. Each person must judge for him- or herself what information from each theory is useful or not useful.

Personality Theories Often Reflect the Biographies of Their Authors

Students sometimes wonder why so many different personality theories exist. One reason is that personality is so complex that different theories can only focus on different aspects of it. Given the fact that personality can be defined and studied in several different ways, the question remains, What causes a particular theorist to choose one approach to defining and studying personality over others? The answer seems to be that, at least in part, personality theories are biographical. That is, they often reflect the significant experiences of the particular theorist. George Atwood and Silvan Tomkins (1976) make this point: "Every theorist of personality views the human condition from the unique perspective of his own individuality. As a consequence, personality theories are strongly influenced by personal and subjective factors" (p. 166). Atwood and Tomkins argue that theories of personality cannot be fully understood without recognizing the biographical contributions to each theory.

A truly unifying theory of personality ought to be able to account not only for the phenomena to which all theories address themselves, but also for the other theories themselves. This is because each of these constructions embodies a vision of the human situation which is rooted in the theorist's own development as a person. . . . If the science of human personality is ever to achieve a greater degree of consensus and generality, it should begin to turn back on itself and question its own psychological foundations. There should be sustained study not only of the phenomena which have always been the province of personality theory, but also of the biasing subjective factors which contribute to the continuing confusion and diversity in the field. (p. 167)

Stolorow and Atwood (1979) apply the analysis suggested in the above quotation to a number of the theories we have covered in this text. Salvatore Maddi (1996) also recognizes the importance of a theorist's personal intuition for determining how he or she views personality. Maddi defines intuition as "an inarticulate, private, and emotional, as well as vivid, immediate, and compelling, sense of the meaning of what is happening" (p. 9).

Does the fact that personality theories reflect the personalities and experiences of their authors invalidate the theories? Not at all. A theory can be valid or invalid, useful or useless, regardless of what motivated its origin. For example, much in Freud's theory reflects his personal experiences and concerns, yet many would agree that his is among the most influential theories ever constructed. We should realize, however, that because any particular theory is partly biographical, it will tend to apply more to certain types of people than to others, and it will ring true to some people more than to others—presumably to those with a personality most like that of the theorist. Perhaps this reason is why, at the end of a course such as this one, different students have different favorite theories. Thus tastes in personality theories might also be biographical. For example, Vyse (1990) found that psychology majors prefer psychological theories perceived as facilitating their self-understanding.

The following observation made by Robinson (1985) pertains to psychoanalytic theory but it could as easily apply to almost any personality theory:

The psychoanalytic account is a story, a narrative, but not a scientific one. It is rather a historical narrative—something of a saga—which is "good" or less than good depending upon the contact it makes with the reader's own experiences and thoughts. We ask of such accounts only whether they make sense, recognizing they are but one of an indefinite number of possible accounts all of which may make as much (or as little) sense. (p. 123)

Much about Personality Remains Unknown

The theories covered in this text, individually or collectively, do not adequately account for personality. Although each theory illuminates part of what we call personality, much remains in darkness. Existing theories need to be extended and new theories need to be developed before we will be able to approximate a thorough understanding of personality.

To test what you have learned about personality and what remains unknown, just attempt one day to account for your own actions and the actions of others by using what you have learned in this text. Perhaps you will have a better understanding of many events now. No doubt, you will encounter examples of repression (evidenced by such examples as slips of the tongue, dreams, and humor) and other ego-defense mechanisms such as projection, identification, and reaction formation. You may find that the emotion-producing symbols found in art, music, and religion reflect our evolutionary experiences as a species. You may see parents instilling either basic anxiety or basic trust in their children. You may conclude that the consistent patterns of behavior observed in people reflect underlying traits, and you may see examples of how reinforcement contingencies influence behavior. You may see people showing favoritism toward their relatives, and you may observe that many apparent acts of altruism are actually selfish. You may see that much of life is a matter of interpretation or attitudinal. You may see different people struggling to satisfy different levels of needs, and perhaps you will see a person who appears to be self-actualizing. You may observe that some people have been more successful than others in developing their own values with which to deal with the world. You may note that you, and others, find meaning in life by embracing personal or collective myths.

At the end of the day, many behaviors that were previously a mystery will have been at least partially explained, but many mysteries will remain. Their solution will require the work and imagination of future personality theorists.

Composite of All Major Theories Best Explains Personality

The position we have taken throughout this text is that all the major personality theories add to our understanding of personality, and therefore it is not necessary to search for the correct theory or even the most correct theory. As mentioned in Chapter 1, just as a carpenter would not attempt to build a house with only one tool, a person cannot hope to understand personality with only one theory. It is nonsensical to say that a screwdriver is any more correct or useful than a hammer. It is simply that different tools have different functions; the same is true for personality theories. In other words, which personality theory is "best" depends on which aspect of personality one is attempting to explain. This position is **eclecticism:** taking the best from several different viewpoints. The eclectic is not bound to any single theory but chooses useful information from any theory or theories.

Is it not possible that society forces people to repress sexual and aggressive urges, and that such repressed urges manifest themselves indirectly in a person's life, as Freud and Dollard and Miller maintain? Is it not possible that we are born with predispositions to respond emotionally to the major categories of existence such as birth, death, and members of the opposite sex, and to symbols of perfection, as Jung suggested? Is it not possible that most of us choose a lifestyle with which to strive for perfection or superiority, and for the betterment of society, as Adler suggested? Does not evidence exist that some neurotics attempt to adjust to life by moving toward people, others by moving away from people, and still others by moving against people, as Horney suggested? Does not evidence exist that life consists of various stages, each characterized by different needs and potential accomplishments, and that one of the most significant events in one's life is the development of an identity, as Erikson suggested? Does it not make sense to say that each person is unique, and that some adult motives are no longer tied to their earlier origins, as Allport proposed? Is it not possible that the many variables affecting human behavior, including constitutional, learning, and situational variables, can be stated in a single equation that can be used in predicting behavior, as Cattell suggests? Is it not reasonable to assume that personality can be described in terms of a few important dimensions that have a substantial biological basis, as Eysenck insisted? Is there not evidence that reinforcement contingencies exert a powerful influence on behavior, as Skinner maintained? Is it not possible to think of the various ego-defense mechanisms and neurotic symptoms as learned, because they temporarily reduce anxiety, as Dollard and Miller suggest? Is it not also possible that we learn some things simply by observing them, and that modeling experiences are extremely important to personality development, as Bandura and Mischel maintain? Is it not possible that various dating, mating, and childrearing practices, the tendency to protect what belongs to us, and differential male–female parenting can be explained, at least in part, by urges within us that have been shaped by natural selection, as the evolutionary psychologists claim? Is it not possible that the reduction of uncertainty is a major motive in human behavior, as Kelly suggested? Does not the possibility exist that much of our behavior is in accordance with our subjective reality rather than with physical reality, as both Kelly and Rogers maintained? Is it not possible to confirm Rogers's contention that because of our need for positive regard and for self-regard many of us internalize conditions of worth that become our frame of reference for living rather than our own organismic valuing process? Is there not evidence for Maslow's contention that the motives of people with their basic needs satisfied are qualitatively different from the motives of people still struggling to satisfy their basic needs? Lastly, is it not possible to find persons attempting to live the type of authentic life that May describes and to find others turning their back on such a life by blindly conforming to values established by others?

Perhaps what the realm of personality theory needs is a grand synthesizer, a person who could coordinate the various terms and concepts from all the various theories. This person would look carefully at all the theories that discuss developmental stages—for example, Freud, Erikson, and Allport—and attempt to derive a more comprehensive picture of personality development. If our contention is true that all of the various theories add something different to our knowledge of personality, it would make sense for a person like Newton to come along and somehow put it all together. Because such a synthesis does not seem possible in the foreseeable future, however, one can only make the best use of the existing paradigms or perhaps create new ones.

You Are the Final Judge

As we have seen, each theory of personality has generated at least some empirical research that supports it. It is also true that at least some empirical research refutes each theory of personality. Because the results of the empirical research performed to evaluate the various theories of personality are equivocal, they cannot be used as a basis for accepting or rejecting a theory. This situation may change as more studies are performed, and they collectively suggest acceptance or rejection of a theory or of parts of a theory. As it is now, however, minimal unambiguous empirical research is available to help decide what is valid or invalid in the realm of personality theory. How, then, does one know what information to accept or reject? It seems that under existing circumstances, Buddha gave the best answer to this question:

> Believe nothing on the faith of traditions, even though they have been held in honour for many generations, and in divers places. Do not believe a thing because many speak of it. Do not believe on the faith of the sages of the past. Do not believe what you have imagined, persuading yourself that a god inspires you. Believe nothing on the sole authority of your masters or priests. After examination, believe what you yourself have tested and found to be reasonable, and conform your conduct thereto. (Hawton, 1948, p. 200)

Summary

Four conclusions seem justified after our review of the major personality theories: (1) Most, if not all, of the theories of personality reflect the biographies of their authors; (2) although the major theories of personality illuminate many aspects of personality, much about personality remains unknown; (3) the best available explanation of personality comes from using the best of all the theories rather than attempting to use one or a few of them; and (4) until more unambiguous empirical research is available, the best one can do is to evaluate the various theories personally, and to accept concepts that make sense and reject those that do not. This guideline means that which theories are found valid and useful theories will vary from person to person.

Experiential Exercises

1. Suppose you are the grand synthesizer mentioned in this chapter; describe how you might go about your task of synthesizing the various personality theories.
2. Review the theory of personality that you formulated as part of the Experiential Exercises for Chapter 1. Reformulate your original theory using what you have learned about personality since your original formulation. Summarize the major differences between your first and second formulations.

References

ADAMS, G. R., & FITCH, S. A. (1982). Ego stage and identity status development: A cross-sequential analysis. *Journal of Personality and Social Psychology, 43,* 547–583.

ADAMS, G. R., RYAN, J. H., HOFFMAN, J. J., DOBSON, W. R., & NIELSEN, E. C. (1985). Ego identity status, conformity behavior, and personality in late adolescence. *Journal of Personality and Social Psychology, 47,* 1091–1104.

ADAMS-WEBBER, J. R. (1979). *Personal construct theory: Concepts and applications.* New York: Wiley.

ADLER, A. (1917). *Study of organ inferiority and its physical compensation: A contribution to clinical medicine* (S. E. Jeliffe, Trans.). New York: Nervous and Mental Disease Publication. (Original work published 1907)

ADLER, A. (1930a). *The education of children.* South Bend, IN: Gateway.

ADLER, A. (1930b). Individual psychology. In C. Murchison (Ed.), *Psychologies of 1930.* Worcester, MA: Clark University Press.

ADLER, A. (1956c). *The individual psychology of Alfred Adler: A systematic presentation of selections from his writings* (H. L. Ansbacher & R. R. Ansbacher, Eds.). New York: Basic Books.

ADLER, A. (1956b). Feeling unmanly as inferiority feeling. In H. L. Ansbacher & R. R. Ansbacher (Eds.), *The individual psychology of Alfred Adler.* New York: Basic Books. (Original work published 1910)

ADLER, A. (1956a). The accentuated dogmatized guiding fiction. In H. L. Ansbacher & R. R. Ansbacher (Eds.), *The individual psychology of Alfred Adler.* New York: Harper. (Original work published 1912)

ADLER, A. (1956d). The use of heredity and environment. In H. L. Ansbacher & R. R. Ansbacher (Eds.), *The individual psychology of Alfred Adler.* New York: Basic Books. (Original work published 1935)

ADLER, A. (1958). *What life should mean to you.* New York: Capricorn. (Original work published 1931)

ADLER, A. (1964a). Problems of neurosis. New York: Harper & Row. (Original work published 1929)

ADLER, A. (1964b). *Social interest: A challenge to mankind.* New York: Capricorn. (Original work published 1933)

ADLER, A. (1979). The structure of neurosis. In H. L. Ansbacher & R. R. Ansbacher (Eds.), *Superiority and social interest: A collection of Alfred Adler's later writings.* New York: Norton. (Original work published 1932)

AGNEW, J. (1985). Childhood disorders. In E. Button (Ed.), *Personal construct theory and mental health: Theory, research, and practice.* Beckenham, UK: Croom Helm.

ALCOCK, J. (2000, April/May). Misbehavior: How Stephen Jay Gould is wrong about evolution. *Boston Review.* Retrieved November 20, 2004, from http://www.pdisci.mit.edu/BostonReview/BR25.2/alcock.html

ALDERFER, C. P. (1972). *Existence, relatedness, and growth needs in organizational settings.* New York: Free Press.

ALLAN, N., & FISHEL, D. (1979). Singles bars. In N. Allan (Ed.), *Urban life styles* (pp. 128–179). Dubuque, IA: William C. Brown.

ALLPORT, G. W. (1937). *Personality: A psychological interpretation.* New York: Holt, Rinehart and Winston.

ALLPORT, G. W. (1942). The use of personal documents in psychological science (*Bulletin 49*). New York: Social Science Research Council.

ALLPORT, G. W. (1950). *The individual and his religion*. New York: Macmillan.

ALLPORT, G. W. (1955). *Becoming: Basic considerations for a psychology of personality*. New Haven, CT: Yale University Press.

ALLPORT, G. W. (1958a). *The nature of prejudice*. Garden City, NY: Doubleday. (Original work published 1954)

ALLPORT, G. W. (1958b). What units shall we employ? In G. Lindzey (Ed.), *Assessment of human motives* (pp. 239–260). New York: Holt, Rinehart and Winston.

ALLPORT, G. W. (1960). *Personality and social encounter: Selected essays*. Boston: Beacon Press.

ALLPORT, G. W. (1961). *Pattern and growth in personality*. New York: Holt, Rinehart and Winston.

ALLPORT, G. W. (1962). The general and the unique in psychological science. *Journal of Personality, 30*, 405–422.

ALLPORT, G. W. (1965). *Letters from Jenny*. New York: Harcourt Brace Jovanovich.

ALLPORT, G. W. (1967). Autobiography. In E. G. Boring & G. Lindzey (Eds.), *A history of psychology in autobiography* (Vol. 5, pp. 1–25). New York: Appleton-Century-Crofts.

ALLPORT, G. W. (1968). *The person in psychology: Selected essays*. Boston: Beacon Press.

ALLPORT, G. W. (1978). *Waiting for the Lord: 33 meditations on God and man*. New York: Macmillan.

ALLPORT, G. W., & ALLPORT, F. H. (1921). Personality traits: Their classification and measurement. *Journal of Abnormal and Social Psychology, 16*, 6–40.

ALLPORT, G. W., & CANTRIL, H. (1934). Judging personality from voice. *Journal of Social Psychology, 5*, 37–55.

ALLPORT, G. W., & ODBERT, H. S. (1936). Trait names: A psycholexical study. *Psychological Monographs, 47*(211), 1–171.

ALLPORT, G. W., & POSTMAN, L. (1947). *The psychology of rumor*. New York: Holt, Rinehart and Winston.

ALLPORT, G. W., & ROSS, J. M. (1967). Personal religious orientation and prejudice. *Journal of Personality and Social Psychology, 5*, 432–443.

ALLPORT, G. W., & VERNON, P. E. (1933). *Studies in expressive movement*. New York: Macmillan.

ALLPORT, G. W., VERNON, P. E., & LINDZEY, G. (1960). *A study of values* (3rd ed.). Boston: Houghton Mifflin.

ALTMAN, K. E. (1973). The relationship between social interest dimensions of early recollections and selected counselor variables. *Dissertation Abstracts International, 34*, 5613A. (University Microfilms No. 74-05, 364)

AMERICAN PSYCHOLOGICAL ASSOCIATION approves FMSF as a sponsor of continuing education programs. (1995, November-December) *False Memory Syndrome Foundation Newsletter* [Online].

AMERICAN PSYCHOLOGIST. (1981). Awards for distinguished scientific contributions: 1980. *American Psychologist, 36*, 27–42.

AMERICAN PSYCHOLOGIST. (1992). Citation for outstanding lifetime contribution to psychology. Presented to Neal E. Miller, August 16, 1991. *American Psychologist, 47*, 847.

ANDERSON, G. H., & KENNEDY, S. H. (1992). *The biology of feast and famine: Relevance to eating disorders*. San Diego, CA: Academic Press.

ANDERSON, J. L., & CRAWFORD, C. B. (1992). Modeling costs and benefits of weight control as a mechanism for reproductive suppression. *Human Nature, 3*, 299–334.

ANDERSON, K. G., KAPLAN, H., LAM, D., & LANCASTER, J. (1999). Parental care by genetic fathers and stepfathers II: Reports by Xhosa high school students. *Evolution and Human Behavior, 20*, 433–451.

ANDERSON, K. G., KAPLAN, H., & LANCASTER, J. (1999). Parental care by genetic fathers and stepfathers I: Reports from Albuquerque men. *Evolution and Human Behavior, 20*, 405–431.

ANNIS, H. M. (1990). Relapse to substance abuse: Empirical findings within a cognitive-social learning approach. *Journal of Psychoactive Drugs, 22*, 117–124.

ANSBACHER, H. L. (1983). Individual psychology. In R. J. Corsini & A. J. Marsella (Eds.), *Personality theories, research, and assessment*. Itasca, IL: Peacock.

ANSBACHER, H. L. (1990). Alfred Adler's influence on the three leading cofounders of humanistic psychology. *Journal of Humanistic Psychology, 30*, 45–53.

APICELLA, C. L., & MARLOWE, F. W. (2004). Perceived mate fidelity and paternal resemblance predict men's investment in children. *Evolution and Human Behavior, 25*, 371–378.

ARAGONA, J., CASSADY, J., & DRABMAN, R. S. (1975). Treating overweight children through parental training and contingency management. *Journal of Applied Behavior Analysis, 8,* 269–278.

ASPY, D. (1972). *Toward a technology for humanizing education.* Champaign, IL: Research Press.

ASPY, D., & ROEBUCK, F. (1974). From human ideas to humane technology and back again, many times. *Education, 95,* 163–171.

ATWOOD, G. E., & TOMKINS, S. (1976). On the subjectivity of personality theory. *Journal of the History of the Behavioral Sciences, 12,* 166–177.

AXELROD, R., & HAMILTON, W. D. (1981). The evolution of cooperation. *Science, 211,* 1390–1396.

AYLLON, T., & AZRIN, N. II. (1965). The measurement and reinforcement of behavior of psychotics. *Journal of the Experimental Analysis of Behavior, 8,* 357–383.

AYLLON, T., & AZRIN, N. H. (1968). *The token economy: A motivational system for therapy and rehabilitation.* New York: Appleton-Century-Crofts.

BAER, J. S., HOLT, C. S., & LICHTENSTEIN, E. (1986). Self-efficacy and smoking reexamined: Construct validity and clinical utility. *Journal of Consulting and Clinical Psychology, 54,* 846–852.

BAILLARGEON, R., GRABER, M., DEVOIS, J., & BLACK, J. (1990). Why do young infants fail to search for hidden objects? *Cognition, 36,* 225–284.

BALDWIN, A. C., CRITELLI, J. W., STEVENS, L. C., & RUSSELL, S. (1986). Androgyny and sex role measurement: A personal construct approach. *Journal of Personality and Social Psychology, 51,* 1081–1088.

BALMARY, M. (1979). *Psychoanalyzing psychoanalysis: Freud and the hidden fault of the father.* Baltimore: Johns Hopkins Press.

BANDURA, A. (1965). Influence of models' reinforcement contingencies on the acquisition of imitative responses. *Journal of Personality and Social Psychology, 1,* 589–595.

BANDURA, A. (1969). *Principles of behavior modification.* New York: Holt, Rinehart and Winston.

BANDURA, A. (1973). *Aggression: A social-learning analysis.* Englewood Cliffs, NJ: Prentice-Hall.

BANDURA, A. (1977). *Social learning theory.* Englewood Cliffs, NJ: Prentice-Hall.

BANDURA, A. (1978). The self system in reciprocal determinism. *American Psychologist, 33,* 344–358.

BANDURA, A. (1982). The psychology of chance encounters and life paths. *American Psychologist, 37,* 747–755.

BANDURA, A. (1986). *Social foundations of thought and action: A social cognitive theory.* Englewood Cliffs, NJ: Prentice-Hall.

BANDURA, A. (1989). Human agency in social cognitive theory. *American Psychologist, 44,* 1175–1184.

BANDURA, A. (1990a). Mechanisms of moral disengagement. In W. Reich (Ed.), *Origins of terrorism: Psychologies, ideologies, states of mind* (pp. 161–191). New York: Cambridge University Press.

BANDURA, A. (1990b). Perceived self-efficacy in the exercise of control over AIDS infection. *Evaluation and Program Planning, 13,* 9–17.

BANDURA, A. (1991). Social cognitive theory of self-regulation. *Organizational Behavior and Human Decision Processes, 50,* 248–287.

BANDURA, A. (Ed.). (1995). *Self-efficacy in changing societies.* New York: Cambridge University Press.

BANDURA, A. (1997). *Self-efficacy: The exercise of control.* New York: W. H. Freeman.

BANDURA, A. (2001). Social cognitive theory: An agentic perspective. *Annual Review of Psychology, 52,* 1–26.

BANDURA, A. (2002a). Growing primacy of human agency in adaptation and change in the electronic era. *European Psychologist, 7,* 2–16.

BANDURA, A. (2002b). Social cognitive theory in cultural context. *Applied Psychology: An International Review [Special issue on Psychology in the Far East, Singapore], 51,* 269–290.

BANDURA, A., ADAMS, N. E., & BEYER, J. (1977). Cognition processes mediating behavioral change. *Journal of Personality and Social Psychology, 35,* 125–139.

BANDURA, A., ADAMS, N. E., HARDY, A. B., & HOWELLS, G. N. (1980). Tests of the generality of self-efficacy theory. *Cognitive Therapy and Research, 4,* 39–66.

BANDURA, A., BLANCHARD, E. B., & RITTER, B. (1969). Relative efficacy of desensitization and modeling approaches for inducing behavioral, affective, and attitudinal changes. *Journal of Personality and Social Psychology, 13,* 173–199.

BANDURA, A., CIOFFI, D., TAYLOR, C. B., & BROUILLARD, M. E. (1988). Perceived self-efficacy in coping with cognitive stressors and opioid activation. *Journal of Personality and Social Psychology, 55,* 479–488.

References **537**

BANDURA, A., & JOURDEN, F. J. (1991). Self-regulatory mechanisms governing the impact of social comparison on complex decision making. *Journal of Personality and Social Psychology, 60,* 941–951.

BANDURA, A., & KUPERS, C. J. (1964). The transmission of patterns of self-reinforcement through modeling. *Journal of Abnormal and Social Psychology, 69,* 1–9.

BANDURA, A., & LOCKE, E. A. (2003). Negative self-efficacy and goal effects revisited. *Journal of Applied Psychology, 88,* 87–99.

BANDURA, A., & MISCHEL, W. (1965). Modification of self-imposed delay of reward through exposure to live and symbolic models. *Journal of Personality and Social Psychology, 2,* 698–705.

BANDURA, A., O'LEARY, A., TAYLOR, C. B., GAUTHIER, J., & GOSSARD, D. (1987). Perceived self-efficacy and pain control: Opioid and nonopioid mechanisms. *Journal of Personality and Social Psychology, 53,* 563–571.

BANDURA, A., REESE, L., & ADAMS, N. E. (1982). Microanalysis of action and fear arousal as a function of differential levels of perceived self-efficacy. *Journal of Personality and Social Psychology, 43,* 5–21.

BANDURA, A., & ROSENTHAL, T. L. (1966). Vicarious classical conditioning as a function of arousal level. *Journal of Personality and Social Psychology, 3,* 54–62.

BANDURA, A., ROSS, D., & ROSS, S. A. (1963). A comparative test of the status envy, social power, and secondary reinforcement theories of identificatory learning. *Journal of Abnormal and Social Psychology, 67,* 527–534.

BANDURA, A., TAYLOR, C. B., WILLIAMS, S. L., MEFFORD, I. N., & BARCHAS, J. D. (1985). Catecholamine secretion as a function of perceived coping self-efficacy. *Journal of Consulting and Clinical Psychology, 53,* 406–414.

BANDURA, A., & WALTERS, R. H. (1959). *Adolescent aggression.* New York: Ronald Press.

BANDURA, A., & WALTERS, R. H. (1963). *Social learning and personality development.* New York: Holt, Rinehart and Winston.

BANDURA, A., & WOOD, R. (1989). Effect of perceived controllability and performance standards on self-regulation of complex decision making. *Journal of Personality and Social Psychology, 56,* 805–814.

BANNISTER, D. (Ed.). (1984). *Further perspectives in personal construct theory.* New York: Academic Press.

BANNISTER, D., ADAMS-WEBBER, J. R., PENN, W. L., & RADLEY, A. R. (1975). Reversing the process of thought-disorder: A serial validation experiment. *British Journal of Social and Clinical Psychology, 14,* 169–180.

BANNISTER, D., & FRANSELLA, F. (1966). A grid test of schizophrenic thought disorder. *British Journal of Social and Clinical Psychology, 5,* 95–102.

BANNISTER, D., & FRANSELLA, F. (1971). *Inquiring man: The theory of personal constructs.* New York: Penguin.

BANNISTER, D., & MAIR, J. M. M. (1968). *The evaluation of personal constructs.* New York: Academic Press.

BARASH, D. P. (1979). The *whisperings within: Evolution and the origin of human nature.* New York: Penguin.

BARON-COHEN, S. (1995). *Mindblindness: An essay on autism and theory of mind.* Cambridge, MA: MIT Press.

BARTOL, C. R., & COSTELLO, N. (1976). Extraversion as a function of temporal duration of electrical shock: An exploratory study. *Perceptual and Motor Skills, 42,* 1174.

BAUMEISTER, R. F., & LEARY, M. R. (1995). The need to belong: Desire for interpersonal attachments as a fundamental human motivation. *Psychological Bulletin, 117,* 497–529.

BECKER, W., MADSEN, C., ARNOLD, C., & THOMAS, D. (1967). The contingent use of teacher attention and praising in reducing classroom behavior problems. *Journal of Special Education, 1,* 287–307.

BELL, R. (1985). *Holy anorexia.* Chicago: University of Chicago Press.

BELL, R. W., & BELL, N. J. (Eds.). (1989). *Sociobiology and the social sciences.* Lubbock: Texas Tech.

BELMONT, L., & MAROLLA, F. A. (1973). Birth order, family size, and intelligence. *Science, 182,* 1096–1101.

BEM, D. J., & ALLEN, A. (1974). On predicting some of the people some of the time: The search for cross-situational consistencies in behavior. *Psychological Review, 81,* 506–520.

BERGER, S. M. (1962). Conditioning through vicarious instigation. *Psychological Review, 69,* 450–466.

BERGIN, A. E., MASTERS, K. S., & RICHARDS, P. S. (1987). Religiousness and mental health reconsidered: A study of an intrinsically religious sample. *Journal of Counseling Psychology, 34,* 197–204.

BERKOWITZ, L. (1989). Frustration–aggression hypothesis: An examination and reformulation. *Psychological Bulletin, 106,* 59–73.

BERRIDGE, K. C., & ROBINSON, T. E. (1995). The mind of an addicted brain: Neural sensitization of wanting versus liking. *Current Directions in Psychological Science, 4,* 71–76.

BETZ, N. E., & HACKETT, G. (1981). The relationship of career-related self-efficacy expectations to perceived career options in women and men. *Journal of Counseling Psychology, 28,* 399–410.

BIERI, J. (1955). Cognitive complexity–simplicity and predictive behavior. *Journal of Abnormal and Social Psychology, 51,* 61–66.

BJORK, D. W. (1997). *B. F. Skinner: A life.* Washington, DC: American Psychological Association.

BLANCHARD, W. H. (1969). Psychodynamic aspects of the peak experience. *Psychoanalytic Review, 46,* 87–112.

BLECHMAN, E. A., TAYLOR, C. J., & SCHRADER, S. M. (1981). Family problem solving versus home notes as early intervention with high-risk children. *Journal of Consulting and Clinical Psychology, 49,* 919–926.

BLOCK, J. (1995). A contrarian view of the five-factor approach to personality description. *Psychological Bulletin, 117,* 187–215.

BLUM, G. (1962). The Blacky test—sections II, IV, and VII. In R. Birney & R. Teevan (Eds.), *Measuring human motivation* (pp. 119–144). New York: Van Nostrand.

BODDEN, J. C. (1970). Cognitive complexity as a factor in appropriate vocational choice. *Journal of Counseling Psychology, 17,* 364–368.

BONETT, R. M. (1994). Marital status and sex: Impact on career self-efficacy. *Journal of Counseling and Development, 73,* 187–190.

BORDAGES, J. W. (1989). Self-actualization and personal autonomy. *Psychological Reports, 64,* 1263–1266.

BORES-RANGEL, E., CHURCH, A. T., SZENDRE, D., & REEVES, C. (1990). Self-efficacy in relation to occupational consideration and academic performance in high school equivalency students. *Journal of Counseling Psychology, 37,* 407–418.

BOSLOUGH, J. (1972, December 24). Reformatory's incentive plan works. *Rocky Mountain News,* p. 13.

BOTTOME, P. (1957). *Alfred Adler: A portrait from life.* New York: Vanguard.

BOUCHARD, T. J., JR. (1984). Twins reared together and apart: What they tell us about human diversity. In S. W. Fox (Ed.), *Individuality and determinism* (pp. 147–184). New York: Plenum Press.

BOUDIN, H. M. (1972). Contingency contracting as a therapeutic tool in the deceleration of amphetamine use. *Behavior Therapy, 3,* 604–608.

BOURNE, E. (1978). The state of research on ego identity: A review and appraisal: I. *Journal of Youth and Adolescence, 7,* 223–251.

BOWERS, K. S. (1973). Situationism in psychology: An analysis and a critique. *Psychological Review, 80,* 307–336.

BRELAND, H. M. (1974). Birth order, family constellation, and verbal achievement. *Child Development, 45,* 1011–1019.

BREUER, J., & FREUD, S. (1955). Studies on hysteria. In *The standard edition* (Vol. 2). London: Hogarth Press. (Original work published 1895)

BRINGMANN, M. W. (1992). Computer-based methods for the analysis and interpretation of personal construct systems. In R. A. Neimeyer & G. J. Neimeyer (Eds.), *Advances in personal construct psychology* (pp. 57–90). Greenwich, CT: JAI Press.

BRONSON, W. C. (1966). Central orientations: A study of behavior organization from childhood to adolescence. *Child Development, 37,* 125–155.

BRONSON, W. C. (1967). Adult derivatives of emotional experiences and reactivity-control: Developmental continuities from childhood to adulthood. *Child Development, 38,* 801–878.

BROWN, R. M., DAHLEN, E., MILLS, C., RICK, J., & BIBLARZ, A. (1999). Evaluation of an evolutionary model of self-preservation and self-destruction. *Suicide and Life-Threatening Behavior, 29,* 58–71.

BRUNER, J. S. (1956). You are your constructs. *Contemporary Psychology, 1,* 355–357.

BUCKMASTER, L. R., & DAVIS, G. A. (1985). ROSE: A measure of self-actualization and its relationship to creativity. *Journal of Creative Behavior, 19,* 30–37.

BUGENTAL, J. F. T. (1996). Rollo May (1909–1994). *American Psychologist, 51,* 418–419.

BUSS, D. M. (1987). Sex differences in human mate selection criteria: An evolutionary perspective. In C. Crawford, M. Smith, & D. Krebs (Eds.), *Sociobiology and psychology: Ideas, issues, and applications* (pp. 335–351). Hillsdale, NJ: Erlbaum.

Buss, D. M. (1988). From vigilance to violence: Mate guarding tactics. *Ethology and Sociobiology, 9,* 292–317.

Buss, D. M. (1989). Sex differences in human mate preferences: Evolutionary hypotheses testing in 37 cultures. *Behavioral and Brain Sciences, 12,* 1–49.

Buss, D. M. (1994). *The evolution of desire: Strategies of human mating.* New York: Basic Books.

Buss, D. M. (1995). Evolutionary psychology: A new paradigm for psychological science. *Psychological inquiry, 6,* 1–49.

Buss, D. M. (1998). The psychology of human mate selection: Exploring the complexity of the strategic repertoire. In C. Crawford & D. L. Krebs (eds.), *Handbook of evolutionary psychology* (pp. 405–429). Mahwah, NJ: Erlbaum.

Buss, D. M. (1999). *Evolutionary psychology: The new science of the mind.* Boston: Allyn & Bacon.

Buss, D. M. (2000). *The dangerous passion: Why jealousy is as necessary as love and sex.* New York: Free Press.

Buss, D. M. (2001). Human nature and culture: An evolutionary psychological perspective. *Journal of Personality, 69,* 955–978.

Buss, D. M. (2003). *The evolution of desire: Strategies of human mating.* New York: Basic Books.

Buss, D. M. (2004). *Evolutionary psychology: The new science of the mind.* Boston: Allyn & Bacon.

Buss, D. M., Haselton, M. G., Shackelford, T. K., Bleske, A. L., & Wakefield, J. C. (1998). Adaptations, exaptations, and spandrels. *American Psychologist, 53,* 533–548.

Buss, D. M., Larsen, R., & Westen, D. (1996). Sex differences in jealousy: Not gone, not forgotten, and not explained by alternative hypotheses. *Psychological Science, 7,* 204–232.

Buss, D. M., Larsen, R., Westen, D., & Semmelroth, J. (1992). Sex differences in jealousy: Evolution, physiology, and psychology. *Psychological Science, 3,* 251–255.

Buss, D. M., & Schmitt, D. P. (1993). Sexual strategies theory: An evolutionary perspective on human mating. *Psychological Review, 100,* 204–232.

Buss, D. M., Shackelford, T. K., Kirkpatrick, L. A., Choe, J., Hasegawa, M., Hasegawa, T., & Bennett, K. (1999). Jealousy and the nature of beliefs about infidelity: Tests of competing hypotheses about sex differences in the United States, Korea, and Japan. *Personal Relationships, 6,* 125–150.

Butler, J. M., & Haigh, G. V. (1954). Changes in the relation between self-concepts and ideal concepts consequent upon client-centered counseling. In C. R. Rogers & R. F. Dymond (Eds.), *Psychotherapy and personality change: Co-ordinated studies in the client-centered approach.* Chicago: University of Chicago Press.

Buttle, F. (1989). The social construction of needs. *Psychology and Marketing, 6,* 199–207.

Button, E. (1985a). Eating disorders: A quest for control. In E. Button (Ed.), *Personal construct theory and mental health: Theory, research and practice* (pp. 153–168). Cambridge, MA: Brookline.

Buunk, B., & Hupka, R. B. (1987). Cross-cultural differences in the elicitation of jealousy. *Journal of Sex Research, 23,* 12–22.

Cantor, N., & Mischel, W. (1979). Prototypes in person perception. In L. Berkowitz (Ed.), *Advances in experimental social psychology* (Vol. 12, pp. 3–52). New York: Academic Press.

Cantor, N., & Zirkel, S. (1990). Personality, cognition, and purposive behavior. In L. A. Pervin (Ed.), *Handbook of personality: Theory and research* (pp. 135–164). New York: Guilford Press.

Caplan, P. J. (1979). Erikson's concept of inner space: A data-based reevaluation. *American Journal of Orthopsychiatry, 49,* 100–108.

Carlson, M., & Mulaik, S. A. (1993). Trait ratings from descriptions of behavior as mediated by components of meaning. *Multivariate Behavioral Research, 26,* 111–159.

Carlson, R. (1980). Studies of Jungian typology: II. Representations of the personal world. *Journal of Personality and Social Psychology, 38,* 801–810.

Carlson, R., & Levy, N. (1973). Studies of Jungian typology: I. Memory, social perception, and social action. *Journal of Personality, 41,* 559–576.

Cartwright, D. S. (1956). Self-consistency as a factor affecting immediate recall. *Journal of Abnormal and Social Psychology, 52,* 212–218.

Cattell, R. B. (1943). The description of personality: Basic traits resolved into clusters. *Journal of Personality and Social Psychology, 38,* 476–506.

Cattell, R. B. (1944). *The culture free test of intelligence.* Champaign, IL: Institute for Personality and Ability Testing.

CATTELL, R. B. (1950). *Personality: A systematic, theoretical, and factual study.* New York: McGraw-Hill.

CATTELL, R. B. (1957). *Personality and motivation structure and measurement.* Yonkers, NY: World.

CATTELL, R. B. (1965). *The scientific analysis of personality.* Baltimore: Penguin.

CATTELL, R. B. (1972). *A new morality from science: Beyondism.* New York: Pergamon.

CATTELL, R. B. (1973). *Personality and mood by questionnaire.* San Francisco: Jossey-Bass.

CATTELL, R. B. (1974). Autobiography. In G. Lindzey (Ed.), *A history of psychology in autobiography* (Vol. 6). Englewood Cliffs, NJ: Prentice-Hall.

CATTELL, R. B. (1975). *Clinical analysis questionnaire (CAQ).* Champaign, IL: Institute for Personality and Ability Testing.

CATTELL, R. B. (1979, 1980). *Personality and learning theory* (Vols. 1 & 2). New York: Springer.

CATTELL, R. B. (1982). *The inheritance of personality and ability.* New York: Academic Press.

CATTELL, R. B. (1987). *Beyondism: Religion from science.* New York: Praeger.

CATTELL, R. B., BREUL, H., & HARTMAN, H. P. (1952). An attempt at a more refined definition of the cultural dimensions of syntality in modern nations. *American Sociological Review, 17,* 408–421.

CATTELL, R. B., EBER, H. W., & TATSUOKA, M. M. (1970). *Handbook for the 16 PF questionnaire.* Champaign, IL: Institute for Personality and Ability Testing.

CATTELL, R. B., & NESSELROADE, J. R. (1967). Likeness and completeness theories examined by sixteen personality factors measured by stably and unstably married couples. *Journal of Personality and Social Psychology, 7,* 351–361.

CATTELL, R. B., SAUNDERS, D. R., & STICE, G. F. (1950). *The 16 personality factor questionnaire.* Champaign, IL: Institute for Personality and Ability Testing.

CATTELL, R. B., SCHUERGER, J. M., & KLEIN, T. W. (1982). Heritabilities of ego strength (factor C), superego strength (factor G), and self-sentiment (factor Q3) by multiple abstract variance analysis. *Journal of Clinical Psychology, 38,* 769–779.

CATTELL, R. B., & WARBURTON, F. W. (1967). *Objective personality and motivation tests: A theoretical and practical compendium.* Urbana: University of Illinois Press.

CHAMOVE, A. S., EYSENCK, H. J., & HARLOW, H. F. (1972). Personality in monkeys: Factor analysis of rhesus social behaviour. *Quarterly Journal of Experimental Psychology, 24,* 496–504.

CHAPMAN, L. J., & CHAPMAN, J. P. (1969). Illusory correlation as an obstacle to the use of valid psychodiagnostic signs. *Journal of Abnormal Psychology, 74,* 271–280.

CHODORKOFF, B. (1954). Self-perception, perceptual defense, and adjustment. *Journal of Abnormal and Social Psychology, 49,* 508–512.

CHODOROW, N. (1989). *Feminism and psychoanalytic thought.* New Haven, CT: Yale University Press.

CHOMSKY, N. A. (1959). A review of verbal behavior by B. F. Skinner. *Language, 35,* 26–58.

CHRONBACK, L. J., & MEEHL, P. E. (1955). Construct validity in psychological tests. *Psychological bulletin, 52,* 281–302.

CIACCIO, N. (1971). A test of Erikson's theory of ego epigenesis. *Developmental Psychology, 4,* 306–311.

CIOFFI, F. (1974). Was Freud a liar? *The Listener, 91,* 172–174.

CIOFFI, F. (1998). *Freud and the question of pseudoscience.* La Salle, IL: Open Court.

CLARIDGE, G. S., DONALD, J. R., & BIRCHALL, P. (1981). Drug tolerance and personality: Some implications for Eysenck's theory. *Personality and Individual Differences, 2,* 153–166.

CLARIDGE, G. S., & ROSS, E. (1973). Sedative drug tolerance in twins. In G. S. Claridge, S. Carter, & W. I. Hume (Eds.), *Personality differences and biological variations.* Oxford: Pergamon.

COAN, R. W. (1966). Child personality and developmental psychology. In R. B. Cattell (Ed.), *Handbook of multivariate experimental psychology* (pp. 732–752). Chicago: Rand McNally.

COILE, D. C., & MILLER, N. E. (1984). How radical animal activists try to mislead humane people. *American Psychologist, 39,* 700–701.

CONLEY, J. J. (1984). The hierarchy of consistency: A review and model of longitudinal findings on adult individual differences in intelligence, personality and self-opinion. *Personality and Individual Differences, 5,* 11–26.

COOK, M., & MINEKA, S. (1990). Selective associations in the observed conditioning of fear in rhesus monkeys. *Journal of Experimental*

Psychology: Animal Behavior Processes, 16, 372–389.

CORDES, C. (1984). Easing toward perfection at Twin Oaks. *APA Monitor, 15*(11), 1, 30–31.

COSMIDES, L. (1985). *Deduction or Darwinian algorithms? An explanation of the "elusive" content effect on the Wason selection task.* Doctoral dissertation, Department of Psychology, Harvard University. (University Microfilms, No. 86-02206)

COSMIDES, L. (1989). The logic of social exchange: Has natural selection shaped how humans reason? Studies with the Wason selection task. *Cognition, 31,* 187–276.

COSMIDES, L., & TOOBY, J. (1987). From evolution to behavior: Evolutionary psychology as the missing link. In J. Dupre (Ed.), *The latest on the best: Essays on evolution and optimality.* Cambridge, MA: MIT Press.

COSMIDES, L., & TOOBY, J. (1989). Evolutionary psychology and the generation of culture, Part II. Case study: A computational theory of social exchange. *Ethology and Sociobiology, 10,* 51–97.

COSMIDES, L., & TOOBY, J. (1992). Cognitive adaptations for social exchange. In J. Barkow, L. Cosmides, & J. Tooby (Eds.), *The adapted mind.* (pp. 163–228) New York: Oxford University Press.

COSMIDES, L., & TOOBY, J. (1997). *Evolutionary psychology: A primer.* Santa Barbara: On-line Center for Evolutionary psycholgy, University of California, Santa Barbara.

COSTA, P. T., JR., & MCCRAE, R. R. (1980). Still stable after all these years: Personality as a key to some issues in adulthood and old age. In P. B. Baltes & O. G. Brim, Jr. (Eds.), *Lifespan development and behavior (Vol. 3,* pp. 65–102). New York: Academic Press.

COSTA, P. T., JR., & MCCRAE, R. R. (1985). *The NEO personality inventory manual.* Odessa, FL: Psychological Assessment Resources.

COSTA, P. T., JR., & WIDIGER, T. A. (EDS.). (2002). *Personality disorders and the five factor model of personality* (2nd ed.). Washington, DC: American Psychological Association.

COTE, J. E., & LEVINE, C. (1983). Marcia and Erikson: The relationships among ego identity status, neuroticism, dogmatism, and purpose in life. *Journal of Youth and Adolescence, 12,* 43–53.

COVERT, M. V., TANGNEY, J. P., MADDUX, J. E., & HELENO, N. M. (2003). Shame-proneness, guilt-proneness, and interpersonal problem solving: A social cognitive analysis. *Journal of Social and Clinical Psychology, 22,* 1–12.

CRAIG, K. D., & WEINSTEIN, M. S. (1965). Conditioning vicarious affective arousal. *Psychological Reports, 17,* 955–963.

CRAIGHEAD, W. E., KAZDIN, A. E., & MAHONEY, M. J. (1976). *Behavior modification: Principles, issues, and applications.* Boston: Houghton Mifflin.

CRAMER, P. (2000). Defense mechanisms in psychology today: Further processes for adaptation. *American Psychologist, 55,* 637–646.

CRAMER, P. (2001). The unconscious status of defense mechanisms. *American Psychologist, 56 (9),* 762–763.

CRANDALL, J. E. (1980). Adler's concept of social interest: Theory, measurement, and implications for adjustment. *Journal of Personality and Social Psychology, 39,* 481–495.

CRANDALL, J. E. (1981). *Theory and measurement of social interest: Empirical tests of Alfred Adler's concept.* New York: Columbia University Press.

CRANDALL, J. E. (1982). Social interest, extreme response style, and implications for adjustment. *Journal of Research in Personality, 16,* 82–89.

CRAWFORD, C. (1987). Sociobiology: Of what value to psychology? In C. Crawford, M. Smith, & D. Krebs (Eds.), *Sociobiology and psychology: Ideas, issues, and applications (pp. 3–30).* Hillsdale, NJ: Erlbaum.

CRAWFORD, C., SMITH, M., & KREBS, D. (EDS.). (1987). *Sociobiology and psychology: Ideas, issues, and applications.* Hillsdale, NJ: Erlbaum.

CREWS, F. (1995). *The memory wars: Freud's legacy in dispute.* New York: New York Review of Books.

CRONBACH, L. J., & MEEHL, P. E. (1955). Construct validity in psychological tests. *Psychological bulletin, 56,* 281–302.

CROSS, H. J., & ALLEN, J. G. (1970). Ego identity status, adjustment, and academic achievement. *Journal of Consulting and Clinical Psychology, 34,* 288.

CRUMBAUGH, J. C. (1968). Cross-validation of Purpose-in-Life Test based on Frankl's concept. *Journal of Individual Psychology, 24,* 74–81.

CSIKSZENTMIHALYI, M. (1975). *Beyond boredom and anxiety.* San Francisco: Jossey-Bass.

CSIKSZENTMIHALYI, M. (1990). *Flow: The psychology of optimal experience.* New York: Harper & Row.

CSIKSZENTMIHALYI, M. (1996). *Creativity: Flow and the psychology of discovery and invention.* New York: HarperCollins.

DALY, M., & WILSON, M. (1982). Whom are newborn babies said to resemble? *Ethology and Sociobiology, 3,* 69–78.

DALY, M., & WILSON, M. (1988). Evolutionary social psychology and family homicide. *Science, 242,* 519–524.

DALY, M., & WILSON, M. (1994). Some differential attributes of lethal assaults on small children by stepfathers versus genetic fathers. *Ethology and Sociobiology, 15,* 207–217.

DALY, M., & WILSON, M. (1997). Crime and conflict: Homicide in evolutionary psychological perspective. *Crime and Justice, 22,* 51–100.

DALY, M., & WILSON, M. (1998). The evolutionary social psychology of family violence. In C. Crawford & D. L. Krebs (Eds.), *Handbook of evolutionary psychology* (pp. 431–456). Mahwah, NJ: Erlbaum.

DALY, M., & WILSON, M. (2001). Risk-taking, intrasexual competition, and homicide. *Nebraska Symposium on Motivation, 47,* 1–36.

DANDES, M. (1966). Psychological health and teaching effectiveness. *Journal of Teaching Education, 17,* 301–306.

DANIELS, M. (1988). The myth of self-actualization. *Journal of Humanistic Psychology, 28,* 7–38.

DARWIN, C. (1859). *The origin of species: By means of natural selection or the preservation of favoured races in the struggle for life.* New York: New American Library.

DARWIN, C. (1871). *The descent of man and selection in relation to sex.* London: Murray.

DAS, A. K. (1989). Beyond self-actualization. *International Journal for the Advancement of Counseling, 12,* 13–27.

DAVIS, A., & DOLLARD, J. (1940). *Children of bondage.* Washington, DC: American Council on Education.

DAVIS, S., THOMAS, R., & WEAVER, M. (1982). Psychology's contemporary and all-time notables: Student, faculty, and chairperson viewpoints. *Bulletin of the Psychonomic Society, 20,* 3–6.

DAVIS-BERMAN, J. (1990). Physical self-efficacy, perceived physical status, and depressive symptomatology in older adults. *Journal of Psychology, 124,* 207–215.

DAVIS-SHARTS, J. (1986). An empirical test of Maslow's theory of need hierarchy using

hologeistic comparison by statistical sampling. *Advances in Nursing Science, 9,* 58–72.

DAWES, A. (1985). Drug dependence. In E. Button (Ed.), *Personal construct theory and mental health: Theory, research, and practice.* Beckenham, UK: Croom Helm.

DAWES, R. M. (2001). *Everyday irrationality: How pseudo-scientists, lunatics, and the rest of us fail to think rationally.* Boulder, CO: Westview Press

DEANGELIS, T. (1994, July). Jung's theories keep pace and remain popular. *APA Monitor, 25,* 41.

DECARVALHO, R. J. (1990a). The growth hypothesis and self-actualization: An existential alternative. *Humanistic Psychologist, 18,* 252–258.

DECARVALHO, R. J. (1990b). A history of the "third force" in psychology. *Journal of Humanistic Psychology, 30,* 22–44.

DECARVALHO, R. J. (1991). Gordon Allport and humanistic psychology. *Journal of Humanistic Psychology, 31,* 8–13.

DE CATANZARO, D. (1987). Evolutionary pressures and limitations to self-preservation. In C. Crawford, M. Smith, & D. Krebs (Eds.), *Sociobiology and psychology: Ideas, issues, and applications* (pp. 311–333). Hillsdale, NJ: Erlbaum.

DERAAD, B. (1998). Five big, Big Five issues. *European Psychologist, 3,* 113–124.

DESTENO, D., BARTLETT, M. Y., BRAVERMAN, J., & SALOVEY, P. (2002). Sex differences in jealousy: Evolutionary mechanism or artifact of measurement? *Journal of personality and social psychology, 83,* 1103–1116.

DIAMOND, M. J., & SHAPIRO, J. L. (1973). Changes in locus of control as a function of encounter group experiences: A study and replication. *Journal of Abnormal Psychology, 82,* 514–518.

DIGMAN, J. M. (1989). Five robust trait dimensions: Development, stability, and utility. *Journal of Personality, 57,* 195–214.

DIGMAN, J. M. (1990). Personality structure: Emergence of the five-factor model. *Annual review of psychology, 41,* 417–440.

DIGMAN, J. M. (1996). The curious history of the five-factor model. In J. S. Wiggins (Ed.), *The five-factor model of personality.* New York: Guilford Press.

DIGMAN, J., & TAKEMOTO-CHOCK, N. (1981). Factors in the natural language of personality: Reanalysis, comparison, and interpretation of six major studies. *Multivariate Behavioral Research, 16,* 149–170.

DIXON, T. M., & BAUMEISTER, R. F. (1991). Escaping the self: The moderating effect of self-complexity. *Personality and Social Psychology Bulletin, 17,* 363–368.

DOBSON, K. S., & BREITER, H. J. (1983). Cognitive assessment of depression: Reliability and validity of three measures. *Journal of Abnormal Psychology, 92,* 107–109.

DOLLARD, J. (1937). *Caste and class in a southern town.* New Haven, CT: Yale University Press.

DOLLARD, J. (1942). *Victory over fear.* New York: Reynal and Hitchcock.

DOLLARD, J. (1943). *Fear in battle.* New Haven, CT: Yale University Press.

DOLLARD, J., DOOB, L. W., MILLER, N. E., MOWRER, O. H., & SEARS, R. R. (1939). *Frustration and aggression.* New Haven, CT: Yale University Press.

DOLLARD, J., & MILLER, N. E. (1950). *Personality and psychotherapy: An analysis in terms of learning, thinking and culture.* New York: McGraw-Hill.

DONAHUE, M. J. (1985). Intrinsic and extrinsic religiousness: Review and meta-analysis. *Journal of Personality and Social Psychology, 48,* 400–419.

DOSAMANTES-ALPERSON, E., & MERRILL, N. (1980). Growth effects of experiential movement psychotherapy. *Psychotherapy: Theory, research, and practice, 17,* 63–68.

DOWNEY, D. B. (2001). Number of siblings and intellectual development: The resource dilution explanation. *American Psychologist, 56,* 497–504.

DRAYCOTT, S. G., & KLINE, P. (1995). The big three or the big five—the EPQ-R vs. the NEO-PI: A research note, replication, and elaboration. *Personality and Individual Differences, 18*(6), 801–804.

DREHER, D. (1995). Toward a person-centered politics: John Vasconcellos. In M. M. Suhd (Ed.), *Carl Rogers and other notables he influenced* (pp. 339–372). Palo Alto, CA: Science and Behavior.

DREIKURS, R. (1957). *Psychology in the classroom.* New York: Harper & Row.

DREIKURS, R. (WITH V. SOLTZ). (1964). *Children: The challenge.* New York: Duell, Sloan & Pearce.

DUCK, S. W. (1979). The personal and interpersonal in construct theory: Social and individual aspects of relationships. In P. Stringer & D. Bannister (Eds.), *Constructs of sociality and individuality* (pp. 279–297). London: Academic Press.

DUDLEY, R. (2000). Evolutionary origins of human alcoholism in primate frugivory. *Quarterly Review of Biology, 75,* 3–15.

DUDLEY, R. (2002). Fermenting fruit and the historical ecology of ethanol ingestion: Is alcoholism in modern humans an evolutionary hangover? *Addiction, 97,* 381.

DUNN, J., & PLOMIN, R. (1990). *Separate lives: Why siblings are so different.* New York: Basic Books.

DUNNETTE, M. D. (1969). People feeling: Joy, more joy, and the "slough of despond." *Journal of Applied Behavioral Science, 5,* 25–44.

EIDELSON, R. J., & EPSTEIN, N. (1982). Cognition and relationship maladjustment: Development of a measure of dysfunctional relationship beliefs. *Journal of Consulting and Clinical Psychology, 50,* 715–720.

ELLENBERGER, H. (1970). *The discovery of the unconscious.* New York: Basic Books.

ELLENBERGER, H. (1972). The story of "Anna O.": A critical review with new data. *Journal of the Behavioral Sciences, 8,* 267–279.

ELLIOTT, C. D. (1971). Noise tolerance and extraversion in children. *British Journal of Psychology, 62,* 375–380.

ELLIS, A. (1970). Tribute to Alfred Adler. *Journal of Individual Psychology, 26,* 11–12.

ELLIS, A., & GREIGER, R. (1977). Handbook of rational emotive therapy. New York: Julian Press.

ELLIS, B. J., & SYMONS, D. (1990). Sex differences in fantasy: An evolutionary psychological approach. *Journal of Sex Research, 27,* 527–556.

ELMS, A. C. (1972). Allport, Freud, and the clean little boy. *The Psychoanalytic Review, 59,* 627–632.

ELMS, A. C. (1981). Skinner's dark year and *Walden Two. American Psychologist, 36,* 470–479.

ENGELHARD, G. (1990). Gender differences in performance on mathematics items: Evidence from the United States and Thailand. *Contemporary Educational Psychology, 15,* 13–26.

EPTING, F. R., & LEITNER, L. M. (1992). Humanistic psychology and personal construct theory. *Humanistic Psychologist, 20,* 243–259.

ERIKSON, E. H. (1959). *Identity and the life cycle.* Selected papers. New York: International Universities Press.

ERIKSON, E. H. (1964). *Insight and responsibility.* New York: Norton.

ERIKSON, E. H. (1968). *Identity, youth, and crisis.* New York: Norton.

ERIKSON, E. H. (1969). *Gandhi's truth: On the origins of militant nonviolence.* New York: Norton.

ERIKSON, E. H. (1975a). *Life history and the historical moment.* New York: Norton.

ERIKSON, E. H. (1975b). Once more the inner space. In E. H. Erikson (Ed.), *Life history and the historical moment.* New York: Norton.

ERIKSON, E. H. (1977). *Toys and reasons: Stages in the ritualization of experience.* New York: Norton.

ERIKSON, E. H. (1982). *The life cycle completed: A review.* New York: Norton.

ERIKSON, E. H. (1985). *Childhood and society.* New York: Norton. (Original work published 1950)

ERNST, C., & ANGST, J. (1983). *Birth order: Its influence on personality.* New York: Springer-Verlag.

ESTERSON, A. (1993). *Seductive mirage: An exploration of the work of Sigmund Freud.* La Salle, IL: Open Court.

ESTERSON, A. (1998). Jeffrey Masson and Freud's seduction theory: A new fable based on old myths. *History of the Human Sciences, 11,* 1–21.

ESTERSON, A. (2001). The mythologizing of psychoanalytic history: Deception and self-deception in Freud's accounts of the seduction theory episode. *History of Psychiatry, 12,* 329–352.

ESTERSON, A. (2002). Misconceptions about Freud's seduction theory: Comment on Gleaves and Hernandez (1999). *History of Psychology, 5,* 85–91.

EVANS, R. I. (1968). *B. F. Skinner: The man and his ideas.* New York: Dutton.

EVANS, R. I. (1976). *The making of psychology: Discussions with creative contributors.* New York: Knopf.

EVANS, R. I. (1978, July). Donald Bannister: On clinical psychology in Britain. *APA Monitor, 9*(7), 6–7.

EVANS, R. I. (1981). *Dialogue with B. F. Skinner.* New York: Praeger.

EVANS, R. I. (1989). *Albert Bandura: The man and his ideas—A dialogue.* New York: Praeger.

EYSENCK, H. J. (1947). *Dimensions of personality.* London: Routledge & Kegan Paul.

EYSENCK, H. J. (1952). *The scientific study of personality.* London: Routledge & Kegan Paul.

EYSENCK, H. J. (1957). *The dynamics of anxiety and hysteria.* London: Routledge & Kegan Paul.

EYSENCK, H. J. (1965). Extraversion and the acquisition of eyeblink and GSR conditioned responses. *Psychological Bulletin, 63,* 258–279.

EYSENCK, H. J. (1967). *The biological basis of personality.* Springfield, IL: Charles C. Thomas.

EYSENCK, H. J. (1970). *The structure of human personality (3rd ed.).* London: Methuen.

EYSENCK, H. J. (1972). *Psychology is about people.* New York: Penguin Books.

EYSENCK, H. J. (1976). *Sex and personality.* London: Open Books.

EYSENCK, H. J. (1977). *Crime and personality* (3rd ed.). London: Routledge & Kegan Paul.

EYSENCK, H. J. (1980). Autobiographical essay. In G. Lindzey (Ed.), *A history of psychology in autobiography* (Vol. VII). (pp. 153–187) San Francisco: W. H. Freeman.

EYSENCK, H. J. (1990a). Biological dimensions of personality. In L. A. Pervin (Ed.), *Handbook of personality: Theory and research.* New York: Guilford Press.

EYSENCK, H. J. (1990b). *Rebel with a cause.* London: W. H. Allen.

EYSENCK, H. J. (1991). Dimensions of personality: 16, 5, or 3?—Criteria for a taxonomic paradigm. *Personality and Individual Differences, 12*(8), 773–790.

EYSENCK, H. J., & EYSENCK, M. W. (1985). *Personality and individual differences.* New York: Plenum Press.

EYSENCK, H. J., & LEVEY, A. (1972). Conditioning, introversion–extraversion and the strength of the nervous system. In V. D. Neblitsyn & J. A. Gray (Eds.), *Biological basis of individual behaviour.* London: Academic Press.

FABER, M. D. (1970). Allport's visit with Freud. *Psychoanalytic Review, 57,* 60–64.

FALBO, T. (1981). Relationships between birth category, achievement, and interpersonal orientation. *Journal of Personality and Social Psychology, 41,* 121–131.

FALSE MEMORY SYNDROME FOUNDATION. (1992, November 5). Information needed in assessing allegations by adults of sex abuse in childhood. *False Memory Syndrome Foundation Newsletter,* p. 5.

FARLEY, F. (2000). Hans J. Eysenck (1916–1997). *American psychologist, 55,* 674–675.

FEIXAS, G., & VILLEGAS, M. (1991). Personal construct analysis of autobiographical texts: A method presentation and case illustration. *International Journal of Personal Construct Psychology, 4,* 51–83.

FERSTER, C. B., & SKINNER, B. F. (1957). *Schedules of reinforcement.* Englewood Cliffs, NJ: Prentice-Hall.

FIEBERT, M. S. (1997). In and out of Freud's shadow: A chronology of Adler's relationship with Freud. *Individual Psychology, 53,* 241–269.

FISHER, D. D. (1990). Emotional construing: A psychobiological model. *International Journal of Personal Construct Psychology, 3,* 183–203.

FISHER, S., & GREENBERG, R. P. (1977). *The scientific credibility of Freud's theories and therapy.* New York: Basic Books.

FORD, K. M., & ADAMS-WEBBER, J. R. (1991). The structure of personal construct systems and the logic of confirmation. *International Journal of Personal Construct Psychology, 4,* 15–41.

FOULDS, M. L. (1969). Self-actualization and the communication of facilitative conditions under counseling. *Journal of Counseling Psychology, 16,* 132–136.

FRANKL, V. E. (1970). Tribute to Alfred Adler. *Journal of Individual Psychology, 26,* 11–12, 146–147.

FRANKL, V. E. (1984). *Man's search for meaning* (rev. ed.). New York: Washington Square Press. (Original work published as *Experiences in a concentration camp,* 1946)

FRANKS, C. M., & LAVERTY, S. G. (1955). Sodium amytal and eyelid conditioning. *Journal of Mental Science, 101,* 654–663.

FRANKS, C. M., & TROUTON, D. (1958). Effects of amobarbital sodium and dexamphetamine sulfate on the conditioning of the eyeblink response. *Journal of Comparative and Physiological Psychology, 51,* 220–222.

FRANSELLA, F., & CRISP, A. H. (1979). Comparisons of weight concepts in groups of neurotic, normal and anorexic females. *British Journal of Psychiatry, 134,* 79–86.

FREDERIKSEN, L. W., JENKINS, J. O., & CARR, C. R. (1976). Indirect modification of adolescent drug abuse using contingency contracting. *Journal of Behavior Therapy and Experimental Psychiatry, 7,* 377–378.

FREEMAN, D. (1983). *Margaret Mead and Samoa: The making and unmaking of an anthropological myth.* Cambridge, MA: Harvard University Press.

FREEMAN, D. (1999). *The fateful hoaxing of Margaret Mead: A historical analysis of her Somoan research.* Boulder, CO: Westview Press.

FREESE, J., POWELL, B., & STEELMAN, L. C. (1999). Rebel without a cause or effect: Birth order and social attitudes. *American Sociological Review, 64,* 207–231.

FREUD, A. (1966). *The ego and the mechanisms of defense* (rev. ed.). New York: International Universities Press. (Original work published 1936)

FREUD, S. (1955a). Beyond the pleasure principle. In J. Strachey (Ed. and Trans.), *The standard edition of the complete psychological works of Sigmund Freud* (Vol. 18). London: Hogarth Press. (Original work published 1920)

FREUD, S. (1955b). A difficulty in the path of psychoanalysis. In J. Strachey (Ed. and Trans.), *The standard edition of the complete psychological works of Sigmund Freud* (Vol. 17, pp. 136–144). London: Hogarth Press. (Original work published 1917)

FREUD, S. (1955c). A note on the prehistory of the technique of analysis. In J. Strachey (Ed. and Trans.), *The standard edition of the complete psychological works of Sigmund Freud* (Vol. 18). London: Hogarth Press. (Original work published 1920)

FREUD, S. (1958). Totem and taboo. In J. Strachey (Ed. and Trans.), *The standard edition of the complete psychological works of Sigmund Freud* (Vol. 13). London: Hogarth Press. (Original work published 1913)

FREUD, S. (1960). Jokes and their relation to the unconscious. In J. Strachey (Ed. and Trans.), *The standard edition of the complete psychological works of Sigmund Freud* (Vol. 8). London: Hogarth Press. (Original work published 1905.)

FREUD, S. (1961a). *Civilization and its discontents.* New York: Norton. (Original work published 1930)

FREUD, S. (1961b). The ego and the id. In J. Strachey (Ed. and Trans.), *The standard edition of the complete psychological works of Sigmund Freud* (Vol. 19, pp. 3–59). London: Hogarth Press. (Original work published 1923)

FREUD, S. (1961c). *The future of an illusion.* New York: Norton. (Original work published 1927)

FREUD, S. (1963). On the beginning of treatment. In J. Strachey (Ed. and Trans.), *The standard edition of the complete psychological works of Sigmund Freud* (Vol. 12). London: Hogarth Press. (Original work published 1913)

FREUD, S. (1964a). Moses and monotheism. In J. Strachey (Ed. and Trans.), *The standard edition of the complete psychological works of Sigmund Freud* (Vol. 23, pp. 3–137). London: Hogarth Press. (Original work published 1939)

FREUD, S. (1964b). *New introductory lectures on psycho-analysis.* New York: Norton. (Original work published 1933)

FREUD, S. (1965a). *The interpretation of dreams.* New York: Norton. (Original work published 1900)

FREUD, S. (1965b). *The psychopathology of everyday life.* New York: Norton. (Original work published 1901)

FREUD, S. (1966a). *The complete introductory lectures on psychoanalysis* (J. Strachey, Ed. and Trans.). New York: Norton. (Original work published 1933)

FREUD, S. (1966c). *On the history of the psychoanalytic movement.* New York: Norton. (Original work published 1914)

FREUD, S. (1966b). *Introductory lectures on psychoanalysis.* New York: Norton. (Original work published 1917)

FREUD, S. (1977). *Five lectures on psycho-analysis.* New York: Norton. (Original work published 1910)

FREY-ROHN, L. (1976). *From Freud to Jung: A comparative study of the psychology of the unconscious.* New York: Dell.

FRICK, W. B. (1989). *Humanistic psychology: Conversations with Abraham Maslow, Gardner Murphy, and Carl Rogers.* Bristol, IN: Wyndham Hall Press.

FRIEDAN, B. (1963). *The feminine mystique.* New York: Norton.

FRIEDMAN, L. J. (1999). *Identity's architect: A biography of Erik H. Erikson.* Cambridge, MA: Harvard University Press.

FROMM, E. (1941). *Escape from freedom.* New York: Henry Holt.

FURNEAUX, W. D. (1957). *Report to the Imperial College of Science and Technology.* London.

GAGNON, J. H., & DAVISON, G. C. (1976). Asylums, the token economy and the merits of mental life. *Behavior Therapy, 7,* 528–534.

GALE, A. (1973). The psychophysiology of individual differences: Studies of extraversion and the EEG. In P. Kline (Ed.), *New approaches in psychological measurement.* New York: Wiley.

GALE, A. (1983). Electroencephalographic studies of extraversion–introversion: A case study in the psychophysiology of individual differences. *Personality and Individual Differences, 4,* 371–380.

GALTON, F. (1884). Measurement of character. *Fortnightly Review, 36,* 179–185.

GANGESTAD, S. W., & THORNHILL, R. (1997). The evolutionary psychology of extrapair sex: The role of fluctuating asymmetry. *Evolution and Human Behavior, 18,* 69–88.

GARCIA, M. E., SCHMITZ, J. M., & DOERFLER, L. A. (1990). A fine-grained analysis of the role of self-efficacy in self-initiated attempts to quit smoking. *Journal of Consulting and Clinical Psychology, 58,* 317–322.

GAY, P. (1988). *Freud: A life for our time.* New York: Norton.

GEEN, R. G., & QUANTY, M. B. (1977). The catharsis of aggression: An evaluation of a hypothesis. In L. Berkowitz (Ed.), *Advances in experimental social psychology* (Vol. 10, pp. 1–37). New York: Academic Press.

GEEN, R. G., STONNER, D., & SHOPE, G. L. (1975). The facilitation of aggression by aggression: Evidence against the catharsis hypothesis. *Journal of Personality and Social Psychology, 31,* 721–726.

GEEN R. G., & THOMAS, S. L. (1986). The immediate effects of media violence on behavior. *Journal of Social Issues, 42*(3), 7–27.

GELFAND, T., & KERR, J. (EDS.). (1992). *Freud and the history of psychoanalysis.* Hillsdale, NJ: Analytic Press.

GENDLIN, E. T. (1988). Carl Rogers (1902–1987). *American Psychologist, 43,* 127–128.

GENDLIN, E. T., BEEBE, J., III, CASSENS, J., KLEIN, M., & OBERLANDER, M. (1968). Focusing ability in psychotherapy, personality, and creativity. In J. M. Schlien (Ed.), *Research in psychotherapy* (Vol. 3). Washington, DC: American Psychological Association.

GENDLIN, E. T., & TOMLINSON, T. M. (1967). The process conception and its measurement. In C. R. Rogers, E. T. Gendlin, D. J. Kiesler, & C. B. Truax (Eds.), *The psychotherapeutic relationship and its impact: A study of psychotherapy with schizophrenics.* Madison: University of Wisconsin Press.

GEWIRTZ, J. L. (1971). Conditional responding as a paradigm for observational, imitative learning and vicarious imitative learning and vicarious reinforcement. In H. W. Reese (Ed.), *Advances in child development and behavior* (pp. 274–304). New York: Academic Press.

GIBSON, H. B. (1981). *Hans Eysenck: The man and his work.* London: Peter Owen.

GIESE, H., & SCHMIDT, A. (1968). *Studenten Sexualitat.* Hamburg: Rowohlt.

GILI-PLANAS, M., ROCA-BENNASAR, M., FERRER-PEREZ, V., BERNARDO, & ARROYO, M. (2001). Suicidal ideation, psychiatric disorder, and medical illness in a community epidemiological study. *Suicide and Life-Threatening Behavior, 31,* 207–213.

GIORGI, A. (1992). The idea of human science. *Humanistic Psychologist, 20,* 202–217.

GLEAVES, D. H., & HERNANDEZ, E. (1999). Recent reformations of Freud's development and abandonment of his seduction theory: Historical/scientific clarification or a continued assault on truth? *History of Psychology, 2,* 324–354.

GLEAVES, D. H., & HERNANDEZ, E. (2002). Wethinks the author doth protest too much: A reply to Esterson (2002). *History of Psychology, 5,* 92–98.

GOLDBERG, L. R. (1990). An alternative "Description of personality": The big-five factor structure. *Journal of Personality and Social Psychology, 59,* 1216–1229.

GOLDBERG, L. R. (1993). The structure of phenotypic personality traits. *American Psychologist, 48,* 1, 26–34.

GOLDSTEIN, A. P., & MICHAELS, G. Y. (1985). Empathy: *Development training and consequences.* Hillsdale, NJ: Erlbaum.

GORDON, R. D. (1985). Dimensions of peak communication experiences: An exploratory study. *Psychological Reports, 57,* 824–826.

GOULD, D., HODGE, K., PETERSON, K., & GIANNINI, J. (1989). An exploratory examination of strategies used by elite coaches to enhance self-efficacy in athletes. *Journal of Sport and Exercise Psychology, 11,* 128–140.

GOULD, S. J. (1997, October 9). Evolutionary psycholgy: An exchange. *New York Review of Books, XLIV,* 53–58.

GOULD, S. J., & LEWONTIN, R. C. (1979). The spandrels of San Marco and the Panglossian paradigm: A critique of the adaptationist programme. *Proceedings of the Royal Society of London, 205,* 581–598.

GRAHAM, W., & BALLOUN, J. (1973). An empirical test of Maslow's need hierarchy theory. *Journal of Humanistic Psychology, 13,* 97–108.

GREENSPOON, J. (1955). The reinforcing effect of two spoken sounds on the frequency of two responses. *American Journal of Psychology, 68,* 409–416.

GREILING, H., & BUSS, D. M. (2000). Women's sexual strategies: The hidden dimension of short-term extra-pair mating. *Personality and Individual differences, 28,* 929–963.

GRUENFELD, D. H. (1995). Status, ideology, and integrative complexity on the U.S. Supreme Court: Rethinking the politics of political decision making. *Journal of Personality and Social Psychology, 68,* 5–20.

GRUSEC, J., & MISCHEL, W. (1966). Model's characteristics as determinants of social learning. *Journal of Personality and Social Psychology, 4,* 211–215.

GUISINGER, S. (2003). Adapted to flee famine: Adding an evolutionary perspective on anorexia nervosa. *Psychological Review, 110,* 745–761.

GUPTA, B. S. (1973). The effects of stimulant and depressant drugs on verbal conditioning. *British Journal of Psychology, 64,* 553–557.

GURMAN, A. S. (1977). The patient's perception of therapeutic relationships. In A. S. Gurman & A. M. Razin (Eds.), *Effective psychotherapy: A handbook of research.* Oxford: Pergamon Press.

GUYDISH, J., JACKSON, T. T., MARKLEY, R. P., & ZELHART, P. F. (1985). George A. Kelly: Pioneer in rural school psychology. *Journal of School Psychology, 23,* 297–304.

HAFNER, J. F., FAKOURI, M. E., & LABRENTZ, H. L. (1982). First memories of "normal" and alcoholic individuals. *Individual Psychology, 38,* 238–244.

HALL, C. S., & LINDZEY, G. (1978). *Theories of personality* (3rd ed.). New York: Wiley.

HALL, C. S., & NORDLY, J. (1973). *A primer of Jungian psychology.* New York: New American Library.

HALL, C. S., & VAN DE CASTLE, R. L. (1965). An empirical investigation of the castration complex in dreams. *Journal of Personality, 33,* 20–29.

HALL, M. H. (1968, July). A conversation with Abraham Maslow. *Psychology Today,* pp. 35–37, 54–57.

HAMILTON, W. D. (1964). The genetical evolution of social behavior I & II. *Journal of Theoretical Biology, 7,* 1–52.

HANNAH, B. (1976). *Jung: His life and his work.* New York: Putnam's.

HARKAVY-FRIEDMAN, J. M., NELSON, E. A., VENARDE, D. F., & MANN, J. J. (2004). Suicidal behavior in schizophrenia and schizoaffective disorder: Examining the role of depression. *Suicidal and Life-Threatening Behavior, 34,* 66–76.

HARPER, R. G., WIENS, A. N., & MATARAZZO, J. D. (1978). *Nonverbal communication: The state of the art.* New York: Wiley.

HARREN, V. A., KASS, R. A., TINSLEY, H. E. A., & MORELAND, J. R. (1979). Influence of gender, sex-role attitudes, and cognitive complexity on gender-dominant career choices. *Journal of Counseling Psychology, 26,* 227–234.

HARRIS, C. R. (2000). Psychophysiological responses to imagined infidelity: The specific innate modular view of jealousy reconsidered. *Journal of Personality and Social Psychology, 78,* 1082–1091.

HARRIS, J. R. (2000). Context-specific learning, personality, and birth order. *Current Directions in Psychological Science. 9,* 174–177.

HARVEY, J. H. (1989). People's naive understandings of their close relationships: Attributional and personal construct perspectives. *International Journal of Personal Construct Psychology, 2,* 37–48.

HASELTON, M. G., & BUSS, D. M. (2000). Error management theory: A new perspective on biases in cross-sex mind reading. *Journal of personality and social psychology, 78,* 81–91.

HASELTON, M. G., & BUSS, D. M. (2001). The affective shift hypothesis: The functions of emotional changes following sexual intercourse. *Personal Relationships, 8,* 357–369.

HASELTON, M. G., BUSS, D. M., & DEKAY, W. T. (1998, July). *A theory of errors in cross-sex mind reading.* Paper presented at the annual meeting of the Human behavior and evolution society, Davis, CA.

HAWTON, H. (1948). *Philosophy for pleasure.* London: Watts.

HAYDEN, B., & NASBY, W. (1977). Interpersonal conceptual structures, predictive accuracy, and social adjustment of emotionally disturbed boys. *Journal of Abnormal Psychology, 86,* 315–320.

HAYDEN, T., & MISCHEL, W. (1976). Maintaining trait consistency in the resolution of behavioral inconsistency: The wolf in sheep's clothing? *Journal of Personality, 44,* 109–132.

HEPPNER, P. P., ROGERS, M. E., & LEE, L. A. (1984). Carl Rogers: Reflections on his life. *Journal of Counseling and Development, 63,* 14–20.

HERGENHAHN, B. R. (1974). *A self-directing introduction to psychological experimentation* (2nd ed.). Monterey, CA: Brooks/Cole.

HERGENHAHN, B. R. (2004). *An introduction to the history of psychology* (5th ed.). Belmont, CA: Wadsworth.

HERGENHAHN, B. R., & OLSON, M. H. (2005). *An introduction to theories of learning* (7th ed.). Upper Saddle River, NJ: Prentice-Hall.

HERMANS, H. J. M. (1988). On the integration of nomothetic and idiographic research in the study of personal meaning. *Journal of Personality, 56,* 785–812.

HERMANS, H. J. M., KEMPEN, J. G., & VAN LOON, R. J. P. (1992). The dialogical self: Beyond individualism and rationalism. *American Psychologist, 47,* 23–33.

HILL, E. M., NOCKS, E. S., & GARDNER, L. (1987). Physical attractiveness: Manipulation by physique and status displays. *Ethology and Sociobiology,* 143–154.

HINDLEY, C. B., & GIUGANINO, B. M. (1982). Continuity of personality patterning from 3 to 15 years in a longitudinal sample. *Personality and Individual Differences, 3,* 127–144.

HIRSCHMÜLLER, A. (1989). *The life and work of Josef Breuer: Physiology and psychoanalysis.* New York: New York University Press.

HOFFMAN, E. (1988). *The right to be human: A biography of Abraham Maslow.* Los Angeles: Jeremy P. Tarcher.

HOLDEN, C. (1987, August). The genetics of personality. *Science, 237,* 598–601.

HOLDEN, G. W., MONCHER, M. S., SCHINKE, S. P., & BARKER, K. M. (1990). Self-efficacy of children and adolescents: A meta–analysis. *Psychological Reports, 66,* 1044–1046.

HOLDSTOCK, T. L., & ROGERS, C. R. (1977). Person-centered theory. In R. J. Corsini (Ed.), *Current personality theories.* Itasca, IL: Peacock.

HOMME, L. E., CSANYI, A., GONZALES, M., & RECHS, J. (1969). *How to use contingency contracting in the classroom.* Champaign, Il: Research Press.

HOOD, R. W., JR. (1970). Religious orientations and the report of religious experiences. *Journal for the Scientific Study of Religion, 9,* 285–291.

HOPKINS, R. J. (1995). Erik Homburger Erikson (1902–1994). *American Psychologist, 50,* 796–797.

HORLEY, J. (1991). Values and beliefs as personal constructs. *International Journal of Personal Construct Psychology, 4,* 1–14.

HORNEY, K. (1937). *The neurotic personality of our time.* New York: Norton.

HORNEY, K. (1939). *New ways in psychoanalysis.* New York: Norton.

HORNEY, K. (1942). *Self-analysis.* New York: Norton.

HORNEY, K. (1945). *Our inner conflicts.* New York: Norton.

HORNEY, K. (1950). *Neurosis and human growth: The struggle toward self-realization.* New York: Norton.

HORNEY, K. (1967). *Feminine psychology.* New York: Norton. (Original work published 1923–1937)

HUBER, J. W., & ALTMAIER, E. M. (1983). An investigation of the self-statement systems of phobic and nonphobic individuals. *Cognitive Therapy and Research, 7,* 355–362.

HUESMANN, L. R., & MALAMUTH, N. M. (1986). Media violence and antisocial behavior. *Journal of Social Issues, 42*(3), 1–6.

HULL, C. L. (1943). *Principles of behavior.* New York: Appleton-Century-Crofts.

HUNDLEBY, J. D., PAWLIK, K., & CATTELL, R. B. (1965). *Personality factors in objective test devices: A critical integration of a quarter of a century's research.* San Diego, CA: Knapp.

HUNT, J. M. (1979). Psychological development: Early experience. *Annual Review of Psychology, 30,* 103–143.

HUNTLEY, C. W., & DAVIS, F. (1983). Undergraduate study of values scores as predictors of occupation twenty-five years later. *Journal of Personality and Social Psychology, 45,* 1148–1155.

ILARDI, R., & MAY, W. (1968). A reliability study of Shostrom's personal orientation inventory. *Journal of Humanistic Psychology, 8,* 68–72.

INGRAM, D. H. (ED.). (1987). *Karen Horney: Final Lectures.* New York: Norton.

ISRAËLS, H., & SCHATZMAN, M. (1993). The seduction theory. *History of Psychiatry, 4,* 23–59.

JACOBSON, N. S. (1978). Specific and nonspecific factors in the effectiveness of a behavioral approach to the treatment of marital discord. *Journal of Consulting and Clinical Psychology, 46,* 442–452.

JAMES, W. (1956). The dilemma of determinism. In W. James, *The will to believe and other essays* (pp. 145–183). New York: Dover. (Original work published 1884)

JANKOWICZ, A. D. (1987). Whatever became of George Kelly? Applications and implications. *American Psychologist, 42,* 481–487.

JENSEN, A. R. (2000). Hans Eysenck: Apostle of the London school. In G. A. Kimble & M. Wertheimer (Eds.), *Portraits of pioneers in psychology* (Vol. 4, pp. 339–357). Washington, DC: American Psychological Association.

JOHNSON, M., & MORTON, J. (1991). *Biology and cognitive development: The case of face recognition.* Oxford: Blackwell

JONES, E. (1953, 1955, 1957). *The life and work of Sigmund Freud* (Vols. 1–3). New York: Basic Books.

JONES, J., EYSENCK, H. J., MARTIN, I., & LEVEY, A. B. (1981). Personality and the topography of the conditioned eyelid response. *Personality and Individual Differences, 2,* 61–84.

JOSEPHS, R., MARKUS, R., & TAFARODI, R. (1992). Gender and self-esteem. *Journal of Personality and Social Psychology, 63,* 391.

JOURARD, S. M. (1974). *Healthy personality: An approach from the viewpoint of humanistic psychology.* New York: Macmillan.

JUNG, C. (1921). *Psychologische typus.* Zurich: Rascher.

JUNG, C. G. (1928). *Contributions to analytical psychology.* New York: Harcourt Brace Jovanovich.

JUNG, C. G. (1933). *Modern man in search of a soul.* New York: Harcourt Brace Jovanovich.

JUNG, C. G. (1936). The psychology of dimentia praecox. New York: Nervous and Mental Disease Publishing Company.

JUNG, C. G. (1953). The psychology of the unconscious. In *The collected works of C. G. Jung* (Vol. 7). Princeton, NJ: Princeton University Press. (Original work published 1912)

JUNG, C. G. (1958). *The undiscovered self.* New York: Mentor.

JUNG, C. G. (1961a). *Memories, dreams, reflections.* New York: Random House.

JUNG, C. G. (1961b). Prefaces to "collected papers on analytical psychology." In *The collected works of C. G. Jung* (Vol. 4). Princeton, NJ: Princeton University Press. (Original work published 1916)

JUNG, C. G. (1961c). The theory of psychoanalysis. In *The collected works of C. G. Jung* (Vol. 4). Princeton, NJ: Princeton University Press. (Original work published 1913)

JUNG, C. G. (1964). *Man and his symbols.* New York: Doubleday.

JUNG, C. G. (1966). Two essays on analytical psychology. In *The collected works of C. G. Jung* (Vol. 7). Princeton, NJ: Princeton University Press. (Original work published 1917)

JUNG, C. G. (1968). *Analytical psychology: Its theory and practice* (The Tavistock Lectures). New York: Pantheon.

JUNG, C. G. (1969). The structure of the psyche. In *The collected works of C. G. Jung* (Vol. 8). Princeton, NJ: Princeton University Press. (Original work published 1931)

JUNG, C. G. (1971). Psychological types. In *The collected works of C. G. Jung* (Vol. 6). Princeton, NJ: Princeton University Press. (Original work published 1921)

JUNG, C. G. (1973a). On the doctrine of complexes. In *The collected works of C. G. Jung* (Vol. 2). Princeton, NJ: Princeton University Press. (Original work published 1913)

JUNG, C. G. (1973b). The psychological diagnosis of evidence. In *The collected works of C. G. Jung* (Vol. 2). Princeton, NJ: Princeton University Press. (Original work published 1909)

JUNG, C. G. (1978). On flying saucers. In *Flying saucers: A modern myth of things seen in the sky* (R. F. C. Hull, Trans.). New York: MJF Books. (Original work published 1954)

KAGAN, J. (1994). *Galen's prophecy.* New York: Basic Books.

KAHN, S., ZIMMERMAN, G., CSIKSZENTMIHALYI, M., & GETZELS, J. W. (1985). Relations between identity in young adulthood and intimacy at midlife. *Journal of Personality and Social Psychology, 49,* 1316–1322.

KANT, I. (1912). *Anthropologie in pragmatischer hinsicht.* Berlin: Bresser Cassiner (Original work published 1798)

KATZ, J. O. (1984). Personal construct theory and the emotions: An interpretation in terms of primitive constructs. *British Journal of Psychology, 75,* 315–327.

KAZDIN, A. E. (1977). *The token economy: A review and evaluation.* New York: Plenum Press.

KAZDIN, A. E. (1989). *Behavior modification in applied settings* (4th ed.). Pacific Grove, CA: Brooks/Cole.

KAZDIN, A. E., & BOOTZIN, R. R. (1972). The token economy: An evaluative review. *Journal of Applied Behavior Analysis, 5,* 343–372.

KAZDIN, A. E., & HERSEN, M. (1980). The current status of behavior therapy. *Behavior Modification, 4,* 283–302.

KEEN, R. (2003). Representation of objects and events: Why do infants look so smart and toddlers look so dumb? *Current Directions in Psychological Science, 12,* 79–83.

KELLEY, M. L., & STOKES, T. F. (1982). Contingency contracting with disadvantaged youths: Improving classroom performance. *Journal of Applied Behavior Analysis, 15,* 447–454.

KELLY, G. A. (1955). *The psychology of personal constructs* (2 vols.). New York: Norton.

KELLY, G. A. (1958). Man's construction of his alternatives. In G. Lindzey (Ed.), *Assessment of human motives.* New York: Holt, Rinehart and Winston.

KELLY, G. A. (1963). *A theory of personality: The psychology of personal constructs.* New York: Norton.

KELLY, G. A. (1964). The language of hypotheses: Man's psychological instrument. *Journal of Individual Psychology, 20,* 137–152.

KELLY, G. A. (1966). A brief introduction to personal construct theory. In D. Bannister (Ed.), *Perspectives in personal construct theory.* London: Academic Press.

KELLY, G. A. (1969). The autobiography of a theory. In B. Maher (Ed.), *Clinical psychology and personality: Selected papers of George Kelly* (pp. 40–65). New York: Wiley.

KELLY, G. A. (1970). A brief introduction to personal construct theory. In D. Bannister (Ed.), *Perspectives in personal construct theory.* New York: Academic Press.

KELLY, G. A. (1980). A psychology of the optimal man. In A. W. Landfield & L. M. Leitner (Eds.), *Personal construct psychology: Psychotherapy and personality.* New York: Wiley.

KENRICK, D. T. (1989). Bridging social psychology and sociobiology: The case of sexual attraction. In R. W. Bell & N. J. Bell (Eds.), *Sociobiology and the social sciences* (pp. 5–23). Lubbock: Texas Tech University Press.

KENRICK, D. T., KEEFE, R. C., GABRIELIDIS, C., & CORNELIUS, J. S. (1996). Adolescents' age preferences for dating partners: Support for an evolutionary model of life-history strategies. *Child Development, 67,* 1499–1511.

KEUTZER, C. S. (1978). Whatever turns you on: Triggers to transcendent experiences. *Journal of Humanistic Psychology, 18,* 77–80.

KIERKEGAARD, S. (1944). *The concept of dread* (W. Lowrie, Trans.). Princeton, NJ: Princeton University Press. (Original work published 1844 as *The concept of anxiety*)

KILMANN, R. H., & TAYLOR, V. A. (1974). A contingency approach to laboratory learning: Psychological types versus experimental norms. *Human Relations, 27,* 891–909.

KIMBLE, M. M. (2000). From "Anna O" to Bertha Pappenheim: Transforming private pain into public action. *History of Psychology, 3,* 20–43.

KINKADE, K. (1973). *A Walden Two experiment.* New York: Morrow.

KIRSCH, T. B. (2000). *The Jungians: A comparative and historical perspective.* Philadelphia: Routledge.

KIRSCHENBAUM, H. (1979). *On becoming Carl Rogers.* New York: Dell.

KITAYAMA, S., & MARKUS, H. R. (1992, May). *Construal of self as cultural frame: Implications for internationalizing psychology.* Paper presented to the Symposium on Internationalization and Higher Education, Ann Arbor, MI.

KLAVETTER, R., & MOGAR, R. (1967). Stability and internal consistency of a measure of self-actualization. *Psychological Reports, 21,* 422–424.

KLINE, P. (1966). Extraversion, neuroticism, and academic performance among Ghanaian university students. *British Journal of Educational Psychology, 36,* 92–94.

KLINE, P. (1972). *Fact and fantasy in Freudian theory.* London: Methuen.

KLUCKHOHN, C., & MURRAY, H. A. (1953). Personality formation: The determinants. In C. Kluckhohn, H. A. Murray, & D. M. Schneider (Eds.), *Personality in nature, society, and culture* (2nd ed., pp. 53–67). New York: Knopf.

KORN, J. H., DAVIS, R., & DAVIS, S. F. (1991). Historians' and chairpersons' judgments of eminence among psychologists. *American Psychologist, 46,* 789–792.

KREBS, D. L. (1998). The evolution of moral behaviors. In C. Crawford & D. L. Krebs (Eds.), *Handbook of evolutionary psychology: Ideas, issues, and applications* (pp. 337–368). Mahwah, NJ: Erlbaum.

KRISHNAMOORTI, K. S., & SHAGASS, C. (1963). Some psychological test correlates of sedation threshold. In J. Wortis (Ed.), *Recent advances in biological psychiatry.* New York: Plenum Press.

KUHN, T. S. (1996). *The structure of scientific revolutions* (3rd ed.). Chicago: University of Chicago Press.

LA CERRA, M. M. (1994). *Evolved mate preferences in women: Psychological adaptations for assessing a man's willingness to invest in offspring.* Unpublished doctoral dissertation, Department of Psychology, University of California, Santa Barbara.

LAMIELL, J. T. (1981). Toward an idiothetic psychology of personality. *American Psychologist, 36,* 276–289.

LANDFIELD, A. W., & EPTING, F. R. (1987). *Personal construct psychology: Clinical and personality assessment.* New York: Human Sciences Press.

LANDFIELD, A. W., & LEITNER, L. M. (EDS.). (1980). *Personal construct psychology: Psychotherapy and personality.* New York: Wiley.

LAVERTY, S. G. (1958). Sodium amytal and extraversion. *Journal of Neurology, Neurosurgery, and Psychiatry, 21,* 50–54.

LEAK, G. K., & CHRISTOPHER, S. B. (1982). Freudian psychoanalysis and sociobiology: A synthesis. *American Psychologist, 37,* 313–322.

LEITNER, L. (1984). The terrors of cognition. In D. Bannister (Ed.), *Further perspectives in personal construct theory.* New York: Academic Press.

LEITNER, L. M., & PFENNINGER, D. T. (1994). Sociality and optimal functioning. *Journal of Constructivist Psychology, 7,* 119–135.

LeMAY, M., & DAMM, V. (1968). The personal orientation inventory as a measure of self-actualization of underachievers. *Measurement and Evaluation in Guidance,* 110–114.

LENT, R. W., BROWN, S. D., & LARKIN, K. C. (1986). Self-efficacy in the prediction of academic performance and perceived career options. *Journal of Counseling Psychology, 33,* 265–269.

LEON, G. R., GILLENN, B., GILLENN, R., & GANZE, M. (1979). Personality, stability, and change over a 30-year period—middle age to old age. *Journal of Consulting and Clinical Psychology, 47,* 517–524.

LESHNER, A. I., & KOOB, G. F. (1999). Drugs of abuse and the brain. *Proceedings of the Association of American Physicians, 111,* 99–108.

LESTER, D., HVEZDA, J., SULLIVAN, S., & PLOURDE, R. (1983). Maslow's hierarchy of needs and psychological health. *Journal of General Psychology, 109,* 83–85.

LEVANT, R. F., & SCHLIEN, J. M. (EDS.). (1984). *Client-centered therapy and the person-centered approach: New directions in theory, research, and practice.* New York: Praeger.

LEWIN, K. (1935). *A dynamic theory of personality.* New York: McGraw-Hill.

LEWONTIN, R. C., ROSE, S., & KAMIN, L. J. (1984). *Not in our genes.* New York: Pantheon.

LINVILLE, P. W. (1985). Self-complexity and affective extremity: Don't put all of your eggs in one cognitive basket. *Social Cognition, 3,* 94–120.

LOFTUS, E. (1993). The reality of repressed memories. *American Psychologist, 48,* 518–537.

LOFTUS, E., & KETCHAM, K. (1994). *The myth of repressed memories and allegations of abuse.* New York: St. Martin's Press.

LOWRY, R. J. (ED.). (1973). *Dominance, self-esteem, self-actualization: Germinal papers of A. H. Maslow.* Monterey, CA: Brooks/Cole.

LOWRY, R. J. (1979). *The journals of A. H. Maslow* (Vols. 1 & 2). Monterey, CA: Brooks/Cole.

LUDVIGH, E. J., & HAPP, D. (1974). Extraversion and preferred level of sensory stimulation. *British Journal of Psychology, 65,* 359–365.

LUMSDEN, C. J., & WILSON, E. O. (1981). *Genes, mind, and culture: The coevolutionary process.* Cambridge, MA: Harvard University Press.

LYNN, R. (1959). Two personality characteristics related to academic achievement. *British Journal of Educational Psychology, 29,* 213–216.

MADDI, S. R. (1996). *Personality theories: A comparative analysis.* Pacific Grove, CA: Brooks/Cole.

MAHONEY, J., & HARNETT, J. (1973). Self-actualization and self-ideal discrepancy. *Journal of Psychology, 85,* 37–42.

MALOTT, R. W., RITTERBY, K., & WOLF, E. L. C. (1973). *An introduction to behavior modification.* Kalamazoo, MI: Behaviordelia.

MANCUSO, J. C., & ADAMS-WEBBER, J. R. (EDS.). (1982). *The construing person.* New York: Praeger.

MANN, R. A. (1972). The behavior-therapeutic use of contingency contracting to control an adult behavior problem: Weight control. *Journal of Applied Behavior Analysis, 5,* 99–109.

MARCIA, J. (1966). Development and validation of ego identity status. *Journal of Personality and Social Psychology, 3,* 551–558.

MARCIA, J., & FRIEDMAN, M. L. (1970). Ego identity status in college women. *Journal of Personality, 38,* 249–263.

MARKS, I. M. (1987). *Fears, phobias, and rituals.* New York: Oxford University Press.

MARKUS, H. R., & KITAYAMA, S. (1991). Culture and the self: Implications for cognition, emotion, and motivation. *Psychological Reports, 98,* 224–253.

MARLOW, F. (1999). Showoffs or providers? The parenting efforts of Hazda men. *Evolution and Human Behavior, 20,* 391–404.

MARROW, A. J., BOWERS, D. G., & SEASHORE, S. E. (1967). *Management by participation.* New York: Harper & Row.

MARX, M. H., & GOODSON, F. E. (EDS.). (1976). *Theories in contemporary psychology* (2nd ed.). New York: Macmillan.

MASLING, J. (ED.). (1983). *Empirical studies of psychoanalytic theories.* Hillsdale, NJ: Analytic Press.

MASLOW, A. H. (1943a). A preface to motivation theory. *Psychosomatic Medicine, 5,* 85–92.

MASLOW, A. H. (1943b). A theory of human motivation. *Psychological Review, 50,* 370–396.

MASLOW, A. H. (1964). *Religions, values and peak experiences.* Columbus: Ohio State University Press.

MASLOW, A. H. (1965). *Eupsychian management: A journal.* Homewood, IL: Irwin-Dorsey.

MASLOW, A. H. (1966). *The psychology of science: A reconnaissance.* New York: Harper & Row.

MASLOW, A. H. (1968). *Toward a psychology of being* (2nd ed.). New York: Van Nostrand.

MASLOW, A. H. (1971). *The farther reaches of human nature.* New York: Penguin.

MASLOW, A. H. (1987). *Motivation and personality* (3rd ed.) (Revised by R. Frager, J. Fadiman, C. McReynolds, & R. Cox). New York: Harper & Row. (Original work published 1954)

MASSARIK, F. (1992). The humanistic core of humanistic/organizational psychology. *Humanist Psychologist, 20,* 389–396.

MASSERMAN, J. H. (1961). *Principles of dynamic psychiatry* (2nd ed.). Philadelphia: Saunders.

MASSON, J. M. (TRANS. & ED.). (1985). *The complete letters of Sigmund Freud to Wilhelm Fliess 1887–1904.* Cambridge, MA: Harvard University Press.

MASTERS, J. C., BURISH, T. G., HOLLON, S. D., & RIMM, D. C. (1987). *Behavior therapy: Techniques and empirical findings* (3rd ed.). Orlando, FL: Harcourt Brace Jovanovich.

MATHES, E. W., ZEVON, M. A., ROTER, P. M., & JOERGER, S. M. (1982). Peak experience tendencies: Scale development and theory testing. *Journal of Humanistic Psychology, 22,* 92–108.

MAY, R. (1939). *The art of counseling: How to give and gain mental health.* Nashville, TN: Abingdon-Cokesbury.

MAY, R. (1940). *The springs of creative living: A study of human nature and God.* New York: Abingdon-Cokesbury.

MAY, R. (1950). *The meaning of anxiety.* New York: Ronald Press.

MAY, R. (1953). *Man's search for himself.* New York: Norton.

MAY, R. (ED.). (1961). *Existential psychology.* New York: Random House.

MAY, R. (1967). *Psychology and the human dilemma.* New York: Van Nostrand.

MAY, R. (1969). *Love and will.* New York: Norton.

MAY, R. (1972). *Power and innocence: A search for the sources of violence.* New York: Norton.

MAY, R. (1973). *Paulus: Reminiscences of a friendship.* New York: Harper & Row.

MAY, R. (1975). *The courage to create.* New York: Norton.

MAY, R. (1981). *Freedom and destiny.* New York: Norton.

MAY, R. (1982). The problem of evil: An open letter to Carl Rogers. *Journal of Humanistic Psychology, 22,* 10–21.

MAY, R. (1983). *The discovery of being: Writings in existential psychology.* New York: Norton.

MAY, R. (1985). *My quest for beauty.* Dallas, TX: Saybrook.

MAY, R. (1986). *Politics and innocence.* Dallas, TX: Saybrook.

MAY, R. (1991). *The cry for myth.* New York: Norton.

MAY, R., ANGEL, E., & ELLENBERGER, H. F. (EDS.). (1958). *Existence: A new dimension in psychiatry and psychology.* New York: Basic Books.

MCBURNEY, D. H., ZAPP, D. J., & STREETER, S. A. (2005). Preferred number of sexual partners: Tails of distributions and tales of mating systems. *Evolution and human Behavior, 26,* 271–278.

MCCANN, J. T., & BIAGGIO, M. K. (1989). Sexual satisfaction in marriage as a function of life meaning. *Archives of Sexual Behavior, 18,* 59–72.

MCCOY, M. M. (1977). A reconstruction of emotion. In D. Bannister (Ed.), *New perspectives in personal construct theory* (pp. 93–124). London: Academic Press.

MCCRAE, R. R., & COSTA, P. T., JR. (1985). Updating Norman's "Adequate taxonomy": Intelligence and personality dimensions in natural language and in questionnaires. *Journal of Personality and Social Psychology, 49,* 710–721.

MCCRAE, R. R., & COSTA, P. T., JR. (1987). Validation of the five-factor model across instruments and observers. *Journal of Personality and Social Psychology, 52,* 81–90.

MCCRAE, R. R., & COSTA, P. T., JR. (1990). *Personality in adulthood.* New York: Guilford Press.

MCCRAE, R. R., & COSTA, P. T., JR. (1996). Toward a new generation of personality theories: Theoretical contexts for the five-factor model. In J. S. Wiggins (Ed.), *The five-factor model of personality.* New York: Guilford Press.

MCCRAE, R. R., & COSTA, P. T., JR. (1997). Personality trait structure as a human universal. *American Psychologist, 52,* 509–516.

MCGAW, W. H., RICE, C. P., & ROGERS, C. R. (1973). *The steel shutter.* LaJolla, CA: Film Center for Studies of the Person.

MCGUIRE, W. (ED.). (1974). *The Freud/Jung Letters.* Princeton, NJ: Princeton University Press.

MCLEOD, C. R., & VODANOVICH, S. J. (1991). The relationship between self-actualization and boredom proneness. *Journal of Social Behavior and Personality, 6,* 137–146.

MCLEOD, J. (1997). *Narrative and psychotherapy.* London: Sage.

MCPHERSON, F. M., & GRAY, A. (1976). Psychological construing and psychological symptoms. *British Journal of Medical Psychology, 49,* 73–79.

MEIER, S. T. (1983). Toward a theory of burnout. *Human Relations, 36,* 899–910.

MIALL, D. S. (1989). Anticipating the self: Toward a personal construct model of emotion. *International Journal of Personal Construct Psychology, 2,* 185–198.

MILLER, G. A. (1965). Some preliminaries to psycholinguistics. *American Psychologist, 20,* 15–20.

MILLER, N. E. (1944). Experimental studies of conflict. In J. M. Hunt (Ed.), *Personality and the behavior disorders* (Vol. 1). New York: Ronald Press.

MILLER, N. E. (1948a). Studies of fear as an acquirable drive: I. Fear as motivation and fear reduction as reinforcement in the learning of new responses. *Journal of Experimental Psychology, 38,* 89–101.

MILLER, N. E. (1959). Liberalization of basic S-R concepts: Extensions to conflict behavior, motivation and social learning. In S. Koch (Ed.), *Psychology: A study of a science* (Vol. 2). New York: McGraw-Hill.

MILLER, N. E. (1964). Some implications of modern behavior theory for personality change and psychotherapy. In P. Worchel & D. Bryne (Eds.), *Personality change.* New York: Wiley.

MILLER, N. E. (1982). Obituary: John Dollard (1900–1980). *American Psychologist, 37,* 587–588.

MILLER, N. E. (1983). Behavioral medicine: Symbiosis between laboratory and clinic. In M. R. Rosenzweig & L. W. Porter (Eds.), *Annual Review of Psychology, 34,* 1–31.

MILLER, N. E. (1984). *Bridges between laboratory and clinic.* New York: Praeger.

MILLER, N. E. (1985). The value of behavioral research on animals. *American Psychologist, 40,* 423–440.

MILLER, N. E. (1991). Commentary on Ulrich: Need to check truthfulness of statements by opponents of animal research. *Psychological Science, 2,* 422–423.

MILLER, N. E. (1992). Introducing and teaching much-needed understanding of the scientific process. *American Psychologist, 47,* 848–850.

MILLER, N. E., & DOLLARD, J. (1941). *Social learning and imitation.* New Haven, CT: Yale University Press.

MILLER, P. M. (1972). The use of behavioral contracting in the treatment of alcoholism: A case report. *Behavior Therapy, 3,* 593–596.

MISCHEL, W. (1958). Preference for delayed reinforcement: An experimental study of cultural observation. *Journal of Abnormal and Social Psychology, 56,* 57–61.

MISCHEL, W. (1961a). Delay of gratification, need for achievement, and acquiesce in another culture. *Journal of Abnormal and Social Psychology, 62,* 543–552.

MISCHEL, W. (1961b). Preference for delayed reinforcement and social responsibility. *Journal of Abnormal and Social Psychology, 62,* 1–7.

MISCHEL, W. (1965). Predicting the success of peace corps volunteers in Nigeria. *Journal of Personality and Social Psychology, 1,* 510–517.

MISCHEL, W. (1968). *Personality and assessment.* New York: Wiley.

MISCHEL, W. (1969). Continuity and change in personality. *American Psychologist, 24,* 1012–1018.

MISCHEL, W. (1977). The interaction of person and situation. In D. Magnusson & N. S. Endler (Eds.), *Personality at the crossroads: Current issues in interactional psychology.* Hillsdale, NJ: Erlbaum.

MISCHEL, W. (1979). On the interface of cognition and personality. *American Psychologist, 34,* 740–754.

MISCHEL, W. (1981). *Introduction to personality* (3rd ed.). New York: Holt, Rinehart and Winston.

MISCHEL, W. (1984). Convergences and challenges in the search for consistency. *American Psychologist, 39,* 351–364.

MISCHEL, W. (1986). *Introduction to personality* (4th ed.). New York: Holt, Rinehart and Winston.

MISCHEL, W. (1990). Personality dispositions revisited and revised: A view after three decades. In L. A. Pervin (Ed.), *Handbook of personality theory and research* (pp. 111–134). New York: Guilford Press.

MISCHEL, W. (1993). *Introduction to personality* (5th ed.). Orlando, FL: Harcourt, Brace, Jovanovich.

MISCHEL, W., & BAKER, N. (1975). Cognitive appraisals and transformations in delay behavior. *Journal of Personality and Social Psychology, 31,* 254–261.

MISCHEL, W., & EBBESEN, E. B. (1970). Attention in delay of gratification. *Journal of Personality and Social Psychology, 16,* 329–337.

MISCHEL, W., EBBESEN, E. B., & ZEISS, A. R. (1972). Cognitive and attentional mechanisms in delay of gratification. *Journal of Personality and Social Psychology, 21,* 204–218.

MISCHEL, W., & LIEBERT, R. M. (1966). Effects of discrepancies between observed and imposed reward criteria on their acquisition and transmission. *Journal of Personality and Social Behavior, 3,* 45–53.

MISCHEL, W., & METZNER, R. (1962). Preference for delayed reward as a function of age, intelligence, and length of the delay interval. *Journal of Abnormal and Social Psychology, 64,* 425–431.

MISCHEL, W., & MOORE, B. (1973). Effects of attention to symbolically presented rewards upon self-control. *Journal of Personality and Social Psychology, 28,* 172–179.

MISCHEL, W., & MOORE, B. (1980). The role of ideation in voluntary delay for symbolically presented rewards. *Cognitive Therapy and Research, 4,* 211–221.

MISCHEL, W., & PEAKE, P. K. (1982). Beyond déjà vu in the search for cross-situational consistency. *Psychological Review, 89,* 730–755.

MISCHEL, W., SHODA, Y., & PEAKE, P. K. (1988). The nature of adolescent competencies predicted by preschool delay of gratification. *Journal of Personality and Social Psychology, 54,* 687–696.

MISCHEL, W., SHODA, Y., & RODRIGUEZ, M. L. (1989). Delay of gratification in children. *Science, 244,* 933–938.

MITCHELL, C., & STUART, R. B. (1984). Effect of self-efficacy on dropout from obesity treatment. *Journal of Consulting and Clinical Psychology, 52,* 1100–1101.

MOGDIL, S., & MOGDIL, C. (EDS.). (1986). *Hans Eysenck: Searching for a scientific basis for human behavior.* London: Falmer Press.

MOORE, B., MISCHEL, W., & ZEISS, A. R. (1976). Comparative effects of the reward stimulus and its cognitive representation in voluntary delay. *Journal of Social Psychology, 34,* 419–424.

MOORE, M. K., & NEIMEYER, R. A. (1991). A confirmatory factor analysis of the Threat Index. *Journal of Personality and Social Psychology, 60,* 122–129.

MORITZ, C. (ED.). (1974). Miller, Neal, E(lgar). In *Current biographical yearbook* (pp. 276–279). New York: W. H. Wilson.

MORUZZI, G., & MAGOUN, H. W. (1949). Brain stem reticular formation and activation of the EEG. *Electroencephalography and Clinical Neurophysiology, 1,* 455–473.

MULTON, K. D., BROWN, S. D., & LENT, R. W. (1991). Relation of self-efficacy beliefs to academic outcomes: A meta-analytic investigation. *Journal of Counseling Psychology, 38,* 30–38.

MURRAY, B. (1996a). British case could set precedent. *APA Monitor, 11,* 10.

MURRAY, B. (1996b). Judges, courts get tough on spanking. *APA Monitor, 11,* 10.

MUSSEN, P., EICHORN, D. H., HANZIK, M. P., BIEHER, S. L., & MEREDITH, W. (1980). Continuity and change in women's characteristics over four decades. *International Journal of Behavioral Development, 3,* 333–347.

MYERS, I. B. (1962). *The Myers–Briggs type indicator manual.* Palo Alto, CA: Consulting Psychologists Press.

NEIMEYER, G. J. (1984). Cognitive complexity and marital satisfaction. *Journal of Social and Clinical Psychology, 2,* 258–263.

NEIMEYER, G. J. (1988). Cognitive integration and differentiation in vocational behavior. *Counseling Psychologist, 16,* 440–475.

NEIMEYER, G. J. (1992a). Personal constructs in career counseling and development. *Journal of Career Development, 18,* 163–173.

NEIMEYER, G. J. (1992b). Personal constructs and vocational structure. In R. A. Neimeyer and

G. J. Neimeyer (Eds.), *Advances in personal construct psychology* (Vol. 2, pp. 91–120). Greenwich, CT: JAI Press.

NEIMEYER, G. J., & HALL, A. G. (1988). Personal identity in disturbed marital relationships. In F. Fransella & L. Thomas (Eds.), *Experimenting with personal construct theory* (pp. 297–307). London: Routledge & Kegan Paul.

NEIMEYER, G. J., & HUDSON, J. E. (1984). Couples' constructs: Personal systems in marital satisfaction. In D. Bannister (Ed.), *Further perspectives in personal construct theory.* New York: Academic Press.

NEIMEYER, G. J., & HUDSON, J. E. (1985). Couples' constructs: Personal systems in marital satisfaction. In D. Bannister (Ed.), *Issues and approaches in personal construct theory* (pp. 127–141). New York: Academic Press.

NEIMEYER, G. J., & KHOUZAM, N. (1985). A repertory grid study of restrained eaters. *British Journal of Medical Psychology, 58,* 365–367.

NEIMEYER, R. A. (1984). Toward a personal construct conceptualization of depression and suicide. In F. R. Epting & R. A. Neimeyer (Eds.), *Personal meanings of death: Applications of personal construct theory to clinical practice* (pp. 127–173). New York: Hemisphere/McGraw-Hill.

NEIMEYER, R. A. (1985a). *The development of personal construct psychology.* Lincoln: University of Nebraska Press.

NEIMEYER, R. A. (1985b). Personal constructs in clinical practice. In P. C. Kendall (Ed.), *Advances in cognitive-behavioral research and therapy* (Vol. 4, pp. 275–339). New York: Academic Press.

NEIMEYER, R. A. (1994). The role of client-generated narratives in psychotherapy. *International Journal of Personal Construct Psychology, 7,* 229–242.

NEIMEYER, R. A., & JACKSON, T. T. (1997). George A. Kelly and the development of personal construct theory. In W. G. Bringmann, H. E. Lück, R. Miller, & C. E. Early (Eds.), *A pictorial history of psychology* (pp. 364–372). Carol Stream, IL: Quintessence.

NEIMEYER, R. A., & MAHONEY, M. J. (EDS.). (1995). *Constructivism in psychotherapy.* Washington, DC: American Psychological Association.

NEIMEYER, R. A., MOORE, M. K., & BAGLEY, K. J. (1988). A preliminary factor structure for the Threat Index. *Death Studies, 12,* 217–225.

NEIMEYER, R. A., & NEIMEYER, G. J. (1985). Disturbed relationships: A personal construct view. In E. Button (Ed.), *Personal construct theory and mental health: Theory, research, and practice.* Beckenham, UK: Croom Helm.

NESSE, R. M. (1984). An evolutionary perspective on psychiatry. *Comparative Psychiatry, 25,* 575–580.

NESSE, R. M. (2002). Evolution and addiction. *Addiction, 97,* 470–471.

NESTLER, E. J., & MALENKA, R. C. (2004). The addicted brain. *Addiction: Scientific American.com.*

NEVILL, D. D., & SCHLECKER, D. I. (1988). The relation of self-efficacy and assertiveness to willingness to engage in traditional/nontraditional career activities. *Psychology of Women Quarterly, 12,* 91–98.

NICHOLSON, I. A. M. (2001). "Giving Up Maleness": Abraham Maslow, masculinity, and the boundaries of psychology. *History of Psychology, 4,* 79–91.

NIEDENTHAL, P. M., SETTERLUND, M. B., & WHERRY, M. B. (1992). Possible self-complexity and affective reactions to goal-relevant evaluation. *Journal of Personality and Social Psychology, 63,* 5–16.

NORMAN, W. T. (1963). Toward an adequate taxonomy of personality attributes: Replicated factor structure in peer nomination personality ratings. *Journal of Abnormal and Social Psychology, 66,* 574–583.

ÖHMAN, A., FLYKT, A., & ESTEVES, F. (2001). Emotion drives attention: Detecting the snake in the grass. *Journal of Experimental Psychology: General, 131,* 466–478.

ÖHMAN, A., & MINEKA, S. (2001). Fear, phobias, and preparedness: Toward an evolved module of fear and fear learning. *Psychological Review, 102,* 483–522.

ÖHMAN, A., & MINEKA, S. (2003). The malicious serpent: Snakes as a prototypical stimulus for an evolved module of fear. *Current Directions in Psychological Science, 12,* 5–9.

O'LEARY, A. (1992). Self-efficacy and health: Behavioral and stress-physiological mediation. *Cognitive Therapy and Research, 16,* 229–245.

OLSON, H. A. (ED.). (1979). *Early recollections: Their use in diagnosis and psychotherapy.* Springfield, IL: Charles C. Thomas.

ORGLER, H. (1963). *Alfred Adler: The man and his work.* New York: Liveright.

OZER, E. M., & BANDURA, A. (1990). Mechanisms governing empowerment effects: A self-efficacy analysis. *Journal of Personality and Social Psychology, 58,* 472–486.

PALMER, E. C., & CARR, K. (1991). Dr. Rogers, meet Mr. Rogers: The theoretical and clinical similarities between Carl and Fred Rogers. *Social Behavior and Personality, 19,* 39–44.

PANKSEPP, J., & PANKSEPP, J. B. (2000). The seven sins of evolutionary psychology. *Evolution and Cognition, 6*(2), 108–131.

PANZARELLA, R. (1980). The phenomenology of aesthetic peak experiences. *Journal of Humanistic Psychology, 20*(1), 69–85.

PARIS, B. J. (1994). *Karen Horney: A psychoanalyst's search for self-understanding.* New Haven, CT: Yale University Press.

PARIS, B. J. (2000). Karen Horney: The three phases of her thought. In G. A. Kimble & M. Wetheimer (Eds.), *Portraits of pioneers in psychology* (Vol. 4, pp. 163–179). Washington, DC: American Psychological Association.

PARKER, A. (1981). The meaning of attempted suicide to young parasuicides: A repertory grid study. *British Journal of Psychiatry, 139,* 306–312.

PAULUS, D. L., TRAPNELL, P. D., & CHEN, D. (1999). Birth order effects on personality and achievement within families. *Psychological Science, 10,* 482–488.

PAVLOV, I. P. (1928). *Lectures on conditioned reflexes* (Vol. 1) (H. Gantt, Trans.). New York: International Publishers.

PAXTON, R. (1980). The effects of a deposit contract as a component in a behavioral programme for stopping smoking. *Behaviour Research and Therapy, 18,* 45–50.

PAXTON, R. (1981). Deposit contracts with smokers: Varying frequency and amount of repayments. *Behaviour Research and Therapy, 19,* 117–123.

PELHAM, B. W. (1993). The idiographic nature of human personality: Examples of the idiographic self-concept. *Journal of Personality and Social Psychology, 64,* 665–677.

PERVIN, L. A. (1984). *Current controversies and issues in personality* (2nd ed.). New York: Wiley.

PERVIN, L. A. (1989). *Personality: Theory and research* (5th ed.). New York: Wiley.

PERVIN, L. A. (2001). *Current controversies and issues in personality* (3rd ed.). New York: Wiley.

PETERSON, D. L., & PFOST, K. S. (1989). Influence of rock videos on attitudes of violence against women. *Psychological Reports, 64,* 319–322.

PIERCE, D. L., SEWELL, K. W., & CROMWELL, R. L. (1992). Schizophrenia and depression: Construing and constructing empirical research. In R. A. Neimeyer & G. J. Neimeyer (Eds.), *Advances in personal construct psychology* (Vol. 2, pp. 151–184). Greenwich, CT: JAI Press.

PIETRZAK, R. H., LAIRD, J. D., STEVENS, D. A., & THOMPSON, N. S. (2002). Sex differences in human jealousy: A coordinated study of forced-choice, continuous rating-scale, and physiological responses on the same subjects. *Evolution and Human Behavior, 23, 83–94.*

PINKER, S. (1997). *How the mind works.* New York: Norton.

POLKINGHORNE, D. E. (1992). Research methodology in humanistic psychology. *Humanistic Psychologist, 20,* 218–242.

POOLE, M. E., & EVANS, G. T. (1989). Adolescents' self perceptions of competence in life skill areas. *Journal* of *Youth and Adolescence, 18,* 147–173.

POPPER, K. (1963). *Conjectures and refutations.* New York: Basic Books.

POWELL, R. A., & BOER, D. P. (1994). Did Freud mislead patients to confabulate memories of abuse? *Psychological Reports, 74,* 1283–1298.

POWER, T., & CHAPLESKI, M. (1986). Childrearing and impulse control in toddlers: A naturalistic investigation. *Developmental Psychology, 22,* 271–275.

PRATT, M. W., PANCER, M., HUNSBERGER, B., & MANCHESTER, J. (1990). Reasoning about the self and relationships in maturity: An integrative complexity analysis of individual differences. *Journal of Personality and Social Psychology, 59,* 575–581.

PRENTICE, A. M., DIAZ, E., GOLDBERG, G. R., JEBB, S. A., COWARD, W. A., & WHITEHEAD, R. G. (1992). Famine and refeeding: Adaptations in energy metabolism. In G. H. Anderson & S. H. Kennedy (Eds.), *The biology of feast and famine: Relevance to eating disorders* (pp. 22–46). San Diego, CA: Academic Press.

PRIVETTE, G., & BUNDRICK, C. M. (1991). Peak experience, peak performance, and flow: Correspondence of personal descriptions and theoretical constructs. *Journal of Social Behavior and Personality, 6,* 169–188.

PROGOFF, I. (1973). *Jung, synchronicity, and human destiny: Noncausal dimensions of human experience.* New York: Dell.

RABINOWITZ, F. E., GOOD, G., & COZAD, L. (1989). Rollo May: A man of meaning and myth.

Journal of Counseling and Development, 67, 436–441.

RAMANAIAH, N. V., HEERBOTH, J. R., & JINKERSON, D. L. (1985). Personality and self-actualizing profiles of assertive people. *Journal of Personality Assessment, 49,* 440–443.

RAVIZZA, K. (1977). Peak experiences in sport. *Journal of Humanistic Psychology, 17*(4), 35–40.

REEVES, C. (1977). *The psychology of Rollo May.* San Francisco: Jossey-Bass.

REGALSKI, J. M., & GUALIN, S. J. C. (1993). Whom are Mexican infants said to resemble? Monitoring and fostering parental confidence in the Yucatan. *Ethology and Sociobiology, 14,* 97–113.

RIGDON, M. A., & EPTING, F. R. (1983). A personal construct perspective on an obsessive client. In J. Adams-Webber & J. C. Mancuso (Eds.), *Applications of personal construct theory.* New York: Academic Press.

RIVERS, P., & LANDFIELD, A. W. (1985). Alcohol abuse. In E. Button (Ed.), *Personal construct theory and mental health: Theory, research, and practice.* Beckenham, UK: Croom Helm.

ROAZEN, P. (1976). *Erik H. Erikson: The power and limits of a vision.* New York: Free Press.

ROAZEN, P. (1980). Erik H. Erikson's America: The political implications of ego psychology. *Journal of the History of the Behavioral Sciences, 16,* 333–341.

ROBINSON, D. N. (1985). *Philosophy of psychology.* New York: Columbia University Press.

ROBINSON, P. J., & WOOD, K. (1984). Fear of death and physical illness: A personal construct approach. In F. R. Epting & R. A. Neimeyer (Eds.), *Personal meanings of death: Applications of personal construct theory to clinical practice.* Washington, DC: Hemisphere.

ROBINSON, T. E., & BERRIDGE, K. C. (2000). The psychology and neurobiology of addiction: An incentive-sensitization view. *Addiction, 95(Suppl. 2),* S91–S117.

ROBINSON, T. E., & BERRIDGE, K. C. (2003). Addiction. *Annual Review of Psychology, 54,* 25–53.

RODGERS, J. L. (2001). What causes birth order-intelligence patterns? The admixture hypothesis, revisited. *American Psychologist, 56,* 505–510.

RODGERS, J. L., CLEVELAND, H. H., VAN DEN OORD, E., & ROWE, D. C. (2000). Resolving the debate over birth order, family size, and intelligence. *American Psychologist, 55,* 599–612.

ROGERS, C. R. (1939). *The clinical treatment of the problem child*. Boston: Houghton Mifflin.

ROGERS, C. R. (1942). *Counseling and psychotherapy: Newer concepts in practice*. Boston: Houghton Mifflin.

ROGERS, C. R. (1951). *Client-centered therapy: Its current practice, implications, and theory*. Boston: Houghton Mifflin.

ROGERS, C. R. (1954b). Toward a theory of creativity. *ETC: A Review of General Semantics, 11,* 249–260.

ROGERS, C. R. (1955). Persons or science? A philosophical question. *American Psychologist, 10,* 267–278.

ROGERS, C. R. (1956b, February). Implications of recent advances in prediction and control of behavior. *Teachers College Record, 57,* 316–322.

ROGERS, C. R. (1956c). Some issues concerning the control of human behavior (Symposium with B. F. Skinner). *Science, 124,* 1057–1066.

ROGERS, C. R. (1959). A theory of therapy, personality, and interpersonal relationships, as developed in the client-centered framework. In S. Koch (Ed.), *Psychology: A study of a science* (Vol. 3). New York: McGraw-Hill.

ROGERS, C. R. (1961). *On becoming a person: A therapist's view of psychotherapy*. Boston: Houghton Mifflin.

ROGERS, C. R. (1963). Actualizing tendency in relation to motives and to consciousness. In M. R. Jones (Ed.), *Nebraska Symposium on Motivation*. Lincoln: University of Nebraska Press.

ROGERS, C. R. (1966). Client-centered therapy. In S. Arieti (Ed.), *American handbook of psychiatry*. New York: Basic Books.

ROGERS, C. R. (1967). Autobiography. In E. G. Boring & G. Lindzey (Eds.), *A history of psychology in autobiography* (Vol. 5). New York: Appleton.

ROGERS, C. R. (1968). Graduate education in psychology: A passionate statement. In W. G. Bennis, E. H. Schein, F. I. Steele, & D. E. Berlew (Eds.), *Interpersonal dynamics* (2nd ed., pp. 687–703). Homewood, IL: Dorsey.

ROGERS, C. R. (1969). *Freedom to learn*. Columbus, OH: Charles E. Merrill.

ROGERS, C. R. (1970). *Carl Rogers on encounter groups*. New York: Harper & Row.

ROGERS, C. R. (1972a). *Becoming partners: Marriage and its alternatives*. New York: Delacorte.

ROGERS, C. R. (1972b). My personal growth. In A. Burton (Ed.), *Twelve therapists*. San Francisco: Jossey-Bass.

ROGERS, C. R. (1973). My philosophy of interpersonal relationships and how it grew. *Journal of Humanistic Psychology, 13,* 3–15.

ROGERS, C. R. (1974). In retrospect: Forty-six years. *American Psychologist, 29,* 115–123.

ROGERS, C. R. (1977). *Carl Rogers on personal power*. New York: Delacorte.

ROGERS, C. R. (1980). *A way of being*. Boston: Houghton Mifflin.

ROGERS, C. R. (1983). *Freedom to learn for the 80s*. Columbus, OH: Charles E. Merrill.

ROGERS, C. R. (1987). The underlying theory: Drawn from experience with individuals and groups. *Counseling and Values, 32,* 38–46.

ROGERS, C. R., & RYBACK, D. (1984). One alternative to nuclear planetary suicide. In R. F. Levant & J. M. Schlien (Eds.), *Client-centered therapy and the person-centered approach: New directions in theory, research, and practice*. New York: Praeger.

ROSE, H., & ROSE, S. (2000). Introduction. In H. Rose & S. Rose (Eds.), *Alas, poor Darwin: Arguments against evolutionary psychology* (pp. 1–13). London: Jonathan Cape.

ROSENBAUM, M., & MUROFF, M. (EDS.). (1984). *Anna O.: Fourteen contemporary reinterpretations*. New York: Free Press.

ROSENBERG, L. A. (1962). Idealization of self and social adjustment. *Journal of Consulting Psychology, 26,* 487.

ROSENTHAL, D. A., GURNEY, R. M., & MOORE, S. M. (1981). From trust to intimacy: A new inventory for examining Erikson's stages of psychosocial development. *Journal of Youth and Adolescence, 10,* 525–537.

ROWE, I., & MARCIA, J. E. (1980). Ego identity status, formal operations, and moral development. *Journal of Youth and Adolescence, 9,* 87–99.

RUBINS, J. L. (1978). *Karen Horney: Gentle rebel of psychoanalysis*. New York: Dial.

RULE, W. R. (1972). The relationship between early recollections and selected counselor and life style characteristics. *Dissertation Abstracts International, 33,* 1448A–1449A. (University Microfilms No. 72-25, 921)

RULE, W. R., & TRAVER, M. D. (1982). Early recollections and expected leisure activities. *Psychological Reports, 51,* 295–301.

RUNCO, M. A., EBERSOLE, P., & MRAZ, W. (1991). Creativity and self-actualization. *Journal of Social Behavior and Personality, 6,* 161–167.

RUNYAN, W. M. (1983). Idiographic goals and methods in the study of lives. *Journal of Personality, 51,* 413–437.

RYCHLAK, J. F. (1988). *The psychology of rigorous humanism* (2nd ed.). New York: New York University Press.

RYCHLAK, J. F. (1991). *Artificial intelligence and human reason: A teleological critique.* New York: Columbia University Press.

RYCHLAK, J. F. (1997). *In defense of human consciousness.* Washington, DC: American Psychological Association.

SAKS, A. M. (1995). Longitudinal field investigation of the moderating and mediating effects of self-efficacy on the relationship between training and newcomer adjustment. *Journal of Applied Psychology, 80,* 211–225.

SALAMONE, J. D., & CORREA, M. (2002). Motivational views of reinforcement: Implications for understanding the behavioral functions of nucleus accumbens dopamine. *Behavioral Brain Research, 137,* 3–25.

SALMON, D., & LEHRER, R. (1989). School consultant's implicit theories of action. *Professional School Psychology, 4,* 173–187.

SANTOGROSSI, D., O'LEARY, K., ROMANCZYK, R., & KAUFMAN, K. (1973). Self-evaluation by adolescents in a psychiatric hospital school token program. *Journal of Applied Behavior Analysis, 6,* 277–287.

SARTRE, J.-P. (1956). Existentialism. In W. Kaufmann (Ed.), *Existentialism from Dostoevsky to Sartre.* New York: Meridian.

SARTRE, J-P. (1957). *Existentialism and human emotions.* New York: Wisdom Library.

SCHAEFER, H. H., & MARTIN, P. L. (1969). *Behavioral therapy.* New York: McGraw-Hill.

SCHATZMAN, M. (1992, March 21). Freud: Who seduced whom? *New Scientist,* pp. 34–37.

SCHIEDEL, D. G., & MARCIA, J. E. (1985). Ego identity, intimacy, sex role orientation, and gender. *Journal of Personality and Social Psychology, 21,* 149–160.

SCHILL, T., MONROE, S., EVANS, R., & RAMANAIAH, N. (1978). The effects of self-verbalization on performance: A test of the rational–emotive position. *Psychotherapy: Theory, research, and practice, 15,* 2–7.

SCHMITT, D. P. (2003). Universal sex differences in the desire for sexual variety: Tests from 52 nations, 5 continents, and 13 islands. *Journal of personality and social psychology, 85*(1), 85–104.

SCHMITT, D. P., & BUSS, D. M. (1996). Strategic self-promotion and competitor derogation: Sex and Context effects on the perceived effectiveness of mate attraction tactics. *Journal of personality and social psychology, 70*(6), 1185–1204.

SCHMITT, D. P., & PILCHER, J. J. (2004). Evaluating evidence of psychological adaptation: How do we know one when we see one? *Psychological science, 15*(10), 643–649.

SCHNEIDER, K. J. (1998). Toward a science of the heart: Romanticism and the revival of psychology. *American Psychologist, 53,* 277–289.

SCHUR, M. (1972). *Freud: Living and dying.* New York: International Universities Press.

SCHÜTZWOHL, A. (2004). Which infidelity type makes you more jealous? Decision strategies in a forced-choice between sexual and emotional infidelity. *Evolutionary psychology, 2,* 121–128.

SCHÜTZWOHL, A. (2005). Sex differences in jealousy: The processing of cues to infidelity. *Evolution and Human Behavior, 26,* 288–299.

SCHÜTZWOHL, A., & KOCH, S. (2004). Sex differences in jealousy: The recall of cues to sexual and emotional infidelity in personally more and less threatening context conditions. *Evolution and Human Behavior, 25,* 249–257.

SELIGMAN, M. E. P., & CSIKSZENTMIHALYI, M. (2000). Positive psychology: An introduction. *American Psychologist, 55,* 5–14.

SEPPA, N. (1997, June). Children's TV remains steeped in violence. *APA Monitor, 28,* 36.

SEWELL, K. W., ADAMS-WEBBER, J., MITTERER, J., & CROMWELL, R. L. (1992). Computerized repertory grids: Review of the literature. *International Journal of Personal Construct Psychology, 5,* 1–23.

SEXTON, T. L., & WHISTON, S. C. (1994). The status of the counseling relationship: An empirical review, theoretical implications, and research directions. *The Counseling Psychologist, 22,* 6–78.

SHAFFER, H. J. (2005). What is addiction?: A perspective. *Harvard Medical School Division on addictions* [Online]. Retrieved November 15, 2004, http://www.hms.harvard.edu/doa/institute

SHAGASS, C., & JONES, A. L. (1958). A neurophysiological test for psychiatric diagnosis: Results in 750 patients. *American Journal of Psychiatry, 114,* 1002–1009.

SHIOMI, K. (1978). Relations of pain threshold and pain tolerance in cold water with scores on Maudsley Personality Inventory and

Manifest Anxiety Scale. *Perceptual and Motor Skills, 47,* 1155–1158.

SHODA, Y., MISCHEL, W., & PEAKE, P. K. (1990). Predicting adolescent cognitive and self-regulatory competencies from preschool delay of gratification: Identifying diagnostic conditions. *Developmental Psychology, 26,* 978–986.

SHOSTROM, E. L. (1963). *Personal orientation inventory.* San Diego, CA: Educational and Industrial Testing Service.

SHOSTROM, E. L. (1964). An inventory for the measurement of self-actualization. *Educational and Psychological Measurement, 24,* 207–218.

SHOSTROM, E. L. (1966). *Manual for the personal orientation inventory (POI): An inventory for the measurement of self-actualization.* San Diego, CA: Educational and Industrial Testing Service.

SHOSTROM, E. L. (1974). *Manual for the personal orientation inventory.* San Diego, CA: Educational and Industrial Testing Service.

SHOSTROM, E. L., KNAPP, L. F., & KNAPP, R. R. (1976). *Actualizing therapy: Foundations for a scientific ethic.* San Diego, CA: Educational and Industrial Testing Service.

SIGNELL, K. (1966). Cognitive complexity in person perception and nation perception: A developmental approach. *Journal of Personality, 34,* 517–537.

SILVERMAN, L. (1976). Psychoanalytic theory: "The reports of my death are greatly exaggerated." *American Psychologist, 31,* 621–637.

SINGH, D. (1993). Adaptive significance of waist-to-hip ratio and female attractiveness. *Journal of Personality and Social Psychology, 65,* 293–307.

SINGH, D. (2000). Waist-to-hip ration: An indicator of female mate value. *International Research Center for Japanese Studies, International symposium. 16,* 79–99.

SINGH, D., & LUIS, S. (1995). Ethnic and gender consensus for the effect of waist-to-hip ratio on judgements of women's attractiveness. *Human Nature, 6,* 51–65.

SINGH, D., & YOUNG, R. K. (1995). Body weight, waist-to-hip ratio, breasts, and hips: Role in judgments of female physical attractiveness and desirability for relationships. *Ethology and Sociobiology, 16,* 483–507.

SKINNER, B. F. (1938). *The behavior of organisms: An experimental analysis.* Englewood Cliffs, NJ: Prentice-Hall.

SKINNER, B. F. (1948). *Walden Two.* New York: Macmillan.

SKINNER, B. F. (1950). Are theories of learning necessary? *Psychological Review, 57,* 193–216.

SKINNER, B. F. (1951). How to teach animals. *Scientific American, 185,* 26–29.

SKINNER, B. F. (1953). *Science and human behavior.* New York: Macmillan.

SKINNER, B. F. (1957). *Verbal behavior.* Englewood Cliffs, NJ: Prentice-Hall.

SKINNER, B. F. (1967). Autobiography. In E. G. Boring & G. Lindzey (Eds.), *A history of psychology in autobiography* (Vol. 5, pp. 387–413). New York: Appleton-Century-Crofts.

SKINNER, B. F. (1971). *Beyond freedom and dignity.* New York: Knopf.

SKINNER, B. F. (1974). *About behaviorism.* New York: Knopf.

SKINNER, B. F. (1976). *Particulars of my life.* New York: Knopf.

SKINNER, B. F. (1978). *Reflections on behaviorism and society.* Englewood Cliffs, NJ: Prentice-Hall.

SKINNER, B. F. (1979). *The shaping of a behaviorist.* New York: Knopf.

SKINNER, B. F. (1983). *A matter of consequences.* New York: Knopf.

SKINNER, B. F. (1990). Can psychology be a science of mind? *American Psychologist, 45,* 1206–1210.

SKINNER, E. A., CHAPMAN, M., & BALTES, P. B. (1988). Control, means–ends, and agency beliefs: A new conceptualization and its measurement during childhood. *Journal of Personality and Social Psychology, 54,* 117–133.

SMITH, H. S., & COHEN, L. H. (1993). Self-complexity and reactions to a relationship breakup. *Journal of Social and Clinical Psychology, 12,* 367–384.

SMITH, J. E., STEFAN, C., KOVALESKI, M., & JOHNSON, G. (1991). Recidivism and dependency in a psychiatric population: An investigation with Kelly's dependency grid. *International Journal of Personal Construct Psychology, 4,* 157–173.

SMITH, T. W. (1983). Changes in irrational beliefs and the outcome of rational–emotive psychotherapy. *Journal of Consulting and Clinical Psychologists, 51,* 156–157.

SOMIT, A., ARWINE, A., & PETERSON, S. A. (1996). *Birth order and political behavior.* Lanham, MD: University Press of America.

SPELTZ, M. L., SHIMAMURA, J. W., & MCREYNOLDS, W. T. (1982). Procedural variations in group contingencies. *Journal of Applied Behavior Analysis, 15,* 533–544.

SPRANGER, E. (1928). *Types of men: The psychology and ethics of personality* (5th ed.) (P. J. W. Pigors, Trans.). Halle: Niemeyer. (Original work published 1913)

STANOVICH, K. E. (2004). *How to think straight about psychology* (7th ed.). Boston: Allyn & Bacon.

STEELMAN, L. C., & POWELL, B. (1985). The social and academic consequences of birth order: Real, artificial, or both. *Journal of Marriage and the Family, 47,* 117–124.

STEIN, K. F. (1994). Complexity of self-schema and responses to disconfirming feedback. *Cognitive Therapy and Research, 18,* 161–178.

STELMACK, R. M., ACHORN, E., & MICHAUD, A. (1977). Extraversion and individual differences in auditory evoked response. *Psychophysiology, 14,* 368–374.

STEPHENSON, W. (1953). *The study of behavior: Q-technique and its methodology.* Chicago: University of Chicago Press.

STERN, P. J. (1976). *C. G. Jung: The haunted prophet.* New York: Dell.

STEVENS, A. (1994). *Jung.* New York: Oxford University Press.

STEVENSON, L., & HABERMAN, D. L. (1998). *Ten theories of human nature* (3rd ed.). New York: Oxford University Press.

STEWART, A. J., FRANZ, C., & LAYTON, L. (1988). The changing self: Using personal documents to study lives. *Journal of Personality, 56,* 41–74.

STEWART, R. A. C. (1968). Academic performance and components of self-actualization. *Perceptual and Motor Skills, 26,* 918.

STEWART, V., & STEWART, A. (1982). *Business applications of repertory grid.* New York: McGraw-Hill.

STOLOROW, R. D., & ATWOOD, G. E. (1979). *Faces in a cloud: Subjectivity in personality theory.* New York: Aronson.

STONE, V. E., COSMIDES, L., TOOBY, J., KROLL, N., & KNIGHT, R. T. (2002). Selective impairment of reasoning about social exchanges in a patient with bilateral limbic system damage. *Proceedings of the National Academy of Sciences, 99,* 11531–11536.

STUART, R. B., & LOTT, L. A. (1972). Behavioral contracting with delinquents: A cautionary note. *Journal Therapy and Experimental Psychiatry, 3,* 161–169.

STUMPHAUZER, J. S. (1972). Increased delay of gratification in young prison inmates through imitation of high delay peer models. *Journal of Personality and Social Psychology, 21,* 10–17.

SUGIYAMA, L., TOOBY, J., & COSMIDES, L. (1995). *Testing for universality: Reasoning adaptations amoung the Achuar of Amazonia.* Meetings of the Human Behavior and Evolution Society, Santa Barbara, CA.

SUINN, R. M., OSBORNE, D., & WINFREE, P. (1962). The self concept and accuracy of recall of inconsistent self-related information. *Journal of Clinical Psychology, 18,* 473–474.

SULLOWAY, F. J. (1979). *Freud, Biologist of the mind: Beyond the psychoanalytic legend.* New York: Basic Books.

SULLOWAY, F. J. (1996). *Born to rebel: Birth order, family dynamics, and creative lives.* New York: Pantheon.

SUTICH, A. (1976). The emergence of the transpersonal orientation: A personal account. *Journal of Transpersonal Psychology, 1,* 5–19.

SWETS, J. A., DAWES, R. M., & MONAHAN, J. (2000). Psychological science can improve diagnostic decisions. *Psychological Science in the Public interest, 1,* 1–26.

SYMONS, D. (1979). *The evolution of human sexuality.* New York: Oxford.

SYMONS, D. (1987). If we're all Darwinians, what's the fuss about? In C. Crawford, M. Smith, & D. Krebs (Eds.), *Sociobiology and psychology: Ideas, issues, and applications* (pp. 121–146). Hillsdale, NJ: Erlbaum.

SYMONDS, A. (1991). Gender issues and Horney's theory. *American Journal of Psychoanalysis, 51,* 301–312.

TALBOT, R., COOPER, C. L., & ELLIS, B. (1991). Uses of the dependency grid for investigating social support in stressful situations. *Stress Medicine, 7,* 171–180.

TANNER, W. P. JR., & SWETS, J. A. (1954). A decision making theory of visual detection. *Psychological reviews, 6,* 401–409.

TELLEGEN, A., LYKKEN, D. T., BOUCHARD, T. J., JR., WILCOX, K. J., SEGAL, N. L., & RICH, S. (1988). Personality similarity in twins reared apart and together. *Journal of Personality and Social Psychology, 54,* 1031–1039.

TESCH, S. A., & WHITBOURNE, S. K. (1982). Intimacy status and identity status in young adults. *Journal of Personality and Social Psychology, 43,* 1041–1051.

TETI, D. M., & GELFAND, D. M. (1991). Behavioral competence among mothers of infants in the first year: The mediational role of maternal self-efficacy. *Child Development, 62,* 918–929.

THOMPSON, G. G. (1968). George Alexander Kelly (1905–1967). *Journal of General Psychology, 79,* 19–24.

THOMPSON, T., & GRABOWSKI, J. (1972). *Reinforcement schedules and multi-operant analysis.* Englewood Cliffs, NJ: Prentice-Hall.

THOMPSON, T., & GRABOWSKI, J. (EDS.). (1977). *Behavior modification of the mentally retarded.* New York: Oxford University Press.

THORNE, F. C. (1975). The life style analysis. *Journal of Clinical Psychology, 31,* 236–240.

THORNE, F. C., & PISHKIN, V. (1973). The existential study. *Journal of Clinical Psychology, 29,* 387–410.

THURSTONE, L. L. (1934). The vectors of mind. *Psychological Review, 41,* 1–32.

TILLICH, P. (1952). *The courage to be.* New Haven, CT: Yale University Press.

TIGER, L. (1979). *Optimism: The biology of hope.* New York: Simon and Schuster.

TRIVERS, R. L. (1971). The evolution of reciprocal altruism. *Quarterly Review of Biology, 46,* 35–57.

TRIVERS, R. L. (1972). Parental investment and sexual selection. In B. Campbell (Ed.), *Sexual selection and the descent of man: 1871–1971* (pp. 136–179). Chicago: Aldine.

TRUAX, C. B., & CARKHUFF, R. R. (1967*). Toward effective counseling and psychotherapy.* Chicago: Aldine.

TRUAX, C. B., & MITCHELL, K. M. (1971). Research on certain therapist interpersonal skills in relation to process and outcome. In A. E. Bergin & S. L. Garfield (Eds.), *Handbook of psychotherapy and behavior change.* New York: Wiley.

TUCKMAN, B. W. (1990). Group versus goal-setting effects on the self-regulated performance of students differing in self-efficacy. *Journal of Experimental Education, 58,* 291–298.

TUPES, E. C., & CHRISTAL, R. E. (1961). *Recurrent personality factors based on trait ratings* (USAF ASD Tech. Rep. No. 61–97). Lackland Air Force Base, TX: U.S. Air Force.

TURNER, C. W., HESSE, B. W., & PETERSON-LEWIS, S. (1986). Naturalistic studies of the long-term effects of television violence. *Journal of Social Issues, 42*(3), 51–73.

TURNER, R. H., & VANDERLIPPE, R. H. (1958). Self-ideal congruence as an index of adjustment. *Journal of Abnormal and Social Psychology, 57,* 202–206.

VACC, N. A., & GREENLEAF, W. (1975). Sequential development of cognitive complexity. *Perceptual and Motor Skills, 41,* 319–322.

VAIHINGER, H. (1952). *The philosophy of "as if": A system of the theoretical, practical and religious fictions of mankind* (C. K. Ogden, Trans.). London: Routledge & Kegan Paul. (Original work published 1911)

VAN DER POST, L. (1975). *Jung and the story of our time.* New York: Pantheon.

VAN HOOFF, J. (1971). *Aspects of social behaviour and communication in humans and higher nonhuman primates.* Rotterdam: Bronder.

VAN KAAM, A. (1966). *Existential foundations of psychology.* Pittsburgh, PA: Duquesne University Press.

VERPLANCK, W. S. (1955). The operant, from rat to man: An introduction to some recent experiments on human behavior. *Transactions of the New York Academy of Science, 17,* 594–601.

VINEY, L. L. (1983). *Images of illness.* Miami, FL: Krieger.

VINEY, L. L. (1984). Concerns about death among severely ill people. In F. R. Epting & R. A. Neimeyer (Eds.), *Personal meanings of death.* Washington, DC: Hemisphere.

VINEY, L. L., ALLWOOD, K., STILLSON, L., & WALMSLEY, R. (1992). Personal construct therapy for HIV and seropositive patients. *Psychotherapy, 29,* 430–437.

VINEY, L. L., BENJAMIN, Y. N., & PRESTON, C. (1989). Mourning and reminiscence: Parallel psychotherapeutic processes for elderly people. *International Journal of Aging and Human Development, 28,* 239–249.

VYSE, S. A. (1990). Adapting a viewpoint: Psychology majors and psychological theory. *Teaching of Psychology, 17,* 227–230.

WAGNER, M. E., & SCHUBERT, H. J. P. (1977). Sibship variables and United States presidents. *Journal of Individual Psychology, 33,* 78–85.

WALKER, B. M. (1990). Construing George Kelly's construing of the person-in-relation. *International Journal of Personal Construct Psychology, 3,* 41–50.

WASON, P. (1966). Reasoning. In B. M. Foss (Ed.), *New horizons in psychology.* London: Penguin.

WATERMAN, A. S. (1982). Identity development from adolescence to adulthood: An extension of theory and a review of research. *Developmental Psychology, 18,* 341–358.

WATERMAN, A. S., GEARY, P. S., & WATERMAN, C. K. (1974). Longitudinal study of changes in ego identity status from the freshman to the senior year at college. *Developmental Psychology, 10,* 387–392.

WATERMAN, C. K., BUEBEL, M. E., & WATERMAN, A. S. (1970). Relationship between resolution of the identity crisis and outcomes of previous psychosocial crises. *Proceedings of the 78th Annual Convention of the American Psychological Association, 5,* 467–468.

WATSON, J. B. (1926). Experimental studies on the growth of the emotions. In C. Murchison (Ed.), *Psychologies of 1925.* Worcester, MA: Clark University Press.

WATSON, P. J., MORRIS, R. J., & HOOD, R. W., JR. (1990). Extrinsic scale factors: Correlations and construction of religious orientation types. *Journal of Psychology and Christianity, 9,* 35–46.

WEBSTER, R. (1995). Why Freud was wrong: Sin, science, and psychoanalysis. New York: Basic Books.

WEHR, G. (1987). *Jung: A biography.* Boston: Shambhala.

WEINBERG, R. S., HUGHES, H. H., CRITELLI, J. W., ENGLAND, R., & JACKSON, A. (1984). Effects of preexisting and manipulated self-efficacy on weight loss in a self-control program. *Journal of Research in Personality, 18,* 352–358.

WEISS, R. L., BIRCHLER, G. R., & VINCENT, J. P. (1974). Contractual models for negotiation training in marital dyads. *Journal of Marriage and the Family, 36,* 321–330.

WEISSTEIN, N. (1975). Psychology constructs the female, or the fantasy life of the male psychologist (with some attention to the fantasies of his friends, the male biologist and the male anthropologist). In I. Cohen (Ed.), *Perspectives on psychology.* New York: Praeger.

WEST, S. (ED.). (1983, September). Personality and prediction: Nomothetic and idiographic approaches. *Journal of Personality* [Special issue], *51*(3).

WESTCOTT, M. (1986). *The feminist legacy of Karen Horney.* New Haven, CT: Yale University Press.

WHITE, M., & EPSTON, D. (1990*). Narrative means to therapeutic ends.* New York: Norton.

WIEDENFELD, S. A., O'LEARY, A., BANDURA, A., BROWN, S., LEVINE, S., & RASKA, K. (1990). Impact of perceived self-efficacy in coping with stressors on components of the immune system. *Journal of Personality and Social Psychology, 59,* 1082–1094.

WIEDERMAN, M. W., & ALLGEIER, E. R. (1992). Gender differences in mate selection criteria:

Sociobiological or socioeconomic explanation? *Ethology and Sociobiology, 13,* 115–124.

WIENER, D. N. (1996). *B. F. Skinner: Benign anarchist.* Needham Heights, MA: Allyn & Bacon.

WIGGINS, J. S. (1968). Personality structure. *Annual review of psychology* (Vol. 19). Palo Alto, CA: Annual Reviews.

WILCOCKS, R. (1994). *Maelzel's chess player: Sigmund Freud and the rhetoric of deceit.* Savage, MD: Rowan & Littlefield.

WILLET, R. A. (1960). Measures of learning and conditioning. In H. J. Eysenck (Ed.), *Experiments in personality* (Vol. 2). London: Routledge & Kegan Paul.

WILLIAMS, D. E., & PAGE, M. M. (1989). A multidimensional measure of Maslow's hierarchy of needs. *Journal of Research in Personality, 23,* 192–213.

WILLIAMS, G. C. (1966). *Adaptation and natural selection.* Princeton, NJ: Princeton University Press.

WILLIAMS, G. C. (1975). *Sex and evolution.* Princeton, NJ: Princeton University Press.

WILSON, C. (1972). *New pathways in psychology: Maslow and the post-Freudian revolution.* New York: Taplinger.

WILSON, E. O. (1975). *Sociobiology: The new synthesis.* Cambridge, MA: Harvard University Press.

WILSON, E. O. (1998). *Consilience: The unity of knowledge.* New York: Knopf.

WILSON, M. (1989). Marital conflict and homicide in evolutionary perspective. In R. W. Bell & N. J. Bell (Eds.), *Sociobiology and the social sciences* (pp. 45–62). Lubbock: Texas Tech University Press.

WILSON, M., & DALY, M. (1994). A lifespan perspective on homicidal violence: The young male syndrome. In C. R. Block & R. L. Block (Eds.), *Proceedings of the 2nd annual workshop of the homicide research working group.* Washington, DC: National Institute of Justice.

WILSON, S. R., & SPENCER, R. C. (1990). Intense personal experiences: Subjective effects, interpretations, and after-effects. *Journal of Clinical Psychology, 46,* 565–573.

WINTER, D. A. (1993). Slot rattling from law enforcement to lawbreaking: A personal construct theory exploration of police stress. *International Journal of Personal Construct Psychology, 6,* 253–267.

WITTELS, F. (1924). *Sigmund Freud: His personality, his teaching, and his school.* London: Allen & Unwin.

WOJCIK, J. V. (1988). Social learning predictors of the avoidance of smoking relapse. *Addictive Behaviors, 13,* 177–180.

WOLPE, J., & PLAUD, J. J. (1997). Pavlov's contributions to behavior therapy: The obvious and the not so obvious. *American Psychologist, 52,* 966–972.

WOOD, R., & BANDURA, A. (1989). Impact of conceptions of ability on self-regulatory mechanisms and complex decision making. *Journal of Personality and Social Psychology, 56,* 407–415.

WOOD, R., BANDURA, A., & BAILEY, T. (1990). Mechanisms governing organizational performance in complex decision-making environments. *Organizational Behavior and Human Decision Processes, 46,* 181–201.

WRIGHT, J. C., & MISCHEL, W. (1987). A conditional approach to dispositional contructs: The local predictability of social behavior. *Journal of Personality and Social Behavior, 53,* 1159–1177.

WRIGHTMAN, L. S. (1981). Personal documents as data in conceptualizing adult personality development. *Personality and Social Psychology Bulletin, 7,* 367–385.

WULFF, D. M. (1991). *Psychology and religion: Classic and contemporary views.* New York: Wiley.

WUNDT, W. (1903). *Grundzuge der physiologischen psychologie* (Vol. 3, 5th ed.). Leipzig: W. Engelmann.

YEAGLE, E. H., PRIVETTE, G., & DUNHAM, F. Y. (1989). Highest happiness: An analysis of artists' peak experience. *Psychological Reports, 65,* 523–530.

YONGE, G. D. (1975). Time experiences, self-actualizing values, and creativity. *Journal of Personality Assessment, 39,* 601–606.

YOUNG-BRUEHL, E. (1988). *Anna Freud: A biography.* New York: Norton.

YOUNG-BRUEHL, E. (1990). *Freud on women: A reader.* New York: Norton.

ZAJONC, R. B. (2001). The family dynamics of intellectual development. *American Psychologist, 56,* 490–496.

ZAJONC, R. B., & MARKUS, G. B. (1975). Birth order and intellectual development. *Psychological Review, 82,* 74–88.

ZAJONC, R. B., MARKUS, H., & MARKUS G. B. (1979). The birth order puzzle. *Journal of Personality and Social Psychology, 37,* 1325–1341.

ZAJONC R. B., & MULLALLY, P. R. (1997). Birth order: Reconciling conflicting effects. *American Psychologist, 52,* 685–699.

ZIMBARDO, P., & RUCH, F. (1977). *Psychology and life* (9th ed.). Glenview, IL: Scott, Foresman.

ZUCKERMAN, M. (1991). *Psychobiology of personality.* New York: Cambridge University Press.

ZUCKERMAN, M. (1995). Good and bad humors: Biochemical bases of personality and its disorders. *Psychological Science, 6,* 325–332.

ZUROFF, D. (1986). Was Gordon Allport a trait theorist? *Journal of Personality and Social Psychology, 51,* 993–1000.

Name Index

Subject Index

Kelly's theory (*cont.*)
  corollaries of
    choice, 413, 435
    commonality, 415, 435
    construction, 410–411, 435
    dichotomy, 412–413, 435
    experience, 414, 435
    fragmentation, 415, 436
    individuality, 411, 436
    modulation, 414–415, 436
    organization, 411–412, 436
    range, 413–414, 436
    sociality, 415–416, 436
  evaluation of, 428–432
    contributions, 430–431
    criticisms, 430
    current status of, 428
    empirical research support-
      ing, 428–430
    summary of, 432–434
Kin selection, 383, 401

Language, importance of in Dol-
    lard and Miller's theory,
    310–311 (*see also* Cue-
    producing responses)
Latency stage of development, 43,
    61
Latent content (of dreams), 47, 61
Learning, 4–5, 344
  as a determinant of personality,
    4–5,
  Kelly's definition of, 442, 436
  structured, 243, 259
Learning dilemma, 300, 324
Letters from Jenny (see Idiogra-
    phic research)
Libido, 30, 61
  Jung's view of, 71, 93
Lexical hypothesis, 247–248, 259
Life-span psychology, 178
Lifestyle, 102–103, 104–106,
    110–111, 121, 124
  mistaken, origins of, 104–106,
    124
  neglecting, 105–106, 124
  physical inferiority, 105, 124
  spoiling or pampering, 105, 124
  types of
    avoiding, 105, 123
    getting-leaning, 105, 124
    ruling-dominant, 105, 124
    socially useful, 105, 125
Long-circuiting, 235, 259
Love, May's views on, 515–517,
    527
  agape, 517, 526
  authentic, 515, 517
  eros, 515–516, 527
  philia, 516–517, 528
  sex, 515, 528

Make-believe, importance of in
    Kelly's theory, 426–427
Mandala, 83–84, 93
Manifest content (of dreams), 47, 61
Masculine protest, 99, 124
Maslow, A. H., biographical
    sketch, 471–475
Maslow's theory, 469–501
  evaluation of, 493–497
    contributions, 497
    criticisms, 496
    empirical research support-
      ing, 493–495
    summary of, 497–499
Mating strategies, 368–378
  long term, females attracting
    males, 373–374
  long term, males attracting fe-
    males, 374
  long term, men's preferences,
    371–373
  long term, women's prefer-
    ences, 369–371
  short term strategies, 375–377
    men's 376–377
    women's 375–376
May, R. R., biographical sketch,
    502–505
May's theory, 502–528
  evaluation of, 521–523
    contributions, 523
    criticisms, 522–523
    empirical research support-
      ing, 521–522
    summary of, 523–526
Metaergs, 233, 259
Metapathology, 482–483, 501
Miller, N. E., biographical sketch,
    294–295
Miller's theory (see Dollard and
    Miller's theory)
Mind-body problem
  proposed solutions to, 9–10,
    19
    epiphenomenalism, 9, 19
    interactionism, 10, 19
    parallelism, 9, 19
    physical monism, 9, 19
Minnesota Multiphasic Personal-
    ity Inventory, 89
Mischel, W., biographical sketch,
    328–329
Mischel's theory (see Bandura and
    Mischel's theory)
Model, 335, 358
Modeling, 338, 347
  types of
    delayed, 338, 358
    live modeling, 347
    participant, 347, 358
    symbolic, 348, 359

Models, news and entertainment
    media as, 337–338
Modern marriage, Rogers's views
    on, 457–458 (*see also*
    Satellite relationships)
Moral anxiety, 34–35, 61
Moral conduct, 342–344, 358 (*see
    also* Self-exonerating
    mechanisms)
Motivation, Kelly's views on, 418
  carrot theories, 418
  jackass theories, 418, 436
  pitchfork theories, 418
  pull theories, 418, 436
  push theories, 418, 436
Motivation, theories of, Allport's
    criteria for determining
    the adequacy of,
    198–199
Multiple Abstract Variance Analy-
    sis (MAVA), 241, 256
Myers-Briggs Type Indicator Test,
    89
Myth,
  importance of in May's theory,
    519–520
Mythical psychology, 254–255

Nativism, 3, 19
Nativism-empiricism controversy,
    3, 19
Natural selection (see Darwin's
    theory of evolution)
Naturalistic fallacy, 385, 401
Nature-nurture controversy (see
    Nativisim-empiricism
    controversy)
Need-directed perception (D-per-
    ception or D-cognition),
    481, 501
Need for positive regard, 445–446,
    468
Need for self-regard, 445–446, 468
Need induction, 197, 215
Need reduction, 197, 235
Negative identity (see Identity,
    negative)
Neglecting, 105, 124
Neurosis,
  Dollard and Miller's views on,
    313–314, 324
Neurotic anxiety, 34, 61, 512,
    527
Neuroticism (N), 236–237, 240,
    242, 244, 246, 247, 259
Neurotic symptom formation,
  Dollard and Miller's explana-
    tion of, 314–315
Neurotic trends (also called neu-
    rotic needs), 131–133,
    151